Rev. vo] 37/UK/1785/27/11 -3/12/04

D1576551

The British Seaborne Empire

THE BRITISH
SEABORNE EMPIRE

Jeremy Black

YALE UNIVERSITY PRESS
NEW HAVEN AND LONDON

For information about this and other Yale University Press publications, please contact:
U.S. Office:sales.press@yale.edu yalebooks.com
Europe Office: sales@yaleup.co.uk www.yalebooks.co.uk

Designed by Sandy Chapman

Printed in Great Britain by St Edmundsbury Press Ltd, Bury St Edmunds

Published with assistance from the Annie Burr Lewis Fund

Library of Congress Cataloging-in-Publication Data

Black, Jeremy.
  The British seaborne empire / by Jeremy Black.
      p. cm.
  Includes bibliographical references (p.   ) and index.
  ISBN 0-300-10386-7 (cl : alk. paper)
    1. Great Britain--Colonies--History, Naval. 2. Great Britain--History, Naval. I. Title.
  DA16.B58 2004
  359'.00941--dc22

                                                                              2004009130

A catalogue record for this book is available from the British Library.

10 9 8 7 6 5 4 3 2 1

For Jan Glete and Larry Sondhaus

CONTENTS

ILLUSTRATIONS

ABBREVIATIONS

Add. Additional Manuscripts
BL. London, British Library
CAB. Cabinet papers
FO. Foreign Office papers
IO. India Office papers
PRO. London, Public Record Office
SP. State papers
WO. War Office papers

PREFACE

The British empire has excited more scholarly attention during and since its demise than it enjoyed during its heyday. This reflects not only the growth in the academic profession over the last four decades, and the fascination of many scholars with decline, but also the extent to which empire as a whole, and the British empire in particular, is held accountable, if not blamed, for much that is unwelcome about the modern world.

This book is not intended as a contribution to that literature. Instead, within a general treatment of British imperial history, I emphasise one particular strand, its seaborne aspect, in order to throw light on the British, the people with whom they came into contact, the process of imperial expansion and the way in which empire was understood. These are big topics, and the process of choosing what to cover in the space available has been far from easy. The appearance of the *Oxford History of the British Empire* in 1998–9[1] ensures that a recent major scholarly treatment exists, and has enabled me to focus on the maritime aspect. Within that, I have been guided by the term British to concentrate on the period from the foundation of the British state in 1707, not least because the earlier period has already been extremely well covered, while the term 'British' empire seems ambiguous if applied to the pre-1707 period. Nevertheless, I have offered a summary of that period, both in order to provide background and also because many themes bridge that divide.

The maritime aspect of the subject deserves particular attention because that dimension of British history is one that may well be sidelined, both because of Britain's role within the European Union and because the immigrant communities whose imperial background press most strongly for attention are not maritime in origin. Sea power, however, made the empire what it was: without sea power there would have been no empire, or at least no empire in the form it actually took. Furthermore, the 'seaborne' character of the British empire captures one aspect of the interdependent character that was important from its outset, and became more so with time.

A major aim of this book is to take the story up to the present day. As a result, more space is devoted to the twentieth than to the nineteenth century. This may seem surprising, but it reflects a wish to focus on the decline of the maritime strand and to consider the continued relevance of the topic. The longevity of the British seaborne empire ensures that the chronological focus of this book is very different from those on the Dutch and Portuguese empires by Charles Boxer and on the Spanish seaborne empire by J. H. Parry. Boxer, for example, chose the dates 1600–1800 for his study of the Dutch seaborne empire, an understandable choice, although one that led him to omit the subsequent history of this empire, particularly its role in what became Indonesia.

Unfashionably, there is also a stress on war and international relations in my book. This approach has been sidelined by important and welcome advances in recent decades in other aspects of imperial history, and has also suffered from a sense that it has somehow all been done. The latter, however, is misleading and underrates the importance of these topics. Imperial conquest does not conform to current mores, and there is profound ambivalence, not to say amnesia, towards Britain's imperial past; but, at the time, victories and conquests were deplored by few. Britain was ruled not by pacifist Quakers, but by a political elite prepared to pursue national interests and destiny across the oceans, and this resonated with the aspirations of the wider political nation. It is truly a world that is lost, but one that cannot be disentangled from the history of the country and people.

In the introduction to their *Historical and Modern Atlas of the British Empire* (1905), C. Grant Robertson and J. G. Bartholomew stated that it was 'a positive duty for every British citizen' to study the history and 'geographical structure' of the empire. Now not only the requisite knowledge but also the relevant cultural parameters that they would have taken for granted are missing. In part, therefore, although readers already well familiar with the subject may find this frustrating, I am offering a narrative account designed to cover both.

This typescript was delivered several years late and I owe a great debt to Robert Baldock for his patient encouragement, and for overcoming my concerns that the topic was too big for me to tackle. I would also like to thank Sandy Chapman for being an exemplary editor. While writing this book, I benefited from the opportunity to lecture at the New Jersey Institute of Technology, the Virginia Historical Society, the University of Hawaii, and Arkansas Tech, Central Arkansas, Hawaii Pacific, Ohio, Ohio State, Old Dominion and Southeastern Louisiana Universities. Much of my interest in the subject stems from lectures by Geoffrey Scammell that I attended as an undergraduate, and it has been a great pleasure to read his subsequent work.

The presence in Exeter of a group of distinguished maritime historians – Nicholas Rodger, Michael Duffy, Roger Morriss and the late Stephen Fisher – and their students, has been a source of great stimulus. It is a great pleasure to dedicate this book to two naval historians whose work I much admire, Jan Glete and Larry Sondhaus. I would like to thank Jan, Larry, Bill Gibson, and four anonymous readers for their comments on an earlier draft, Grayson Ditchfield and James Murray Howard for commenting on part of the draft and Peter Ackroyd for a piece of useful stylistic advice.

I owe a great debt to those who have invited me to various parts of what was once Britain's seaborne empire. I have enjoyed visiting Singapore and Vancouver, Wellington and New York, Sydney and Boston, and many other fascinating places. Pride of place goes to a family holiday in 2002 to Nova Scotia and Prince Edward Island, not so much because I enjoyed both places and people, but rather because I was with those who are dearest to me.

Introduction
EUROPE AND THE OCEANS

There was built into English foreign policy a duality of ocean and continent. In normal, peaceful times the dominant influence, the dominant
attraction was that of the ocean. In times of European crisis . . . the influence of the continent was the more powerful . . .

R. B. Wernham, *The Making of Elizabethan Foreign Policy, 1558–1603*
(Berkeley, 1980), p. 95.

At the start of a new millennium, it is all too easy to forget that what made
Europe distinctive in world history was its ability to use the oceans in order
to create the first trading systems and empires able to span the world. Easy
to forget in part because of the nature of Europe now, but also because of
the way in which the European identity is currently understood.

Now, Europe's attitude towards the outside world is defeatist. Some
Europeans are clearly unhappy about the strength of American power,
military, political, economic and cultural, and see themselves as under threat
from it, a situation that was exposed, and accentuated, in 2002–4, during the
debate over policy towards Iraq; although the roots of difference went far
deeper, and related, in particular, to an ambivalence about change and an
uneasiness with the impression of European powerlessness in the face of
American strength. Furthermore, European societies have found it difficult
to respond to large-scale immigration, and to associated debates about
national identity and its relationship with problematic, but potent, concepts,
especially ethnicity, race and national culture. Such concerns affect the
response to history, and there is particular sensitivity about past links with
areas, many of them former colonies, from which large numbers of immigrants have come and with which current relations are often strained.

Yet, there is also a more profound problem. The European Union, a body
created, as the European Economic Community, in 1957, and which Britain
joined in 1973, represents a view of Europe not only today and for the
future, but also for the past. This view is one that sees European identity as
central to the real interests and histories of European peoples and countries,

and this encourages an emphasis on links within Europe, a process that has
gained strength with the fall of the Iron Curtain in 1989–91, and the subsequent attempt to incorporate Eastern Europe into the political, economic
and military structures of Western Europe. The attempt has a clear cultural
correlate, as it seeks to persuade the peoples of Western Europe that
they are European, and that their countries have a European identity and
destiny.

WHICH EUROPE?

To modern readers, this may seem a matter of stating the obvious, but,
in fact, primarily owing to two factors, this is far from the case. First, for
much of the last 600 years, a large part of Eastern Europe has been part of
a very different cultural (and political) world, that of the Ottoman Empire,
an Islamic imperial state with its capital at Constantinople (Istanbul) that
spent much of the period in conflict with Christian powers. Although
modern scholarship can search for parallels between (Christian) European
governments and societies, and those in the Ottoman Empire, to contemporaries the Empire was not so much non-European as anti-European. It
defined that which was not European, both tyranny and Islam, and presented both as a threat.[1] Indeed, in 1521, Ottoman forces captured Belgrade,
while at Mohacs in 1526, the main Ottoman army, commanded by the
Sultan, Suleyman the Magnificent, destroyed the Hungarian army. In 1529
and 1683, the Ottomans besieged Vienna, and in 1565 Valetta (albeit unsuccessfully on all three occasions), and, in 1739, they regained Belgrade, having
lost the city in 1717.

Second, if 'Europe' did not extend into the Ottoman world, it did spread
across the oceans. In the sixteenth century, the Spaniards rapidly established
themselves as the leading imperial power (whether European or non-
European) in the Americas, while Portugal became the leading maritime
power in the Indian Ocean. Other European peoples followed, particularly
the Dutch, French and English, although the list of those that founded
colonies includes Denmark, Sweden and Brandenburg-Prussia, while Austria
(i.e. the Austrian branch of the Habsburgs) also established, in the
eighteenth-century, Ostend Company, a trans-oceanic trading company.
Even the Baltic duchy of Courland, a weak state, but a maritime one, sought
to join in this great expansion in the seventeenth century.

The conventional account of imperial expansion has been affected by
important strands of scholarship in recent decades. First, there has been an
emphasis on the degree to which European expansion relied on the
co-operation of non-Europeans, particularly in South Asia and in the

Atlantic slave trade. In the former case, this has been linked to a stress on the limited impact of the Europeans in the sixteenth and seventeenth centuries, for example of their trade in the Indian Ocean. Second, the collapse of European colonialism in the twentieth century helped accentuate the effect of the global approach to history by suggesting that European expansion was only one stage in the history of the world, an important one, but, nevertheless, only a phase, and one followed by 'post-colonialism' in history and literature. While true, this underrates the qualitative and quantitative difference between European expansion and that of other empires, and the impact of European expansion, not only on areas that were conquered, but also on societies elsewhere across the world, especially those (the majority) involved in commercial transactions.

The great expansion changed the world, but it also altered Europe. This was true both of the Europe from which trade, territorial control and colonisers came, and the rest of Europe which was affected by the expansion, for example through the provision of trans-oceanic goods such as sugar and tea, as well as, directly or indirectly, by shifts in advantage and interest stemming from these changes. By 1750, as a result both of Ottoman conquests and of the great expansion, London, Paris and Madrid had more in common with colonial centres, such as Philadelphia, Québec and Havana, than they did with cities under Ottoman rule, such as Belgrade, Bucharest and Sofia. Furthermore, this situation remained the case over the following century, while, with a different geography, it was to resume during the Cold War. Relations between Western Europe and the trans-oceanic European world were affected, from 1775, by successful moves for independence on the part of settler populations, first in Britain's North American colonies and then in Latin America, but their links with Western Europe remained strong. This was even more the case when, as in Australia, Canada and New Zealand, political and governmental relations between colonies and the imperial power were lessened peaceably and gradually.

It is this tradition that is questioned directly by the creation of a new European history, for, alongside the challenge to the individual states of the European Union that has attracted most attention, and caused particular controversy in Britain, has come a determination to marginalise the residue and influence of empire, so that past links are treated as anachronistic, if not undesirable. These processes influence both present policy and cultural formation: in the case of the former, there has been the successful downplaying of economic links with former colonies, a shift highlighted by the fate of New Zealand lamb imports to Britain in the 1970s, once the agricultural protectionism of the European Economic Community had been implemented, and by Britain's difficulties in retaining preferential terms for banana imports from its former West Indies colonies while, in the case of cultural formation, it is Europe and the Oceans that has become the forgotten theme.

Other factors also lead to the same neglect, the changing nature of transport, both of people and of goods, being one of the most important. The aeroplane has altered the movement of both, and has transformed people's conception of space – diminishing, if not destroying, their awareness of distance. Initially, air transport had only a minor impact on long-distance travel, and, in the inter-war period (1918–39), there were no scheduled services across the Atlantic, and those to Australia or South Africa were expensive. Most travellers continued to go by ship, as did the vast majority of freight. The situation altered after the Second World War with the introduction and spread of jet aircraft. Travel by ship decreased, especially on prestige routes, such as those across the North Atlantic and to Australia. Across the North Atlantic, air travel was greater than sea travel from 1957, and by 1959 was nearly twice as great.[2] The nodal points of travel, the places where people were introduced to new worlds, ceased to be ports and became airports, and, instead of being glimpsed from the horizon, and fringed by water, the earth was scrutinised from up-high. Thus, at the same time as more Europeans travelled outside Europe than ever before, their relationship with the outside world was no longer refracted across the sea. Liverpool, Plymouth, Southampton and other ports ceased to be the gateways to new worlds, and their traffic and image were greatly affected as a consequence. More mundanely, airports, such as Heathrow in Britain, became crucial to international trade, particularly in terms of value rather than volume.

IMPERIAL HISTORY

If Europe and the Oceans, and European imperialism, are indeed major themes in the history of the last half-millennium,[3] that does not mean that they are equally pertinent for all European countries. For Poland or the Czech Republic, they are distinctly marginal, and essentially of importance for their impact on other European states; while, for those countries that were imperial powers, the lasting impact has varied greatly, both on them and on the areas that were under their sway.

For both imperial powers and the areas that they influenced, there is the problem of how best to define empire. A recent collection offers the definition of 'a state established by conquest that has sovereignty over subcontinental or continental-sized territories and incorporates millions or tens of millions of people within a unified and centralised administrative system. The state supports itself through a system of tribute or direct taxation of its component parts and maintains a large permanent military force to protect its marked frontiers and preserve internal order'.[4] There is also an account of secondary or mimicking shadow empires, including maritime trade empires, which are held to be inherently weaker. In the case of the British Empire, it is argued that a trade empire 'evolved' into a primary empire with colonial dependencies 'ruled directly from London'.[5]

This approach, however, is problematic, for it is far from clear that there is an essential or primary state of imperial power. Rather than adopting such a typology, it is necessary, instead, to consider each empire in terms of its own period, while also accepting that it is valuable to supplement this approach by an analysis that employs modern terms, however anachronistic their application may seem. The idea that a maritime trade empire was in some fashion secondary is unhelpful: the English, later British, government was generally far more interested in an 'empire of commerce' than in one of colonisation.[6] For example, for the mid-eighteenth century, the focus tends to be on the conquests of Bengal and Canada, yet, as has been pointed out, 'perceptions or notions of national identity may have increasingly revolved around Britain's status as a global power, but colonial acquisition was simply one of many expressions of this', and the emphasis was placed on the maritime nature of Britain's Empire.[7] The contemporary presentation of British power as unacquisitive in territorial terms was strengthened by the view that in North America the British were settling empty lands, in the sense of territories that were actually uninhabited or not being properly looked after by their native inhabitants; the last seen as either a denial of the gifts of Providence or, in secular terms, as an aspect of a less developed society.

At the same time, the notion of a British Empire stemming from the British Isles, which entailed, variously, the suzerainty of the English Crown in the British Isles, dynastic links between England and Scotland, and the English conquest of Ireland, provided a territorial component to imperial ideology as developed in the sixteenth century. It was used in this geographical sense by Humphrey Llwyd in 1572, although John Dee later in the decade saw the Empire as including the surrounding seas as well as the Atlantic coastline of North America 'discovered' by English explorers.[8]

The word empire in seventeenth- and eighteenth-century England was commonly applied to describe authority or control over trade and the sea as much as, if not more than, colonial control, and this approach helps explain the purpose of naval activity: Nicholas Rodger has shown how trade concerns explain a focus on the use of naval power for dominance in European waters, rather than trans-oceanic power projection.[9] More generally, a stress on what contemporaries meant by empire directs attention to government attitudes and to how far the metropolitan context shifted, and the important consequences these had for policy. At the same time, from the perspective of areas that experienced British activity, whether in trade or conquest, and, especially conquest, if followed by settlement, the extent to which imperial and naval policy focused on the threat from France is of secondary importance. This is an aspect of one of the tensions in imperial history, between centre and periphery, that helps to make the subject so dynamic; and indeed the way in which imperial history is capable of so many interpretations is a product of the manifold impact of empire. Analogously, there is an equivalent need for care in too readily applying theories of decline to changes in British power over the last century.

Different interpretations are not only a matter of present judgement, but were also seen in the past, as policy was considered and debated. Thus, in 1787, the Foreign Secretary, Francis, Marquess of Carmarthen, complained that, in the House of Lords, the Lord Chancellor, Edward, Lord Thurlow, had 'reprobated any shadow of right to our settlements on the Mosquito Shore at any time and treated the soidisant subjects in that quarter (perhaps with justice at least) as a set of buccaneers merely subsisting by smuggling'. The government indeed had promised, in a convention signed the previous year with Spain, that it would evacuate and demolish all fortifications on the Spanish–claimed Mosquito Coast (the Caribbean coast of modern Nicaragua), a step regretted by Carmarthen, and in 1787 2,211 settlers, mostly slaves, moved from the Black River settlements to Belize.[10] Thurlow was not unique in his approach. Alongside support for expansion, there was, throughout British imperial history, caution, if not opposition, that stemmed from a variety of causes, which can be crudely categorised as specific and prudential, or general and ideological. Similarly, support for initiatives varied and, although the distinction was not always clear, and there was an overlap, there was a tension between schemes for territorial expansion, which frequently involved speculative gains, and the quest for assured profit that was pushed hard by established commercial interests. Thus, the initiative by a merchant, Francis Light, that led in 1786 to the occupation of the island of Penang as a base on the route to China, was countered by the East India Company's refusal to heed his suggestions and the requests from Malay princes that Britain establish a presence elsewhere; and by its reluctance to help the Sultan of Kedah, with whom the Penang negotiations had been conducted, against his aggressive opponents.[11] Variations on this dispute were played out on numerous occasions.

It is particularly important to note the extent of debate over goals and methods, because it underlines not only the difficulty of moving from events to analysis, but also the problem of where best to place the emphasis when considering the nature of British imperialism. For example, to suggest that, in the nineteenth century, Britain's naval hegemony was more important to her great power status than her colonial expansionism may make more sense if relations with France or China are considered than if developments in Africa and India are discussed.

France, Spain and Britain were the European maritime imperial powers that had the most lasting impact; although, in terms of a (so far) permanent extension of territorial control, it was Russia, in Siberia, that was most successful of the European empires. Of the major maritime imperial powers, France continues to make a major effort to capitalise on past imperial strength in order to sustain and spread cultural influence, particularly in sub-Saharan Africa, but the dual effects of French territorial losses to Britain in the wars of 1689–1815 and the traumatic nature of the end of Empire in some of her colonies, especially in Indo-China and Algeria, gravely compromised this influence. With the exception of the British in lightly populated Australasia, Spain (with the addition of Portugal in Brazil) was the European imperial power that had the greatest impact on an individual continent (South America), in large part because of the length of its imperial control and its ability, in part through syncretism, to convert the indigenous population to Christianity. Spanish political and economic influence, however, were gravely lessened after independence by Spain's weakness on both counts. Furthermore, although the cultural legacy of Spain in Latin America remains very strong, it is indirect, and, instead, the impact of the USA there is far more powerful.

THE DISTINCTIVENESS OF THE BRITISH EMPIRE

The last is also true for much of what was the British Empire. The relationship between Britain and empire is regarded as different to that of other European states for a number of reasons. The most frequently cited, both during the period of empire and subsequently, was that the limited authority and power of government within Britain greatly affected the character of British imperialism, especially, but not only, in the case of colonies that received a large number of British settlers, although the benign implications of this interpretation have been challenged by those understandably concerned to emphasise the often harsh impact of European (including British) imperialism on native peoples. Nevertheless, the commercial focus or, at least, nexus of much British imperial activity was such that the role of the state was less than for Portuguese, Spanish and French activity. All countries had a role for private adventurers, but the opportunity for personal, or, at least, corporate, profit played a particularly important role in British imperialism, as seen, for example, with the slave trade. Corporate profit was also a driving force in Dutch imperialism.

There are other distinctive aspects of British imperialism that repay attention, one of the most important being that Britain is an island, and the
resulting economic, political and strategic consequences. Britain's position as
an island helped ensure that fishing and foreign trade played a major role
in its history, while the role of the sea was fostered by the nature of the
offshore waters and the role of oceanic currents, both of which ensured a
rich and varied fish life. The Gulf Stream is the most important of these
currents, bringing warm waters from the Caribbean to British shores, and
helping ensure that the climate is far more temperate than other areas at
the same latitude, such as Sakhalin and Kamchatka in East Asia, and Labrador
on the eastern shore of North America.

The expansion of the country was also in no small part due to the economic development and power that the importing and exporting of goods
made possible. An emphasis on trade helped lead to the greater sophistication of the economy, in particular the development of the financial sector
and the growth of overseas shipping, both of which, in turn, helped trade.
Trade, however, also posed problems, including the commerce protection
that required naval strength and commitment, although the provision of both
in turn fostered trade. Dependence upon the import of foreign foodstuffs,
at the same time, helped make the country vulnerable during both the First
and Second World Wars and the Cold War.

Trade was crucial to Britain's maritime position, and became an iconic
aspect of the British Empire, indeed the iconic aspect as far as many Britons
and foreigners were concerned. When, in 1933, Carl Paul Jennewein produced a bronze sculptural relief above the main entrance of the British
Empire Building constructed the previous year at 620 Fifth Avenue as part
of the Rockefeller Center in New York, the emphasis was economic: on the
products and people of the Empire, with figures for cotton and tobacco,
both bare-breasted women, as well as for wool, sugar, coal, salt, wheat and
fish, and a navigator at the bottom. The stone panel, or cartouche, above
the doorway depicted the royal coat of arms. In contrast, the French Building's bronze panel, created by Alfred Janniot in 1934, showed figures of
poetry, beauty and elegance; while the cartouche symbolised freedom. In
light of its earlier role in the end of the slave trade and the subsequent
spread of Dominion status to some colonies, the British Empire also had
claims to be a force for freedom; but, by the 1930s, it was widely seen as a
trading force. This was reasonable in light of the longstanding strength of
the commercial theme in British imperial history; although it helped ensure
that, when trade declined, relatively little was left. Against this view, it is
possible to argue that the use of imperial energy and resources to defend
freedom from Nazism was a culmination, justification and even a destiny
for the British Empire.

Island status was also important to British imperialism from the outset, not least because it made Britain difficult to conquer. There were successful invasions, particularly those by the Roman Emperor Claudius in 43 and the Norman William the Conqueror in 1066, both of which led to longlasting conquests, and, less clearly because he was welcomed by many, by William III of Orange in 1688. But it was more difficult to invade a country by sea than by land, and this proved crucial to national safety after English forces (or, earlier, the forces of the King of England) had been defeated on the Continent, as when King John lost Normandy to Philip Augustus, King of France in 1204, as well as after defeat in the Low Countries by France in 1794 and by Germany in 1940. Invasion attempts that were thwarted by British naval power and/or the weather included those in 1588, 1692, 1696, 1708, 1744, 1745–6, 1759 and 1805.

Britain's island existence also engendered an insularity that made for suspicious minds when it came to relationships with Continental Europe. The late nineteenth-century tradition of 'splendid isolation' in foreign policy may be regarded as the precursor of Britain's present status as the 'awkward partner' within the European Union.

The legacy of British imperial rule varied greatly and this resonates in modern world politics. British control of many territories – of the nineteenth-century empire, let alone colonies gained after the First World War – was more shortlived than was true of its Spanish counterpart. In many of these territories, British settlement was also limited. The combined effect was of a less profound and lasting impact than in former settlement colonies – Australia, Canada, New Zealand – mostly also occupied during the nineteenth century, but where the bulk of the present population is not of indigenous descent. These were to be the colonies that lent themselves to a process of autonomy through self-government (the acquisition of Dominion status), as it proved easiest to ensure, and justify, such a development in colonies where at least part of the population were British subjects living abroad. Dominion status was also seen as a key to imperial strength, and, indeed, in his *Britain and the British Seas* (1902), Halford Mackinder, a Liberal Imperialist who played a key role in the development of the concept and practice of geopolitics, claimed,

> The whole course of future history depends on whether the Old Britain besides the Narrow Seas have enough of virility and imagination to withstand the challenge of her naval supremacy, until such time as the daughter nations shall have grown to maturity, and the British Navy shall have expanded into the Navy of the Britains.[12]

The situation was different in colonies where the population lacked the rights or claims of Britons, and, in these, authority remained as a tool of imperial administrators, and institutions of representative and responsible government were granted more reluctantly. Furthermore, it would be misleading to neglect the extent to which, thanks in part to ethnic and social stereotyping and policies, the practice of representative government in the Dominions did not match modern liberal suppositions of acceptable conduct.

It would also be misleading to see the difference between the Dominions and the other colonies in terms of more, or less, 'seaborne' or maritime characteristics. Although Australia remained far more a series of coastal societies, each based on the port-capitals of individual states (Adelaide, Brisbane, Hobart, Melbourne, Perth and Sydney), than its shape on the map would suggest, the Canadian Prairies were part of a continental culture, while the Maritime Provinces in Atlantic Canada failed to retain their relative demographic and economic importance and, instead, inland Ontario became the key province in eastern Canada. Furthermore, in terms of economic interests, strategic concerns and racial composition, the British seaborne empire was as much a matter of Accra and Georgetown, Durban and Singapore, Lagos and Hong Kong, Colombo and Mombasa, Bombay and Penang, as of Auckland and Vancouver, or Halifax and Perth. Thus, nuances, rather than stark contrasts, are the order of the day.

IMAGES OF EMPIRE

Nuances are less obviously the case with images of the British Empire. British colonies in Africa and South Asia, especially India, are generally seen in terms of images of the interior, as in E. M. Forster's successful novel *A Passage to India* (1924), of which the three parts are 'Mosque, Caves, Temple'; while, although not set in a British colony, Joseph Conrad's novel *Heart of Darkness* (1902) was a potent and influential depiction of Africa in terms of the savagery of its 'inscrutable' jungle, an intense counterpart to the mystery of the interior seen in Henry Rider Haggard's *King Solomon's Mines* (1885), its sequel *Allan Quatermain* (1887) and *She: A History of Adventure* (1887), works that enjoyed considerable popularity as adventure stories until the late twentieth century. Haggard, who served in South Africa in 1875–9 and 1880–81, taking part in the annexation of the Transvaal, also wrote a Zulu trilogy: *Marie* (1912), *Child of Storm* (1913) and *Finished* (1917), as well as writing non-fiction works on South Africa. Haggard's work, like that of Kipling, is also notable for the respect it showed for native traditions and culture. Imperial images often reflect such respect and show the breadth of the Empire and the diversity of the areas Britain had acquired. The focus on the interior has been taken further in the world of film and television, as in the 1983 Merchant Ivory Productions film of Ruth Jhabvala's novel about British women in India, *Heat and Dust* (1975).

Yet such images of the interior provide a less-than-full account of the British imperial presence, much of which focused on port cities and rested on maritime and naval hegemony. Indeed, the Polish-born Conrad (1857–1924) became a naturalised British subject in 1886, having worked on British merchantmen from 1878, and his experiences of the sea and empire, which took him to Bombay in 1884 and subsequently to Singapore, were reflected in a series of novels including *The Nigger of the 'Narcissus'* (1897), *Lord Jim* (1900), *Youth* (1902), *Victory* (1915) and *The Shadow Line* (1917). At a different level and with reference to India, Sardar Panikkar, an Indian court adviser who subsequently became Indian ambassador to China, wrote in 1945 that from the early sixteenth century, 'the future of India has been determined not on the land frontiers, but on the oceanic expanse which washes the three sides of India';[13] from the eighteenth century, this had been dominated by Britain.

The oceans and their shores, rather than the mysterious interiors of continents, certainly dominated the English perception of the trans-oceanic world in the sixteenth, seventeenth and eighteenth centuries, climaxing with the fascination in the Pacific in the age of Captain Cook and continuing into the nineteenth century with Franklin in the Arctic and Ross in the Antarctic. The oceans offered much more than fascination. In England, from the late sixteenth century, maritime conflict and imperial strength were seen as important to national morale and reputation and led first the English and then others to a sense of English and, later, British exceptionalism. William Gordon, a diplomat travelling through Germany in 1764, found that victory over France and Spain in the Seven Years' War (1756–63) had 'struck such an awe upon all foreigners, that they look upon us as a race of people superior to the rest of mankind'.[14]

Such victories continued to resonate into the early twentieth century, but have ceased to do so today. The bells of victory that rang out over Britain in 1759, as the British won major victories at sea (Lagos and Quiberon Bay) and in Germany (Minden), Canada (Québec) and the West Indies (capture of Guadeloupe), still resonated when Julian Corbett (1854–1922) published *The Seven Years War* in 1907 and he could address an audience that took imperial heroism, adventure and expansion for granted. Having already published biographies of two prominent naval figures from the glorious past, George Monck (1889) and Francis Drake (1890), Corbett had moved on, with his *Drake and the Tudor Navy* (1898) and *The Successors of Drake* (1900), to offer a more searching account of naval capability and limitations, while his view that an understanding of the past was of current relevance was seen in *England in the Mediterranean* (1904) and *Some Principles of Maritime Strategy* (1911).[15]

As an alternative to Lord Tebbit's subsequent cricket test for national loyalty (whether spectators applauded England or, if immigrants, foreign teams), Corbett's account in *The Seven Years War* of James Wolfe's triumph in the Québec campaign of 1759 would offer those brought up with Edwardian values a quickening of the breath. Corbett was at pains to stress cohesion and coordination as a cause of success: 'So in the moment of triumph the last touch was given to that remarkable harmony between the services, both in spirit and action, which had been the conspicuous feature of the campaign, and the main cause of its success. As it began, so it ended'.[16] Yet, as a measure of the world that has passed, Corbett and the Seven Years' War are scarcely household names now. More generally, as Paul Kennedy pointed out in his perceptive lecture 'The Boundaries of Naval History', the British nation now has far less public and political interest in matters maritime and naval than has been the case since the fifteenth century;[17] and there is no sign of this changing.

As a reminder, however, of the former strength of the sea and shipping in the British imagination, and the variety of images that could be conjured up, it is appropriate to turn to J[oseph] M[allard] W[illiam] Turner (1775–1851). A painter of imperial themes, interested in the clash between Rome and Carthage, which was widely seen as prefiguring that between Britain and France, Turner marked Nelson's victories over the French at the Nile (1798) and Trafalgar (1805) with paintings displayed the following years. The former has disappeared but the latter, seen as a British epic picture, is an important part of the Tate Gallery's collection. It shows both victory and the heroic death enacted on the ship, offering a focused concentration lacking from a genre that usually depicted naval battles on a larger scale. Turner's personal interest led him to sketch the *Victory* as she returned from the battle and to make detailed studies on the ship; he also painted *The 'Victory' beating up the Channel on its return from Trafalgar*. A different account of Britain's maritime role was offered in Turner's *Slavers throwing overboard the Dead and Dying – Typhon [sic] coming on* (1840). This powerful work, full of dramatic colour and based on the Liverpool slaver the *Zong*, was described by Ruskin in *Modern Painters* (1843) as displaying the power and majesty 'of the open, deep, illimitable sea!', and can be seen as a condemnation of the slave trade, in which Britain had been prominent, but also a tribute to the British role in the abolition of both the trade and slavery itself. Queen Victoria's husband, Prince Albert, was the President of the Anti-Slavery League.

Other maritime images of empire were provided, in the inter-war period, in the advertising posters of the Empire Marketing Board, which was established in 1926 and lasted until 1933. In focusing on the mutual dependence of the empire at home and overseas, there was a stress in these posters on lines of communication, which were very much maritime. Thus, MacDonald Gill's poster *Highways of Empire* (1927) concentrated on maritime links, as opposed to rail links such as those across Canada. Charles Dixon's *The River Mersey: The Western Gateway of Empire* (1928), a portrayal of bustling energy, complemented the series that year on *The Empire's Highway to India* by Charles Pears, which depicted Gibraltar, Malta, the Suez Canal, Aden and Bombay, made reference to India as the biggest customer for British goods and had a military theme, with the Gibraltar poster showing a warship while its Malta counterpart had a RAF plane flying over a merchantman leaving Valetta.[18]

The character of these posters matched those produced in the inter-war period by railway lines and the Shell petrol company, for, just as the latter produced attractive images of Britain in order to tempt travellers, so the posters of imperial links and products were at once the description of what was useful and a lyrical depiction, the aesthetic quality of which contributed to this sense of natural usefulness. There was no more reason to see these posters as anachronistic than to regard those of Britain (which in some ways demonstrated the values of the National Governments of 1931–40) in the same light. Perhaps the most popular and commonplace images of empire in Britain were those that ordinary people came into contact with: buildings, such as the Dominion High Commissions in London and, even more, advertising imagery, for example tea pickers illustrated on Brooke Bond PG Tips boxes, or soldiers and tents on Camp coffee.

At the same time, it is necessary to note the degree to which the view on the periphery could be much harsher. Dean Mahomet (1759–1851), an Indian quartermaster with the Bengal army of the East India Company, recorded the advance of a brigade from Bihar to Calcutta in 1772–3 and the response to resistance by the hill people of the passes through which Bengal was entered. After the 'licentious savages' had attacked those cutting grass and gathering fuel for the camp, two companies of sepoys advanced:

> Our men, arranged in military order, fired . . . the greater part of them [savages], after a feeble resistance with their bows, arrows, and swords, giving way to our superior courage and discipline, fled . . . two hundred . . . prisoners . . . severely punished for their crimes; some having their ears and noses cut off, and others hung in gibbets.[19]

As a reminder of the variety of experience summarised by the term empire, Mahomet came to Britain in 1784, married an Irish woman, became an assistant to Sir Basil Cochrane at his vapour bath in London, established the

Hindoostane Coffee House in the capital in 1810 and subsequently opened
Mahomet's Baths, which was patronised by such leading figures as Sir
Robert Peel.

Although Mahomet's description did not present the 'savages' as posing
much opposition, military operations frequently required considerable
bravery, and the individual and collective factors that produced and sustained
this were important to the success of empire. As troops approached the
Egyptian coast in a landing contested by the French in 1801, 'the enemy
commenced their attack upon us with round shot and shell which as we
approached nearer was changed into the hottest discharges imaginable of
grape, canister and musquetry without our being able to make any return.
In spite of this destructive opposition the boats still advanced.'[20] And the
landing was successful, as was the subsequent campaign against the French
in Egypt which culminated in their surrender, lessening the threat of French
activity between the Mediterranean and India. A different form of bravery,
less immediately spectacular but more consistent in the longer term, was
required from those who took to the ocean in small ships, vulnerable to the
perils of the sea, whether for fishing, trade or migration.

BRITAIN AND THE USA: TWO EMPIRES

The geographical range of the British Empire is such that its study is an
important element in world history, while, in addition, the indirect impact
of Britain, through its role in the early history of the contemporary world's
major power, the USA, is also crucial – although this also serves as a
reminder of the difficulty of separating out 'the empire' for analysis. Many
of the liberal ideas that played a central role in British assumptions in the
nineteenth century were taken up by American writers and policymakers
from the 1940s, in part, initially, in criticism of the protectionism then shown
by the British Empire. There was a focus on free trade, and the unfettered
movement of money, as political and economic goods, and thus as central
goals for government; and the American, and, earlier, British, pursuit of a
benign and mutually beneficial world order reflected an imperium,
rather than an empire simply of control, constraint and coercion. In the
American case, however, a democratic objective played a major role,
although, earlier, this had not been prominent in nineteenth-century
American expansionism. As Andrew Bacevich has pointed out, echoing
observations that can be made about British imperialism,

the politicoeconomic concept to which the United States adheres today
has not changed in a century: the familiar quest for an 'open world,' the

overriding imperative of commercial integration, confidence that technology endows the United States with a privileged position in that order,
and the expectation that American military might will preserve order and
enforce the rules. Those policies reflect a single-minded determination
to extend and perpetuate American political, economic, and cultural
hegemony – usually referred to as leadership – on a global scale . . . The
question is what sort of empire they intend theirs to be.[21]

In studying the British seaborne empire, there is the unique possibility of
considering two consecutive leading world powers, indeed the two powers
that moulded the modern world, and, for that reason among others, had a
special relationship. None of that, however, seemed even a distant prospect
when maritime expansion began from Britain.

I

THE ORIGINS OF EMPIRE

Wind, rain, and thunder, remember, earthly man
Is but a substance that must yield to you;
And I, as fits my nature, do obey you.
Alas, the sea hath cast me on the rocks,
Wash'd me from shore to shore, and left me breath
Nothing to think on but ensuing death.
Let it suffice the greatness of your powers
To have bereft a prince of all his fortunes.
    The shipwrecked Pericles from the play *Pericles, Prince of Tyre* (c. 1608)
        by William Shakespeare and, probably, George Wilkins, II, i.

The most recent treatment of the origins of the British Empire correctly points out that the British 'role in long-distance voyaging was relatively modest before the close of the sixteenth century',[1] and, essentially, offers an account of the late sixteenth and seventeenth centuries. That is clearly appropriate as far as trans-oceanic activity was concerned, and it was from that that the British seaborne empire derived. However, there is an additional story, of empire within the British Isles and, indeed, Western Europe, that repays attention.

There might appear to be no connection between this and the later seaborne empire. Indeed, it has been argued that the failure of the kings of England to sustain their inherited territorial position in France was a precondition of imperial expansion; an argument I shall return to. In practice, however, there were connections, however tenuous they might appear, between trans-oceanic and earlier imperial activity; and this was true not only of Britain but also of Europe as a whole. In particular, medieval practices and ideas of imperial rule, territorial expansion, commercial ambition and maritime activity all continued within Europe, and were also transposed outside the Continent during what is termed the early modern period, roughly 1500 to 1750.

As far as Continental Europe was concerned, this legacy was a complex one. To modern observers, the most dramatic aspect was the crossing of the Atlantic by the Norsemen in the early eleventh century, via Iceland (which they had colonised in the ninth century) and Greenland (colonised in the tenth century). This was an impressive feat of seamanship and endurance and the settlements established across the North Atlantic represented the furthest reaches of European power until the fifteenth century. However, the lasting impact of these voyages and settlements was limited. Affected by disease, native hostility, climatic difficulties and deterioration, and an inability to sustain them, the settlements in North America and Greenland were abandoned, after the early eleventh century and in around 1500 respectively, and, within the ambit of European expansion, the Norse world dwindled into a sideshow. There were still distant fishing and whaling voyages, for example to Spitsbergen, but the basis for sustained long-range trade and territorial expansion was lacking. There were too few people, the climate and sailing conditions were · hostile in the high latitudes, and the Danish state (which ruled Norway and dominated Iceland) lacked both the resources and the will to pursue options. Instead, there were more promising opportunities for Denmark in Scandinavia, the Baltic and Germany, and this became more the case in the sixteenth century as the Reformation threw open the lands of the Baltic Crusading orders in the Eastern Baltic for conquest. The impact on Britain of Norse expansion was the knowledge of the fisheries off Iceland, which helped attract boats across that stretch of the North Atlantic in the late Middle Ages.

Maritime expansion was also important in the medieval Mediterranean, where it was crucial to the recapture of islands such as the Balearics, Sicily and Crete from Islamic control, and, from the late eleventh century, to the projection of Christian forces in the Crusades on a long, but ultimately unsuccessful, series of expeditions to Palestine and North Africa. Trade, naval power, territorial control and imperial rule were all linked most clearly in the position of both Venice and Genoa, each of which controlled a far-flung maritime empire, and Venice was to provide a model of maritime expansion (and political organisation) subsequently cited in England as an alternative to the territorial conquest associated with the Spanish trans-oceanic empire. As such, Venice and the United Provinces (the Dutch) offered a goal and means of empire that could be readily assimilated to important themes within English political culture in the seventeenth century, especially the quest for commercial profit and an anti-authoritarian ethos, at least in so far as royal power was concerned.

Northern European shipping played a role in the conflict with Islam, transporting Crusaders from Dartmouth to Lisbon in 1147 and on the

Third Crusade in 1190, and there were important economic links between northern Europe and the Mediterranean. However, this relationship was largely controlled by Italians, and the Mediterranean was not a sphere for northern European territorial expansion. Richard I, the 'Lion Heart' (r. 1189–99) might play a prominent martial role in the politics of Cyprus and Palestine, but it was shortlived, although the future Edward I also went Crusading to Palestine. French interest in the Mediterranean was more sustained, especially in the thirteenth century. Subsequently, the Aragonese spread their power across the Mediterranean. England did not really play a role there in the fourteenth and fifteenth centuries, except indirectly through the impact of wars between England and France: the Hundred Years' War.

The medieval interaction of naval power, trade and territorial control was also seen in the Baltic. In particular, it was linked to the eastward expansion of German power, a multifaceted process that included the subjugation of native peoples by German Crusading orders, the spread of Christianity and the development of a commercial world controlled by the Hanseatic cities and their shipping.

THE BRITISH LEGACY

The British Isles were not separate from this process of European maritime imperialism; indeed the very uncertainty of their political fate rested in part on the impact of this imperialism. The land-bridge that joined England to the Continent across the southern North Sea had been cut in about 6500 BCE, as the sea level rose with the melting of the ice at the close of the Ice Age. As an island group (albeit one in which most of the land is occupied by two large islands), the British Isles were linked by maritime routes, and it was through such routes that commercial, political and other links with the rest of Europe were developed. Thanks to these links, Britain had more in common with the rest of north-west Europe than did the latter with the remainder of Europe. There were similarities in terms of the peoples, demography, environment and technology, and local museums in Brittany, the Netherlands and Britain show immediately that the similarities of material culture were far more obvious than the differences. Indeed cycles of exchange helped link Europe's Atlantic coastlands.[2]

The history of the British Isles interacted with particular maritime routes, as links were created and sundered. Roman rule meant a focus on links across the Channel, as Britain was exposed to the naval strength of an imperial power able to afford maritime ambitions. Southern England was invaded by Julius Caesar in 55 and 54 BCE, and the Romans benefited from their opponents' inability to contest the passage of the Channel. This was also the case in 43 CE when the Emperor Claudius began what was to be the Roman conquest of England, Wales and southern Scotland; although not Highland Scotland or Ireland. In 83 or 84 CE the first circumnavigation of Britain was allegedly undertaken by the Roman fleet, and Roman naval activity was certainly important in the acquisition of geographical information about the British Isles, as well as in military operations.[3]

Britain's active role within the trading system of the Roman Empire, as an exporter of silver, lead, gold and iron, encouraged the development of a commercial infrastructure. The greater quantity of archaeological material from England in the Roman period than hitherto suggests a society that was producing and trading far more goods than its Iron Age predecessor, although the archaeological evidence is of greater value for some commodities than others. London developed as the major port, and, in the late Roman period, the use of vessels of up to 200 tons was common.

The end of Roman rule resulted from, and led to, a shift in the character and direction of Britain's maritime links, with the North Sea playing a more important role. Maritime attacks by Saxons from northern Germany and southern Scandinavia had led, by 270, to the construction by the Romans of a chain of forts from Brancaster, Norfolk to Portchester, Hampshire: a 'Saxon Shore' designed to protect vulnerable harbours and estuaries. Nevertheless, the combination of external attack and, more seriously, divisions within the Roman Empire led to the end of the latter in Britain in 409–10, and this was exploited by the Angles, Saxons and Jutes who crossed the North Sea and conquered most of England in the fifth to seventh centuries. There was also a new political world in what became Scotland as a result of the crossing of the North Channel by Scots from Ireland who settled in Argyll.

The subsequent coalescence of kingdoms in England and Scotland, however, owed little to maritime links. Instead, although they traded with the Mediterranean, a process that left a rich legacy in the ship burials of Sutton Hoo (c. 630) and Snape, these were kingdoms based on territorial control of land, while expansion was mostly across land frontiers. This was true of what became in the seventh century the three major kingdoms in England: Northumbria, Mercia and Wessex, although Northumbria also conquered the islands of Anglesey and Man. A small number of major ports – Ipswich, London, Southampton and York – nevertheless, developed spectacularly in the eighth century, as trade became more regular.

The impact of seaborne power was to be felt far more directly by the inhabitants of Britain owing to the attacks of the Vikings (Danes and Norwegians) from the late eighth century. Possibly with limited land available for colonisation in Scandinavia, they were motivated by opportunities for raiding and settlement in more prosperous and fertile lands that were vulnerable to the amphibious operations that the Norsemen could mount so well. Viking longboats, with their sails, stepped masts, true keels and steering rudders, although shallow and open, were effective ocean-going ships, able to take to the Atlantic, but also capable, thanks to their shallow draught, of being rowed in coastal waters and up rivers, even if there was only three feet of water. Thus, in Britain, the Vikings used island bases, such as the Isle of Sheppey, while in Ireland, where the wealthy monasteries attracted attack, the numerous rivers and lakes facilitated Viking movements.

The impact of the Vikings demonstrated the importance of the sea as a basis for political as well as economic links, and the British Isles in this period can be seen in part as an amalgam of regions centred on bodies of water: the English Channel, the Irish Sea and the North Sea. In turn, these maritime regions can be divided for purposes of study, especially the last: the southern North Sea was linked to the Channel and looked to the Low Countries, while the more open northern North Sea linked Britain and Scandinavia. To the west, the Irish Sea, a 'Celto-Norse lake' in the tenth century, became a basis for Norwegian hegemony in both political and economic spheres, while the attempt of the kings of York and Dublin to run a commercial and political empire from the mid-ninth to the mid-tenth century indicates the importance of the maritime dimension. To the north, the Norwegian Earls of Orkney ruled the Scottish mainland as far south as the River Oykell in Sutherland

Successful in England in the mid-ninth century against East Anglia, Yorkshire and Mercia, the Vikings were eventually stopped in 878 by King Alfred of Wessex (r. 871–99). This was a victory won on land at Edington, but Alfred subsequently created a navy so as to be able to challenge Viking control of the sea, although, owing to the nature of the sources, there is need for caution about his, and the navy's, role and impact.[4] This navy was apparently raised on a sophisticated system by which a large number of warships were provided on a quota basis.

Naval power played a role in the subsequent creation of the English state, as Alfred's successors, Edward the Elder (r. 899–924), Athelstan (r. 924–39) and Edmund (r. 939–46), drove back the Danes and Norwegians in the tenth century. The rulers of Wessex brought modern England under their authority, but their legitimacy rested in part on the notion of reconquest, which was especially appropriate in the sense that Christian territory was being regained. In 973, at Bath, Edgar was the first monarch to be crowned as King of the English; although earlier monarchs had used the title. The West Saxon rulers also laid claim to the overlordship of all Britain, and naval power enabled them to exercise a degree of hegemony over their British neighbours and to play a role in international relations. This power was not to be maintained by the Normans, and the proportion of national resources devoted to naval power was not to return to Anglo-Saxon levels until the reign of Elizabeth I (r. 1558–1603) or possibly the 1650s.[5]

FROM THE ELEVENTH TO THE FIFTEENTH CENTURIES

The sea again served as the basis for the subordination of much of Britain to foreign control during the Middle Ages. King Swein of Denmark led serious attacks in 1003–6 and 1013 and his son Cnut became King of England (r. 1016–35), while, after the death of Cnut's older brother, Harold, King of Denmark, in 1019, England became part of a Scandinavian multiple kingdom under Cnut. In modern geopolitical terms, this multi-national kingdom could be described as an empire, and an expanding one, although imperial institutions were not created. Cnut conquered Norway and, in 1031, advanced to the River Tay, receiving the submission of Malcolm II of Scotland.

The return of the house of Wessex to rule in England, in the person of Edward the Confessor (r. 1042–66), brought to a close England's part in a Scandinavian empire; as the home-grown character of English empire was revived. Under Edward, the royal titles of King of the English and of Britain were used indifferently, and, although Ireland was completely independent, Wales and Scotland were in part dependent. The power of the state was supported by naval strength, not least in successful operations in Wales and Scotland.[6]

Seaborne conquest was again at issue in 1066. The Scandinavian attempt, under King Harald Hardrada of Norway, to gain power was defeated at Stamford Bridge near York, but the Normans, under William the Conqueror, succeeded at Hastings. The hazards of attempts at seaborne conquest, even across the Channel, were seen in the temporary isolation of William's ship en route to Pevensey. Like Cnut, William seized a kingdom and a throne. He claimed to be Edward's rightful successor, replacing the usurper Harold, and may have initially not intended to introduce sweeping changes, but the scale of resistance to the consolidation of Norman rule led him to drive forward the process of Normanisation. Unlike Cnut's seizure, that by William was followed by a social revolution that stemmed from the impo-sition of a new and foreign ruling order, and this was a different form of empire to that of pretensions to overlordship.

In some respects, the Norman conquest of England provided one model for imperial expansion, and was indeed to be seen in this light during the heyday of British imperialism, although the concept of empire was one that was problematic as the position and pretensions of the Holy Roman Empire dominated the ideology and vocabulary of empire in Western and Central Europe, while those of Byzantium (the Eastern Roman Empire) had the same role further east.[7] As with the Norman conquests of Sicily from the Arabs, and of Apulia and Calabria in south Italy from the Byzantine Empire, in the late eleventh century a small group of invaders seized power in England, replacing the social elite. There was no mass displacement of the original population and much of the earlier administrative structure – Old English, Byzantine or Arab – continued, although it was now used for the benefit of new rulers.

In England, these rulers had a particular territorial problem, the defence of the Duchy of Normandy against its neighbours. This helped determine English territorial interests throughout the Middle Ages, and ensured that the composite state, of which England was a part, was concerned about land frontiers, however much maritime routes across the Channel were the crucial link within the state. The continuous military effort that war on the Continent entailed was also to be a central theme in domestic history, not least because it was instrumental in the development of English government.

War on the Continent also compromised attempts to spread the power of the Kings of England within the British Isles, attempts that illustrated the variety of motives for, and means of, imperial expansion. In Wales and Ireland, Anglo-Norman aristocrats pursued their own territorial interests, exploiting divisions between the local rulers and, in both cases, the English crown sought to impose its authority, although, in each case, its writ ran only in some areas. In Scotland, by contrast, English expansion was initiated by the monarch, in this case Edward I (r. 1272–1307), and this was symbolised when Edward adjudicated between the claimants to the Scottish throne and John Balliol, his choice, swore fealty and did homage.[8]

The hegemony of the King of England over the British Isles seemed established, but was rapidly rejected in Scotland and Edward and his successors proved unable to sustain control. Their failure, and that of English control in fourteenth-century Ireland, a commitment that also rested heavily on sea power, throws light on the limitations of imperial expansion. The Edwards relied in Scotland, and in most of Ireland, not on colonisation, but on collaboration, and it proved impossible to maintain the necessary level. Furthermore, military intervention faced formidable logistical problems. More seriously, from the late 1330s, Edward III (r. 1327–77) was most concerned about his ambitions in France; and the resulting commitment was also of great importance to his successors. Like earlier struggles with France, for example that during the reign of King John (1199–1216), this led to the build-up of naval strength. The sweeping victory over a French fleet at Sluys in 1340 was subsequently to be seen as a key date in the list of English naval triumphs. Naval strength enabled the English to mount sustained attempts at conquest in France, Henry V (r. 1413–22) building up a notable fleet based at Southampton.[9] Dramatic successes in France, especially on the battlefields of Crécy (1346), Poitiers (1356) and Agincourt (1415), were, however, followed by total failure, culminating in the loss of Normandy and Gascony to Charles VII of France in 1449–51 and in defeat at Castillon in 1453.

The complete failure of the attempt on the French throne was important to the development of English nationhood and government and provided a backdrop to trans-oceanic ambitions. The cross-border interests and nobility that had resulted from the Norman Conquest, and, subsequently, from England's place within the Plantagenet amalgamation of distinctive territories, had inhibited the political consequences of an increasingly apparent national consciousness, although the relationship was more complex because the war with France that stemmed from the links had also encouraged this consciousness – not least by leading to xenophobia, royal war-propaganda, military service (and also resistance to it), national taxation and the enhanced role of Parliament. As a result of the demands of war finance in the particular circumstances of English politics, the need for parliamentary consent for taxation was confirmed. These facets of the English state were eventually all to be important to British seaborne empire and also to contribute to its image.

English medieval overseas trade was focused on the export first of wool and then of cloth to nearby areas of Europe. The English had developed breeds of sheep with particularly good wool, much sought after by the cloth-manufacturing centres of Flanders, but, from the fourteenth century, the wool was increasingly exported in the form of cloth. Wool and cloth exports helped accentuate the relative wealth of south-eastern England, the role of shipping, and the importance of east-coast ports such as Great Yarmouth and Boston, which, until the close of the thirteenth century, exported more wool than any other port in England. Vital to government finances, these exports also helped to finance England's wars with France, and they continued after these wars had been lost. However, the strength of the economy rested on more than a desirable export sector. Agricultural development led to a major rise in the population in the thirteenth century, as well as in the percentage involved in industry and services, and, as society became more complex, there were increases in monetary transactions, the volume of the currency, economic diversification, the number of markets and towns, and trade, both domestic and foreign. Markets linked the localities into wider commercial networks, transmitting goods, demands, information and innovation,[10] and this system was to be important when the stimulus of trans-oceanic opportunities became available in the sixteenth century, as was the development of shipping and seamanship, in particular the marked rise, thanks to a major increase in overseas trade in the early decades of the sixteenth century, in native shipping.[11] There was money available for invest-ment, merchants seeking export markets and new sources for imports, and commercial networks that ensured that risks were worth taking and that opportunities could be turned into profit.

After 1453 the English Crown was shut out from the Continent. Although Calais, originally conquered by Edward III, was held until 1558, and the Channel Isles, the last of the Norman legacy, are still held by the Crown, France was lost: one of the crucial political legacies of the medieval period. This was not, however, a legacy that monarchs were keen to accept. The claim to the French throne was abandoned only in the reign of George III (1760–1820); and Edward IV in 1475, Henry VII in 1492 and Henry VIII campaigned there, the last waging a series of wars, the first in 1511–14, with conflict resuming in 1522 and the last, which started in 1544 finishing only in 1550, in the reign of Edward VI. However, these campaigns had no lasting success: the Norman duchy, the Angevin Empire and Lancastrian France had all gone, and the consolidation of France meant that these could not be revived. The more insular, and in some aspects even isolationist, character of England and its politics after 1453 was one of the keys to its subsequent domestic and international development, although a loss of Continental empire was not a necessary precondition for trans-oceanic expansion. Spain gained both an Italian and an American Empire in 1492–1559.

AN IMPERIAL REALM

During that time, the British polities – the Crowns of England and Scotland, and the semi-autonomous lords, both there and, more particularly, in Ireland – did not benefit from European expansion. Instead, this period was principally important for subsequent British imperialism because it wit-nessed the Protestant Reformation, which in England led to the assertion of an imperial theme for English monarchy as the authority of the papacy was challenged. Henry VIII's acquisition, as 'Supreme Head', of jurisdiction over the Church was accompanied by the statement that England was an empire, and thus jurisdictionally self-sufficient, with an imperial Crown allegedly descended from that of the Roman Emperor Constantine, a figure of great symbolic potency. A crucial piece of legislation, the Act in Restraint of Appeals [to Rome] of 1533, declared 'that this realm of England is an empire', and was the first claim of imperial status for the realm, rather than the Crown.[12]

Despite the fact that it was to be strongly contested, the Reformation (both in England and Scotland) was important to the process of national redefinition, and a major theme in English and, later, British discussion of the empire was to be its Protestant character; although the failure of the Reformation in Ireland helped ensure that it played a seriously divisive role there for the empire in the short and long terms, and eventually permanently. It was not only that the ruler of England was now head of the Church, but also that the Church was now depicted as representative of a chosen people with a sense of divine mandate, for Protestant England was seen as God's New Israel, a Protestant people and state, with all the possibilities that this entailed of defining purposes and identities separate to those of the rest of Christendom.

The Reformation helped ensure enmity between England (and later Britain) and the leading European imperial powers, because Spain, Portugal and France remained Catholic, and religious tensions became more serious owing to the Counter-Reformation of the late sixteenth and seventeenth centuries. This lent a religious dimension to imperial competition that was to be very important to the domestic understanding of empire, both then and subsequently, and also helped encourage the rethinking of territorial ambitions that was so important to England's changing role in the world. In turn, the nature of empire played a key role in domestic developments, although, for the sixteenth and early seventeenth centuries, this was largely a matter of omission: the English and Scottish monarchies had not gained great wealth as a result of European trans-oceanic expansion.

FACING THE ATLANTIC

The peoples of the British Isles were far less favourably situated for such activity than the Iberians. To sail west was to be exposed to prevailing westerlies in those latitudes, whereas, further south, the Iberians benefited greatly from supporting winds when they sailed to the Caribbean. As a result, the peoples of the British Isles had only limited experience of deep-sea navigation, and, in addition, they lacked the 'stepping stones' into the Atlantic provided to the Portuguese and Spaniards by the islands of the Azores, Madeira and the Canaries; as the Vikings had earlier with the islands of the Faeroes, Iceland and Greenland. There was also nothing comparable to the tradition of expansion at the expense of the heathen that the Portuguese and Spaniards had acquired from their long wars against the Muslims, and which they subsequently pursued first in the islands off the north-west coast of Africa, and then further afield, down the coast of Africa and then across the Atlantic and into the Indian Ocean.

Nevertheless, Britain's island character ensured that maritime traditions were well developed; aside from the importance of fishing[13] and foreign trade, the difficulties of land transport, not least the draught animals required to pull laden wagons, led to an emphasis on coastal transport, and this was accentuated by the lack of bridging points near estuaries, and by the role of ferries. For example, there was no road crossing of the River Tamar downriver of Gunnislake until the Tamar Bridge at Saltash was opened in 1961. River and sea systems, transport and commercial, were not separate but part of a shared maritime world,[14] and, because ships were small, seagoing vessels could go far inland, making towns distant from the sea, such as Bristol, Lincoln, Norwich and York, ports, while many harbours handled foreign trade; in contrast to the nineteenth century, when the greater size of merchantmen led to the concentration of long-distance trade on fewer harbours with the necessary facilities.

Inshore maritime experience was far more readily translated to deep-sea activities than is the case today, and by the late fifteenth century, over a hundred English boats per year were braving the Northern Atlantic, and round trips lasting six months, to sail to Iceland in order to fish or to buy cod. These voyages encouraged developments in English shipbuilding, and also led to greater knowledge of currents and winds in the North Atlantic, in particular of the brief season of easterlies from March to May, which permitted ships to sail to Iceland. This trade was dominated by Hull, East Anglia, especially King's Lynn, and Bristol, but with a role some years also for a range of other ports including Boston, Dartmouth, Grimsby, Newcastle and Scarborough. As was typical of much European expansion, violence was involved in this activity, not only the killing of fish, but also armed struggles with Hanseatic competition and with the Danish overlords of Iceland.[15]

The English also benefited from developments in shipping that helped them take part in trans-oceanic expansion, first across the Atlantic and eventually to southern Asia. Late fourteenth- and fifteenth-century improvements in ship construction and navigation included the fusion of Atlantic and Mediterranean techniques of hull construction and lateen- and square-rigging, the spread of the sternpost rudder and advances in location-finding at sea. The number of masts on large English ships rose from one to three in the fifteenth century, increasing the range of choices for rigging and providing a crucial margin of safety in the event of damage to one mast, while developments in rigging, including an increase in the number of sails per mast and the variety of sail shapes, permitted greater speed, a better ability to sail close to the wind and improved manoeuvrability, although the latter was limited by a difficulty in tacking close to the wind.[16]

Navigational expertise also increased. Thanks to the use of the magnetic compass, the spread from Mediterranean Europe of astrolabes, cross-staffs and quadrants, which made it possible to assess the angle in the sky of heavenly bodies, and other developments in navigation, such as the solution in 1484 to the problem of measuring latitude south of the Equator, it was possible to chart the sea and to assemble knowledge about it, and therefore to have greater understanding than before over the relationship between the enormity of the ocean and the transience of man. Control, however, would be an inappropriate term, given the vulnerability of ships and sailors, and the number of ships that were lost is a ready testimony to a range of problems that included inadequate pumps, weak anchors, vulnerable rudders and difficulties with seams and caulking, the last ensuring that ships were not reliably watertight.

In the last quarter of the fifteenth century, there were increasing signs of English participation in long-range naval activity. Edward IV (r. 1461–83) was interested in trade and shipping, encouraged the development of both and responded to merchants' requests by unsuccessfully pressing Pope Sixtus IV in 1481 to reject the Portuguese claim of a monopoly over the trade to West Africa. It is possible that Thomas Croft and others whom Edward licensed as traders the previous year may have sailed to North America, but the evidence is slim.[17] Fishing expeditions from Bristol may have reached Newfoundland's offshore Grand Banks, if not North America, in the 1480s or 1490s, but the first precise information relates to the Italian John Cabot, who sailed west from Bristol in the *Mathew* in 1497 hoping to reach the wealth of East Asia reported by Marco Polo and others, but arriving instead, probably, in Newfoundland, his 'new found land'. Cabot had been convinced that it would be easier to sail to Asia in higher latitudes, only to find not the prosperous and developed society he had sought, but, rather, plentiful cod. In 1498, Cabot set out on another voyage, again with backing from Henry VII (who regretted his failure to heed Columbus's request for support), but this time with five ships in order to enable him to trade on the Asian coastline he claimed to have discovered the previous year. Little is known of this expedition, from which only one heavily damaged ship returned, and it is possible that the rest of the fleet, including Cabot, fell victim to a savage storm.[18]

Other expeditions were mounted in 1501–5, in order both to explore and to trade. The first led to knowledge of parts of the North American coastline from Labrador probably to Cape Cod, but made it clear that China had not been reached. In 1508, Cabot's son Sebastian set out to find a passage to Asia around the new continent and may have reached Hudson Strait before wintering further south, possibly in Chesapeake Bay, and returning to find Henry VII dead, his pension (salary) revoked and Henry VIII uninterested in supporting trans-Atlantic voyages. Instead, Henry focused his glory on Continental power politics, with a strong additional interest in expanding his power and authority in Ireland and, in the 1540s, subjugating Scotland.

Nevertheless, by spreading knowledge of the Newfoundland fisheries, these voyages contributed to England's interest in the region and the route was soon followed by numerous English fishermen. The role and impact of the fishermen who sailed to Newfoundland has not received adequate attention in general surveys of the development of empire,[19] but, building on the methods of the Icelandic fishery, which continued strong into the seventeenth century, the Newfoundland fisheries eventually led large numbers of ships and men to cross the Atlantic and return each year, and this resulted in two important foundations for future activity: first, knowledge about Atlantic navigation, specifically the currents, winds and coastlines of the North Atlantic, and, second, a sense that sailing across the Atlantic was normal. The Portuguese, French and Basques were initially most active in the Newfoundland fisheries, but the English came to play a more prominent role from the 1570s, and, by the end of the century, several hundred English ships were sailing there each year. The conflict between England and Philip II of Spain (from 1580 also Philip I of Portugal) was also played out in these distant waters, with the English and French winning.

Cod was the principal target, and was brought back in sufficient quantities to undermine the North Sea and Icelandic cod fisheries, although the movement of fish shoals may also have played a role. The Newfoundland fisheries involved not only fishing but also activity on land, especially the salting and drying necessary to preserve the catch, activities that led to the development of a coastal infrastructure, with wharves, washing cages, drying platforms and oil vats for the cod liver oil.[20] Salting and drying also increased the labour demand of the fishery and as this could not rely on the Beothuk Natives, who were few in number and in competition with the Europeans for the fish, there was a reliance on labour from south-west England. This helped spread the impact of maritime activity, because, aside from experienced or 'specialised' fishermen, there was also a tapping of the general labour market that took advantage of the widespread need for money and of the extent to which fishing was also part of a less specialised labour world. Thus, farmers and tradesmen turned to the sea in order to supplement their income, and the Newfoundland fisheries helped to introduce the seasonal migration of labour that was so important to English labour and to the trans-oceanic world, although the lengths of the voyages ensured that the ships and seamen were less available for other activities than was generally the case with fishing. The labour needs of the fisheries and the length of the voyages also increased the requirement for capital.

With time, the fisheries became more complex, as sources for fish and technical and market possibilities were probed and investment was directed to what was proving an important source of profit. Initially, boats sailed from England, moored in harbours and then sent out shallops (25- to 30-foot

boats that had been transported in sections) to fish, while, once caught, the
cod was salted lightly, washed and dried. Some ships, however, came to sail
to the offshore banks where they preserved the cod in the hold by heavily
salting it, the 'wet' or 'green' fishery which led to a more perishable product,
but required less labour. The need for salt, which was obtained from Iberia
or the Mediterranean, increased the diverse sailing patterns that the fisheries
gave rise to, as well as underlining the capital needs of the industry. These
capital needs extended the impact of the fisheries within Britain, and,
although boats and men came often from small ports, merchants in larger
ones, especially, increasingly, London, were important in financing and marketing the trade. This was to look towards a degree of specialisation by the
late seventeenth century, with the use then of bigger ships based in a smaller
number of large ports. The fish trade was not simply bilateral, as, benefiting greatly from the injunctions on Catholics not to eat meat on Fridays
and in particular seasons, fish was exported also to Spain, Portugal and Italy,[21]
playing an important role in English trade.

Fishing was associated with national strength, and encouraged to that
end. Fish days were extended in England as part of an attempt to use legislation to strengthen naval capacity: in 1563, Wednesday fish days were added
to existing Fridays and Saturdays. The Act also contained other measures
designed to encourage the fish industry, for example a ban on tolls for
landing fish.[22] With their deep-sea range, the Newfoundland fisheries were
seen as particularly important to the strategic strength of the country, as a
'nursery' of sailors,[23] for war and peace, while the fish caught provided food
not only for the fishermen but also for the navy. Although largely separate
from subsequent patterns of Atlantic trade, the Newfoundland fisheries
helped establish methods of organisation, particularly capital support, that
were to be important to other trades.

Despite the fishing wealth of Newfoundland's waters, John Cabot's
voyages were very much on the margins of profitable activity. Not only did
English expeditions fail to discover a direct route across the Atlantic to
'Cathay' (China) or, subsequently, a north-west or a north-east passage – a
route to the wealth of East Asia round North America or North Asia;
they also missed out on the compensation of American bullion that was to
bring such wealth to the Crown of Spain and to help finance its policies
in Europe. In addition, English commercial penetration of the Indian Ocean
began only after the Portuguese were well established there. Thus, the British
monarchies (England and Scotland) failed to gain an infusion of trans-
oceanic wealth, especially American bullion, except vicariously through
English attacks on Spanish settlements and trade, and the latter helped ensure
that violence became important to the character of English trans-oceanic
enterprise.

The potential domestic consequences of such an infusion are suggested by Portugal, where the later discovery of gold in Minas Gerias, part of Portuguese Brazil, ensured that there was no need for the Crown to call the Cortes between 1698 and 1820. Indeed, the possible impact on British governmental independence and policy of trans-oceanic wealth, in the shape of revenues from India, was to be stressed in the late eighteenth century by critics of measures to increase ministerial control of the East India Company, such as Charles James Fox's India Bill of 1783.

THE DEVELOPMENT OF A NAVY

Naval strength entailed a commitment of resources that was often greater than that required for warfare on land, in part because the wooden warship equipped with cannon was the single most costly, powerful and technologically advanced weapons system of the period. Warships provided effective mobile artillery platforms that lacked an equivalent on land, and an individual vessel might carry a heavy firepower capacity comparable with that of an entire army. The introduction of large numbers of cannon on individual ships made maritime technology more complex and increased the operational and fighting demands on crews, while the construction, equipment, manning, supply and maintenance of a fleet required considerable financial and logistical efforts.[24] The construction of large warships using largely unmechanised processes was an immense task that required large quantities of wood and formidable capital investment, but ships generally had a life of only 20 to 30 years. Maintenance was also expensive, as wood and canvas rotted and iron corroded, so that warships demanded not only, by the standards of the day, technologically advanced yards for their construction, but also permanent institutions to manage them. Indeed, the construction and logistical infrastructure of a fleet constituted the most impressive industrial activity of the sixteenth century, with a requirement for a commensurate administrative effort to support it and a dependence on skilled labour.

Naval requirements changed with developments in warships as well as new demands upon naval power, not least the capacity to engage in distant operations. Balancing speed, armament types and numbers, sea-keeping quality, optimum size of crew, draught and cargo capacity (even for warships), involved difficult choices, not least with reference to the anticipated form of conflict. In the medieval period, it had been common to grapple and board rival warships, and boarding was not suddenly replaced by firepower, as the capture of prizes was an important goal. Even during the Armada engagements, there was a determination by the English to capture vessels, and the rich booty from the *Rosario* demonstrated why. Equally, the Spaniards tried hard to capture the *Revenge* off the Azores in 1591 by boarding her. Instead of a sudden replacement in tactics, there was a long transition during which boarding followed a missile exchange, now conducted by gunpowder weaponry that involved different fighting requirements. Furthermore, a growing emphasis on cannon and their capability for ship destruction had implications for construction, armament, supply and tactics. Heavy guns were carried by English warships from the early 1510s. Carvel building (the edge-forming of hull planks over frames), which spread from the Mediterranean to the Atlantic and Baltic from the late fifteenth century, replaced the clinker system of shipbuilding using overlapping planks, contributing significantly to the development of hulls that were stronger, larger and better able to carry heavy guns.[25] The development of Henry VIII's fleet was in part a response to the building of warships by France and Scotland, and, in 1513, French galleys carrying cannon showed their ship-killing capability at the expense of the English fleet off Brest.

The rising importance of firepower led to a shift towards stand-off tactics in which ships did not come into direct contact and boarding became impossible. The Portuguese were the first systematically to exploit heavy cannon to fight stand-off actions against superior enemies, a development often incorrectly claimed for the English at the time of the Spanish Armada (1588). The shift towards stand-off tactics can be seen by contrasting the Anglo-French war of 1511–14, in which the fleets fought in the Channel in the traditional way and the major clash off Brest in 1513 involved grappling and boarding,[26] with the gunnery duel in which they engaged off Portsmouth in 1545. This shift had important implications for naval battle tactics (although truly effective ways of deploying naval firepower were not found until the seventeenth century), and it further encouraged the development of warships primarily as artillery platforms.

A revolution in naval warfare centred on the development of the more powerful 'ship-killing' warships has been discerned.[27] It is unclear, however, whether the focus should be on shipping or weaponry, and it is also necessary to note the importance of earlier, fifteenth-century developments, especially the successive shifts in gunpowder weaponry on board ship and their initial use as anti-personnel weapons.[28] The manufacture of large cast-iron weapons was initially beyond the technological scope of the period, but, from the mid-fifteenth century, firepower was increased with the development of large cannon cast from lighter, more durable and workable 'brass', which was actually bronze, an alloy of copper and tin. They were thick enough to withstand the high pressure from large powder charges and able to fire iron shot with a high muzzle velocity and great penetrative force. The stone shot used in early cannon was phased out. From the 1540s, cast-iron cannon were produced in England, but, though inexpensive, they could burst when overheated through rapid firing, and a list of the cannon on English warships at sea in 1595 revealed that 80 per cent were bronze and only 20 per cent cast iron.[29]

English naval development continued to owe much to competition with France, with which conflict was frequent from the 1540s to the 1560s, while, subsequently, the threat from Spain dominated attention. Like Francis I of France and James IV of Scotland, Henry VIII (r. 1509–47) had built large warships, such as the *Henry Grace à Dieu* (*Great Harry*), which had a 1514 specification of 186 guns, but these were as much statements of royal power, even fashion, as functional warships. However, in the 1570s, the English constructed purpose-built warships along new technological lines. Essentially for the defensive task of dominating the English Channel, they were hired out by Elizabeth I for commerce raiding on an *ad hoc* basis. These warships, like the merchantmen that were being built in increasing numbers from the 1570s, were smaller than some of the very large ships constructed under Henry VIII, bringing advantages in terms of enhanced manoeuvrability, the ability to enter more anchorages and the spread of risk.[30]

THE BRITISH ISLES AND THE IMPERIAL QUEST

Naval power was also important to the attempts by the English Crown to enforce imperial pretensions in the British Isles. It was significant in operations against Scotland, especially during the reign of Edward VI (1547–53), taking a tactical role in providing firepower at the Battle of Pinkie (1547) and, more generally, enhancing English operational capability by providing power projection and logistical support and attempting blockade and commerce raiding along Scotland's coasts, even in winter weather. After war with Scotland ended, Edward's government maintained the navy, an important continuity of strength in peacetime. Subsequently, an English fleet played a crucial part in 1560 in the defeat of the French attempt to suppress the Protestant Lords of Congregation who had rebelled against Mary Queen of Scots, then also, as wife of Francis II, Queen of France. The English under William Winter cut links across the Firth of Forth, before successfully blockading Leith. The English land assault on Leith failed, but the naval blockade led the French to negotiate the withdrawal of their force.[31]

Naval strength and maritime capability were also central to the English ability to operate across the Irish Sea, the most important area of English imperial expansion during the sixteenth century. Henry VIII had sought to maintain his father's policy of increasing Tudor control in Ireland without launching major initiatives, but the Reformation altered the situation. In

1534, Thomas, Earl of Kildare rebelled, offering the overlordship of Ireland
to the Pope or the Emperor Charles v, in place of the schismatic Henry,
only to be defeated. Henry was declared 'Supreme Head' of the Irish
Church, and exchanged the title of Lord of Ireland for King, while Gaelic
nobles were offered English law and charters for their lands, an attempt to
incorporate them peacefully into the structure of governmental control.
Such a conciliatory policy was to be abandoned after Henry's death, but it
already faced formidable difficulties given the precarious nature of royal
control over much of the island.

Under his successors, this policy was replaced by that of the 'plantation'
of areas with English settlers. This increased the security of the Crown's
position, but the expropriation of Gaelic landowners heightened its
unpopularity. From the late 1560s, English rule in Ireland became increasingly military in character and intention, leading to fresh attempts to extend
and enforce control, at the expense of Gaelic Irish opposition but also with
little support from the Anglo-Irish. Authority, albeit with considerable
difficulty, was nevertheless extended into outlying areas, such as Sligo,
Fermanagh and Monaghan. This was not, however, a conducive environment for the expansion of Protestantism, and, as Catholic energies were
revived by the Counter-Reformation, religious differences became a more
important feature of the situation, symbolising, reflecting and strengthening
a political rift, and the hatred felt, between what were increasingly seen
as conquerors and a subject population. In the long-term, this was to undermine imperial rule in Ireland, while, in the short and medium term, religious tension helped give it much of its character, not least a frequently
embattled sense of identity,[32] and this was important because policies and
habits of authority developed there were to be used in more distant English
(later British) imperialism, while the Protestant aristocracy and gentry established there were to play a disproportionately large role in imperial rule.[33]

Irish resistance in the late sixteenth century culminated in a major rising,
finally suppressed in 1603, in which English naval power lessened the ability
of Spain to intervene on behalf of the Irish and was crucial to English
logistics and operational capability. Conflict in Ireland, however, also showed
the difficulties of operating against a different naval system, in this case the
shallow-draught Viking-style longships of the Western Islemen, notably the
MacDonalds, which were employed to transport mercenary redshanks from
the Isles into Ulster, using Lough Foyle as their landing area in pursuit of
an attempt to create a viable position outside the control of the Crowns of
Scotland and England.[34] Attempts by English sailing warships to intercept
the fleets were unsuccessful, as were those to penetrate into the lochs of the
Mull of Kintyre to attack the vessels at source, and only the occupation of
Lough Foyle by the English finally solved the problem. The navy played a

more successful and important strategic role in the successful campaign against Spanish and Irish forces at Kinsale in 1601, blockading the Spanish garrison in Kinsale.

For the first time, the entire island had been conquered, and this was followed by the imposition of English law and custom in Ulster and by the confiscation of much of it. Whereas, in the sixteenth century, owing to the costs of conflict and expenditure, Ireland was a cause of expenditure, rather than profit, for the Crown, in the early seventeenth century, there were significant gains. However, little of the benefit went to the Crown: the gains were principally in the form of land, and, as also later with imperial settlement policies, that had to be made attractive to settlers. Some of the less fertile portion of Ulster was granted to the native Irish, but the rest was allocated to English and Scottish settlers, Crown officials, the established (Protestant) Church and, in return for financial support for the plantation, the City of London, the financial resources, enterprising energy and political connections of which were to be crucial to much of the dynamic of empire. Large portions of Antrim and Down in Ulster were granted as private plantations and settled largely by Scots, for whom Ireland was more important as a sphere for expansion than it had been in the sixteenth century, so by 1618, there were about 40,000 Scots in Ulster. Other plantations were established further south, in, for example, Wexford, Leitrim, Westmeath and Longford. Across much of Ireland, therefore, the British Empire became a matter of the dispossession of native landowners, while, in Ulster, the native population as a whole saw their position deteriorate as large numbers of Protestants were settled.[35] Expansion in Ireland was an important background to trans-oceanic colonisation, helping to mould attitudes towards territorial control and non-Protestants; and, in some cases, similar groups were involved in sponsoring activity.

TENSION WITH SPAIN

The English conquest of Ireland was also a defeat for Spain, part of a struggle that, at times, spanned the oceans. Alliance with Spain and Portugal earlier in the century, which culminated in the marriage, in 1554, of Queen Mary of England (r. 1553–8) to Philip II of Spain, had tempered government support for trans-oceanic expansion, although this was not its sole effect on England's overseas position. The marriage led, in 1557, to England's participating in Philip's war with France. The following year, at Gravelines, English warships under Captain John Malen helped the Spaniards defeat the French. However, in January 1558, French forces had bombarded Calais, England's last foothold on mainland France, into surrender.[36]

Irrespective of England's diplomatic position, there was growing interest in distant prospects, and clashes occurred in the 1550s and 1560s, as merchants unsuccessfully attempted to break into Portugal's trade with West Africa. Naval officers invested in the West African voyages dispatched in 1562 and 1563 and the merchants involved probably hired the warships that helped provide protection.[37] This is a reminder of the need not to separate public and private, official and unofficial, too clearly in accounts of empire. Similarly, in 1562–3, when Ambrose, Earl of Warwick, Governor of Le Havre, then under English occupation, had granted letters of marque to privateers, the sailors of the West Country were only too willing to take them up. This relationship between public and private was important to English transoceanic activity, as an unwillingness by the Crown to confront directly the imperial interests of Portugal and Spain encouraged a reliance on unofficial or semi-official action such as privateering.

In the 1560s, the attempt to take a share in the profitable slave trade between Africa and the Spanish New World was an important aspect of a search for overseas opportunities that in part reflected difficulties with trade to the Low Countries and in which trade with West Africa and the search for bullion took precedence over interest in settlement in the New World. The prime area of competition over Spanish claims in North America occurred in Florida, but the principals were France and Spain, and, although an English expedition there was mounted in 1565, the inability to find gold led to a failure to establish a settlement. Again no fort was built in West Africa, where most English voyages in this period were for pepper, hides, wax, ivory and in search of gold, rather than for slaves. Nevertheless, John Hawkins sold slaves to the Spanish West Indies until, at San Juan de Ulúa (near Vera Cruz in modern Mexico), in 1568, the presence of the Viceroy of New Spain led to a Spanish attack on what was, in the official view, an unwelcome interloper, helping ensure that the venture made a large loss.

English trade with West Africa did not focus on the slave trade until the mid-seventeenth century, and, instead, the range of commodities sought indicated the varied search for opportunities that was so important to the quest for profit, and that reflected the absence of specialisation in trade. The goods imported were in part designed to contribute to English industry: the cloth industry, the most important in England, benefited from gum Arabic, used for sizing cloth, and, from the 1600s, redwood, employed for dyeing it. Such imports contributed to the diversity of commercial links with the outer world, the growing interdependence that trade brought, and the proportion of the population affected, at least indirectly, by trans-oceanic activity.

Privateering also led the Scots and English to more distant waters. As associates of the French, Scottish ships had taken part in attacks on the

Spanish New World from at least 1547, while privateering voyages led the
English into waters that were new to them, including, in 1555, the earliest
recorded occasion of an English voyage into the southern hemisphere. In
turn, mercantile horizons expanded.

As tension between England and Spain rose in the 1570s, privateering
attacks on Spanish trade and settlements in the New World became more
common,[38] while greater lawlessness at sea affected those who tried to maintain a peaceful trade. William Winter raided the Spanish base in Florida at
St. Augustine in 1571, while Francis Drake attacked the Spanish silver route
across the Panama isthmus in 1571–3, although he encountered serious
difficulties, including yellow fever and a stronger resistance than had been
anticipated. In 1576, his former companion John Oxenham was defeated
when he sought to capture Panama. At this stage, however, as England
and Spain were not at war, Elizabeth I (r. 1558–1603) was hesitant about
overly offending Spain, especially as relations improved in the mid-1570s.
For example, Sir Richard Grenville's attempt to mount an expedition
in 1574–5, probably in order to establish a colony in the southern reaches
of South America, was unwelcome to the government, while, although
Elizabeth invested in Drake's 1577 voyage to the Pacific, he was not given
a formal commission.

In 1577–80, Drake became the first Englishman to circumnavigate the
world, a formidable feat of seamanship that included only the second passage
of the Straits of Magellan, and one that yielded an excellent return to the
investors, particularly for Elizabeth. Spanish shipping and positions in the
Pacific were not expecting attack, and Drake made a number of profitable
seizures. He fulfilled his goal of plunder, but did not further the cause of
English settlement, although he sailed up the Californian coast and claimed
it as 'Nova Albion' for Elizabeth. In April 1581, she knighted him on board
his ship, the *Golden Hind*, at Deptford, an important display of approval,[39]
and one that was subsequently to be seen as an important symbolic moment
in English imperialism, one that linked personal heroism, enterprise and
bellicosity with monarchy and Protestantism.

WAR WITH SPAIN, 1585–1604

Drake played a major role in the war with Spain that broke out in 1585 as
English support for the Dutch Protestant rebels against Philip II increased
the tension between the two powers, much of which derived from attacks
on Spain's position in the New World. This conflict, which lasted until 1604,
brought only limited success for England, although the Dutch secured their
independence, and this major defeat for Spain made it a less potent threat

to England; at the same time, however, creating a new competitor in the form of the Dutch. In the New World, the sacking of Spanish settlements, most spectacularly Santo Domingo, Cartagena and St. Augustine by Drake in 1585, yielded only transient gains and was increasingly thwarted by the strength of Spain's imperial defences; although these attacks increased collective experience of long-distance operations, and also helped create an enticing image of national interest and heroism. Drake was certainly ambitious not only for short-term profit but also for the seizure of imperial bases: both Havana and Panama.[40] Drake was long a lodestar of English manliness, and *Under Drake's Flag* (1883) was to be the title of one of George Alfred Henty's popular adventure stories for boys. 'Drake's Drum' was the most popular work in *Admirals All and Other Verses* (1897), Henry Newbolt's highly patriotic and very successful collection of verse. Including the promise of timeless success 'If the Dons sight Devon, I'll quit the port o'Heaven,/An' drum them up the Channel as we drummed them long ago', 'Drake's Drum' was subsequently set to music by Charles Stanford in *Songs of the Sea*.

The most important Elizabethan naval success was defensive – the defeat of the Spanish Armada. Spain now had an enemy that could be attacked decisively only by sea, but Philip II's attempt at a large-scale invasion of England was delayed by the immensity of the necessary preparations, and postponed because, in 1587, Drake successfully attacked the Spanish base at Cadiz. The following year, the Armada proceeded up the Channel to Calais, harried by long-range English naval gunnery, which did little damage and did not break the tight Spanish formation. With the advantage of superior sailing qualities and compact four-wheeled gun-carriages (many of the Spanish guns were on cumbersome carriages designed for use on land), which allowed a high rate of fire, the English fleet suffered even slighter damage, although it was threatened by a shortage of ammunition. The Armada was designed to cover an invasion from the Spanish Netherlands by the Spanish Army of Flanders, which was commanded by the Duke of Parma, but the details of how the two elements were to co-operate had not been adequately worked out and Philip had underestimated the difficulties facing Parma, who could not leave port until after the English and Dutch blockading squadrons had been defeated. Instead, the Spanish fleet was disrupted off Calais by an English night attack using fireships, and the English fleet then inflicted considerable damage in a running battle off Gravelines, in which the brunt of the battle was borne by the galleons of the Portuguese navy in Spanish service, which were experienced in stand-off gunnery. A strong south-westerly wind, seen as a 'Protestant wind', drove the Armada into the North Sea, and, with no clear objective after Parma's failed embarkation, the Spanish fleet returned home round Scotland and

Ireland, losing many ships to unseasonably violent storms that drove vessels onto the rocky coasts.[41]

An attack on Lisbon in 1589, seen as a counter-strike to the Armada, failed, however, in large part owing to a lack of surprise that stemmed from the problem of multiple aims and objectives. It is worth discussing, still, as a reminder of the extent to which English maritime activity and force projection were not a simple story of heroic success. Funded as a joint stock enterprise, in part because expenditure on the fleet in 1588 had resulted in shortages of money, Elizabeth's aims, to destroy the remnants of the Spanish fleet, were at variance with those of the force commanders, Drake and Sir John Norris, while the presence of the Portuguese pretender Dom Antonio offered the prospect of driving Philip II from Portugal and gaining commercial access to Lisbon, and through it to Portugal's trans-oceanic trading networks, which led to substantial funding put up by London merchants. The result was the worst possible compromise. An attack on Corunna, in deference to Elizabeth's instructions, destroyed three Armada survivors, but this gave away the essential element of surprise while failing to satisfy Elizabeth's minimum goal, which would have required attacks on the ships sheltering in Santander and San Sebastian, ports deeper into the Bay of Biscay. The English force then made a successful landing at Peniche about 50 miles from Lisbon, only to find that hopes that the countryside would rise in support of Dom Antonio proved unfounded, while the landing gave away the tactical initiative to the Spaniards. As Norris and the army trekked across the broken country to Lisbon, losing men all the time to heat exhaustion, Drake sailed to the Tagus narrows but failed to force the forts guarding the entrance to Lisbon.

The problem of multiple aims and objectives was that ultimately nothing of substance was achieved. The Armada survivors were refitted and formed the basis of a revived Spanish fleet; the English expeditionary force was decimated by disease; the nascent Portuguese resistance was crushed; the operation failed to cover its cost; and Drake and Norris lost their reputations and the favour of the Queen. The expedition probably offered the best strategic opportunity of the entire war with Spain, but lack of vision or conviction on the part of Elizabeth limited its potential for success, and lack of conviction on the part of the commanders squandered the opportunities that a large force with surprise on its side could have achieved. Had Lisbon been taken, it might have been possible to derive strategic benefit, in terms of overturning Philip's position in Portugal.

Nevertheless, building on a military tradition that had developed steadily throughout the century, the English acquired considerable expertise in maritime expeditionary warfare during the war with Spain, and the threat of another Armada led to a pre-emptive strike being launched against

Cadiz in 1596 by a large Anglo-Dutch amphibious force in one of the most impressive operations of the era. The attackers were fortunate: not only was the Spanish fleet dispersed by storms, but they gained surprise, helping them to fight their way into a defended anchorage under the guns of the city defences and to carry out a successful opposed landing, followed by the storming of the city walls. The concentration on the landing, nevertheless, allowed a fleet of merchant vessels sheltering in the inner harbour to be burnt by the Spaniards, with the loss of much valuable booty for the expeditionary force. The loot from the city was still immense, but the commanders failed to control their troops and Elizabeth did not obtain her share of the proceeds.

Lengthy sea lines of communication, however, helped ensure that it was impossible to turn this victory to strategic advantage. Neither the Earl of Essex at Cadiz nor Henry, 3rd Earl of Cumberland at San Juan, Puerto Rico in 1598 could sustain a garrison in the cities they had captured: it was beyond the capability of sixteenth-century logistics, and therefore the overall result was minimal, and degenerated into acrimonious arguments with Elizabeth over the division of the booty. As with the successful attack on Corunna in 1589, such amphibious operations led to no permanent gain, and there was no establishment of any equivalent to the Portuguese bases in Africa or the Indian Ocean, or to the earlier English position at Calais; nor was any attempted.

The English naval effort was an uneasy co-operation between government and private maritime interests, which worked effectively against the Armada in 1588 but less so in offensive operations when disparate goals became more apparent, as in the Lisbon operation of 1589. Elizabeth backed a major shipbuilding programme after the defeat of the Armada which led to an increase in the size of the royal fleet, but she continued to try to make the maritime war pay for itself. Improved Spanish fortress defences and a fleet of purpose-built warships meant, however, that the English failed to intercept the *flota* (the treasure fleet), although they came close to it on several occasions, in the process capturing the East Indiaman, the *Madre de Dios*, but losing the *Revenge*. In the West Indies, an attempt by Drake and Hawkins at the head of a fleet of 27 ships to seize a major position, San Juan, Puerto Rico, was thwarted in November 1595 by a lack of surprise and the improved naval and fortress defences. Hawkins died at sea in November, while Drake, whose expedition had failed to take over the Panama isthmus, died of dysentery the following January, although Cumberland, using an indirect approach, did manage to capture San Juan in 1598, when he attacked the landward approaches to the city.[42]

Elizabeth's encouragement of privateering was, in part, a product of the weakness of the state and the need to tap any military resources that might

be available, even at the cost of very limited control. Nevertheless, the ability
to draw on privateers, which reflected a more general mingling of public
and private naval warfare, was an important aspect of English naval capability, providing both tactical expertise and an indispensable pool of highly
capable leaders and battle-trained seamen; the Spaniards had no equivalent
source of manpower to draw on. Moreover, building on 'a long tradition of
war and trade by sea', the creation of large fleets using partnership arrangements with commercial and investment interests, and the use of maritime
capability by state-sponsored piracy showed a degree of organisational flexibility that also helped ensure that there was a very diverse naval heritage.[43]
Prize goods provided a crucial source of capital for ports such as
Barnstaple, and much of it was invested in new shipping, particularly in large
ships capable of long-distance voyages. The resulting demand for mature
timber, for both warships and merchantmen, helped spread on land the
impact of naval warfare and trade. This demand led also to a concern about
timber supplies, and the state of English forestry was to be a longlasting
theme of discussion.

Although co-operation with private maritime interests was important, it
is also appropriate to emphasise the extent to which the navy had become
stronger during the century, as well as the achievement of sustaining it
during the long war with Spain from 1585 to 1604, much of which was a
period of fiscal crisis. The defeat of the Armada underlined the growing
technical skill of English seamanship and naval warfare, including the
advanced state of English gunnery. At the time of her death in 1603,
Elizabeth owned between 40 and 45 ships, most of them in a good condition, and, aside from the *Revenge*, only a few small ships had been lost in
action.[44]

British naval strength came almost entirely from the English, and
the Scots were not involved in the war with Spain. Although James IV
(r. 1488–1513) had built up a strong navy, the conflicts of the 1540s to
1560s, both with England and civil wars, had led to the disappearance of
the Scottish fleet and the country lacked the maritime strength to provide
a substitute from privateers and other parts of the world of commerce.

THE SEA ROUTE TO THE INDIAN OCEAN

England's war with Spain helped open the sea route to South Asia, while,
in turn, the search for profit encouraged the establishment of links with
distant markets; in this, trade with the Indian Ocean mirrored the attempt
to develop links with West Africa and the Mediterranean which led, in the
latter case, to the establishment of the Turkey Company in 1581, renamed

the Levant Company in 1592.[45] The first English ships in the Indian Ocean arrived in 1591, and the *Edward Bonaventure*, captained by James Lancaster, captured three Portuguese ships in 1592 (from 1580 to 1640 the King of Spain was also King of Portugal). Lancaster went on to command a fleet that seized the Portuguese base of Pernambuco in Brazil with great booty in 1595 and the first fleet of the East India Company. The basis of England's, and later Britain's, Asian empire, in 1600 this Company was granted a royal charter to trade with South and South-East Asia and the East Indies, principally to obtain spices. The Company was a chartered monopoly that used the joint stock method to spread the considerable risks of long-distance trade among a number of investors, and thus drew on the wealthy mercantile world of London, already a financial centre of European importance by the 1550s,[46] the commercial entrepôt between England and the wider world, and the source of the crucial investment required for long-distance enterprise. The initial stock was £30,000, but the 101 investors were confident that they could profit from a monopoly in trade between England and South Asia. The recent successes of Dutch traders demonstrated that it had become possible and profitable to challenge the Portuguese monopoly on the sea route to the East Indies, and thus to avoid the dependence on intermediaries experienced by those who had traded overland via Russia or the Ottoman (Turkish) Empire,[47] both routes that the English were developing. Merchants from the Levant Company provided much of the leadership and capital for the East India Company. The first voyage organised by the Company, four ships led by Lancaster, sailed in 1601, returning in 1603 with pepper purchased from Aceh in Sumatra and Bantam in Java. From 1607, ships were also sent to Surat in India; the first, the *Hector*, arrived there in 1608. Five years later, the Mughal Emperor, Jahangir, granted the Company the right to trade there.

Trade with South Asia challenged Portugal's control of much of India's trade with Europe, and in this case, as in others, trade was not readily separable from force; indeed each, in part, was an application of the other, understandably for the English throughout the sixteenth century, as merchants coming late into a trans-oceanic world already dominated by others sought to carve out a niche. The emphasis on force, specifically on privateering, was not readily compatible with the agriculture necessary if colonisation was to be sustained, but this was not a prime goal beyond Ireland, and only very limited numbers of settlers were available for North America in the sixteenth century. Force had also been crucial to the establishment of empires by Portugal and Spain. The relationship between English trade and force was not restricted to the struggle with Spain: for example, the rapid development of successful Dutch and English armed merchantmen for trade in dangerous areas, especially the Mediterranean and the East Indies, was closely connected with the spread of cheap, small and medium cast-iron guns. English and Dutch success at sea enabled both powers to take a leading position in trade, much of it armed, between northern and southern Europe. The expansion in this and other trades also helped finance an important expansion in shipbuilding.

COLONISATION IN NORTH AMERICA

There was considerable interest in developing new trade routes through exploration, although the search for a north-east passage to the riches of the East Indies delayed the quest for the north-west passage. Sir Hugh Willoughby died in 1552 on the coast of Lapland, but Richard Chancellor reached the White Sea, before travelling to Moscow, opening up a tenuous trade route. This was explored further by Anthony Jenkinson in 1558–62 when he travelled thence to Central Asia and to Persia on behalf of the Muscovy Company, established in 1555, which developed economic links with Russia but not a territorial position.[48] The Siberian coast and the nearby Arctic islands were not a promising destination for the establishment of bases nor for colonisation, and, instead, furs were to be obtained from trading with the Russians.

From 1576, explorers again probed icy seas to the north-west of Newfoundland in pursuit of what was hoped would be the tremendous commercial opportunity of a north-west passage. Martin Frobisher, John Davis and Henry Hudson entered major bodies of water – Baffin Bay and Hudson Bay – and, in 1576, Frobisher found what he called Frobisher Strait, which he saw as the opening to the route to 'the West Sea' and 'Cathay' (China); in fact, he had found a bay on the coast of Baffin Island, now named Frobisher Bay. Frobisher also thought he had discovered a gold-bearing ore, and this was the focus of expeditions in 1577 and 1578, in the second of which he entered Hudson Strait. The ore was mined and a large quantity was brought back, but it was discovered to be iron pyrites (fool's gold), and this collapse led to the failure of the Company of Cathay which had provided the finance for the expeditions.[49] John Davis found Cumberland Sound in 1585 and Davis Strait in 1587, while Henry Hudson wintered in Hudson Bay in 1611–12 before being cast adrift by his mutinous crew the following June. In the 1610s, Thomas Button and William Baffin, and, in the 1630s, Luke Foxe and Thomas James, established that the passages that had been discovered led to further shores, not open ocean, but these voyages accumulated valuable information that was to be used by those who sought economic benefit, especially in furs and whales.

Further south, Newfoundland was not to be the only target for British fishermen. The discovery of fish stocks off the coast of New England, possibly as early as 1597, led to a similar pattern of activity, with offshore fishing and an onshore settlement, at Sagadahoc in Maine in 1608, although this was soon abandoned. That did not, however, mean the end of fishing off New England, and, while southern New England came to be dominated by nonconformist settlers, fishermen remained more important further north. Their 'stations' are far less well documented than the Massachusetts 'Pilgrims', an instance of the varied existence of sources for the different types and characters of imperialism, but there was a big one, established by Robert Trelawny, a Plymouth merchant, at Richmond Island from the late 1620s until his death in 1644.[50]

Humphrey Gilbert had claimed Newfoundland for Elizabeth I in 1583, but it proved hard to transform a scattering of fishing stations into an England settlement colony. In 1610, the Newfoundland Company established a settlement at Cupid's Cove in Conception Bay, and, thereafter, the Company granted land to settlers on the Avalon peninsula, but it proved difficult to make a success of them. The hopes outlined in a pamphlet by John Mason, the Governor of the Conception Bay settlement, *Brief Discourse of the New-found-land with the Situation, Temperature, and Commodities thereof inciting our Nation to go forward in that hopeful plantation begun* (1620), proved deceptive, as the climate was too harsh for farming. By 1630, the colony at Cupid's Cove contained only a few settlers, while George, 1st Lord Baltimore, who came to Newfoundland in 1627 to help the colony he had founded at Ferryland in 1621, found the climate unpleasant and turned his interest to more clement climes further south: ultimately obtaining a charter for Maryland where he established a colony in 1634. Nevertheless, the seaborne empire relied on flexibility and probing limits, and the New-foundland settlements showed that it was possible to overwinter there, which provided the basis for a strengthening of the fisheries as the fishing season was extended.[51]

The English also made efforts to establish a colony on the eastern seaboard of the North American mainland, naming it Virginia in honour of the unmarried Elizabeth. In 1585, 108 colonists were landed on Roanoke Island, in what is now North Carolina, but they found it difficult to feed themselves, had tense relations with the native population and were taken off the following year. Another attempt was made in 1588, but when a relief ship arrived in 1590 it found the village deserted: disease, starvation or Native Americans may have wiped out the colonists. Nevertheless, the positive impression created by Thomas Hariot's *A Brief and True Report of the New Found Land of Virginia* (1588) and other reports encouraged fresh efforts to establish a colony.[52]

It was not until a base was established by the Virginia Company at Jamestown in the Chesapeake in 1607 that a permanent English colony was founded on the eastern seaboard. Spain regarded this colony as an invasion of its rights and protested about its foundation, but, although the defences at Jamestown were prepared to resist Spanish attack, it did not come: Virginia was too distant from the centres of Spanish power. Despite heavy initial losses of settlers, largely owing to the impact of disease in an unfamiliar environment,[53] the colony expanded as a result of the continued arrival of new settlers and the willingness to put an emphasis on growing food, and, after much bloodshed, Native resistance was overcome in 1622–4 and 1644. Disappointingly, no gold or silver was found there. Nor was it possible to trade with the Spanish colonies in order to obtain sugar and tobacco that could be profitably sold in England, as Spain was determined to exclude foreign traders. The bankrupt Virginia Company failed in 1624, but the colony was continued with a royal governor.

Further north, a settlement created in 1602 by Bartholomew Gosnold, on an island near what he had named Cape Cod, suffered because of Gosnold's failure to develop initial trading contacts with the Natives and, in the face of the latter's hostility, it had to be abandoned.[54] In 1620, however, the Pilgrim Fathers, a group of Protestant nonconformist separatists who had leased a concession from the New England Company, sailed on the *Mayflower*, made a landing at Cape Cod and established a settlement at New Plymouth, beginning the development of a colony in New England – a term first used in 1614 by Captain John Smith when he described the coastline north of the Hudson and popularised by his *Description of New England* (1616). The settlers sought to create a godly agrarian world, and believed their righteousness made them more entitled to the land than the Natives, although it was not only Protestant nonconformist settlers who saw Natives as savages.[55] The settlers were helped greatly by the impact on the Natives of what was probably plague in 1616–18 and smallpox in 1634.

The separatists were followed by other settlers who although not separatists were also zealous for a godly commonwealth and were increasingly uncomfortable with William Laud's High Church activism in England, and these more mainstream Protestants, sponsored by the Massachusetts Bay Company established in 1629, founded Boston in 1630. Thanks to settlement in the 1630s, when migration to the American colonies was far greater than in the 1620s, this colony expanded rapidly and the Natives were unable to confront the growth of the English presence. The settlers' brutal defeat of the Pequots in a brief war in 1637 confirmed the Puritans' position and their conviction of divine support. Settlement spread, for example in the Connecticut River Valley from 1634, and, with it, a new landscape of English townships and agrarian control was created.[56] By 1642 there were over 15,000 English settlers in New England, and by 1650 nearly 23,000; although more settlers went to the Chesapeake and to the West Indies. An emphasis on spreading settlement can lead to an underrating of the role of ports, especially Boston, and, more particularly, the importance of the beginning of the annual sailing season and the arrival of ships that brought immigrants, products, money and news: their likely arrival was the focus of continual discussion and concern.

The bleaker environment of eastern Canada, however, proved unpropitious for Sir William Alexander of Menstrie who, in 1621, was granted a charter giving him and his heirs a claim to a New Scotland in what are now the Maritime Provinces of Canada. The charter was renewed by Charles I in 1625, but it proved impossible to establish a successful settlement on the south shore of the Bay of Fundy. A ship sent in 1622 left the colonists in Newfoundland, and by 1623 only ten of them were willing to continue. Their experience of Nova Scotia did not persuade them to stay. Alexander's son, also William, established a colony at Port Royal in the Bay of Fundy in 1629 but, like Québec, which had been captured from France, it was handed over to France in 1632 as part of the peace agreement. The French had already captured the settlement established in 1629 at Port aux Balemes in Cape Breton. Although, in 1633, he gained the title Viscount Canada, Alexander died bankrupt in 1640 and it was the French who founded a settlement at Port Royal that lasted.[57]

The West Indies

Further south, English settlements were also established on islands that the Spaniards had not colonised; although this was not an easy process. Settlements were founded on St. Lucia in 1605 and Grenada in 1609, but opposition from native Caribs helped lead to their failure. Bermuda, an island in the Atlantic that was remote from other islands, was discovered in 1609, helping inspire Shakespeare's play *The Tempest*, and settled in 1612, becoming a successful colony where tobacco cultivation was swiftly introduced. The settlement of Bermuda, which was taken over by the Crown when the Virginia Company failed, was followed by the establishment of lasting colonies in the West Indies: St. Christopher (Kitts, 1624), Barbados (1627), Nevis (1628) and Antigua and Montserrat (1632). An attempt upon the Spaniards on Trinidad in 1626 failed, however, and the Puritan-run colony on Providence Island off the coast of Nicaragua did not last. As England was at war with Spain, and also France in the 1620s, there was a congruence of bellicosity with schemes for new colonies.

The colonies established were to be important bases for subsequent expansion. Without these, it would have been far more difficult to make subsequent gains at the expense of Spain and, later, France. Colonies also

helped in a transfer of English energy in the Caribbean from buccaneering
to a more regulated process of activity and expansion; although buccaneering remained important to the established authorities in the second half of
the century.[58] Furthermore, the opportunities of, and profits derived from,
colonies helped make their development and the acquisition of new ones
normative, while, although disease hit hard, the presence of settlers permitted a process of acclimatisation and the development, among survivors,
of a degree of immunity to tropical diseases that provided an important
local resource for future aggression and development.

The Caribbean islands were no mere adjunct to North America. They
generated more wealth and, indeed, until the 1660s attracted more settlers,
Barbados proving the most popular destination. These islands were rapidly
used for commercial agriculture and the labour-intensive nature of the
resulting plantation economies led to a need for settlers, at this stage largely
labourers provided by contracts of indenture, a practice of labour provision
and control transplanted from England.[59] Tobacco and cotton were the
initial crops, but, from the 1640s, there was a shift to sugar, particularly on
Barbados. Sugar was to lead to slaves, but it is important not to see this as
the inevitable economic and social pattern of the colonies in the West Indies.
Instead, a more mixed economic pattern that was less capital-intensive was
initially dominant, and it continued to be important even after there was an
emphasis on sugar. Tobacco also became the major crop around Chesapeake
Bay, in Virginia and Maryland, and its limited capital requirements and high
profitability encouraged settlers and investment. New settlers also provided
the colonies with vital assistance against the inroads of war and disease. These
were not the only problems facing the colonies, although the settlers were
not fully aware of their responsibility for deleterious change. The troubling
impact of the rats that were unwittingly introduced by the English to
Bermuda was an instance of a wider and more devastating ecological impact:
European diseases ravaged native societies, while hunting and the introduction of new species harmed indigenous animals. The feral hogs on St. Kitts
and Barbados were hunted to extinction.[60]

A WIDER WORLD AND THE LIFE OF SAILORS

There was a growing awareness in England of the nature and opportunities
of the wider world. The Drake Cup at his house at Buckland Abbey was
engraved with a version of Mercator's world map of 1587, and, in about
1596, London audiences heard of Shakespeare's Antonio, the merchant of
Venice: 'He hath an argosy bound to Tripolis, another to the Indies . . . he
hath a third at Mexico, a fourth for England' (I, iii). In Shakespeare's

King Henry VIII (1613), the porter at the Palace-Yard, wondering why there was so much noise, added sexual interest and rivalry to the outside world: 'have we some strange Indian with the great tool come to court, the women so besiege us?' (v, iv). Attempts to understand the wider world led to the study of geography, which offered a new ideal of science as a tool for understanding and controlling nature. Service of the state fostered an interest in mathematical geography, while descriptive geography encouraged readers to regard the world as a source of wondrous tales and new goods, and there was a close relationship between the study of geography and the development of ideas of English power and imperial growth.[61] A sense of maritime destiny was pressed in a number of publications, including John Dee's *General and Rare Memorials pertaining to the Perfect Art of Navigation* (1577) and Richard Hakluyt's *Principal Navigations, Voiages, Traffiques and Discoveries of the English Nation* (1598–1600). Hakluyt's work served in its field a function akin to John Foxe's *Book of Martyrs* (1563), which provided an account of England as a kingdom that had been in the forefront of the advance towards Christian truth. The impact of such works is difficult to assess, but they offered those open to the culture of print an awareness of the oceans and the overseas world that provided a potent vision of present interest and future glory.

A focus on ideas of maritime destiny and, more generally, on a 'top-down' approach to trade, empire and sea power needs to be complemented by an awareness of the nature of maritime life. The extent to which working conditions on land were often grim did not lessen the difficulties posed by life at sea, although it does provide a useful benchmark for comparison. The nature of life at sea varied greatly, although, to lessen this variety, there was an important degree of movement between the sectors of the maritime community, lessening the distinctive nature of any one individual's work. Furthermore, seamen were not passive – they had a strong concept of the value of their work and were ready to defend their interests, both through group solidarity and by means of individual firmness. Solidarity reflected the trust and co-operation necessary to achieve teamwork tasks, but also the particular character of maritime life, which, to some degree, was cut off from life on land. For example, the network of credit and debt that was crucial to so many sailors was primarily shipboard, or otherways limited to the maritime community.

War with Spain interrupted the conventions of maritime life brutally, as impressment obliged seamen to serve for low wages in dangerous conditions while wartime commanders did not seek the consensus sought by peacetime captains and, far from being a short conflict, this war posed lengthy demands on sailors. In 1590, the government tried, unsuccessfully, to confine all sailors to their home ports in case they were required for naval duty, and the burden of naval service was exacerbated by the failure to pay sailors, or by payment in arrears, and, even had they been paid, the wages were low, although naval pay was raised in 1582. Low pay contributed to a bitterness and level of evasion and desertion that are aspects generally neglected in heroic accounts of the navy.

Other aspects of naval service that were less than welcome included poor food, inadequate hygiene and high levels of sickness and death, for example on the fleet that had fought the Armada in 1588 once the Spanish ships had been driven away. Serious diseases included scurvy, which reflected the lack of vitamin C in the diet of seamen, dysentery, typhus and plague. Aside from the impact of vitamin deficiencies, especially on long voyages, the crowded and dirty nature of shipboard life and infestations of lice, fleas and rats helped the spread of infectious disease. The inadequate nature of the food provided on ships made a significant contribution to the problem, as malnutrition lessened resistance to disease. Health was also affected by a lack of fresh water and by the nature of the clothing of sailors: generally scanty and often wet and encrusted with salt. Although the impact of vitamin deficiencies could not have been appreciated, the dangerous consequences of a lack of adequate food and clothing were realised, but acceptable provision proved beyond the resources of the government, while its reliance on impressment to provide sailors ensured that there appeared no need to offer good conditions.[62]

Different environments added specific problems, such as the danger and hardships of Arctic whaling, and tropical voyages proved particularly detrimental to health. This needs to be set alongside the heroic portrayal of naval endeavour and action. Anson's celebrated three years and nine months circumnavigation of the world in 1740–44 cost over 1,300 dead from disease and only four from combat; just 145 men and one of the eight ships returned.

THE EARLY STUARTS, 1603–38

In the early seventeenth century, the Crown moved away from the Elizabethan interest in distant waters. Empire, instead, was very much a theme focused on the possibilities for a kingdom of Great Britain created by the accession of James VI of Scotland to the throne of England as James I (r. 1603–25), although James's hopes of a 'union of love', or at least a measure of administrative and economic union, were not realised, and separate parliamentary, ecclesiastical and legal systems continued: there were fears in England about the legal and constitutional implications of any union, and the Westminster Parliament rejected a parliamentary or legal bond with Scotland.[63] The circle of James's eldest son, Prince Henry, included men with an interest in geography and imperial expansion, but he predeceased his father and, in the 1620s, James and his successor, Charles I (r. 1625–49), focused their attention on European power politics.

With the Treaty of London of 1604, James had brought the war with Spain to an end, the government of Philip III refusing to accept the English demand that they be free to trade and settle in parts of the world claimed by Spain but where she had not hitherto established bases. In practice, privateering by both powers continued and the concept of no peace 'beyond the Line' legitimated this state of semi-warfare while simultaneously both restricting it geographically to an anarchic trans-oceanic world, for example in West Africa, and separating it from full-scale conflict. As a result, James was able to preserve the peace. At the same time, peaceful trade increased 'beyond the Line', although there was often an undercurrent of potential force.

Under James, who was genuinely committed to peace,[64] the navy stagnated and was badly affected by corrupt administration, and, although English colonies were founded in North America, and he left his name on the map with Jamestown in Virginia, concern about the response of France and Spain, and a lack of royal support, harmed colonisation attempts in the period, such as the Amazon Company established in 1619. However, the inherent difficulties of the task help explain the failure of the schemes for a colony on the Amazon, as well as of Sir Walter Raleigh's better-known plans for Guiana. The expedition he organised in 1617 attacked the Spaniards, ignoring the King's insistence that it was not to do so; and it did not find any gold mines. Raleigh was beheaded on his return.[65]

The focus of maritime concern had switched in the 1610s, as piracy, an activity dominated by the English and Dutch, was taken over by the 'Barbary' pirates of North Africa, especially Algiers, seeking slaves and loot. The Newfoundland fishery was soon a victim and there were also raids in British waters, especially off south-west England in 1625–6.[66] In response in 1620, a fleet of six of James's ships and 12 armed merchantmen under Sir Robert Mansell was sent to Algiers, but the Algerians chose to rely on their strong defences, rather than fighting, and, in 1621, neither blockade nor fireship attack proved successful in forcing Algiers to acceptable terms.

Closer to home, relations with the Dutch were put under pressure in large part as a result of envy of growing Dutch maritime prosperity and strength. This was given political force, under James, by an attempt to define a notion of coastal waters under state control, a concept taken from Scots law, and to link it to the English move to force other powers to accept their position in the 'Narrow Seas' by saluting the flag.

In the 1620s, war with Spain and then France developed into conflict outside Europe, including the capture of Québec in 1629 by the Scots captain David Kirke, but, although competition with the French added a new dimension to the English Atlantic world, for it was no longer centred on hostility towards Spain, neither James nor Charles was particularly interested and Québec was returned to France in 1632. In contrast, the Dutch were able to benefit from their resumption of conflict with Spain in 1621 in order to make a major effort to seize Spanish and Portuguese colonies. England was unable to grasp a similar opportunity, although in 1622 the East India Company helped Shah Abbas I of Persia capture the Portuguese base of Hormuz in the Persian Gulf and, in return, gained favourable terms in trade with Persia.

In Europe, amphibious expeditions against Cadiz (1625) and La Rochelle (1627) were embarrassingly unsuccessful. The withdrawal of royal support for the navy by James, and his antagonism towards piracy and privateering, had removed an underpinning of naval capacity, and the expeditions of the 1620s showed that, within 20 years, English naval capability had been severely diminished, with a dramatic decrease in the competence of its commanders and a serious failure in logistics.

Charles I negotiated peace, and from 1633 built up the navy. In 1637, a small successful expedition was mounted against the Moroccan pirate base of Sallee (now Rabat), but pirate raids continued, and the large ships of the English fleet were not designed for trade protection.[67] Charles dissociated himself in the 1630s from the idea of maritime expansion at the expense of Spain, preferring to align himself with her, and, partly as a result, disputes over financing the navy, by means of Ship Money from 1634, accentuated distrust of Charles. The idea of a Protestant foreign policy and a triumphant naval war with Spain remained potent,[68] and the Providence Island Company from its base off the coast of modern Nicaragua kept alive the idea of profitable piratical opposition to Spain,[69] but Charles was not interested.

By the 1630s, however, the imperial community had developed a powerful momentum of its own, with the East India Company and the North American colonies owing relatively little to the Crown. James I sent Sir Thomas Roe as ambassador to the Mughal Emperor and he was there from 1615 to 1618, but the East India Company's position in Asia depended on its own resources and efforts, and, after initial difficulties, it raised nearly £3 million in its first 30 years. Thanks to the autonomous structure of the Company, it was able to use the profits of its trade to support a forceful stance, as when it repelled Portuguese attacks off Surat in 1612 and 1615 and, in co-operation with Abbas I of Persia, attacked the Portugal at Hormuz, these the most prominent of a series of clashes.[70] The Company also found itself in conflict with the Dutch over the spice trade to the East Indies, most violently in 1618–23, an instance of the declining centrality of relations with Spain, and also had to establish relations with local powers, not least in order to benefit from the 'country trade' between Asian ports.

Whereas considerable profits had been made in the 1600s, the situation in the 1620s and 1630s was less favourable, and a failure to live up to expectations led to the abandonment of trading bases in Japan, Siam (Thailand) and what is now Malaya in 1623. Dutch competition in the East Indies affected profits, and the position did not improve until the 1660s. In 1623, ten English merchants on the spice island of Amboyna in the Moluccas were massacred by the Dutch, but the Company had already decided to withdraw from the Moluccas, although it maintained an important role in the East Indies spice trade, especially through Macassar in the Celebes, Bantam on Java and bases on Sumatra. At the same time, the Company, whose monopoly was reaffirmed by Charles 1 in 1632, developed its interests in India, especially in the import of cotton textiles, initially from Gujarat, and subsequently from the Coromandel Coast, at first from Masulipatam and, from 1639, from Madras, where a fortified position was established. Also in the 1630s, the Company of Merchants Trading to Guinea, which, in 1631, was given a monopoly, established factories on the Gold Coast, initially at Komenda and subsequently at Kormantin, which was fortified from 1638, and Winneba.

Although the Crown did not direct overseas enterprise, it did play a role in the granting of monopoly rights, which were useful in encouraging finance from mercantile sources. However, the costs of these rights and the obligations that went with them also proved a burden, and helped ensure a judgement of opportunities largely in terms of short-term gain. As a result, unprofitable trades were abandoned, such as that to the Gambia in 1618–21 launched by the Company of Adventurers of London Trading to the Parts of Africa (the Guinea Company), which was granted a monopoly by James 1 in 1618. Monopolies were unwelcome to other interests; the Russia Company's monopoly of whaling secured in 1577 being contested by force by other merchants, such as those from Hull, although it was the Dutch who competed with the English in whaling in the following century.

CIVIL WARS

The limited role of the Crown in supporting trans-oceanic activity helped lessen the impact on Britain's overseas position of the civil wars that broke out in 1639, but this impact was still serious. Moreover, the challenge to established assumptions about the conduct of government posed both by Charles I and by some of his critics manifested itself in the colonies as well as in the British Isles. In 1638, Massachusetts refused an order to submit its charter for scrutiny and slighted the condemnation of the charter by the Privy Council. Charles was considering a forceful response when the crisis of authority in Scotland gathered pace. Within New England, there were also tensions over authority, with Connecticut and Rhode Island being founded as breakaway settlements from Massachusetts in response to differences over Church government.

The Bishops' Wars between England and Scotland in 1639–40 were followed by the Irish rising of 1641, which indicated the tensions that had been building up under the imperial order in Ireland. Driven by anger at their treatment by Protestant overlords and settlers, and under serious economic pressure, the Catholic Irish rebelled and slaughtered many of the Anglo-Scottish settlers, overrunning Ulster. The issue of control over the troops to be sent to Ireland helped lead to the breakdown of relations between Charles I and the Westminster Parliament and to the outbreak of civil war in England. The English Civil Wars of 1642–6 and 1648, were matched by civil wars in Ireland and Scotland, and wars between the Commonwealth (Parliamentary) regime in England and both the Irish (1649–52) and the Scots (1650–52).

The general crisis of the British Empire continued until 1652, by which time the forces of the Commonwealth regime in England had overcome resistance throughout the British Isles. From the outset of the First English Civil War, naval power was important to the survival and success of the Parliamentary cause. The fleet was brought under Parliamentary control in March 1642, and an attempt to restore royal control was thwarted that July: Charles I's departure from London had left the Royalists in the fleet in a weak position and this was exploited in order to replace Royalist captains by more politically reliable (and experienced) seamen from the mercantile marine. On behalf of Parliament, the navy was put under the command of Robert, 2nd Earl of Warwick, who had played a major role in privateering in the 1610s and 1620s and in the early settlement of New England. Under his command, the navy helped maintain the commercial buoyancy of London, the centre of the rebellion, and this was crucial to the revenues on which the Parliamentary cause depended. The navy was also operationally important, especially in making it possible to supply isolated strongholds such as Hull, Lyme Regis, Milford Haven, Pembroke and Plymouth. Their retention by Parliament made it difficult for the Royalists to exploit local strength and successes and to concentrate their forces on targets closer to London, and also prevented the Royalists from gaining important positions that would have increased their maritime presence. The navy was also used to threaten Royalist supply links, although it was not able to prevent the movement of Royalist troops from Ireland to both England and Scotland, as the operational difficulties of seeking to project power into the Irish Sea, which was distant from the navy's leading bases, were serious. In turn, the Royalists challenged the Parliamentarians by licensing a large number of privateers, which posed a major problem for trade and made the Parliamentary fleet's task of commerce protection difficult. The small Royalist fleet created after the capture of Bristol in 1643 was not strong enough to contest control of the sea by battle.

After the First Civil War ended in 1646, the Parliamentary navy was affected by the political chaos of the following years, as victory accentuated Parliamentary disunity, especially over Church government and negotiations with Charles I. In 1647, Colonel Thomas Rainsborough, a radical, was appointed commander of the navy, but his unpopularity there helped lead the navy to divide in 1648 when the Second Civil War broke out. Rainsborough was rejected and 12 warships blockaded the Thames on behalf of Charles, but, without control of an anchorage and threatened with a squadron under Warwick, who had returned to command on behalf of Parliament, the Royalist ships lifted the blockade and sailed to Holland; the threat of another Royalist blockade played a role in the Stuart restoration in 1660.

Like the 'Glorious Revolution' of 1688–9, the civil wars remind one that a change of regime in England meant also a change of regime in the colonies. The civil wars affected English imperialism both because they led to serious and sustained conflict in the leading colony, Ireland (although less so in the New World), and because they ensured that domestic support for imperial expansion markedly slackened, although a raiding expedition of seven ships under Captain William Jackson, sent to the Caribbean in 1642 by Warwick, captured Jamaica temporarily during the course of its successful cruise.[71] At the close of the 1640s, many colonies were still not under the control of the new republican regime in England, accentuating the already-pronounced variety of the empire, which has led to the description of the English Atlantic world of the 1630s as 'a series of disparate and chaotic colonial adventures';[72] although the drive to end Royalism was to lead the regime to enforce control.

Fortunately for the English, they were not alone in their problems. Civil wars in France and in Spain's European empire also broke out in the period 1640–52, and although France gave refuge to Charles, Prince of Wales, neither was in a position to exploit English difficulties. The Dutch, however, with their efficient, and therefore low-priced, shipping came to play an increasing role in the economy of English colonies, providing both shipping

links to Europe and working capital. The civil wars also hit English overseas activity by dividing merchant communities, by causing fiscal instability
and by reducing the money available for investment in trade and colonisation, with varied effects in individual trades.[73] For example, as trade with
Asia had, in large part, to be paid for with bullion exports, the disruption
of financial and economic systems within England and the English Atlantic
made it harder to obtain bullion. In addition, the overthrow of Crown
authority challenged the monopoly rights that rested on it, so that the privileges of the East India Company were attacked by mercantile competitors
and its monopoly rights were infringed, while the Guinea Company lost
its monopoly of the trade on the Gold Coast. Colonial enterprise, however,
continued during the civil wars. Unsuccessful attempts were made by
London merchants under Maurice Thompson to establish a colony on
Madagascar, while, on the Gold Coast, factories were established at Anomabu
(1639), Takoradi (1645) and Cape Coast (1650) and interloping merchants
were active; another factory was founded on the Benin Coast.

West Africa, like the Indian Ocean, was seen principally in terms of competitive relations with other European powers, particularly the Dutch, and,
more generally, the distant world was conceived of principally as an extension of the nearby, especially of its problems, configurations and patterns of
causality. Thus, the Ottoman Empire in the seventeenth and eighteenth
century tended to be seen by the English foremost as a sphere of commercial competition with France.

By 1650, it appeared that despite overseas possessions, particularly in
North America and the West Indies, a commercial profile absent 60 years
earlier and a large fleet, the English would nevertheless remain marginal, or,
at best, a minor element in the major expansion of European trans-oceanic
power. The English had acquired considerable navigational experience[74] and
had created completely new maritime links, particularly to New England,
but these were of minor significance compared with those of other powers.
Although responsible, in the person of Sir William Alexander for Nova
Scotia, and with both a Scottish Guinea Company founded in 1634 and
operating on the Gold Coast and trade developing with the North
American colonies, Scotland's role was far less than that of England, and its
Guinea Company, which, in fact, was largely London-based, had only limited
success.[75]

Furthermore, in 1650, empire still primarily meant the British Isles, as
was driven home by Oliver Cromwell's campaigns in Ireland and Scotland
on behalf of the Commonwealth regime. The ships that had carried his
force to Ireland in August 1649, and those that enabled him to outflank the
Scots at Stirling, and to cross the Firth of Forth the following summer,
seemed the most apparent means of Britain's seaborne empire. Neverthe-

less, the striking political, social and religious developments of the 1640s led to the creation of a new state that was to be particularly dynamic in the 1650s, while, although less clearly, it also influenced the eventual nature of English and, later, British imperial imperatives.

2

Growing Strength, 1650–1750

'Behold, ev'n to remoter Shores
a Conquering Navy proudly spread'.

John Dryden, *Threnodia Augustalis* (1685)

To close the previous chapter by mentioning the power projection provided by maritime 'lift' in 1649–50, and then to look forward a century, is to suggest an easy parallel: with the warships that, in 1746, helped the forces under William, Duke of Cumberland, the second son of George II, in his successful Scottish campaign against the Jacobites under Charles Edward Stuart (Bonnie Prince Charlie), the son of the Stuart claimant 'James III and VIII'. And yet a very different parallel can also be offered, between the capture of Jamaica from Spain in 1655 and that of Louisbourg on Cape Breton Island from France 90 years later. Both were products of an ability to project British power in the New World, and each was a success won at the expense of a leading imperial power.

To push the parallel further, each was also linked to failure. Oliver Cromwell's Western Design had focused on the far more prosperous and important Spanish colony of Hispaniola, which remained outside the English grasp, while the gain of Louisbourg was seen as a stage in the conquest of New France: Canada. Far from that being the case, however, plans for an expedition to seize Québec were abandoned and, indeed, at the Congress of Aix-la-Chapelle of 1748, the government agreed to return Louisbourg (which a French fleet, wracked by disease, had failed to regain in 1746). This return led to bitter denunciations. Louisbourg had been presented by the press as a British objective, and had been contrasted with the government's unpopular concern to fight the French in the Low Countries. The *Universal Spectator* of 27 July 1745 stated, 'It is presumed our success at Cape Breton, which the French have so much interest in defending, will encourage us to some farther attempts upon their settlements in America: By which we might much more effectively distress them, and serve ourselves, than by showing them our backsides in Flanders'. Reprinting an item from the

London news, the *Newcastle Courant* of 5 March 1748 asked 'whether Quebec, St. Augustine, Havana, St. Domingue or Martinique, be not of more importance to us than Tournai, Mons, Namur, Brussels, Antwerp, or Bergen-op-Zoom'.

The government was unimpressed, and its policy over the next eight years focused on trying to build up a powerful collective security system in Continental Europe, rather than planning how best to conquer the Bourbons' overseas empires. Indeed, in 1750, the government accepted a trade treaty with Spain in which the Spanish claim to a right to search British merchantmen, the cause of war between the two powers in 1739, was not explicitly denied. William Pitt the Elder, the Paymaster General, defended the treaty in Parliament in 1751, arguing that he had been wrong in 1739 to criticise Sir Robert Walpole, then head of the Whig ministry, for failing to secure the same repudiation: 'I have considered public affairs more coolly and am convinced that the claim of *no search* respecting British vessels near the coast of Spanish America can never be obtained, unless Spain were reduced as to consent to any terms her conqueror might think proper to impose'.[1] A century later, during the heyday of self-confident gunboat diplomacy, Viscount Palmerston would never have conceded such limits.

Parallels, however, can suggest a misleading degree of continuity. There was, throughout the period 1650–1750, a central concern with Continental power politics (particularly during the reigns of William III, George I and George II, all of whom were also Continental rulers), but that did not preclude an increase in trans-oceanic territorial control, settlement and trade, nor a greater interest in imperial themes. A sense of opportunity was captured in the claim in *The Map of Virginia* (1651) by John Ferrar (also spelt Farrer) that the New Albion discovered by Drake in the Pacific on his circumnavigation of the world was close by on the other side of the Appalachians, and that it could be reached in ten days march from the head of the James River through valleys 'beautified' with rivers.

If Britain did not, in 1650–1750, enjoy the clear colonial, commercial and maritime predominance that she was to wield for most of the following two centuries, the century 1650–1750 nevertheless was a formative period in the development of the British seaborne empire. Britishness was an important aspect of this development. The defeat of successive Jacobite risings secured both the exclusion of the male line of the Stuarts, which was a result of the Glorious Revolution of 1688–9, and the parliamentary union of England and Scotland that came into effect in 1707, providing a more secure home base and also underlining the self-image of the British state in terms of Protestantism, liberty, limited government, commerce, prosperity and a commitment to the value of change. There was also a willingness to embrace new solutions and an absence of complacency that were to be important to the practice and ethos of imperial expansion.

FISHERIES AND TRADE

Colonial gains tend to be placed first in discussion of trans-oceanic activity, but it is worth contextualising them by considering the gains as an aspect of a dynamic period of expansion that included increased trade, settlement and knowledge, each of which productively interacted with the others. A common factor was provided by the 'shrinking' of the British Atlantic as a result of significant improvements, such as the development of postal services, and the introduction of the helm wheel soon after 1700, which dramatically increased rudder control on large ships by removing the need to steer with the tiller. In addition, the average annual number of trans-Atlantic British voyages doubled between 1675 and 1740, and the number of ships that extended or ignored the 'optimum' shipping seasons also increased on several major routes. Links became more frequent and easier and average peacetime passages from England to Newfoundland were five weeks, from the eastern Caribbean colonies to England eight weeks, and from Jamaica to England fourteen.[2] Sailings reflected commercial opportunity, not government permission, although the ability of the navy to ensure the peacetime safety of the seas enabled ships to sail with fewer cannon and thus to need a smaller crew, a measure that helped the profitability of shipping.[3] A reduction in the time ships spent in harbour and a fall in the cost of credit and insurance, as well as the costs of packaging and storing goods, were also important to greater profitability.[4]

Improved trans-Atlantic passages benefited both the fisheries and trade. The former were part of a complex trading system that indicated the multiple opportunities provided by trans-oceanic activity and the resources that were tapped. The fisheries relied on ships, men and food from southern England, food from Ireland, salt from Iberia and France, and some products from the New World, principally rum, molasses and sugar from the West Indies, either directly or via New England, from which bread and timber were also imported. In turn, the cod that was caught was sent to Iberia and Italy, while, in small amounts, cod liver oil was sent to England. This complex trading system required a large amount of capital. The ships and sailors came from southern England, principally Dartmouth, Bideford and Plymouth, which was very important to the local shipbuilding industries, but also indicated the separate strands of trans-oceanic activity. Bristol and London, which played a prominent role in other trades, did not do so in the Newfoundland fishery.

The growing complexity and opportunities of the fisheries were also indicated by the increased role of overwintering (spending the winter on the Newfoundland coast). Furthermore, by the early eighteenth century, a fishery on the offshore Grand Banks based in Newfoundland had developed and supplemented the inshore fishery. Overwintering also indicated the tensions that could arise from trans-oceanic activity, in particular rivalry, real or apparent, between British-based and colonial activity. The British-based fishery saw Newfoundland as a source of competition, particularly over the fishing sites, but also for labour, and resisted any recognition of the permanence of settlement. There was also concern that Newfoundland would form direct links with foreign markets and suppliers, and, indeed, in 1671, settlers were urged to move to Jamaica. In response, it was argued that Newfoundland provided an opportunity for settlement, that this offered possibilities for the fishery, and that it was necessary to thwart French expansion. Although not formally a colony, the English settlements in Newfoundland grew, their development helped by their relatively unregulated nature – the absence of customs officials and the limited implementation there of the Navigation Acts led to the growth of free trade, which contrasted markedly with the situation in New France. A system of naval government based in St. John's proved sufficient and lasted until representative government was established in 1832.[5]

In discussions of the British Empire, the fisheries tend to disappear after the sixteenth century, and the attention devoted to them here might appear strange, which is unfortunate, as they were important for two reasons. First, the fisheries provided a 'nursery' for seamen, essential for fulfilling the labour demands of sailing ships, particularly in the North Atlantic. Second, the continued value, until the end of the eighteenth century, of English participation in the Newfoundland fishery is a salutary reminder of the multiple narratives of empire. The rise of the sugar and slave economy in the British Atlantic was very significant, but it should not be allowed to crowd out other aspects of that world, nor its impact in Britain. Fishery itself was a varied activity. While the Newfoundland fishery flourished, that to Iceland declined in the late seventeenth century. At the turn of the eighteenth century, a new industry was developing, as whaling vessels from North Sea ports such as Aberdeen and Hull hunted their prey, first off the coast of Greenland and later in Pacific waters.[6]

Trade has a somewhat arid feel to many modern readers, the term unfortunately suggesting a tedious array of statistics. To say that trade was the lifeblood of empire is to testify to the extent to which individual voyages carried not only migrants and officials, letters and publications, but also the goods that made the entire system of exchange work. Statistics summarise this effort, but they can convey only in part the challenge faced by sailors,

navigators and captains, as well as the difficulties that buyers and sellers had
to confront, and especially the willingness to leave home and family for prolonged periods: a stark contrast to workers in arable farming who lived and
worked in their extended family and rarely travelled far from home. Trade
also helped create the character of empire, which involved the impact of
centre on periphery, and periphery on centre, as well as that of periphery
on periphery.

The upward trend of the trade statistics was particularly impressive as
much of the European economy was stagnant during the century. Thus, for
example, at a time of low inflation, the value of London's imports from the
East India Company and the English plantations nearly doubled from the
1660s to the end of the century, while the percentage of London's total
imports by value from these areas rose from 24 to 34 in the same period.[7]
Such statistics reflected the rise in direct trade, rather than using intermediary traders, particularly the Dutch, and intermediary ports. Helped in part
by Dutch investment after the Glorious Revolution of 1688–9,[8] an important aspect of a growing Anglo-Dutch co-operation,[9] London's role in the
multi-centred trading system was becoming more prominent. Direct trading
required more capital resources and expenditure and a more sophisticated
organisational structure, but it enabled the British to bear the bulk of the
transaction costs themselves and also to take much of the profit. This can
be seen with the India trade, which was largely financed with returns for
bullion that could be obtained only from profits on other trades. More generally, far from being compartmentalised, the British trading system had
important financial as well as economic interdependencies. Indeed, British
re-exports rose from £2.13 million in 1700 to £2.30 million in 1720,
and £3.23 million in 1750, as imported goods, such as tobacco from the
Chesapeake or sugar from the West Indies, were re-exported to Continental Europe. Imports of tobacco through Liverpool rose in weight from
1.49 million pounds in 1689–96 to 2.86 million pounds in 1703–12.[10]

Government sought to help trade. The Navigation Acts of 1650 and 1651,
which excluded other powers from the trade of the English colonies, and
restricted most of the trade of England, Wales and Ireland to nationals, were
reprised in the Navigation Act of 1660 and the Staple Act of 1663. Customs
revenues were helped by the prohibition of exports direct from the colonies
to foreign markets, and, instead, the requirement that they be exported to
England or one of its colonies. It was laid down in 1660 that all foreign-
built ships in English ownership should be registered and, two years later,
the purchase of Dutch ships was hindered when an Act decreed that ships
of foreign build not registered by that date were to be deemed alien and
to be subject to alien duties.[11] Union with Scotland in 1707 ended its exclusion from what had been an English empire, as the Navigation Acts now

encompassed Scotland, and this was to be important to the dynamic of British imperialism. Not only were British entrepreneurs protected from foreign competition by the Navigation Acts, they also benefited from the absence of local tariffs.

Aside from measures to encourage shipping, there was also assistance for exports, as trade took precedence over short-term financial considerations. In 1722, the export duties on most British-manufactured products were abolished and import duties on foreign raw materials required for these products were reduced or abolished. Exports to the colonies rose, average annual British exports to North America rising from £0.27 million in 1701–5 to £1.3 million in 1751–55.[12] The British West Indies remained an important market for most of the period, reflecting their profitability as a plantation economy as well as their role as entrepôts for a contraband trade with Spanish America. This helped provide a crucial infusion of bullion into the British trading system, as well as contrasting with the British determination to use navigation laws to prevent Europeans from challenging their own monopolistic claims.[13]

A discussion of government support has to include not only peacetime but also wartime measures. Here the growth in naval strength discussed in the next chapter was of great importance, but so also was its application. Trade protection was a crucial goal, but it entailed policy choices and different levels of commitment. Naval protection became more regular and consistent with time, with convoys for defence and squadrons for attacking opposing naval forces including privateers. In the Mediterranean, this tasking was fully operational by the time of the Second Anglo-Dutch War (1665–7) and this cut shipping losses, as well as increasing the efficiency of the commercial system by creating a clear distinction between mercantile and military shipping, and thus increasing the appeal of investing in trade.[14]

The expansion of trade helped shipping, and English shipping tonnage rose from 162,000 in 1660, to 340,000 in 1686, and 2,477,000 tons in 1815, an expansion that was linked to a growth in the maritime labour force that helped the wartime manning of the navy. The focus on more distant trades played a major role in this expansion, while the development of particular trades led to the use of larger vessels and the building of purpose-built ones,[15] both of which increased the profitability of trade. The growth of foreign trade and of shipping also benefited from the increase in domestic trade, and there was a relationship between the two, with domestic trade moving goods for or from foreign trade and coastal traffic becoming more important as the national economy was increasingly integrated, while coastal trade also helped strengthen the shipping industry.

Losses to storm, shipwreck and privateers ensured that it was necessary to build if only to maintain shipping capacity, but greater demand meant that shipbuilding was far more than just for replacement. The need for ships was not met by imports, and the Navigation Acts ensured that it was not met by hiring foreign carriers. Furthermore, long-distance trade entailed particular requirements for shipbuilding, both in Britain, where most large ships were built on the Thames, and in the colonies, especially Boston. Shipbuilding was therefore associated with the continued process of differentiation that characterised British industry and the development of the urban hierarchy. Outside London, there was a shift in shipbuilding from East Anglia to north-east England. The Union also created opportunities for Scottish shipbuilding: the number of ships from Glasgow rose from 30 in the late 1680s to 70 by the 1730s, while overseas, shipbuilding also began in North America and, to a lesser extent, Bermuda, Barbados and Jamaica, the first locally built ocean-going ship from there sailing for London in 1660.[16]

The increase in the range as well as the volume of exports to the colonies helped spread the benefit of empire throughout different areas of British industry and was particularly important to the development of the iron and textile industries, while, aside from advantages in terms of sales, there were also significant qualitative changes, not least those that flowed from the economies of scale made possible by exports.[17] Such production and trade also brought turnover and profit that provided crucial investment capital, so that, although colonial trade might be an enclave activity centred on ports, such as Whitehaven, the profits gained as a result acted as stimuli for other economic sectors, providing both liquidity for bankers and investment capital. One extreme example of 'enclave' activity was provided by the wrecks of merchantmen, and the *Albemarle*, a diamond-carrying East Indiaman wrecked off Cornwall in 1708, provided a considerable boost to the local economy, both legally and illegally.

Trade also affected diet and health. Sugar and tobacco came from the colonies and were seen as beneficial as they helped to finance their import of British manufactured goods. Although sugar was initially a luxury item, the average retail price fell considerably in the second half of the seventeenth century and it became important to the British diet, partly replacing honey as a sweetener for food and drink. In 1702, John Evelyn had at Falmouth, 'a small bowl of punch made with Brazil sugar'. The addition of sugar to hot drinks increased their popularity: chocolate was altered by sugar, making it a sweet rather than a bitter drink, and so the import of its main ingredient, cacao, grew. Cacao plantations were established on Jamaica in the 1660s, and this encouraged consumption, although by the 1680s its place on the island had been superseded by sugar. As the consumption of caffeine drinks rose, so demand for sugar increased, while, in Britain, the new drinks led to the production, purchase and use of new goods, such as teapots. Hot drink utensils were appearing in Kentish inventories by 1685, but not in

Staffordshire until 1725. Sugar was also added to jam, cakes, biscuits and medicine. Between 1663 and 1775, the consumption of muscovado sugar in
England and Wales increased twenty-fold, while British rum consumption
rose from the 207 gallons imported in 1698 to an annual average of 2 million
gallons in 1771–5.[18] The profits of the sugar trade helped lead Bristol to a
mercantile standing and prosperity, reflected in the rebuilding of the Council
House in 1704 and to the building of the New Exchange, designed by John
Wood the Elder, the leading architect of elegant gentility in Bath, which
opened in 1743. Trade thus helped to transform, as well as to create, aspects
of British life a long way removed from military and political history, but
there was no compartmentalisation, and just as wars affected the flow of
goods, so this flow, in turn, partly depended on the factors that contributed
to slavery and the slave trade.

Trade links with the non-British world were very varied, and much trade
took place far from the oceans, although the importance of water transport
as a means to overcome problems of distance and load was demonstrated
by the use of river and lake routes. In North America, where British merchants increasingly traded among Native groups west of the Appalachians,
they established temporary posts in the 1720s on the upper Ohio River and
on an eastern tributary of the Wabash River, while, in 1725, the Iroquois
permitted the Governor of New York to construct a stone fort at Oswego,
the first British base on the Great Lakes, and it served to extend their trading
network, for example into southern Ontario. This trade might appear to
have little to do with maritime commerce, but was in large part only possible within an oceanic system: goods and products took on meaning within
it, while much of what was sold to Natives had come from overseas. Thus
the inexpensive rum that was available at Oswego had come from the British
colonies in the West Indies. Furthermore, naval power played a major role
in developments far from the ocean. The British capture of Louisbourg in
1745 allowed them to blockade the St. Lawrence, destroying the basis of the
French fur trade, because Native alliances were sustained by presents and
trade goods. As a result of the blockade, British fur traders were able to
undersell the French dramatically, and this encouraged both the Miami and
the Huron to break with the French.

The ability to profit from multiple links was crucial to the success of
trading systems. Thus, the northern American colonies provided goods, such
as timber, for the colonies further south, both in North America and in the
West Indies, leading to a mutual dependence that was particularly marked
on the part of the northern colonies, which lacked a profitable product
to export to Britain comparable with tobacco or sugar. To a considerable
extent, effective imperial regulation sought to foster such multiple linkages,
albeit within a political culture that placed a high premium not only on the

role of government but also on a regulatory system that presumed an inherent competition between different powers and therefore sought to foster protectionism.

Furthermore, colonial production or services, particularly shipping, could be restricted to benefit Britain. This was readily apparent in the case of Ireland, the trade of which was dominated by the British market, and the terms of the trade set in London. One of pastoral Ireland's major activities was affected by the restrictive Cattle Acts of 1666–7, Irish exports suffering until they were suspended in 1758–9, while Irish exports of wool and woollen textiles to foreign and colonial markets were banned in 1699. Although the percentage of Irish exports going to the New World colonies rose, helping tie Ireland into the increasingly multiple linkages of the empire, most of this trade depended on English intermediaries and Irish expatriates, especially in London where George II's wife, Caroline of Ansbach, dressed in Irish linen in an attempt to boost sales. Restrictions were not only imposed on Irish production. The Navigation Acts were particularly directed against the Dutch, but the Sugar Act of 1733, which sought to protect the exports of the British West Indian islands from French competition, and was passed in response to lobbying by merchants trading there, were unwelcome to the British colonies in North America which unsuccessfully petitioned Parliament against them.[19] In 1750, in order to help British exports, the making of steel, the refining of iron, and the manufacture of finished articles from iron, were prohibited in the North American colonies.

Aside from seeking to control colonial trade, successive British governments, especially in the sixteenth and seventeenth centuries, saw monopoly chartered companies as ways to harness and control private enterprise. These companies, however, faced serious criticism, especially from those excluded from their benefits, principally the merchants of secondary ports.[20] The Royal African Company, chartered in 1672, and its predecessor, the Company of Royal Adventurers Trading into Africa, chartered in 1660 (it went bankrupt in 1672), made a major effort to develop a monopoly trade with West Africa. The strong interest of courtiers, especially James, Duke of York, later James II, and Prince Rupert of the Rhine, in the trade helped ensure political support, and was important to the deterioration of England's relations with the Dutch, which contributed to the outbreak of the second Anglo-Dutch war (see pp. 91–2). The role of the Royal African Company was criticised widely, and its position deteriorated after the Glorious Revolution of 1688–9. The freeing of the African trade from the Company's control by the Ten Per Cent Act in 1698 (thus named because the merchants had to pay a 10 per cent duty to maintain the Company's forts) legalised the position of interlopers, and the Company became insolvent in 1708. The opening up of the trade helped Bristol merchants develop the triangular trade in which they took textiles, alcohol, metal goods, guns and gunpowder to West Africa, and used them there to purchase slaves, which they took to the New World, purchasing colonial products there.[21] Another monopoly, the Hudson's Bay Company, whose first expedition was dispatched in 1668, was attacked for allegedly failing to uphold national interests in the face of French competition and for a lack of interest in expanding into the interior of Canada. This criticism led to a parliamentary inquiry in 1749.

The joint-stock capitalisation of a company, the approach used to accumulate capital and spread risk for some trades, was not the financial and organisational method that was to dominate the Atlantic trades, and the result of this played an important role in the flexibility of the latter. After 1689, only the Hudson's Bay trade was a successful monopoly in the British Atlantic world.

The situation was very different further east, and company monopoly, after a brief hiatus, was maintained: hostility to the East India Company led, in 1698, to the establishment of an additional East India Company, but, in 1709, the two companies, which were serving only to damage each other's interests, merged. The Company represented English interests not only in India but also around the Indian Ocean and in neighbouring seas, with a presence in the East Indies, especially Sumatra, and the Persian Gulf, while, to provide a base en route, the Company took control of St. Helena in the South Atlantic in 1673; the Dutch had established a position at Cape Town in 1652. The Company benefited greatly from the rise in the import of tea: from 1717, Company ships began a regular cycle of trade direct to China in order to obtain tea, and, whereas in the 1720s almost nine million pounds of tea were landed, by the 1750s more than 37 million pounds came to Britain, the price falling by roughly a half over that period.

Manufactured imports were less welcome in Britain as they competed with native producers, and, as a result, the import of printed calicoes was restricted in 1700. The 1721 ban on the wearing of imported printed fabrics, passed in order to protect native manufacturers of wool and silk stuffs from the competition of Indian calicoes imported by the Company, stimulated the growth of a British cotton industry. As yet, British producers did not enjoy the advantage over imports that mechanisation was to bring in the nineteenth century, but they were able to profit from printing the imported fabrics.[22]

Although the East India Company remained important, the idea of privileged companies declined with that of royal authority unconstrained by parliamentary supervision. After the removal of James II and VII in the Glorious Revolution, the relationship between government and trade no longer focused on the Court, and, instead, mercantile business and merchant representation played a growing role in the House of Commons, as part of a close relationship between trade and government in which merchants influenced policy.[23] In Somerset, the wool traders petitioned Parliament successfully in the 1690s for an Act to make the River Tone navigable to Bridgewater in order to allow traders access to the shipping of the British Channel. The political contours and context of mercantilism were now very different to those of court-focused and directed oligarchy. At the same time, the growing celebration, especially from the 1730s but with earlier anticipation, of the patriot merchant, inherently a self-reliant individual, helped make trade a potent political goal and platform, and was directly linked to the pursuit of maritime hegemony and imperial advantage.

The close relations between trade and the wars that followed the Glorious Revolution were seen in particular in the privateering through which Britain attacked the trade of its opponents and in the pursuit of colonial sources for products. Privateering entailed a fusion of patriotism and profit, and the prospect of the latter helped mobilise support for imperial warfare within the mercantile community, in both Britain and in the colonies.[24] In turn, Britain, in wartime, suffered serious blows from privateering. French bases, especially St. Malo and Dunkirk, proved difficult to contain, and this led to higher insurance premiums, danger money for sailors and the need to resort to convoys, while the damage to the economy and public finances helped cause the financial crisis of 1696. Privateers were a threat to the trade of the empire not only in home waters, but also across the world, so that the East India Company lost the *Samuel* off Cape Town in 1692 and the *Canterbury* in the Straits of Malacca in 1703. The French used regular warships as well as privateers to attack British trade, and, in 1693, over 80 merchantmen were lost when the Smyrna (Izmir) convoy bringing home goods from Turkey was intercepted by the Brest fleet off Lagos in Portugal, a blow that caused a political crisis. Attacks continued to be a problem in the wars of the mid-eighteenth century. In the 1740s, during the War of the Austrian Succession, French and Spanish privateers inflicted serious losses on the agricultural staple trades of the Carolinas, the Chesapeake and, especially, the Caribbean, and in 1747–8 they brought Philadelphia's trade to a halt.[25]

Such attacks underlined the importance of naval protection for British trade and the extent to which commercial prosperity, and thus growth, depended on security rather than on technological changes in shipping. The role of the navy was particularly clear in North Africa, as naval officers played a crucial role in relations with the Barbary states. For example, Captain George Delaval was sent on two missions to Sultan Isma'il as-Samin of Morocco: in 1700 he negotiated a treaty for the redemption of captives, and in 1708 an agreement not to molest each other's ships. Captain Padden concluded a truce with Morocco in 1713, Commodore Augustus Keppel reached an agreement with Algiers in 1751, and Commodore Sir Roger Curtis was ordered in 1783 to renew the treaty of friendship with Morocco.[26]

The political, governmental and financial changes that followed the Glorious Revolution, including the establishment of the Board of Trade and Plantations in 1696, also played a major role in fostering trade. The stabilisation of financial markets in London after the foundation of the Bank of England in 1694, and Britain's success in gaining access to South American bullion, especially gold from Brazil, a colony of Portugal, with which she was allied from 1703, were crucial in developing the finance and infrastructure for credit. By providing the funds and instruments for long-term credit, the so-called Financial Revolution underwrote British participation in an Atlantic economy that ran on borrowed capital, and this was important to the growth of shipping as well as to the development of tobacco production round the Chesapeake, sugar production in the West Indies and the slave trade that provided the manpower necessary for both.

THE SLAVE TRADE AND SLAVERY

Trade was linked to migration (another fundamental lifeblood of empire), through the trade in human beings, slavery, one of the most emotive issues in history. To point out that slavery has been a constant for most of human history, and that it has been practised by many societies, is not intended to minimise the suffering and impact of the Atlantic slave trade, which had important consequences for the British economy,[27] and fundamental demographic, cultural and social effects on Africa and on many of the British colonies in the New World. These effects reach to the present day, nowhere more so than in the continued relevance of slavery for modern debate over racism and its impact. Historically, there was no necessary relationship between slavery and racism, and enslavement was often a penalty for illegal behaviour, but there was a deeper identity of racialism and slavery, for enslavement was frequently the response to the 'other', to other peoples (irrespective of their skin colour), and other creatures. Thus, treating conquered peoples and their offspring as slaves seemed as logical to many as treating animals such as horses as slaves; the latter, beasts of burden, were also the creation of God, but their very openness to enslavement apparently demonstrated a natural and necessary fate. The treatment of (white) indentured servants, who agreed to provide several years service in return for the cost of their passage to the New World, is sometimes regarded as a form of slavery, but legal reality and the cultural context were very different; and the greater number of these servants who escaped, compared with slaves, reflected their different circumstances, their ability to find new opportunities and the greater effort put into recapturing escaped slaves.

The Native (pre-European) population in North America and the West Indies had fallen dramatically as a result of European illnesses, especially smallpox and measles, and, as most of the surviving Natives lived outside regions under the control of imperial powers, they did not provide a possible labour force in North America. Instead, slaves came to provide the labour force across much of the British New World. Whether brought from abroad or born in the colonies, they were more malleable than indentured servants. The English slave trade had initially been dominated by the attempt to supply Portuguese and Spanish colonies with labour, and thus obtain bullion or goods readily sold in England, but, as the English colonies expanded, the supply of slaves was increasingly focused on the latter. Providing slaves to the colonies of other powers nevertheless remained important; in 1713, Britain gained the *asiento* contract to transport slaves from West Africa to Spanish America, a lucrative opening into the protected trade of the Spanish Empire, and many slaves sold in the West Indies, for example in Jamaica, were resold to Spanish colonies.[28] Brazil was also a market, and there was concern in 1723 about possible Portuguese competition in the supply of slaves.[29] However, for British, as for French, merchants, the core trade was that of selling slaves to their own colonies.

The British transported even more slaves than the French. Between 1691 and 1779, British ships transported 2,141,900 slaves from African ports, and British colonial ships took another 124,000.[30] London dominated the trade until the 1710s when it was replaced by Bristol, while Liverpool took the leading position from the 1740s. In 1725, Bristol ships carried about 17,000 slaves and, between 1727 and 1769, 39 slavers were built there, while, by 1752, Liverpool had 88 slavers, with a combined capacity of over 25,000 slaves. Most of the slaves transported ended up in the West Indies colonies, where, despite a high death rate, the number of slaves rose from about 15,000 in 1650 to about 115,000 fifty years later, a rate of increase that greatly outpaced that of British settlers. Most labour in North America then was indentured, but the number of slaves there rose from about 20,000 in 1700 to over 300,000 by 1763, particularly as first South Carolina and then Georgia were developed as plantation economies.

The slave trade was integral to the commercial economy and shipping world of the British Atlantic, crucial to entrepreneurial circles in Britain, and to the financial world there, and had a range of influences elsewhere in Britain, particularly, but not only, in the ports. Not only were the large ports of Liverpool, Bristol, Glasgow and London involved in the trade, but also smaller ports, such as Barnstaple, Bideford, Dartmouth, Exeter, Lancaster, Plymouth, Poole, Topsham and Whitehaven.[31] However, the development of this and other Atlantic trades contributed to the decline of the importance of ports that could not play a role in them, so that, whereas, for example, Great Yarmouth, King's Lynn and Ipswich had been well-placed on the North Sea to take a major role in England's foreign trade in the Middle Ages, by the seventeenth century they were essential, instead, only for coastal trade, not least the movement of coal south from the Tyne. This was also part of a more profound geographical shift towards Atlantic trade and connections, so that, by 1750, Bristol had replaced Norwich as the second most populous city in England.

Returns from slave-trading ventures were risky, but also sufficiently attractive to keep some existing investors in the trade and to entice new investors to join up, and the returns could enable men of marginal status to prosper sufficiently to enter the merchants class. Furthermore, the triangular pattern of Atlantic trade – goods, both British manufactures and imports such as East India Company textiles, from Britain to Africa, slaves to the New World, and colonial products such as sugar and tobacco to Britain – was practicable for small-scale operators, as the outlay of funds required was less than for the trade to the East Indies, while the triangular trade offered considerable flexibility so that, for example, when sugar became harder to obtain from the West Indies, Lancaster's traders found other imports in which to invest their proceeds from slave sales, particularly mahogany, rum and dyewoods, each of which was in demand in Britain. This enabled them to maximise their profits on each leg of their enterprise, which was particularly important for marginal operators trading in a competitive field, while, when competition did eventually make the slave trade less viable at Lancaster, the contracts and experiences forged by the African trade meant that other opportunities were on offer to merchants.[32] The triangular trade was not the sole commercial system that was developed to help finance and exploit slavery. Supplying food and other products to the slave plantations was also important, and this included the development of a trade in salt cod from Newfoundland to the West Indies and to Charleston, the port for South Carolina.

The slave trade, nevertheless, involved serious commercial risks, created for example by a lack of sufficient slaves or, alternatively, by the glutting of markets. The slave trade was expensive to enter, while, on the whole, it did not bring great profits, which may explain why the majority of British ships involved made only one voyage in the trade. Whitehaven merchants largely abandoned the trade after 1769, and there were also problems for more prominent slaving ports, for example Bristol in the early 1730s, which was hit by shortages of slaves, falling profits on colonial re-exports, as prices dropped, and deteriorating relations with Spain.[33] More generally, concern about the profitability of the trade was a major factor in the pronounced variation in the number of voyages per year from individual ports. This concern was an aspect of what has been presented as a distinctive system of economic activity and thought, based on the uncertainty of trade, credit and politics, that was the product of capitalism and the new demands of the Atlantic economy.[34]

Profitability was also hit by the human cost of slavery, in the shape of the high death-rate on the Atlantic crossing. At the individual level, the reality of slavery was of the trauma of capture by African chieftains, sale to British merchants and transportation: violence, shock, hardship and disruption. Individuals were taken from their families and communities, and many died in the process of capture, in the drive to the coast, in the port towns where they were crowded together in hazardous circumstances, on the ships that transported them across the Atlantic, and soon after arrival, as the entire process exposed slaves to unaccustomed levels and types of disease. There are no precise figures for deaths, but it has been suggested that 10 per cent died on the Atlantic crossing, where they were crowded together and in poor, especially insanitary, conditions, and, although with time the percentage who died fell appreciably, this was owing to shorter journey times rather than improved conditions. Many of the officers and crew involved in the trade also died, including 10 to 15 per cent of the Liverpool captains who sailed from 1785 to 1807,[35] in part as a consequence of their exposure to tropical diseases.

The price for male slaves was greater than that for females, both on the African coast and in the New World, and more males than females were imported, reflecting the role of demand factors in the trade, specifically the hard physical nature of the work that was expected. Once arrived, conditions for the slaves could be very bleak, both psychologically and in terms of the labour regime: they lost their names and their identities were challenged. The labour regime in sugar and rice cultivation was particularly arduous and deadly; tobacco and cacao less so. Hacking down sugar cane – crucial to the production process – was back-breaking work and required a large, expendable and easily replaced labour force that slavery provided more effectively than indentured labour, which was not only less malleable but less ecologically attuned to the working environment. Captain William Freeman, who from 1670 developed a sugar plantation on the West Indies island of Montserrat, before becoming a London merchant, claimed that 'land without slaves is a dead stock'.[36] Colonies that shifted from tobacco to sugar saw a marked increase in the slave population and less of a reliance on indentured labour: on Montserrat, 40 per cent of the 4,500 population in 1678 was non-white; but this grew to 80 per cent of the 7,200 population in 1729. Slaves had difficult and frequently harsh living conditions; aside from the nature of their work, they were less well fed, housed and clothed than the white population, and, partly as a result of these conditions, were more affected by disease. This was particularly true of the West Indies, but less so of the Chesapeake, where tobacco cultivation combined with a more favourable environment to produce less hostile conditions.

The profits and possibilities brought by slavery and the slave trade readily explain both, but it would be wrong to present the complex dynamics of enslavement simply in terms of rising demand for labour in the New World. Accounts focusing on Western economic domination in Africa, and/or the gun-slave cycle, by which slaves were obtained from African rulers in return for European guns, are inadequate, not least because it was not until after the Industrial Revolution had transformed Britain's economy that traders could exert significant economic pressure on Africans, while weapon sales do not provide the key to the trade. Instead, it is necessary to focus on the supply of labour, as well as the means for satisfying demand, and also to offer a specific examination of the slave-supplying regions in order to suggest the danger of broad generalisations. What emerges clearly is a politics of frequent conflict within Africa that produced slaves. A breakdown of order was instrumental in providing large numbers of slaves in Congo, while, on the Gold Coast, wars and banditry also resulted in the sale of large numbers. In the area of the Bight of Benin, instability emerged from the expansionism of Dahomey, while, near Angola, the expansionism of the Lunda Empire produced slaves; although fighting was also often linked to serious droughts. Enslavement was thus common, but the widespread belief among many Africans exported as slaves that they had been sold to cannibals to be cooked and eaten possibly expressed a wider opposition to the cannibalistic social politics of selling slaves to foreigners.[37]

If so, it had little effect on African polities, for African rulers proved more than willing to sell captives, and the slave trade would not have been possible without their active co-operation. Indeed, the slave trade encapsulated much of the reality of the British impact in the world: it was destructive, served the needs of a European-dominated global economy and would have been impossible without local support, the last a point that is unacceptable to many modern critics of imperialism. In practice, the global economy pressed on the local, and the local served the global. The British territorial presence in West Africa was very limited, posts were not held by sovereign right but by agreement with local rulers – rent or tribute was paid for several posts, and the officials of the Royal African Company sought to maintain a beneficial relationship with numerous local caboceers (leaders) and penyins (elders) through an elaborate and costly system of presents and jobs.

The crucial role of local co-operation in the slave trade was more generally true of British trans-oceanic activity in this period, for example of

trade in the Indian Ocean,[38] and any discussion of relations in terms of conflict alone is unhelpful. Instead, economic, cultural, religious and political
ties crossed British/non-British divides, turning them into zones of interaction in which symbiosis, synergy and exchange are analytical terms that
are as helpful as conflict and war. Furthermore, much of the violence across
these divides involved an important measure of co-operation. If this helps
locate the slave trade, it does not lessen its horror; and, as on other occasions in British imperial expansion, co-operation in no way entails the
benefit of all concerned. Instead, in this case, slavery entailed the interaction of the Western economic order and the dynamics of African warfare at
the cost of the victims of the latter.

Many slaves soon died as a result of the crossing or the punishing and
unfamiliar work regime, but the flood of arrivals Africanised the areas to
which they came, because slaves used their African culture to adapt to the
New World. African 'nations' emerged in the New World, but they did not
correspond well to political or social units in Africa, in that they were based
on language alone. This sustained African culture in America, although
ethnic ties and identities were eroded when the percentage of those born
in Africa decreased in slave communities.[39] The development of new ties
among slaves was mediated through the differing circumstances of slave life;
owing to the varied demands of tobacco and rice cultivation, and related
environmental and social characteristics, slaves in the Chesapeake were more
affected by white life, living in close proximity to owners in relatively small
farms, whereas, in the rice lands of South Carolina, there were fewer, but
larger plantations, the percentage of slaves was greater and the higher death
rate ensured that there were more imported African slaves compared with
the American-born slaves who were more important in the Chesapeake. As
a consequence, in South Carolina, slaves were more autonomous and more
influenced by African culture and material life, and relations between slaves
and whites remained more antipathetical than where they lived in closer
proximity,[40] although it is not easy to assess slave attitudes. The slave situation in Jamaica, where slaves were also treated harshly, was more similar to
South Carolina than the Chesapeake; among both slaves and whites in
Jamaica the majority were immigrants.[41]

The differing needs for slaves were not solely geographical, as opinion
among planters was divided. For example, late in the eighteenth century, in
South Carolina, Georgia and East Florida, the better established commercial agriculture was, the more its participants wanted to reform or diversify
it, especially to prevent greater dependence on slavery; while, conversely,
newer settlers welcomed such dependence.[42]

In slave-holding areas, there were both slave risings and problems created
by escaping slaves. In 1739, in the Stono rising in South Carolina, 100 slaves

rose and killed 20 colonists before being defeated by the militia and their Native allies.[43] Circumstances did not favour slave risings, as the whites limited the availability of firearms to slaves and made efforts to prevent them plotting; they were unable to co-ordinate action except in very small areas. Flight was a more common form of resistance, and it led, in Jamaica, to unsuccessful expeditions against the Maroons – runaway slaves who controlled much of the mountainous interior – which were followed in 1738 and 1739 by treaties that granted the Maroons land and autonomy.[44]

MIGRATIONS

Enslavement was not the only way in which force played a major role in the migrations in the British Atlantic. The dispatch of convicts to provide a labour force was also important, and was a pointed instance of how colonies were supposed to accommodate what was seen as surplus population. Many of those defeated in Monmouth's Rebellion in 1685 were transported, especially to Jamaica. Concern about rising crime after the War of the Spanish Succession (1702–13), when demobilisation released large numbers of fit men trained to violence into a labour market that could not cope, led to the Transportation Act of 1718 which, for the first time, allowed for transportation, not only as part of the pardoning process in the case of capital offences, but as a penalty for a wide range of non-capital crimes, including grand larceny – the theft of property between a shilling (five new pence) and £2 (worth about £10 to £200 in 2004 values). Parliament went on to pass another sixteen Acts between 1720 and 1763 that established transportation as a penalty for crimes from perjury to poaching, and, as a result, as many as 50,000 convicts were transported from the British Isles to America and the West Indies in 1718–75: well over 30,000 from England, with more than 13,000 from Ireland, and nearly 700 from Scotland to America. The shipboard mortality rate was about 14 per cent, a number comparable with the cruel treatment of Africans sent as slaves – infectious disease in the crowded conditions was, again, the major problem. The majority of the convicts sent to America went to Virginia and Maryland, with most of the rest being sent to Pennsylvania; very few were sent to New England,[45] reflecting, but also accentuating, the contrasting social character and political culture of the colonies, particularly the lesser role of social distinction and control in New England. An analysis of indentured servants leaving Liverpool in 1697 to 1707 also demonstrates this.[46] Alongside slaves, the use of convicts testified to the widespread belief that coercion was the only way to deal with the labour needs of settlement colonies, as coercion made possible the diligent and purposeful supervision required for the proper improvement of the colonies, and, possibly of both slaves and convicts.

Alongside those who were compelled to travel and work in order to serve the needs of the imperial economy and state, came the voluntary migrants. The number of British emigrants to the New World far outnumbered those to South Asia and West Africa, neither of which attracted settlers, and this emigration greatly accentuated the impact of earlier migration, increasing the number and percentage of non-Natives in the British New World. The pace of settlement was higher in the British than in the French North American colonies, because the opportunities in the British colonies were as much a matter of governmental attitude as of agricultural and urban possibilities. The British were particularly tolerant of religious groups outside the established Churches, although the position in individual colonies varied: in Virginia, in 1643, Puritan nonconformity was banned, whereas, six years later, Lord Baltimore, the Catholic proprietor of Maryland, had the Assembly enact a law of toleration.

The overall contrast with French intolerance helped to ensure that, by 1700, despite the fact that Britain's population was only about a quarter of that of France and the number of French inhabitants in Canada had risen to about 10,000, there were about 210,000 Europeans in British North America. In part, the expansion in numbers in British North America reflected the conquest of New Netherland (which had, in the 1650s, already acquired the New Sweden established from 1638 in the Delaware Valley), a conquest organised as two colonies, New York and New Jersey, each of which gained representative assemblies, which had been absent under the Dutch. In addition, there was a burst of colonisation with the settlement of Carolina (1663), Delaware (1664) and Pennsylvania (1681).

Much of the French population was ready to migrate within France but, in contrast, in Britain, not only was there a high degree of internal migration, but also there was a greater willingness to emigrate to, or act as an entrepreneur in, distant areas. Compared with France and Spain, the population, on average, lived closer to the sea, a consequence of Britain's island nature, and, for those in port cities and coastal regions, maritime activity played a role in the popular consciousness that was very different from the situation today.

Emigration followed possibilities created by trade and other contacts. Voluntary emigration was a cumulative process, as it made particular use of networks of family, friends and other contacts, especially neighbourhood and religious groups, which provided the collective solidarity that helped individuals overcome the hardships and anxieties of migration and settlement. Voluntary settlement was also encouraged by particular sponsors, especially the proprietors of colonies, for example the Trustees of Georgia. All these factors combined to produce a mass of information about options regarding work and settlement overseas, although it was difficult to distinguish fact from rumour, for empire always attracted projectors and flourished on rumour.[47]

The disparity between European migration to the British and French colonies became more marked during the eighteenth century, with consequences felt when the two powers clashed in North America. Canada had only about 56,000 inhabitants of French origin in 1740, whereas, by then, British North America had nearly a million people of European background, reflecting the willingness to accept both a high rate of migration from the British Isles and non-British immigrants. The poverty of some settlers did not discourage others from migrating, because wage rates were higher in the New World than in the British Isles, and an Act of Parliament of 1697 which allowed people to seek work outside their own parish if they carried a certificate made the poor more mobile and encouraged the migration of indentured servants to America[48] and the West Indies.

It is too easy to lose sight of the latter. Indeed, between 30,000 and 50,000 white migrants arrived in Jamaica in the first half of the eighteenth century. Aside from the importance of the island as an entrepôt for Spanish America,[49] the cultivated area on Jamaica increased greatly; tellingly, this information refers to the land under imperial control, not that tilled by escaped slaves. But for disease, this migration would have led to a British New World demographically dominated by the West Indies, where the British presence was expanded by the settlement of Jamaica and the Cayman Islands from 1655, the Virgin Islands from 1666, and the Bahamas from 1670, although much immigration by both white migrants and slaves was to already established colonies. If migrants in the West Indies had multiplied at the same rate as emigrants to the mainland, their population by 1760 would have been nearly 3 million, compared with only 1.7 million in British North America, and if the rate had been the same as that of migrants to the southern plantation colonies in North America, the figures would have been equal. Conversely, death rates comparable with those in the British West Indies would have left a mainland population of less than 200,000 in 1760, of whom only about 50,000 lived in the northern colonies. In Jamaica, white death rates were higher than those of slaves, and this ensured that the colony could not become a settler society with a large, locally born white population. Yellow fever, which first struck in 1694, was a particular scourge and was especially virulent in those previously unexposed to the disease, while malaria was also a serious problem.[50]

Whereas, in the seventeenth century, English migrants dominated emigration from the British Isles to the New World, in the eighteenth there was also extensive emigration from Scotland and Ireland, especially in response to economic difficulties in both.[51] This emigration helps provide a key to the detailed patchwork of settlement, not least in religious terms: much of the emigration from both Scotland and Ireland, the latter referred to today in the USA as Scots-Irish, was of Presbyterians, and they had a different religious culture to the Anglicans (later Episcopalians) who were particularly prominent in Virginia. The Presbyterians had a strong sense of community, but they lacked the emphasis on hierarchical authority seen among Anglicans. Particular links and opportunities played an important role in the detailed pattern of migrating, as with the heavy preponderance of Orcadians in the factories of the Hudson's Bay Company: the Company's ships took on water in the Orkneys en route to Hudson's Bay.

Furthermore, emigration to the British colonies from outside the British Isles affected both the general character of the colonies and specific locations. Germans were particularly concentrated in Pennsylvania, but not only there. In North Carolina in 1710, a group of German and Swiss immigrants established the town of New Bern, which was so successful that it became the capital of the colony in 1770, and, by then, maybe as much as 30 per cent of the colony's population was of German descent.[52] Many had come from the Rhineland, where, in the Palatinate, there had been serious persecution of Protestants in the 1700s and 1710s. Religious refugees were particularly encouraged in Georgia (where the first settlement was established in 1733), enabling the fledgling colony to anchor Britain's presence between Carolina and Florida: many of these refugees came from the Archbishopric of Salzburg, indicating the importance of colonisation in the British Empire for ordinary people far distant from the Atlantic coast. Under the Plantation Act of 1745, it was possible for all, bar Catholics, to become eligible for naturalisation after seven years in a British colony.

These migrants helped push forward the frontier of settlement, taking advantage of the new land made available by Native American defeats, and earlier territorial claims were given a degree of substance by this advance. In 1663, Charles II had granted to eight supporters the proprietorship of a colony from the Atlantic to the Pacific, between 31° and 36°N, 'and that the country . . . may be dignified by us . . . we of our grace . . . call it the Province of Carolina'. Two years later, the bounds were extended to 29° to 36°30′N. The assertion of claims rested in part on a conviction that the apparent Native inability or unwillingness to settle and develop lands, left them free for imperial acquisition and improvement.[53] This was a self-serving belief, but it stemmed from a powerful conviction of human responsibility to make the best use of the gifts and opportunities given by God, a religious conviction that helped condition moral, judicial and social assumptions within Britain and her colonies. Applied in the colonies, in a Christian context that was determined by British norms, these attitudes provided ready guidelines by which most commentators judged Native mores and practices inadequate, and a similar stance was adopted towards those mores regarded as inherent to slave society. Thus religion helped provide a ranking of peoples and a justification for settlement that prefigured what has been referred to as the Social Darwinism seen in the late nineteenth-century heyday of imperialism.

Although the creation of the colony of Carolina was intended to free the area from dependence on the colony of Virginia as much as to deny Native interests, it indicated the extent to which British territorial claims bore no relation to the frontier of settlement. This became less the case with expansion in the eighteenth century, which was largely a matter of initiatives by colonists. Conflict with the French interacted with tension and conflict with Native Americans, especially arising from the land hunger that the demographic growth of the British colonies exacerbated. The Tuscaroras responded to the advance of settlers by raiding settlements in North Carolina in 1711. Counter attacks that year and in 1712 failed, but, in 1713, with the support of a larger allied Native American force, the Tuscaroras were defeated and nearly 600 were killed or enslaved, a defeat that was followed by the advance of British settlement to the Blue Ridge Mountains.

Further south, provoked by exploitation by Carolina merchants and landowners, the Yamasee of the Lower Savannah River attacked South Carolina in 1715, raiding to within 12 miles of Charleston, while other tribes, including the Lower Creek, Cherokee and Catawba, provided them with support. The initial South Carolina military response was unsuccessful, but the Native alliance was not sustained and Native disunity greatly helped the colonists. The Cherokee came round to help the Carolinians in 1716, and, in 1717, the Creek deserted the Yamasee. Defeat had a major demographic impact on the Natives, and, from 1715, most of the Yamasee were killed or enslaved by the colonial militia.

After 1730, as readily cultivatable land grew scarcer in Maryland, Pennsylvania and Virginia, settlers travelled down the Great Philadelphia Wagon Road, through the Shenandoah Valley and the James River and Roanoke Gaps, to enter the Piedmont of North and South Carolina, a migration stream that was different in its composition from that which supplied people to the Tidewater, or coastal plain, of both colonies, and one that drove up the population: that of North Carolina from 30,000 whites and 6,000 blacks in 1730, to 255,000 whites and 10,000 blacks in 1775. These figures reflect the extent to which North Carolina was not a plantation society like South Carolina, and, indeed, underlining the variety of colonial economies, timber products were among its more important exports. Settlement also furthered the process of re-naming that was such an important legacy of empire. Thus, Denys Rolle, a Devon landowner, established Rollestown in East Florida in the 1760s, and, when he was offered land in the Bahamas after Spain regained the colony at the close of the War of American Independence, established Rolleville and Rolletown. The surname Rolle survives among the descendants of his slaves,[54] and other slave-owners have left a similar legacy.

FRONTIER SOCIETIES

Discussion of advancing frontiers of settlement can underplay the extent to which the British Empire involved co-operation as well as conflict, and can thus lead to a simplification of frontier society and 'the frontier'. Frontier society is an aspect of empire that receives insufficient attention because better records survive for those of the colonial populations who lived in port cities and plantations, and they, and their trade with Britain, engaged most fully the attention of the British government. Another reason for the underrating of frontier society is that its economy and society were inherently unstable and prone to be absorbed by the controls, practices and ethos of more colonised areas, especially as immigration gathered pace. Thus, in the lower Mississippi valley, a frontier exchange economy involving Native Americans and white traders lasted into the 1760s when new rulers in Louisiana (Spain) and West Florida (Britain) took measures to increase the number of colonial inhabitants, both white settlers and black slaves.[55]

Nevertheless, however unstable, frontier societies were not some mere fag-end of empire. Instead, the phrase encapsulates complex relationships, both between British colonists and non-Europeans, and between colonists and their government, and these societies have been presented as providing what has been termed a 'middle ground' of shared cultural space between colonists and Natives. In this space, individuals and groups have been seen as playing an active role in organising relations, instead of being simply victims of a distant imperial power, and this is part of an understanding of empire in terms of processes rather than structures, and processes in which those immediately engaged in colonisation played a crucial role.[56]

Many individuals prominent in the 'middle ground' alongside the Thirteen Colonies were the product of British–Native marriages, which helped them to act as translators and to play a major role in trade. Such intermarriage was also very important in other frontier areas such as Hudson Bay and West Africa,[57] and, as more mixed-race children were born, so the prospects of marrying mixed-race women increased. However, the process of participation in the 'middle ground', and, more generally, in the imperial system was both unstable and unequal. Mixed-race heterosexual relationships faced growing opposition in the empire to what was seen as concubinage,[58] and there was also an instability in political relations, seen, for example in King Philip's War in which the Native view that the sovereignty of their tribal units could be incorporated into the English political system clashed with an English and, even more, colonists' perception of Natives as subjects.[59]

This unstable ambiguity was not limited to relations with Natives. There were also differences between governmental views and colonists, both those who lived in settled communities and others who were more clearly independent, such as privateers. For many privateers, both war and peace were periods of opportunity, and they were as prepared to attack compatriots as the subjects of other rulers, which helped lead to a shift in government attitudes, for piracy at the expense of compatriots was different from buccaneering at the cost of enemies. Piracy was a particular opportunity and problem in the late seventeenth and early eighteenth centuries, not least as a consequence of demobilisation at the close of the War of the Spanish Succession. Firm government action in the 1710s and 1720s, based on parliamentary legislation in 1700 and 1708, transformed the situation, indicating the value government offered ship-owners and merchants in terms of an ability to deliver protection. In 1718, 'Blackbeard' (Edward Teach), who had held Charleston to ransom earlier in the year, died after being trapped on the North Carolina coast, while, four years later, another British warship defeated the two ships of Bartholomew Roberts off West Africa, killing Roberts.[60] Trade protection was thereafter to be a major function of the peacetime navy, and while the need for action was episodic, it still had to be borne in mind, the obligation growing as imperial interests and responsibilities spread.

Piracy has been presented as an aspect of a wider proletarian hostility within the empire to the forces of power, profit and order, the last seen as the enforcement of the cruel 'anarchy of the global market'.[61] With its wide-ranging links and capacity to draw on support from, and interact with, groups and mercantile circles, piracy can also appear as a form of counter-empire within the British maritime world, particularly the British Atlantic. Nevertheless, although there was indeed social tension within the empire, it would be mistaken to see this in terms of clashing worlds. Instead, there was a continuum of relations, with multiple links, including the attempt to transplant British customs and pratices,[62] as well as serious discords.

This was true not only of maritime life but also of the settler population. Much of this was poor and lacking in power. Many settlers were indentured servants, most of whom went as labourers. In return for their passage, indentured servants bound themselves to service for a number of years, and they were traded like slaves.[63] Furthermore, some settlers were badly off wage labourers or impoverished farmers. Although they had opportunities to challenge their conditions by abandoning their employment or by labour protest, and cannot really be considered as white slaves, their circumstances were often difficult,[64] and it is important to remember the role of social tensions within settler communities alongside the race relations that attract so much modern attention. In North America and the West Indies, yeomen clashed with gentry over a range of issues, including political representation and economic interests. Furthermore, racial issues were often driven by social tensions within the settler community. Opposition to the import of slaves and a desire to drive Natives from the land both, in part, reflected the particular interests of poor whites.[65]

COLONISTS AND GOVERNMENT

Tensions between colonists and government reflected the politics of the homeland as well as a complex interaction of links and differences played out against a background of social developments in the colonies. As far as links are concerned, it is too easy to underrate the Englishness or Britishness of early colonial history: in the case of the Thirteen Colonies which were, in 1776, to declare independence from the British Crown, it is understandable both that knowledge of eventual independence colours the analysis, and that the experience of emigration and the conditions encountered in the colonies are assumed to have constituted a radical break. This is mistaken, as the evolution of colonial societies was greatly affected by British assumptions, although this should not be presented as a passive process, for the impact of the local environment and economy were important, not least in creating very different worlds of work, with consequent social relations. In addition, far from there being uniform views and experiences, the variety of settler communities interacted with that of British patterns of behaviour and thought.

Thus, New England, with its Puritan separatism, urban character, and (albeit limited) democratic practices, in part drew on different traditions to the society that was established round the Chesapeake. To understand both it is necessary to appreciate the varied character of English social development. In the case of seventeenth-century Maryland and Virginia, most settlers were English by birth and upbringing, they established a society based on English laws, government and economic organisation, and brought traditional English attitudes towards the social order and religious practices, although ones that differed from those that influenced New England. However, in the case of the Chesapeake, immigration from England greatly slackened from the 1690s, and social contrasts became more marked, and this was linked to a demographic shift in which, thanks to a decline in death rates, the percentage of native-born inhabitants rose, ensuring a better balance of men and women, early marriages and thus more children. A greater separateness from England emerged, but this was less the case with colonies subsequently settled, such as Georgia and (East and West) Florida. There was also considerable variety among the West Ladies' colonies.[66]

The politics of the homeland were important in the development of British colonies, and their history in the seventeenth century reflected the instability of the homeland, for, in both, this was an era of rapid change that challenged existing ideas and institutions and ensured that developments occurred against a background of instability and crisis. Rather than thinking primarily in terms of a tension between colonial autonomy and English (later British) authority, differing political positions spanned the Atlantic, so that, under Charles II, the formal authority of the Crown over the governments of Barbados and Massachusetts was increased, while, in 1677–9, abortive plans were drafted to make legislation in Virginia and Jamaica dependent on the assent of Parliament. From his accession in 1685, James II of England and VII of Scotland's attempt to impose autocracy clashed, in both Britain and the colonies, with the corporate ideal of government, as well as with a Protestant suspicion of the intentions of the Catholic monarch, and the overthrow of James in the Glorious Revolution of 1688–9 was popular with colonial elites not only because it promised to roll back Stuart autocracy, but also because it provided legitimation for America's evolving politics.[67] James had created a Dominion of New England (1686–9) that had sought to give force to royal edicts and to overcome colonial autonomy, so that the Navigation Acts, which had been ignored by a number of the colonies, were enforced. As an aspect of the Glorious Revolution, royal governors were overthrown in Boston, New York, Maryland and Antigua in 1689,[68] and the Dominion disintegrated as colonists restored the governments replaced by James. This overthrow, like subsequent defeats in Britain for Jacobitism – attempts at Stuart revival – helped strengthen the community of sentiment that spanned the Atlantic.

The Glorious Revolution was followed in both England and the colonies by the implementation of a new order that included a measure of religious toleration as well as an extension of government based on the Westminster Parliament; Ireland and Scotland still had their separate parliaments. This extension was seen with the revised Navigation Act of 1696, that authorised colonial vice-admiralty courts and with the creation in 1700 of a General Post Office that had branches in the colonies. Furthermore, the spread of a measure of religious toleration (markedly so in contrast with the French and Spanish Empires) led to pressure on colonial assemblies to copy the Toleration Act of 1689, and also to the Naturalization Act of 1740, which offered to foreign Protestants and Jews in the colonies the rights of British subjects.

This parliamentary assertiveness added a dimension to the relations between Crown and colonies that had, in other respects, been modified in favour of co-operation, not only by the reaction to James II, but also because the series of wars with France between 1689 and 1763 put a premium on colonial assistance. The contiguity or proximity of British colonies with Bourbon possessions in North America and the West Indies was particularly important in this respect: colonial military assistance was both necessary and possible, although the pressure of war led also to a more active imperial grip in colonies deemed of strategic importance. Alongside respect for established rights, pressure for co-operation helped ensure the failure of the Board of Trade's attempt in 1701–2 to bring all the remaining chartered colonies under the direct control of the Crown.

In addition to changes in authority to match those in England, there was also conflict specific to the colonies, especially in 1676, when a serious rising occurred among part of the settler population in Virginia: Bacon's Rebellion. When many of the militia supported the rebellion, the governor, Sir William Berkeley, a wealthy landowner who represented elite interests, turned to local loyalists, but he was unable to hold Jamestown, and the rebellion collapsed only when Bacon died.[69] There was a parallel 'Huy and Crye' rebellion in Maryland in 1676, directed against the autocratic and pro-Catholic policies of the proprietor, Lord Baltimore.

Less dramatically, governors clashed with assemblies that, on the whole, displayed more independence than the English (later British) House of Commons showed in the eighteenth century. There was a strong sense of local rights and privileges that were seen as the local and necessary encapsulation of British liberties, while disputes over the power and pretensions of governors were widespread and frequent, so that, in 1708, Nathaniel Johnson, Governor of Carolina, imprisoned Thomas Nairne, the province's first Indian agent, for complaining about his abuse of commercial links with the Natives, while, two years later, Daniel Parke, the Governor of the Leeward Islands, was lynched by colonists in Antigua when he sought to overawe complaints with a display of military strength, and no one was punished. The expansion of territorial claims and settlement was a particular source of dispute in the North American colonies, as it brought issues of both authority and interest into play, while support for imperial defence was also an issue in all colonies. In 1703, Colonel Dudley, the Governor of Massachusetts, traced his difficulties to the character of the colony's political culture, specifically the extent of representation, claiming that as the colony's Council was

of the people's choice . . . they are more careful of their election than of the Queen's service and satisfaction, in so much that I have only power to deny anything offered me that is amiss in the Assembly, but no assistance to bring to pass what is necessary for the service, which will be in a great measure altered when Her Majesty will please to assume her just power to name her own Council here as in all the other governments in America.[70]

By mid-century, the British Empire was, while still in flux, becoming more defined and populous: Philadelphia had grown from a population of 2,500 in 1685 to about 25,000 by 1760. An urban hierarchy had emerged clearly among the settlements and economic links had developed between colonies, while those between them and the British Isles had strengthened and become more varied. As in Spanish America, a sense of community, separate from, but not opposed to, that of Britain, was increasingly apparent; this sense superimposed on the multitude of identities that colonial life and settlement gave rise to. The foundation of a colonial press was a clear sign of this. English newspapers were shipped across the Atlantic, but, as early as 1704, Boston had the *Boston News Letter*, the first regular newspaper in British North America published by authority (although, in 1690, the unlicensed *Public Occurrences Foreign and Domestic* had been published there, only to be swiftly suppressed). The press communicated both pressures for a separate sense of identity and those for Anglicisation, both a sense of distinction from Britain and yet being part of a trans-Atlantic world, as indeed the press was, for newspapers were a major component in the trans-Atlantic information system, and both in the colonies and in Britain reported the voyages of individual ships, with predictions of arrival dates and, sometimes, information about cargoes. In addition, many printers crossed the Atlantic to the Thirteen Colonies and the West Indies.[71]

EXPLORATION

In turn, the ready availability of colonial news provided British publications with information about a trans-oceanic world that was of increasing interest. The nature of this news varied: alongside prosaic information about political and other developments, there was the playing out of moral themes that the exoticism of colonial life permitted. Thus, the tale of 'Inkle and Yarico', published in the leading English periodical, the *Spectator*, on 13 March 1711, was one of humanity affronted, and morality breached, by slavery:

Mr. Thomas Inkle, an ambitious young English trader cast ashore in the Americas, is saved from violent death at the hands of savages by the endearments of Yarico, a beautiful Indian maiden. Their romantic

intimacy in the forest moves Inkle to pledge that, were his life to be preserved, he would return with her to England, supposedly as his wife. The
lovers' tender liaison progresses over several months until she succeeds in
signalling a passing English ship. They are rescued by the crew, and with
vows to each other intact, they embark for Barbados. Yet when they reach
the island Inkle's former mercantile instincts are callously revived, for he
sells her into slavery, at once raising the price he demands when he learns
that Yarico is carrying his child.

This was but a stage in a tale that had surfaced in Richard Ligon's *History
of the Island of Barbadoes* (1657),[72] but the popularity of the story reflected
the way in which the trans-oceanic world could provide a setting for moral
challenges. Knowledge of this world, which owed much to the interlinking
of travel and publication, also expanded the horizon of British readers.
North America, for example, had different flora and fauna to that of Europe,
as was shown in publications such as Mark Catesby's well-received *The
Natural History of Carolina, Florida and the Bahama Islands* (1731–47), which
was based on his travels in 1712–25.[73] Exploration provided a staple for the
British (and colonial) world of print, as travel literature offered vivid
accounts for a society interested in novelty, while individual works were
given further prominence by being republished in collected works, such as
Thomas Astley's *New General Collection of Voyages and Travels* (1745).

English voyagers played a prominent role in spreading knowledge about
the Pacific, which the Spaniards sought to close to other Europeans. In
1680, reflecting the continued role of force, a band of buccaneers under
Bartholomew Sharp crossed the Isthmus of Darien from the Atlantic to the
Pacific. Using a Spanish vessel they had seized off Panama, they then
attacked Spanish shipping, before navigating the waters south of Cape Horn
from west to east (the first English expedition to do so) and returning to
England in 1682. The band included Basil Ringrose, who both wrote a
journal of the expedition that was published in an altered form in 1685 (in
the second volume of the 1684 London edition of Exquemelin's *Bucaniers
of America*), and compiled a substantial 'waggoner' – a description in the form
of sailing directions – to much of the coast he sailed along as well as to
some parts he never visited. This stemmed from the *derrotero*, or sets of
official manuscript sailing directions, illustrated by a large number of coastal
charts, that Sharp seized from a captured Spanish ship in 1681 and that he
presented to Charles II in order to win royal favour. Such atlases had been
regarded by the Spaniards as too confidential to go into print.[74]

Some of the information reported by voyagers was inaccurate. In 1687,
the buccaneer Edward David allegedly discovered 'Davis's Land' in the
south-east Pacific between the Galapagos Islands and South America. The

printed account of the expedition spread the news, Davis's Land was recorded on maps, and it was suggested that it was the outlier of Terra Australis (southern land), the vast continent in southern latitudes that was generally believed to lie to the south of Magellan's westward route across the Pacific in 1520–21, and that was assumed to be necessary to balance the land masses of the northern hemisphere. Later explorers searched in vain for Davis's Land, which was probably the small island of Sala-y-Gómez and a cloud bank to the west suggesting land,[75] providing a salutary reminder of the need to qualify what might otherwise be a heroic interpretation of exploration in terms of the steady increase of knowledge.

William Dampier was a particularly prominent figure in exploration, not least thanks to coverage in the world of print. A buccaneer, who in 1679 pillaged the Pacific coast of South America, Dampier sailed to the west coast of New Holland (Australia) in the *Cygnet* in 1688, where his observations included details of the tides. Government interest led to Dampier being subsequently sent out in command of an expedition that was intended to bring back more knowledge about the continent, and in 1699–1700, in the *Roebuck*, Dampier sailed along parts of the coast of Australia and New Guinea and discovered that New Britain was an island, although he did not fulfil his plan to sail along the east coast of Australia. Like earlier Dutch explorers, Dampier found nothing in Australia of apparent value, but publications spread news of the Pacific. He published the very successful *New Voyage Round the World* (1697), *A Discourse of Winds* (1699) and a *Voyage to New Holland in the Year 1699* (1703–9). An artist accompanied the voyage of 1699–1700 and his drawings were published in the book, while Dampier's voyage also led to the naming of islands, such as New Britain, New Ireland, New Hanover and Rooke Island, and of features, such as Cape St. George, Cape Orford, Cape King William, Cape Anne, St. George's Channel and Montagu Harbour, while, with Cape Dampier, Dampier Strait and Dampier Island, the explorer himself was not forgotten.[76]

In the same period, the astronomer Edmund Halley explored the South Atlantic in the *Paramore*, acquiring valuable information. He produced his chart of trade winds in 1689, the first scientific astronomical tables in 1693 and his 'General Chart' of compass variations in 1701, all important tools for navigators. His interest in the transit of Venus looked towards James Cook's first voyage to the Pacific in 1769–70.

Contemporary interest in distant seas also affected the world of fiction, particularly in Gulliver's voyage to Lilliput, which was located in the South Pacific, while Daniel Defoe's *Robinson Crusoe* was based on the marooning of the privateer Alexander Selkirk on Juan Férnandez in 1704–9. Narratives such as those by Dampier, as well as Lionel Wafer's *A New Voyage and Description of the Isthmus of Panama* (1699), William Funnell's *A Voyage Round the*

World (1707) and Edward Cooke's *A Voyage to the South Sea and Round the World* (1712), helped create a sense of the Pacific as an ocean open to profitable British penetration, and one that could be seized from the real and imagined grasp of Spain,[77] and this fuelled support for the speculative frenzy focused on the South Sea Company.

Maritime exploration attracted most attention, but it was not the only type. The search for fur took traders well beyond their bases on Hudson Bay. The most far-flung in the late seventeenth century was that of Henry Kelsey, a member of the Hudson Bay Company base at Fort York, who, in 1690, joined a group of Crees on their return from trading on the Bay and, by his return in 1692, had crossed the Saskatchewan River and become the first white man to reach the great grasslands of western Canada. Like other overland journeys, Kelsey's was dependent on native support and knowledge.

Compared with what was to come in the second half of the eighteenth century, there was relatively little exploration in the first half. The quest for information about the Pacific remained important, and it was seen as attractive for whaling, but Spain maintained its effort to thwart attempts to enter the ocean from around South America. In 1749, the Spanish government objected to British plans for an expedition to the Pacific and the establishment of a base on the then uninhabited Falkland Islands that would support further voyages in southern latitudes. The recent war, however, had provided an opportunity for Anson to enter the Pacific and profitably attack Spanish commerce.

The quest for the Pacific also encouraged attempts to discover a navigable north-west passage above North America. Several efforts were made from Hudson Bay. James Knight failed in 1719, but, in 1741, the Admiralty sent the *Discovery* and *Furnace* to Hudson Bay under Christopher Middleton. The following year, he sailed further north along the west coast of the Bay than any previous European explorer, but could not find the entrance to a passage. The naming of Repulse Bay testified to Middleton's frustration. In 1746–7, William Moor, who was sent by the Northwest Committee organised by Arthur Dobbs, a critic of the Hudson Bay Company, also failed;[78] although these voyages did leave a scattering of the names of British ministers along the coast of Hudson Bay, for example Chesterfield Inlet and Wager Bay.

These voyages provided knowledge to fill in the map, although it proved easier to give detailed shape to coastlines than to interiors. In his *New Set of Maps Both of Ancient and Present Geography* (Oxford, 1700), Edward Wells, an Oxford academic, revealed contemporary knowledge as far more extensive: the New World was presented as 'unknown' to the ancients, unless it was their Atlantis, and even so, they could not map it, whereas, as Wells showed, the moderns could. However, longitudinal mapping faced problems, because, as yet, there were no clocks accurate enough to give a ship's meridianal position. As a result, many islands were placed too far to the west or the east, and, combined with the failure of captains to know where their ships were, this caused shipwrecks. In 1741, Anson nearly ran aground on Tierra del Fuego; dead reckoning had put his position more than 300 miles out to sea. With the aid of declination tables, the suns and stars could be used to calculate latitude, although the instruments in general use had limitations,[79] but longitude could not be checked by observation while at sea. In 1714, Parliament established a Board of Longitude and offered a substantial reward for the discovery of a method for determining longitude at sea, the French following suit in 1715. However, it proved difficult to make progress, and, in his series *A Rake's Progress* (1735), the painter William Hogarth presented a madman trying to solve the problems of longitude on the madhouse wall. This seemed an appropriate response to the difficulties of engaging with the intellectual problems posed by the now-global character of Britain's maritime ambitions.

3

COLONIAL EXPANSION AND THE STRUGGLE FOR MARITIME DOMINANCE, 1650–1750

During Charles II's Royal Entry into London in 1661, a figure representing Father Thames as well as three 'sailors' took part in an entertainment outside East India House to celebrate English naval power.[1] The linkage of trade and naval strength was appropriate, but spreading territorial control was also at issue. Activity in the form of trade, migration, settlement and knowledge, was linked to the expansion of empire, either as ostensible control, in the form of claims to territory, or in terms of more realistic criteria, both at the expense of non-European peoples and at the cost of other European powers. The English had been less active and successful in trans-oceanic expansion in the late fifteenth and sixteenth century than both Portugal and Spain, and, as a result, their expansion, like that, earlier, of the Dutch, was largely at the expense of already existing European empires. Rivalry with other European powers led, in the century 1650–1750, to war with the Dutch, Spain and France.

BRITAIN AND PORTUGAL

Portugal, in contrast, was Britain's ally for most of the period, which, in large part, reflected the animosity between Portugal and its more powerful neighbour, Spain: the two were at war in 1640–68 and 1703–13 and relations were tense for much of the rest of the century. Portuguese independence from Spain was important to British security: earlier, Philip II's control of Portugal had posed a major maritime threat. The animosity between Portugal and Spain provided both England and France with the possibility of gaining allies, a situation that matched the practice of imperial politics outside Europe, at least in so far as the search for co-operation and the attempt to create and manipulate alliances were concerned. Poor relations between England, and later Britain, and Spain encouraged good ones with Portugal, making redundant suggestions of colonialization in southern Brazil;[2] although other issues also played a role in these good relations, ranging from the dynastic link provided by Charles II's marriage with Catherine of Braganza in 1662, to the growth in trade. Catherine's dowry brought Charles Bombay and Tangier, although, in the face of Moorish hostility, the latter was abandoned in 1684.[3] Alongside the services of Indian sailors and soldiers, the co-operation of Portuguese merchants and mariners was important to the British presence in the Indian Ocean;[4] while trade with Portugal enabled Britain to profit from its most important colony, Brazil, which, in the early eighteenth century, became Europe's principal source of gold.

WARS WITH THE DUTCH

Relations with the Dutch were also to become close, but, at the outset of the period, they were very different. The rivalry with the Dutch helped determine English commercial activity, ensuring, for example, that the English were on the whole excluded from South-East Asia and the East Indies, whereas they were far more successful with India. Conflict with the Dutch was to play a major role in the development and assertion of English maritime strength, and there were three Anglo-Dutch wars between 1652 and 1674. The first (1652–4) revealed the extent to which English naval power had been developed by the republican 'Rump' government that had toppled Charles I, and, indeed, by 1650, the English navy had become the largest in the world, a development that was to be continued by the subsequent Cromwellian regime. Between 1649 and 1660, some 216 vessels were added to the fleet, many of which were prizes, but half the fruits of a shipbuilding programme. The earlier dependence, in part, on the use for conflict of large merchantmen ended with the establishment of a substantial state navy, which, in 1653, employed almost 20,000 men.[5] One of its roles was to ensure, in 1652, that, in the aftermath of the Civil War, Virginia, and, following its example, Barbados, Maryland, Bermuda and Antigua, submitted to the Rump, which they had refused to do in 1650–51.

Traditionally explained as a mercantilist struggle largely owing to commercial and colonial rivalry, the first Anglo-Dutch war has more recently been discussed in terms of the hostility of one Protestant, republican regime towards a less rigorous counterpart.[6] This was a war of fleet actions in European waters, as well as of commerce raiding and colonial strikes, while attempts to preserve or cut trade links, crucial to the financial and military viability of the two powers, also played a major role. In 1652, the English won battles off Dover and the Kentish Knock, but were badly defeated by a larger Dutch fleet off Dungeness. In 1653, they won again in a battle fought from Portland to Calais (the Three Days Battle), and in another at the Texel in which the Dutch admiral, Tromp, was killed, and the sole major Dutch victory that year was the destruction of an English squadron off the Mediterranean port of Livorno. The English victories closed the English Channel to Dutch trade and this helped lead the Dutch to peace.

Being larger than the Dutch (and with a higher ratio of cannon per ton) made the English warships particularly effective, but their size meant they were unable to mount a close blockade of the Dutch ports. The English navy had many ships that could carry full batteries of 32- or 18-pounders, while the Dutch had only a few that could carry batteries of 18- and 24-pounders. Size gave a double advantage: the English had a large number of guns of sufficient power to disable and even sink Dutch warships and armed merchantmen, of which few were larger than 700 tonnes, while the Dutch had hardly any guns that could inflict large-scale destruction on the large number of English ships of 700–1,400 tonnes. Larger ships meant bigger scantlings (standard dimensions) and a generally more robust hull and rig which could resist gunfire more effectively.

It is also important to understand the constraints of naval warfare in the age of sail. Lacking, by modern standards, deep keels, sailing vessels suffered from limited seaworthiness, while the operational problems of working sailing ships for combat were very different from those that steam-powered vessels were to encounter. The optimal conditions for sailing ships were to come from windward in a force 4–6 wind across a sea that was relatively flat; it was more difficult to range guns in a swell. Limitations on manoeuvrability ensured that ships were deployed in line in order to maximize their firepower, and skill in handling ships entailed getting wind behind the top-sails. In 1653, the English fleet was ordered in its fighting instructions to provide mutual support, and, while this was not an order to fight in line ahead, it encouraged the line formation that maximised broadside power. Fighting instructions and line tactics instilled discipline and encouraged a new stage in organisational cohesion that permitted more effective fire-power. The stress on cohesion reflected a move away from battle as a series of struggles between individual ships, and represented a transfer of military models to naval war, as commanders with experience of combat on land sought to apply its lessons and to devise a formation that permitted control and co-operation during the battle. The nature of conflict at sea made it difficult, however, to maintain cohesion once ships became closely engaged and, as battles arose from chance encounters, much had to be left to the discretion of commanders whose ability to control a battle was limited.[7]

Having replaced the Rump Parliament, Oliver Cromwell was happy to negotiate peace with the Dutch, but he subsequently used the navy elsewhere. Without it, there could have been no Western Design against Hispaniola in 1654–5, and this Design and Cromwell's readmission of the Jews to England have both been seen as aspects of 'a millennial moment', a salutary reminder of the variety of drives that lay behind imperial activity, for, in 1654, Cromwell had cited divine support to counter criticism of the proposed war with Spain.[8] This support was not forthcoming in Hispaniola, but Robert Blake, the leading English admiral of the period, destroyed a Barbary pirate squadron with minimal losses at Porto Farina on the Tunisian coast in 1655, blockaded the Spanish coast in the winter of 1656–7 and defeated a Spanish fleet in the Canaries in 1657, the year in which the plate fleet was also captured. Naval power also enabled the English to intimidate John IV of Portugal into accepting English terms in 1654 and 1656, and to play a role in the Baltic rivalry of Denmark and Sweden, although the international context was important: Dutch intervention was more important in the Baltic, while, more generally, Cromwell benefited from the war between France and Spain that had been declared in 1635 and that lasted until 1659, obviating the possibility of foreign intervention in the civil wars.[9]

In the 1660s, under Charles II (r. 1660–85), conflict with the Dutch resumed, because although neither Charles nor the Dutch government sought war, certain political groups believed they could obtain their ends through firmness. In English court circles, there was hostility to the Dutch both as republicans and because of their toleration of a variety of Protestant sects, while war offered chances of employment for those who had fought since 1642 and for whom peace offered penury, or at least diminished opportunities. War also lured politicians with the prospect of gaining office or promotion. The government hoped that a forceful approach would secure peace on their own terms, but they had underestimated the determination of the Dutch.

Conflict was set off by the valuable trade of West Africa, the source of slaves, a prize that caused a struggle for control between the Company of Royal Adventurers Trading into Africa, chartered in December 1660, and the Dutch West India Company. In early 1661, the English Company sent out a small expedition using royal vessels under the command of the aggressive Captain Robert Holmes, a protégé of James, Duke of York, the Lord High Admiral, later King James II. Holmes seized two islands in the mouth of the Gambia and attacked nearby Dutch forts, but the Dutch reacted sharply, seizing English ships and in June 1663 capturing the English base at Cape Coast. In November 1663, Holmes was sent to support the Company, and to maintain the rights of English subjects by force, and, in early 1664, he seized the major Dutch settlements on the Gold Coast, before sailing to North America, capturing New Amsterdam and renaming it New York. However, a Dutch fleet under de Ruyter recaptured the African settlements and Dutch complaints led to Holmes being committed to the Tower.[10]

The Dutch wished to avoid war, but the English were no longer willing to restrict hostilities to distant seas, where it was easier to present violent acts as unsanctioned or irrelevant to European diplomacy. In August 1664, Thomas Allin was sent to command in the Mediterranean, with instructions to seize Dutch warships and, if possible, their Smyrna fleet, a convoy of merchantmen from Asia Minor whose valuable cargoes provided a major inducement in the shape of booty and goods whose sale would help to fund English activities. The opportunistic, not to say piratical, nature of English policy was amply demonstrated by Allin's attack on a Dutch merchant fleet off Gibraltar in December 1664; from then on Dutch merchantmen were seized in large numbers, and, on 4 March 1665, Charles II declared war.

The war was not a great success for the English, who were affected by the strengthening of the Dutch fleet: a large number of warships were constructed in the 1650s and 1660s, and the size of the Dutch warships now began to match the English. The English were also handicapped by the international situation, specifically French support for the Dutch: France declared war in January 1666, although the French did not campaign vigorously other than in the West Indies. The honours at sea were divided between England and the Dutch. As in the first war, most of the naval conflict occurred in the Channel and the North Sea. In the first major battle of the war, in Sole Bay off Southwold in June 1665, James, Duke of York, defeated Jacob van Wassenaer-Obdam, whose flagship was destroyed by an explosion. Obdam's leadership was poor, but the English were unable to exploit the victory. A year later, in the Four Days' Battle, between the Downs and Dunkirk, the more numerous Dutch won after taking heavy losses in broadside exchanges: the English under George Monck had engaged, rather than wait for a supporting squadron under Prince Rupert. As an indication of the degree to which neither side enjoyed a clear superiority, in July 1666 the two English commanders attacked and defeated the Dutch under Michiel De Ruyter at the Two Days' Battle. The English also attacked Dutch merchantmen, although it proved impossible to mount an effective blockade, while, in turn, Dutch privateers devastated English trade.

Although Parliament voted the unprecedented sum of £2.5 million, there was no money for a long war, and credit proved increasingly difficult to obtain. The financial burden of the war forced the English to lay up their larger ships in 1667 and to focus instead on commerce raiding, but the Dutch used the opportunity to attack the major English base at Chatham: they captured the magazines at Sheerness, broke the protective boom across the River Medway and burnt six deserted ships of the line before towing away Monck's flagship, the *Royal Charles*. Another Dutch squadron captured Surinam on the coast of South America. The Treaty of Breda of July 1667 confirmed English possession of New York, but the Chatham debacle left an impression of English weakness, as, in the West Indies, did French seizure of English islands in 1666. The eventual peace restored these islands, but left Surinam with the Dutch and acknowledged French control of Acadia (later Nova Scotia).

In the next conflict, in 1672–4, the Dutch faced a more difficult situation as Charles II had formed an alliance with his cousin Louis XIV (r. 1643–1715) of France, who had greatly built up his fleet. Much of the conflict continued to be in home waters and, by maintaining a fleet 'in being', the Dutch made it impossible for their opponents to attack their coast and launch an invasion. In May 1672, de Ruyter surprised James's force in Southwold Bay, inflicting much damage and delaying a planned attack on the Dutch coast, and in 1673 he skilfully fought off a superior Anglo-French fleet. In addition, the Dutch continued to attack English and French shipping in the Caribbean and off North America, and also recaptured New York, although the town was returned by the Peace of Westminster (February 1674), in which Charles abandoned his alliance with France.[11]

Thanks to French and Dutch shipbuilding, England had declined from leading to third most important naval power, but, in turn, her naval strength greatly revived thanks to a major shipbuilding programme in 1677–80 after new taxation was agreed in 1677. However, the French navy remained larger in the 1680s.

The next Anglo-Dutch conflict occurred in 1688 when, taking advantage of opposition within England to the pro-Catholic and autocratic policies of James II (and VII of Scotland), William III of Orange invaded in order to gain British resources for use in an impending struggle with his bitter rival, Louis XIV. This could have been a major naval conflict, as the English fleet had been prepared to repel the invasion fleet on behalf of his uncle and father-in-law, James II. William's first sailing, in mid-October, encountered a great storm and returned to harbour next day, with the loss of many supplies, including over a thousand horses: they were especially liable to break their legs in storms because ships were not stabilised. After a week of ship repairs, the same fleet set sail once more. William's second attempt was more successful: a strong north-easterly wind prevented the English fleet, then lying at the Gunfleet off Harwich, from leaving their anchorage, and this allowed William to sail into the Channel. By the time the fleet's commander, George, Lord Dartmouth, finally sailed on 3 November, the main Dutch fleet was already past Dover. William landed at Brixham in Devon on 5 November, at a time that the pursuing fleet was no nearer than Beachy

Head. Even so, a successful attack on the Dutch fleet would have weakened William, but, at a Council of War on 5 November, the English captains decided not to attack what they believed would be a larger Dutch force and, thereafter, first storms and then bad weather prevented the English fleet from acting until it surrendered to William's authority on 13 December. This was the most ignominious campaign in English naval history, a campaign that was flawed from the outset by a defensive, reactive mentality that owed something to England being formally at peace, and much to division and discontent with James II among the captains.[12] The failure of the English navy to act was crucial to what became known as the Glorious Revolution: once he had landed, William rapidly overthrew James, who was weakened by a lack of support from key political figures and by his own collapse of nerve.

WARS WITH FRANCE, 1689–1713

Thereafter, it was France that became Britain's leading maritime rival. William was Louis's most prominent opponent and his overthrow of James II and VII inaugurated a series of wars between Britain and France, first from 1689 until 1697, and then again in 1702–13, 1743–8, 1754–63, 1778–83 and 1793–1815; although the wars that broke out in 1743 and 1754 were not declared until 1744 and 1756. These were wars waged in Europe, North America, the West Indies, West Africa and India, and, at sea, in home, European and trans-oceanic waters.

The shift from the Dutch to France and also, after 1700 when a Bourbon succeeded to the throne, Spain as enemies, affected the tasks and structure of English naval power. Whereas naval conflict with the Dutch focused on the southern North Sea and the English Channel, with France and Spain it was much more far-flung, especially after 1689–92 when there was a concentration on Channel waters and those south of Ireland. This shift in focus led to different operational demands, which had an impact on ship design and naval support. English naval power was given a westward orientation with the development of Portsmouth and Plymouth, which supplemented the late seventeenth-century concentration of naval facilities on the Medway and the Thames, at Chatham, Sheerness, Deptford and Woolwich. In 1691, contracts for work on the dry dock at Plymouth were changed so that it would be able to take the biggest ships of the line, becoming a front-line operational facility.[13] Although the French launched more warships than England in the early 1690s, England, thanks to an Act of 1691 sponsoring new construction, had a definite lead in new launchings over both the Dutch and the French from 1695.

The naval struggle was crucial to the support and pursuit of empire not only because of operations in trans-oceanic waters, but also because the ability to stage expeditions there in large part rested on success in winning the struggle for naval dominance in home waters. Furthermore, this dominance was vital to the more central question of empire: the ability of a state based in southern England to retain control over the British Isles, where the navy played a crucial role in the conquest of Ireland from James II and in thwarting subsequent Jacobite plans, including those supported by France and Spain. This role was dramatised on 28 July 1689 when Londonderry, then under siege by supporters of James, was relieved by the fleet from siege after the boom across the River Foyle blocking the harbour had been broken, an episode that was to be the iconic moment of naval history for Ulster's Protestants. More significantly, William III's control of the Irish Sea enabled him to overcome the logistical problems of supplying a large force in Ireland. The fleet thus made possible a focusing of resources, providing not just mobility, but also a local concentration of strength sufficient to achieve military goals. Naval strength also explains the wide-ranging reach of English forces, most impressively with the expedition, under John Churchill, Earl of Marlborough, in the autumn of 1690, that led to the capture of Cork and Kinsale, the major ports on the south coast, which made French reinforcement of the Irish more difficult. In September 1691, the last Irish Catholic stronghold, Limerick, fell: its siege on land had been supported by a naval squadron at the mouth of the Shannon that blocked the prospect of French reinforcements.

Jacobite hopes of a French-backed invasion of England or Scotland, to reverse the verdict of 1688, were also thwarted. Initially, the naval situation had been parlous for William, owing in large part to the size of the French navy in the 1680s and early 1690s, a reminder of the extent to which the English move toward a stronger empire was threatened by the pace of developments in other powers. In the indecisive battle of Bantry Bay (1 May 1689), Admiral Herbert and 22 ships of the line were unable to defeat a French fleet of 24 ships of the line under Château-Renault covering a landing of troops at Kinsale and Bantry Bay. Thereafter, the English had to return to Portsmouth for repairs, because there was no dry docking in the Channel further west. This gave the French a major advantage as, from their bases at Brest and Rochefort, they could challenge the English in the Channel and in Irish waters, and also attack shipping routes. Two months later, the French threat was accentuated when the able Count of Tourville evaded the English fleet off Brittany to lead much of the Toulon fleet into Brest, creating a threatening concentration of French strength. In 1690, the French fleet successfully escorted another force of troops to Ireland, and were victorious in a battle off Beachy Head on 30 June, but, although

English coastal positions could now be attacked, there was no force available to invade England: Louis XIV was more concerned about French operations in the Spanish Netherlands (modern Belgium).

It was not until 1692 that the French prepared an invasion of England,
but this was compromised by a loss of secrecy, delays in the preparations, a
failure to unite their naval forces and rigid instructions enforcing conflict
even if the fleet was outnumbered. A far larger Anglo–Dutch fleet under
Admiral Edward Russell attacked the French on 29 May 1692 off Barfleur
on the Cotentin peninsula. The French fought well before withdrawing, but
many of their damaged warships, which had taken shelter in the bay of
La Hogue, were attacked and burned there on 2 June by small boats sent
in by Vice-Admiral Sir George Rooke.[14]

This was not the last French invasion attempt. Preparations were
made in 1696, but were thwarted by the assembly of a large English fleet.
In 1708, during the War of the Spanish Succession, 'James III and VIII',
the Stuart claimant, and 5,000 French troops tried to invade Scotland from
Dunkirk, evading the British blockading squadron in the mist, but the pursuing British warships deterred the French from landing in the Firth of
Forth. In 1719, a Spanish invasion fleet was dispersed off Cape Finisterre by
a violent storm, and only a small force was landed in Scotland by a separate squadron. In 1744, a storm in the Channel put paid to a major French
invasion plan. In the winter of 1745–6, French plans to invade in support
of Bonnie Prince Charlie, then in command of a Jacobite rebellion, were
thwarted by the British navy as well as the weather, and, in 1759, the last
plan for a French invasion on behalf of the Jacobites fell victim to the British
fleet in the battle of Quiberon Bay. Thus the navy played a crucial role in
thwarting Jacobitism, a goal that was linked to its mission to dominate home
waters.

The use of naval power by Britain in these waters was not only defensive. It also served for amphibious attacks and force projection. The privateering harbour of St. Malo and the naval base of Brest were attacked
unsuccessfully in 1692 and 1694 respectively, a policy replaced by the less
costly one of bombarding French ports – such as St. Malo in 1693 and 1695,
Dunkirk in 1695, and Calais in 1696 – but these attacks had only a limited
impact and did not distract the French from their campaigns in the Spanish
Netherlands.

In contrast, the dispatch of a large fleet under Russell to the Mediterranean in 1694 was followed by its wintering at the allied port of Cadiz, a
new achievement for English force projection. The interests of Austria,
France and Spain in the Western Mediterranean ensured that it was the
cockpit of European diplomacy, and, in the half-century from 1694, it was
to be a major sphere of British naval power, which helped set the pattern

for public assumptions about British naval capability. English warships had been to the Mediterranean before, especially under Robert Blake in the 1650s and, thereafter, to protect trade against the Barbary pirates of North Africa, but from 1694 such naval deployment was more closely linked to strategic confrontations with other European states, leading to battles with the French (Malaga in 1704 and Mincora in 1756), Spain (Cape Passaro in 1718), and a Franco-Spanish fleet (Toulon in 1744). This force projection led to the capture of what became colonies, Gibraltar in 1704 and Minorca in 1708, and this imperial expansion in turn ensured the continuation of naval deployment in the region.[15]

Concern about trans-oceanic interests and possessions also increased during 1689–1713. Anxiety was particularly intense during the negotiations over a possible future partition of the Spanish Empire in 1698–1700 and in the subsequent war (the War of the Spanish Succession) that began, for England, in 1702, but even in the Nine Years' War with France (1689–97) there was heightened concern about the colonies, especially over North America and West Indies. In the former, 'English' activity was almost entirely locally generated, with scant direction or assistance from England itself. Instead, maritime attacks by the New England colonies played an important role, and in May 1690 an expedition of eight ships and 700 men under Sir William Phips sent by the Court of Massachusetts successfully captured an unprepared and poorly defended Port Royal in Acadia (now Nova Scotia), the fort being burnt down. That July, however, an expedition of 32 New England ships and 2,200 troops failed at Québec owing to adverse winds, a shortage of ammunition and an epidemic of smallpox. Phips visited England in 1691 and pressed on William III the need to continue the attack on Canada and the value of its fur and fisheries, but, despite plans, no more attacks on Québec were launched, because it was peripheral to the concerns of English government, politicians and public opinion; they were more focused on Europe, and, within the New World, the West Indies. The French took most of the English bases in Newfoundland in 1696, including St. John's, which was burnt, but an English expedition in 1697 rebuilt the latter, adding barracks and defences.

Fighting in the Caribbean in 1689–97 was also a matter of local initiatives and occasional interventions by metropolitan forces. St. Kitts, taken by the French in 1689, could not be retaken until English reinforcements arrived in 1690, although this force consisted of only eight small ships of the line, a contrast to the large fleets deployed in home waters. In 1691, the strength of the fortifications of Guadeloupe, the arrival of a French squadron and disease among the English troops and sailors led to the abandonment of the expedition sent there, while yellow fever and poor leadership thwarted an expedition to Martinique in 1693.

The operations in the West Indies did not determine the outcome of the war. Conflict there still bore many of the characteristics of buccaneering, while, although English forces were able to launch major attacks, they found it much more difficult to sustain operations in the face of opposition and the logistical and ecological problems of campaigning there. In 1697, a small squadron under Vice-Admiral Neville was sent to the Caribbean, but disease claimed Neville, all his captains and half of the sailors. Nevertheless, although the effectiveness of operations varied, there was a common theme of gaining the initiative, mounting attacks, protecting English trade and attacking that of France. There was a much greater willingness to commit forces to the West Indies than to send them to conquer Canada: the former were a more attractive target in economic terms and also seemed more vulnerable.

The war was also affected by a bitter debate about strategy, one that was linked to very different views on national interest. The extent to which the war effort should involve major commitments to the defence of the Low Countries, as William III wanted, as opposed to the maritime strategy of coastal attacks on France and colonial conquest, as advocated by many opposition politicians, was controversial, and increasingly so as a result of the costly nature of the conflict and its limited success. In his *Discourses on the Publick Revenues* (1698), the political economist and MP Charles Davenant complained of the cost of keeping forces in the Low Countries, and suggested that in any future war England should restrict herself to a maritime role. The stress on the national character of maritime goals was deliberately employed by 'blue water' critics of the government during the reigns of William III (r. 1689–1702), George I (r. 1714–27) and George II (r. 1727–60) as a counterpoint to the monarchs' and their ministers' supposedly non-national pursuit of particular interests, in the first case continental interventionism and, in the other two, such interventionism combined with aggrandisement for the Electorate of Hanover. This helped ensure that the navy, which, under the Tudors and Stuarts, particularly Henry VIII, Charles I and James II, had been a tool of royal policy, was now seen as more truly national; and, although this distinction was not always clearly drawn, the different nuances were readily apparent in contemporary polemics and politics. The Crown's need for parliamentary funds for the navy contributed to its national character, but the ability to use this need to provide the basis for criticism of royal policies played as important a role in establishing this character, because it led to a contrasting of navy and army, with the latter presented as less national in its goals. The particular use of the navy was also scrutinised critically. In the early 1690s, Parliament's consideration of the conduct of the war led to discussion of naval operations and issues such as the number of French warships that survived their defeat at Barfleur, the failure of the proposed English 'descent' (amphibious operation) of 1692 and the Smryna convoy disaster of 1693. Complaints led to William dismissing first Admiral Edward Russell and then the Tory admirals.

Despite failures in protection, the trade secured by naval power certainly contributed to the nation's ability to bear the burden of war, making it possible to finance the huge remittances of money made necessary by the war in the Low Countries. There were many pressures, and over-borrowing in 1693–4 and 1696 hit foreign credit,[16] but England was in a better shape to sustain the war than other powers, because of her trade and her administrative developments, especially the establishment, in 1694, of the Bank of England and a funded national debt.[17]

War resumed in 1702, this time, in the War of the Spanish Succession, with both France and Spain. Spain's colonial position ensured that transoceanic concerns played a role in the build-up towards war, as they had not done in 1689. William III had negotiated two partition treaties for the Spanish inheritance, the first, in 1698, allocating the Spanish colonies, with most of the rest of the inheritance, to Joseph Ferdinand, the child heir to the Elector of Bavaria. After Joseph Ferdinand died in 1699, the second treaty, signed in March 1700, left Spain and her overseas empire to the Holy Roman Emperor's younger son, Archduke Charles, thus restricting the French claimant to gains in Europe. However, in November 1700, Charles II of Spain died, leaving his entire inheritance to Philip, Duke of Anjou, the second grandson of Louis XIV. Philip accepted the will, leading to an increase in Anglo-French tension that was to help propel England into war. Concern about French commercial opportunities in the Spanish Empire played a role in rising English anger, as the French were granted concessions, including, in August 1701, the *asiento*, the monopoly to supply the Empire with slaves. The following month, when England joined with Austria and the Dutch in the Alliance of The Hague, creating the diplomatic basis for action against France, the agreement stipulated that the Crowns of France and Spain were to be kept separate, that French trade to the Spanish Indies was to be forbidden, and that, in the anticipated war, England and the Dutch were to retain any conquests they made there.

In order to thwart the French, the bulk of English military activity focused on Europe, not the colonies. The concentration of French military expenditure on the army helped ensure that English naval strength was not seriously contested, enabling the English to inhibit French invasion planning, to maintain control of maritime routes to the Low Countries, the crucial axis of the alliance, and to project power, especially into the Mediterranean. But for the English navy, there would have been no war in Iberia, not least because the threat of naval action, underlined by the fleet's success in attacking a Spanish squadron at Vigo in 1702, led Portugal to abandon its French alliance in 1703. Thanks to the fleet, an amphibious expedition was able to capture Gibraltar in 1704, and to thwart French attempts to regain it in 1704–5. Naval strength made possible the dispatch of British troops to support the Habsburg claim to Spain, and the fleet performed a major operational role, being crucial to the capture of Barcelona in 1705 and of Minorca and Sardinia in 1708. The improvement in British naval capability was demonstrated again with the development of revictualling at sea in order to support a fleet maintaining watch on Brest, although manning the navy remained a serious problem.[18] Naval strength also secured for Britain its substantial trade surplus, and this, in turn, provided the financial security that permitted the payment of subsidies to Savoy-Piedmont, Denmark, Hesse-Cassel, Prussia, Austria, Portugal, Saxony and Trier, and thus helped maintain opposition to France on land in Europe.

French naval weakness from the outset of the war gave the English a greater freedom to mount trans-oceanic expeditions than in the Nine Years' War. Under Vice-Admiral John Benbow, 22 warships were sent to the Caribbean in 1701, although an attack on French warships convoying the Spanish treasure ships was thwarted off Santa Marta in 1702. St. Kitts was captured in 1702, but Guadeloupe resisted attack in 1703, while, in Florida, an attempt to capture St. Augustine, the major Spanish base, failed in 1702. Spanish warships from Cuba relieved the garrison, indicating the importance to operations on land of the situation at sea. Further north, there was bitter fighting in Newfoundland, in which, from 1706, the French largely took the initiative. Neither side there, however, won lasting success, or received adequate support from regular forces.

On the mainland, the French pressed the New England settlements, largely by arming a Native American tribe, the Abenakis of Vermont. In response, the New Englanders struck at French bases, but they were happier mounting amphibious attacks than engaging in frontier warfare, a harsher course where they had to face Natives, the rigours of the terrain, and their opponents' effective transport system, which was based on birchwood canoes. In 1704, a 550-strong Massachusetts force attacked Castine, but decided that Port Royal was too formidable a target. The latter was attacked without success by a New England force in 1707, increasing pressure for the use of regulars, although that was delayed by the demands of the European theatre, which consistently received greater priority. Nevertheless, in 1710, 400 British marines joined with 7,500 militia to capture Port Royal, and, instead of burning down the settlement and then leaving with the loot, the captors left a garrison in what was renamed Annapolis Royal in honour of Queen Anne. British power was thus clearly established in Nova Scotia.

In 1711, the new Tory government sent a major force to attack Québec. This expedition, the largest hitherto to North America, was designed to improve Britain's position in negotiations with France, to distract attention from the Duke of Marlborough's campaigns in the Low Countries, which had been supported by the previous, Whig, government, and to vindicate the maritime focus and 'blue water' policies advocated by the Tories. Preparations, however, were hasty and the government relied too much upon their own over-optimistic assumptions of logistical support from New England. Despite difficult relations between the New Englanders and the British commanders, a large force was assembled at Boston, including over 1,000 militia, but, on 23–4 August 1711, a night-time error in navigation led to eight transport ships and nearly 900 men being lost on rocks near the Ile des Oeufs in the St. Lawrence estuary, and the expedition was abandoned.

Canada had not fallen, but the Peace of Utrecht of 1713 left Britain with the gains of Gibraltar and Minorca in Europe, an important extension of maritime power, and also with Nova Scotia, Newfoundland and Hudson's Bay in North America, increasing the British stake there and weakening the defences of New France: given that in any future war, the British would only have a certain number of years for campaigning, they could only benefit from not needing to capture Port Royal again. The war and the subsequent peace settlement left Britain dominant in North American Atlantic waters, but there were still unsettled issues, as well as a French presence that provided opportunities to weaken the British. For example, in Newfoundland, the French retained (until they were exchanged for concessions in Africa in 1904) seasonal shore rights from Port Riche to Cape Bonavista, which supported the continued French presence in the Newfoundland fishery, while the French settlers in Nova Scotia, the Acadians, maintained a French interest in the colony. The peace settlement also left Britain with the *asiento*, the right to supply slaves to the Spanish Empire and a limited, though potentially profitable, right to trade there.

Britain in 1713 was far stronger than she had been in 1688, and this increased confidence in her maritime destiny. Britain's naval dominance was celebrated in the Royal Hospital for Seamen for which the Tudor palace at Greenwich had been rebuilt: in 1708, James Thornhill was commissioned to paint the Great Hall, and he provided a triumphant work, proclaiming British power and making reference to naval success and power, not least with a list of naval victories appearing as part of the group portrait of the Hanoverian royal family. Thornhill, who under George I became Serjeant-Painter to the King and the King's History Painter, was the first native artist to be knighted. Over the following decades, the British used their navy in pursuit of political objectives across Europe. When war began with Spain in 1718, the navy was employed most spectacularly with the defeat off Cape Passaro in Sicily in July 1718 of a poorly deployed Spanish fleet and the capture of seven ships of the line.[19] This led to euphoria about British naval capabilities, the *Weekly Journal*, a Whig London newspaper, claiming in its issue of 18 October 1718, 'This single action renders the King of Great Britain as much master of the Mediterranean as he has always been acknowledged to be sovereign over the British seas'. The commitment to the Mediterranean led to the development of naval facilities at Gibraltar and at Port Mahon, Minorca; although the bold proposal of Lord Tyrawly, the martial envoy in Lisbon, that the British conquer Majorca and also use the navy to back a Moroccan invasion of southern Spain,[20] was not pursued.

In practice, the use or threat of naval power did not lead to the Spaniards abandoning Sicily in 1718, nor to Peter the Great being willing in 1719–21 to respond to British pressure and return his Baltic conquests from Sweden, but it did ensure that Britain could take a major role in European power politics, including in disputes over control of distant territory. The *Weekly Medley* claimed on 19 July 1729 that 'the British squadron without going out of our ports can incomparably hasten matters towards a conclusion much quicker than bare negotiations', and, although the situation was rarely that simple, naval strength was seen as an important factor, especially in the confrontation with Austria, Russia and Spain in 1726–7. Again, in 1734–5, there was an impressive naval armament, in order to give force to British threats to go to war if their attempt to mediate the War of the Polish Succession was unsuccessful. The armament was trumpeted by the government in Parliament, the press, and to foreign envoys, whom they invited to visit the fleet at Spithead in the summer of 1735. In order to assist Portugal against a feared Spanish attack, a large squadron was dispatched to the Tagus in 1735, where it remained for over a year, proof that the ministry was not intimidated by the Bourbons, was willing to assist an ally and was able to deploy a fleet at a distance.

WAR WITH THE BOURBONS, 1739–1748

Although Britain and France were at peace for three decades after the Peace of Utrecht was negotiated, and were even allies from 1716 and 1731, they still competed actively in production and trade, especially in the West Indies and with Spanish America, while the expansion of their rival trading networks in the North American interior, where intra-Native and intra-European rivalries were closely connected, involved the use of force. British activity was a matter of initiative by settlers, the government taking little interest in the interior of North America, whereas, in contrast, the French authorities followed an active policy of expanding their power in the interior, which was to lead to conflict in 1754; although the two powers had earlier fought in 1743–8 as a result of rivalry in Europe when they had taken opposite sides in the War of the Austrian Succession.

Britain had already become involved in war with Spain in 1739, the War of Jenkins' Ear, which arose from the response to Spain's attempts to prevent illicit trade with its New World colonies, most famously with the ear allegedly removed from the captured Captain Robert Jenkins;[21] it was also suggested that he had been castrated. This war was subsumed into the Anglo-French conflict that began in 1743, because Spain was an ally of France. War with Spain was largely waged in the New World, was primarily a maritime and amphibious struggle, and helped encourage a maritime vision of British power. In 1739, at the outset of the war, Vice-Admiral Edward Vernon, with six ships of the line, attacked the port of Porto-Bello on the isthmus of Panama, a region of great significance for British maritime endeavour. The port was defended by three well-sited fortresses, but, becalmed alongside the first, the warships silenced the Spaniards with a heavy fire before landing sailors and marines who climbed through the embrasures and took the surrender of the position. The other forts and the town then surrendered.

This was a glorious episode, extensively reported in the press and reproduced in other media, and it created high expectations about the outcome of action in the Caribbean. In the volatile political atmosphere, the government felt it necessary to respond, but the situation was far less promising than was generally believed in Britain. Vernon had destroyed the fortifications of Porto Bello, for he was in no position to retain them, while, more generally, the resilience of the Spanish Empire was much underrated. In 1741, a major expedition was launched against Cartagena, on the coast of modern Colombia, but, although carefully planned, it failed. This was in part owing to an inability to mobilize sufficient resources, but also because of operational problems, some of which derived from a serious lack of co-operation by army and naval commanders, as well as from the debilitating impact of disease on the British force. Later success during the Seven Years' War (1756–63) was not a result of innovative strategy, but rather greater resources and better co-operation between army and navy commanders. Attacks on Santiago de Cuba and Panama after the debacle at Cartagena also failed.[22]

This was not the end of amphibious operations in the Caribbean during this war, but, from 1743, military and naval resources were concentrated on the threats from France in Europe and in home waters, and the war with Spain became a side-show. Nevertheless, the conflict had indicated the development of British capability in the region: a naval base had been established at English Harbour, Antigua from 1728, and others at Port Antonio (from 1729) and Port Royal (from 1735) on Jamaica, and the naval administration was able to ensure that warships could operate effectively in these distant waters.[23] In 1748, Captain Charles Knowles captured Port Louis on French-ruled Saint-Domingue by sailing his ships close into the defending fort and bombarding it into ruins.

In North America, fighting with France during the War of the Austrian Succession was largely restricted to the Atlantic littoral, in part because of the nature of the military aid sent from the metropolis: naval rather than army. Sea power could both bring targets within range and permit the concentrated application of force, and, in 1745, there was an attack on Louisbourg, the major French base on Île Royale (Cape Breton Island), which challenged both British control of Nova Scotia/Acadia and New England interests in fishing, trade and territorial expansion. As a result, the government of Massachusetts organised a force of 3,000 militia under William Pepperell, which was transported by New England ships and supported by the Leeward Islands squadron under Commodore Peter Warren. Louisbourg was the best-fortified position in New France, but the combined efforts of the Massachusetts forces and the navy led to its fall: Warren blockaded the harbour and the New England militia was able to land safely in Gabarus, advance on Louisbourg and begin a bombardment that eventually breached the walls. After his blockade had reduced the food available to the defenders, sapping their already low morale, Warren was able to force his way into the harbour.

The growing divergence between British colonial and naval success and the dismal progress of the campaigns in the Low Countries led to the hope that naval success could compensate for Continental defeats, which placed a new politico-strategic responsibility on the navy, for it was now required to obtain trans-oceanic conquests, an obligation that necessitated a mastery of home and European waters that would permit the dispatch of naval forces to support amphibious operations. In part, these ideas were long-standing and reflected a traditional optimistic public assessment of naval capability, but the political need for them can be traced to 1745, for it was then that the hopes of defeating France on the Continent that had been so marked in 1742–3, especially after victory at Dettingen in 1743, were replaced by the realisation that it would be difficult to stop the French triumphing by land. Once Cape Breton had been captured, the proposal for its exchange for French gains in the Austrian Netherlands as part of a peace emerged speedily, placing an immediate strategic task on the navy, the defence of Cape Breton.

The British were less successful in India, where their forces were inadequate: in 1740, the East India Company controlled only 2,000 troops throughout India and their fortresses were in poor condition. In 1746, Madras was lost to the French, although they failed to press on to capture Cuddalore and Fort St. David.

In European waters, however, the British established a clear superiority over the French with two victories off Cape Finisterre in 1747. The French could not keep their fleet in Brest safe (but also a threat to the British) if they wished to maintain an imperial commercial system, but their attempts to escort trade with the New World and the East Indies exposed their warships to attack and led to these striking successes. On 3 May 1747, Vice-Admiral George Anson defeated an outnumbered French fleet. Rather than fight in line, Anson ordered his captains to close with the French as fast as they could, and therefore fight in a series of individual actions, in order to prevent the French from escaping under cover of darkness. On 14 October 1747, Rear-Admiral Edward Hawke followed Anson's tactics, and, although the French fought well, the British benefited from having taken the initiative and from abandoning the rigid tactics of a line in order to direct heavier concentrations of gunfire on individual French ships, leading to the surrender of six of the French ships and the French loss of 4,000 sailors, a crucial limitation of their maritime strength.

As the French fleet thereafter could no longer escort major convoys bound for French colonies, the logic of the French imperial system had been destroyed and the British victories contributed both to a serious crisis in French finances and to a sense that the war should be brought to an end. The trade war on the Bourbons was worldwide, did great damage to their commerce and was eagerly followed in Britain. The most spectacular episode occurred in 1743 when Anson captured the treasure-laden Manila galleon off the Philippines, a move that, like the capture of Porto-Bello, suggested that the age of Drake had been revived, but, although not with this effect, such actions were not unique: in January 1745 three large French East Indiamen were captured in the East Indies.

Irrespective of the trade war, the navy had fulfilled its role in European waters by helping thwart French schemes to assist the Jacobites both in 1744 and in the winter of 1745–6 when the balance of naval power gave the royal army an important margin of capability in its operations against Bonnie Prince Charlie. This helped ensure the failure of Jacobite schemes, and thus the consolidation of the British solution established by the parliamentary union of 1707.[24]

The decline in the naval strength of Britain's major maritime ally (from 1689), the Dutch, accentuated the importance of British naval power. In the abortive defensive treaty of 1678, the ratio of Dutch to English capital ships had been fixed at 3 : 4, and in 1689, this was lowered to 3 : 5, but, during the Spanish Succession War (1702–13), the Dutch were generally more than half-way below their quota, and their ships often arrived late. Over the following decades, Dutch naval strength was called upon on a number of occasions, such as the naval mobilisation at Spithead in 1729 to intimidate Spain, but the Dutch were progressively less important, and were of little assistance at sea during the War of the Austrian Succession. In the Seven Years' War, the Dutch were neutral, and in the War of American Independence opposed to Britain, the Fourth Anglo-Dutch War breaking out in 1780.

The War of the Austrian Succession showed that, despite British naval strength and achievements, 'blue water' policies could not secure either the specific objectives that the Continental strategy was designed to protect, essentially the Low Countries and Hanover, or more general goals, summarised by the vague notion of the balance of power (in Europe). However, in domestic political terms, it was a more acceptable strategy, while it also lessened the need for co-operation with allies; and a shift towards 'blue water' attitudes became more apparent from mid-century.

CONFLICT WITH NON-EUROPEANS

There was also conflict with non-European powers and peoples in the second half of the seventeenth century. English territorial control did not increase greatly in India or West Africa, but unlike in North America, the establishment of factories (trading bases) was the goal. In India, a number of factories were established, but they were held as tenancies from the territorial princes, although in 1661 Charles II gained Bombay as a sovereign territory as part of the dowry of his Portuguese wife. However, in 1686 when Aurangzeb, the Mughal Emperor, vigorously pursued a dispute with the East India Company, the weakness of the English position was fully demonstrated: a powerful force advanced against Hooghly, the English base in the Bay of Bengal, and the English under Job Charnock, without cavalry or field guns, were pushed back and evacuated by sea to Madras. Another Mughal force attacked Bombay (taken over by the East India Company from the Crown in 1668), forcing the English to retreat into the fort and then surrender. The English were able to continue trading only after they apologised for their conduct in 1690 and paid an indemnity. In contrast with North America, they were vastly outnumbered.

Most of the conflict with non-Europeans occurred in North America, the most serious, in 1675-6 in New England, being known as King Philip's War after the English name for Metacomet, the Sachem (chief) of the Wampanoags, and was unrelated to England's rivalry with other European powers. The English had few regular troops in the colonies, and, as a result, in this war, as in other conflicts with Native Americans prior to the 1760s, the colonists had to rely on their own forces and on whatever Native support they could win. In King Philip's War, the colonists were outmatched in forest combat by hostile Natives, who had adopted firearms, until they began to copy their enemy's tactics and to make good use of their Native allies; their opponents suffered from Mohawk hostility, disease, starvation, lack of ammunition and relentless pressure,[25] and, once defeated, became serfs to English settlers.[26] The colonists also had to rely on their own forces in campaigns against the Pamunkey, Occaneechee and Susquehannock in Virginia in the 1670s.

In the first half of the eighteenth century, conflict in North America was again important (see p. 77), although there was also fighting in West Africa and India. In the former, cannon drove off Dahomey forces that attacked the British fort at Glehue in 1728. In India, unsuccessful attacks were mounted by East India Company forces against Gheria, Khanderi and Colaba, coastal forts on the Konkan coast of the Maratha naval commander Kanhoji Angria, who launched piratical attacks on the Company's trade. Angria's ships avoided battle and the thick walls of his forts saw off poorly conducted attacks, and in 1721, despite the involvement of the navy, naval bombardment failed to destroy Colaba. The British made little impact until, after Kanhoji had died in 1729, his navy was divided between his sons, and a policy developed of seeking to exploit their rivalries and of gaining local allies against one of them.[27] Fortunately for the British, none of the Indian rulers of the period devoted major efforts to building up naval strength, so that, in mid-century, the dispatch of a British squadron to India in 1754 represented an important factor in regional power politics.

IMPERIAL DESTINY

In 1750, Richard Rolt, a popular historian, claimed that France, which he saw as a threat, 'could only promise Great Britain what Polythemus did to Ulysses, "To be the last devoured"'.[28] It is salutary to break at mid-century, because this throws a question mark against the usual emphasis on a seamless web in British development, and, instead, directs attention to conjunctures and turning points in the development of empire. The Seven Years' War (1756–63), is an important instance of the latter, but the engagement with trans-oceanic conquest also stemmed in large part from the greater emphasis on such concerns seen in public debate from the late 1730s. The ability to strike a resonance when presenting issues in terms of national interest was important, for, in the mid-1730s, the opposition press had tried, and failed, to work up a storm about the Walpole ministry's failure to come to the assistance of Austria, as it was obliged by treaty to do, against the Bourbons in the War of the Polish Succession (1733–5), a conflict that was far more widespread than its title might suggest, and that left France with the reversion to Lorraine.

British relations with Spain, in contrast, proved a different matter and the mid-century emphasis on empire initially focused on the traditional topics of trade, Spain and the West Indies, and only later on land, France and the North American interior. Spanish attacks on British merchants in the West Indies, who, the Spaniards claimed with a great deal of truth, sought illicitly to breach the Spanish commercial monopoly in their empire, had been an important political issue in the late 1720s, particularly in the parliamentary session of 1729, and this issue was revived a decade later when sustained pressure from mercantile groups and an opposition press and parliamentary campaign had a significant effect. The government negotiated a settlement with Spain, the Convention of the Pardo, but disputes over its implementation interacted with the impact on the ministry of the domestic debate, and, despite Walpole's opposition, war broke out in 1739.[29]

Vernon's early triumph in capturing Porto Bello in November 1739 led to a wave of jingoism that encouraged the political commitment of military resources to empire,[30] and entrenched the account of national interest and destiny that opposition writers and politicians had affirmed in the late 1730s, in criticism of what was presented as Walpole's appeasement. In his poem *London*, published anonymously in May 1738, the young Samuel Johnson idealised past naval triumphs, using Elizabeth I's successful stand against Spain in the assault:

> In pleasing Dreams the blissful Age renew,
> And call Britannia's Glories back to view;
> Behold her Cross triumphant on the Main,
> The Guard of Commerce, and the Dread of *Spain*,
> Ere Masquerades debauch'd, Excise oppress'd,
> Or *English* Honour grew a standing Jest.[31]

The xenophobic assault on Spain and France was also linked to Protestantism and to migration in the development of concepts of Britishness and the British Empire as a political community encompassing England, Wales, Scotland, Protestant Ireland and the British possessions in the New World.[32] This development was long drawn out, in part because the conceptual language of Britishness and that of empire was used until the seventeenth century to describe more restricted communities within the British Isles: England (and Wales) and Scotland, or the three and Ireland. The relationship between these communities altered greatly in 1689–1746, and this was an important aspect not only of the development of their joint, and separate, senses of identity, but also, especially to critics, of an imperialism in process, in both Scotland and Ireland.

The Union of 1707 between England (and Wales) and Scotland, far from being inevitable, arose essentially from recent English concern about the possible hazards posed by an autonomous, if not independent, Scotland. Despite the serious weakness of the Scottish economy, there was only limited support for the measure in Scotland, and its passage through the Scottish Parliament depended in part on corruption. As a result of the union, Scotland retained a different national Church and legal and educational systems, and continued to be governed by Scots,[33] but the sense of separate identity was weakened, while Scots came to play a major role in the expansion of empire, not least through disproportionate service in the army and the East India Company.[34] In the Highlands, the transition was far bleaker, as the suppression of the 1745 Jacobite rising was followed by a harsh pacification of what was seen as a barbarous threat that involved the breaking up of the clan system as part of an attempt to alter the politics and society of the region. This was the imperial episode to which the government devoted the most attention in the 1740s. Power was affirmed by roadbuilding and fortification. Indeed, empire was expressed and defended by building, most dramatically near Inverness. William Skinner, who was sent to Scotland in 1746 as Chief Engineer of North Britain, proposed a major new fort on the coast at Arderseer Point which would control the northern end of the Great Glen and block any foreign intervention there, as well as being reinforceable by sea. Fort George, a 'state-of-the-art' bastioned fortification, took a decade to construct, costing over £100,000. That it never heard a shot fired in anger can be seen as part of its success, but was more truly a product of the navy's successive triumphs in defeating or deterring invasion.

In the first half of the eighteenth century, the languages of Britishness and empire also provided the conception of a larger community, with the full range of English-speaking territories in the western hemisphere being members of a single body, the Empire, a potent ideology that accorded with other developments within British public culture, specifically an emphasis on the linkage of Protestantism, trade, maritime range and liberty, their role in British identity, and their positive synergy. The vision and, increasingly, reality of a maritime commercial empire identified the success of a trading nation with the liberty of its government, and distinguished this process (in a positive fashion) from territorial conquest. British writers saw this, as ensuring that the corruptions and debilities discerned in Classical and modern republics, and associated with a lack of liberty and with conquest, need not destroy British liberties. This approach integrated the British world and yet also created tensions within it, as the Patriot ideologies that drew on notions of Britishness and the proper operation of empire were defined differently in Ireland and, eventually, the Thirteen Colonies that were to become the USA.[35]

The British perception of their empire also led to the exposition of the theme of a chosen people in the form of a clear expression of superiority over other empires; and Spain was increasingly seen as offering a model of imperial rule that should not be emulated.[36] In 1739, in condemning the Convention of the Pardo as ignominious and a betrayal of national interests, William Pitt the Elder, then making his name as a vigorous opposition parliamentarian, also objected to referring Britain's right to freedom of navigation to negotiators, because, he told the House of Commons, this was treating as equal two very different situations:

> On the part of Spain, an usurpation, an inhuman tyranny claimed and exercised over the American Seas; on the part of England, an undoubted right by treaties and from God and Nature, declared and asserted in the resolutions of Parliament.[37]

The positive presentation of empire was enhanced as trans-oceanic victories, most obviously Vernon's at Porto-Bello and Anson's success in capturing the Manila galleon with its fabulous cargo in the Pacific,[38] brought more of the world within Britain's real and imaginative grasp. Greater interest was not restricted to mercantile and political circles, nor to the depiction of warships and other maritime themes on canvas,[39] and it was no coincidence that 'Rule Britannia' was matched by 'God Save The King', earlier a tune sung by Jacobites, but now a popular and loyal song. The commemoration of Vernon's success in 1739 and thereafter can be traced through society. In Durham, Dove and Booth increased attendance at their 'mathematical lectures' by promising to exhibit fireworks in honour of Vernon's birthday immediately afterwards, while, across the country, Vernon ceramics constituted the most prolific output of commemorative pieces since the beginning of the century. One of the inexpensive London newspapers, the *Penny London Post*, devoted several issues in March 1749 to printing Vernon's speech on the encouragement of naval service. Maritime mastery was increasingly seen as Britain's destiny, part of the identity of people, state and empire. The foundation in 1749 of the Free British Fishery Society, specifically an attempt to establish a successful deep-sea British herring fishery, testified to the importance of hopes about fishing to the cause of the patriotic renewal of national strength.[40] Ten years earlier, a former sea captain and shipbuilder Thomas Coram had established the Foundling Hospital in London, combining male philanthropy with patriotism, not least because the foundlings were seen as future sailors.

It is worth pausing at this point in the account of Britain's maritime strength and imperial expansion to consider its global significance. Britain in the Seven Years' War (1756–63) was to use its position as Europe's, and therefore the world's, leading naval power to help defeat the French and become the most active European empire, and, as a consequence, theorists of 'leadership long cycle' discuss the period in terms of British power: 'The management of intercontinental questions of political economy depends on the extent to which capabilities of global reach are concentrated in the control of the world system's lead economy. Historically, one state, the "world power", has emerged from periods of intense conflict in a position of naval and commercial-industrial pre-eminence'.[41] However, while Britain was indeed the dominant naval power, it is less clear that this made it the world power, in so far as the definition given above assumes a single hierarchy of strength that is in fact inappropriate for a world that had multiple power systems as well as economies that were only partially integrated.

British expansion in the middle third of the century was, nevertheless, of particular note. Furthermore, there was no comparison between the trans-oceanic colonisation and power-projection of the Atlantic European powers, especially Britain, and the more land-based character of Eastern European and non-European powers, including those, such as China and the Ottoman Empire, with a lengthy coastline. China overcame the Zunghars of Xinjiang in the 1750s, demonstrating an impressive logistical capability that was the product of a sophisticated administrative system,[42] but neither China nor Japan made an impact in the Pacific, either by launching voyages of exploration or by creating settlement colonies across the Pacific or around its rim. Although this absence from the oceans appears a failure in Atlanticist terms, it is necessary to note the continued importance of Asian merchants in maritime trade, and to stress the role of overland economic links. This was true of the trade from India to the Near East via Kandahar in the seventeenth century, which helped account for the struggle between Mughals and Safavids for control of the city.[43]

Britain's rise to leading imperial status depended not only upon her position within the European power system but also the relationship of the latter to non-European systems. Despite eighteenth-century interest in the strength of different political systems, it is difficult to discern how far Britain's relative success stemmed from the character of her system and how far from the more contingent application of power in particular circumstances. Certainly, comparisons of Chinese and Christian European government have not made it clear that a particular type of state structure was necessary, for example, to the large-scale coal mining that Britain, but not China, pursued, or, more generally to the modernisation seen as crucial to the West's ability to become central to global economic links, and thus to the process and profits of globalisation.[44]

This globalisation also brought profit to societies with whom the Europeans traded, and there was a strong degree of mutual dependence, but it was Westerners, and especially the British, who organised the new systems, and this altered Britain's attitude to the non-European countries with which it had relations: mutual dependence and power projection were in a dynamic tension, frequently shifting in balance. Rivalry with the Bourbons led to an emphasis in Britain on power projection which helped reshape the terms of mutual dependence with non-European countries, although the nature and chronology of this reshaping varied greatly, as the contrast between British relations with China and India, and, later, China and Japan, indicated. In the mid-eighteenth century, the overcoming of the French in India and North America and British expansion in India were to lead to a closer interest in non-European society. After France was defeated in the Napoleonic Wars, this process became stronger, but it was to recede as imperial challenges within the Western world in the late nineteenth century coincided with a rise in racialist attitudes and a stress on the apparent merits of Westernisation.

4
THE BATTLE FOR PRIMACY, 1750–1815

They have stood out to sea again, but how far, or where, they are going remains to be known – From their entire command of the water they derive immense advantages, and distress us much by harassing and marching our troops from post to post – I wish we could fix on their destination – in such case, I should hope we would be prepared to receive them.

> George Washington on Howe's force, then sailing from Staten Island towards the Chesapeake, August 1777.[1]

The Jamaica letters delivered this day mention, that their chief complaints originated in want of slaves to work the plantations; which, however, as peace is now concluded, they hoped to receive a supply of from Africa.

Several planters belonging to the British islands in the West Indies, particularly those of the greatest property, are preparing to sell off their estates in that part, to enable them to make purchases on the continent of America.

> *Edinburgh Advertiser*, 17 June 1783.

I have rather a predilection to it, unless something better calculated to obtain the commerce and navigation of the Eastern Seas could be secured to us, for surely the obtaining of these objects are very important.

> Henry Dundas, a member of the Board of Control for India, about Penang, Britain's first position in the Malayan peninsula, 1787.[2]

If turning points are to be sought, then this was a period full of them. Victory over the Bourbons (France and Spain) in the Seven Years' War (1756–63) made Britain the leading maritime and colonial power, defeat in the War of American Independence (1775–83) led to the permanent loss of the Thirteen Colonies, and eventual success against France in the French

Revolutionary and Napoleonic Wars (1793–1802, 1803–1814, 1815) re-affirmed British dominance. It is therefore easy to see why empire in this period is presented in terms of conflict and conquest, which will receive full weight in the following chapter, but another theme is that conquests alone would have been of only limited benefit but for the continued dynamics of trade and settlement, although it is necessary to note the absence of any 'coherent, structured, overall imperial plan or policy'.[3] In addition, the psychological processes of empire require attention in order to understand its impact in the British Isles and elsewhere.

THE STRUGGLE WITH FRANCE, 1750–1763

The conflicts of the opening decade and a half of the period deserve attention first, not only because of their importance in terms of territory gained, but, also, as they help explain the flowering of interest in empire that came subsequently, an outburst of energy that included Pacific exploration, a new prominence for empire in the world of print, and new schemes for imperial government, although the last were to help cause crisis in North America.

The Congress of Aix-la-Chapelle of 1748 had failed to settle differences between Britain and France over North American boundaries, and the issue was referred to commissioners, who, however, could not settle the matter. Meanwhile, growing French assertiveness helped lead to crisis. Interest in the containment of the British colonies led the French, in 1749, to send a small force into the Ohio Valley, where, the previous year, the British government had given the Ohio Company, a group of Virginia landowners and London merchants, title to half a million acres. In 1752–4, the French drove out British traders, intimidated Britain's Native American allies and constructed forts between Lake Erie and the junction of the Allegheny and Monongahela Rivers. The recovery of French activity threatened to exclude the British not only from the Ohio Valley, but also from the entire interior of the continent: by 1753, a line of French posts lay across canoe routes to Hudson Bay. Both sides were convinced that the other was stirring up Native hostility and acting in a hostile fashion.[4]

The French were also taking an assertive role in India. Dupleix, Governor of Pondicherry from 1742, followed an expansionist and inter-ventionist policy, becoming a player in the volatile situation created by the decline of Mughal power and, in particular, the disputes over control of Hyderabad and the Carnatic (the major territories in south-central and south-eastern India). In 1749, the Nizam of Hyderabad, a protégé of the British, was defeated and killed by a mixed French-local force, and a

Frenchman, Charles de Bussy, became the key adviser to his two successors. The French made important territorial and revenue gains in Hyderabad, while, separately, a French protégé was recognised as the Nawab of the Carnatic.

At that stage, it seemed possible that France would, at the very least, contain Britain in both North America and India, if not become the dominant power in both. Moreover, thanks to an influx of funds, the French fleet had been built up since 1749 and its infrastructure had been improved. France's alliance with Spain, while not as close as it had been, was a factor that the British had to consider, and France's alliance with Prussia threatened the King's German possession, the Electorate of Hanover. There was nothing inevitable about Britain's eventual success over France, although she had two very important advantages in the leading navy in the world and a far more populous colonial base than France in North America.

The French position unravelled first in India. Attacking the Maratha Confederacy, the most dynamic force in India, proved a serious mistake, because, despite a victory in December 1751, it was difficult to obtain any lasting victory over the Marathas, while the French were unable to concentrate their own, or their allies', forces to fight those of the British East India Company under Robert Clive that undermined the French position in the Carnatic. The British had supported a rival to the French-backed Nawab, sending forces to assist him at Trichinopoly, about 200 miles to the south of the capital, Arcot. When Trichinopoly was besieged in 1751, Clive led a diversionary force of 500 men that captured Arcot in a surprise attack and then held the fort against a 50-day siege by an Indian force of about 10,000. After the siege was raised, Clive defeated the besiegers. This was a victory that was to resonate in British storytelling as long as the British dominated India, as a crucial instance of skilful heroism against terrible odds, but it is one that scarcely echoes now.

These defeats wrecked the momentum and appearance of success on which Dupleix depended, and his alliance system collapsed. The British exploited the situation thanks to the creation of a field army in the Carnatic by Stringer Lawrence, the able and energetic commander of the forces of the Madras Presidency of the Company. This army ensured that the Company was not restricted militarily to a few coastal positions, and enabled it to take a more pro-active role in politics. Dupleix's failure to regain Trichinopoly in 1753, and his demands for men and money, led to his recall by the French East India Company in 1754 and a provisional peace was reached with the British that winter, leaving Britain the dominant European power in south India.

In North America, owing to the assertive French stance, it proved harder for both sides to disengage. Although the British government had no wish for war, it could not accept French claims in the Ohio Valley. British complaints, however, were rejected, and on 17 April 1754 a 500-strong French force made the small colonial garrison of 40 men in Fort Prince George (near Pittsburg) surrender. The following month, George Washington advanced into the contested area at the head of a small force of Virginia militia, defeating a smaller French detachment on 28 May. The French, in turn, advanced in greater numbers, and on 3 July Washington was obliged to surrender at Fort Necessity, while later that summer French-backed Natives raided British settlements, advancing to within 15 miles of Albany. At that point, the British had fewer than 900 troops in North America.

Domestic political pressures, and their own interest in the place of North America in competition between Britain and France, obliged the government to adopt a firm attitude in 1755, and regulars were dispatched to mount attacks on French bases. The most successful were those in which naval power could be used: attacks on the French forts that threatened Nova Scotia. The British marked their presence by renaming the captured forts, and, more harshly, by deporting the Acadians from Nova Scotia: ruled by Britain since 1713, they were suspected of disloyalty. Another force, however, largely of regulars under the inexperienced Major-General Edward Braddock, had already been ambushed and defeated on 9 July near Fort Duquesne by the outnumbered French and their Native allies. Braddock's army, fresh from Britain, lacked experience of North American operations, and Braddock had deprived himself of the possibility of effective Native support by refusing support from Shingas, the Delaware chief, who had sought a promise that the Ohio region should remain in Native hands. These actions were supported by an attempt by the navy to stop the French reinforcing Canada. This led to the largely unsuccessful interception in the fog of the French squadron on 10 June 1755 that caused the French government to order their envoy to leave London; although war was not formally declared until 1756.

For Britain, North America was the most important sphere for hostilities in the early stages of the Seven Years' War, reflecting the eagerness to strike at the French there, although it was also necessary to consider challenges to the British position in Europe. There were concerns about a possible French invasion of England, and in 1756 the Mediterranean colony of Minorca, conquered from Spain in 1708, was lost to a French expeditionary force, while British naval power was humiliated when, in conflict nearby with a French fleet, Admiral Byng, who had been sent to relieve the defenders, failed to sustain the attack and instead withdrew.

There were also defeats on land in North America. The new French commander, Louis Joseph, Marquis de Montcalm, who had no experience in North American warfare, decided that it was best to take the initiative, and thus counter the British numerical advantage in North America, by

achieving a local superiority in strength. In August 1756, he captured Forts
Ontario, George and Oswego, taking 1,620 prisoners for the loss of only 30
men, and driving the British from Lake Ontario. That year, the British did
not mount an effective response in North America. The government was
weak and demoralised, and also concerned about the defence of Britain from
possible French invasion, while differences over the reimbursement and
control of colonial troops hit co-operation in North America. In 1757, in
contrast, a large fleet was sent to Halifax, but it was deterred from pressing
on to Louisbourg by the presence of a French squadron and poor weather.
Instead, Montcalm advanced again and captured Fort William Henry at the
head of Lake George.

An unimpressed William Pitt the Elder who, as one of the two Secre-
taries of State, was the key figure in planning war policy in 1757–61, was
determined to do better. For 1758, he planned a three-pronged offensive on
New France, and, although that on the fort of Carillon (Ticonderoga),
which controlled the axis of advance via Lake Champlain, was a costly
failure, Louisbourg fell to a successfully organised amphibious operation,
while a force, mostly of American provincials, captured Fort Duquesne,
today's Pittsburg. Viewed from Europe, this was a two-sided conflict,
whereas, on the ground, the shifting support and fears of Native groups
could be decisive. The French position was weakened when Pennsylvanian
authorities promised the Native Americans that they would not claim land
west of the Appalachians and the consequent shift of Native support obliged
the French to give up the Ohio region.

In 1759, the British concentrated on the St. Lawrence, where their naval
power could be used most effectively. Already, in August 1758, an amphibious force had captured Île Saint-Jean, which became Prince Edward Island,
and its population was largely deported to France. The importance of the
colonial contribution was shown in 1759, when American troops garrisoned
Louisbourg, freeing regulars for the advance on Québec. Benefiting from
reliable pilots and nearby harbour facilities at Halifax, both of which had
been lacking when attempts had been mounted in 1690 and 1711, the navy
convoyed a force under James Wolfe to near Québec. He arrived there on
26 June 1759, but the natural strength of the position, French fortifications
and the adept nature of Montcalm's dispositions thwarted him for over two
months, and, as winter approached, failure seemed imminent, leading Wolfe
to risk a bold move. James Cook had thoroughly surveyed the river, and
the army was skilfully transported up-river of Québec. Having scaled the
cliffs early on 13 September and driven off the French pickets, the British
advanced to the Plains of Abraham at the south-west of the city. Instead of
remaining in the city, Montcalm advanced to the attack, but the French
columns were hit by British volley fire before being driven back by a

bayonet charge. Wolfe and Montcalm were both fatally wounded in the battle. French morale was shattered and Québec surrendered, although, as a reminder of the role of contingency, a relief force was advancing on the city. That year, other British forces advanced to Lake Ontario and captured Fort Niagara, Carillon and Crown Point.

The capture of Québec was not the end of New France, and in early 1760 the substantial French army still in Canada advanced to regain it, defeating the British on the Plains of Abraham at the battle of Sainte-Foy on 28 April. The city was then besieged, but, once the ice on the St. Lawrence had melted, the British fleet was able to bring relief: the empire was literally shipborne, and, as the ice receded, the stretch of maritime power reached even further into North America. The French raised the siege and fell back on Montréal, but in the summer of 1760 a three-pronged British advance, from Québec, Crown Point and Lake Ontario, finally triumphed, and on 8 September 1760 the Marquis de Vaudreuil, the Governor-General of New France, and the 3,520 French in Montréal surrendered to Amherst's force of 17,000. Canada had fallen.

Meanwhile, the British had been victorious elsewhere. In India, Dupleix's failure provided them with the opportunity to tackle opposition from native powers, and in 1755–6 land and naval forces captured the Angria strongholds and destroyed their fleet, the British benefiting from Maratha support. The British position was soon after challenged in Bengal in East India, when in 1756 the newly acceded Nawab, Siraj-ud-daula, stormed poorly defended and fortified Fort William at Calcutta after a brief siege. He confined his captives in the 'Black Hole', an episode that was to resonate in Britain, entering the language and forming notions about the nobility of British conduct. It also created an impression of countervailing cruelty that contributed to the British sense of the morality of their imperial mission and was to help shape the response to the atrocities committed on British civilians during the Indian Mutiny.

Clive, then Lieutenant-Governor of Fort St. David, and Rear-Admiral Charles Watson, were now instructed to retake Calcutta. Clive was in command of 850 British soldiers and 2,100 sepoys (Indians), an important deployment of British strength, and this force reached Bengal in late December 1756 and regained Fort William, largely thanks to the guns of Watson's squadron. Concerned about the French presence in Bengal, Clive also attacked their fort at Chandernagore, with crucial support from the warships, made possible by excellent navigation in the difficult waters of the Hooghly River. Clive then marched inland towards the Nawab's capital of Murshidabad. The Nawab stationed his army to block Clive's advance near the village of Plassey, and the two forces met on 23 June 1757. The poorly commanded and divided Indians, about 50,000 men, were routed by Clive's

3,000-strong force, which was superior in disciplined firepower. Clive's men suffered about 60 casualties, the Nawab only about 500 dead; but the political consequences were important, because soon after the Nawab was killed and replaced by a British protégé. The path from Plassey to British control of Bengal, Bihar and Orissa was not complete until 1765, and was far from smooth – the British had to face both attempts to reimpose a Muslim ascendancy and the problems of establishing a stable regime there – but the situation in India had been radically transformed. The British conquest was attributed, not unreasonably, by contemporary Persian-language histories not to British military superiority, but to the factionalism and moral decline of the ruling Indian families of the region.

At sea, the British had been challenged in the Seven Years' War by the pre-war increase in Bourbon naval strength. Together, France and Spain launched warships with a total displacement of around 250,000 tons in 1746–55, while Britain launched only 90,000, losing its previous superiority over the combined Bourbon powers. Fortunately for Britain, Spain did not join in the war until 1762, and by then France had been defeated at sea. In the late nineteenth century, the notion of command of the seas was much discussed (on A. T. Mahan's inspiration) in navalist literature. Its value as a concept at that point is open to debate, but it was certainly questionable prior to the development of steam power. Wind-powered warships were dependent both tactically and strategically on the weather, although its impact could be lessened by good seamanship and, as a result, skill and experience were important elements in relative effectiveness. Nevertheless, ships could only sail up to a certain angle to the wind, and too much or insufficient wind were serious problems. Furthermore, reliance on the wind alone made inshore naval operations much more chancy undertakings than they were to be in the steam era. However, there were specialised wooden sailing ships, in particular bomb ketches, designed with coastal operations in shallow waters during the sailing era foremost in mind, and it is possible to adduce examples of successful campaigns in precisely such waters – such as the Chesapeake campaign of 1814 – so it is important not to exaggerate the operational limitations caused by wind and, particularly, wood. Nonetheless it was far harder to counteract the impact of current and tide before the advent of steam power than after. French ships could readily leave Brest, their major Atlantic port, only when the wind blew from the east. The fact that at best it did so only intermittently helped British blockaders. Comparisons with steam power could not be made in the mid-eighteenth century, though, and the British navy of the period was state-of-the-art.

In addition to the problem of the force that moved ships, there were serious limitations in the contemporary surveillance and command and control capabilities of naval power, which made it very difficult to 'see' or

control in any strategic sense, and certainly limited the value of any blockade. It was generally possible for a lookout to see only about 15 miles from
the top of the main mast in fine weather, which had implications not only
for operations between fleets, but also for trade protection, making it difficult to counteract privateers. Logistical factors were also an important
limiting factor on blockading operations. Only with Portsmouth and
Plymouth close at hand could the British maintain an effective blockade of
the French Channel and Atlantic ports.

After being checked off Minorca in 1756, and assuaging its anger and
shame by a show-trial that led to the shooting of Byng, the British navy
became increasingly effective, and from 1758 its ability to act as an offensive strategic force and as a restraint on French trade was fully demonstrated.
This was a cumulative process, as French effectiveness declined with the
capture of sailors, leading to strains in its smaller maritime labour pool.
British expeditionary forces in North America, West Africa and the West
Indies were ably supported by the navy, while French trade was put under
steadily greater pressure, both in European waters and further afield,
affecting French power. For example, British ships in the Gulf of Mexico
captured most ships bound for New Orleans, and weakened the French
colony of Louisiana, not least by increasing discontent among the Native
Americans.

The large number of warships captured by Britain and incorporated into
her navy played a major role in affecting the balance of naval strength, and
also aided the process by which the British changed the nature of their navy,
copying the large Bourbon two-deckers, which were more manoeuvrable
than the small three-decker 80- and 90-gun ships that had been so important earlier in the century. The new ships were better sailers and fighters,
both manoeuvrable and capable of holding their own in the punishing
artillery duels of the line of battle engagements that the British preferred
to conduct at close range, in contrast to the French preference for long-
range fire.

The crucial naval victories occurred in 1759, when French plans for an
invasion of Britain were wrecked. The division of the French navy between
an Atlantic fleet at Brest and a Mediterranean fleet at Toulon made it difficult for them to concentrate the necessary covering force for an invasion,
and, although the Toulon fleet managed to leave the Mediterranean, it was
defeated by the pursuing fleet under Edward Boscawen near Lagos on the
Portuguese coast on 18–19 August. On the 19th, Boscawen violated Portuguese neutrality in order to attack the French fleet that had taken refuge
in Portuguese waters, and the outnumbered French lost five warships.

Bad weather forced Edward Hawke, the chief exponent of close block-
age, to lift his blockade of Brest in November 1759. The French fleet under

the Marquis de Conflans was able to leave the harbour but, before sailing to Britain, had first to meet troop transports off Morbihan, and this led to a delay that gave the British their opportunity. Conflans was trapped off the Breton coast, and took refuge in Quiberon Bay, counting on its shoal waters and strong swell to deter Hawke's ships. Although he had scant knowledge of the Bay's rocks, Hawke launched a bold attack on 20 November. With sails set, despite the ferocity of the wind which was blowing at nearly 40 knots, his ships sailed into the confined space of the bay and forced a general action in which superior gunnery and seamanship led to victory.[5]

After the British victory, much of what was left of the Brest fleet took refuge in the River Vilaine, and stayed there for the remainder of the war. Others took refuge in Rochefort, political and financial support for the navy ebbed and the British were left to take the initiative at sea. Thus, the French navy did not disrupt the successful attack on Belle Isle in 1761 or the dispatch of troops to help Portugal successfully against a Bourbon invasion in 1762, despite the fact that both enterprises were vulnerable to naval forces based in Brittany. A squadron under Commodore Augustus Keppel covered the Belle Isle expedition, while in 1762 a fleet based at Gibraltar under Admiral Saunders discouraged a junction between Bourbon naval forces in the Atlantic and the Mediterranean. More generally, British warships were increasingly successful both in limiting French privateering and in damaging French trade.

Naval victory over France was not a result of superior weaponry. One crucial factor was, despite a higher joint French and Spanish investment immediately prior to the Seven Years' War, a level of continuous commitment and expenditure helped to ensure that a high level of both was regarded as normal and necessary and that naval strength never collapsed. Thanks to its relative security, Britain could afford to prioritise the navy above the army in a way that continental powers could not. Also important were the inculcation of an ethos and policy that combined the strategic offensive with tactical aggression and, within the constraints of the naval warfare and technology of the period, an effective use of the warships. This was facilitated by an impressive logistical system that rested on public support and was capable of sustaining an unprecedented degree of trans-Atlantic power projection.[6] In addition, British naval commanders generally sought battle and took the initiative, and were therefore best placed to obtain propitious circumstances. An experienced admiral, George, Lord Anson, was First Lord of the Admiralty in 1751–62, while admirals such as Boscawen, Hawke, Pocock and Rodney were bold and effective commanders. Manning, however, was a serious problem. Impressment – forced service – led not only to individual hardship and the disruption of trade, but also to problems of desertion. Unlike the army, which for operations in Europe, North America, and India relied in large part on assistance from subsidised allies, colonial militia, Native Americans and hired Indians, the navy did not deal with its manning problem by hiring large numbers of foreigners. Indeed, a significant difference between British naval and army strength was that the former was essentially self-reliant, with the important exception of Baltic naval stores for ship construction and maintenance. As a result, the government had greater control over naval operations.

The political context was also crucial to naval success. It explains the willingness of the political nation to spend substantial sums in order to gain and sustain naval superiority. Investment in the dockyards was considerable, and the workforce at Plymouth rose from 54 in 1691 to 1,837 in 1759, while a continuous pattern of support underwrote improvements in operational practice. In addition, political support was not restricted to the protection of home waters and trade, but also encompassed action in distant waters. The contrast between the limited public support for operations in Mediterranean waters during the War of the Austrian Succession and the popularity of naval operations off Canada during the Seven Years' War was clear, and it was not only the greater success of the latter that was important – there was a powerful sense that colonial operations were serving national interests. The damaging accusations of surrender to the views of allies or the Hanoverian interests of the monarch, that had so often compromised the public reputation of operations in European waters during the first half of the century, for example the victory over the Spaniards off Sicily's Cape Passaro in 1718, were now absent.

The crucial figure here was William Pitt the Elder. He appealed neither to a desire to uphold the Hanoverian dynasty nor to a wish to give priority to the fighting in Europe but rather to a sense of national destiny that defined Britain as a maritime power with trans-oceanic concerns. Such interests and identities had been offered before, but mostly in terms of rhetoric, as in the campaign against Walpole in 1738–9. With Pitt in government, they came centre stage to national policy, as well as being actively propagated both by his vigorous speeches in the House of Commons and in sympathetic publications, such as the *Monitor*, a London newspaper that pressed the case for the links between maritime power, commercial expansion and colonial conquest.[7] Pitt freed Britain from the mesmerised state of 1756, when the prospect of French invasion had led to an essentially reactive strategy. Instead, he committed British troops to Germany from 1758, in support of both Frederick II of Prussia and Hanover, and supported trans-oceanic amphibious operations.

It has been argued that a commitment of troops to the Continent was an essential part of any 'blue water' strategy, in that French strength was thereby diverted from the maritime struggle, and that this was demonstrated by the contrasting results of the Seven Years' War when Britain had an ally and the War of the American Independence, when she was isolated.[8] This argument, which prefigures later strategic debates, underrates, however, the precarious nature of Britain's 'Continental' strategy in the Seven Years' War and the reluctance with which troops were sent to help Prussia. The argument that they would help bring victory in North America was made for domestic political consumption, largely in order to clear Pitt of the charge of hypocrisy; and any treatment of the war as a strategic success for Britain that fails to place weight on the failures of 1756–7, the vulnerability of Hanover, Prussia, and, in 1762, Portugal, and the threat until 1759 of a French invasion, is misleading. As Frederick II of Prussia pointed out to Earl Cornwallis in 1785, with reference to the Seven Years' War, Britain and Prussia were not a match for the Bourbons, Austria and Russia, and 'although from some fortunate circumstances such a contest had been maintained, it was not a game to play often'.[9]

Naval superiority was one of these circumstances, permitting the pursuit of objectives both in Europe, such as the attack on Belle Isle, and the dispatch of forces to Portugal and across the world. Forts St. Louis and Gorée, the French trade and slaving bases in West Africa, were easily taken, in May and December 1758 respectively. They were poorly fortified and inadequately garrisoned, lacked hinterlands that could provide support and were particularly exposed to naval attack, but the major French positions in the West Indies were better fortified. Nevertheless, Guadeloupe fell in 1759, Dominica in 1761, and Martinique, Grenada, St. Lucia and St. Vincent in 1762. In India, the French had taken the initiative in 1758, sending an expedition to the Carnatic that captured Fort St. David and besieged Madras, but the British regained the initiative the following year, capturing Masulipatam, a crucial point on the east coast of India, defeating the French at Wandewash in 1760 and successfully besieging the leading French base, Pondicherry, in 1760–61.

The effectiveness of British amphibious operations was demonstrated most dramatically against Spain, which came to the help of France in 1762. These successes were a sharp contrast with earlier failures during the War of the Austrian Succession: there was to be no repetition of the failure at Cartagena in 1741. The major British effort was directed against Havana, the principal Spanish position in the West Indies and their leading naval base in the New World, and a force of 12,000 men, covered by 22 ships of the line, landed on 7 June. While the troops set up siegeworks in the bare rock, a third of the force was lost to malaria and yellow fever, but the storming of Fort Moro, which dominated the harbour, was followed by the city's surrender on 13 August. The expedition against Manila, the capital of the Philippines, was on a smaller scale, but the city fell on 6 October and its capture encouraged British interest in the Pacific that did not cease when it was returned to Spain in 1764.[10]

The navy was able to do far less, however, for Britain's ally, Frederick the Great of Prussia. His pressure for the dispatch of a fleet to the Baltic was fruitless, but, more seriously Britain was having to confront a shift in the European international agenda from the issues that had dominated the first half of the century, especially the fate of Italy, in which Britain's naval power brought her a role, to a new set of problems in the second half – the Austro-Prussian struggle, the fate of Poland, the Balkan question – in which this power was of little consequence. This shift in Continental alignments and priorities ensured that Britain became less important in European international relations and as an ally. While Britain had struggled to create an Atlantic empire, other states had grown in strength thanks in part to major earlier gains of contiguous territory, and the Austrian acquisition of Hungary, the Russian of Baltic territories and Ukraine, and the Prussian of Silesia had led both to a new diplomatic agenda and to new resources for pursuing it. As a result, Britain, at the same time that it became more powerful on the oceans, became less so in Europe, a situation that was to last until the French Revolutionaries and, even more, Napoleon forced Austria, Russia and Prussia to pay more attention to Europe's Western Question, the dominance of Western Europe, in which Britain indeed could play a role.

The Seven Years' War closed with the Peace of Paris, signed on 10 February 1763. Britain returned many of its conquests, including Guadeloupe, Martinique, Gorée, Pondicherry, Cuba and the Philippines, but it retained others, including Canada, Senegal, Grenada, Tobago, Dominica and St. Vincent, and gained, in return for Cuba, East and West Florida from Spain, providing a new sphere for British expansion and settlement, particularly for plantation agriculture. Although not free from serious controversy, thanks to the extent to which the 1762 victories had raised public expectations of much harsher terms on France and particularly because the French were allowed to regain their position in the Newfoundland fisheries, the terms fortified the impression created by the war: that Britannia ruled the waves.

There had, initially, been no plan to conquer the French Empire, still less that of Spain, understandably so as in 1755 the conquest of French India, Canada, West Africa and much of the French West Indies seemed unrealistic. Yet, once won, gains appeared both necessary and natural. Indeed, in 1776 Benjamin Franklin referred to Britain's 'fondness for conquest as a warlike nation'.[11] As optimism about British naval capability grew, this helped to make a maritime foreign policy appear normative. Empire gained lent a celebratory goal to the recent war that underlined the nature of heroism and gave it an imperial turn. Wolfe joined the pantheon of national greatness and was commemorated on canvas and with the Québec

Monument at Studley Royal as well as a 100-foot column at Stowe. At a more mundane level, where bravery was not celebrated in this fashion, the war saw Britishness in action. Scots and Irish represented more than half the total number of soldiers, while, in the 1757 return, the English and Welsh contributed just 30 per cent of the manpower. Irish recruitment remained high into the nineteenth century, with more Irishmen than Englishmen in the army in 1830, although the percentage fell with the population of Ireland later in the century.[12]

The reconceptualisation of Britain, and her role in the world, was one of the major changes that took place in mid-century, and the fusion of Protestantism, economic growth and military success produced a surge in confidence that helped the British to feel that modern Britain defined civilisation. The choice in policy was no longer largely seen, as in the 1700s, in terms of Whiggish Continental interventionism versus a Tory, agrarian withdrawal from abroad, albeit one that was tempered by a degree of 'blue water' raiding and cheap colonialism, and, instead, 'blue water' was transformed into Britain's destiny. Any single explanation of what was a complex and multi-faceted shift needs to be qualified by an awareness of the interaction of shifts in attitude with changes in political contexts and policies, and, in particular, political leadership by Pitt, and George III's determination, in the early 1760s, to break with Continental (European) interventionism, played a major role. The failure, in 1755–6, of the European collective security system pressed as crucial to British interests by Thomas, Duke of Newcastle, the leading minister since 1754 and the effective director of foreign policy since 1744, was crucial to the development of a more aggressive maritime policy, as this was a failure not only of policy, but also of Europe as a definition of British identity and interest.[13]

The Seven Years' War had been waged by a society that understood the politics of economic competition: the furs of Canada, the fish of Newfoundland, the sugar of the West Indies and the trade of West Africa and India had all been at stake, and trade interests were frequently mentioned in the press. Nevertheless, at least initially in the war, colonial gain was not the theme of policy; and, instead, as also on later occasions, the preservation of colonial possessions, really or apparently endangered, was a much more important objective. Ironically, the bulk of British colonial gains were acquired in the Seven Years', French Revolutionary and Napoleonic Wars, conflicts whose initial purposes were not major colonial conquests.

EXPLORATION

The apparent maritime destiny of the country affected foreign policy and British public culture in the three decades after the Seven Years' War, as successive governments were wary of commitments in European power politics (as opposed to gaining alliances that would help weaken the Bourbons in confrontation outside Europe); while the public was increasingly interested in the trans-oceanic world. This was encouraged by the fame of maritime exploration, which owed much to publications such as Alexander Dalrymple's *Account of the Discoveries Made in the South Pacific Ocean* (1767), a copy of which was taken on Cook's first voyage, and, more successfully, his *Historical Collection of the Several Voyages in the South Pacific Ocean* (1770–71).

The British indeed took the leading place in maritime exploration, with the Admiralty taking the key organisational role. In 1767, Samuel Wallis, a naval officer, entered the Pacific through the Straits of Magellan on HMS *Dolphin*. Sailing then on a course different from that of his predecessors, who had followed the route established by the Spaniards, Wallis was able to 'discover' many Pacific islands, including Tahiti, which he called King George the Third's Island, before going on to complete a circumnavigation of the world. After their ships had passed through the Straits of Magellan, Wallis was separated from Lieutenant Philip Carteret and HMS *Swallow*, which crossed the Pacific further south than any other explorer, 'discovered' a large number of islands, including Pitcairn, and extended the British naming of much of the world, with Osnaburg, Duke of Gloucester and Queen Charlotte Islands, each named after a member of the royal family, as well as Gower's, Simpson's, Carteret's, Hardy's, Wallis's and Leigh's islands, and those of Sandwich, Byron, New Hanover, the Duke of Portland and the Admiralty. Wallis and Carteret did not repeat their voyages, and their reputation was soon to be overshadowed, but they were important, not least in demonstrating anew that circumnavigations could be successful and could lead to 'discoveries'. The pace of competition with France heated up as Louis Antoine de Bougainville circumnavigated the globe in 1767–9, and his *Voyage autour du Monde* (1771) appeared in an English edition the following year.

In 1769, Captain James Cook was sent to Tahiti in HMS *Endeavour* to observe Venus's transit across the sun, as part of a collaborative international observation that involved 151 observers from the world of European science, but his secret orders – to search for the southern continent – helped lead him even further afield and were responsible for his sailing into the history books. He conducted the first circuit and charting of New Zealand and the first voyage along the east coast of Australia: to approach Australasia from the east was not easy, because the prevailing westerly winds combined with the Humboldt current to push ships north as they rounded South America and entered the South Pacific. In 1770, Cook landed in Botany Bay, the first European to land on the east coast of Australia, and claimed the territory for George III. Then, after having run aground on the Great Barrier Reef and repairing the *Endeavour,* Cook sailed through the Torres Strait, showing that New Guinea and Australia were separate islands, before reaching the Dutch base of Batavia (modern Djakarta).

On his second voyage, with two ships in 1772–5, Cook's repeated efforts to find the southern continent, efforts that included the first crossing of the Antarctic Circle, failed. He had sailed to 71° 10′S, farther than any known voyage hitherto, when he encountered the ice outlier of Antarctica, and reported that it was not a hidden world of balmy fertility. Nevertheless, New Caledonia was 'discovered' by Cook in 1774, while knowledge of the Southern Pacific and Southern Atlantic was increased, and his energetic determination to keep his men healthy ensured that, as on the other two voyages, no hands were lost to scurvy. On his third voyage (1776–9), Cook, in 1778, sailed to a new farthest north – 70° 44′N at Icy Cape, Alaska – proved that pack ice blocked any possible north-west passage from the Atlantic to the Pacific to the north of North America and 'discovered' Christmas Island and Hawaii, where he was to be killed in a clash that contributed to disillusionment with the apparently paradisical character of the South Seas. Cook had continued the process of British imperial naming, his including the Hervey Islands and Palmerston Atoll.

Voyages to the Pacific benefited from the growth in the number and manoeuvrability of bigger ships and from advances in navigation, hull design and rigging: changes in sail plans made ships easier to handle, improved their performance and required less manpower, and thus food and water, a crucial consideration on long journeys. Such changes are a reminder of the importance of incremental developments within a given technology, as opposed to the more spectacular paradigm shifts to new technologies, an instance of which was to occur with steam power in the nineteenth century.[14]

Pacific explorers had a greater impact on the public imagination than their overland counterparts, Cook being presented as an exemplary national hero,[15] but explorers expanded the bounds of British North America, especially Samuel Hearne, who followed the Coppermine River to its mouth in 1771 and saw the Arctic, while others travelled out from British positions in Asia, including George Bogle and Alexander Hamilton, who were sent to Tibet in 1774 in an attempt to establish relations. There was only limited exploration in Africa, although James Bruce's tour of Ethiopia helped to increase interest in its interior. He wished to gain fame by discovering the source of the Nile and reached the springs of the Blue Nile in 1770.

Cook's second and third voyages had benefited from John Harrison's invention, in 1761–2, of an accurate chronometer to measure longitude, which erred by only 18 miles in measurement of the distance of a return journey to Jamaica. Such calculations depended on the precise measurement of local time in relation to the time at the Greenwich meridian. Navigators were therefore able to calculate their positions far more precisely, which made it easier for map-makers to understand, assess and reconcile the work of their predecessors. Maps of the West Indies and North America had come to play a greater role in atlases published in the first half of the century – for example those produced in London by Moll, Senec and Bowen – and this markedly gathered pace with the Seven Years' War, and then the War of American Independence. Thus, Thomas Jefferys published a number of atlases, including *A General Topography of North America and the West Indies* (1768) and *The American Atlas or, a Geographical Description of the Whole Continent of America* (1776). Other visual images stemmed from painters, especially William Hodges, who accompanied Cook on his second circumnavigation, painting sites such as Table Bay and Easter Island. He first exhibited at the Royal Academy with Pacific views. Aside from publications on the Pacific and New World, more was published on India from mid-century as part of a determination to acquire and record knowledge[16], while the pace at which information became more rapidly and regularly available increased, in large part in response to public interest, so that Henry Vansittart's *Narrative of Transactions in Bengal, 1760–1764* was published in 1766.

TRADE

Aside from information about empire, there was also more trade and migration in the late eighteenth century than before. Statistics have to be used with care – allegedly, half the tea and tobacco consumed in Britain was provided by smugglers, an indication of the varied consequences of transoceanic links – but they indicated growth. Exports rose from £12.7 million in 1750 to £14.3 million in 1770 and £18.9 million in 1790, and that during a period of only modest inflation, while the value of colonial re-exports rose from £3.23 million in 1750 to £4.76 million in 1780. More trade meant more ships, and English shipping tonnage rose from 421,000 in 1751 to 523,000 in 1764, 608,000 in 1775 and 752,000 in 1786. Ports thrived and expanded. In Liverpool, the Old Dock was followed by the Salthouse Dock (1753), St. George's (1771) and Duke's (1773), while, in Lancaster, an Act of Parliament of 1749 enabled the new Port Commission, in which slave traders played a major role, to develop St. George's Quay (1750–55), and this was followed by a Custom House in 1764 and the New Quay in 1767.

The markets and products of the trans-oceanic world were increasingly important to the British economy, and the linked interest in empire and trade also had a political impact, helping to create an image of national identity that was focused on maritime and imperial themes.[17] Although it is important not to exaggerate the importance of trans-oceanic markets for British products, the combination of these markets and trans-oceanic imports made a major contribution to economic activity, growth, sophistication and ethos,[18] and this was not restricted to coastal regions. Kendal was an English inland town that did not have close links to a major port, yet, in his *Tour of Scotland 1769* (1771), Thomas Pennant recorded how trade had encouraged industry there, leading to the integration of the town into the British-directed global economy:

> The number of inhabitants is about seven thousand; chiefly engaged in manufactures of . . . a coarse sort of woollen cloth called cottons sent to Glasgow, and from thence to Virginia for the use of the Negroes . . . the manufactures employ great quantities of wool from Scotland and Durham.

Thanks to demand from the East India Company, exports of serges from Exeter rose from 163,000 pieces in 1745 to 390,000 in 1777.

As trade increased, the investment networks on which it drew strengthened. Long-distance trade and the multiple linkages of British commerce had far greater capital requirements than short-distance trade, and, as a result, its expansion was in part dependent on a more sophisticated capital structure. As such, trade was an aspect of a wider economic development linked to capital flows and investment opportunities, as seen, for example, in mining. In turn, this development created increased demand for shipping.

The impact of trade and empire on ports, however, was varied. Portsmouth was a major naval base, but other aspects of its maritime activity were also significant, especially the development by the East India Company of its most influential and sophisticated outport or provincial depot, which had a number of consequences, including investment in Company stock, the provision of crew for the ships and troops for the Company army and the growing numbers of Company officers who gravitated towards Hampshire's coastal communities for rest and recuperation. The town's role as a local commercial nexus also led to the development of a confident, cohesive and affluent mercantile community that was linked to its prominence in trans-oceanic trade. Portsmouth's relationship with the navy was less happy: while there were times when town and navy appreciated the value of a mutually beneficial relationship, attitudes towards each other hardened, in part because of manning problems, pay differentials, the availability of materials and the provision of repair work in Portsmouth, but also because of disputes over convoying requirements and responsibilities. In addition, there was a local war between smugglers and revenue men.[19]

The nature of the impact of empire, the navy and maritime trade on other ports varied greatly – Bristol, for example, had a different relationship with the navy from Plymouth, where the need to import naval stores helped make the port the most important in Devon. Bristol's dominance of trans-Atlantic trade was successfully challenged by Liverpool and Glasgow, but the city still saw important growth in the processing of colonial goods. It had a tobacco industry, for example milling snuff, as well as sugar-refining with a peak of 16 refineries. In 1731, chocolate and cocoa-making began in Bristol, and there were at least three cotton mills. All the leading Irish towns were ports, their prosperity dependent on the growing commercialisation of an economy with greater links to the overseas world, not least through the supply of provisions to the navy, especially from Cork.

Shifts in the hierarchy of ports were quite pronounced, and were not restricted to the rankings of Bristol, Glasgow and Liverpool, for instead, there was a more general process of change that was the product of the interplay of such factors as entrepreneurial initiative and capital availability. Whereas, for example, in the 1670s ships from Dartmouth, Plymouth and Bideford had dominated the Newfoundland fishery, by the 1770s the leading ports were Dartmouth, Exeter and Poole. Devon's foreign trade grew, but it became proportionately less important within Britain, which, in part, reflected the absence of a dynamic coal-based hinterland to match those accessible to Glasgow and Liverpool, while, in addition, there was nothing to match the re-export trade seen at these ports as well as at Whitehaven. Bideford played a role in the tobacco trade, but it could not sustain it, and, from the 1750s, the Devon fleet increasingly concentrated on coastal vessels, which, however, lacked the profitability of foreign commerce.

A focus on Atlantic ports should not lead to a neglect of the continued importance of London. Alongside nearby trades, such as Baltic imports, particularly timber for the shipbuilding that remained important on the Thames, came products from across the oceans, including timber from North America and tea and other goods from India.[20]

Aside for its importance for the ports themselves, the impact of empire also affected their hinterlands. Thanks to the possibilities for increasing integration offered by turnpike roads and canals, this meant, in practice, most of England, as well as Central Scotland. In the latter, the investment of profits from the tobacco trade, which Glasgow dominated, substantially funded the development of the chemical industry. Similarly, the liquidity of banks, such as the Edinburgh-based Royal Bank, was increased by the profits of the tobacco merchants, and this was important for the funding of economic expansion.

Much of the expansion in long-distance trade was with the British colonies in North America and the West Indies, for both of which trade with Britain was crucial.[21] With the exception of the Hudson's Bay Company, this was an area open to free trade within the protectionist terms of the British imperial system, and once trades had been established their growth vindicated the critique of commercial monopolies offered by Adam Smith in his *Inquiry into the Nature and Causes of the Wealth of Nations* (1776):

> By a perpetual monopoly, all the other subjects of the state are taxed very absurdly in two different ways; first, by the high price of goods, which, in the case of a free trade, they could buy much cheaper; and, secondly, by their total exclusion from a branch of business, which it might be both convenient and profitable for many of them to carry on.[22]

Indeed, the efficiency of the private sector of the economy was at least as important as the protectionism of mercantilism to British trans-Atlantic trade and settlement.[23] Smith himself taught at the university in Glasgow, Scotland's foremost port.

Trans-oceanic trade affected not only Britain's national economy, it also continued to transform the diet of Britons at home and in the colonies. In 1772 alone, the British officially imported 12 million pounds of tea (much was also smuggled in), and this was complemented by the large quantities of sugar imported. This global system continued to have a harsh side. The transport of slaves increased and, in 1750–79, there were about 1,909 slave-trade sailings from Liverpool, 869 from London and 624 from Bristol.[24] Concern about slave resistance remained an undercurrent of colonial rule. In Pensacola in West Florida, which was under British rule from 1763 until regained by Spain in 1781, no slave was allowed out without his owner's written permission, and meetings of more than six slaves were forbidden after 9 pm.[25]

Although less stark, the disruptive character of British imperialism was again evident in South Asia. In Bengal, where the East India Company gained effective authority in 1765, it can be seen as a new force trying to define mutually beneficial commercial links, but the emphasis can also be on an exploitation that brought high taxation, deflation and famine.[26] British administration of Bengal apparently also revealed the different attitudes of the natives and the British to authority and profit, which were shown in the implementation of the law and in financial control over markets and trade. The idea of a capitalistic market economy, it has been suggested, was more important to the British (an argument that may underrate the role and sophistication of Indian banking networks), and the entry of the East India Company into regional trade involved coercion: the colonial confrontation between British power and native interests was thus partly a prolonged contest over the habits, terms and meanings of goods, markets and people, which together linked authority, patronage and material culture in Bengal. Once Company power was forcibly established, there was an alteration in the political economy of trade, as control over customs was monopolised by the Company, the authority of local landed chiefs was banished from rivers, ferries and tollways and intermediate controls over markets were ended; as a consequence, the colonial marketplace was opened up to the freer flow of imperial commodities and investment, long-distance trade rose and prices became more uniform. The gathering of information was central to this policy, and published lists of prices challenged the immense variety of wholesale and retail rates that had once characterised markets where trade was subject to different political authorities.[27] It was not only local chiefs who suffered: the treatment of native labour by the Company could also be harsh.

At the same time, although the British organised, taxed and exploited (each of these descriptions is appropriate, but, if only one is used, a single, misleading resonance is struck) trade, this process could only work if it satisfied non-Western interests and attracted their merchants. In 1772, Dean Mahomet, an Indian in the service of an officer of the Bengal army, wrote of Calcutta, the port that the British made the capital of Bengal, 'the greatest concourse of English, French, Dutch, Armenians, Abyssinians, and Jews, assemble here; besides merchants, manufacturers, and tradesmen, from the most remote parts of India'.[28] However, mutual interest was capable of many definitions, and as British power increased, the terms of this relationship were more slanted to the benefit of the British. British power in India was focused on the ports: the three Presidencies were based at Bombay, Calcutta and Madras.

THE AMERICAN REVOLUTION

In British North America, this process of definition was, increasingly, between settlers and the representatives of the imperial government; although Native Americans remained an important element in frontier zones, creating problems in relations between government and settlers, who resented the 1763 Royal Proclamation establishing a line beyond which colonial settlement was prohibited. In 1771 the Cherokee, who owed money to a consortium of traders, ceded a large amount of land along tributaries of the Savannah River in Georgia. Governor James Wright argued, however, that such a cession could legally be conducted only with the government. This occurred in 1773 when the land was formally ceded to Georgia, which reimbursed the traders, intending to compensate itself by selling the land to settlers.[29] This tension was an echo of that between medieval monarchs and nobles seeking territory in Wales and Ireland.

Anger over the 1763 proclamation was part of a more general tension between backcountry settlers and government. Reluctant to pay taxes, settlers in backcountry areas complained about royal officials and linked interests, based in ports and colonial centres – complaints against authority that were to continue after royal power had ceased with independence. In North Carolina in 1766–70, the colony's government was resisted by back-country farmers who sought to 'regulate' local officials, but the Regulators' attack on regressive taxation and a lack of consultation was unsuccessful and they were defeated in battle.

Tension was not limited to backcountry areas, for there was a more wide-spread colonial concern with the attempts of the British government after the Seven Years' War to reform the workings of empire and, at least partly, to seek an imperial solution for the accumulated debts of war. The increased interest that British politicians took in the country's imperial position was unwelcome to many colonists.[30] The varied character of the Empire was such that the change in government policy was felt very differently, espe-cially in India and North America. The administration of the territories acquired by the East India Company was left to the Company, but it became apparent that it could not cope with the burden and obvious that the real and potential importance of the Company to national finances required gov-ernment intervention. In the absence of settlers, this was primarily set by financial constraints: government, Parliament and Company wanted the cost of maintaining the Indian empire as a whole to be less than that of the rev-enues from it, which were seen as crucial. In December 1782, Sir John Macpherson claimed 'India has sent in specie and in goods and in drafts upon foreign nations to England since the year 1757 upwards of 50 millions sterling upon balance of account with Britain.'[31]

In 1773, this policy directly interacted with issues of authority in America, and the character of the Empire there, when the government passed a Tea Act that allowed the Company to sell its tea directly to con-signees in America, a measure designed to cut the cost of tea there and thus boost sales. However, the Act was condemned by Patriot activists unwilling to accept Parliament's right to impose direct taxes on the American colonies. Ten thousand pounds' worth of tea was seized from three ships in Boston Harbour by Sons of Liberty, led by Samuel Adams, and thrown into the water. Colonial protestors who in 1765 and 1768 had reacted to British economic impositions by agreeing temporarily to halt the import of British goods had fashioned in New England's largest port a powerful symbol of resistance. A fresh non-importation movement followed in 1774–6.

The Boston Tea Party dramatised the breakdown of imperial authority for at least some of the colonists, a breakdown that was the first stage in a more general collapse in European control in the New World over the following 125 years, but rather than suggesting any inevitable clash, it is necessary to underline the continued similarities between the societies of Britain and British North America and the colonists' sense of themselves as British,[32] to explain why the process of reaching and endlessly redefining a consensus that underlay and often constituted government in this period broke down, and to consider why this process did not break down for large numbers of colonists, both in the Thirteen Colonies and elsewhere, for example in the West Indies. The origins of the American Revolution looked back to seventeenth-century British traditions of resistance to unreasonable royal demands, and in some respects it was a second version of the Civil War and a war of religion, one in which the principal source of support for royal authority (from within the colonies) again came from Anglican Loyalists. Many colonists, however, resisted Parliament's efforts to project its sovereign authority across the Atlantic, efforts that were seen as natural in Britain in order to secure both the liberty of the subject and the coherence of the Empire.[33] The debate over the terms of empire that grew out of the Seven Years' War had become, in North America, an effort to limit the exercise of state power by defining and asserting the natural and constitutional rights of individuals and groups within the body politic, but disagreements over the colonial bond cut to the core of the nature of the Empire, which was that of a reciprocal benefit controlled by the state, as expressed through the sovereignty of Parliament.

Tensions also arose from other developments within the colonies, not least the disruptive consequences of rapid population growth, as well as the Great Awakening in religious consciousness, and challenges to established patterns and practices of authority and social influence. Nevertheless, the American Revolution occurred not because of a general desire to fight for liberty, but rather as a hesitant, if not unwilling, response to the confused tergiversations of British policy, as remedies for the fiscal burden of imperial defence were sought in the context of heavy national indebtedness, apparently pointing the way to new forms of imperial governance. This led to a pervasiveness and depth of alienation that was underrated in Britain.

There were variations in the degree of hostility shown to imperial pretensions, with most hostility from the colonies where there was a lower rate of recent immigration, especially New England and Virginia, while, in contrast, colonies with higher percentages of immigrants, such as New York, contained more Loyalists. This was particularly true of East and West Florida, whose European population almost entirely changed with the end of Spanish rule, and Nova Scotia, where there was a significant rise in population in the 1760s and early 1770s. The Floridas, the West Indies and the colonies that were to become Canada, did not rebel, and government-sponsored anglicisation did not lead to rebellion in conquered Québec, where, indeed, it was tempered by concern for the position of the Catholic Church.[34]

A lack of understanding of American colonial society and aspirations on the part of the government played a major role in the developing crisis and was exacerbated in 1774 by the view that concessions would be seen as weakness, leading to fresh demands; earlier, in the 1760s, the unwillingness to resort to coercion had contributed to serious indecision in the government's handling of the situation. Whatever the view on conessions, there was no support for independence, and even William Pitt the Elder, now 1st Earl of Chatham, a supporter of conciliating the Americans, was fixedly against independence, as it would destroy the integrity of the Empire and the political, strategic and economic interdependency he saw and advocated. Like most politicians and commentators, Chatham felt that economic and political strength were related, that the monopoly of American trade supported British power, and that, without political links, it would be impossible to maintain economic relationships, a view almost unanimously held in Britain, where the splitting of the British Atlantic was seen as an opportunity for France.

Fighting began in 1775, with a British attempt to seize a cache of arms reported to be at Concord. The shedding of blood outraged New England and a substantial army of volunteers soon encircled the British force in Boston. Elsewhere in the Thirteen Colonies, British authority collapsed: owing to the concentration of troops in Boston, governors elsewhere were provided with insufficient military support. Although initially successful, an American invasion of Canada failed to capture Québec, but, by the end of March 1776, after the evacuation of Boston, in response to the threat to the harbour posed by new American artillery positions, there were no British troops in the Thirteen Colonies. The war seemed completely won.

In 1776, however, the Empire struck back, opening the second stage of the war. The melting of the ice on the St. Lawrence enabled a fleet to relieve Québec, the Americans were subsequently defeated at Trois Rivières and they were driven from Canada. The main British army landed on Staten Island on 3 July, defeated the Americans at Long Island on 27 August, and captured New York. However, although there were to be further important British successes, including the capture of Philadelphia (1777), Savannah (1778) and Charleston (1780), each reflecting the amphibious capability stemming from naval strength, it proved impossible either to secure a decisive victory in the field over the main American field army or to negotiate a settlement. American determination remained high and France entered the war on the American side in 1778.

At sea, the war had already exposed the limitations of British naval power. The concentration of naval vessels in Boston harbour and along the New England coast, as occurred in 1774–5, was achieved only by leaving the rest of the American coast largely unsupervised, and thus permitting trade to continue essentially without imperial regulation and restrictions.[35] Once war had broken out, the navy proved unable to protect trade from American privateers in American, Caribbean, Nova Scotian and European waters, and also failed to block the crucial supply of European munitions to the revolutionaries, although it was able to provide crucial support for the army, in the shape of amphibious capability and logistics – this was very much a case of joint operations. This capability enabled the British to take the initiative, at least in so far as amphibious operations were concerned, and despite the serious damage to its infrastructure caused by the revolution, the navy used its blockade to inflict considerable damage on the revolutionary economy.[36] Jack the Painter, a Scot who sought to help the American cause, was striking at an appropriate target when he set fire to Portsmouth's naval ropehouse in December 1776.

French entry into the war, followed by that of Spain (1779) and the Dutch (1780), altered the situation. British warships were redeployed, as Britain responded to the integration of the American conflict into a wider struggle in which the naval balance in American waters was interrelated with that in European and, more obviously, Caribbean waters. By 1780, thanks to shipbuilding after the Seven Years' War, France and Spain had a combined quantitative superiority in naval tonnage of about 25 per cent, and, partly as a result, Britain gained control of neither European nor American waters and was unable to repeat its success in the earlier war. The problem of numbers of warships interacted with disputes over strategy, as the desirability of blockading French ports, for which there were arguably too few ships, clashed with the prudent argument of John, 4th Earl of Sandwich, the First Lord of the Admiralty, that naval strength should be concentrated in home waters, not only to deter invasion but also to permit a serious challenge to the main French fleet, which was based at Brest, and thus to gain a position of naval dominance. This would be compromised by dispersing much of the fleet among distant stations, where it could support amphibious operations and protect trade, but not materially affect the struggle for naval dominance. The commanders of those distant stations were difficult to control effectively and they jealously guarded their autonomy and resources, producing an inflexibility that was ill-suited to the need to react to French initiatives. However, keeping a close eye on Brest, but leaving the Toulon fleet free to sail to North America, which it did in 1778, carried with it the risk that naval control of American waters would be lost. If the French made such an attempt, a matching squadron could theoretically be sent in pursuit, although it was possible that the French fleet might inflict serious damage before the British arrived.

The failure to defeat the Brest fleet in an indecisive battle off Ushant on 27 July 1778, was followed in 1779 by a Bourbon attempt to invade Britain. This was thwarted by disease and poor organisation, rather than British naval action, and there was no repetition of the crushing of the French fleet seen when invasion had been attempted in 1759. The French were more successful at sea than in the Seven Years' War, in part because of determined and effective leadership, and they also mounted a series of amphibious expeditions, capturing Grenada (1779), St. Vincent (1779), Tobago (1781) and Minorca (1782) and destroying British bases on Hudson's Bay (1782). In 1781, the French fleet played a crucial role in the campaign in North America, barring the entrance to the Chesapeake where a British army had established its base at Yorktown. Because the British had not transferred a matching number of warships from the Caribbean, the French had a temporary superiority in numbers, which helped them thwart the poorly commanded British attempt to defeat them off the Virginia Capes (5 September): instead of taking the risky course of ordering a general chase on the French van as it sailed in disordered haste from the Chesapeake, Admiral Graves manoeuvred so as to bring all his ships opposite the French line of battle, which had been given time to form.[37]

As the inconclusive battle prevented the relief of the army at Yorktown, it was instrumental in its surrender the following month, and in the subsequent unravelling of political support for the war within Britain. This is a reminder of the fine margin on which the seaborne empire rested. As in 1588, 1692, 1759, 1805, 1916, 1943 and other occasions, there was nothing inevitable about the translation of naval superiority, whether British or that of Britain's opponents, into victory. Naval success in 1781 could have easily led to the relief of Cornwallis's army, which, while not bringing victory in America, would have prevented defeat.

It was not until 12 April 1782 that the British won a naval victory to rank with those of 1759. Off the Îles des Saintes, south of Guadeloupe, the location of the battle a testimony to the importance of trans-oceanic operations, the outnumbered French fleet was soundly defeated with the capture of five ships of the line, including the flagship and the capture of Grasse, the admiral. Thanks in part to innovations that increased the ease of serving cannon, of firing them instantaneously and the possible angles of training them, including improvements in flintlocks, tin tubes, flannel cartridges, wedges to absorb recoil and steel compression springs, British cannon fire was particularly effective, while a vigorous head-on attack, rather than sailing in parallel lines, was mounted on the French line. Seen as a saviour of national pride, Admiral Rodney became a hero. In Bristol, his Lordship made his triumphal entry into the City to dine by invitation with the Society of Merchants at their hall in King Street . . . several hundred of the citizens met and formed a magnificent cavalcade consisting of equestrians and carriages forming a long line interspersed with bands of music embosomed in laurels in boats placed upon wheeled carriages. Also three persons in the characters and costumes of Mars, Britannia and Minerva seated upon thrones likewise upon wheeled carriages with their attendants at their feet. In the cavalcade was a vessel about 40 tons burthen drawn also upon a wheeled carriage by horses (having swivels on board which were fired occasionally) . . . every insignia and trophy that could add splendour to the scene were resorted to. The cavalcade passed through the principal streets of the city amidst the acclamations of the spectators, the music playing, bells ringing, flags flying and guns firing, [word obscure] by the smiles and the waving handkerchiefs of the fair lasses of Bristol.[38]

The war placed wide-ranging demands on British forces, for there was fighting not only in the New World and in Europe, where Gibraltar was unsuccessfully besieged (1779–83), but also in West Africa and South Asia. There the British captured French and Dutch bases in India, Sri Lanka and Sumatra, but were challenged in 1782–3 by a French squadron under Suffren that provided support for Haider Ali, Sultan of Mysore, who had invaded the Carnatic in 1780. The British had already found the Marathas a difficult foe in Western India in 1778–82, with the surrounded Bombay army forced, at Wadgaon in 1779, to negotiate its retreat. In southern India, Haider and his son and successor Tipu pressed the British hard, and they were happy to end the war, by the Treaty of Mangalore of March 1784, on the basis of *status quo ante bellum* (a return to the situation prior to the war). Suffren's operations had indicated the vulnerability of the British position and its dependence on naval strength. In 1781, his arrival thwarted a British attempt to capture Cape Town, and, from February 1782 until June 1783, Suffren fought a series of battles with Vice-Admiral Sir Edward Hughes in the Bay of Bengal and off Sri Lanka. He was able to put great pressure on the British position, not least by forcing the garrison in Trincomalee to capitulate in 1782. When the war ended, Suffren was planning an attack on Madras. Suffren, who had to cope without a well-equipped local base, showed that the British navy was not inherently bound to triumph.[39]

In September 1783, the War of American Independence ended with the Peace of Versailles. France won minor gains, including Tobago, Senegal and consent to the fortification of Dunkirk, while Spain obtained Florida, East and West, and Minorca. The most important loss was the Thirteen Colonies, which, in the long term, permanently changed the course of world history.

Contemporaries suspected that this loss would mark a fundamental weakening of the Empire and be followed by French challenges to British power elsewhere, especially in Canada and India. Typically, the Native Americans were not represented in the negotiations that also reapportioned their land.[40]

Despite the loss of the Thirteen Colonies, the Empire had shown considerable resilience in the war. In the teeth of a powerful American-European-Indian range of enemies, Britain had held on to Canada, Jamaica, Gibraltar and Madras, and the British position in Canada was greatly strengthened by the approximately 68,000 Loyalists who emigrated there from the Thirteen Colonies, especially as tensions between them and the French Canadians were contained. The British Isles themselves had not been invaded, there had been no rebellion in Ireland and the French fleet had been defeated in 1782. Nevertheless, although the crisis was to be short-lived, it posed important questions about Britain's strength as a world power. All such powers have faced such questions, as the USA did at the time of its failure in the Vietnam War, but the loss of Britain's American colonies was a more fundamental challenge, as it revealed important deficiencies in the incorporating character of British Empire, deficiencies that were to be tested thereafter in relations with Ireland. In addition, the war suggested that the clear-cut victory over France (and Spain) in the Seven Years' War was as much the result of the particular circumstances of the conflict as of inherent British strength, which opens up basic questions relating to the respective roles of structure and process.

The British had fought the War of American Independence without allies, but the suggestion that the absence of a diversionary war on the Continent helped lead to failure underrates both the difficulty of achieving victory over the Americans (which had eluded Britain *prior* to the French intervention) and, also, British resilience in the face of Bourbon efforts in the later conflict. Even had they been allied to Britain and not diverted her strength to support their own goals, neither Austria, Prussia nor Russia were in a position to help in a war fought at sea and in the colonies, and the war that broke out, in the extraordinary circumstances of an American rebellion, placed wholly unexpected military burdens on Britain.

BRITAIN AND NON-WESTERN POWERS

The naval history of Britain in the period covered by this chapter is generally discussed in terms of the challenge from other Western forces, but this leaves out of the equation the 'dog that did not bark in the night' in the shape of the failure of non-Western powers to contest British strength at sea. Thus, in the difficult conflict with native Caribs on St. Vincent in

1772–3, the British benefited from their ability to move forces from elsewhere in the West Indies and from North America, and did not need to fear disruption in this from the Caribs, nor attacks on other British islands.

The British did encounter hostile naval forces in India, however. In 1756, Charles Watson reported from captured Gheria that he had discovered plentiful artillery, and that Tulajee Angria had been building a 40-gun warship. In 1775, two British warships encountered a Maratha squadron 'of five large ships and two ketches with some gallivats', the large ships mounting 26 to 40 guns and the ketches two guns. The Maratha ships scattered and the British ships engaged the largest being fired on, 'but far short of what might reasonably have been expected from a vessel of her force'. Maratha hopes of boarding a British warship were thwarted by its gunfire, and the Maratha ship blew up with no British casualties. Five years later, Hughes found Haidar Ali's fleet off Mangalore. Covered by gunfire, and in the face of fire from coastal positions, the ships' boats of the British squadron moved in and successfully boarded the two leading Mysore warships, boats of 26 and 24 guns. In 1783, John Macpherson, a senior official of the East India Company, wrote that British forces had taken ports belonging to Mysore, 'in some of which we have found the materials and great advancement of a very considerable naval power'.[41]

Such developments indicate the potential for Indian naval power, but they are striking in their rarity. In South Asia, with the exception of the Omani Arabs, who made less of an impact in the late eighteenth century than a century earlier, native rulers focused on shallow-draft ships best suited to inshore naval capability, in so far as they were interested in naval strength. Both the Mughals and the Marathas had land-based military systems, and this was also true of less powerful rulers. Mysore was very much a land power, and its fleet was lightly gunned and small. Asian rulers were impressed when shown European warships, because they had seen nothing like them, and in 1755 Watson was delighted to show his flagship, HMS *Kent*, to the Nawab of the Carnatic. In particular, local warships could not match the firepower of the British ones. After bombarding Gheria and setting ablaze Tulajee Angria's fleet, overcoming fire from both, Watson noted 'the hulls, masts and rigging of the ships are so little damaged, that if there was a necessity we should be able to proceed to sea in twenty four hours'.[42]

However, logistical limitations, along with disease and climate, substantially affected British force projection. Naval operations, especially in the Indian Ocean and the Caribbean, remained greatly conditioned by climate and disease. Despite improvements in some spheres, the general conditions of service at sea remained bleak. In addition to suffering from cramped living conditions and poor sanitation, common sailors remained poorly fed, lacking fresh fruit and vegetables and thus vitamin C.

Moreover, the unmatched strength of European warships in Asian, African, Australasian and Pacific waters did not necessarily mean that they could achieve what they wanted. Their limitations as large, wind-driven wooden warships included serious problems with operating in shallow waters, while their size was such that, in the absence of wind, although they could be towed by rowers in the ships' boats, they lacked the flexibility of the far smaller fighting rowboats seen, for example, in Madagascar and Hawaii. However, in deep water there was no effective opposition to European warships, and this tactical advantage was enhanced by the operational range stemming from their size and cargo-carrying capacity, and a ratio between supplies and sailors that was far more favourable than ships depending on rowers.

China, Japan and Korea, particularly China in the early fifteenth century, had all had a formidable naval capacity for at least part of the period 1400–1600, and they had the administrative sophistication to accumulate and deploy resources for military development; indeed, by the period 1680–1760 China was the world's most successful empire in terms of expansion on land, driving back the Russians from the Amur valley and conquering Mongolia, Tibet, Xinjiang and Chinese Turkestan. China did not, however, mount comparable efforts during the remainder of the century. There were local struggles on parts of the southern frontier – unsuccessful in Burma in the 1760s and Tongking (northern Vietnam) in 1788–9, and successful against Nepal in 1792, but the Manchu Chinese state was no successor to the medieval steppe empires of the Mongols and Timur: there was no drive to conquer Japan, as the Mongols had sought to do in the thirteenth century, and the frontier with Russia fixed in 1685 and 1729 was seen as acceptable. Yet, it is difficult to see China in terms of failure. Indeed, the Chinese population may have risen from 150 million in 1650 to 300 million in 1800, both figures greater than the population of European Christendom. Defeat in IndoChina was a blow, but it was distant from the centre of Chinese concern, which was the Beijing-Xinjiang axis.

In 1792, China consolidated its position in Tibet, ending a challenge from the expanding power of the Gurkhas of Nepal by sending a force to capture Katmandu. The British in India, who had approached Nepal for trade, felt it prudent to ignore a Gurkha request for assistance, instead restricting themselves to offering mediation, but they had no need to fear Chinese naval power. Indeed, the naval strength of any Asian state did not become a factor until the rapid development of that of Japan in the early twentieth century. Once Anglo-Japanese relations had deteriorated in the 1920s, this abruptly changed the assumptions of British naval power. Prior to that, however, the British, in Asian waters, had only had to consider the navies of other Western powers, ensuring that the focus of naval conflict was in European waters,

for, if their opponents could not prevail there, at least to the extent of maintaining communications, they would not be in a position to sustain a serious
challenge to the British in more distant waters. This was to be demonstrated
anew in war with France in 1793–1815.

A DECADE OF NEW BEGINNINGS, 1783–1793

At the time of the loss of the Thirteen Colonies, there were dire predictions that the rest of Britain's Empire would soon disintegrate, but in fact
it was to revive rapidly. As far as the Thirteen Colonies were concerned,
their loss greatly altered the character of the Empire, but the swift resumption of commercial links with the newly independent state greatly lessened
the potential damage and contrasted with the failure of French trade with
Haiti to recover after its revolution in the 1790s.[43] Average annual British
exports to North America, which had been £1.3 million in 1751–5, rose to
over £2 million in 1786–90. The new state was populous, still needed access
to Britain's credit (often generously supplied) and lacked the range of British
industrial production, and so the business networks that had developed in
range and intensity prior to the war, as Britain took a greater role in the
Atlantic economy,[44] reknit swiftly. American ships and shipbuilding had been
important to the pre-war maritime capacity of the British Atlantic, and, after
independence, their merchants and ships were to compete strongly with the
British in a number of markets, including the West Indies and those round
the Pacific. Nevertheless, the resumption of trade with America was particularly fortunate for Britain, as Western and Central Europe experienced
difficult industrial and commercial conditions in the 1780s. Thanks in part
to the recovery in trade with North America, British exports rose in value
from £14.3 million in 1770 to £18.9 million in 1790.

Although commercial relations were re-established quickly, independence
led to an acceleration of the process of differentiation that both characterised
and challenged the Anglo-American world. As this diversity was not new,
but had started as early as the foundation of British North America, it is
important not to exaggerate the role of independence in this process, not
least because the end of political links also, in some respects, lessened tensions in the Anglo-American world. The role of British investment might
suggest that the new state was, at least in some respects, part of what was
to be termed the informal empire, but this does less than justice to the
strains in the relationship.[45]

Relations were also improved with Ireland, which had not rebelled but
where the American War of Independence had helped provoke a political
crisis whereby Protestant nationalists had pressed the case for legislative

independence. Once peace had returned, relations with Britain became less tense, although the Pitt government's attempt in 1785 to secure closer commercial relations failed. Aside from the competing economic interests involved, trade was not sufficient as a bond.[46]

The absence of further rebellion provided a good basis for the continued imperial competition with France, which was seen across the range of government concern, especially in diplomacy and naval policy, and was also fully reflected in the press. The *Morning Post* of 17 March 1786 noted

> By the last accounts from Halifax . . . we learn . . . Capt. Stanhope, of the Mercury man of war, with four frigates, to cruise on the Banks of Newfoundland, in order to prevent the French from making encroachments on the British fisheries.

The government negotiated a trade treaty with France in 1786, the Eden Treaty, but it was extensively criticised and the two states came close to war over the United Provinces (Dutch) in 1787. In that crisis, the rapid preparation of the fleet was an important factor, although the decisive military stroke was a Prussian invasion that swiftly overcame the Patriots, France's Dutch allies.

In part as a response to the loss of America, there was a major attempt to explore trans-oceanic possibilities over the following decade. Although the West Indies remained pre-eminent 'as an imperial enterprise',[47] India was the pivot of much activity, and was also important to the changing conception of empire. The gain of an Indian-based Oriental Empire from the 1750s encouraged comparison with imperial Rome because, unlike Britain's North American Empire, but like that of imperial Rome, the new British Empire in India had no ethnic underpinning and was clearly imperial. Writers in the tradition of civic humanism and, later, Romantic writers such as Byron, Shelley and de Quincey, searched for points of reference around which to discuss and resonate their anxieties about the effects of empire upon metropolitan culture, and imperial Rome was the obvious parallel.[48] Wealth, especially from India, was seen as a source of political corruption and pernicious, effeminate luxury. Thus, the *Dorchester and Sherborne Journal* of 2 July 1802 stated that the electors of Shaftesbury would 'soon be free, and once more relieved from Asiatic bondage', because the political interest of Paul Benfield, the recent MP who had made his money corruptly in India, had collapsed.

The fate of British India also involved the British position in the China trade, as well as attempts to challenge the Dutch, particularly in Sumatra and Sri Lanka, the possibility of Pacific expansion and the future of the maritime route to India, all of which widened the area that came within the imperial scan. The plan to develop a base on the south-west coast of Africa on the route to India led to the *Nautilus* survey of the coast north of St. Helena Bay in 1786, although it was found unsatisfactory as an area for colonisation, even for convicts. This was not the only disappointment, as, to open up the 'Middle Passage' to India, the Court of Directors of the East India Company in 1785 ordered that a base be established at Diego Garcia in the Chagos Archipelago, which was seen as a source of refreshments for ships en route to India. However, the *Admiral Hughes*, which reached the island in 1786, found plenty of rats but no grain or local building supplies, and later that year the settlement was evacuated.

Further east, concern about competition with France led to interest in the establishment of naval bases in the Andaman or Nicobar Islands, or on St. Matthew's Island (off the Kra Isthmus in modern Thailand), Sumatra or Jung Saylang in the Mergui Archipelago. In the event, the wild, in British eyes, Andaman Islands were claimed in 1789, and Port Cornwallis, named after William Cornwallis, Commander-in-Chief in the East Indies, was established as a base. Earlier, local initiative by a merchant, Francis Light, led to the occupation of the island of Penang as a base on the route to China, a move designed, in part, to check French ambitions to the east of the Bay of Bengal. The island was renamed Prince of Wales Island when the flag was hoisted, and it was to be the basis for Britain's subsequent expansion in Malaya.

Maritime exploration was one index of Anglo-Bourbon competition. In 1784–9, France sent ten naval expeditions into the Indian and Pacific Oceans, but British activity came to be more important, a development dramatised in the Nootka Sound crisis of 1790. The publication in 1784 of the narrative of Cook's last voyage, *A Voyage to the Pacific Ocean*, which included his account of his voyage along the north-west coast of North America, inspired three other British projects for developing the fur trade with the Orient from that coast and also for searching for a north-west passage. In 1786, expeditions reached Nootka Sound on Vancouver Island, and in 1788 John Meares obtained permission from the local inhabitants to establish a trading depot at Friendly Cove. The new base and the prospect of profits excited both mercantile and official interest, but they were thwarted by Spanish action initially designed to block a reported Russian plan to claim the area. In July 1789, the commander of a Spanish warship who had been sent there responded to an assertion of British rights by pulling down the British flag and seizing the British ships in Nootka Sound. Separately, two months earlier, owing to the clash between the respective interests of the Spanish claim that their sovereignty extended over uninhabited coastline and the British determination to expand a 'Southern Fishery' in the waters of the South Atlantic and South Pacific, two London ships had been detained sealing off Penguin Island near Puerto Deseado in what the Spaniards saw as their waters.

The news of Nootka Sound reached London in January 1790, and led to demands for redress supported by a major naval armament. In response, the Spaniards armed and sought French support under the Family Compact between the Bourbon ruling houses. In Britain, the crisis saw the expression of robust public confidence in naval strength. A caricature published in July 1790, *The British Tar's Laughing-stock, or The Royal Quixote*, an attack on Charles IV of Spain, included the verse, 'Our British tars shall crop your ears,/And drive your Fleets to hell'. British hopes of imperial prospects rose, one diplomat, Robert Liston, writing of a possible north-west passage from near Nootka to Hudson's Bay and of a large inland sea like the Baltic or the Mediterranean, adding 'if the coasts of this new Mediterranean are of a rich sort, producing ship-timber, and peopled with a race of men wishing to exchange furs for our woollens and other manufactures, we cannot give up such an extensive prospect for the increase of our trade'.[49]

By October 1790, the British had 43 ships of the line and 10 frigates ready at Spithead. In the event, Spain backed down, accepting a settlement that established the rights of the British to settle to the north of the areas occupied by Spain in April 1789 (which included most of the coast of modern California): the coast of what is now British Columbia, Washington and Oregon, the Russians already being in Alaska. British whalers and traders were to be able to operate 'in the Pacific Ocean or in the South Seas, or in landing on the coasts of those seas in places not already occupied, or for the purpose of carrying on their commerce with the natives of the country or of making establishments there'.[50] This furthered the goal of using a British presence in the Pacific as the basis for an exchange of European, American and Asian goods.[51] The British government, however, had not gained all the points it had sought, as British merchants were not to be allowed to trade directly with Spanish America, which remained within the protectionist framework of the Spanish Empire, and the demand for specific borders had been avoided, although British policy had been motivated largely by a concern to vindicate their principles of colonial sovereignty, rather than specifically to secure new dominions. The opposition criticised the terms, but the resolution of the crisis was generally seen as a triumph. French weakness, in the early stages of the French Revolution, had played a crucial role in the crisis and this led to a situation in which the British clearly became the leading power in the Pacific.

This was exploited as naval officers accumulated information and made claims. In the waters of the south-west Pacific, the British added to their Empire Lord Howe Island (1788), the Chatham Islands (1791) and Pitt Island (1791), while Captain William Bligh made intelligible charts of Fiji, the

Banks group and Aitutaki in the Cooks, Captain Lever 'discovered' the Kermadecs and Penrhyn Island, and Captains Gilbert and Marshall the islands that bear their names, and in 1789 Lieutenant John Shortland coasted the shores of Guadalcanal and San Cristobal. Commander George Vancouver, who had been on Cook's second and third voyages, was sent to the Pacific in 1791 in order to carry out survey work and to secure Britain's possession of the Nootka Sound coastline. He explored part of the coast of New Zealand, 'discovered' the Chathams and charted the Snares, as well as thoroughly surveying the Pacific coastline of modern Canada and Alaska in 1792–4, showing that there was no water passage between the Atlantic and the Pacific south of the Arctic. Vancouver was accompanied by the naturalist Archibald Menzies who, also, had already visited the Pacific, and he brought back a large number of plants, as well as descriptions of new animals and an account of mountains in Hawaii.[52] In addition, the East India Company was responsible for surveying, the Bombay Marine, for example, for surveys of the Pellew Islands in 1790–93 and New Guinea that were intended to provide information on routes to China, particularly if there was a sea passage through New Guinea.[53]

These voyages were matched by land exploration. Alexander Mackenzie travelled from Fort Chipewyan to the Arctic in 1789, and in 1792–3 crossed North America from the Atlantic to the Pacific. In 1788, Sir Joseph Banks, who had sailed on Cook's first voyage and was now President of the Royal Society, played a major role in founding the Association for Promoting the Discovery of the Interior Parts of Africa, or African Association, a society of British societists and scholars that sponsored exploration, seeking to use the trans-Saharan trade routes to send explorers into the African interior, and also to explore it from the River Gambia. Daniel Houghton, an ex-army officer, went further beyond the Senegal into the interior than previous European travellers, but his efforts to open a trade route were unsuccessful, and he was robbed and died in 1791, well short of his goal, Timbuktu. Exploration brought knowledge, much of which was made available through publication. For example, William Paterson (1755–1810), an army officer with a strong interest in botany, travelled extensively in southern Africa in 1777–9, reaching the Orange River, and his *Narrative of Four Journeys into the Country of the Hottentots and Caffravia* (1789) was dedicated to Banks. As an instance of the range of British imperial activity, Paterson went on to serve in India and Australia, where he ascended the rapids on the Hawkesbury River, and eventually became Lieutenant-Governor; a keen collector of botanical specimens, he named a river, a mountain and a creek in Australia after himself.

The foundation of a British settlement in Australia owed much to the loss of America, which had brought transportation to an end and led to a crime wave as a substantial number of major offenders were released into the community. After considering transportation to Africa (the Irish government meanwhile sent convicts to Newfoundland, Nova Scotia, Cape Breton Island and Barbuda), the government decided, in 1786, to found the colony of New South Wales in Australia in order to provide a penal colony, and the first settlers were landed in January 1788. The government also hoped for geopolitical advantage: aside from pre-empting the French, who indeed reached Botany Bay six days later, it planned a base that would project British power into the southern hemisphere and provide naval supplies.[54] Initially, the high hopes were to be disappointed, as the harsh climate and difficult ground vegetation created problems, as did scurvy, and a failure to provide and produce sufficient supplies ensured that there were grave difficulties until the Second Fleet arrived in 1790. Thereafter, the situation improved: more fertile soils were cultivated and Port Jackson on Sydney Cove (the latter named after the Home Secretary) became an important calling-place for whalers and sealers. After the first two fleets, Irish convicts were also accepted.[55] The resonance of Australia in the British imagination was varied. The focus was on the penal colony, but the influence was far-flung, including the naming of sites, for example 'Botany Bay' among the copses in the Quorn hunting country of high Leicestershire.

Another aspect of greater British interest in the opposite side of the world was an increased engagement with China, from which tea imports grew greatly, to more than 13 million pounds in 1788 and to 17.25 million of the 19.5 million sold at Canton in 1791, stimulating, in turn, exports from India to China. The wide-ranging impact of China also ensured greater interest in South-East Asia, while in 1788 the East India Company drew up a project for an agreement with the Spanish Royal Philippine Company in which Manila was to become a free port enabling the British to trade indirectly with South America and, as a result, to obtain silver that could be used in the China trade. A more direct engagement with China included plans in 1787 to negotiate for the establishment of a commercial base in China, but, although the Qianlong emperor was impressed by the model of the British warship he was shown, the MacCartney mission of 1792–4 failed to realise hopes for an enhanced commercial relationship.[56]

A very different settlement had been founded in West Africa in 1787, at what was symbolically termed Freetown. The settlers came from London's blacks, of whom some had come to England in the course of their working lives, individually as seamen or as servants, although the great majority of those who became involved in the Sierra Leone expedition were Loyalists from the War of Independence. Most were poor, in their twenties and lived in the East End, and, since there were relatively few women among them, or among the already established black community in England, a significant number took white wives. The great majority of newspaper items about the expedition were sympathetic in tone and, combined with intermarriage and the good public response to the appeal for money to help poor blacks, this suggests that racial hostility may have been less common than has often been assumed. Both the Committee for the Relief of the Black Poor and key government supporters appear to have been motivated by humanitarianism springing from Christian convictions, gratitude towards Loyalist blacks and abolitionist sympathies, and the settlement explicitly forbade slavery. Freetown was long to remain a symbol of this idealism, although the settlement experienced many difficulties and in 1808 the Sierre Leone Company transferred the colony to Crown government.[57]

The rise of the anti-slavery movement was one of the most important developments within the Empire. Christian assumptions about the unity of mankind and the need to gather Africans to Christ played a major role in influencing British opinion, while commercial benefits from the abolition of the slave trade were also predicted by some commentators, Malachy Postlethwayt arguing in his *The Universal Dictionary of Trade and Commerce* (4th edition, 1774), that the slave trade stirred-up conflict among African rulers and thus obstructed both British trade and 'the civilising of these people'.[58] The ruling in the Somerset case of 1772 that West Indian slave owners could not forcibly take their slaves from England, and therefore that slavery was unenforceable there, reflected the growing prominence of the issue and in 1787 the Society for the Abolition of the Slave Trade, a national lobbying group, was established. Its pressure helped lead to the Dolben Act of 1788 by which conditions on the slave ships were regulated.

The abolitionist movement was linked to a major expansion of missionary activity. The long-established Societies for Promotion of Christian Knowledge (founded in 1698) and the Propagation of the Gospel in Foreign Parts (1701), were joined by the Baptist Missionary Society (1792), the London Missionary Society (1795), the Anglican Church Missionary Society (1795), the Scottish Missionary Society (1799), the Church Missionary Society (1799) and the Wesleyan Missionary Society (1813). Evangelicalism was also related to exploration, both aspects of 'the national mission to save the debased savages from themselves', a mission that took on added force in the context of conflict with France.[59] Missionary activity reached out to many corners of the world, the missionaries sent out from the homeland by sea. In 1807, the Church Missionary Society (until 1812 the Society for Missions to Africa and the East), sent out Robert Morrison to proselytise in China, but he was not allowed to penetrate beyond the permitted foreign trading areas, and the situation did not change until after the Treaty of Nanjing in 1842. The British and Foreign Bible Society, established in 1804, spread the word in another way. Missionary activity was to play a major role in the post-Napoleonic Empire, helping to contribute to a sense of superiority that appeared entirely appropriate in the most powerful empire the world had hitherto seen, and that stemmed in large part from the powerful Evangelical theme in early nineteenth-century British society.

In the 1780s and 1790s, pressure to abolish the slave trade was hindered by the importance of the plantations of the West Indies to the British economy, as well as by the opposition of George III and the House of Lords, and by the conservative response to agitation for reform that followed the outbreak of the French Revolution.[60] The growing crisis of the French state in the 1780s had suggested either that it would become stronger, most probably under a popular reform monarchy, or sink into chaos. As the failure of the Estates General to end the crisis in 1789 appeared to lessen the chances of the first, so the British Empire seemed relatively stronger, and this helped lead to success in the confrontation with Spain over Nootka Sound in 1790. However, the steadily more radical French regime did surprisingly well when war with Austria and Prussia began in 1792. The overrunning of the Austrian Netherlands (Belgium) that November and the subsequent threat to Britain's Dutch ally led to a crisis in Anglo-French relations that was exacerbated by mutual distrust stemming from hostility towards the other's political system: France had become a republic in 1792, and the radicalism of the Revolution challenged the social and political norms of the bulk of the British establishment, not least because of the stress in British public culture on organic change, the rule of law and moderation.

WAR WITH FRANCE, 1793–1815

Britain entered the war against Revolutionary France in February 1793, but the powerful coalition arrayed against France was defeated in 1794 and collapsed in 1795, the British army being driven out of the United Provinces. Having established a puppet regime in the United Provinces in 1795, the French were also able to force Spain into an alliance in 1796. These steps made the naval situation far more serious for Britain, but, from the outset of the war, the British had again needed to dominate the seas in order to provide home security, to protect trade and to make it possible to mount attacks both in Europe and across the oceans. The protection of trade was particularly important to the securing of empire, because the value of colonies and trading stations was largely a function of their ability to trade, and once war had broken out naval power ensured that Britain gained most of the wealth of long-range European trade, a vital key to the ability to finance the war effort and to provide the financial support that helped keep allies in the war.

Victory in the first naval battle of the war, the Glorious First of June (1 June 1794), enabled Britain to grasp the controlling maritime position: Richard, Earl Howe, with 25 ships of the line, attacked a French fleet of 26 of the line under Louis Thomas Villaret-Joyeuse, sent to escort a grain convoy from America into Brest. Howe, who had gained the weather gauge as a result of skilful seamanship, was unable fully to execute his plan for all his ships to cut the French line, so that each passed under the stern of a French ship and engaged it from leeward, but enough ships succeeded and British gunnery was sufficiently superior, and at close range for long enough, to lead to the sinking of one French ship, the capture of six and 5,000 casualties, the last important given the difficulties of obtaining skilled manpower. The vital convoy did, however, reach France.

When Spain joined France in 1796, the British navy cut its links with its colonies, but also withdrew from the Mediterranean; instead using Lisbon and the estuary of the River Tagus as a base. In 1797, the British could not mount a response when the French invaded Venice, seizing its navy and its bases in the Ionian Isles, such as Corfu, and the British garrison on Elba was also evacuated. Given the bleakness of the naval position, it was scarcely surprising that Britain sought peace, although talks at Lille broke down as a result of the British refusal to return all their colonial conquests and of the intransigence of the French government.

The dangerous situation was eased by the difficulties in achieving co-operation and co-ordination between the French, Dutch and Spanish fleets, by the mismanagement of French expeditions against Ireland and by a series of British naval victories in which France and her allies were outfought. In these battles, the fighting quality of individual British ships was combined with a bold command culture that emphasised manoeuvre and seizing the initiative in order to close with the opposing fleet and defeat it in detail after it had been divided by intersecting the opposing line, tactics recommended by the influential *Essay on Naval Tactics* by John Clerk of Elden, a work that greatly impressed Horatio Nelson. Off Cape St. Vincent, a larger and far more heavily gunned Spanish fleet was defeated on 14 February 1797, as the British brought their strength against part of the opposing fleet and used their greatly superior rate of fire to deadly effect in individual ship encounters. Four of the Spanish ships of the line were captured, ten more were badly damaged and their fleet was driven back into Cadiz, ending the plan for them to join the French at Brest. At the battle of Camperdown in the North Sea on 11 October 1797, the Dutch fleet was defeated, with the loss of seven of the line, British victory owing much to its gun-power, although Dutch gunnery skill was such that British killed and wounded were proportionately closer to that of their opponent than in any other fleet action of the war.

The most dramatic victory was won by Rear-Admiral Sir Horatio Nelson (1758–1805), who had already taken a prominent role at St. Vincent. The eldest son of a Norfolk clergyman, Nelson had entered the navy under the auspices of an uncle, and after serving in the Caribbean, the North Sea and North American waters during the War of American Independence he was sent to the Mediterranean in 1793. There Nelson took part in the conquest of Corsica in 1794, losing the sight of his right eye, while in 1797 he lost his right arm in a mis-managed amphibious attack at Tenerife in the Canary Islands. In 1798, the government felt able to send a fleet back into the Mediterranean where it could observe the French fleet in Toulon, only for a strong northerly gale to drive Nelson away, enabling the French to launch their expedition to conquer Egypt, then an autonomous part of the Ottoman (Turkish) Empire. After a long search, Nelson found the French fleet anchored in Aboukir Bay, but by then Napoleon and his army had already begun the conquest of Egypt.

At dusk on 1 August 1798, in the battle of the Nile, Nelson unexpectedly attacked the French on both sides: on the shallow inshore side of their line, where the French were not prepared to resist, as well as simultaneously on the other side. British seamanship was superior, the well-drilled gun crews outshot the French, who were not only poorly deployed but also failed to respond adequately to the attack, and Nelson had ably prepared his captains to act vigorously and in co-operation in all possible eventualities, and had fully explained his tactics to them. The dangerous commitment made by the dispatch of a fleet to the Mediterranean, not least the weakening of the fleet in home waters, was justified by a sweeping victory that had a major impact on British morale, and it was celebrated in a variety of ways: a local dining club constructed a Naval Temple on the Kymin in South Wales, while on their Thoresby estate in Nottinghamshire the Manners family laid out a plantation in the order of Nelson's line of battle.

There were also vigorous attacks in the 1790s on French colonies, which seemed the most profitable and appropriate way to strike at France (especially after British forces were driven from the Continent), the best way to make effective use of the striking power of the navy and the means of stopping French attacks on British colonies. The most important French colonies were in the West Indies, and the British made a formidable effort there, Tobago being captured in 1793, and Martinique, St. Lucia and Guadeloupe following in 1794. However, weakened by disease and affected by the French ability to win support by abolishing slavery, the British lost Guadeloupe (December 1794) and St. Lucia (May 1795), were driven back on St. Domingue and in 1795 were faced with slave rebellions in Grenada, St. Vincent, Dominica and Jamaica.

This was a crisis for the Empire that was far more serious than the expulsion of forces from the Low Countries, and that threatened to rank with the loss of the Thirteen Colonies, because the West Indies was important to British trade and public finances. In late 1795, 33,000 troops, from over half the line regiments in the army, were sent there. Demerara and St. Lucia were captured in 1796 and the rebellions were suppressed, while in 1797 Trinidad was taken from Spain, the Dutch colonies of Surinam (1799) and Curaçao (1800) following. However, the British lost 45,000 troops in the West Indies in 1793–1801, over 95 per cent to disease, particularly yellow fever and malaria; casualty rates that affected morale, leading to desertion and mutiny. Nevertheless, had the British not followed a policy of conquest in the West Indies they would still have had to deploy sizeable forces there in order to protect colonies from local revolt and French attack, and the best way to prevent such attack was to seize the French colonies themselves.[61]

Other expeditions seized many of the colonial bases of France and her allies distant from the Caribbean. In India, Pondicherry and Chandernagore were captured from France in 1793, while in the Indian Ocean the Seychelles were taken in 1794 and in West Africa the slaving base of Gorée fell in 1800. After the United Provinces fell to France, the British conquered much of the Dutch Empire: the bases in India, as well as Cape Town, Malacca and Padang in Sumatra in 1795, the Dutch positions in Sri Lanka and the Moluccas in 1796 and other bases in the East Indies in 1797 and 1801. Success on land followed skilful amphibious operations that were the highpoint of good co-ordination between army and navy, although naval activities were greatly affected by the prevailing winds and an absence of sufficient frigates and sloops. Naval success also played an important background role. Trinidad was captured after four Spanish ships of the line and a frigate had been surprised by a British squadron. The Spaniards abandoned and set fire to their ships, and the destruction of Spanish naval power in the eastern Caribbean helped the British. British naval strength also lessened the risk from counterattacks. In 1796, the Dutch sent a fleet to regain Cape Town, but it was caught at anchor in Saldanha Bay by a greatly stronger British fleet and surrendered without a fight.

Repeated successes still left much of the French, Dutch and, in particular, Spanish Empires outside British control, but, thanks to these gains, the British were clearly in a position of maritime and colonial dominance. In 1798, Geoffrey Mowbray claimed 'our navy keeps every one of our enemies bound in chains upon their own coasts',[62] a situation that was important for the protection of British commerce and the harrying of that of their opponents. Doing so hit their opponents' finances. On 16–17 October 1799, off Cape Finisterre, four frigates captured two Spanish frigates, each bearing bullion from the New World; the following April the blockading squadron off Cadiz captured nearly all of a large Spanish convoy and in 1804 it took three Spanish frigates carrying bullion.

Maritime dominance also ensured that the British–Irish Act of Union of 1800 could come into effect (on 1 January 1801) and be consolidated without disruption by France: there was no repetition of the unsuccessful French intervention on behalf of the failed Irish rebellion of 1798 and in 1800 the British introduced a close blockade of Brest, further ensuring control of Irish waters. The Act abolished the separate Irish Parliament in return for Irish representation at Westminster: 100 new MPs and 32 new peers, but William Pitt the Younger's attempt to follow Union by admitting Catholics to Parliament and to most public offices was thwarted by George III, who argued that this would breach his promise in his coronation oath to protect the position of the Church of England. Catholics could not become MPs in the new Parliament until 1829, and this may have undermined the Union, although a fair share of informed British political opinion thought it could go forward on that narrow basis.[63] In the meanwhile, Irish soldiers, including Catholics, played an important role in the British army, while Irish provisions were crucial to the logistics of British naval power.

With naval strength and a good network of bases, the British were able to mount trans-oceanic operations with little fear of interruption, and the range of British naval activity expanded. Thus, in 1799, warships were sent to the Red Sea in order to deter any possible French threat from Egypt to India, while the campaign of 1801, in which the British invaded Egypt, defeating the French, indicated the far-flung nature of British military power: the main strike force reached Egypt via the Mediterranean while other forces sailed from India and the Cape of Good Hope, marched across the desert from the Red Sea in the summer of 1801 and then sailed down the Nile in time to take part in the capture of Alexandria. The decision to send so many troops to Egypt was an important strategic choice that reflected the weight of imperial commitments and was dependent on the strength of British naval power.

Closer to home, the British navy in 1801 took action against the threatening Northern Confederacy of Baltic powers, which was seen as a challenge to British strategic and commercial interests. Denmark, an important naval power, rejected an ultimatum to leave the Confederacy and the British responded with naval action. At the battle of Copenhagen on 2 April 1801, Nelson, who after sounding and buoying the channels by night had sailed his division down the dangerous Hollaender Deep, in order to be able to attack from an unexpected direction, was again successful at the expense of an anchored line, this time that of the Danish fleet. Heavy Danish fire led Nelson's commander, Sir Hyde Parker, to order him to 'discontinue the action' if he felt it appropriate, but Nelson continued the attack and the Danes were battered into accepting a truce.

Despite her naval victories, the Peace of Amiens of 1802 reflected Britain's isolation after Austria had been driven from the war the previous year, bringing the War of the Second Coalition to an end on the European mainland, and the wish for peace of the Addington government that had replaced that of Pitt in 1801. All gains from France, Spain and the Dutch were to be restored, except Trinidad and the Dutch bases in Sri Lanka, terms that were bitterly criticised in Parliament and viewed by the government as little more than a truce. The aggressive policies on the Continent of Napoleon, who had seized power in France in 1799, especially his refusal to withdraw his forces from the Dutch Republic and his prohibition on British commerce, exacerbated British distrust, and the naval situation was instrumental in the resumption of hostilities in 1803, because the British government refused to surrender Malta as it was obliged to do by the Peace of Amiens. Captured in 1800, the new base at Malta was valued highly because the British had already been compelled to give up other bases in the Mediterranean: Toulon, Corsica and Elba. This was even more the case in 1802, when Minorca was given up under the Peace of Amiens, ending its periods as a British colony (1708–56, 1763–82 and 1798–1802). With the resumption of war, the colonial world had to be conquered anew by Britain, but the task was easier because the army and navy were both prepared, while their opponents' fleets had not recovered from recent maulings. St. Lucia, Tobago, Demarara, Essequibo and Surinam were all seized in 1803–4.

The British advantage was to be secured by naval victory. In 1805, Napoleon prepared an invasion of England for which he required naval superiority in the Channel. He planned for his squadrons to evade the British blockade, sail to the West Indies, join at Martinique and then return as a united force able to cover a landing in Kent. Although French squadrons escaped from Toulon and Rochefort, the Brest squadron was restrained by a close blockade. Villeneuve and the Toulon squadron, which had sailed to Martinique, sailed back to Europe, where it was checked by a smaller fleet under Sir Robert Calder west of Cape Finisterre on 22 July, and instead of trying to fight his way into the Channel Villeneuve took shelter in Cadiz.

Napoleon cancelled his invasion plans and launched his forces against Austria, which he was to crush at Ulm and Austerlitz, and when the Franco-Spanish fleet of 33 of the line set sail on 19–20 October it was for Italian waters in order to support French operations against Austria and her allies in Italy. The fleet was intercepted by Nelson and 27 of the line off Cape Trafalgar and he attacked in two divisions in order to penetrate his opponents' line and split it into smaller groups that could be attacked in strength. By using his windward position to attack his opponents' rear and centre, Nelson achieved numerical superiority, as their foremost ships could not intervene effectively. The Franco-Spanish line was penetrated as planned, making it difficult for Villeneuve to retreat or regroup, and the battle became a series of small struggles in which British gunnery and seamanship prevailed. Nineteen French and Spanish ships of the line were captured or destroyed, and their fleet suffered 14,000 casualties, whereas the British dead and wounded totalled 1,690, including Nelson, who was mortally wounded by a French sharpshooter.

After Trafalgar, the British enjoyed a clear superiority in ships of the line, although Napoleon's victories over Austria, Prussia and Russia in 1805–7 ensured that the War of the Third Coalition ended in Europe with France in an even stronger position. Napoleon sought after Trafalgar, with some success, to rebuild his fleet, and by 1809 his Toulon fleet was nearly as large as the British blockaders, but his naval strength had been badly affected by losses of sailors. Furthermore, owing to Napoleon's attempt in 1808 to take over Spain and put his brother Joseph on its throne, he replaced his alliance with Spain with what became an intractable counter-insurgency conflict that was made far worse for France by the intervention of British forces based in Portugal where their intervention thwarted a French conquest. The loss of the Spanish fleet by France was an important side-effect of this conflict for Britain, while six French ships of the line sheltering in Cadiz and Vigo surrendered to the Spaniards in 1808 and Napoleon's plan to take over the Spanish overseas empire was made redundant by both Spanish hostility and British naval power. The British kept the Portuguese and Danish fleets out of French hands, the former by persuasion and the latter by force, while Russia's Black Sea fleet, then in the Tagus, was blockaded until the British were able to seize it. By 1810, Britain had 50 per cent of the ships of the line in the world; up from 29 per cent in 1790.

Britain's proportion of world mercantile shipping also grew. The rise in trade led to an increase in demand for shipping and in the prices for ships, which encouraged both shipbuilding and ship repair. Effective convoying ensured that ships could be constructed with reference to the goods to be carried, rather than their defensive characteristics: re-established in 1793, convoys were made compulsory in 1798. Britain's maritime strength thwarted Napoleon's attempt, with the Continental System declared by the Berlin Decree of November 1806, to sever her trade with the Continent. The Berlin Decree, expanded by the Edict of Fontainbleau in 1807 and the two Decrees of Berlin of that year, announced a blockade of Britain, the confiscation of all British goods and the arrest of all Britons and were for France's allies as much as France. Instead, the attempt to enforce the blockade helped make alliance with France unpopular, and was repeatedly challenged by the continuance of trade under the shelter of British naval power.[64] Furthermore, the profits from trade enabled Britain to finance her war effort and to make loans and grants to European allies. In contrast, a strategy of economic warfare based on naval blockade of France and her allies became feasible for Britain, and the precariousness of the French economic system was exposed.

The navy had numerous tasks in European waters after Trafalgar. It had to convoy British trade and offer protection against French privateers, as well as attack enemy trade wherever it could be found. The blockade of French ports also helped provide cover for amphibious operations. In home waters, this meant the Walcheren expedition of 1809, an unsuccessful attempt on the French naval base of Antwerp. In the Mediterranean, the navy sought to blockade Toulon as the first line of defence for British and allied interests, such as the protection of Sicily, and in addition the blockade was intended to complement more offensive steps, including intervention in Iberia and moves to limit French influence in the eastern Mediterranean, which included Vice-Admiral Sir John Duckworth's unsuccessful attempt to obtain the surrender of the Turkish fleet in 1807. Duckworth sailed through the Dardanelles on 19 February 1807, destroying a squadron of Turkish frigates, but the Turks refused to yield to his intimidation and when, on 3 March, Duckworth returned through the straits he ran the gauntlet of Turkish cannon, firing some shots of up to 800 pounds – one took away the wheel of HMS *Canopus*. Turkish resistance had been stiffened with French assistance and the operation also suffered from unfavourable winds and Duckworth's indecision.

The British also had defensive and offensive objectives in the Baltic. Concern about the Danish fleet led to a successful joint attack on Copenhagen in 1807: the British fleet under Admiral James Gambier helped bombard the city and the Danish fleet soon after surrendered, while the following year warships were sent into the Baltic in order to assist Sweden against attack by Denmark and Russia and on 25 August two British ships of the line helped 11 Swedish counterparts defeat nine Russian ships off south-west Finland. In 1809, Vice-Admiral Sir James Saumarez led a powerful fleet to the Gulf of Finland, thus preventing the Russians from taking naval action against Sweden. However, naval pressure could achieve only so much: the Russians had already conquered Finland, and were able to force the Swedes to accept a dictated peace. Thereafter, as Sweden was forced into the French camp, Saumarez took steps to protect British trade and, crucially, naval stores: much of the timber, tallow, pitch, tar, iron and hemp required for the navy came from the Baltic.

The general situation was more favourable than in 1795–1805, particularly after the Spanish navy and naval bases were denied France in 1808, although there were fewer opportunities than earlier to increase the size of the navy by adding French prizes. The blockaded French navy was no longer a force that was combat-ready, as the longer it remained in harbour the more its efficiency declined: officers and crews had less operational experience. It remained difficult to predict French moves when at sea, but the French were less able to gain the initiative than hitherto.

The French and allied squadrons that did sail out were generally defeated, and these frequently overlooked, post-Trafalgar engagements were important because a run of French success would have challenged British naval control. Samuel Hood and the blockading squadron off Rochefort on 25 September 1805 attacked a French frigate squadron bound for the West Indies with reinforcements: four of the five frigates were captured, although Hood had to have his arm amputated after his elbow was smashed by a musket shot. On 6 February 1806, Duckworth and seven of the line engaged a French squadron of five of the line that had escaped from Rochefort off Saint Domingue in the West Indies. The superior British gunnery brought Duckworth a complete victory: three of the French ships were captured and two driven ashore and burnt. During the battle, a portrait of Nelson was displayed on HMS *Superb*. Warren on 13 March 1806 captured two warships sailing back from the East Indies as they neared France. Further afield, the Dutch squadron in the Indian Ocean was destroyed at Gressie on 11 December 1807. On 4 April 1808, an escorted Spanish convoy was intercepted off Rota near Cadiz, the escorts dispersed and much of the convoy seized. A French squadron in Basque Roads was attacked by fireships on the night of 11–12 April 1809, and, although the French warships incurred no damage, many ran aground in escaping the threat; they were attacked on 12 April and four were destroyed.

Two years later, on 13 March 1811, a squadron of four frigates under Captain William Hoste, one of Nelson's protégés, engaged a French squadron of six frigates under Dubourdieu off the Adriatic island of Lissa, a British base that the French were trying to seize. As the French approached, Hoste hoisted the signal 'remember Nelson' to the cheers of his crew. Thanks to superior seamanship and gunnery, the French were defeated with the loss of three frigates. Frequently, foreign warships had to be attacked while inshore or protected by coastal positions, a situation that enhanced the value of Britain's clear superiority in vessels other than ships of the line. In August 1806, the Spanish frigate *Pomona* anchored off Havana close to a shore battery was captured by two British frigates.

These engagements were the highpoints of a prolonged and often arduous process of blockade in which British squadrons policed the seas of Europe and, to a lesser extent, the oceans of the world. The history of these squadrons was often that of storms and of disappointed hopes of engaging the French. Blockade was not easy and this was especially true off Toulon owing to the prevailing winds. Blockading squadrons could be driven off station by wind and weather: this was the case with the small watching squadron off Toulon when the French sailed in May 1798, while the exposure of warships to the constant battering of wind and wave placed a major strain on an increasingly ageing fleet. The Channel fleet, for example, was dispersed by a strong gale on 3 January 1804, and the blockade of Le Havre lifted, although that of Brest was swiftly resumed. The weather claimed and damaged more ships than the French: out of the 317 warships lost in 1803–15, 223 were wrecked or foundered, including, in December 1811, HMS *Amazon*, with the loss of all bar twelve of the crew of 850, and HMS *Defence* when they were driven onto the Danish coast in a storm. Tropical stations could be particularly dangerous and in 1807 Troubridge and HMS *Blenheim* disappeared in a storm off Madagascar.

Fog was also a problem, particularly for blockaders. It could cover French movements, as when the Brest fleet sailed in April 1798, and, once a fleet had sailed, it was impossible to know where it had gone: in this case the British were unsure whether the French would head for Ireland or the Mediterranean. In January 1808, the French Rochefort squadron evaded the British blockaders in bad weather and poor visibility and sailed to Toulon, making the concentration of French warships there more serious. Fog was also a hazard to British warships. HMS *Venerable*, part of the squadron covering Brest, sank on the Devon coast in 1804 after running ashore in a thick fog.

The poorly charted nature of inshore waters was a problem that led to ships running aground, nearly 400 men drowning in March 1801 when HMS *Invincible* ran aground near Great Yarmouth. It was particularly easy to do so when enforcing blockades, and shoals were also a problem when attacking enemy warships sheltering in coastal waters. Fire at sea was another hazard, HMS *Queen Charlotte*, flagship of the Mediterranean fleet, being destroyed off Livorno in 1800 with the loss of nearly 700 men.

Despite the burdens of blockade, the very presence of blockading squadrons was crucial as they prevented French squadrons from uniting and becoming a more serious threat and limited the supplies they could receive. The threat posed by the united Franco-Spanish fleet in Cadiz in 1805 was a salutary reminder of the need to keep French squadrons separated, as Villeneuve would have had more ships in his force had he been able to join with the Brest fleet.

After Trafalgar, the British presence off Spain and in the Mediterranean was maintained by Vice Admiral Cuthbert Collingwood, who had received a peerage for his role as second in command at Trafalgar. In 1805–7, he blockaded Cadiz, but then moved into the Mediterranean where his main concern was the French fleet in Toulon. Threatening Sicily, this fleet forced the British to adopt a defensive strategy, but at least after Trafalgar this was based on clear maritime dominance. In 1808, Collingwood failed to intercept Ganteaume when he relieved the French garrison on Corfu, largely because he received news of French moves only belatedly and responded in an overly cautious fashion, but the blockade of Toulon was more successful the following year, and on 26 October two ships of the line attempting to carry supplies to Barcelona were driven on shore and destroyed. Concern about the Toulon fleet, however, continued strong, and at times, not least because of a shortage of frigates and the range of commitments, the British fleet seem stretched. Nevertheless, the Toulon fleet did not escape and attack Wellington's position at Lisbon, as was feared in 1811, while a sortie from Toulon was turned back in 1812, and despite the problems of British naval power in the Mediterranean there was no retreat from the sea as there had been in 1796.[65] This led to the spread of British influence around the sea. In 1810, George, 4th Earl of Aberdeen, who had spent much time in Greece then part of the Ottoman (Turkish) Empire, argued that there was considerable interest in independence there, and that Britain should encourage it, adding 'a French connection, from the absence of naval intercourse and protection, is much less desired than the friendship of this country'.[66]

The responsibilities of fleet command in the Mediterranean were primarily determined by the need to respond to the possibility of French sorties. A more aggressive note was struck by junior commanders, such as Thomas Cochrane, and this helped shape subsequent heroic images of naval action. As captain of the frigate HMS *Pallas* in the Bay of Biscay, Cochrane harried French trade and destroyed corvettes, while in 1808 as captain of the frigate *Impérieuse*, he attacked semaphore stations, fortifications, lighthouses, batteries and bridges on the coasts of southern France and Catalonia. William Hoste also had the active time that being detached on independent cruises permitted. As commander of the frigate HMS *Amphion* and later the HMS *Bacchante*, he operated against French bases on the coast of Calabria in 1806 and in 1808–14 ravaged French trade in the Adriatic and attacked coastal positions. Both Cochrane and Hoste showed their flexibility and all-round military skills by also operating successfully on land, although only so much could be achieved against superior French forces. Nevertheless, British naval activities harassed the French and forced them to deploy considerable forces to garrison their coasts, a counterpart to the commercial challenge posed by British contraband. Attacks on coastal shipping and positions required less military effort and resources than amphibious operations, put the French onto the defensive, and, in some cases, were operationally significant: a squadron under Vice-Admiral Thomas Freemantle drove the French from much of the Dalmatian coast, playing a major role in the capture of Fiume in 1813 and Trieste in 1814.

In the Atlantic, Channel and North Sea, there were fewer opportunities for operations against coastal positions, but there were many small-ship actions against warships and French privateers. Aside from blockade and inshore attacks, the navy also played a major role in supporting operations in the Peninsular War (1808–14). This involved the transport of men and supplies for the British forces and also of supplies for their Portuguese and Spanish allies. Amphibious operations on the north coast of Spain in 1812 were particularly important.[67]

British naval hegemony rested on a sophisticated and well-financed administrative structure, a large fleet drawing on the manpower resources of a substantial mercantile marine, although there were never enough sailors, and an ability to win engagements that reflected widely diffused quantities of seamanship and gunnery, a skilled and determined corps of captains, a relatively meritocratic promotion system and able leadership. This was true not only of command at sea, as with Nelson's innovative tactics and ability to inspire his captains, the 'band of brothers', but also of effective leadership of the navy as an institution. The strengthening of the navy in the 1780s, not least thanks to the successful administration of Sir Charles Middleton, Comptroller of the Navy Board from 1778 to 1790, helped once war broke out in 1793, and able administrators such as Samuel Bentham and John Payne did much to develop the organisation and infrastructure of the navy.[68] At a time when warships were made of wood and enjoyed a useful life ranging from eight to fifteen years, depending substantially on the temperature of the waters in which they served, a constant commitment was required to ensure that an ageing fleet was replenished successfully, and in terms of expensive equipment, this commitment was certainly larger than for the army.[69] Middleton, created Lord Barham in 1805, was an effective First Lord in 1805–6, and played an important role both in developing organisational efficiency and in providing able and effective leadership during the Trafalgar campaign. Efficient dockyard operations and victualling, the conquest of scurvy and the establishment of new standards in the officer corps, were fundamental to the success of the blockade of France and her allies. More specifically, signalling at sea, crucial to operational effectiveness, communications and co-ordinated action, improved from the 1780s, as a quick and flexible numerical system of signals was developed. The strength of the British economy was also vital to naval warfare, although expenditure on the navy, and, more generally, on the war, pushed up the national debt and strained the monetary system, depressing general standards of consumption and distorting trade and manufacturing, even though certain activities, such as shipbuilding and metallurgy,[70] benefited. Merchants were affected by privateering, convoying and a higher insurance rate. The developing coal and iron industries were directly linked to naval capability, providing yet another instance of the penetration of maritime concerns and interests far from the coast: progress in metallurgy, which bound together England, Scotland and Wales, improved British gunnery, helping to ensure that enemy ships were reduced to wrecks in a comparatively short time. More generally, resources permitted, and administrative systems supported, the maintenance both of the largest and most effective battlefleet in the world and of a crucially large number of smaller warships.

Despite the relative strength of Britain's overall naval capacity, there were some serious problems. The hardships of naval service for ordinary seamen, especially dissatisfaction over pay, led to mutinies in 1797. The Spithead fleet refused to sail, there was trouble in St. Vincent's fleet off Cadiz and, most seriously, that at the Nore began to blockade the Thames until quelled by firm action.[71] Later mutinies were on a smaller scale and more specific in their grievances. In 1801, the crew of some of the ships ordered to sail for the Caribbean mutinied, only for the mutiny to be crushed and the ringleaders executed. The 1797 crisis left a bitter legacy of distrust, so that alongside heroic verses celebrating triumphs can be noted the following on Sir John Colpoys:

> The murdering Colpoys, Vice-Admiral of the Blue,
> Gave order to fire on the *London's* crew;
> While the enemy of Britain was ploughing the sea,
> He, like a base coward, let them get away
> When the French and their transports sailed for Bantry Bay.

At a different level, the extensive and costly programme of repair, refitting and construction faced serious deficiencies in the dockyards and in supplies, especially of timber, and a rapid rise in the demand for timber led to the use of inferior, including unseasoned, stock, and thus to warships rotting rapidly. Part of the strain was met by adding captured warships to the fleet. The hostility to naval contractors of Earl St. Vincent, First Lord of the Admiralty in 1801–4, limited the rate of construction and repair and placed the navy in a difficult position in 1804, but the reversal of this policy when St. Vincent resigned ensured that by the end of 1808 the commissioned fleet totalled 113 of the line and 596 other ships. This expansion increased the number of sailors required and by 1810 the navy and marines contained over 142,000 men, in comparison with its peacetime strength of 20,000 in 1792.

The infrastructure of naval power improved and became more far-flung as new naval facilities were developed both in Britain and abroad, for example at Malta, where Nelson established a ropeworks. Cape Town,

Madras, Bermuda, Barbados, Trincomalee and Bombay were developed as naval bases, while two new deep docks were created at Portsmouth in 1796–1800. Such developments had significant effects on society and the economy. Plymouth's importance as a naval base led to a growth in its population, so that whereas Exeter had been the leading town in Devon by population in the mid-eighteenth century, by the census of 1801 that of 'Plymouth' (Plymouth, Stonehouse and Devonport) was more than twice as large. The presence of a large fleet in the Western Approaches provided jobs in the dockyard as well as a ready market for local farmers and businessmen, but that helped drive up the cost of food, leading to riots in 1795.

Thanks to her naval resources, Britain was able to turn tactical triumphs to strategic advantage, successive victories, particularly Trafalgar, conditioned British and foreign expectations, and the latter affected French naval strategy, or rather the absence of it, for most of the war. Confidence is a vital military resource, and victory both brought it to Britain and denied it to France. This was crucial because British naval resources were stretched. Despite the size of the navy, there were too few ships and sailors for the myriad tasks expected of it, and the situation could become hazardous if the French acted in strength. In December 1809, HMS *Junon* sailing from Halifax to the West Indies was attacked, heavily battered and successfully boarded by four French frigates near Guadeloupe. However, the successive capture of French overseas bases lessened their ability to challenge the British.

IMPERIAL ACTIVITY, 1800–1815

Naval superiority enabled the pursuit of colonial gains, ensuring that the British could defend far-flung positions with relatively few troops as well as conducting offensive operations. Thus, successes in the West Indies owed much to the end of the French attempt to reinforce them with the naval victory in Basque Roads in 1809: success in European waters was linked to naval superiority in distant seas. The navy also provided crucial cannon and manpower for sieges.

Cape Town was captured from the Dutch after a brisk campaign in 1806; the Dutch West Indies islands of St. Croix, St. Thomas and St. Johns in 1807; Martinique and Cayenne in 1809; Fort Louis on the Senegal river, the French positions in Santo Domingo, Guadeloupe, Réunion, Mauritius and the Dutch bases of the Moluccas and Sulawesi and Aceh in 1810; Batavia (now Djakarta), the leading Dutch position in the East Indies and a potential threat to the China trade, and Timor in 1811; and Bali in 1814. Some of the conquests were not simply the recapture of earlier gains ceded at

Amiens, and the fall of Batavia totally altered the situation in the East Indies. Successive victories enhanced the geopolitics of British strength.[72] The French naval presence in the Indian Ocean was destroyed with the fall of Réunion and Mauritius; Mauritius had been an important base for French warships and privateers in successive wars, and a threat to the British naval position in Indian waters. The initial attempt on Mauritius failed in August 1810 in the battle of Grand Port, when a British frigate squadron under Samuel Pym was badly battered by heavier French ships, and then had to surrender when a French squadron appeared. The fighting quality of the French accentuated the rash character of Pym's bold leadership, while the battle indicated the danger of overconfident, dispersed British forces being defeated by French squadrons enjoying a local superiority. The situation was remedied when the British warships that had helped in the conquest of Réunion in July arrived, and the British were able to begin a close blockade of the French base.

Conquest was followed by the introduction of British government, the integration of new ports into the British maritime system and cultural developments, including the establishment of the Church of England, missionary activity and the launching of English-language newspapers such as the *Royal Essequebo and Demerary Gazette* (1796), the *Trinidad Weekly Courant* (1800), the *Cape Town Gazette and African Advertiser* (1800) and the *Ceylon Government Gazette* (1802).[73] Such papers provided information of government and for trade, and it also kept the colonies informed of news from Britain, the first issue of the *Cape Town Gazette* noting 'In consequence of the non-arrival of any ships from England for so long a time, we feel disappointed at not being able to lay before our readers any thing particularly interesting'.

The British were not successful everywhere. In July 1806, in an unauthorised expedition that took advantage of the presence of sizeable forces in newly captured Cape Town, Buenos Aires fell to a force of about 1,200 men, apparently opening up a vast new sphere for imperial expansion. Hopes of freeing South America for British trade and of spreading power by means of expeditions to Chile and Mexico spread throughout Britain. However, in the meantime the small British garrison was forced to surrender in August in the face of a major popular rising. After a larger force was sent to capture the city anew, Montevideo was successfully stormed in February 1807, and on 5 July about 8,000 troops attacked Buenos Aires, only to find the town strongly defended.

The attacking columns were isolated in the barricaded streets, and having suffered 3,000 casualties the commander agreed to an exchange of prisoners and the evacuation of the Plate estuary, including Montevideo. This expedition was not one that left much of a record in the annals of empire, but it provided an important indicator of the limitations of seaborne power. Although the British deployed a substantial force, enjoyed good naval support and did not face an ecosystem as hostile as that in the West Indies, they were confronted by a hostile population that did not want to exchange Spanish rule for foreign and Protestant control. This was crucial to the battle, and even had the British won they would have faced a sullen population and been obliged to use large numbers of troops to extend and maintain control, which was very different from the situation in the French overseas empire where there was no large, hostile population and where the defenders were gravely weakened by the consequences of British naval power.

In 1807, as in Sudan later in the century, the British also discovered in Egypt the risks of pressing on with inadequate knowledge in the face of hostile local forces. To block the danger that the French might establish a presence, an expedition was sent to Alexandria, which, vulnerable to naval attack, surrendered quickly. However, two overland attempts on Rosetta, a crucial point for trade on the Nile, were defeated with heavy casualties, and the British soon after abandoned Alexandria.

This failure throws the success of inland expeditions in India into greater prominence. There, the fusion of European training and Indian manpower was an opportunity grasped, and the mostly Indian East India Company army, 18,200 strong in 1763, was 154,500 strong by 1805. This was to be the basis of British military strength in Asia during the nineteenth century. In 1799, the threat from Tipu Sultan of Mysore was ended when his capital, Seringapatam, was stormed, Tipu dying in the defence. The rest of Mysore surrendered soon after and the British restored the dynasty displaced by Tipu's father, Haidar Ali. Although independent territories were annexed by the East India Company, Mysore was left landlocked and the new ruler was forbidden to maintain an army. In 1803, when war broke out in western India with the Marathas, Arthur Wellesley, later Duke of Wellington, a master of methodical, yet rapid, warfare, defeated Maratha forces at Assaye and Argaon, while further north victories over the Marathas by Gerard Lake outside Delhi and at Laswari were followed by another at Farruckhabad in 1804. The Mughal Emperor, Shah Alan II, sought British protection in 1803. However, the 'invincible army . . . strong executive power' model sought by proponents of military power[74] was very costly and clashed with the preference of the East India Company for profit.

Supported by the resources of the fertile areas of India, Bengal and the Carnatic, not least by their banking networks, British power in India was not only a landward asset but also a seaborne one. In a way that was unprecedented in Indian history, forces from India were sent to Egypt in 1801, to Sri Lanka in 1803 and again, more successfully, in 1815, and to

Batavia in 1811, as well as 10,000 troops to Mauritius in 1810. India was the base for seaborne action against both European and non-European powers, the Sri Lankan kingdom of Kandy proving a prime instance of the latter, as was intervention in the Persian Gulf, where British sensitivity was increased by the Franco-Persian alliance of 1807, which encouraged the British, in 1809, to sack the Wahabi base of Ras-ul-Khymah in the Persian Gulf, from which Wahabi pirates had attacked East Indiamen and British warships in the Arabian Gulf. This expedition freed British trade from attack until a fresh pirate campaign began in 1816, leading to another British expedition in 1819–20.[75] The growing British naval and mercantile presence in the Indian Ocean owed much to shipyards in India, where merchantmen averaging 600–800 tonnes and capable of carrying very large cargoes were constructed, as well as warships. British commercial penetration of South and South-East Asia and the Far East was aided by naval strength: occupation, as of Java in 1811–16, was important, but developing trade was not just a function of conquest, as the growing penetration of the Manila market showed.

Competition with France helped drive forward ideas for imperial expansion. Thus, in 1812, when Major-General Charles Stevenson proposed that Britain acquire Timbuktu he referred to the danger that France would establish 'a chain of posts from the Upper Senegal to the Niger' and from there threaten Egypt, as well as to the prospects of exports, imports and African gold, of growing wood for shipbuilding and of raising African troops.[76]

By 1815, when Napoleon was finally defeated at Waterloo, Britain was the strongest power around the Indian Ocean, as well as on the oceans themselves. Aside from the major British contribution at Waterloo, the other forces deployed against Napoleon had been heavily subsidised by Britain. Napoleon himself surrendered to Admiral Henry Hotham on board HMS *Bellerophon*, leading Captain Stanhouse to write to his wife, 'I have just returned from dining with Napoleon Bonaparte, can it be possible?', and was imprisoned by the British on St. Helena, an island in the distant South Atlantic, while British naval dominance made his imprisonment secure.

In the meanwhile, her dominant position had served to ensure that Britain took the leading role in exploration, trade and the assembling of knowledge about the world. This left its mark in the imperial capital where there was a major expansion in shipping and docks: the London Dock was excavated in 1801, followed by the West India Docks in 1802, the East India Docks in 1805 and the start of work on the Surrey Commercial Docks in 1807, all important developments in the commercial infrastructure of the Empire. Elsewhere, the war led to an expansion of shipbuilding, both for the navy and for trade. Thus, Robert Davy, who developed shipbuilding at

Topsham from 1806, built 19 warships, as well as merchantmen, and was to find his output fall during the post-war slump.[77]

The expansion of trade and shipping was not without serious problems, including credit availability, many of which were the consequences of the economic difficulties of the wartime years. These difficulties had more beneficial consequences for another branch of the maritime world, the fisheries, as, concerned about the pauperisation of the labouring poor, the Association for the Relief and Benefit of the Manufacturing and Labouring Poor undertook, in 1812, to buy fish in order to sell it to the poor at a much reduced rate. Initially beginning with 10–20,000 mackerel daily, the Association moved on to contract for 200 tons of corned or salted cod and 400,000 corned herrings, to form, in 1813, the Fish Association for the Benefit of the Community, and to press for the abolition of the duty on salt, a measure finally obtained in 1824.[78]

EXPLORATION

As a more dramatic sign of maritime activity, the contrast between oceanic exploration by Britain and other powers became very marked after 1793 as the French overseas empire was destroyed. This was most clearly seen in seas close to British colonies, and brought information of value for navigators, as when George Bass and Matthew Flinders circumnavigated Tasmania in 1798–9, establishing that it was an island, and therefore that ships sailing to Sydney from around the Cape of Good Hope did not need to round Tasmania, but, instead, could shorten their journey by going through the Bass Strait. Instructed to carry out an accurate survey of Australia's coast, Flinders explored its southern coast in 1801–2, and, although his mission was affected by scurvy, was responsible for its first circumnavigation in 1802–3.[79]

The navy's Hydrographic Office, founded in 1795, was responsible for co-ordinating much surveying, and British ships charted large portions of the world's coastlines during this period. Reiterated voyages that probed every inlet and charted each mile of shore were as important as the more dramatic voyages of discovery that brought initial knowledge, not least in rectifying errors. For example, Cook's voyages had provided a significant body of information, and Arthur Phillip used Cook's chart when he sailed into Botany Bay in 1788. However, Cook had provided an outline of coasts, rather than exact charting, so that in 1794 Vancouver discovered that the body of water in southern Alaska named 'Cook's River' by Cook in 1778 was in fact an inlet, while Cook's mapping of New Zealand presented the Banks peninsula inaccurately as an island, and incorrectly had Stewart Island as part of the mainland; the island was charted by William Stewart, first officer of HMS *Pegasus* in 1809, and is still named after him, rather than going by the native name of Rakiura. The value of experience brought by repeated voyages was seen not only with charting, but also with Vancouver's ability to build upon Cook's programme of maintaining sanitation and good diet in order to fight scurvy and other diseases.

Furthermore, Britain's maritime dominance helped ensure that the British took the leading role in overland exploration in this period. In Africa, aside from the journeys of Mungo Park in West Africa in 1795–7 and 1805–6, Friedrich Hornemann in 1800 became the first European to cross the Sahara, doing so with the support of the African Association. Information from explorers was swiftly disseminated by publications, atlases and paintings,[80] and there was an emphasis on new knowledge, so that the *New Map of South America*, published in 1794 by Robert Wilkinson of London, continued in its title, *Drawn from the Latest Discoveries*. Officials encouraged mapping. John Barrow, private secretary to Lord Macartney, Governor of Cape Colony, was instructed by the governor to gather topographic knowledge so that he could draw up a map, which he did in 1801, and, later, as Second Secretary in the Admiralty, Barrow was to be a keen supporter of polar exploration. Systematic British surveying and mapping of India followed the appointment of James Rennell in 1767 as the first Surveyor-General of the Bengal Presidency and, based on a series of survey journeys, he produced his *Bengal Atlas*, and followed this in 1783 with the more general *Memoir of a Map of Hindostan; or the Mogul's Empire*. Formal trigonometrical surveys followed, with William Lambton, who began the triangulation of India in 1800, playing a prominent role.

Economic entrepreneurs followed exploration, when they were not responsible for it. The first British sealing operation off New Zealand was established in 1792, and the first British sealing station began operating on the east coast of New Zealand a decade later. The search for seals led to the 'discovery' of sealing islands, such as Antipodes Island in 1800, Auckland Island in 1806 and both Campbell and Macquarie Islands in 1810. Other voyages sought to supply the new colony in New South Wales until it could feed itself; traders imported pork from Pacific islands, especially Tahiti.

On the opposite side of the Pacific, on the north-west coast of North America, British traders competed with Americans and Russians, and the trade (as elsewhere) was both destructive and enriching for the natives. The traders wanted sea-otter pelts and offered trinkets, beads, copper, iron, firearms, textiles and alcohol in exchange. Aside from coastal trade, the Montréal-based North West Company developed trading networks in the interior of North America, making extensive use of waterway systems, but trade brought the disruption and suffering that stemmed from alcoholism, firearms and smallpox.

Not all pressure was so insistent. In October 1793, Captain John Hayes hoisted the British flag on the north-west coast of New Guinea and took possession, on behalf of George III, of what he called 'New Albion', the first European post on the island. This was a privately funded expedition, backed by two merchants in Bengal, in search of valuable nutmeg. The local Papuan people were welcoming, but the Governor-General of India, Sir John Shore, and his council, sceptical about the economic prospects, refused to support the new settlement at Fort Coronation, and in 1795 it was abandoned.[81] Five years earlier, the East India Company had not persisted in its interest in a base on the Pellew (Palau, Belau) Islands, 1,000 kilometres north of New Guinea to supply ships sailing to China.

ENDING THE SLAVE TRADE

One of the major forms of entrepreneurship, the slave trade, was banned in 1807, following recent upsurges of abolitionism. In 1805, William Pitt the Younger issued orders-in-council that banned the import of slaves into newly captured territories after 1807 and, in the meantime, limited the introduction of slaves to 30 per cent of the number already there. This legislation was taken much further by the next government, the Ministry of all the Talents, which, in 1806, supported the Foreign Slave Trade Act, ending the supply of slaves to conquered territories and foreign colonies, presenting this as a way to limit the economic strength of these territories at the end of the war. The end of the process occurred when the Abolition Act of 1807 banned slave-trading by British subjects and the import of slaves into the older colonies, and, in 1811, participation in the slave trade was made a felony. Britain also used her international strength to put pressure on other states to abolish or limit the slave trade, for not only did it now seem morally wrong, but it was also seen as giving an advantage to rival plantation economies. In 1810, pressure was exerted on Portugal, then very much a dependent ally, to restrict the slave trade as a preparation for abolition, while in 1815 the returned Bourbon regime in France was persuaded to ban the slave trade and under British pressure the Congress of Vienna issued a declaration against the trade.[82]

These moves were to be seen as an aspect of the moral superiority of British imperialism, but this has to be qualified. First, slavery had not been abolished, and although demand for slave labour was, in large part, met from the children of existing slaves, the now illegal slave trade continued, albeit no longer very extensively to the British West Indies. On Mauritius, which was captured from France in 1810, however, the trade continued with the connivance of the first two British governors, and sugar production there considerably expanded after 1825.[83] Indeed, there is a sense that the slave world was being strengthened at the same time that it was dissolving. This was true not only of Mauritius but also of the colonies of Demerara-Essequibo and Berbice, seized from the Dutch in 1803, where plantation agriculture, the large-scale importation of African slaves and a switch from cotton and coffee to sugar followed British conquest. Thus, those colonies were more like those of the late seventeenth-century West Indies than the more mature slave societies of the West Indies of the period where a lower percentage of the slaves were African-born and where the work regime was less cruel.[84]

Second, abolition can be presented as a response to economic developments, rather than as a product of ideological pressures, although in fact the slave trade was increasingly valuable at the time of its abolition. Indeed popular pressure, combined with intellectual currents, notably Evangelicalism, were the key factors in Britain, when the decision for abolition was taken (see also p. 180). Nevertheless, racism remained strong, and was brutally displayed in the colonies, for example in the murderous treatment of the Aborigines of Tasmania,[85] and in the brutal suppression of slave rebellions on Barbados in 1816, in Demerara in 1823 and on Jamaica in 1831–2.[86]

CONCLUSIONS

The importance to Britain of her maritime position helped ensure that relief at naval success led to a clear air of triumphalism, while, in both victory and defeat, maritime themes were stressed. John Bacon produced a statue of George III in the courtyard of Somerset House in a Roman costume holding the rudder of a ship attended by a majestic lion and above a colossal figure of Father Thames. In James Barry's paintings in the Society for the Encouragement of Arts, Commerce and Manufactures (1777–83), the figure of Father Thames was presented as a reborn Neptune,[87] although such celebration was contested in France where Charles-Jean Benard designed a triumphal arch in 1784 to commemorate the Treaty of Versailles and the freeing of France from British naval tyranny.[88]

In the event, this 'tyranny' was reimposed a decade later, and thanks to naval strength and victories Britain was able to act as a great power and to do so successfully. At one of the peaks of its power, the navy faced worldwide responsibilities as a result of interrelated expectations in the military, diplomatic and commercial spheres, and fulfilled the hopes placed upon it. However, just as with the defeat of the Spanish Armada, naval victory did not lead to the overthrow of Britain's enemy. Instead, just as there was a synergy in British amphibious operations, with land and sea forces co-operating, and in her trans-oceanic commercial activities, with trade reliant on foreign suppliers and markets, so Britain's military capability was effective in the crucial period of Napoleonic decline, 1812–14, as part of an international league in which the major blows against France were struck on land, and by Britain's allies. This reflected a long-term limitation in naval capability: its inability to determine the policies of land powers, as was seen in the failure to coerce Russia in 1720–21 and 1791, and which was to lead Palmerston to observe in 1864, 'ships sailing on the sea cannot stop armies on land'. The consequences of this were to become apparent in Britain's military posture and alliance commitments in the two twentieth-century world wars.

British military power rested on four fundamental capabilities: the successful suppression of internal revolt (except in America), a small but highly trained army that could engage its larger enemies in Europe, naval dominance and successful trans-oceanic land warfare. There was nothing inevitable about how these capabilities emerged or interrelated, for they were forged by circumstance from experiment and hard fighting. Particular circumstances, especially command decisions and skills, were important, not least in explaining why Britain's performance was better in 1702–13, 1756–63 and 1803–15 than in 1689–97, 1739–48 and 1793–1802. A thriving market economy and effective public finances were vital aids, but wars had to be fought. In turn, these conflicts affected Britain, its economy, society and politics, and by 1815, thanks to success in war, Britain's maritime strength had brought her the most far-flung empire in the world, and established her in a position with which no European power could seriously compete.

5
THE WORLD POWER, 1815–1901

Master followed me into the kitchen and told me I had better go to my work than meddle my tongue. I answered him, 'I am doing my work, and you come to trouble me; I was not speaking to you.' Then he went to the store and took a horsewhip and began to flog me. I asked him for what he flogged me; he said for badness.

Complaint by slave called Princess.[1]

... when he swelled with song again, and poured with all his soul the green meadows, the quiet brooks, the honey clover, and the English Spring, the rugged mouths opened ... these shaggy men, full of oaths and strife and cupidity, had once been white-headed boys, and had strolled about the English fields ... the past shone out in the song-shine; they came back, bright as the immortal notes that lighted them, those faded pictures and those fleeted days; the cottage, the old mother's tears when he left her without one grain of sorrow ...

Charles Reade (1814–81), who was ranked with Charles Dickens and George Eliot by contemporaries, describing a caged English skylark singing before Australian miners in chapter 63 of his novel *It is Never Too Late to Mend* (1856). Reade, who had never been to Australia, used this novel to condemn the viciousness of both transportation and prison. He returned to the theme of Australian convicts in his novel *Foul Play* (1869).

Nineteenth-century empire is generally seen in terms of power and expansion on land. The dominant image is of a line or square of redcoats confronting charging natives. The geographical focus is on India and, towards the close of the century, Africa. Ideas associated with David Livingstone or Rudyard Kipling are those of the interior: the dark forests of Africa for the former, distant hill-stations and mountain valleys for the latter. All of these were indeed important, but they draw attention from the naval power on which the British position rested, and that provided a consistent goal throughout the period, linking the years immediately after Waterloo to the late Victorian era. Expansion on land relied on *Pax Britannica* at sea, naval hegemony providing the secure background to force projection. This hegemony combined with industrial growth and a liberal entrepreneurial ethos to encourage and sustain the commitment to free trade and a liberal international order that was to be a defining feature of nineteenth-century British imperialism. This commitment to free trade was also to be of great importance for economic growth across the world, although the 'globalisation', or, at least, openness to markets, it fostered also caused major problems of adjustment, and the benefits it brought were spread very unequally. Trade, rather than costly expansion on land, was the source of Britain's status as the world's wealthiest nation, and thus of her power, more particularly the resources that were to underwrite government revenues, while maritime strength was also crucial to the image of British power.

WAR, 1812–1826

This was seen at the outset of the period. The end of the Napoleonic wars in 1815 provided the opportunity to reduce the navy, by the sale or breaking up of warships and the laying off of officers and crew, some of whom found opportunities in the navies of the newly independent Latin American republics.[2] The varied consequences of the end of the wars included the end of impressments and action against the Barbary States of North Africa, whose piracy was seen as an attack not only on British interests but also on the general freedom of navigation and trade with which the British associated themselves. In 1816, Admiral Lord Exmouth, the Commander-in-Chief in the Mediterranean, who from 1811, during the Napoleonic Wars, had been responsible for the blockade of Toulon, was ordered to deploy the fleet to Algiers, Tripoli and Tunis, in order to force them to release British subjects. The last two agreed, but the Dey of Algiers refused. It was agreed to allow the Dey to send an embassy to London, but the continuation of Algerine piracy led the government to order the enforcement of its views, and Exmouth returned to Algiers with five ships of the line and sixteen other warships, as well as with the support of a Dutch frigate squadron. Arriving on 27 August 1816, Exmouth demanded the end of Christian slavery in Algiers, and, when no answer was returned, began fire. After a bombardment of nearly eight hours, in which 40,000 round-shot and shells were fired, the Algerine ships were destroyed, the batteries were silenced and much of the city was in ruins; although not without the cost of 818 British casualties. The Dey yielded and over 1,600 slaves, mostly from Spain and the Italian principalities, were freed. This was seen, in both Britain and Europe, as a great triumph, Exmouth was made a viscount and voted the freedom of the City of London, and his victory was commemorated in paintings, including those of Chambers and Whitcombe, as well as in other formats. European honours included membership of chivalric orders in Naples, Sardinia, Spain and the Netherlands, and a cameo from Pope Pius VII.[3]

This triumph did not end piracy, but it established a pattern of glorious and successful conduct on behalf not only of British interests but also those of what the British saw as the civilised world. Unlike operations on land, some of which had to be presented as glorious failures, and few of which could be seen as of general value to humanity, it was possible to present the *Pax Britannica* at sea as invariably successful and praiseworthy. Furthermore, at Algiers the British fleet had assumed a responsibility formerly undertaken by the Bourbon powers in particular, and its success contrasted markedly with Spanish failure there in 1784. In 1819, a British squadron returned anew, and in 1824, the threat of naval bombardment led the Dey of Algiers to capitulate anew to British demands. This expedition included HMS *Lightning*, a wooden steam-powered paddleship equipped with three guns launched at Deptford in 1822, the first operational deployment of a British steamship. As with other naval expeditions, that of 1824 was reported extensively in the press, and not only in the London newspapers; for example, the *Birmingham Chronicle* of 26 February took its report from an item in the *Royal Cornwall Gazette* based on a warship arrived in Falmouth. Also in 1824, the Bey of Tunis was made to stop the sale of Christian slaves, while in 1828 Tangier was blockaded after the capture of two British merchantmen.

On the eve of Exmouth's expedition, the international peace Congress of Vienna (1814–15) had set the seal on Britain's triumph over France and marked the beginning of a period in which the British Empire was faced with no effective threats. In the peace settlement, British control of a host of wartime gains, including Cape Colony, the Seychelles, Mauritius, Trinidad, Tobago, St. Lucia, Malta, the Ionian Islands, Sri Lanka, Essequibo and Demerara (the last two the basis of British Guiana), were all recognised. Britain ruled far more than just the waves, and this was a far more widely flung congeries of possessions than any other empire in the world, either then or previously. This was also very much an empire that had been tested in war, and that, if necessary, was ready for further conflict. Britain's gains ensured that she had a system of bases to protect her trade while denying positions that would be a threat in hostile hands. British naval interests have also been seen as playing a role in the European territorial settlement, with shipbuilding ports that would be a threat in French hands put in those of British allies: Trieste and Venice with Austria, Genoa with the Kingdom of Sardinia, and Antwerp with the new Kingdom of the United Netherlands.[4]

While this factor did play a role, especially for Antwerp, far more was involved in the peace terms, and it is important not to exaggerate Britain's ability to dictate those terms. Furthermore, concerned about Russian intentions, Britain was willing, from 1814, to respond to a French desire for better relations.[5]

Before his return in 1815 launched the short Waterloo campaign, which did not involve naval conflict, Napoleon had already been driven by advancing Austrian and Prussian armies into abdication and exile in 1814, which had provided an opportunity for the British to tackle more vigorously a number of enemies. A major effort was made to bring to a successful conclusion the war with the USA, that had started, in 1812, in large part because a series of disputes, especially over maritime rights and British policy in frontier regions, had been exacerbated by American bellicosity and a lack of British finesse. Poorly executed American invasions on Canada in 1812 and 1813 were thwarted, thanks in large part to Canadian loyalty, and in 1814 the British riposte came. A large force was sent to North America, and attacks were launched on the Canadian frontier and in the Chesapeake and Gulf of Mexico. These expeditions reflected Britain's amphibious capability, but they led to no permanent gains and were memorable for the burning of Washington, the unsuccessful bombardment of Fort McHenry at Baltimore and in 1815 the British defeat outside New Orleans.

Public recollection of the naval war is dominated by the loss of three frigates to the more heavily gunned USS *Constitution* and USS *United States* in 1812, and the British, indeed, initially suffered from over-confidence, inaccurate gunnery and ships that were simply less powerful and less well-prepared than those of their opponents. Although the Americans had no ships of the line, and their total fleet at the outset contained only 17 ships, they did have the most powerful frigates in the world, while the British were initially affected by insufficient ships and seamen, the product, at root, of the strategic overreach stemming from war against the USA and France.[6] However, the other British losses were all of smaller vessels, while British gunnery improved during the war as, more generally, did their naval effectiveness. Over half the American navy was destroyed in the war; losses would probably have been greater had not the British navy been greatly distracted by the war in Europe.

Notwithstanding British control of Halifax, Bermuda and Jamaica, the navy, as in the War of American Independence, lacked the requisite support bases to mount an effective blockade of the entire coast. Blockade, nevertheless, greatly harmed the American economy and also thwarted the American plan for a small squadron to cruise off Nova Scotia and the St. Lawrence to intercept British supply ships. Furthermore, Britain retained and used amphibious capability until the end of the war — when hostilities ceased, an expedition was being planned against first Savannah and then Charleston, both of which were already blockaded.[7]

The British were also successful in South Asia. In 1815, the kingdom of Kandy in Ceylon (Sri Lanka) was conquered, the first time it had been overthrown by a European power, while victories in 1815 and 1816 brought the war with the Gurkhas of Nepal, declared in 1814, to a successful conclusion. In addition, in India, the Marathas were rapidly crushed in a new war in 1817–18, thanks to victories at Kirkee, Sitabaldi, Mahidpur, Koregaon and Satara. The subsequent treaties led to major gains of territory and the remaining Maratha leaders had to accept terms that brought them under British protection.

This sustained burst of warfare was not to last. Instead, although great care is necessary in suggesting coherence, let alone central direction, in imperial policy,[8] Britain, both ministries and public opinion, was cautious about expanding its overseas territorial power in the years after the Congress of Vienna. The cost of the long period of war since 1793 had led to a massive rise in the national debt, the consequences of which were exacerbated by post-war depression and by a reluctance to pay taxes, but the fiscal situation alone was not responsible for this more cautious position, for there was now also far less reason to fear competition from France.

Britain still took an active role in international crises, such as that over Belgium in the 1830s, and her naval power helped her to do so, as in 1823, when troops were sent to Portugal in the face of a Spanish-supported insurrection, and in 1849, when a fleet was sent to provide the Ottomans (Turks) with a demonstration of support against Austro-Russian pressure. Nevertheless, Britain was not directly involved in war on the Continent until 1854 or from the close of the Crimean War in 1856 until 1914, and British politicians preferred to avoid commitments to other European powers that might lead to war.[9]

Turning away from Europe's conflicts gave Britain the opportunity to expand elsewhere, as did British naval dominance, although there was no overall plan for colonial conquest. British naval strength also played a crucial role in relations with other European powers. Thus, the prospect of naval intervention helped protect the newly independent Latin American states from Spanish *revanche*, while it also underlined the dependency of the Dutch East Indies on Britain. Java and other conquests were returned to the Dutch in 1816, and in 1824 a treaty between the two powers established a frontier of influence along the Straits of Malacca with Singapore, which the British had gained in 1819, and Malacca was acknowledged as British in return for Bencoolen in Sumatra, which was ceded to the Dutch.[10]

There was no foreign power in the first half of the century, especially in 1815–30, able, if it wished, to provide large-scale support to non-Western opponents of Britain, for example Burma in the 1820s. Burmese expansion, especially the annexation of Manipur in 1819 and of Assam in 1821, was seen as a challenge to both the East India Company's position in Bengal and its determination to support nearby protectorates, and differing notions of sovereignty and borders created a serious problem between the two powers, particularly over the Burmese pursuit of Arakanese rebels into Bengal.[11] In the resulting First Burmese War of 1824–6, Britain's amphibious power ensured that it was possible to avoid fighting solely in the difficult jungles of the frontier zone (where British forces indeed advanced in 1824 and 1826), and instead to strike directly at Burmese centres of power. Rangoon fell to assault on 10 May 1824 by a force sent from the Andaman Islands; and, from Rangoon, a force was sent on to Martaban, although the British, in turn, were besieged in Rangoon in the second half of 1824. However, the garrison resisted both siege and the inroads of disease, finally smashing the Burmese investment on 15 December. Amphibious British attacks were also launched on Ye, Tavoy and Mergui in Tenasserim in 1824 – this was the most effective way to seize the province – and on Negrais Island and Myohaung in 1825. In 1825–6, the British advanced, against firm opposition, up the River Irrawady to Mandalay, benefiting from the effective use of their fleet and from the disciplined firepower of their infantry. Thanks to the use of the steam-powered paddle-tug *Diana*, ships were towed up river and provided both firepower and men for a naval brigade.

In the subsequent peace, Britain was ceded Arakan and Tenasserim, which helped ensure that the subsequent development of an independent Burma was limited, while these gains also eased the path for later British expansion in Burma and Malaya. Following the successes in South Asia of the late 1810s, victory in the war confirmed a perception of military prowess, although the war had been costly in casualties and expenditure: 15,000 British and Indian soldiers died, mostly of disease, and £5 million was spent.

The importance of amphibious capability to British success in the First Burmese War was underlined by the failure elsewhere of expeditions into the interior. In 1820, Captain Thomas Perronet Thompson, the commander of the Bombay Army's garrison at Ras-ul-Khymah in the Persian Gulf, was badly defeated by the Bani Bu Ali, desert Arabs whom he had accused of piracy. Thompson was reprimanded for rashness at the subsequent court martial, and the British presence was wound down when the base on Qeshm island near the mouth of the Gulf was abandoned in 1823. A year later, the 5,000-strong Royal African Colonial Corps under Colonel Sir Charles Maccarthy, Governor of Sierra Leone, was destroyed by a larger, more enthusiastic and well-equipped Asante army. Maccarthy's head, a war trophy, was used as a ceremonial drinking cup, a lurid demonstration of British overreach, and his replacement, Major-General Charles Turner, recommended total withdrawal from the Gold Coast, although, in the end, Cape Coast Castle and Accra were retained.[12] Such episodes are worth recalling not only as instances of imperial failure, but also as demonstrations of the major contrast in the early decades of the century between strength at sea and vulnerability on land.

Penetration of Burma up the Irrawady, nevertheless indicated a new capability and interest for British expansion, the use of steamships for river navigation. The British had earlier used river routes, most obviously the St. Lawrence, but deep-draught wooden sailing ships faced serious problems in this task, as a result of their draught, wooden bottoms and reliance on the wind, whereas steamers had shallower draught, were not reliant on the wind and were increasingly made with iron bottoms. The notion of river navigation as subject to international control had been part of the Vienna peace settlement, leading to agreements for the Rhine, Main, Moselle, Meuse, Neckar and Scheldt; this idea was taken forward in the nineteenth century, particularly in China, as the British sought to use rivers for both trade and power projection that was sometimes linked directly to the protection of trade. Rivers were also explored in order to probe the possibility of new trade routes. In 1835–6, on an expedition that received £20,000 of government support, Francis Chesney used two steamers, the *Tigris*, which sank, and the *Euphrates*, to explore the River Euphrates in pursuit of a new shorter route to India via Syria and the Persian Gulf. This was taken further from the 1850s with plans to build a railway along the route, although these were not pursued.[13]

The use of rivers was limited by rapids and shallows, so that rapids on the Zambezi thwarted Livingstone's attempt to use the steamer *Ma-Robert* in 1858, while three years later his attempt to ascend the Rovuma and the Zambezi in the *Pioneer* was thwarted by the depth of water it required. Nevertheless, problems with river steamers reflected the nature of the waterways rather than any inherent deficiencies of steam power. Indeed, river steamers proved of great value for military, economic and administrative purposes, and as a sign of Britain's presence. As with warships at sea, the use of a river steamer in part rested on the multiple purposes that it could serve.[14]

IMAGES OF EMPIRE

One of the most prominent figures in nineteenth-century popular literature, Frederick Marryat (1792–1848) saw service in the First Burmese War. A veteran of the Napoleonic wars, Marryat was senior naval officer at Rangoon in 1824, and the following year was the naval commander of a successful expedition up the Bassein river. Marryat, who resigned in 1830, made his name with *The Naval Officer or Scenes and Adventures in the Life of Frank Mildmay* (1829), a narrative of naval exploits based on his experiences which was a tremendous literary and financial success. Other naval adventures followed, including *The King's Own* (1830) and *Peter Simple* (1834), which drew on Marryat's service in the Napoleonic Wars against the French under the daring Captain Thomas Cochrane, as well as *Jacob Faithful* (1834), *Mr. Midshipman Easy* (1836), *The Pirate, and the Three Cutters* (1836), *The Phantom Ship* (1839) and *The Privateer's Man* (1846). For children, Marryat wrote *Masterman Ready, or the Wreck of the Pacific* (1841), a tale of a marooned family. Marryat presented maritime life as exciting, both in his accounts of Napoleonic operations and in his novels about subsequent events.[15]

It was not only the readers of novels who were given reason to celebrate Britain's success, for a sense of Britain as naturally a major and triumphant military power followed the Napoleonic Wars. Multi-volume naval histories by William James, Edward Brenton and William Goldsmith that appeared in 1822–6 celebrated recent achievements and sought to appeal to the next generation.[16] Nelson and Wellington were remembered for their personal heroism, their military skill, their triumph over Napoleonic France and for the manner in which they strengthened nationalistic pride. Wellington, the victor of the Maratha and Peninsular wars and of Waterloo, was Prime Minister in 1828–30, and London's Trafalgar Square, begun in the 1820s, soared with Nelson's column, which was topped by the 18-foot-high statue of Nelson by Edward Baily, whose father had been a carver of ships' figureheads in Bristol. The bronze lions around Nelson's column, sculpted by Victoria's favourite painter, Sir Edwin Landseer, followed in 1867, completing the heart of empire. Nelson monuments were also erected in Dublin and Edinburgh, while his victorious death at Trafalgar was commemorated in annual dinners, paintings and engravings, most famously with Arthur William Davis's *Death of Nelson in the Cockpit of HMS Victory*, which was reproduced in a popular engraving. Robert Southey's successful *Life of Nelson* (1813) helped develop the patriot ideal, and reflected the extent to which patriotism was in part expressed in a sense of exemplary national character.[17] William Huggins, who had been a sailor in the service of the East India Company and was marine painter to George IV and William IV, painted three large paintings of Trafalgar for William, the 'Sailor King', who was popularly portrayed in naval uniform, while Daniel Maclise (1806–70), now largely unknown but much applauded in his day as a great artist, received £7,000 for painting *Wellington and Blücher at Waterloo* (1861) and *The Death of Nelson* (1864) for the Houses of Parliament, these works being thought an appropriate inspiration and backdrop for the empire's legislators. References to Nelson were frequent whenever the navy was discussed.

Edmund, 1st Lord Lyons (1790–1858), who was applauded for his boldness in the attack on Sevastopol in 1854, liked the comparison. Warships were named after the victories, warships and admirals associated with Nelson. Thus, the battleships the *Nile* and the *Trafalgar* were built in 1886–91.

The commemoration of naval glory led also to a geography of sites of remembered triumph. In 1823, the Painted Hall of the Greenwich Naval Hospital was established as a national gallery of marine paintings to mark the services of the navy. George IV provided over 30 canvases from the Royal Collection, and the gallery was soon receiving up to 50,000 visitors a year.[18] The Hardy Monument in Dorset was erected by public subscription in 1846 to commemorate the Flag Captain of HMS *Victory* at Trafalgar, although it is symptomatic of modern interest and knowledge that visitors to the area today assume that the monument commemorates the late-Victorian novelist, not the naval captain. Wellington was to be commemorated with the dramatic Wellington Monument on the Blackdown Hills; begun in 1817, the 175-foot obelisk was completed in 1854.

The naming of empire also reflected the pantheon of imperial glory. New Zealand added the towns of Nelson and Wellington to Hawke's Bay, while in Britain and elsewhere the empire was commemorated in the names of the streets of new residential areas and of public houses, the naming of the latter after imperial triumphs and heroes an indicator of the social range of the celebration of war and empire. The military and imperial leaders and heroes who followed Nelson and Wellington were similarly remembered. Thus Napier, Wolseley, Gordon and Roberts joined sites of martial glory, the Almas, Inkermans and Omdurmans, that survive as street names to this day. The navy, however, was under-represented in this process, especially outside naval bases, because Britain was not involved in any major naval struggle until 1914; her imperial position rested on naval strength, but the resulting conflicts were waged largely on land.

EMPIRE AND MORALITY

Morality shared with remembered triumph in a potent psychological brew. Divine sanction was seen both in victory over France and in subsequent greatness, and in his 'Ode for the Day of General Thanksgiving' for victory, held on 18 January 1816, William Wordsworth urged 'this favoured Nation' to 'be conscious of thy moving spirit . . . thy protecting care' (lines 189–200). A sense of mission was important alongside triumphalism, racialism and cultural arrogance: these together contributed to a view that Britain was bringing civilisation to a benighted world and was therefore fulfilling a prov-idential purpose, indeed, in some overblown comments, the providential purpose. The result was a commitment, varied but insistent, to the imperial mission that encouraged persistence in the face of adversity. More generally, the cultural manifestations and images of empire usually associated with the later 'Age of Imperialism' in the late-Victorian and Edwardian period did not begin then.

The abolition of slavery in the colonies as a result of the Emancipation Act of 1833 contributed powerfully to this sense of superiority; not least because France did not follow until 1848, the Dutch until 1863, the USA until 1865 and Brazil until 1889. Britain expended much diplomatic capital on moves against the trade, so that the granting of recognition to the states that arose from the collapse of Spain's empire in Latin America depended on their abolition of the slave trade, while recognition of the Republic of Texas in 1840 was made on the same basis, and pressure was exerted on other states, including France and the USA, to implement their bans on the trade.

The end of both the slave trade and slavery has been ascribed by some commentators to a lack of profitability caused by a developing economy, rather than to humanitarianism,[19] but this view underplays the multiplicity of factors that contributed to it. There are, indeed, indications that slave plantations in the West Indies remained profitable,[20] while the plantation economy represented an important asset base, and the limited convertibility of assets did not encourage disinvestments from slavery: too much money was tied up in mortgages and annuities that were difficult to liquidate in a hurry, and the planters had a good case for the generous compensation they received.[21] Instead of problems within the slave economy, it is more appropriate to look at the outside pressures towards abolition. In the Empire, and especially in Britain itself, these included, and contributed, to a marginalisation of groups, especially West Indian planters, that had encouraged and profited from British, and indeed European, demand for tropical goods.[22] Furthermore, the reforming, liberal middle-class culture that had become so important in Britain regarded slavery as abhorrent, anachronistic and associated with everything it deplored. Thus, the Whig ministry that pushed through the Great Reform Act of 1832 that revised the electoral franchise to the benefit of the middle class also ended slavery, and many Whig candidates included an anti-slavery platform in their electoral addresses.[23]

Some radical MPs were critics of imperial government, in certain cases taking up anti-imperial themes that had characterised radical writers the previous century. James Silk Buckingham (1786–1855), who, as MP for Sheffield 1832–7, was a pioneer temperance reformer and pressed for major changes in naval life – the abolition of both the press gang and flogging – had established the *Calcutta Journal* in 1818, but his criticism of the administration of Bengal led, in 1823, to his expulsion and the closure of his paper.

1 and 2 *An English Ship Running Towards a Rocky Coast* (above), attributed to Tobias Flessiers, *c.* 1652–65,
indicates clearly the perils of storms at sea, which the birds flying high in the centre of the picture find it
easier to avoid. The sails are shown being hurriedly furled, the men in the rigging attempting to stop the
ship heading for the rocks. The companion piece, *An English Ship Leaving the Coast* (below), shows a ship
in calm conditions.

3 (*right*)   *Captain James Cook*,
Nathaniel Dance, 1775–6. The
Explorer as Hero. Cook
wearing captain's full-dress
uniform holding his own chart
of the Southern Ocean and
pointing to the east coast of
Australia. Cook sat for this
portrait, commissioned by
Sir Joseph Banks, 'for a few
hours before dinner' on 25 May
1776. The large burn scar on his
right hand was omitted.

4 (*below*)   HMS *Resolution and*
HMS *Adventure with Fishing
Craft in Matavai Bay*, William
Hodges, 1776. Appointed by the
Admiralty to record the places
discovered on Cook's second
voyage, Hodges produced the
drawings that became the basis
of the engravings in the official
account of the voyage, as well
as oils. Hodge's painting
provides a vivid display of the
range of British naval power.

5 *The* Victory *Returning from Trafalgar*, J. M. W. Turner, 1806. The totemic character of Nelson's death extended to the *Victory* and Turner made a special trip to sketch the ship as she entered the Medway with Nelson's body in December 1805. He made a large number of detailed studies on board, one of which he used for this painting.

6 *The Battle of Navarino, 20 October 1827*, Thomas Luny, 1828. A graphic, smoke-shrouded depiction of the last British fleet action fought under sail, showing Codrington's flagship, the *Asia*, right of centre, in close action with the flagship of the Egyptian admiral. In the left of the picture is the burning ship of the Turkish flagship, and on the far left the port side of HMS *Genoa*.

7   Detail of *The Death of Nelson*, Daniel Maclise, 1859–64. A totemic moment frequently depicted in the nineteenth century as a sign of victorious self-sacrifice: martyrdom in the cause of national defence. Other maritime moments painted by Maclise included a smaller version, *Here Nelson fell*, as well as *Elizabeth at Tilbury* and *Blake at Tunis*.

8   *The Port of London*, Charles William Wyllie. The largest port complex in the world in the nineteenth century, albeit a declining centre of shipbuilding. The psychological consequences of the nearness of the centres of power, finance and trade were considerable.

9   *HMS Dreadnought*, 1906. A demonstration of manufacturing capability, organisational efficiency and fiscal strength that launched a naval race with Germany won by Britain.

10   *Engaging the Enemy*, Charles William Wyllie, 1914–18. The advent of aircraft marked a shift in naval warfare although its impact was far more apparent in the Second World War. Scenes of naval combat enjoyed a market after the First World War, although it proved impossible to give conflict with submarines the drama of warfare in the age of sail.

11   *Battlecruisers: The Second Cruiser Squadron*, William Lionel Wyllie. Britain lost three of the four battlecruisers sunk during the First World War, but owing to the strength of the British navy at the outset – the numbers of ships seen in this and other paintings – it was able to cope with such losses and remain the leading and most active naval power. All three were lost at Jutland as a result of terrible magazine explosions that claimed 3,339 lives: only 28 men survived.

12   *Amphibious Capability*. Trawler with troops passing HMS *Implacable*, 1915. The *Implacable*, a pre-dreadnought battleship, fell victim to a mine during the unsuccessful attempt to force the Dardanelles on 18 March. As a consequence, the emphasis switched to a landing.

14   *Seaside as sex interest.* 'Blackpool', painting by Fortunino Matania for the London, Midland and Scottish Railway for a poster promoting holidays to the expanding Lancashire resort, 1937.

15 *The Empire Strikes Back*, briefly. Helicopter and landing craft assault, Suez operation, 1956.

16 (*below*) *Economic Links*. Indian tea pickers advertising Brooke Bond.

17 (*right*) *Private Eye*, 2 April 1976. The photograph of a German warship scuttled at Scapa Flow in 1919, an unintended comment on the decline of British power as Harold Wilson hands over a bankrupt Britain to James Callaghan.

Back in London, Buckingham founded the *Oriental Herald and Colonial Review* (1824–9), while his books included a study of *Canada* (1843). Such careers are a reminder of the variety of responses created by imperial expansion.

The sense of moral purpose behind British policy rested on naval power, and was given a powerful naval dimension by the anti-slavery patrols off Africa and Brazil and in the West Indies. The most important active naval force in the first half of the century was that based in West Africa (until 1840 part of the Cape Command), which freed slaves and took them to Freetown in Sierra Leone, and the anti-slavery commitment led to a major expansion of this force from the 1820s to the 1840s. Warships based in Cape Town also played a major role, and anti-slavery patrols were extended south of the Equator in 1839 enabling Britain to enforce the outlawing of the slave trade Brazil had promised in 1825, but failed to implement.

The achievements of the warships were celebrated in Britain, so that the capture of the slave schooner *Bolodora* by HMS *Pickle* in 1829 led to a painting by William Huggins that was engraved by Edward Duncan. Anti-slaving activities were not restricted to the Atlantic, but were also important in the Indian Ocean and in East Asian waters. Thus, in 1821–3, the frigate HMS *Menai*, based at Mauritius, took action against slavers. As slaving was largely brought to an end in the Atlantic in the 1860s, so the struggle against it in East African waters became more prominent, with the Cape Squadron being allocated to the task, and, in 1864, merged with the East Indies Squadron. This struggle with Arab slavers was presented in an heroic light and fully covered in British publications, including newspapers, and was also considered worth publishing books about, as in Captain George Sulivan's *Dhow Chasing in Zanzibar Waters* (1873) and Captain Philip Colomb's *Slave Catching in the Indian Ocean* (1873).

Opposition to slavery was not restricted to the sea, but encouraged moral activism towards Africa, especially hostility to the slave trade in Central and East Africa. This hostility had a number of consequences, including the development of a British presence in Zanzibar[24] and a strengthening of the determination to blaze the trail for Christian grace and morality, seen for example in the actions of, and response to, David Livingstone, who helped secure British pressure to persuade the Sultan of Zanzibar to outlaw the slave trade in 1873. HMS *London*, an old ship of the line, was sent to Zanzibar to enforce this, and the acquisition from Germany of Zanzibar itself as a colony in 1890, in exchange for Heligoland, led to the end of the trade.

Similar popular attention was also devoted to operations against piracy, which was often focused on slave-raiding, and some of these attacks directly served British interests. In 1843–9, HMS *Dido* and other warships joined James Brooke in stamping out pirates who resisted his influence. Having helped suppress a rebellion, Brooke had been appointed Rajah of Sarawak by the Sultan of Brunei in 1841. His career illustrated the interlinked range of British activities, for alongside individual entrepreneurship, which led to Sarawak being recognised as an independent state in 1863, came the search for economic opportunity, the application of naval power, particularly at the expense of pirates, and missionary work. Brooke's position had been strengthened and validated by government appointments: Agent with the Sultan of Brunei in 1844, and Commissioner and Consul-General to the Sultan and Independent Chiefs of Borneo in 1848. However, Brooke's activities and those of British warships led to political controversy, with radicals attacking Brooke in the Commons for illegal conduct, only for him to be defended by Palmerston and for the critics to lose the parliamentary division.

British intervention in struggles for independence also rested on naval power, the most dramatic being the Greek War of Independence. The Greek rebellion against Ottoman (Turkish) rule that began in 1821 attracted support in fashionable, especially liberal, British and Continental circles, but in 1826 the rebellion was almost suppressed by the Ottomans, with crucial support from Egypt, which was still technically part of the Ottoman Empire. This encouraged the intervention of the great powers, and in the Treaty of London of 1827, Britain, France and Russia decreed an armistice, only for this to be rejected by the Ottomans and for an Anglo–French–Russian fleet under British command to be instructed to enforce it. The fleet's subsequent victory at the battle of Navarino Bay on 20 October had paradoxical consequences for the British government. It led to concern about the responsibility for starting the battle, and exacerbated governmental anxiety about Russian expansionism. In contrast, the general public response was that of pleasure at naval success. The victory was commemorated on canvas, for example by Thomas Luny, and Codrington, the commander, was also honoured abroad – receiving chivalric orders in France, Greece and Russia. His reception in St. Petersburg in 1830 and in Paris in 1831 was a testimony to the regard for British naval power and indicated the extent to which it gave Britain a continuing major role in great power diplomacy.

As another very different instance of the ambiguous consequences of an act of morality, the end of slavery did not completely transform labour relations in British colonies. Control over labour continued, many former slaves being pressed into continuing to work in sugar production, while labour continued to flow to the colonies: in place of slaves, the British West Indies and other colonies received cheap Indian indentured labour, although sugar production declined,[25] while British investors continued to support other slave systems. Nevertheless, the former plantation societies of the West Indies and British Guiana became far less important to the British economy, and, as their exports declined, so they were less able to attract investment, afford imports and develop social capital; and this had an impact on the living standards of the bulk of the population of these colonies. Furthermore, the decline of the plantation economies helped ensure that the share of the empire in British trade declined. In 1815, the West Indies had been the leading imperial market for British exports, but it was passed by 1840, by India, Australia and Canada, in that order,[26] and the role of the West Indies in British shipping needs also declined.

The end of slavery also did not mark the close of the powerful racism of the period, as was to be seen in the background to and, even more, the harsh and illegal suppression of the Morant Bay uprising in Jamaica in 1865. This racism drew on the notion of sharply distinguished races, and supposed differences between them, that could be classified in a hierarchy whose genesis was traced back to the sons of Adam. Race was seen in physical attributes, particularly skin colour, but was linked also to alleged moral and intellectual characteristics, and to stages in sociological development, encouraging a sense of fixed identity as part of a compartmentalised view of mankind, rather than an acceptance of an inherent unity and of shared characteristics. Religious and biological explanations of apparent differences between races, with blacks as the children of the cursed Ham, were important.

Aside from the assessment of the inherent characteristics of the other peoples, a belief in progress, and in the association of reason with European, if not British, culture necessarily encouraged a hierarchy dominated by the British, and thus a treatment of others as inferior and in need of enlightenment, a process greatly encouraged by Britain's leading role in technological advance and scientific understanding.[27] The specific benefits of the latter for Britain's imperial expansion included a greater understanding of disease and improved weapons for the struggle with it. This culminated in 1898 with the establishment of the Royal Army Medical Corps, and in the Boer War of 1899–1902 the death rates among non-battle casualties were lower than in earlier imperial operations; although, thanks to cholera, dysentery and typhoid, more British and imperial troops still died from disease than in battle.[28]

The characteristics and development of other people were understood in terms of the suppositions of British culture, and this led to, and supported, the process of hierarchisation, which was true also of the developing idea of cultural relativism. The teleology of British thought was captured by Edward Quin in his influential *Historical Atlas in a Series of Maps of the World, as Known at Different Periods* (1830), which offered a diffusionist model in which the centres of colour that comprised Europe impacted

on the world. What was 'unknown' by Europeans (and the Classical civi-
lizations they acknowledged as roots) was enveloped in darkness: black and
grey clouds. Quin claimed

> there has always been, in every age of the world, parts of the earth, not
> unknown to the geographer or the historian, but classed, by their want
> of civilization, of regular government, and of known and recognized
> limits, under the general description of *barbarous countries*. Such as Scythia
> through all antiquity, and such is the interior of Africa at the present
> moment . . . tribes having no settled form of government, or political
> existence, or known territorial limits. These tracts of country, therefore,
> we have covered . . . with a flat olive shading . . . which designates . . .
> barbarous and uncivilized countries.[29]

This approach was linked to the idea that the British Empire was both
apogee and conclusion of the historical process, and the product of both
Classical and Christian civilisation. There was a fascination with Classical
Rome, seen, for example, in paintings and in the success of novels such as
Bulwer Lytton's *Last Days of Pompeii* (1834), and Classical Rome and modern
Britain were often compared directly, as in the preface to Charles Pearson's
Historical Maps of England (1869) when, in a discussion of the size of the
indigenous population, he wrote 'our troops have repeatedly fought in India
against greater odds than the Romans ever encountered in the conquest of
Britain'. The past also echoed British greatness, as when Mehmet Ali, ruler
of Egypt, presented an obelisk known as Cleopatra's Needle to George IV
in 1820 (it was erected on the north bank of the Thames), and when the
collecting instinct filled museums. This was true for Classical antiquities, but
also for societies and environments across the world.

   The variety of collecting (and classification) was related to the range of
Britain's engagement with the trans-oceanic world. Lieutenant-General
Augustus Pitt-Rivers (1827–1900) served abroad as a soldier, became a noted
collector of ethnographic material and in 1882 donated his collection
as the basis of the Pitt-Rivers Museum in Oxford,[30] while the London
Zoological Gardens displayed animals from around the world, and their
images were reproduced in illustrated magazines. There was a particular fascination with the animals of the Tropics and, especially, of areas of British
rule and expansion. In addition, plant-hunters enriched gardens with plants
never seen before in Britain. Arboreta, such as that at Westonbirt, displayed
trees from far-flung places, and at Killerton these included a Californian
giant redwood named Wellingtonia after the 1st Duke because it stood so
high above its fellows. The role of botanic collecting and gardens in expanding knowledge was co-ordinated by the Royal Botanic Gardens at Kew, and

gardens modelled on it could be found throughout the empire, more particularly the other four designated as regal botanic gardens: at Calcutta, Pamplemousses (Mauritius), Peradeniya (Ceylon/Sri Lanka) and Trinidad.

To modern eyes, a far less attractive form of collecting was provided by that of hunting trophies. Empire provided an unprecedented opportunity for hunting. This was taken up with relish not only by individual hunters, for whom it served to display prowess and skill, but also by a press that was keen to recount their achievements,[31] and by writers of adventure stories such as Robert Ballantyne in *The Gorilla Hunters* (1861). The activities of hunters, particularly their 'bags', were recorded in photographs, and photography was also used to capture and classify images of imperial people. Clashes with the latter provided part of the narrative of hunters' accounts, whether in publications or in lectures.[32]

EXPLORATION

Attitudes towards the rest of the world contributed to the heroic account of exploration in which the British remained particularly active. The extent of British maritime power and the range of her territorial presence was such that, after peace with France and the USA returned in 1815, Britain continued to dominate oceanic exploration, and, indeed, it helped provide employment for the remaining naval officers. John Franklin of the Royal Navy, sent to descend the Coppermine River and then explore the Arctic coast of North America, from the west, charted nearly 1,000 kilometres of coastline in 1821, leaving a legacy of placenames, including Banks Peninsula, Bathurst Inlet and Warrender Bay, and knowledge of the region increased with the Dease expedition of 1836–9 which explored the coast near the Mackenzie delta. Further east, in 1818 John Ross explored openings to the west from Baffin Bay, and in 1819–20 William Parry unsuccessfully attempted to find a north-west passage through McClure Strait. In 1827, Parry tried to reach the North Pole from Spitsbergen, but his sledge-mounted boats did not cover more than a fraction of the distance.

The British were also active on land, both where they had a colonial presence and elsewhere. In the latter case, there was important exploration in the interior of North Africa. In 1821–5, Hugh Clapperton, Dixon Denham and Walter Oudney travelled from Tripoli across the Sahara to Lake Chad, Denham proving that the River Niger did not link with Lake Chad. Nevertheless, much of the interior of Africa remained unexplored until later in the century, and this was especially so in the vast tract between Sudan and southern Africa. In 1816, an expedition sought to travel up the Congo River in order to discover if it was the outlet of the River Niger. Led by

Commodore James Tuckey, this was a failure that at once showed the growing capability of British society and the limitations of expansionism. Tuckey was in command of the *Congo*, the first steamship on an African river, but the boat did not operate correctly, the expedition was blocked by difficult cataracts on the river and Tuckey and many of his men died of disease. No further progress was to be made until 1877, when Stanley completed the first descent of the Congo. Tuckey's very career showed the range of British activity. Born in 1776, he worked on a merchantman in the Caribbean before serving in the navy off Sri Lanka (1795) and in the East Indies and the Red Sea (1800) and going to New South Wales to establish a colony at Port Phillip (1802–4), where he made a survey of the nearby coastline. As with many travellers, Tuckey published a travelogue: *Account of a Voyage to Establish a Colony at Port Phillip* (1805).

Steamships symbolised progress and also provided a new means of transport for explorers. A case in point was the expedition up the Niger in 1832–4 that was organised by Macgregor Laird (1805–74), a member of the prominent shipbuilding family. This expedition included the *Alburka*, a paddle-wheel steamer, and the first iron vessel to make an ocean crossing. Subsequently, Laird founded the African Steamship Company, which was intended to develop trade along the coast of West Africa, and also sought with the use of steamships to make the Niger a commercial thoroughfare for British trade, as well as undermining the slave trade. Although still in large part dependent on their sails, steamers there and elsewhere were to play a crucial role in the expansion of the British presence.[33] Likewise, the navy played an important role in helping explorers. For example, warships carried supplies for and transported Livingstone, including from Africa to Mauritius in 1856 and from Liverpool to Africa in 1858.

Exploration was a powerful contribution to the sense of the British as the purposeful bringers of knowledge and the standard-bearers of a single world order of beneficial purpose and consequences, and in 1830 the Royal Geographical Society was established as a focus of exploration. Britain's colonial presence was closely linked to exploration, as in Australia, where, moving inland from Sydney, a route was found across the Blue Mountains in 1813, and at the close of the 1820s Charles Sturt explored much of south-eastern Australia, paving the way for the foundation of the colony of South Australia in 1836. Exploration was also related to the systematisation and dissemination of knowledge. Once a way had been found across the Blue Mountains, Governor Macquarie commissioned the surveying and building of a road to the Bathurst Plains, where he established a government settlement in 1815. An active process of land grants helped encourage expansion, and the government sought to control this by organising surveys, under John Oxley and Thomas Mitchell, that served as the basis for an expansion of government structures: 19 countries were declared in New South Wales in 1826. The same process was seen in Tasmania.

MAPPING

Mapping served to help Britain understand its conquests and played a role in legitimating its presence. In particular, mapping helped the British organise their control and perception of India, and George Everest, who became Superintendent of the Trigonometrical Survey in 1823, and Surveyor-General in 1830, employed a grid covering the entire subcontinent; William Lambton had earlier laid down the 'Great Arc', the central north–south axis for the grid. Also in 1823, and based on the Trigonometrical Survey, the *Indian Atlas* of J. and C. Walker was commissioned by the East India Company. Produced at a scale of four miles to one inch, this topographic map series offered an impressive range of detail, although it was not finished until the twentieth century. By providing accurate guidance to space, the Trigonometrical Survey offered a more precise basis for taxation. Mapping also supported the mental world of empire, and in India the Trigonometrical Survey helped present British rule as scientific, rational and thus liberal, in stark contrast to Asian rule, which the British stereotyped as mystical, irrational and despotic. The process of surveying for the Trigonometrical Survey showed the nature of British dominance, for, whereas Colin Mackenzie had used locally produced compasses and Mughal land records, and had appreciated his Indian informants, now the British came to discard information from Indian sources, carried out most of the surveying and provided the precision measuring devices, with Indians largely employed as labourers, guards and bearers. Underlying the unreasonably low opinion held by the British of the Indians' worth as surveyors were some basic assumptions about their alleged inability to conceive of space and distance in European terms. The native cartographic tradition was indeed very different and there was no comparable emphasis on fixed scales: instead, the tradition focused on routes, not areas.

Whatever the nature of indigenous spatiality, it was subordinated to imperial cartography after the arrival of British power, and the maps that were produced for government and personal purchasers ignored or underrated native peoples and states, presenting areas such as sub-Saharan Africa as open to appropriation. This mapping helped to legitimate British expansion by making the world appear empty, or at least uncivilised, unless under British control. The drawing of straight lines on maps, without regard to ethnic, linguistic, religious, economic or political alignments and practices, let alone drainage patterns, land forms and biological provinces, was a statement of political control, and an exercise of its use to deny existing indigenous practices and to assert the legitimacy only of the new, and only of a new that derived directly from British control.[34] Across the Empire, this imposition of a European grid of knowledge reproduction followed an earlier stage in which there was greater use of native information,[35] so that, in 1829–33, John Ross's search for the north-west passage had been helped by native cartographic and navigational knowledge.

Knowledge focused on utility: channels to navigate, harbours to use as ports, lands to cultivate and so on. Oceanic voyages identified resources, such as whales and seals, that could be exploited. More specifically, knowledge served the cause of the imperial state. William Moorcroft, who travelled widely into Central Asia in the 1810s and 1820s, crossing the Himalayas in 1812 and reaching Bukhara in 1825, did so, at least officially, in order to find horses for the army of the East India Company, and also to find out about the wool of the Shawl goat.[36]

More significantly, the charting of coastal waters by the British navy continued, helping provide vital charts for merchantmen. For example, a coastal survey of 1822–4 brought back much information about East Africa. In 1829, Francis Beaufort, a frigate captain during the Napoleonic period, became Hydrographer to the Navy, a post he held until 1855. Soon after his appointment, Beaufort plotted on a map of the world the coasts already covered by surveys. Concerned by the large number not yet tackled, he pressed on to fill the gaps. The results were seen in individual careers. Thus, Edward Belcher surveyed the coast of West Africa in the early 1830s, an area of growing concern as the British sought to suppress the slave trade, while, later in the decade, he surveyed the Pacific coast of South America, such surveying being an aspect of what has been seen as the British 'informal empire' in Latin America, and, as commander of HMS *Samarang* in 1842–7, the coasts of Borneo, the Philippines and Taiwan. Belcher's predecessor as commander of HMS *Sulphur*, Frederick Beechey, had surveyed the north coast of Africa, as well as the Pacific coast of South America. Both Beechey and Belcher built up public interest by publishing narratives of their surveying expeditions, Belcher's appearing in 1843 as a *Narrative of a Voyage round the World, performed in Her Majesty's ship Sulphur*. Charles Darwin served on HMS *Beagle* in her surveying voyage to South America and the Pacific in 1831–6. The *Beagle* had already been used in a survey of the Magellan Strait in 1826, and in 1837–43 it surveyed Australian coastal waters, while in 1848 HMS *Acheron* began the first systematic survey of New Zealand waters, being succeeded in 1851–5 by HMS *Pandora*, which produced detailed harbour charts. The two ships covered nearly all the coast and sent 250 maps to the Hydrographic Office. The East India Company was also responsible for surveying, its ship *Palinurus* surveying the Red Sea in 1829–34. In addition, the science of oceanography developed, with the British taking the leading role in understanding the oceans and in systematising the subject.[37]

For the British, power was a matter of territory and wealth, both of which required knowledge in the form of locational specificity, and the construction and acquisition of that knowledge were parts of a more general process by which the British sought to understand the world in their own terms, which were those of Western science. Terminology can convey different meanings here and elsewhere; for example, instead of 'understand', it is possible to use the term 'grasp'. Thus the physical geography of the world was measured: seas charted, heights gauged, depths plumbed and rainfall and temperature graphed, and all were integrated, so that the world was increasingly understood in terms of a British matrix of knowledge. Areas were given an aggregate assessment – for example, wet, hot, mountainous, forested – that reflected and denoted value and values to the British, and similarly, regions were grouped together, most prominently as continents, in response to British ideas. For example, the East Indies was classified as part of Asia, and not grouped with Australia.

This was also the period in which specific parts of maps of the world were coloured red to denote the Empire. This began in the first half of the century, and Henry Teesdale's *New British Atlas* (1831) was one of the first recorded examples of the use of red to show British possessions, while the 1841 edition of this atlas was the first to use the red convention for all British colonies. The colour was probably chosen for its striking effect. It came into general usage after 1850, with the development of chromolithography (colour printing), and was popularised by school wall maps and atlases. Foreign atlases, however, continued to use other colours for the British Empire.

The demand for more accessible and easy to assess and apply information was wide-ranging, and covered cartography, dictionaries, encyclopedias and a range of other systems for organising, transforming, displaying, storing and communicating information, which were central to the public engagement with empire. It was believed necessary and appropriate to communicate information about the empire to the public. Information was deployed in order to further what was defined as orderly, rational progress, and advances in knowledge interacted. There was, for example, much more, and better, information to be found in nineteenth-century maps and graphs than ever before, reflecting the greatly increased knowledge that had been accumulated and systematised. In turn, cartographers, geologists and statisticians found means of representing such information in more precise and accurate graphical forms: visual narration giving way to scientific system.[38] This information was accumulated, classified and applied with reference to British concepts, for example of land as property, and this helped imperialism in a number of ways, not least by sustaining the distinctions drawn between wilderness and civilisation, and between progress and failure.[39]

MISSIONARIES

Aside from abolitionism and knowledge, missionary activity was important to the sense of British superiority, and of a providential role for Britain. Missionary work seemed necessary to fulfil this role, while, at the same time, the reputation in Britain of missionary work helped to disseminate ideas of empire.[40] The mission societies provided the opportunity for individual missionaries to expand the reach of British society. Robert Moffat (1795–1883), who became a missionary for the London Missionary Society in 1816, went beyond the frontier of Cape Colony, north into what is now Namibia. Nine years later, he laid out a new mission station at Kuruman. Moffat learned the Sechwana language and translated part of the Bible into it. In 1828, he erected a church and a schoolhouse at the mission, and, in 1830, the government allowed its printing office to be used to print Moffat's translation. Moffat was to be father-in-law to the greatest explorer of Africa, David Livingstone.

The relationship between missionaries and British officials was often ambivalent, and there was a fair amount of mutual mistrust. Governmental tolerance of other religions, which contributed to this ambivalence, was seen in Queen Victoria's Proclamation to the People of India in 1858 which repudiated any right or desire to impose on the faith of her subjects and promised all, irrespective of religion, the rights of law. Missionaries were also often ambivalent about, if not opposed to, British settlement, for example in New Zealand, as they saw it as likely to harm native interests and hinder conversion. However, missionary activity spread British influence, not least as it frequently competed with indigenous or rival Western activity, and the creation of mission schools was particularly important, as English was taught side by side with Protestantism. These schools were heavily dependent on funds from Britain, as was the Colonial Bishoprics Fund which greatly expanded the institutional structure of the Anglican church from the 1840s. Missionary activity also played an important role in French imperialism.

The forcible abolition of *Suttee*, suicide by burning of Hindu widows, in Bengal in 1829, and the spread of British law and legal practice, were other aspects of a diverse process of moral utilitarianism that was important to the sense of mission and superiority. The Empire, not imperial rule by others, but the British Empire, was held to equate with civilisation. This displayed a confidence reflected in the Great Exhibition of 1851 and elsewhere.

For example, in the notes to accompany the globe he exhibited in a large circular building in Leicester Square in 1851–62, James Wyld, an active parliamentarian, reflected a widespread British confidence in their superiority and rule:

> What comparisons suggest themselves between the condition of the Pacific region in the time of Cook and now? What was then held by illiterate savages now constitutes the rising communities of New South Wales . . . the civilising sway of the English crown . . . an empire more extended than is governed by any other sceptre.[41]

DOMINION STATUS

The sense of national distinctiveness and mission was also expressed in the export of the British constitution, an export symbolised by the construction of Parliament buildings such as that for Canada in Ottawa that drew on the neo-Gothic example of the new Houses of Parliament in Westminster. A considerable measure of domestic self-government had been the case for the long-established colonies of white settlement, and this had been extended in Canada, especially with the Canada Act of 1791, although Newfoundland did not gain representative government until the control of the fishing admirals was replaced in 1832.

Internal self-government was expanded from the mid-nineteenth century with the development of an extended form of self-government known as responsible government. This reflected population growth in the settlement colonies. The growth of 'responsible government' meant that colonial governors were henceforth to become politically 'responsible' to locally elected legislatures, rather than to London, a process that reflected the institutionalising of a comparable parliamentary arrangement in Victorian Britain. In most of these areas, the population of European settlers and their descendants had become far larger than the indigenous populations.

'Responsible government' was first applied when Lower (Québec) and Upper (Ontario) Canada were joined together in the Province of Canada in 1841; a capital was chosen at Bytown (Ottawa) in 1857. Other colonies followed: Nova Scotia in 1848, Prince Edward Island in 1851, New Zealand in 1852, New Brunswick in 1854, Newfoundland, New South Wales, Victoria, Tasmania and South Australia in 1855, Queensland in 1859, the Cape in 1872, Western Australia in 1890 and Natal in 1893. Dominion status took this forward and the Dominion of Canada was established by the British North America Act in 1867 when Canada joined Nova Scotia and New Brunswick. The Dominion of Australia followed in 1900.

The development of 'responsible government' was an important aspect of the extent to which imperial expansion and governance tested assumptions about how best to devise and sustain political arrangements: the principle of self-government acknowledged in Canada in the 1840s and in the Australian Colonies Act of 1850 had left unclear the best way to secure workable self-government, but this was unsurprising as there was a far from fixed sense about the best political system for Britain. Although the Colonial Laws Validity Act of 1865 declared colonial legislation that clashed with that from Westminster invalid, the Act was only rarely invoked.

Canada expanded greatly after Confederation. Under the Rupert's Land Act of 1868, the lands of the Hudson's Bay Company were transferred to Canada in 1870, extending it into the Arctic and the Rockies. In 1870, Manitoba was established as the fifth province, British Columbia following in 1871 and Prince Edward Island in 1873. Newfoundland, however, remained outside this process. An Order in Council of 1880 transferred to Canada all British islands in North America, bar Newfoundland and its dependencies. It needs hardly be said that the Native population was not consulted.

TRADE

Alongside ideology, trade and migration were key dynamics and processes of empire, while free trade was a crucial aspect of British imperial ideology from mid-century. Mission, confidence and self-interest were linked in the development of the ideal of free trade, which was presented in moral as well as economic terms. Economic liberalism was seen as the best way to improve relations between peoples, and protectionism as an unnatural restraint; and economic liberalism, which entailed an openness to British products, was presented as a corollary to an openness to best practice in all respects. Monopolies within the British Empire found their position challenged and, eventually, abolished, and partly in response to the attack on the position of the East India Company, whose monopoly over the China (but not the India) trade had been confirmed in 1813, a greater emphasis on speed characterised trade with the Far East, and in 1817 the fully laden China fleet sailed from Canton River to the Channel in 109 days. The Company finally lost its rights in 1858, while those of the Hudson's Bay Company were limited. Nevertheless, the investment requirements of cutting-edge trade (in the form of shipping), mining and industry limited the number of entrants and, in some fields, created quasi-monopolistic companies.

The pressure for free trade focused on the Corn Laws, protectionist measures to safeguard British agriculture that were repealed by Peel in 1846 in response to pressure, particularly from industrial interests, for cheaper food for the workers, which was seen as a way to secure domestic peace and restrain industrial wages. The abolition of the Corn Laws split the Tory party and created a furore that led to the general collapse of protectionism, with the repeal of most of the Navigation Acts in 1849, although this resulted in a major fall in the percentage of British trade carried in British ships. The end of protection for British coastal trade followed in 1854. Free trade also meant the dismantling of imperial preference, with the ending of tariffs and other measures that had helped ensure markets in Britain for West Indian sugar and Canadian timber, although this process met with opposition from interested groups, who sought to mobilise support through petitions.[42]

Free trade was also introduced to the colonies, helping to lead both to greater direct integration into the world economy and to more exposure to economic change.[43] In turn, economic liberalism had an impact in neighbouring regions. Singapore's role as a free-trade entrepôt was particularly important in South-East Asia, fostering the local cultivation of plantation products such as pepper and ensuring its position as the crucial intermediary between China and the Indian Ocean, and this to the benefit of British commercial interests.

As the leading industrial producer, the British needed other states to open their markets, and vulnerable foreign powers were persuaded or forced into accepting free-trade agreements that did so: Turkey in 1838, Egypt and Persia in 1841 and China in 1842. Morocco (1856), Thailand (1857) and Japan (1860) followed. Free trade also influenced British policy in Europe, with favour shown to efforts to encourage it. Thus, initial concerns about the German Customs Union (*Zollverein*) of 1834 were replaced by a more supportive approach as it was seen as a step to dismantling protectionist barriers in north Germany, and, by the late 1850s, the British government was increasingly trying to shape free trade in Europe through negotiations. This led to the Anglo-French trade treaty in 1860 and to treaties with the German Customs Union in 1865;[44] although France soon came to take the major role in spreading free trade in Europe.[45]

A different form of free trade was pushed by smugglers. The naval blockade of France during the Napoleonic Wars, particularly the construction of a chain of naval signal stations on the English coast, had afflicted smugglers, while the establishment in 1810 of a Preventive Water Guard did not help. Smuggling revived with the coming of peace, but in 1822 the Coast Guard was founded, and this led to a new coastal order with smugglers facing increasing difficulties;[46] although changes in taxation policy, with the dropping of duties, were also important: official free trade hit smugglers.

Imperial trade was responsible for less than half of Britain's exports and imports, but it was still of great economic importance under both categories and contributed to specialisation across the range of British economic activity. Furthermore, by cutting the cost of trade, British shipping also fostered economic specialisation, and therefore growth, although the benefits of this were spread very unequally and British trade itself had to respond to major shifts in market competition. For example, the difficulty of competing in Europe and the USA, and of expanding sales in traditional colonial markets in Canada and the West Indies, ensured that the bulk of the rise in exports in 1816–42 was obtained from markets in Africa, Asia and Latin America. Aside from colonies, these markets were, in large part, made up of areas that have been described in terms of an informal empire comprising economically subordinate but not politically controlled territories, although that concept aggregates a great variety of experience and is a matter of controversy.[47]

Parts of Latin America, much of which the British navy had helped protect from Spanish reconquest, comprised an important part of this informal empire. The sources of British influence were varied, and not limited to trade and finance:[48] some of the expatriates and naval mercenaries who had played a prominent role in the Wars for Independence, then settled down to establish prominent naval and/or mercantile families, intermingling with the locals and embedding a British connection in the life of these new countries, while British political and economic ideas and practice were admired by Latin American reformers, such as Bernardino Rivadavia, in what became Argentina, and this helped ensure that Britain's commercial role was widely accepted.[49] In addition, British entrepreneurs, such as Thomas Brassey, played a major role in the development of Argentinian railways.[50]

Naval power continued to underline British influence in Latin America, and it led to the direct expansion of power in the Falkland Islands, where the British thwarted both Argentina and the USA, and established control in 1833. The government was concerned about the potential threat that the Falklands in other hands might pose to British seaborne and political interests in South America and the southern oceans, and Viscount Palmerston, Secretary of State for Foreign Affairs in 1830–34, 1835–41 and 1846–51, was influenced by the views of William Gore Ouseley, envoy in Rio de Janeiro, who argued that, if the Falklands were developed as a centre for trade, ship repair and shipbuilding, they would assist the steady ascendancy of British seaborne activities. The American government, whose role in Latin America the British had been concerned about after the Monroe Doctrine declared in 1823, was reluctant to co-operate with Argentina against Britain.[51]

In Argentina, the *British Packet and Argentine News* was an established weekly by 1835, with a strong mercantile emphasis, regularly reporting the movement of foreign ships and the current prices of such commodities as skins, wool and salt. English became the language of business, the language

of profit, across most of the world, a development that owed much to expatriate communities and to the role of British finance and shipping. The
world of print, however, was not accessible to all. Newspapers aimed at
emancipated slaves began to appear, but the Jamaican *West Indian* (1838)
proved short-lived, possibly because it did not serve a sufficiently profitable
market to attract much advertising.[52] In contrast, Lieutenant Hugh Pearce
Pearson, sending news home of the Indian Mutiny, told his parents, 'the
Friend of India . . . is a paper you can rely upon as containing the puckah
news and is the *Times* of India'.[53]

A major difference between Britain and Continental countries, especially
in the mid-nineteenth century, was that Britain traded abroad far more than
they did, and far more widely. Having applied new technology to industrial
production more successfully than other European states, the British were
producing more goods, more efficiently than their rivals, and, as a result,
Britain was best placed to benefit from the major expansion of the global
economy, that itself owed much to Britain. Her leading industrial sectors,
textiles and metal products, were dependent on export markets, while coal
exported from ports such as Cardiff, Seaham, Hartlepool and Sunderland
powered locomotives and forges overseas. Coal exports were particularly
important for South Wales, which provided about 30 per cent of British coal
exports in 1870 and 40 per cent of the much greater total in 1910. Coal
from South Wales was particularly useful for steam-raising.

In the scholarship, alongside, and in part in opposition to, the emphasis
on the export of coal and manufactured goods, has come a stress on
'gentlemanly capitalism', and on the role of finance and services, such as
shipping and insurance, in the British imperial economy. This has been
linked to the suggestion that the key figures in this economy, and, more
generally, in the development of empire, were the products of public schools,
with 'gentlemanly' values, heavily based in south-east England, rather than
coal and factory-interests in northern England, Scotland and Wales.[54] This
approach offers a way to link the British presence in colonies with that in
the 'informal empire' that was not under territorial control, as British investment capital, both in foreign bonds and direct investments, mercantile credit
and expertise, especially railway engineering and mining expertise, played a
major role in many parts of the world, with America being the biggest recip-
ient of investment, for example in mining.[55] Sterling was the major currency used in international trade and finance, banking houses such as Barings
provided the credit for the development of railways abroad, as with America's
first railroad, the Baltimore and Ohio; and banking offices were opened in
colonial centres such as Singapore. Within the 'formal' empire, imperial
control and governmental support encouraged investment in what might
otherwise have been regarded as overly risky countries,[56] while, in the

'informal' empire, the prospect of British governmental assistance was an important help.

Continental economies were more self-sufficient; what foreign trade they did was mainly with other European countries, including Britain. This was related to other aspects of Britain's distinctiveness: her outward-lookingness and internationalism; her interest in peace, which was believed to create the best conditions for trade; and her opposition to a large and expensive army, and therefore to conscription. Although Britain's economic development was not dependent on empire, and compared with trade with Europe and the USA, the loss of which was very important in this respect, the formal empire played only a relatively small role in the export/import economy, it was still an important one. The Empire took about 35 per cent of British exports in the last quarter of the century, and although many of the new acquisitions in that period, for example Burma and East Africa, proved relatively unrewarding in terms of trade, they contributed to a sense of commercial strength, and were at least denied to rivals. Earlier, those who had pushed for free trade the hardest, for example Richard Cobden and John Bright, were most hostile to the formal empire as it was and also opposed to its expansion.

British colonies were affected by the pressures that operated within the Western trading world, specifically the search for markets and materials. Thus, British industries sought raw material for the textile industries required to clothe the growing population. It became economic to bring fine wool from Australia, which led to major developments in the 1820s, as the expansion of grazing land was encouraged, and helped provide a dynamic behind British expansion in south-east Australia and Tasmania. This process caused conflict with local peoples: in Tasmania, the spread of sheep ranching clashed with Aboriginal migration paths, leading to the Black War of the 1820s. Until the American Civil War (1861–5) most cotton came from the southern states of the USA, but the Union blockade led to a major increase in imports from Egypt and, in particular, India. Thanks to investment in technological developments in Britain, it also became possible to sell cotton products back to India, and India's role as the major market for exports of cotton textiles ensured that it took about a third of the rapidly growing exports to the Empire in the second half of the century.

More generally, the dynamic of economic change in response to the British-centred globalism led to significant economic and social disruption, both within British colonies and in other areas, not least as the production of cash crops for export was fostered. The growth in the global economy and its inherent volatility ensured a powerful element of instability, as shifts in relative economic strength became more rapid and were more widespread in their effects. Existing economic activities and practices were made less profitable, if not redundant, and trade routes shifted. Thus in the Philippines, a Spanish colony but one where British capital and trade was important, there was a shift from trade with Mexico, no longer part of the Spanish Empire, to links via the Indian Ocean, including the import of textiles.

In colonies, there was a related desire on the part of administrators and exponents of progress to control social and economic practices in order to improve economic possibilities, and thus there was a preference for settled agriculture and communities, rather than for more nomadic activities and lifestyles. In many areas, this led to a decline of tribal peoples and others who could, or did, not respond to new cash crops. Hostility towards indigenous lifestyles varied, however, and was more pronounced in Australia than in Canada.

The Empire became more important to the British diet during the century, but in a very different way from the earlier impact of the import of sugar. Britain became a more central part of a developing global agrarian system. This reflected the end of protection for British agriculture, with the repeal of the Corn Laws in 1846. It was also the consequence of the technological changes, barbed wire, long-distance railways, large steamships and refrigerated holds, that led both to the development of agricultural production for the British market in other temperate climates, and to the ability to move products rapidly without spoilage. Some food was imported from the Continent, especially fruit and vegetables, grain from Germany, Poland and Ukraine, and Danish bacon by the end of the century, but Canada was the crucial source of wheat, Argentina of beef, and Australia and New Zealand of wool and mutton, Australian frozen meat arriving in London from 1879.

From the 1860s, cheap grain imports greatly affected British agriculture, and imports led to a severe and sustained agricultural depression from the 1870s that was to have an important impact on the nature of British society, helping to lead to the relative decline of rural regions and thus accentuating the impact of industrialisation. Imports also included products that did not compete with what could be produced in Britain, such as rubber from Malaya, oil-seeds from West Africa, tin from Malaya and jute from India. Tea from Ceylon and India replaced imports from China, helping bring more profit to the empire, and to make the Home and Colonial Stores of Julius Drewe, who encouraged the shift, a lot of money. Although there was continuing growth of food and raw material imports from the Empire, the share of Britain's imports from there fell as a result of a major rise in the import of manufactured goods, mostly from Western Europe. Some of the food and raw material imports were for re-export, especially Australian wool to Europe.

The extent to which Britain became a vital market for foreign producers of food had a great impact on the Empire, and also encouraged British emigration to the expanding agrarian export regions in Australasia and Canada. About half of all Canadian exports by value in 1891–1915 were wheat and flour for Britain, and timber was also important. In the last two decades of the century, exports of salmon from the Canadian Pacific and of cheese developed. The former reflected the capacity created by canning. The import of fish was in part a result of the decline of long-distance British fishing. Investment was directed towards trade, rather than long-distance fishing, while the demand for fish in the expanding British cities could in large part be met from less distant waters, not least from the North Sea in which there was a major expansion of herring fishing. The British cod fishery on the Grand Banks off Newfoundland had collapsed in the early nineteenth century, being replaced by fishing by those resident in Newfoundland. In the second half of the century, as Canadian fishing as a whole rose in value, with Britain a major market for fish and lobster exports from Newfoundland and Canada, the role of American and French fishermen in this fishery became more important. Nevertheless, the British fishing industry in the late nineteenth century was in a much better state than it would be in a century later: Greenland whaling was a source of profit, for example releasing much capital into the Shetland economy, while the introduction of steam fishing boats from 1877 made it easier to exploit North Atlantic fishing grounds.

COMMUNICATIONS

The development of rail traffic did not undermine the seaborne character of the Empire as rail helped funnel goods to the ports: it led to a focus on particular ports, not to the end of maritime influence. Where, however, within a country, sea and rail transport competed, as with the movement of coal from Newcastle to London, rail eventually won, although its victory was often hard-fought and took time. In 1855, three million tons of coal were moved by sea to London, and only 1.2 million by rail, only in 1869 was coal brought by sea matched by that moved by rail, and, in 1879, although 6.6 million tons was transported to London by rail, some 3.5 million still entered the Thames by sea.

Railways were all-weather. Their extension over, or under, water by bridge or tunnel, altered both local and national geography and diminished in-shore shipping, especially ferries. In Britain, this was true of the Britannia Tubular Bridge across the Menai Strait (1849) and the bridges across the Tay estuary (1877) and the Firth of Forth (1890), and in Canada the Victoria Bridge across the St. Lawrence River at Montréal (1860). By hitting coastal and river traffic, rail lessened maritime resources and skills, particularly at the local level. For example, in Wales the opening of the railway to Barmouth in 1867 wrecked the lighterage carriage up-river to Dolgellau: in 1866, 167 ships entered and left the port, but only 11 in 1876. Coastal shipping remained important for certain commodities, such as coal and grain, in some places, so that Poole's trade, for example, was increasingly dominated by clay shipments, but the relative role of such shipping markedly decreased, while the hinterlands of lesser ports contracted. The decline of such ports meant that the impact of the sea outside port cities and fishing areas was markedly lessened.[57] Railways also offered a powerful aesthetic of movement that was removed from that of the sea. Hitherto, ships had been the fastest, and most impressive, form of movement, but their impact was now lessened.

There was also a heroic dimension to railway construction. In Canada, where waterways were affected by winter freezing, a rail route from coast to coast was opened in 1885. This had been a stipulation when British Columbia joined the Canadian Confederation in 1871, and the railway was designed to create a west–east link from ocean to ocean, and thus overcome the north–south nature of the topography, which, it was feared, would increase American influence. By opening up areas, and, in many cases, directly encouraging immigrants, rail links also stimulated settlement in the interior of colonies, for example on the Canadian Prairies and in Australia beyond the Blue Mountains, as well as leading to the integration of already settled regions to the global economy, as in India. Whereas many early rail links had supplemented traditional maritime coastal routes, in particular by providing shortcuts across peninsulas, railways were increasingly developed as internal systems, as with the links from Bombay to Madras, and to Calcutta via Delhi. They also helped in the development of new maritime routes. The ocean-to-ocean rail route in Canada was followed by the establishment of a steamship route across the Pacific from Vancouver to Sydney and Melbourne, which was also an instance of the degree to which communication routes that did not focus on London were opened up between parts of the Empire. Telegrams had a similar synergy, with land systems of overhead wires linked by undersea cables. The Pacific Cable was opened in 1902.

At the same time, engineering directly enhanced maritime links with the construction of the Suez Canal, which was opened in 1869 and over which Britain purchased a controlling interest in 1875. This reduced the sailing distance from Britain to India by about 4,500 miles, and also cut the distances to points further east, such as Singapore and Shanghai, leading to a cut in freight costs and an increase in trade, so that direct trade between London and the Persian ports trebled between 1873 and 1878: the first steamship from Britain to Bushire via the Suez Canal had sailed in 1870. The tonnage of British shipping in the Persian Gulf was listed as 1,200 tons in 1876, but in 1889, 113,000 of the 115,000 tons of shipping that cleared from Bushire was British. Viscount Curzon argued that 'this astonishing growth' could be attributed 'to the immense reduction of distance by the Suez Canal route . . . and, above all, to the vast improvement in steam service and the cheapening of maritime freights', and by 1900, 321 out of 327 steamers entering Persian Gulf ports were British, while in 1901, £3,300,000 of the trade of the ports (the total value of which was £3,600,000) was British.[58] Owing to the opening of the Suez Canal, naval bases in the Mediterranean, especially Malta, also became more important.

London was the centre of the imperial trading system, one that was speeded up by steamships and telegraphs and that benefited from the fall in shipping freight rates.[59] Ships bringing goods from all over the world docked there, and the dockyards expanded greatly, reducing congestion in the Thames, making it easier to control trade and to cut pilfering, and responding to the needs of the larger iron and, later, steel merchantmen. The St. Katharine Docks, opened in 1828, were followed by the Poplar Docks (1852), Royal Victoria Dock (1855), Millwall Dock (1868), Royal Albert Dock (1880) and Tilbury Docks (1886), in total a major investment, and the royal nomenclature reflecting their grandeur and the official endorsement of their purpose.

Other dockyards and port cities also expanded. In 1801, Liverpool's population stood at 82,000; within 50 years, this had grown to 376,000, while for Glasgow the figures were 77,000 and 357,000. In Sunderland, a quarter of the men over 20 in the town in 1861 were employed in shipping. The rapidly expanding ports had a bleak side, however, with a decline in the quality of life, particularly as a result of overcrowding. Multiple-occupancy was combined with indifferently built houses, and the result was insanitary housing conditions. Plymouth, a major manning port for the navy, was hit hard by cholera in 1832, while in 1841 Liverpool was the most densely populated urban space in the world, with 138,224 people per square mile, and mortality rates were fearfully high: in 1840, Liverpool's was 34.4 per 1,000. Glasgow had annual average death rates of 33 per 1,000 in 1835–9, the highest in Scotland: it was hit by typhus in 1817–18 and 1837, and by cholera in 1832. Port cities existed to serve the needs of sailors as well as merchants: at Liverpool, about 30,000 sailors were ashore at any one time, leading to a major rise in prostitution: from about 300 brothels in 1836 to 538 in 1846, while, in 1857, there were at least 200 regular prostitutes under the age of 12 in the city. Other port cities, both commercial and naval,[60] had similar districts and services.

The wealth and problems of ports were clearly seen at Dundee: its quay developed to take ships bringing jute from Calcutta for the factories in the city that made it into sacks, carpets and lineoleum. These products were then shipped to foreign markets, and that made the city synonymous with jute, but the city's people faced disease and high infant mortality. The wealth and employment produced by the jute trade and industry was a graphic instance of the impact of empire in Scotland, an impact that included emigration and career opportunities, military service and the spread of ideas about how best to rule and convert imperial territories. The consequences were less apparent in Wales, but ports also expanded there, although they were less focused on trans-oceanic opportunities. In the decade after 1856, coal exports from South Wales led to the opening of the Bute East, Roath Basin and Penarth docks at Cardiff. Improved lighthouses were another aspect of the willingness to invest in developing the maritime infrastructure; the fourth Eddystone lighthouse, built between 1878 and 1882, cost £59,250.

Dockyards were also developed in British colonies, such as Singapore, where a dry dock was built in the 1850s. The concentration of harbour facilities in the British Isles, as larger iron, and later steel, ships required deeper anchorages, more sophisticated purpose-built facilities for particular goods and linkages with the rail system, was matched in the colonies, and cities such as Bombay and Halifax developed as major ports serving a world trading system.[61] In turn, this development led to labour requirements and social changes that helped alter local attitudes and structures.

While Britain had the largest merchant fleet in the world, creating problems in manning that fostered the training ship movement,[62] some of its colonies were also important shippers, and in 1867 the Canadian sailing-ship fleet was the third largest in the world after Britain and the USA. This fleet also helped sustain links with Britain, and the major destination of ships leaving Canada in the 1860s and 1870s was Britain. Sailing ships built in Canada were sold to British shippers, playing a major role for example in the trade with Liverpool, while many officers and men on Canadian boats came from Britain. Sailing ships, however, were to decline in the face of the increasing cost-efficiency of steamships, with the Canadian shipping industry declining from the 1880s. At the close of the century, the largest business in New Zealand was the Dunedin-based Union Steam Ship Company; founded by Dunedin and Glasgow entrepreneurs in 1875, its shareholding was predominantly British from the 1880s. Aside from British capital, the Company benefited from the demands and opportunities provided by the Empire: in addition to links with Australia, there were also routes to Fiji from 1881 (sugar imports) and to Calcutta from 1887 (tea and jute being imported), while routes from Melbourne to Fiji, and from Brisbane to Vancouver, began in 1882 and 1901 respectively.

This network was an aspect of the developing importance of economic links between imperial possessions, links largely conducted by sea, that can be magnified if the 'informal' empire is also considered. Thus, China had been brought into the British commercial world in large part alongside India. From the 1810s, the British financed imports from China, which were largely of tea and silk, by exporting opium there from India, and this also helped to provide a means by which the government of India, and the import of British goods there, were financed, and thanks to which funds were transferred from India to Britain: the export of opium peaked in 1879. In the Indian Ocean, the shift from sailing to steamships ended dependence on monsoon routes and seasons.[63]

The development of trans-oceanic steamship systems reflected the economic return from trade, especially from predictable crossings, but government subsidies also played a part in the shape of mail contracts. The resulting communication system directly helped the cause of commerce,[64] but, in addition, other goods as well as people were also carried by the mail ships. The 1839 mail contract between the government and the Halifax merchant and whaler Samuel Cunard for services to Halifax, Boston and Québec required that the ships be able to act as troop ships and to carry the necessary armament. The maiden voyage, in 1840, in the *Britannia*, marked the beginning of steam postal services across the Atlantic, and, by the end of the decade, the service had increased to satisfy the government's demand for a weekly mail. In 1855, an iron boat, the *Persia*, was brought into the run, and in 1862, the *China*, the first big boat to cross the Atlantic using a screw-drive rather than a paddle-wheel.

The major role of shipbuilding in the British economy underlined the importance of Britain's active part in framing its maritime destiny. The loss of America had led to a reduction of just over a third in the merchant fleet,[65] but this was rectified by rapid and extensive shipbuilding that owed much to the opportunities provided by the curtailment of other European merchant navies in the French Revolutionary and Napoleonic Wars; although the situation deteriorated after peace returned. The Navigation Acts also helped by maintaining imperial trades for British shipping, and ensured that imperial expansion, for example to include Australia, also helped shipping; although the protection provided by these Acts was eroded as attempts were made, particularly from 1815, to open up shipping, in part in order to win concessions, and most of the Acts were finally repealed in 1849.[66]

The switch from timber to iron ships helped shipping and the shipbuilding industry greatly, as Britain had major competitive advantages for ships built of iron and powered by coal, and this helped ensure a rise in shipbuilding and an increase in the percentage of trade carried in British ships, a process further assisted by the disruption to American shipping

caused by the American Civil War (1861–5), which ended the serious competition experienced in the 1850s. Similarly, shipbuilding had benefited from
the impact of the American War of Independence on colonial-built ships.
The switch to iron meant that it was no longer necessary to rely on timber
imports, and also led to a new geography of shipbuilding, with the focus
on the Clyde and the Tyne and the Wear and a decline in some traditional
centres, such as Devon; although the capitalisation and new requirements
stemming from the building of bigger ships once iron replaced wood were
also important. The tonnage launched rose, so that whereas in the 1840s,
Irish shipbuilding had centred on Cork, where a tonnage of about 2,000
was being launched annually, by the 1900s the figure for Belfast was 150,000
annually, and in 1912, the major yard there, Harland and Wolff, launched the
Titanic. In contrast, in 1881, 341,000 tons were launched on the Clyde and
308,000 on the Tyne and Wear combined, and in 1914, the figures were
757,000 and 666,000. At Sunderland, on the Wear, 2,500 tons had been
launched annually before war with France began in 1793, but by the 1830s,
the annual average was over 30,000, by 1850, Sunderland was the world's
leading shipbuilding town, by the 1860s an annual average of over 60,000
tons was being launched, and by the 1890s, 190,000. Barrow-in-Furness, the
Humber and the Mersey were also important centres of shipbuilding, while
London ceased to be a major centre, although warships were still being built
there in the 1870s, including for the Brazilian and Ottoman navies.

Shipyards employed large numbers of people, as did ancillary concerns,
such as engine-makers and steelworks. Whereas there were 4,000 workers
in Scottish shipbuilding in 1841, the number had risen to 51,000 by 1911.
Such figures encouraged labour flows and transformed local and regional
economies. Most of the tonnage built in British yards was for British and
imperial shippers, but a significant amount was for foreign concerns, and
this contributed greatly to British exports. Thus, the Birkenhead firm of
John Laird built the *John Randolph* in 1834, a paddle steamer sent across the
Atlantic in parts that was the first iron vessel in American waters, as well,
in 1837, as a steamer for the Nile for Mehmet Ali. Shipping services were
also important to invisible exports.

MIGRATION

Migration was another important dynamic process that provided multiple
links within the Empire, and, for the settlement colonies, it had the
greatest lasting impact – 22,600,000 people left the British Isles in
1815–1914. In 1815–30, a period of post-war depression and apparent over-
population, when emigration was seen as a useful device for Britain,[67] the

majority of emigrants from the British Isles went to Canada; while most immigrants there came from the British Isles. The population of Upper Canada rose from 60,000 in 1811 to 150,000 by 1824. This growth was sustained by the Canada Company, a private enterprise established by John Galt and chartered in 1825. Investors in the company provided the capital with which just over a million hectares of land were purchased at 3s 6d (17.5 new pence) per acre, and also an annual subvention to government costs, while the Company laid out townships and attracted settlers. Emigration from the British Isles strengthened the British character of Canada, so that from 1832 to 1867 Montréal took on an English-speaking majority.[68]

Thanks to trans-oceanic steamship services, the average ocean crossing between England and Halifax fell from 40 days in 1837 to 12 days westbound in 1852; and scheduled passenger services linked Halifax to other ports in Nova Scotia as well as to New Brunswick and Newfoundland. Steamships cut the cost of migration and helped ensure that a high rate of emigration spread from the Atlantic to encompass Australasia. Steamships also altered the financial structure of emigration, as the size and cost of these new ships ensured a need for more investment capital, and thus for a greater numbers of passengers, so that a number of large shipping companies, such as Cunard and White Star, came to play a more dominant role in transporting emigrants, and also joined those playing an active part in encouraging emigration. This was the obvious way in which emigration relied on Britain's maritime position, but, in the background, there was also a naval element. Had ships been attacked by pirates, for example in the Indian Ocean en route to Australasia, this would have lessened the appeal of distant voyages. At times, especially in the initial stages of emigration, there were more direct links. Thus, indicating the variety of tasks undertaken by warships, in 1820 Fairfax Moresby, commander of HMS *Menai*, a frigate based at Cape Town, surveyed Algoa Bay (on which Port Elizabeth sits), arranged the landing of settlers, and organised the colony.

Compared with Canada, the number of emigrants was lower to more distant Australia, which suffered from its reputation as a penal destination – a total of 158,000 convicts were sent there,[69] and it was also a dumping ground for other unwanted groups, such as demobilised troops. However, numbers received a boost in 1829 when Britain annexed Western Australia and established its first settlement there as the centre of a free colony. Furthermore, the sale (as opposed to grant) of Crown lands was seen as a way to encourage settlement by providing funds to pay transport costs, and the establishment in 1830 of the National Colonisation Society by Edward Gibbon Wakefield was designed, at a time of growing economic expansion in Britain, to encourage more selective emigration, and thus to enhance the value of colonies. Wakefield's ideas influenced bounty policies introduced in

1832 and 1836, and were taken up by the South Australian Association which founded a colony in 1836. To this day, the centre of Adelaide (named after the wife of William IV) reflects the planning and ethos of the founders of South Australia. The New Zealand Association followed in 1837.

The role of convicts in imperial settlement diminished, as no more were sent to New South Wales after 1840, or to Tasmania after 1852, and although Western Australia had responded to labour shortages in 1850 by requesting convicts, this was opposed by the colonies further east and none were sent after 1868. The debate over the value of convicts highlighted differences over the best way to populate colonies, and whether migration was good for Britain and/or the colonies, and the extent to which government should take a role. Convicts were also transported between colonies, for example from South Asia to Aden, the Andaman Islands, Bencoolen on Sumatra, Burma, Mauritius and the Straits Settlements (Penang, Malacca, Singapore): the 1,500 convicts sent to Mauritius in 1815–36 were used as labour for public works.[70]

Emigration to Australia benefited not only from government financial assistance but also from the sense of opportunity focused on gold discoveries, and these were also of importance for migration to South Africa in the 1890s. However, emigration was not simply to the Empire. Between 1815 and 1901, the USA took over eight million immigrants from the British Isles – more than the entire movement to the Empire, and a reflection of the way in which the British government, which discouraged this emigration, played only a partial role in shaping migration patterns, although state financial support for colonisation and regulation of shipping by Passenger Acts were of some, albeit limited, importance.[71] Emigration from Ireland to the USA owed much to the famine in Ireland that resulted from the potato blight that began in 1845 and was followed by disastrous crops in 1846 and 1848. About 800,000 people died as a result of starvation, or diseases made more effective by malnutrition, and the government's attempts to bring relief had little effect. Migration was to be one of the defining factors in the Irish experience in the nineteenth century.[72]

Whereas, in the 1870s, it took ten days to sail to New York, it took 90 to sail to Wellington in New Zealand, and cost nearly four times as much. Nevertheless, the assisted immigration scheme introduced by the New Zealand government in 1870, and an aspect of the way in which colonial governments came to take a greater role in migration policy, led to an immigration peak there in the 1870s. However, some of those who emigrated to the Empire did not stay. The USA took a large number of immigrants from Canada, such that, in the 1870s and 1880s, Canada had more emigrants than immigrants,[73] and, as a result, its rise in population then, and into the early twentieth century, relied more on natural increase than on net migration.

The late 1880s also saw net emigration from New Zealand in response to the economic difficulties of the period.

This reflected the degree to which migration responded to opportunities. In some cases, the intention from the outset had been to return to Britain having made money, and this became simpler as steamships made movement easier, and, in this respect, migration to the Empire was part of the more general pattern of migration. Most migrants, however, did not return, and this contributed to the emotional wrench of emigration and to the psychological character of the Empire (and of the English-speaking world) as a separated family, a concept that was actively propagated, both in Britain and in the colonies that looked toward the notion of a Commonwealth. The wrench was diminished by this character and by specific aspects of emigration, including the degree to which it took place within, or with regard to, friendship, family, locality or occupational networks; while, although most migrants, especially towards the end of the century, were single (as well as young and male), many also migrated within family groups.

The impact of emigration on the British Isles varied greatly, reflecting the range of local circumstances. Ireland, from which there was particularly large-scale emigration to the USA after the potato famine, provided the largest number of migrants from Western and Central Europe for most of the period 1861–1913. In addition, more than half of the natural increase of population in Scotland left, and a higher rate of emigration than from England and Wales led Scotland to have a lower rate of population growth. Scottish emigration reflected the limited agrarian opportunities in Scotland, that in part were the product of tight social control, landlord policy and the periodic downturns in demand for industrial labour. In the Highlands and Islands of Scotland, emigration was frequently linked to the clearances pushed through by landlords in order to enable them to use their land for other purposes, especially sheep and hunting. Some of the migration was voluntary and assisted by the landlords, but in other cases there was compulsion and scant assistance, and the entire process was a bitter one.[74]

In Cornwall, where serious falls in the prices of copper and tin in the late 1860s and 1870s, in part owing to growing world competition, led to a decline in the number of mines, there was heavy emigration, and by 1891, the Cornish diaspora amounted to about 210,000, roughly 42 per cent of all the Cornish-born population at that time. About 45 per cent of this diaspora were living in England and Wales, but the rest were spread over much of the world, mostly in Australia, North America and South Africa.[75] With their mining experience, the Cornish were particularly prone to settle in mining areas.[76]

Within England, however, Cornwall was exceptional. The percentage of the English population that emigrated was lower than those for Scotland

and Ireland, although, as also there, there were important variations, both by region and by period. The impact of the agricultural depression from the 1870s ensured that rural areas, especially in the 1880s, saw much emigration, and encouraged calls for state-support for it, although the majority of English emigrants were young townspeople seeking economic opportunity. Popular in fiction – the financially embarrassed Algernon in *The Importance of Being Earnest* (1895) faced the choice of this world, the next world or Australia – remittance men were not all that common, although the Empire did provide opportunities for many who could not fulfil their social expectations in Britain.

Thanks to immigration, both Canada and the USA were to have thriving Welsh communities. Michael D. Jones, a committed nationalist, undertook an ill-fated attempt to establish a Welsh community in Patagonia in 1865: this, however, proved more difficult than expected and did not fulfil the hopes of those involved. Jones's project reflected the way in which migration, and more generally the Empire, provided an opportunity for individuals and groups to try to pursue hopes and implement ideas, which provided much of the energy of empire, and it was certainly important to migration, for example with the sponsoring and organisation by the Salvation Army of the emigration to Canada of 200,000 people between 1890 and 1930 in pursuit of the view of William Booth that it offered the prospect of a virtuous regeneration.

Migration more generally illustrated the polycentric character of the Empire, as some important population flows within it did not involve the British Isles. Australia, for example, was a source of New Zealand immigrants, India was important for British Guiana, the West Indies, East and South Africa, Sri Lanka, Burma, Malaya and Fiji, while Pacific islanders were used, often virtually as slaves, for work on the Queensland plantations, although, alongside stress on disruption and hardship, it is important to note that the opportunities for employment provided by migration were also welcomed, or at least accepted, by many. Much of this migration was initially designed to replace or supplement the earlier movement of slaves to colonies where there was reliance on them for plantation labour, so that in 1840, there was an unsuccessful effort to obtain indentured labour for Mauritius from Madagascar, but increasingly migration was designed to provide labour across the Empire, including in colonies such as Queensland where there had not been slavery. These labour flows complemented those of white migrants from the British Isles and elsewhere providing manpower for arduous labour in difficult environments, such as the Queensland sugar plantations,[77] and were important to the development of cash crops, such as the expansion of Malayan rubber production in the 1900s, which owed much to labour from South India. Most of this labour was recruited by means of long-term contracts of indenture.[78] The destination of such migration varied, with an emphasis on Mauritius until 1866, then on British Guiana and Trinidad, and from 1890, increasingly on Africa (mostly Natal), Queensland and Fiji.[79]

Although China was an important source of migrants, especially for the Transvaal gold mines after the Boer War, most migrants were within the Empire, and these labour flows helped make it more effective as a series of regional economies and, to a lesser extent, as an economic unit. Labour, entrepreneurial initiative and energy, and capital were all provided, and the Indian Ocean, in particular, became both more diverse and more integrated as a result of this diaspora. In part, it built on existing links, for example between India and both Burma and the Persian Gulf, but there were also vital new links, such as that between India and South Africa.

This was an important aspect of the degree to which the nineteenth-century empire encompassed a powerful dynamic centred on the Indian Ocean that, to a considerable extent, replaced the seventeenth- and eighteenth-century focus on the North Atlantic (including the Caribbean). To a certain extent, the nature of this dynamic has been lost, or at least minimised, as a result of referring to it as India, which suggests a landward configuration that corresponds to important parts of the British role. It also underrates the place of the Indian economy and port cities within a dynamic oceanic system that although centred on nearby waters – the Arabian Sea, the Persian Gulf and the Bay of Bengal – stretched out not only to East Africa, South-East Asia and China, but also to Madagascar, where Britain had growing interests (although not sufficient to pre-empt French conquest), Australasia, into the Pacific and, less prominently, into the Atlantic. This system represented both the refraction of earlier maritime networks through British rule and also the powerful contribution of British imperial expansion and enterprise.

Migration flows within the Empire were increasingly debated by the population of settlement colonies, for, while they sought immigrants from Britain, they were also able to make critical comments both on their suitability and on the extent to which migration was a reflection of British society. As such, immigration both joined and separated, and immigrants were increasingly expected to see themselves as members of more confident communities within the Empire. The history of migration, as of trade, in this period therefore is paradoxically one of growing links but also of a stronger sense of distinct identities and interests.

6

NAVAL STRENGTH AND IMPERIAL EXPANSION, 1815–1901

NAVAL POWER, 1815–1871

Trade, migration and other movements took part within an imperial system protected by the Royal Navy, and, in turn, made the maintenance of sea power more important. Successive victories during the French Revolutionary and Napoleonic Wars conditioned British and foreign expectations about the nature of naval power and of Britain's maritime role, and allowed her, throughout a great part of the nineteenth century, to get from much of the world some official support for, and more grudging unofficial recognition of, *Pax Britannica*, the doctrine of the Royal Navy keeping the peace of the seas for all to benefit, although sometimes in dubious circumstances. Indeed, the navy provided much of the character of British imperial power, as when it sought to end the slave trade and to suppress piracy,[1] while the use of the navy in 1850 to blockade Greece in the Don Pacifico affair, in order to force the payment of damages to a British passport holder whose property had been damaged in an anti-semitic riot in Athens, was defended by Palmerston in Parliament with reference to the role of Britain as offering guarantees equivalent to those of the *Pax Romana* of Classical fame, a potent reference point for British aspirations. The navy also backed the cause of free trade, so that in September 1864 in Japan, British, Dutch and French warships co-operated in acting against batteries erected by the Prince of Nagato that had closed the use of the Straits of Shimonoseki by foreign shipping, thus obstructing the route between China and Yokohama: the British contributed the largest force, and the effective bombardment was supported by landing parties that spiked the guns.[2]

The ability and readiness of the navy to achieve its goals depended on the changing international context and on a willingness to respond to developments in naval technology that was an indication of the strength of the economy and the willingness to spend money on the navy. Steam power, in which Britain led the world, transformed naval capability, just as it did trade and much of the economy; the steam engine, developed in the eighteenth century, was harnessed to the cause of marine propulsion, part of the process by which the stationary steam engine acquired a locomotive capability. On land, the British led with the development of steam-powered trains. Ironically, in contrast, the first steam warship, *Demologos* (Voice of the People), later renamed *Fulton*, was laid down in 1814 in order to provide defence against British naval power: for the protection of New York Harbour. However, the British rapidly developed a steam capability at sea. Their industrial capacity ensured that, even when other countries took the lead in technological innovation, Britain would be best placed to catch up and to develop what seemed appropriate. Thus, it was possible to spend £150,000 on building HMS *Victoria*, the largest wooden screw warship built: launched in 1859, it mounted 131 guns. This material flexibility and power enabled the navy to cope with the absence of any comparable lead in formal training or doctrine; although the deficiencies in formal training were more than compensated for by the extensive practical experience that stemmed from the range of Britain's commitments.

The navy at first leased small private steamships for use as tugs, but in 1821 the tug *Monkey* was bought, providing the navy with its first owned steamship. In 1822, the *Comet*, the first steamer built for naval service, followed. Again, it was a small ship – brig-sized and for use as a tug, reflecting the manoeuvrability provided by steam power. Four British-built paddle steamers were used for the new Greek fleet from 1827, and they encouraged interest in steam power among serving British officers. HMS *Columbia*, which entered service in 1829, was the first armed steamship in the British navy, and the following year the first purpose-built steam warship, HMS *Dee*, entered service.

Early steamships suffered from slow speed, a high rate of coal consumption and the problems posed by side and paddle wheels, which included their vulnerability to fire and the space taken up by wheels and coal-bunkers: the wheels ensured that steamships carried few guns (the *Columbia* only two), so that had it come to conflict with a ship of the line it was thought that the outgunned steamer would be sunk. There was also a reluctance to throw away the existing British lead in sail-warships by embracing the new technology.[3]

However, steam power replaced dependence on the wind, making journey times more predictable and quicker (a requirement for both the merchant and the royal navy), and increased the manoeuvrability of ships, making it easier to sound inshore and hazardous waters, and to attack opposing fleets in anchorages. This made a major difference in the struggle against the slave trade, as slavers were fast, manoeuvrable and difficult to capture, and could take shelter in inshore waters. It was also necessary, in the 1840s, to respond to the use of steamships by slavers. The ability of ships to operate in rivers and during bad weather was also enhanced by steam power,[4] and this was demonstrated in the First Burmese War of 1824–6 when the 60-horsepower engine of the East India Company's steamer *Diana*, a 100-ton paddle tug built in India in 1823, allowed her to operate on the swiftly flowing Irrawady. The *Diana* towed sailing ships, destroyed the Burmese war boats and was crucial to the successful British advance 400 miles up-river, which led the Burmese to negotiate and accept British terms.

On the high seas, steamships showed that they were able to cope with bad weather. The *Nemesis*, a 700-ton British iron-hulled paddle steamer, built at Birkenhead by John Laird for the East India Company, sailed through the winter gales off the Cape of Good Hope to China in 1840 and was the first such warship to reach Macao, although two lesser warships had crossed the Pacific from Chile the same year. The rapid acceptance of steamships into the pantheon of British naval greatness was seen in the response to the destruction by *Nemesis* of 11 war junks in January 1841 near Canton, in what the British significantly named Anson's Bay: Edward Duncan painted a celebratory canvas, although the focus was on the destruction, rather than on the *Nemesis*, while Captain William Hall was rewarded with promotion. British steam technology was also important for other powers, providing the engines for the *Sphinx*, France's first successful steam warship, and for the steamships built by Russia for her Black Sea Fleet.

In the 1840s, the screw propeller (placed at the stern) offered a better alternative to the paddle wheel, by making it possible to carry a full broadside armament, and this made the tactical advantages of steam clear-cut; screw steamers were also more mobile. In 1845, Sir George Cockburn, an experienced admiral, pressed for the change, referring to the process of experimentation: 'The proof we have lately had of the efficiency of the screw as a propellor on board the *Rattler* . . . with all these efforts and improvements in continued progress, in which we are decidedly taking the lead, and are therefore in advance, I feel very confident'.[5] The sloop *Rattler*, launched in 1843, was followed in 1846 by the frigate *Amphion*, and the British quickly followed suit when the French ordered the *Napoléon*, the first screw ship of the line, in 1847, converting HMS *Ajax* to screw propulsion that year, albeit amidst great anxiety as there was political pressure for a shift to steam in the battle fleet. Alongside new ships, there were conversions, encouraged by cost factors, and while, by the start of 1854, France had the *Napoléon* and eight conversions, the British, who outspent them heavily in 1848–51, had constructed three new screw ships of the line and converted another seven.

Naval capability was further improved by the introduction of heavier guns. In 1826, the British decided to introduce 32-pounders for all their ships of the line, and they demonstrated their effectiveness the following year when, thanks largely to superior British gunnery, an Anglo-French-Russian fleet under Sir Edward Codrington destroyed the Ottoman and Egyptian fleets at the battle of Navarino Bay on 20 October 1827, the last great battle of the Age of Fighting Sail, and one in which the Western fatalities were far lower than those of their opponents: 177 to several thousand. This battle was crucial to the success of the fight for Greek independence against Ottoman rule and also underlined that, irrespective of war with France, Britain's naval power had a major role in the Mediterranean, a role that had been demonstrated when Algiers was bombarded in 1816. British warships subsequently took part in operations in Greece, and in 1833 Prince Otto of Bavaria, its newly chosen king, was escorted from Trieste to Athens by HMS *Madagascar*.

Developments in naval ordnance, particularly the introduction in the 1820s of exploding shells in place of solid shot, posed a terrible threat to wooden ships. Colonel Henri-Joseph Paixhans, who developed the necessary type of gun, pressed for the combination of his new ordnance with steamship technology. His supporters hoped that the new technology would enable France to threaten British naval hegemony, but the French at first found it difficult to manufacture reliable shell-firing guns (or, indeed, a sufficient number of good steam engines), and in 1838, a year after the French, the British adopted the shell gun as part of their standard armament. The new naval capability was demonstrated when a British fleet bombarded Acre in 1840: steamers showed their ability to operate inshore, while a shell caused the explosion of the fortress's main magazine. Having had about 40,000 rounds fired at it, the garrison was forced out, a decisive blow in the expulsion of Egyptian forces from Syria: the British, concerned about Egyptian expansionism and French ambitions, had intervened to maintain Ottoman rule in the area, and Austria and the Turks contributed warships to the preponderantly British fleet.[6] The following year, during the Opium War, steamers towed into position the British warships that breached the forts defending the Pearl River below Canton.

Shells helped lead to their antidote, armoured warships. The first iron-clad warship was French, inspired by the success of French iron-plated floating gun platforms off Kinburn in 1855. Laid down in March 1858, and launched in November 1859, the 5,630 ton *Gloire* was merely a wooden frigate fitted with 4.5-inch-thick metal plates, since the French were handicapped by a lack of iron-working facilities. Nevertheless, Napoleon III, who was determined to challenge the British, ordered five more ironclads in 1858 and they were commissioned in 1862.

Worried that their naval lead was being destroyed, the British matched *Gloire* with an armoured frigate, HMS *Warrior*, laid down in May 1859 and completed in October 1861. With its iron hull and displacement of 9,140 tons, this was more significant than the *Gloire*, and, built at the Thames Iron Works, testified to British manufacturing capability: the *Warrior* could also make 14 knots (compared with the *Gloire's* 13) and carry 200 tons more coal, thus having a greater range. The *Warrior*, which cost £377,000 to build, was a revolutionary ship design, actually a true iron (as opposed to iron-clad) ship, with watertight compartments below, the first large sea-going iron-hulled warship.

Nevertheless, both ships retained sail rigs, as did most early steamers. The British remained confident in the capability of their sailing ships of the line, and they stayed in use both in the Crimean War and thereafter, not least because the strategic advantage of steam was less clear-cut than the tactical one, although it had become equally apparent in European waters by about 1875. Improvements in engine design and technology increased power and cut coal consumption and thus the need for coaling, making steamships more attractive. In his *On Naval Warfare under Steam* (1858), General Sir Howard Douglas had claimed 'the employment of steam as motive power in the warlike navies of all maritime nations, is a vast and sudden change in the means of engaging in action on the seas, which must produce an entire revolution in naval warfare'. In the 1860s, high-pressure boilers were combined with the compound engine, and in 1874, the triple-expansion marine engine was introduced, although it was not used in warships until the 1880s. It was to be followed by the water tube boiler. By 1885, only distant service ships still required sail. HMS *Imperieuse*, the last big British warship designed with the ability to sail, was laid down in 1881, although it speedily lost its big rig.

This and other changes transformed the economics of naval power. Not only did steam power and iron push up the cost of building and using ships, but successive developments made it difficult to justify keeping old warships on the reserve list, which had been the established practice during the eighteenth century and had helped ensure that so many ships of the line could be listed as available for service during the French Revolutionary and Napoleonic Wars. Thus HMS *Victory* had been launched in 1765. This practice continued after 1815 and to help protect ships from rain some were provided with roofs; however, the accelerating process of continual technical change cut the fighting life of warships and made it less viable to retain them on the reserve list.

The shift to iron reflected not simply the vulnerability of wooden ships to shellfire, but also success in overcoming the problems that had delayed the use of iron, including its effect on magnetic compasses, the fact that iron

hulls fouled very much worse than those that were copper-bottomed and
the difficulties of securing sufficient consistency and quality in the iron. The
ability to overcome these problems reflected the strength of the British
economy in the acquisition and application of relevant knowledge. Iron
ships were structurally stronger and made redundant the wooden screw
steamers built in large numbers in the 1850s and the very beginning of the
1860s; Britain's last wooden screw ship of the line entered service in 1861,
and, having gained the lead in iron ships, the British retained it, ensuring a
major advantage over the French navy. Continuing developments in naval
ordnance were also important, and British industrial capability was shown
with the development, in place of the early shell guns, of 7-inch Armstrong
breech-loading rifled guns; although because these were found too unreli-
able, as their screwed breech-blocks blew out, the British reverted for a while
from the early 1860s to muzzle-loading guns.[7]

Discussion about the best characteristics for warships and their armament
and the most appropriate fleet structure also reflected the geopolitical situation facing Britain.[8] Although France for some of the century appeared
a threat, as Germany was to do in the 1900s and early 1910s, unlike for the
American Empire of the late twentieth century, there was no Cold War with
a powerful rival state and ideology willing and able to mount challenges
across the world, nor any system of alliances and commitments comparable
with that of the Americans, especially spanning the North Atlantic; nor was
there any need to appear to operate within any equivalent to the international order presided over by the United Nations. Instead, the British relied
on their own efforts as they decided how far to regard other states as challenges, and how best to confront them. From 1815 until the revival of French
naval strength from the mid-1820s, the Admiralty saw the American fleet as
its most likely rival, but Anglo-American relations improved in the aftermath of the War of 1812–15, while the two powers implicitly co-operated
on crucial issues – not least in opposing Spanish attempts to reimpose
control in Latin America, where neither attempted to win colonies – and
also collaborated to suppress the slave trade. The Spaniards tried to build up
a fleet to help their unsuccessful struggle against revolution in Latin America,
but it was far smaller than that of Britain, and conflict was avoided. The
size of the British fleet was reduced and its cost and manpower requirements were cut by keeping most of the ships of the line in reserve. This
reserve – 84 ships of the line in 1817 – was the deterrent on which British
naval strength rested, and although new ships of the line and frigates were
not built in sufficient quantities to replace the wartime bulge as the latter
was reduced by scrapping and sale, nevertheless, the navy remained clearly
the largest in the world, while the use of seasoned timber ensured that the
new ships were more long lasting than many built in the wartime rush.

Force projection in nearby seas and distant oceans against smugglers, pirates and slavers, and to show the flag, for example patrolling fishing grounds off Newfoundland, did not require the mobilisation of this fleet, but instead relied on the use of smaller warships, particularly frigates, which had lesser requirements in terms of manpower and supplies. Operations against pirates and slavers represented an important opportunity to foster combat experience and seamanship and to further British interests. Thus in the late 1820s, naval action against pirates on the Perak coast south of Penang was in part intended to help the Sultan, while in 1831 and 1838 British opposition to what were presented as piratical attacks on the Sultanate of Kedah were important to its politics, and in the early 1830s action against pirates was intended to affect those of Kelantan and Terengganu. As a result, naval power enabled the British to extend their influence in Malaya way beyond their Straits Settlements – Penang, Singapore and Malacca – while, combined with these positions, it gave Britain the dominant position on the route between the Indian Ocean and the Far East.

Naval action was usually small-scale, and for the protection of commerce (a goal directly assisted when specie was carried for merchants), but, on occasion, it served more strategic goals, as in November 1862 when Kuala Terengganu was bombarded in an unsuccessful attempt to influence the civil war in the Sultanate of Pahang in which the Sultan of Terengganu was backing the candidate opposed by the governor of the Straits Settlements. As an instructive sign of the sometime reluctance of the British government to accept naval action at the behest of the periphery, it responded to complaints from Siam and acknowledged Siamese suzerainty in Terengganu.

Events in distant waters were dependent in large part on the naval and geopolitical position closer to Britain. From the 1820s, there was growing concern about what was seen as French aggression – in Spain in the 1820s, and, more seriously, in the Near East in 1840; although there was also co-operation extending to joint military operations, for example in Greece in 1827, and in blockading the Dutch fleet in 1830–33 in order to force the Dutch to accept Belgian independence. As relations deteriorated, France, however, became the major naval threat to Britain, and was also seen as an imperial rival. British concern about French ambitions registered around the world, leading, for example, to the mapping of the Suez isthmus in 1836, to naval demonstrations off Tunis in 1836 and 1837 and to the annexation of New Zealand in 1840, while French expansion in Indo-China, especially the prospect that Danang, seized by France in 1858, would become, as an eastern Cherbourg, a threatening base on the route to China, led to a stronger British interest in northern Borneo, not least in the development of a naval base at Labuan, which Britain gained from Brunei in 1846.[9]

There was also worry about the French ability to take advantage of changes in naval technology. In 1845, Cockburn wrote, 'from the period when the first large seagoing steam vessel was successfully completed, it became evident to everybody that a facility never before existing, must be afforded thereby for sudden invasion of this country [from France]'.[10] The previous year François, Prince of Joinville, the son of King Louis Philippe and a key French admiral, published *De l'état des forces navales de la France*, a work that presented steamships as both the key measure of naval strength and a means by which France could challenge Britain at sea. Britain, in fact, had a major lead in naval steamships, but signs of French naval ambitions combined with international disputes between the two powers, for example over Tahiti in 1842–4, to create a sense of vulnerability that Viscount Palmerston spoke to in Parliament when he referred to the Channel as a 'steam bridge' able to serve the cause of French invasion.

In response to the French development of Cherbourg as a naval base and to their construction of steam-powered warships, the British created a naval base at Portland to cover the south coast of England between the existing bases of Plymouth and Portsmouth. The defences of the coast, especially round the Solent and on the Channel Isles were also improved. Nevertheless, despite much concern within Britain, and periodic invasion panics, especially in 1842–5 and on occasion during the years when Napoleon III controlled France (1848–70),[11] there was no war between the two powers. France's defeat by Prussia in 1870–71 confirmed the naval superiority already demonstrated by Britain in the iron-clad-building race of 1858–61, as it led France to focus on strengthening its army for a future war with Prussia. As a result, the British government felt able to reduce its naval shipbuilding and to retain fewer large ships in service, measures that helped public finances.

Naval technology, however, continued to change. The tension between armour and armament, weight and manoeuvrability, not least the mutually interacting need for more effective guns and stronger armour, led to changes in armour, and the iron, or in some cases in the 1870s the composite iron and wood, navy was followed, after the introduction of compound armour plate in 1877, by the iron and steel navy. The British continued to make large hull components, like the keel, stern post and stern, out of iron until the 1880s, but there were also moves towards the first all-steel warships in the 1870s: two all-steel cruisers were completed for the navy in 1879. There were also important changes in armament. In place of warships designed to fire broadsides, came guns mounted in centreline turrets that were designed to fire end-on as well as to turn. This shift, which was the idea of Edward Reed, owed much to, and in turn contributed to, the changing surface of ships: masts were eliminated and a single superstructure put in the centre, with turrets built fore and aft. The practice of locating heavy guns in an armoured casement began with the British *Research* in 1864 and was followed in 1866 by the larger *Bellerophon,* a battleship protected by six inches of armour plating.

The increasing size and cost of armoured battleships encouraged, however, consideration of substitutes, while there was also a need to respond to developments in weaponry, some commentators wondering if battleships had a future in the face of torpedoes. In 1864, the modern self-propelled torpedo originated, with the invention of a submerged self-propelled torpedo driven by compressed air and armed with an explosive charge at the head. The first steam-powered submarine was launched in 1879, and the British pioneered steam torpedo boats, launching HMS *Lightning* in 1876: the boat could make 19 knots. The vulnerability of battleships to underwater weapons led, in the late 1870s and early 1880s, to growing doubts about their viability, challenging Britain, which had a marked lead in these warships, although the British continued to lay down battleships.

IMPERIAL EXPANSION, 1830–1875

After the First Burmese War of 1824–6, landward advances in India were important. In these, naval power could be directly useful, as when Karachi fell to amphibious attack in 1839, but the intervention in Afghanistan in 1839–42, the conquests of Sind and Gwalior in 1843, and the First (1845–6) and Second (1848–9) Anglo-Sikh Wars, were army operations. Elsewhere in Asia, naval power was far more important, in the Persian Gulf to stop what was seen as the piracy of the Qasimi Arabs,[12] in Malayan waters, and in Britain's first war with China: the Opium War of 1839–42 arose from the Chinese attempt to enforce their prohibition on the import of opium, the profit from the rising export of which was important to the financing of British imports from Asia, while the seizure of opium held by British merchants and their expulsion from Canton led to pressure within Britain for a response. The pressure for compensation was backed up by force and conflict developed from the Chinese demand for the handing over of a British seaman accused of murdering a Chinaman. This was a conflict focused on maritime power projection, and Britain's naval position ensured that reinforcements could be sent, especially in 1840 and 1842, and thus that the British could enjoy and use the initiative. By 1842, the British deployed 12,000 troops, 25 sail-powered warships and 14 steamers, but, more particularly, naval power gave them the ability to decide where to apply this strength, and thus to use it for maximum effect. This was done by blockading the major Chinese positions and by focusing, in 1842, on the Yangzi, eventually proceeding up the river to the capital, Nanjing, an advance dependent on the steamers. Successes, including the capture, assault or blockade of the Pearl (Zhu) River forts, Amoy, Canton, Chinkiang, Chusan, Ningpo and Shanghai by amphibious forces, led China to cede Hong Kong by the Treaty of Nanjing of 1842: it had been seized the previous year. Lower tariffs on British goods were enforced at the expense of China's right to regulate its economy and society, while compensation was granted for the opium destroyed in 1839, and a number of ports were opened to British trade.

In another first for a European power, Aden, which had defied Portuguese attack in the sixteenth century, was annexed in 1839: naval strength was combined with the use of troops from India, and Aden was placed until the government of Bombay, being transferred to that of India in 1932.[13] This annexation was an aspect of a wide-ranging British commitment to the Near East in response to Mehmet Ali of Egypt, who, in the 1830s, had built a large battle fleet with French technical support, launching ships of the line (ten of them very large) and also defeating the Ottomans on land. However, in the face of British action, he was unable to sustain his position in Syria. In 1840, a British squadron blockaded the Egyptian fleet in Alexandria, while British and Austrian warships and marines helped overthrow the Egyptian position in Lebanon and Syria. Sidon was stormed, the marines joined the Ottomans in defeating the Egyptian army at Boharsef and Acre was heavily bombarded. Mehmet agreed to evacuate Syria, while the British application of pressure following the occupation of Aden led, in 1840, to the Egyptian evacuation of Yemen. In South Africa, the British expanded inland from Cape Colony, annexing Natal in 1845 and British Kaffraria in 1847.

The Opium War was the first time a West European state had waged war on China, the first European victory over the Chinese, and one achieved in China itself. Combined with the successful British intervention against Egyptian forces in Lebanon and Palestine in 1840, an impressive demonstration of power against a modernising and empire-building non-Western power, this suggests that a 'tipping power' towards British dominance had occurred. In 1807, British forces in Egypt had been defeated at Rosetta, while in 1809 the Chinese had rejected the suggestion of a British presence in Macao to protect the Portuguese colony against possible French attacks, but by the 1840s the situation was very different. In part, this reflected the extent to which British military resources in the 1800s had been devoted to conflict with France, but there had also been, subsequently, an important enhancement in British military capability, both in absolute terms and relative to that of leading non-Western powers.

Equilibrium in Europe between the major powers provided opportunity for British expansion abroad, but where war did not occur is as interesting as where expansion was pursued. Despite serious differences, conflict was avoided with the USA. In peace-talks in 1814, British negotiators had demanded from the USA, the exclusion of American warships from the Great Lakes, British freedom to navigate the Mississippi River and a major Native American buffer state in the Old Northwest (between the Appalachians and the Great Lakes). None of these demands were to be met, but there was to be no attempt to prepare for British expansion in a future conflict, and instead British defensive success in Canada during the War of 1812–15, combined with the setbacks, or worse, with their attacks on America during the war, encouraged post-war conciliation of the USA, seen both in the willingness to accept the Monroe Doctrine for Latin America, and in the settlement of frontier disputes. The Treaty of Ghent, which had ended the War of 1812, had provided for adjustments of boundary disputes and in 1818 a convention extended the frontier along the 49th parallel from the Lake of the Woods to the Rockies, with the Oregon Territory to the west to be jointly administered by Britain and America for ten years. This administration, which was extended indefinitely in 1827, and, in practice, until the Oregon Boundary Treaty of 1846, excluded the two other powers that bordered the region, Mexico and Russian-ruled Alaska, as well as the Native population who were treated as passive recipients of the largesse of enlightened Western rule.[14]

The British took a dynamic role in the Oregon Territory. The Hudson's Bay Company established many bases below the 49th parallel, including Forts Boise, Colville, Flathead, George, Nez Percés, Nisqually, Okanagan, Umpqua and Vancouver; several were on or south of the Columbia River, including Fort Nez Percés, established in 1818, and Fort Vancouver in 1825. The Company dominated international trade from the region with direct sailings from London, and its presence clashed with American ambitions for the Territory. These were not the only areas of tension. A dispute over the Maine frontier led, in 1838, to the bloodless 'Aroostook War' between Maine and New Brunswick, and in 1839 to American strategic planning for war.[15] These disputes drew on political concerns: Democratic expansionists saw Britain as a threat and there was unfounded concern about British meddling in Texas when it was an independent state.[16] American concern about the possibility of war with Britain and of a British invasion led to investment in coastal fortifications, and in the 1830s and 1840s led Brigadier-General Edmund Gaines to press for a rail system, built by the federal government and able rapidly to move militia from the interior.

In turn, British concern about war with the USA led to defence planning for Canada. Rumours of American invasion preparations, for example in Tennessee and New York in late 1845, were followed carefully, there was concern about the British position on the Great Lakes, not least in response to the number of steamships that the Americans had available, and the eventual location of the capital at inland Ottawa was a defensive measure to overcome the vulnerability of Toronto, Kingston and Montréal to attack. The British relied not only on their garrison and navy but also on local military support, a system that was to define the Empire. Loyalists played a major role in suppressing insurrection in Canada in 1837–8 that arose from anger about land tenure, although the inter-connected nature of British military power and its dependence on the navy was shown with the role of the navy in moving troops within British North America – from Halifax to St. John's, New Brunswick and Québec – and to there from the West Indies, Gibraltar (units en route home from Corfu) and the British Isles. Warships also carried specie for the Commissariat. The vessels used as troopships included large warships.[17]

In the 1840s, a report by Wellington, then Commander-in-Chief of the Army, on the defence of Canada led to a government response acknowledging deficiencies:

> concur with your Grace in attaching the greatest importance to a well organised and well disciplined militia, in support of any force which this country may employ in the event of a war in Canada; and I have not failed to press this subject earnestly on the consideration of the Governor General. In the last session I regret to say that he failed in inducing the legislature to make provision by law for this important object.[18]

In America, James Polk campaigned for the presidency in 1844 on the platform '54° 40′ or fight', a stark settlement of the Oregon issue, but compromise proved possible. Already, the Ashburton–Webster Treaty of 1842 had settled disputes over the Maine, New Hampshire and Minnesota boundaries, and, once elected, Polk was willing to settle in 1846 without British Columbia or Vancouver Island,[19] so that the longest frontier of a British colony was established peacefully. Had there been a war, it would have been, on the part of Britain, largely naval and amphibious in character.

Palmerston, foreign secretary in 1846–51 and prime minister in 1855–8 and 1859–65, took care to try to ease tensions with France, and the two powers co-operated in war with Russia, the Crimean War of 1854–6, an attempt to limit Russian expansion at the expense of the Ottoman (Turkish) Empire, an advance the British saw as a threat to their position in India. The Russian navy had been bold and completely successful at the expense of the Ottomans off Sinope on 30 November 1853, but felt totally outclassed by the Anglo-French fleet that entered the Black Sea in 1854, initially in order to prevent a Russian attack on Constantinople, but subsequently to cover the troops sent first to Varna in order to put pressure on the Russian forces in the Balkans and, once these had retreated, to the Crimea in order to attack Sevastopol, the base of the Russian Black Sea Fleet. The Russians had more warships in the Baltic, but there also they did not challenge the allies: the Russians initially had no screw ships of the line. In contrast, the British fleet sent to the Baltic in 1854 included no fewer than nine steam battleships, two designed as steam battleships and the other seven converted from sailing ships of the line, as well as six sailing ships of the line and four 60-gun steam blockships, with another four, plus four screw battleships and ten sailing ships of the line, following later in the year; although the fleet achieved little in the Baltic.

The allied navies, which were able to blockade Russia, were essentially opposed to Russian coastal defences, and, indeed, their bombardments of Odessa and Sevastopol in 1854 underlined the vulnerability of wooden warships to effective defensive fire from shore batteries, not least the use of red-hot shot. In 1855, however, when the British sent a large squadron to attack the Russian supply lines through the Sea of Azov, the Russians abandoned the forts protecting the Straits of Kerch and the British were able to devastate shipping in the Sea. Also that year, the British Baltic fleet successfully bombarded Sveaborg, the fort that guarded the approach to Helsinki (then ruled by Russia), destroying not only fortifications but also six ships of the line and 17 smaller warships sheltering in the harbour. The use by the British of 16 mortar vessels and 16 screw gunboats, which presented a smaller target to the batteries and came close inshore, was important. The ability of the British to operate in the Crimea reflected their maritime capability: the army was both transported and maintained there, and the formidable logistical burden, which included the supply of 1,350,000 artillery rounds for the Anglo-French siege of Sevastopol, was maintained. This was underlined by the battles of Balaclava and Inkerman (in which the Naval Brigade took a prominent role), which arose from the Russian attempts to breach the supply route back to the coast.

Russia's failure to defend its coastlines led it to accept the demilitarisation of the Black Sea in the Treaty of Paris of 1856; had it not done so, the British were preparing for an Anglo-French attack on Kronstadt and St. Petersburg and had ordered large numbers of screw gunboats and mortar boats, as well as iron-plated wooden floating batteries comparable with those successfully used by the French when an Anglo-French squadron bombarded Kinburn on the Black Sea in October 1855.

The Crimean War was a triumph for maritime power over a Continental Empire. All such contests involve specific characteristics that make comparison difficult, but it is still instructive to consider not just the general point but also the nature of these specific characteristics. Victory for the maritime powers owed much to the combination of their limited

goals, principally securing Ottoman territorial integrity, and to Russian isolation. By 1856, the alliance of Britain, France, Sardinia and the Ottomans
looked set to expand, possibly to include Austria and Sweden. In addition,
Russian industrialisation was not yet developed to the scale it would soon
reach, while Russia also suffered from very poor communications. The
sparseness of Russian railways was such that the advantages brought by steam
power were largely enjoyed by the Allies, while, aside from affecting the efficiency of the Russian economy, this sparseness made it difficult to apply
and support military power, especially at the periphery.

Nevertheless, the war had also indicated the extent to which threats to
Britain's imperial position were perceived. Rear-Admiral Sir James Stirling,
who in 1854 had been appointed Commander-in-Chief of the China and
East Indies Station, feared Russian pressure on China and Japan via
Manchuria, as well as the impact of the visit of an American squadron under
Commodore Matthew Perry to Japan in 1853–4. In 1855, Stirling argued in
a 'Memoir on the Maritime Policy of England in the Eastern Seas', read by
Palmerston the following year, that an expansionist Russia was a major threat
to British interests in the East, not least as capturing the coast of Chinese
Manchuria would free her from the constraints of ice. As a result, he felt
that Britain had to take a pro-active role in organising China; failure to do
so, he warned, would open India to the threat of a Russian-dominated
China. What this required, however, was formidable: Stirling urged the
opening of all Chinese and Korean ports to Britain, the repression of piracy,
the protection of the coasting trade by the navy, and the expansion of the
naval base at Hong Kong so as to: 'maintain an undeniable superiority over
all other nations: In other words we must establish a Maritime Empire with
all its concomitant adjuncts of Naval Positions, Postal Communications,
Hydrographical Surveys, and Steam Factories and Dock Yards'.[20] More of
this was to be realised than Stirling possibly anticipated.

In the 1850s, aside from the Crimean War, the British were most heavily
engaged in South Asia. India again served as the basis of British expansion,
while the governments of India and Bombay had political responsibility for
British interests around much of the Indian Ocean. Lower Burma was
annexed in 1852, a move that was criticised by Cobden, although it was not
'pacified' until 1857, and, within India, Nagpur, Jhansi and Berar followed
in 1853 and Awadh (Oudh) in 1856. The Indian Mutiny of 1857–9, in which
most of the Bengal Army in the Ganges Valley mutinied, largely in response
to a maladroit command that paid insufficient attention to religious sensi-
tivities, was a serious challenge and victory was seen as crucial to British
prestige and power in India. Control of the seaways helped the British
deploy reinforcements: thus HMS *Shannon*, a 51-gun steam frigate, sailed
from Singapore to Hong Kong and took aboard 300 marines and carried

them to Calcutta, where they helped to secure the city. The *Shannon*'s boats, cannon and crew were then formed into a Naval Brigade, as were those of HMS *Pearl*, a steam corvette that had brought troops from Singapore. Naval artillery provided close fire-support, especially at Cawnpore and Lucknow. The Mutiny led to a major constitutional change: the East India Company had continued to play a major role in the government of India, but, in 1858, the Crown assumed full sovereignty.

Naval power was more directly valuable against Persia in 1856–7. Employing their amphibious capability, the British took further their role in the Persian Gulf when they staged a successful landing, seized Persian positions, defeated the Persians at Khush-āb (1857) and intimidated Persia into evacuating Herat in Afghanistan. Thus, naval power secured a political settlement far from the sea: there was concern about the impact of Persian expansion on Afghanistan's ability to act as a buffer for India.

A second war with China was a more formidable challenge. Britain pressed for an extension of commercial rights, while the Chinese refused to accept a revision of the Treaty of Nanjing of 1842. The incident that led to hostilities was the arrest in Canton on charges of piracy of the crew of the *Arrow*, a Hong Kong ship with a Chinese crew said to be flying the British flag, although, whether it was or not, it had no right to do so. This crisis was exploited by Henry Parkes, acting Consul in Canton, and by Palmerston, both of whom sought conflict.[21] Initially, the British relied on a naval response, seizing the forts on the approach to Canton, but the need to divert troops to deal with the Indian Mutiny made it difficult to take matters further, until, with French reinforcements, it was possible to capture Canton at the close of 1857. In 1858, attention shifted to north China and an attempt to put pressure on Beijing. Bombardment by screw gunboats led to the capture of the forts at Taku that protected the mouth of the Peiho river, and the allies advanced up the river as far as Tientsin when the Chinese accepted terms. Once they had removed their troops, however, China rejected the treaty and conflict recommenced, initially, in June 1859, with different results at the Taku forts: the British found Chinese fire as accurate as their own and three British screw gunboats were sunk by the Chinese – owing to the shallows, the ships of the line and frigates had to stand off out of range of the forts, a sobering example of the weakness of the small but heavily armed wooden screw gunboat that was all the rage after its successes in the Crimean War at Kinburn and Sveaborg in 1855. Furthermore, the earthen Chinese fortifications absorbed British shot. In 1860, however, a fresh attack by a larger Anglo-French force led to the fall of the Taku forts, after which the force advanced to occupy Beijing, an important symbolic step, and a blow at the heart of Chinese prestige. The subsequent Chinese capitulation was followed by a treaty that led to the opening of China to trade and missionaries and the expansion of Hong Kong to include the Kowloon peninsula. Hankou and Tientsin swiftly became 'treaty ports', where the British presence included concessionary areas.

China focused many of the aspirations of empire. Trade and missionary activity were both important, but so was a conviction that the British presence could help ensure a beneficial modernisation. More generally, like other European imperial powers, the British sought to impose their definitions and rules, as well as their interests, and to deny that non-European powers and peoples had any that were comparable or of equal validity. This did not only entail attacks on piracy and the slave trade, for the advance of British power, and its increased territorialisation, brought British concepts of sovereignty, suzerainty, governance, frontiers and conflict into dispute with those of other societies. Thus, in India, Awadh was seized under the pretext that it was misruled.

In China, however, empire was not accompanied by colonisation. As such, British impact was less sweeping than in settlement colonies, while there was not an experience of rule comparable with the situation in much of South Asia and Africa. Nevertheless, China was important to the history of the seaborne empire, not least because the absence of territorial control ensured that the emphasis there remained much more on maritime power; the British presence was focused on ports, where British power played the greatest role in securing a treatment of economic interests that would not otherwise have been acceptable to the Chinese government. It was not only in China that the British government was anxious to restrict colonialism: in 1847, Palmerston had turned down the idea of establishing a colony in Abyssinia (modern Ethiopia) and in 1859 he took the same attitude towards Egypt. The emphasis here was on trade and the means to secure it, not on land.

The situation was very different in the settlement colonies. Indigenous resistance was overcome in Australia, although less easily and completely in New Zealand. In Australia, the Aborigines were hit hard by Western diseases, especially smallpox and influenza, which not only killed many but also affected social patterns and lowered morale. Their resistance was also affected by the very fragmented nature of the Aboriginal 'nation', which greatly lessened the prospect of co-operation. By the second half of the century, the settlers enjoyed an important technological advantage, thanks to the spread of breech-loading rifles, and were able to make rapid advances, especially in Queensland. Much of the treatment of the Aborigines was harsh and many were hunted and killed as if little different from wild animals.[22]

British expansion in New Zealand indicated the global reach of its maritime-borne power, but also that progress was far from easy. The Maoris used well-sited trench and *pa* (fort) systems that were difficult to bombard or storm, and they inflicted serious defeats on the British. Without either side winning a decisive victory, a ceasefire was negotiated in 1861. Further north, conflict broke out in 1863, as the British sought to expand their control over land to the south of Auckland. This war involved road and fort construction, and the deployment of up to 9,000 troops, as well as local colonists. As the conflict spread in 1865, the British responded by constructing forts at river mouths on the contested west coast of North Island. Maori forces defeated colonial forces in 1868, but their support ebbed in 1869 and the colonists were able to regain ground. Also on North Island in 1868, another Maori leader, Te Kooti, launched a vigorous attack on colonial settlements. The response was largely by colonial and allied Maori forces, as most regular units had now left. By 1872, Te Kooti had clearly lost. Militarily, the mobility of the colonial forces, including the Arawa Flying Column, was combined with a process of steady entrenchment. Roads, telegraph lines and armed constabulary stations, practical and physical manifestations of control, were all constructed.[23]

In West Africa, Lagos, a major slaving port, was attacked in 1851, with the steamship *Penelope* playing a prominent role, and the slaving facilities were destroyed. Lagos was annexed in 1861, although an expedition against the Asante (Ashanti), one of the more militarily powerful of all African people, in 1864 was wrecked by disease. In 1871, the Dutch sold their forts on the Gold Coast to Britain without any heed to the views of the King of Asante, Kofi Kakari, who saw these forts as trading bases under Asante sovereignty. Furthermore, British pressure for free trade clashed with the Asante defence of controlled monopolies. Resentful of this, and of past Asante success, the British failed to heed Asante views, leading to a war that was welcomed by Edward Cardwell, the Secretary of State for War, Lord Kimberley, the Colonial Secretary, and General Sir Garnet Wolseley. In 1873–4, a new expedition, in which the Asante were outgunned and the well-prepared British force benefited from the assistance of other African peoples, especially the Fante, led to the seizure and burning down of the Asante capital, Kumasi.[24]

Meanwhile, another major African kingdom, Abyssinia (Ethiopia), had been brought low by British power in 1868. In a methodically planned campaign under Napier, the commander of the Bombay army, an expedition entered the Red Sea and a 13,000-strong force landed and marched from the coast into the mountains, defeating the Abyssinians at Arogee, storming the fortress of Magdala and rescuing imprisoned British hostages. Emperor Tewodros II committed suicide.[25] The British then withdrew, and Abyssinia remained independent.

Elsewhere, British governments also showed caution in limiting intervention. The navy had been challenged by the prospect of war with the

Union side in the American Civil War (1861–5). Relations were tense, as the British government expressed sympathy for the Confederacy, and there was anger about the Union blockade, which hit British trade links.[26] The British fleet in North American and Caribbean waters was strengthened. However, opinion within Britain was divided,[27] there were powerful voices for caution, and, to Confederate disappointment, the controversial building of Confederate warships by private British shipyards was banned in 1863 and war was avoided. In March 1863 the French envoy in Washington suggested to his British counterpart that the two powers bring the war to a close by recognising the Confederacy, but the British envoy retorted that Britain was against interfering by force.[28] British entry would have transformed the situation at sea. American naval strength should not be exaggerated, as their iron-clads were not really suited for distant service on the high seas, while American ships would also have been inferior in battle conditions, because their naval ordnance had too low a muzzle velocity to be effective against British armour, and American armour was inferior because of the incapacity to roll thick iron plates.[29] The Union fleet would probably have been badly battered in any war, although the fast wooden screw steamers authorised by Congress in 1864 would have been a threat to British trade, and led to the British building fast unarmoured iron-hulled warships in response.

The rapid demobilisation of the Union fleet after the war improved the British position. There was to be no conflict between the two powers over Canada or over American colonial ambitions, because the Americans chose not to use their military strength for expansionist ends, other than against Native Americans. Instead, Anglo-American differences were settled by the Treaty of Washington of 1871 and this permitted a reduction in the British military presence, with garrisons in Canada restricted to the naval bases of Esquimalt on Vancouver Island and Halifax, both important coaling stations for the navy, and Halifax protected by an impressive system of artillery batteries. This reduction was an important aspect of a major shift in defence priorities, as troops were recalled from self-governing colonies, the last British soldiers in Australia leaving in 1870, a policy seen as Fortress England by critics, and the colonies were encouraged to develop their forces, a process that bore fruit with the assistance they provided to Britain in the Boer War of 1899–1902, but that also made the colonies important as providing coaling stations rather than being the sites of British garrisons.[30]

Aside from not intervening in the American Civil War, there was also caution about Latin America. Instability in Mexico and repudiation of international debts had led Britain, France and Spain to intervene in order to secure repayment, and their troops landed at its main port, Vera Cruz, in

December 1861 to January 1862, but the Mexicans did not change their policy. The French increased their force, and eventually tried (and failed) to establish a client government, but the British had already joined the Spaniards in evacuating their troops in 1862.

More generally, the British role in supporting independence for Latin America helped delimit the Empire. South America was the only one of the three inhabited continents entirely or partly in the southern hemisphere in which Britain did not become a major colonial power. British Guiana became an important plantation colony, especially for the production of sugar, and expanded into the interior, but this expansion was challenged by Venezuela and the colony remained relatively small. In the West Indies, there were few opportunities for British expansion, and in the 1890s Spanish weakness was to be exploited by the USA, not Britain: in 1898, Cuba and Puerto Rico were conquered by the former. Partly for these reasons, the British presence in the region became proportionately less important in the Empire: the existing colonies were not stepping stones to anywhere, while economic opportunities were greater in the USA, Canada and the independent republics of Latin America.

NAVAL POWER, 1871–1884

In the 1870s, in face of the weakness of other navies, there had been only limited governmental concern about naval strength or public interest in naval issues,[31] although a war scare with the Russians over their advances at the expense of the Ottoman Empire in 1877–8 led to the reinforcement of British forces in the Mediterranean, with Indian units swiftly sent to Malta via the Suez Canal and the dispatch of a fleet to Constantinople through the Dardanelles in February 1878 as a response to the movement of Russian troops to near Constantinople. From Malta, troops were sent with Turkish permission to occupy Cyprus. It became a British protectorate, but was not annexed until 1914. As a first step in 1878, the navy took formal possession of the island.[32] Russia, whose fleet was still quite weak, backed down, but the risk had been demonstrated and the subsequent Russian determination to build up their Black Sea Fleet led to greater British concern about the Eastern Mediterranean. The importance of this region had been accen-tuated by the opening of the Suez Canal in 1869. Britain's interest in Egypt had been strengthened in 1875 by the purchase of the shares of the Egyptian Khedive (Viceroy for the nominal sovereign, the Ottoman Sultan) in the Suez Canal Company, which amounted to 44 per cent of the total share capital.

From 1884, concern about France and Russia mounted, but already the development of British trade and the Empire had led to an emphasis on the value of a powerful navy as the best means to secure national interests. This was propagated in Parliament, newspapers and other publications, as in Captain J. C. R. (John Charles Ready) Colomb's *The Protection of our Commerce and Distribution of our Naval Forces Considered* (1867). The position of the navy was affirmed from a different direction when the future George V, then the second son of Edward, Prince of Wales, entered the navy in 1877. He left only when his older brother, the Duke of Clarence, died in 1892.

For French strategists, the extent of the British Empire apparently represented an opportunity. From the 1690s, the French saw themselves facing the British with their superior naval resources, but with a greater reliance on overseas trade, and this frequently led to a French emphasis on commerce raiding, the latest iteration of which was *La Guerre Maritime et Les Ports Françaises* (1882) and *De la Guerre Navale* (1885) by Admiral Théophile Aube, who was navy minister in 1886–7. He and the so-called *Jeune École* pressed for unarmoured, and thus fast, light cruisers, able to attack British commerce, rather than the more heavily armoured battleships with their need for large quantities of coal. Aube also favoured the torpedo boat, claiming that it nullified the power of British battleships, and this led the British, in response, to build both cruisers and torpedo boats.

The British, indeed, had to protect their massive overseas trade and the sea routes to their global empire and be ready to face all comers, and so had to maintain the biggest navy in the world, as well as, more specifically, to meet the threat from the ideas of the *Jeune École* by building fast steel cruisers. In the 1880s, British expenditure was close to the combined figure of the next two high-spending powers, France and Russia. Unlike France and Russia, but like the USA and Japan, Britain was not threatened overland, and so all three could concentrate their defence spending on their navies. The British navy was helped by its peacetime victory in the competition with the French for naval enhancement in the 1860s, and also by the consequences of the Franco–Prussian War (1870–71) for French military priorities: there was a determined effort thereafter to strengthen both the army and fortifications facing Germany.

Deployed across the world, the British navy faced the dilemma of maintaining fairly distinct forces in home waters and on colonial/overseas stations. The former was an armoured battleship-centred fleet, while the latter was a hodgepodge of unarmoured ships and gunboats whose fighting value was relatively far less, but which, nevertheless, were fit-for-purpose against likely opponents, such as the lightly armed pirate fleets of China and Borneo.[33] An iron hull was a problem on tropical stations, as it required cleaning more often than wooden hulls, and there were no large dry docks available there for such cleaning. Fully rigged screw steamers continued to be used to show the flag on distant stations, their speed helping provide a strategic reach that ensured a response to imperial crises, while their rig reduced dependence on coal supplies,[34] but, thanks to improved communications, including the opening of the Suez Canal, the number of ships on foreign stations fell by 40 per cent in 1865–76. The diversity of ship type was ultimately addressed by the extension of the network of coaling stations, so that steam-powered armoured warships could be used in deep waters across the world, an extension advocated in 1881–2 in reports produced by the Carnarvon Commission established in 1879.

Both before and after this extension, often relatively small British warships played a major role inshore on colonial/overseas stations. In 1849, three British warships destroyed 23 Chinese pirate junks in two battles, and one of them, a sloop, went on that year, without any British casualties, to destroy 58 pirate junks mounting about 1,200 guns.[35] Similarly, small forces of gunboats enforced British interests in Melanesia[36] and on the coast of British Columbia, destroying canoes and villages in punitive action.[37] The war with piracy led to wide-ranging and continuing operations by the British navy, for example in the Straits of Malacca and in the waters off the Arabian peninsula, and was also an important aspect of the deterrent capacity of naval power. In addition, river steamers were very important on Chinese and African rivers, such as the Yangzi, the Niger and the Nile.

IMPERIAL EXPANSION, 1875–1901

Imperial advance was not without its defeats, particularly in 1879 when the initial British attack on the Zulus failed because the advancing columns were unable to offer mutual support and the Zulus brought overwhelming force against one of the columns, wiping it out at Isandlwana. However, the British went on to inflict heavy and decisive defeats on the Zulus. Similarly, in the Second Afghan War (1878–80), defeat at Maiwand in 1879 was followed by victory outside Kandahar in 1880. Nevertheless, the combination of the replacement of Disraeli's Conservative government in 1880 by a Liberal ministry opposed to bold expansionism, and the political and logistical problems of operating in Afghanistan, a truly hostile interior, challenged the efficacy of the 'Forward Policy' that the government of India had been pursuing, and encouraged the British to draw back, evacuating Kandahar, and, instead, to stabilise their position to the east, on the 'North-West Frontier'. There the pacification of Baluchistan by Sir Robert Sandeman in the 1870s offered a model for other frontier regions. Winning local allies played a crucial role, but so also, as the Punjab Irregular Force repeatedly showed, did an ability to adapt to local military conditions.

The conquest of Egypt in 1882 demonstrated the dual effectiveness of navy and army. In the face of a surge of nationalist opposition that toppled the Khedive, the Gladstone government was initially unwilling to intervene, although the British were concerned to protect their interests, especially their financial presence in a heavily indebted state, and to gain physical control of the Suez Canal. The murder of 50 of Alexandria's European residents on 11 June led to a more active British stance: the navy joined in an international mission to evacuate the city's foreigners, while Gladstone ordered Admiral Sir Beauchamp Seymour, the commander of the British warships, to stop any strengthening of the city's defences. On 11 July, in response to such work, Seymour entered the harbour and bombarded its defences: 14 ships with powerful guns, including HMS *Inflexible* which had four 16-inch guns, inflicted great damage (although many of the shells missed), with few British casualties. The battle was not particularly illustrative of the problems facing naval power at the time – the central battery ships forcing the harbour did not have to face mines or torpedoes, and the guns of the shore batteries were not particularly well handled by the Egyptians – but British naval force projection was generally helped by such a capability advantage over non-Europeans. Having taken the initiative, the British landed 15,000 troops who, at Tel el Kebir on 13 September, routed the Egyptian army.

A quasi-protectorate over Egypt was established, and this was seen as important in thwarting French plans in the Mediterranean, as well as in securing Britain's position on the route to India via the Suez Canal, and thus protecting South-West Asia from Russian expansion. The Suez Canal gave Britain dominance over a crucial sea lane, one that could be more readily controlled than the routes that passed Cape Town, Singapore and the Falklands. However, intervention in Egypt was to lead to an initially unsuccessful commitment in Sudan; an aspect of the way in which maritime interests could lead to a role that was both far inland and very difficult. Naval interests in the shape of the Suez Canal route to India and the defence of the Eastern Mediterranean, were to become fused with military concerns in the shape of supplies to India, and the eventual need to quash first the threat from the Mahdists of Sudan and then French expansionism.

The 1880s and 1890s brought a major burst of territorial expansion, such that by 1900 the British had an empire covering a fifth of the world's land surface and including 400 million people (many of them in India); whereas that of France, the second-largest Western maritime empire, included only 52 million inhabitants. It is easy to underrate Britain's colonial wars as none was a war for survival or transformed British society, but their cumulative impact for Britain was important, not least culturally, and their individual impact on other societies formative. Britain's role was part of the wider story of European imperialism, but it was larger than that of any other state, and the greater British ability and willingness to support territorial expansion affected not only Britain and the areas she seized, but also other powers, both imperial and non-imperial.

The British saw their successive military triumphs as a demonstration of innate superiority, an approach that led them to underrate the successes of opposition, as with the Maori.[38] The standard image was of well-disciplined British formations using ordered fire power, and of non-Western hordes employing shock tactics; not a valid description of the wide variety of non-Western fighting methods, but one that accorded with the cultural requirements of many British commentators. Better weaponry, an aspect of British technological prowess and manufacturing capability, certainly played a major role. The fictional Captain Blood famously observed, in Hillaire Belloc's poetic attack on the rapacity, cruelty and dishonesty of imperial adventures, *The Modern Traveller* (1898), 'Whatever happens we have got/The Maxim Gun; and they have not'.[39] In 1889, indeed, the British had adopted a fully automatic machine-gun developed by Hiram Maxim that could fire 600 rounds per minute, employing the recoil to eject the empty cartridge case, replace it and fire; and this was used in the Matabele War of 1893–4, the Chitral Campaign on the North-West Frontier in 1895 and at Omdurman in 1898. Across much of Africa, however, the breech-loading rifle was, in fact, more significant, while artillery was also important. As was characteristic of British military activity, there was a process of challenge and response with weaponry, so that, in the mountainous terrain of the North-West Frontier of India, a practical engineered solution was devised for the limitations of artillery: mobile screw-guns, light, carried in sections and then screwed together for firing, were found best.

The ability to outgun opponents was important, as was the organisational system with which the technology was applied. General Stockley Warren felt that at the battle of Mazina of 1880 'the immense superiority of controlled volley firing, over independent blazing away, was clearly demonstrated'. He noted that the Afghans had effective Snider rifles, but felt that the bayonet charges, artillery and 'heavy volleys' of the British were crucial to the outcome.[40] In the Sudan, at Atbara in 1898, the advancing Anglo-Egyptian forces lost 81 men with a further 487 wounded, compared with their opponents' 3,000 killed and 4,000 wounded. Later in the year, at Omdurman, British rifles, machine guns and artillery, including high-angle howitzers, devastated the attacking Mahdists, Winston Churchill, who was present, writing 'It was a matter of machinery'. The Anglo-Egyptian forces suffered 49 killed and 382 wounded, and their opponents about 11,000 and

16,000; although it is important to note the extent to which the Mahdists' inappropriate strategy and tactics, not least the decision to fight a pitched battle and the frontal advance across flat ground, contributed greatly to British victory.[41]

Logistics were also very significant to British success around the world. Steamships, railways and telegraph lines combined to facilitate the transfer and return of forces, permitting a greater integration of military structures in Britain and the colonies. Railways played a major role in structuring and linking imperial space and were important in deploying troops towards areas of operation. Railway-building on the North-West Frontier in the 1890s reached to within 70 miles of Kandahar, while, in 1896, the army invading Sudan built a railway straight across the desert from Waida Halfa to Abu Hamed, which was pushed on to Atbara in 1898 and was vital in the supply of British forces. By 1900, 20,000 miles of railway had been constructed in India, a major commitment of capital, and in East Africa the railway from Mombasa on the Indian Ocean to Lake Victoria was completed the following year.[42] The use of gunboats, made in Britain in numbered sections, on the Nile in 1896–8 was also important, providing firepower and mobility, and, although far from the sea, was an instance of the waterborne power of the Empire. After the victory at Omdurman, the gunboats served to help extend British power into southern Sudan, and, crucially, to take Kitchener to confront the smaller French expedition that had reached Fashoda overland.

Telegraph systems were also part of the infrastructure of empire, facilitating the more rapid transmission of messages, and being developed to bind the Empire together. The British, with the most far-flung imperial system, preferred trans-oceanic overland telegraph links in order to limit the possible interference of foreigners in their communications.[43] As another instance of the combination of knowledge, engineering and capital, the construction of an infrastructure of sanitation, offering pure water, effective sewage systems and sanatoria, greatly increased the survival rates of British troops, administrators and settlers, and transformed the demographics of empire.

The political context was also important to the expansion of control. The British were able to use large numbers of indigenous mercenary soldiers to aid their imperial advance, particularly in India and also where Indian troops could be used outside India, so that in 1878 the war scare with Russia led to the dispatch from India of drafts of troops as far as Malta. Once the Punjab had been conquered in the 1840s, its Sikh troops provided a significant accession of strength, while, as an instance of the potential ratio of strength, the British successfully invaded Hunza on the North-West Frontier of India in 1891, with 1,000 Gurkha and Kashmiri troops under 16 British officers. In Africa, there was also an important use of indigenous troops: in Nigeria, the West African Frontier Force, at Omdurman, the Sudanese brigades in Kitchener's force, which played a crucial role, and, in Somaliland, native levies and Indian and African troops, as well as British forces.

The ability to win local support was in part a product of local rivalries, which greatly helped the British in many cases, although it also ensured a degree of instability in imperial control. The British benefited in their imperial conquest and rule, across its span, from their ability to elicit – by coercion or more willingly – local support, which in large part arose from divisions within polities, reflecting the fact that many were composite states. For example, the Zulu Civil War that followed conflict with Britain in 1879 provided the British with co-operative chiefs. The British also benefited from the multipolar character of power in many areas, such as West Africa and the Malayan peninsula, and their consequent ability to tackle problems in a sequential or separate fashion, rather than to have to face a powerful regional opposition.

Their skill in eliciting local support was demonstrated in South-West Asia, where the East India Company had gained Aden in 1839, and a series of islands off the Arabian peninsula had been annexed: the Kuria Muria Islands in 1854, Perim in 1857, Kamaran in 1858 and Socotra in 1886. On the mainland of Arabia, Ottoman (Turkish) pretensions were curtailed as a series of local emirs were recognised as independent under British protection: on the 'Pirate Coast' (Trucial Oman, now the United Arab Emirates) from 1820, in part the consequence of a punitive expedition against piracy, as well as Bahrain from 1811, Oman from 1891 and Kuwait from 1899; while, to the south-west of Oman, Hadhramaut became a protectorate in 1888 and the hinterland of Aden followed in 1903.

The British came to the task of imperial expansion in the late nineteenth century with considerable experience of treating with non-Western peoples and of fighting outside Europe, experience that encompassed the recruitment, training and use of local levies and allied forces, the development of logistical capability and combined operations using coastal and river vessels. The role of commanders and officials on the spot was important, and often aggressive,[44] so that Sir Bartle Frere, Governor of Cape Province and Commander-in-Chief for South Africa, adopted an aggressive stance towards the Zulus in 1878, launching an offensive the following January against the wishes of the Colonial Secretary, while Brigadier-General Frederick Lugard, High Commissioner for the Protectorate of Northern Nigeria, pressed by the government to keep the peace with the Sokoto caliphate, was determined on war and got it in 1902. The pretext was the murder of a British officer and the failure to hand over the murderers, but other justifications included the continuation of slave raiding.

However, men on the spot played a smaller role than in earlier centuries: autonomous armed forces were less important than hitherto, while advances in communications, especially the telegraph, further increased the control of central governments by reducing the ability of frontier commanders to determine the content and flow of information. In addition, opportunities for entrepreneurs were less extensive than they had been for James Brooke as he established his position in Sarawak in the 1840s. His nephew and, from 1868, successor in Sarawak, Charles Brooke, had to cope with a government in London that was now opposed to expansion at the expense of Brunei, and instead, in 1888, protectorate agreements with Brunei, Sarawak and North Borneo (Sabah), the territory created by the British North Borneo Company, fixed the territorial situation in Borneo and thus lessened the possibility of tension with both Brunei and the European imperial power on the island, the Dutch.

Attitudes within Britain were important to the spread of empire. There was a greater emphasis than hitherto on territorial control, and sovereignty became more crucial than informal influence, in part because the profit motive was subordinated to geopolitics. Much imperial expansion from 1880 arose directly from the response to the real or apparent plans of other imperial powers, although the search for markets was also important and imperialists such as Cecil Rhodes and Lugard, who developed British power in Southern Africa and Nigeria respectively, were proponents of both business and great power rivalry. For Rhodes, the quest for new deposits of diamonds and gold, and for better terms for the mining of existing deposits, served British political interests and geopolitical needs, a quest that led him to support the idea of a railway from Cape Town to Cairo, linking two British-governed positions in order to dominate trade and to thwart other European powers.[45]

The sense of imperial mission, often linked to, or expressed in, racial and cultural arrogance, was characteristic not only of expatriate Britons but also of the Dominions, and it was displayed particularly clearly by the Australians, in their interior and in the south-west Pacific. For both New Zealand and Australia, there was a mix of commercial and strategic interests, not least concern about French and German expansion, as well as missionary activity, and a sense of racial and cultural superiority, seen for example with Richard Seddon, New Zealand Prime Minister from 1893 to 1906. This expansion encouraged a longstanding interest in the development of colonial naval power that owed much, as in 1885, to fear of Russian attack. The Crimean War had led the Governor of Victoria to order the purchase of a steamship, HMCS *Victoria*, for the colony's defence, and it was subsequently made available to help in the Waikato War in New Zealand, ferrying troops and attacking Maori *pa*. As a result of the Colonial Naval Defence Act of

1865, Victoria, the wealthiest Australian colony, ordered the building in Britain of another warship, the *Cerberus*, which arrived in 1871; although other colonies did not follow suit. In 1881, the Australian colonies pressed for a stronger British naval presence, but were unwilling to pay for it. However, the Colonial Conference held in London in 1887 accepted the idea of corporate imperial defence and agreed that more British warships should be employed to defend Australian maritime trade, while Australia and New Zealand, in return, were to provide annual payments.[46] In New Zealand, there was support for expansion in the western Pacific, particularly Samoa, while Australian interest in the region led the government of Queensland to try to annex eastern New Guinea in 1883, a step that the British government refused to support. Competition with Germany led to a more assertive British position and, having established British New Guinea, it was transferred to Australia in 1902–6.

Instead of open conflict between themselves, European powers, fearing that opportunities for expansion would soon be over, tried to pre-empt their rivals by grabbing territory, and the doctrine of 'effective occupation', developed at the Berlin Congress of colonial powers in 1884–5, encouraged a speeding up of the process of annexation. There had been British anxiety about French intentions for much of the century, especially in the Pacific and Egypt, but these became more pronounced in the 1880s and 1890s. Concern about French ambitions led to the British capture of Mandalay in 1885 and the annexation of Upper Burma the following year, although much of it was brought under only limited control and the British had to deploy 40,000 troops and military police for several years to confront a serious insurrection. Similarly, French and German expansion in Africa led Britain to take counter-measures, although economic factors, such as the search for markets and the wish to secure raw materials, for example palm oil, also played an important role. Having abandoned Sudan in 1885, the British invaded it in 1896 in order to pre-empt the French, and this led to confrontation at Fashoda in 1898. German moves in East Africa led Britain to establish its power in Uganda in the 1890s, German interest in New Guinea led Britain and the Dutch to assert claims and British expansion in Somaliland was, in part, a consequence of concern about French schemes in the region. The Russian advance into Central Asia led to British responses in Persia and Afghanistan and on the North-West Frontier of India.[47] Conversely, Spanish concern about British interest in the Sultanate of Sulu in the southern Philippines led to a Spanish expedition to Sulu in the 1870s and to an agreement with Britain in 1885, and alleged British ambitions were used to justify French expansion in West Africa in the 1880s and 1890s.

Unsurprisingly, there has been an extensive debate about the reasons for British imperial expansion in the late nineteenth century, much of which relates to matters of emphasis, although, more generally, the debate would benefit from greater comparative consideration within the context of general European imperial expansion. The extent to which imperial expansion was welcomed and planned has been debated, as has been the respective role of metropolitan drives and pressures from the periphery (in the shape both of British agents on the spot and of native peoples), and the roles of great power rivalry, economic interests and idealistic considerations. Clearly, factors varied by ministry, colony and period, but maritime strength was a crucial underpinner, as was the ready availability of credit, much of which stemmed from Britain's position in what was a maritime global economy. The existence of 'bridgeheads' in the shape of already existing colonies, the legacy of military success down to 1815, was also very important to creating interests, interest groups and expertise that aided expansion,[48] and this matched the position with the major burst of activity and expansion in the 1750s.

The combined effect of the drive from the centre and local initiatives from the imperial periphery was a major increase in British territorial power, although there was some governmental and political concern about these rising commitments, for example in Uganda. In West Africa, the British occupied the interior of Gambia in 1887–9, campaigned successfully against the Asante in 1895–6 and annexed Asante in 1901 after a rebellion had been crushed, captured Benin, defeated the Yorubas in Nigeria and established the protectorates of northern and southern Nigeria in 1900. In Sudan, the Mahdi's successor, the Khalifa Abdullahi, was defeated and killed at Umm Diwaykarat in 1899. In southern Africa, Rhodes's British South Africa Company played the major role in expanding British and Cape interests, a position legitimated by a royal charter of 1889. Rhodes became Prime Minister of the Cape Colony in 1890, and that year a Pioneer Column was sent to seize what became Southern Rhodesia (now Zimbabwe). The conquest of Northern Rhodesia (Zambia), part of Rhodes's 'Cape to Cairo' plan for British rule, followed, and resistance by the Ndebele and Shona was suppressed. In the Pacific, where Fiji had been annexed in 1875, islands and island groups were swiftly divided up, eastern New Guinea between Britain and Germany in 1884, while, as an instance of the political compromises and governmental experimentation that accompanied imperialism, New Hebrides became an Anglo-French condominium in 1906. Protectorates were declared over the Gilbert and Ellice islands in 1892 and the Solomon Islands the following year, the skill with which the expansionist Sir John Thurston, the High Commissioner for the Western Pacific, played on fears that otherwise the French would act playing a key role.[49]

In some areas, British advances led to religious–cultural disquiet and disorientation that produced movements of religious reaction; this was true of

Sudan and of the Pathans of the North-West Frontier in the 1890s, and was also the case in parts of sub-Saharan Africa, for example in Matabeleland in 1896. These and other conflicts have been reinterpreted in recent decades, as the effective denial of sovereignty to many non-European polities for long ensured that conflict with them was treated as little different from the suppression of rebellion, but shifts in assessment stemming from decolonisation have ensured that what were previously regarded as rebellions or lawlessness are now termed wars.

There were also areas where British imperial power was not expressed as territorial control, most obviously East Asia, where Japan, Korea and China did not become colonies, while the Japanese, not the British, conquered Taiwan. In China, the British acquired 'concessions', territory in the leading open ports placed under the authority of their consuls, and in 1898 leased Hong Kong's New Territories and the area of Wei-hai-wei, but these did not serve as the basis for an expansion of power and certainly not one comparable with the situation in Malaya and north Borneo. The British, nevertheless, had considerable influence in areas they did not conquer, including in the provision of naval power. William Armstrong (1810–1900), the British armaments king of his age, built warships on the Tyne for foreign powers including Argentina, Austria-Hungary, Brazil, Chile, China, Italy, Japan and Romania, and entertained foreign rulers seeking arms deals, including the Shah of Persia in 1889 and the King of Siam. However, regardless of the value of British exports, finance and protection, it would be wrong to use these as evidence of informal empire without noting, at the same time, that Britain's roles were usually accepted on terms and were subject to negotiation. More generally, with both formal and informal empire, a sense of uneasiness affected many of the Britons involved, and this was an aspect of the extent to which empires transmuted into each other as new imperial forces were used as well as yielded to, a process of nuance, if not uncertainty, captured by those who described the imperial process in terms of sexual ambiguity, and that was to be repeated in the twentieth century as American hegemony replaced British power.

THE BOER WAR

The period closed with a difficult war in southern Africa, the (Second) Boer War of 1899–1902, which challenged confidence in imperial strength, purpose and morality, although its eventual successful outcome also showed British resolve and resources. Britain's opponents were the Afrikaners, whites of Dutch descent, who had established the republics of Transvaal and Orange Free State to the north of the British possessions in South Africa. Their nationalism and fierce independence led them to oppose Britain's attempts to dominate both them and southern Africa as a whole, and in 1899 the two republics declared war on Britain. The conflict is often seen as a classic instance of capitalist-driven empire-building, but many capitalists with interests in the region concerned themselves with politics and war only when aggressive business methods did not meet their needs, and although the Boer War might never have happened had it not been for the gold and diamonds of the region upsetting the economic balance of power, it is necessary to be cautious before ascribing too much to the capitalists: those in business were less important than government figures concerned about power and prestige rather than profits. Alfred Milner, the aggressive Governor of Cape Colony from 1897 to 1901, was essentially driven by political considerations and his own ambition, and British ministers were greatly influenced by the fear that gold and diamond discoveries would enhance Boer power and ensure that the Boers would work with Britain's imperial rivals, especially the newly arrived Germans in South-West Africa, and threaten its strategic interests at the Cape; although in August 1898 Germany agreed to leave South Africa to British interests. As with the Indian Mutiny, the British were able to face a major imperial crisis without foreign intervention, although there was some concern that the French might exploit the situation.[50] In 1899, ministers in London thought the Boers were bluffing and would not put up much of a fight if war followed; while the failure of the British government to send sufficient reinforcements persuaded the Boers to think it was the British who were bluffing.

The British had already experienced the consequences of their own military blunders and the skill of Boer fire power at the battle of Majuba Hill of 1881 in the First Boer War, which had led them to acknowledge Boer independence, reversing the annexation of Transvaal in 1877. Sir William Butler, the Commander-in-Chief of British forces in South Africa, warned against fighting the Boers anew, only for his views to lead to his recall in 1899. Now, by taking the initiative and fighting well, the Boers inflicted a string of defeats in December 1899 and January 1900. However, more effective generalship under Lord Roberts and his Chief of Staff, and, later, successor, Horatio Kitchener, changed the situation in the spring and summer of 1900, as the British seized and maintained the initiative, overrunning the Orange Free State and Transvaal. Unchallenged control of the South African ports allowed Britain to bring its strength to bear and ensured that foreign intervention was not possible, while the merchant marine played a major role in providing supplies and transport.[51] The navy also blockaded Delagoa Bay to prevent supplies from reaching the Transvaal via the neutral Portuguese colony of Mozambique, and provided more direct support in the shape of naval artillery mounted on wheels and used to help the army.

Furthermore, the railways that ran inland from the ports facilitated the deployment of the very extensive military resources brought into southern Africa. Income tax, however, had to be doubled in Britain to pay for the war, and government borrowing also rose greatly, ensuring that the Conservative government's policy of low taxation, especially low income tax, and financial retrenchment, had to be abandoned under the pressure of imperial protection and expansion. Aside from the dispatch of much of the regular army, reservists, volunteer service companies and yeomanry regiments from the British Isles, the Empire, particularly Cape Colony, Australia (16,175 men), Canada and New Zealand (6,500 men),[52] also sent troops, which was a reflection of its polycentric character and also helped foster Dominion nationalism within the Empire. The colonial commanders were given considerable independence.[53]

THE SHIFT TO BATTLESHIPS

Imperial competition encouraged and highlighted the British determination to maintain their naval lead, while the process and pressures of technological enhancement continued. HMS *Inflexible*, launched in 1881, was the first battleship fitted with vertical compound engines as well as electric power for lighting, including searchlights, although these features led to its hitherto unmatched cost – £812,000 – and to a construction period of seven years. However, the power of the ship, with its four 16-inch guns, ensured that it was the prototype for four others laid down in the late 1870s, none of which had masts. The marine turbine engine, which raised efficiency and cut costs, was invented by Sir Charles Parsons in 1884, the new water-tube boiler technology of the early 1880s was introduced in large ships, and nickel-steel armoured warships were developed in the 1890s. Better engines increased the speed of heavy warships, which was seen as an important response to the threat from torpedo boats, and helped with the problem of ship design: juggling the three desirable, but mutually antagonistic qualities required of weapons platform: speed, armament and armour. The eight 14,150-ton battleships of the *Royal Sovereign* class laid down under the Naval Defence Act of 1889, the largest yet built, were capable of 18 knots. Nickel-steel gave extra protection without added weight, making it unnecessary to dispense with heavier guns in order to obtain greater speed and encouraging the construction of bigger ships, a process that required a sophisticated shipbuilding industry and much expenditure.

This protection was a necessary response to the development of chrome steel shells and armour-piercing shell caps, while the latter had increased the effectiveness of major pieces of naval ordnance, and thus provided a greater role for large ships able to carry such guns. The 110-ton, nearly 44-foot long, Armstrong breech-loading guns manufactured for HMS *Victoria*, which was built in 1885–91, were the largest and most powerful in the world. In 1890, the British introduced a more powerful 'smokeless' powder, cordite, which had a nitroglycerine base, and, because it burned more slowly and accurately, this propellant was responsible for an increase in barrel length and gun range; and in the 1890s, the British built nine battleships of the *Majestic* class: fitted with nickel-steel armour, these were the first ships to carry cordite-using big guns mounted in fully armoured centre-line turrets, the first of the group, built in only 22 months, being launched in 1895.

There was a renewed emphasis on battleships in naval doctrine in the 1890s. In part, the changes in warship capability mentioned above were crucial, as, despite the earlier appearance of steam, iron armour and breech-loading guns, the true ocean-going modern (all-steam) battleship did not really emerge until the 1890s. Growing awareness of the possibility of thwarting torpedoes involving torpedo nets, and thick belt armour around the waterline, as well as electric searchlights and quick-firing medium-calibre guns that could provide a secondary armament for use against torpedo boats, were also important, although the threat from torpedoes was enhanced by the launching of destroyers, boats equipped with both them and guns. These advances reflected British industrial capability; Armstrong was at the fore-front of technological application as well as shipbuilding, and his Elswick Ordnance Company was responsible for a marked improvement in the rate of fire of the quick firers of the secondary armament: in 1887, he demon-strated a 4.7-inch gun capable of firing ten rounds in 47.5 seconds.

There was also a shift in thought about naval warfare, particularly in response to *The Influence of Sea Power upon History, 1660–1783* (1890) by the American naval strategist Alfred Thayer Mahan, who emphasised the impor-tance of command of the sea and saw the destruction of the opponent's battle fleet as the means to achieve it. Commerce raiding was presented as less important to victory, and as a consequence Mahan put an emphasis on battleships, not cruisers. The favourable response to his work encouraged big-ship construction. In Britain, Rear-Admiral Philip Colomb's *Naval Warfare: Its Ruling Principles and Practice Historically Treated* (1891) similarly put an emphasis on command of the sea, and the role of the navy in the devel-opment and defence of trade and empire was emphasised alike by strategists and naval historians, underplaying its historical part in defence from inva-sion, a task that no longer seemed so necessary.[54]

In 1885, the invasion that seemed threatened was that of India by Russia, as the Penjdeh Crisis, arising from Russian expansionism at the expense of Afghan interests, led to British disillusionment with Russian assurances, to the placing of the navy on full alert and to consideration of plans for a naval attack on Russia, including a bombardment of Kronstadt, Russia's Baltic naval base, and amphibious operations against Batum on the Black Sea and Vladivostok, the latter to be preceded by the establishment of a base in Korea. However, the extent to which the navy could be used to help the defence of India's landward frontier was unclear, and the prospect of repeating naval power projection into the Black Sea was thwarted by opposition from the Ottoman Empire and Germany. There was also concern about India's sea defences. General Frederick Roberts, Commander-in-Chief of the Madras army 1881–5, who became Commander-in-Chief in India in 1885, noted in a memorandum that October that the ports were poorly defended, adding:

> What we require is long reaching guns for our batteries, both land and floating, and swift powerful torpedo boats. In addition, and this I believe will prove the most efficient defence, our ports should be protected by one or two swift steamers with long range guns.

Fortunately, the Penjdeh crisis was rapidly settled.[55]

Earlier, the defence of India had appeared to require the capacity to mount a counter-offensive from Alexandretta in the eastern Mediterranean, a position that could be supported only by sea.[56] More generally, the defence of India was linked to concern about the Mediterranean, for Russian naval power would have to be repelled there. The prospect of the Russians forcing the Bosphorus and Dardanelles and entering the Mediterranean led to a focus on the naval defence of the latter. A war scare with France followed in 1888.

Concern about foreign naval threats led to the development, in Britain and elsewhere, of 'navalism' – vocal pressure for a naval build-up – and also influenced the government. 'The Truth about the Navy', W. T. Stead's campaign in the *Pall Mall Gazette* in September 1884, was followed, later in the decade, by parliamentary and newspaper pressure for more ships. By pushing naval readiness to the fore as an issue, public pressure led to greater readiness to pay for the fleet, and in 1889 the Naval Defence Act led to an official commitment to a two-power standard, so that Britain should be in a position to fight the second and third largest naval powers combined with a prospect of success. This was an expensive task: £21.5 million was allocated to achieve this goal within five years.[57]

However, in the last decades of the century, in addition to the challenge from France and Russia, the traditional naval ranking, Britain, France and Russia, was challenged by the emergence of Germany, the USA and Japan, now major industrial powers with navalist ambitions. Thus, despite a substantial rise in the naval estimates, from £11 million in 1883 to £18.7 million in 1896, and a significantly larger number of battleships – 38 in 1883, 62 in service or construction in 1897 – the relative size of the navy declined.[58] British naval construction was driven most by closer Franco-Russian co-operation, which included an alliance in 1892, the first alliance between the second and third strongest naval powers that Britain had had to face since the Franco-Spanish co-operation of the Napoleonic period, and by the expansion of the Russian navy. This led to the Spencer programme, approved in December 1893, under which the *Majestic* class was built, and the extent of anxiety about naval strength, specifically of supporting French action in the Mediterranean in the event of a Russian attack on the Ottoman Empire, led to all the ships being laid down within 15 months. This anxiety also led to the building of new battleships after the *Majestic* class entered service, ensuring that Britain more than met the two-power standard: 20, each modelled on the *Majestic* class, were laid down in 1896–1901, while ten armoured cruisers were laid down in 1898–9. The eight battleships of the 15,585-ton *King Edward VII* class started in 1902–4 followed, as did 22 armoured cruisers laid down in 1899–1904.

American diplomatic support for Venezuela in her 1895–6 border dispute with Britain over the border of British Guiana led, however, to concern that the two-power standard would not be enough, but such fears were not fulfilled in 1898, when, in the Fashoda crisis with France, which stemmed from competing interests in Africa, the British mounted an impressive display of naval power in Atlantic and Mediterranean waters, the crisis did not widen and France backed down. In fact, despite their treaty, Franco-Russian naval co-operation was limited. To strengthen Britain's position in the Mediterranean, and make it easier to handle larger ships, work started in Gibraltar in 1895 on a mole and an extension of the dockyard,[59] while concern with the Mediterranean axis led to the deepening of the Suez Canal in 1898. Anxiety was not limited to the Mediterranean. Already in 1885, a permanent interdepartmental Colonial Defence Committee had been established in order to keep an eye on colonial security, and, two years later, imperial defence, understood principally in terms of the defence of the navy's coaling stations, was a major topic for the meeting of colonial government leaders in London.[60]

In 1895, in his *History of the Foreign Policy of Great Britain*, Captain Montagu Burrows R.N. (1819–1905), Chichele Professor of Modern History at Oxford, had seen sea power as the vital defence of national interests. Burrows, who also wrote a biography of Hawke, saw Britain's destiny as

prescribed by nature and approved by experience . . . This fortress-isle of Britain, safely intrenched by stormy seas, confronting the broadest face of the Continent, and, later on, almost surrounding it with her fleets, was,

and was not, a part of Europe according as she willed . . . her strong position as an extra-Continental Power, – a position which, as her navy, her
commerce, and her colonies grew, expanded into that of a world-wide
maritime empire'.[61]

ATTITUDES TO EMPIRE

For long, most British scholars treated British imperialism as different in
type from its Continental counterparts – more hesitant, commercial, moral
and defensive – but this approach, or aspects of it, is increasingly questioned.
There is also debate about the domestic political resonance of empire, which
was not simply a matter of power politics, military interests, elite careers and
an ideology of mission and progress that appealed to the propertied and
proselytising.[62] Instead, the missionary activity of religious groups reflected
and developed an activism among wide sections of the public, while, most
clearly in the final decades of the century, empire had relevance and meaning
throughout society. This was reflected in the jingoistic strains of popular
culture: adventure stories, the ballads of the music hall and the images
depicted on advertisements for mass-produced goods. George Alfred Henty
(1832–1902), who had been a war correspondent on the expeditions to
Ethiopia in 1868 and against the Asante in 1873–4, following the heroes
of empire, Napier and Wolseley, also wrote popular adventure stories
for children, such as *Under Drake's Flag* (1883) and *With Clive in India: or the
Beginnings of an Empire* (1884), which enjoyed substantial sales. In the preface
of his *With Wolfe in Canada: The Winning of a Continent* (1887), Henty stressed
Britain's trans-oceanic destiny, adding in a passage that distinguished Britain
from France, and was ironic given the course of British policy over the
following century, 'Never was the short-sightedness of human beings
shown more distinctly than when France wasted her strength and treasure
in a sterile contest on the continent of Europe, and permitted, with
scarce an effort, her North American colonies to be torn from her'. Henty
brought his imperial manliness up to date with imperial expansion in *With
Kitchener in the Soudan* (1903).[63]

The reputation of soldier heroes, such as Robert Napier, Garnet
Wolseley, Frederick Roberts, Horatio Kitchener and Charles Gordon, fed a
tradition of exemplary imperial masculinity, a combination of Anglo-Saxon
authority, superiority and martial prowess, with Protestant religious zeal
and moral righteousness.[64] This might seem ironic given allegations of
Kitchener's homosexuality, but the emphasis was on public appearance.
Gordon's death at Khartoum in 1885 at the hands of the Mahdists provided
Victorians with an epic of manly sacrifice, while the virtue of fortitude

was the lesson drawn from heroic sieges, such as Lucknow (1857), Rorke's Drift (1878), Chitral (1895) and Mafeking (1900). In turn, the popularity of empire-building contributed to that of both generals and soldiers,[65] and although naval successes were fewer than prior to 1815, they were celebrated, while the legacy of Nelson was commemorated frequently. The inspiration of imperial manliness and the role of empire-building in the development of national character was to be taken forward by Robert Baden-Powell (1857–1941), a hero of the Boer War who in 1908 founded the Boy Scouts.[66]

The sieges of the Indian Mutiny and the Boer War offered drama for the entire country and, in the developing imperial press system,[67] for the empire. Newspapers spent substantial sums on the telegraphy that brought news of imperial conflict, and war correspondents rose to the challenge posed by newspaper proprietors, offering an heroic and uncritical account of imperial conflict, which was matched in open-air spectacles, and, in turn, by the newly developed cinema. Jack Hunt, a private in the Scots Guards, described the British entry into Pretoria in 1900 in a letter to his brother: 'When we marched into the market square headed by Lord Roberts to raise the flag they took our photo by the cinematograph so I expect you will see it on some of the music halls in London'.[68] Empire was indeed staged actively, in music-hall, melodrama, blackface minstrelsy and exhibitions, such as *The Empire of India* exhibition in London in 1895, or the *Stanley and Africa* exhibition five years earlier.[69]

Such coverage does not imply that imperialism was popular with all the working class, for many workers appear to have been pretty apathetic and recruitment for the army was a major problem. The London crowds that applauded the relief of Mafeking in 1900 were mainly clerks and medical students, rather than labourers, while those who volunteered to serve in South Africa were not a representative cross-section. Nevertheless, all were exposed to an educational and print culture that took empire for granted and that regarded empire-building as part of the British national character. Maps such as George Parkin's *The British Empire Map of the World on Mercator's Projection* (Edinburgh, 1893) encouraged pride in the breadth of the Empire, while William Ernest Henley (1849–1903) began *England, my England*, a poem that speaks the values of the age,

> What have I done for you,
> England, my England?
> What is there I would not do,
> England, my own?
> With your glorious eyes austere,
> As the Lord were walking near,

> Whispering terrible things and dear
> As the Song on your bugles blown,
> England –
> Round the world on your bugles blown!

He continued by referring to 'Such a breed of mighty men', presenting England as 'You whose mail'd hand keeps the keys/Of such teeming destinies' and began the last verse 'Mother of ships whose might,/England, my England,/Is the fierce old Sea's delight'. Henley also used his editorship of the *Scots Observer* (later *National Observer*) in 1889–94 to give voice to his Tory imperialism, and published the young Kipling – the latter's barrack-room ballads *Fuzzy-Wuzzy*, *Gunga Din* and *Mandalay* appearing in the review in 1890. Henley also played a role in Britain's maritime image: an amputee, he was the model for Long John Silver in Robert Louis Stevenson's *Treasure Island* (1883). As a reminder of the range of response to empire, Stevenson (1850–1894), in search of better health, spent the last years of his life in Samoa, becoming a bitter critic of Western colonial exploitation in *The Beach of Falesá* (1893) and *The Ebb-Tide* (1894).

Despite criticism of imperialism, the sea and ships offered potent images of national strength and mission. These were captured most vividly on canvas by Turner, and industriously, if less memorably, by a host of painters whose works were also engraved, such as William Wyllie. Images of ships and shipping hung on the walls of clubs and cottages, while the activities of Naval Brigades were also celebrated, as in W. H. Overend's painting of a sketch by the war artist Melton Prior, *Blue Jackets to the Front!*, which showed a resolute and eager group of sailors in 1884 running forward with a light gun past the bodies of dead Sudanese warriors. Sailors also played a positive role in music-hall songs and in operettas, as with the patriotic robustness and pride-in-nation displayed in Gilbert and Sullivan's popular comic-operatta HMS *Pinafore* (1878): 'His bosom should heave and his heart should glow,/And his fist be ever ready for a knock-down blow'. Whereas, owing to their recruitment patterns, army regiments had strong local roots, the navy was more clearly a national force. Sailors and the navy also came to play a major role in the world of things, appearing as pottery figures and on tins and featuring prominently in advertisements, for example for tobacco, which was presented by such an association in masculine terms, the sailor being linked to strong tobacco. Advertising was linked by the celebration of naval power and heritage, which took many forms, including a benign view of naval heroes, not least the defence of Sir John Hawkins from being the founder of the slave trade.[70] Alfred, Lord Tennyson, the Poet Laureate, in *The Revenge* (1880), took an important role in the celebration of the bravery of Elizabethan Seadogs:

And the sun went down, and the stars came out far over the
   summer sea,
But never a moment ceased the fight of the one and the fifty-three.
. . .
God of battles, was ever a battle like this in the world before.

The poetic appeal of the sea was also demonstrated in Kipling's *The Seven
Seas* (1896), a work that reflected a shift in the writer's interests, also seen
in his *A Fleet in Being* (1899), away from India and towards a maritime
concept of empire.[71] Henry Newbolt's popular collections of poetry –
Admirals All and Other Verses (1897) and *The Island Race* (1898) – linked
maritime destiny with manly patriotism. Less poetically, over 2.5 million
visitors thronged the naval exhibition on the Thames embankment in
London in May to October 1891, while, three years later, the Navy League
was formed in order to orchestrate public pressure for naval strength, part
of the competitive navalism of the period. Interest in the heritage led to
the foundation of the Navy Records Society in 1893.[72]

The Golden and Diamond jubilees of Queen Victoria, in 1887 and 1897
respectively, showed how much empire was part of British identity and ceremonial. Each was marked by major fleet reviews at Spithead, the latter, in
which 165 warships, all from the home station, took part, being particularly
spectacular as the ships were deployed in five lines and covered over
30 miles. Within Britain, the jubilees saw much striking of imperial themes
and, indeed, in 1876 Victoria had become the first Empress of India. In 1896,
the Earl of Meath launched Empire Day on 24 May, Victoria's birthday.

Identity and ceremonial were for the Empire as well as Britain, and in
settlement colonies there was a ready transfusion of both, not least in sport.
In other colonies, however, there was a need to incorporate existing hierarchies, interests and rituals, which was particularly pronounced in India,
where the princely dynasties that had gained effective independence with
the decline of the Mughal Empire in the eighteenth century, only to be
overawed by the British, were wooed from the 1870s by the creation of an
anglicised princely hierarchy that gave them roles and honours, such as the
orders of the Star of India and the Indian Empire, in accordance with British
models and interests, a process that was also to be followed in Malaya. This
led to a stress on status, not race,[73] that is easy to criticise, not least because
an emphasis on inherited privilege served as a brake on inculcating values
of economic, social and political development, but it was also a response to
the large amount of India that had been left under princely rule, and helped
consolidate the 'internal frontier' of imperialism.[74] Furthermore, the search
for support in India and elsewhere was a multi-layered one, extending

to the co-option or creation of professional and administrative groups able to meet local as well as imperial needs.

CONCLUSIONS

When Queen Victoria died in 1901, there was much talk of Britain as the uniquely successful imperial power, but at the same time the Empire itself was in flux. Thanks, in part, to the diffusion within the Empire of British notions of community, identity and political action, and British practices of politicisation, specifically democratisation, there was opposition to imperial control, although it was limited in scope. The Indian National Congress was formed in 1885 and the Egyptian National Party in 1897, but simultaneously there was a considerable measure of compliance with British rule, in part reflecting the co-option of traditional local elites, as in much of India. Imperial power also provided opportunities for those who were upwardly mobile, and, in particular, the products of new Western-style educational institutions found opportunities in government and commerce.

The granting of Dominion status to 'settlement colonies' became a peaceful evolutionary route to independence, reducing what might otherwise have been difficulties in relations with Australasia and Canada, and sustaining the organic notions of national strength that had contributed to support for imperial expansion. Canada became a Dominion in 1867, Australia in 1901 and New Zealand in 1907; in the first two cases, the creation of statehood out of what had been a group of disparate colonies. Colonial and Imperial conferences from 1887 helped give the Dominions a voice in imperial policy. They were prefigured from 1867 by the Lambeth Conferences of colonial bishops, which provided a system of consultation that helped support the continued acknowledgement of the spiritual authority and leadership of Archbishops of Canterbury.

It was far from clear how empire would develop, and different goals and strategies were actively pushed. Pressure, in Ireland and Britain, for 'Home Rule' for Ireland reflected the widespread support among politicians expressing, and accommodating, aspirations for autonomy while keeping Ireland in the Empire, but the measure was defeated in 1886 and 1893 as a result of the strength of unionist feeling at Westminster. Alongside the support, at the start of the twentieth century, for close links with 'white' colonies, which were pushed by Joseph Chamberlain and the tariff reformers, there was also interest in the development of a powerful Asiatic Empire, which was advocated by George, Lord Curzon, Viceroy of India from 1898 to 1905. He pressed a forward policy – in Tibet, on the North-West Frontier of India, and in the Persian Gulf – and sought to strengthen British government of India, not least by stabilising it in a conservative fashion through closer alliance with the native princes.

There were also serious questions confronting British naval power. The isolation of the British Empire in the Boer War had been accompanied by much international criticism, and in 1899 there were disturbing rumours about the prospect of French and Russian military support, possibly with German backing. The navy responded by focusing on being able to defend the route from Britain to South Africa, but the crisis underlined the sense of vulnerability frequently expressed over the previous two decades. Already, in 1885, at the time of the Penjdeh crisis, the prospect of responding successfully to any Russian advance into Afghanistan was felt to be lessened both by the commitment of British forces to Sudan, and by the need to retain troops in India in order to prevent a rebellion; and this was before the added threat that followed when France allied with Russia. As the twentieth century began, there were differing indications of the future of the British Empire and of the strength of its naval power. In 1901, the 2nd Earl of Selborne, the First Lord of the Admiralty, wrote to Curzon,

> I would not quarrel with the United States if I could possibly avoid it. It has not dawned on our countrymen yet, but doubtless it has on you as it has on me, that, if the Americans chose to pay for what they can easily afford, they can gradually build up a Navy, firstly as large and then larger than ours and I am not sure they will not do it.[75]

7
EMPIRE UNDER CHALLENGE, 1901–1918

War will come like the Day of Judgement . . . there will be no more time for building submarines than there will be for repentance . . . The finality of a modern sea fight – once beaten, the war is finished.

> Sir John Fisher, First Lord of the Admiralty[1]

The maintenance of naval supremacy is our whole foundation. Upon it stands not the Empire only, not merely the great commercial prosperity of our people, not merely a fine place in the world's affairs. Upon our naval supremacy stands our lives and the freedom we have guarded for nearly a thousand years.

> Winston Churchill, newly appointed First Lord of the Admiralty,
> Lord Mayor's Banquet, London, 9 November 1911

They shall not return to us, the resolute, the young,
The eager and whole-hearted whom we gave.

> *Mesopotamia* (1917), Kipling's comment on the debacle of the Kut
> campaign in 1915

Challenge was scarcely a novelty for the British Empire. At the military level, there had been a series of invasion threats and attempts from the sixteenth century, culminating in the crisis of 1805, while, in ideological, religious and cultural terms, all of which were inter-related, there had also been serious challenges, many linked to these invasion threats, in the same period. In some respects, the crisis of empire in the early twentieth century can be seen as a return to an earlier situation after a Regency and Victorian highnoon of security. Indeed, in the Second World War, Sir Arthur Bryant, a crypto-Fascist, was able to position himself as a patriot by publishing works on the struggle with Napoleon that were clearly designed to highlight this sense of parallel.[2] This approach is lent further support by the work on leading powers by political scientists, who tend to propound a cyclical theory of rise and fall, while, although not expressed in these terms, the sense of recurrence taps into a more profound organic understanding of nationhood, an understanding that dominated much earlier thought about empires.

Whereas commentators in the eighteenth century focused on the moral aspects of strength and ideology, and saw the seeds of imperial decline in self-indulgence and a lack of public spirit, their twentieth-century counterparts were predisposed to search out economic causes for decline, and here a crisis can, and could, be discerned from the late nineteenth century, in large part because of American and German economic growth, in both quantitative and qualitative terms. No longer the world's leading economic power, how could Britain expect to be the leading empire? This argument can then be traced forward to note the interaction between economic decline and the strains of international competition, as war placed a formidable burden on the economy and, even more, the public finances, while the difficulties of both made it harder to sustain Britain's imperial position. Thus, for example, the decline in British industrial capacity in the inter-war period, especially in shipbuilding and related industries, made it more difficult to meet the challenge of defeating Germany and Japan at sea during the Second World War.

THE EMPIRE BEFORE THE FIRST WORLD WAR, 1901–1914

While there is much to this analysis, it is important not to anticipate decline and crisis. Although, for example, manufacturing in Britain was hit hard from the 1880s, with the Sunderland shipyards suffering empty order books and wage cuts, and much of British agriculture in severe difficulties, the economy still had considerable potential at the beginning of the century. Aside from her major, sometimes leading, role in the production of goods such as coal, textiles, steel, iron and ships, Britain was also playing a major part in the development of new sectors: in the growth of production in chemicals and in new consumer products, such as motor cars and telephones.

In 1902, Arthur Benson's words for 'Land of Hope and Glory', the first of Edward Elgar's *Pomp and Circumstance* marches, were first heard as part of the Coronation Ode for Edward VII (r. 1901–10). They promised a steadily 'wider' empire. The Empire was indeed not only the most extensive and populous in the world, but was still expanding rapidly, although in the case of Elgar (who had not written the marches with the expectation that words would be set to them), there is little sign that he was a militarist.[3] The Empire also dominated the production of many important goods, while imperial products were processed, manufactured and marketed in Britain, and it was from there that the finance for their exploitation and transport came. In an industrial system where metal bashing played a major role, the British benefited from the availability of iron, and from their ability to import copper from Canada and tin from Malaya. Britain also dominated the export of coal, the major energy source, while her finances benefited from South African gold, as there was a greater demand for gold (with which most currencies were convertible) than was available, and, in 1914, largely thanks to heavy investment, 40 per cent of the world's gold came from the Transvaal. Furthermore, British manufactures flowed to imperial markets. In 1896, 27 per cent of the exports of the British cotton industry went to India, while by 1913 India's trade with Britain was worth £120 million, and that year 14.7 per cent of Britain's gross national product was exported. In addition to trades focused on Britain, important economic links developed within the Empire with many consequences: for example, the export of rice from Burma to India led to a substantial expansion in the acreage under rice in Burma, with important environmental effects in the Irrawaddy delta.

If, by the 1900s, Britain's share in world trade had fallen, that trade was now far larger, and the decline was only a relative, not an absolute, fall. Partly as a result, dock facilities expanded, and the 1911 census recorded 167,000 men employed in the ports. In northern Lincolnshire, where Grimsby's capacity had been expanded with the opening of the Alexandra Dock in 1880, a completely new dock was opened at Immingham in 1912. Moreover, as the largest overseas investor in the world, with a third of her wealth invested abroad in 1913, Britain was able to benefit from economic growth elsewhere, while, at the centre of the world's financial and communications system, Britain benefited from the expansion of the service sector, and global commodity prices, shipping rates and insurance premiums were all set in London. The pound sterling was the international reserve currency in a global financial system that relied on a fixed exchange rate regime, while Britain's financial strength helped ensure political influence.[4]

Britain was still the greatest merchant shipper and shipbuilder in the world. In his poem 'Cargoes' (1903), John Masefield, who was to become Poet Laureate in 1930, was able to present the three ages of marine trade through a 'Quinquireme of Nineveh', a 'Stately Spanish galleon', and, lastly, a 'Dirty British coaster', carrying a cargo of British exports. Masefield (1878–1967) had become a sailor in the merchant navy at the age of 13, being sent to Chile, but in 1895, on his second voyage, he deserted in New York. Nevertheless, the sea played a major role in his writings and his first major collection of poems, *Salt-Water Ballads* (1902), included, in 'Sea Fever', one of the most memorable accounts of the appeal of the sea: 'I must go down to the sea again, to the lonely sea and the sky'; while a lengthy sea-voyage featured in his narrative poem 'Dauber' (1913). The reach of

Masefield is suggested by the way in which learning poems such as 'Cargoes' and 'Sea Fever' was required of generations of schoolchildren, including myself in the early 1960s. Masefield's successors as Poet Laureate have lacked his maritime interests, but in his day Masefield was not alone – Henry Newbolt, for example, produced popular collections of poetry including *The Sailing of the Long-Ships* (1902) and *Songs of Memory and Hope* (1909), while his history *The Year of Trafalgar* (1905) captured the mood of national celebration at the time of the battle's centenary. Newbolt was later an offi-cial war historian, writing *The Naval History of the Great War* (1920), and his famous poems include 'The Fighting Téméraire'.

'Sea Fever' testified to the appeal of sailing: 'all I ask is a tall ship and a star to steer her by'. Despite the continued importance of sailboats, espe-cially for much local trade, it was the world of steam that was the focus of maritime industry. In 1892–4, Britain had built 82 per cent of the world's ships, and in 1910–14 the proportion was still 62 per cent.[5] Because the British were the biggest shippers in the world, the Empire's total being about 45 per cent of world tonnage and the UK's 39 per cent, the merchant marine created extensive employment opportunities. Most of these were taken by Britons, 119,000 in shipping according to the 1911 census (with 155,000 in shipbuilding), although recruitment from the Empire was also important and helped increase racial diversity in Britain as large communities of Lascar (Indian) or Chinese seamen were established in port areas, for example on the Clyde, the Tyne and the Thames. This was the first large-scale exposure of Britons to non-Europeans, certainly outside London.

Income from shipping services made a major contribution to British finances, as did the sale of ships to foreign shippers. Although there were already signs of problems in shipbuilding,[6] the launching of big ships, such as the *Aquitania* into the purposely deepened and widened river at Clydebank in 1913, an episode that reflected the combined resources of industry and capital, were impressive occasions that captured the public imagination. So also, with an even stronger burst of patriotism, was the launching of warships. Less dramatic were the successes of trans–oceanic businesses such as the Royal Niger Company which specialised in the import of palm oil from Nigeria for soap manufacture.

At a more mundane level, but one that brought far more people into contact with the sea, the fishing industry was in a buoyant state as far as the fishing of waters round the British Isles was concerned, and the 1911 census recorded 53,000 men employed in the industry. The domestic market for fish had been expanded by the spread of the rail system, so that fish could be sped by train to urban markets, and this and the opportunities pro-vided by the application of steam power encouraged investment, especially in larger boats. Furthermore, the integration of the industry assisted the process by which boats moved between fishing areas, as with Scottish ships following the herring in the North Sea, or Lowestoft herring boats moving south-west after the East Anglian 'Home Fishing' was over. Fish was also exported, for example herring to northern Europe.[7]

Despite pressure in particular sectors, Britain was doing well in the liberal international economic order, and the adoption of the Greenwich meridian was a symbolic indication of this success. The maritime powers had used different standard meridians: for the British, it passed through Greenwich, for the French Paris, the Dutch Amsterdam, the Spaniards Tenerife, and the Portuguese Cape St. Vincent, while, in 1850, Congress decided that the National Observatory should be the standard meridian for the USA. Consistency was established with difficulty, and then only as a grudging acknowledgement of the need for uniformity and of Britain's maritime dominance. An international meeting of 1884 chose the Greenwich meridian as the zero meridian for time-keeping and for the determination of longitude, the French abandoned the Paris meridian in 1911, and the American Act of 1850 was repealed in 1912.[8] The standardisation of the zero meridian was an important aspect of a more general consequence of British power in terms of the implementation of British norms, for example in legal disputes. This was pressed furthest within the Empire with the use of standard weights and measures and with the development of currency and postal links.

Maritime images remained important in the symbolisation of British power. In 1913, the so-called Sea Horses design, Britannia in a chariot pulled across the waters by horses, was used for the high value George v stamps that were issued. A more dramatic impression of Britain's worldwide energy was provided in 1912 by Captain Scott's unsuccessful attempt to be the first to the South Pole, and by Shackleton's polar expedition in 1914, both presented as heroic epics.[9]

Migration patterns were another aspect of a dynamic empire. There was an emigration surge in the 1900s, and although the numbers emigrating to the USA did not drop, they were of decreasing significance as a greater percentage went to the colonies, particularly Canada; although emigration from there to the USA was important.[10]

The Empire also posed economic problems for Britain, providing direct competition for much of her agriculture, while, to a certain extent, imperial markets lessened the pressure to improve the industrial base in order to succeed in more difficult markets, especially in Continental Europe and the USA. Competition from outside the Empire, particularly from the rapidly growing economies of Germany and the USA, nevertheless encouraged calls for the replacement of free trade through tariff reform (protectionism) in order to create a self-sufficient imperial trading block. In 1902, Joseph

Chamberlain, the Liberal Unionist Colonial Secretary and an advocate of an empire based on co-operation, told the Colonial Conference:

> The weary Titan staggers under the too vast orb of its fate. We have borne the burden for many years. We think that it is time that our children should assist us to support it . . . If you are prepared at any time to take any share in the burdens of Empire, we are prepared to meet you with any proposal for giving you a corresponding vote in the policy of the Empire.[11]

He also presented an account of branches of the economy that were withering, or under pressure from international competition. Chamberlain's hope of imperial federation, to be achieved through imperial preference and protection foundered, however, upon British hostility to tariffs on food imports and upon residual faith in free trade. Yet, although rejected, with the rest of the Unionist (Conservative and Liberal Unionist) programme, by the electorate in 1906 and 1910, this was largely owing to Liberal success in arguing that Chamberlain's policies would lead to more expensive food, rather than hostility to the idea of an imperial bloc.[12] The Dominions Royal Commission, established after the Imperial Conference of 1911 in order to investigate the economic potential of the Dominions, was scarcely a fulfilment of Chamberlain's hopes.

Much else was involved in the Unionist defeats, not least the sense that the Unionist government of 1895–1905 had become tired and support, in 1910, for Liberal social welfare policies, but Chamberlain's failure invites consideration of the strength and depth of imperial sentiment both within Britain and in the colonies, and on how Britons and colonists identified themselves: nationally, imperially or a compound of both. There has been considerable debate over the imperial content of such varied but apparently emblematic works and events as Elgar's music and the celebrations of the relief of Mafeking in 1900. These and other episodes can be seen as patriotic, chauvinistic and national, rather than imperial, or it could be argued that such a distinction is of limited value, not least because the Empire was seen as both product and part of the nation.

Indeed, the British nation was not regarded as limited to one state or country, and the values that accrued to empire offered therefore an extensive fluidity that encompassed Britons abroad, although they could also serve to exclude immigrants. The relationship between national and imperial identity can be seen in a number of respects, not least the freedom to move within the Empire and the character of voluntarist bodies pledged to imperial and national assertion, such as the Tariff Reform League, the Navy League and the Emigration Committee of the Royal Colonial Institute.[13]

If such bodies were dominated by the middle class, that was more generally true of the voluntarist sector, including female voluntarist societies. The relationship between empire and issues of gender has engaged considerable scholarly concern in recent years, and works on empire now routinely (and profitably) address it.[14] There was in the Victorian and Edwardian period a potent image of empire as masculine or, rather, pertaining to values, such as fortitude, seen as masculine, but that did not exclude an explicit role for women, alongside the reality of their largely unacknowledged activities as wives, mothers and workers, all of which contributed greatly. The Victoria League, which was the leading voluntarist movement in this sphere, supported female emigration and served to underline the role of empire as a place of domesticity, family and the virtues of home, as well as the masculine assertion more prominently discussed and celebrated.[15]

There were also significant political differences over empire, although the opposition of some prominent Liberals, such as David Lloyd George, to the Boer War benefited the Unionists under Robert, 3rd Marquess of Salisbury when a 'khaki election' was held in October 1900, as most of the electorate then had no doubts about the expansion of empire, and, in that election, only 184 Liberals were elected and no fewer than 163 government supporters were elected unopposed. The detention of Boer civilians in camps where 27,927 died from disease was criticised, but was less emotive an issue for contemporary Britons than was subsequently suggested by the misleading comparison with Nazi Germany implied by the use of the term concentration camps to describe the policies of both.

Attitudes to empire were closely related to domestic politics, with the important link being supplied by Ireland, the future status of which contributed strongly to crises in politics and national identity in the early 1910s.[16] The Liberal Unionists, who had abandoned the Liberals to join the Conservatives in opposition to Irish Home Rule, such as Chamberlain, tended to press hard for measures to strengthen the Empire: for consolidation if not expansion. They and the Conservatives felt that what they saw as a Liberal threat to the Empire was a matter of Liberal views on domestic politics, Ireland and colonial policy,[17] and the progressive Liberal criticism of J. A. Hobson's *Imperialism: A Study* (1902) was unwelcome to them. At the same time, the support of Liberal Unionists and Conservative paternalists for social welfare in large part rested on a desire to strengthen the country and, with it, the Empire, rather than on individual amelioration. A preoccupation with national degeneration dated back to the 1880s and focused on the alleged degeneration rising from the country's increasingly urban and industrial nature. Poor urban housing, sanitation and nutrition were widely blamed for the physical weakness of much of the country, and this was seen as a threat to the Empire. Both army and police were concerned about the health of recruits.

Despite the strength of the Empire, there was a mounting sense of challenge, as the imperial competitiveness of the late nineteenth century ensured that Britain's commitments and opportunities around the world put her into competition with other Western powers, especially France, Germany, Russia and the USA. France and Russia appeared the most acute threats in the 1890s, and in 1898, in the Fashoda Crisis, Britain came near to war with France over Sudan. There were also a number of issues in dispute in the New World with the USA, particularly the Canadian frontier, while growing American assertiveness challenged British interests in Latin America and the Pacific. However, Britain managed her disputes with the USA skilfully and accepted American hegemony in the Western hemisphere, in part by being more conciliatory over the Canadian–American frontier and the dispute over seal fishing rights in the Bering Sea than the Canadians would have preferred,[18] and, in turn, the Americans did not seek to overthrow the British Empire, so that, in 1908, the Committee of Imperial Defence and the Foreign Office concluded that the possibility of war with the USA was remote;[19] although that was not to prevent American contingency plans for the invasion of Canada.

Competition over empire changed in character in the 1900s, as areas of expansion had already been allocated or, increasingly, were delimited. In 1898, the grave Portuguese financial crisis had led to a secret Anglo-German treaty allocating Angola and Mozambique, the major Portuguese colonies in Africa, in the event of Portugal wishing to sell them, which in fact she was not to do, while, in West Africa, the Anglo-French Treaty of 1898, which divided Hausaland, led to a joint frontier commission in 1906–8 that produced the modern boundary between Niger and Nigeria; and the Nigeria–Cameroon Boundary Commission followed in 1912–13. This process was repeated throughout the world. In addition, non-Western powers such as China, Persia, Thailand and Turkey were pressed into agreeing to Western demands about disputed frontiers, and, in this, the British proved forceful. In 1909, the Malay sultanates of Kedah, Kelantan, Terengganu and Perlis were transferred from Siamese (Thai) to British protection, while British determination to protect the Suez Canal led to a demarcation of the Egyptian–Turkish frontier on British terms in 1906, and Britain and Turkey also reached agreement on their respective spheres of influence in Arabia, drawing boundaries known as the Blue (1913) and Violet (1914) Lines. In 1913, the British obtained Turkish agreement on a boundary with Persia, where Britain had important economic and strategic interests, and this led to the Constantinople Protocol of that year, which clarified the delimitation, and to a Frontier Commission that continued its work until the outbreak of the First World War, and, in 1913–14, the British imposed the McMahon Line as the Indian–Tibetan border.

Elsewhere pressure was more forceful. In 1904, a British force advanced to Lhasa, the capital of Tibet, in order to dictate terms. En route, at Guru, it opened fire on Tibetans who were unwilling to disarm, and in large part owing to their two Maxim guns, four cannon and effective rifles, the British killed nearly 700 Tibetans without any losses of their own. Thanks to the resources of the Empire, this advance was supported by 10,000 coolies (human porters), 7,000 mules, 5,000 bullocks and over 4,000 yaks. The previous year, the British had smashed the army of the Emirate of Sokoto at Burmi in Nigeria, with vastly disproportionate casualties, and had brought resistance in northern Nigeria to an end, while in Kenya in 1905 the field force sent to suppress resistance among the nomadic Nandi used its ten Maxims to cause heavy casualties. In a subsequent expedition, 407 Embu were killed, but only two among the field force. However, victory did not end difficulties, for the expansion of imperial rule from the late nineteenth century posed anew the problem of how best to govern newly gained lands.

As the British crossed the Himalayas on the way to Lhasa, British ministers and commentators were also having to consider a threat nearer home: Germany. Unification in 1866–71 had produced an assertive state that was increasingly regarded by Britain as a challenge, and in terms of containment. Alongside anxiety about her apparently dominant position in Europe, came concern about German naval and commercial policy, and over her colonial ambitions in Africa, China and the Pacific.[20] A German threat also became a theme in imaginative literature, and a projected German invasion was central to *The Riddle of the Sands* (1903), a very successful novel by Erskine Childers that was first planned in 1897, a year in which the Germans indeed discussed such a project.[21] German naval expansion, which had begun in 1898 and was intended to produce a fleet capable of making Germany a world power,[22] worried the British government.

Britain also came to play a greater role in international power politics, turning away from the non-interventionism, indeed isolationism, that had characterised her policy, especially since the Crimean War of 1854–6, and acknowledging that alliances served her interests and the pursuit of stability. Alliance with Japan in 1902, which took far further the 1894 treaty of commerce and navigation, helped Britain do so by reducing her exposure in Far Eastern waters. The alliance obliged the signatories to provide help if the other was attacked by two or more powers, thus bringing Japan into the equation against France and Russia. There were also secret agreements to align naval signal systems and for wartime logistical co-operation. The alliance had a more direct benefit, as it was followed by the recall of the five battleships on the China station.

Britain and France moved closer together with an *entente* in 1904. This was an understanding, not an alliance, and did not include mandatory provisions such as were included in the Anglo-Japanese Alliance of 1902. Thereafter, co-operation with France came to play a bigger role in British thinking. This has recently excited controversy as revisionists have argued that it would have been more appropriate to remain neutral and disengaged from the Continent, and that this would have left the Empire in a better shape, an assessment that underrates the extent to which German attitudes aroused alarm in Britain. The defeat of France's ally, Russia, in the Russo-Japanese war of 1904–5, a defeat that owed much to the successful adoption of Western, especially British, naval techniques by the Japanese, badly damaged the Russian navy and weakened Russia as a balancing element within Europe, exposing France to German diplomatic pressure and creating British alarm about German intentions, especially in the First Moroccan Crisis of 1905–6. This crisis, provoked by Germany, was followed by Anglo-French staff talks aimed at dealing with a German threat, and their consequences were to play a major role in leading Britain towards the First World War. In 1907, British military manoeuvres were conducted for the first time on the basis that Germany, not France, was the enemy,[23] while, that year, fears of Germany also contributed to an Anglo-Russian *entente*. Thus, Britain moved closer to a power with whom it had competed for hegemony in South Asia for decades, and, indeed, the *entente* involved a delimitation of their spheres of influence in Persia, a country in which they had long competed.

THE NAVAL RACE

Ententes were not alliances, but Britain's changing international position affected her naval deployment and grand strategy. Whereas any conflict with France and Russia would require squadrons around the world, not least in the Mediterranean (an area of concern during the Fashoda Crisis in 1898) and the Pacific, confrontation with Germany, a state with a smaller empire than France, encouraged the focus on home waters already desirable for reasons of cost and already facilitated by alliance with Japan. The worldwide nature of the British naval presence was important in one particular respect, in that it encouraged recruitment.[24] The emphasis, however, not least in the 'hierarchy of language' in strategic plans for the navy and other documents, put a clear stress on the defence of the British Isles, and the Dominions were treated as secondary.[25] In turn, the Dominions pursued their own naval views: at the 1911 Imperial Conference, both Australia and Canada expressed their opposition to a single Imperial navy (the Royal Australian Navy was founded in 1911), while in 1913 Liberal opposition in the Senate thwarted the plan of the Canadian government to order three capital ships, a measure that would have contributed to imperial naval strength.

At the Admiralty, Sir John ('Jacky') Fisher, the First Sea Lord from 1904 to 1910 and again from 1914 to 1915, had originally planned a focus in naval construction on battle-cruisers, a new type of ship designed to have more firepower than existing battleships or cruisers, but to be quicker than battleships owing to reduced armour and the use of Parsons turbine engines. It has been argued that he saw the new battleship HMS *Dreadnought*, launched in 1906, as a one-off, but, instead, confrontation with Germany encouraged an emphasis on battleships, not on the global range offered by battle-cruisers. Furthermore, Japanese victories over the Russians at the battles of the Yellow Sea (1904) and Tsushima (1905), in which the damage was inflicted by big guns and the Japanese scored hits from unprecedented distances, led many to conclude (correctly) that future battleship engagements would be fought at great distance, reinforcing the case for the heavily armoured all-big-gun (12-inch) battleship. This approach is not accepted by all scholars, but HMS *Dreadnought* was certainly to be the first of a new class of battleship, its guns able to fire two rounds per minute, and the first capital ship in the world to be powered by the marine turbine engine. Completed in 14 months, her construction reflected the industrial and organisational efficiency of British shipbuilding.

HMS *Dreadnought* was faster and more heavily gunned than any other battleship then sailing, and made the earlier arithmetic of relative naval power redundant, encouraging the Germans to respond with the construction of powerful battleships: four were begun in the summer of 1907,[26] and, in a naval race with Britain, Germany built up the world's second largest battle fleet. However, as the British were determined to stay ahead, willing to pay to do so, and had the necessary shipbuilding capacity, German shipbuilding simply encouraged the laying down of more dreadnoughts, as new battleships were now called. The naval race continued because attempts in 1909–10 and 1912 to negotiate a treaty fixing the ratio of strength between both navies failed, in part because of the obduracy of Kaiser Wilhelm II; although it has been argued that the Germans had given up on the naval arms race by 1912 as they were running out of the financial resources necessary to keep up and, believing a war in Europe to be imminent, instead began to focus more emphatically on land warfare. At the same time that they laid down dreadnoughts, the British scrapped large numbers of warships now seen as obsolete, not least as showing the flag on distant stations no longer seemed important.

In combination with the commitment of the Liberal government to social reform, particularly the Old Age Pensions Act of 1908, the naval race put a strain on British public finances that helped provoke a political and constitutional crisis in 1909–11, with David Lloyd George's People's Budget, with its higher taxes, being rejected by the House of Lords in November 1909. Conservative defeats in the two general elections of 1910, which ensured the failure of Chamberlain's hopes for tariff reform, led to the Lords losing their veto on legislation by the Parliament Act of 1911. Lloyd George had declared in a speech at Newcastle, on the shipbuilding Tyne, that 'a fully equipped duke costs as much to keep up as two Dreadnoughts'. A very different testimony to the importance of the navy, and its ability to link new money and established institutions, was shown in 1911 when the University of Cambridge accepted the Vere Harmsworth professorship of naval history.

By the outbreak of the First World War, the British had 21 dreadnoughts in service, and the Germans 14. Twelve and five respectively were under construction, although numbers were to be affected by Britain seizing ships being prepared for delivery to Turkey and Chile. The British also had more battle-cruisers (eight compared to Germany's four) in service. Germany's failure in this race, which helped lead Admiral Tirpitz, the State Secretary of the Navy Office, to feel that the fleet was not yet ready for war, was to ensure a shift to submarine attack by Germany after war broke out, although numbers of warships were not the sole issue, not least because the British suffered from a weaker system of range plotting and fire control for naval gunfire, and less effective torpedoes and mines. In 1909, the British had also begun a new base at Rosyth on the Firth of Forth, designed to help the major home force, the Grand Fleet, contest the North Sea, and including three dry docks able to take dreadnoughts, although the lack of a comparable base further south on the east coast was a major problem both in protecting the coastline from attack and in responding rapidly to German naval moves.

The focus on competition helped navalism to retain a central position in British political culture. This was seen in particular with the launching of ships, which, as earlier clearly from the 1780s,[27] were public acts marked by much celebration and pride. Large numbers of groups were represented in these massive public rituals,[28] and their impact was furthered by the press, illustrated magazines, souvenirs and the cinema. The newly launched warships were celebrated as products of industrial might that would serve the Empire, and indeed represented it; although their deployment in home waters made this imperial identity problematic. Furthermore, the focus on naval competition with Germany, while intended to provide a deterrent that would make war less likely, was also linked to a commitment to European power politics that made participation in war there more probable, and thus accentuated the effects of preparing the navy for war.

Voices were already raised to suggest that navalism was becoming redundant, as the argument that the development of rail had altered the paradigm of economic potential away from maritime power, expressed by the geographer Halford Mackinder in his *Britain and the British Seas* (1902), seemed borne out by the economic growth of the USA and Germany. More radically, manned and powered air flight from 1903 appeared as an augury of a very different world, and suggested that the maritime geopolitics of British imperial power might be made redundant. Even if navies were still crucial to power, there was the question of the impact of new naval technology, particularly in the shape of the submarine. H. O. Arnold-Forster, Parliamentary Secretary to the Admiralty, had offered reassurance in 1901:

> The submarine is, in fact, the true reply to the submarine . . . That provided we are as well equipped in the matter of submarines as our neighbours, the introduction of this new weapon, so far from being a disadvantage to us, will strengthen our position. We have no desire to invade any other country: it is important that we ourselves should not be invaded. If the submarine proves as formidable as some authorities think is likely to be the case, the bombardment of our ports, and the landing of troops on our shores will become absolutely impossible. The same reasoning applies to every part of our empire which is approachable by water only.

Others were less confident. In 1902, Fisher, then Second Sea Lord, saw submarines as an instance of the competitive enhancement of weaponry that he felt Britain had been falling behind in, like the introduction of the gyroscope:

> The great principle to be invariably followed by us is that no naval weapon of any description must be adopted by foreign navies, without exhaustive trials of it on our part, to ascertain its capabilities and possibilities in a future naval war, and to make provision accordingly. We cannot afford to leave anything to be a matter of opinion which affects, in the slightest degree, the fighting efficiency of the fleet.[29]

A memorandum 'The oil engine and the submarine' among the material relating to the 1912 Royal Commission on Fuel and Engines, in the papers of Vice-Admiral John Jellicoe, Commander of the Second Division in the Home Fleet, asked:

> What is it that the coming of the submarine really means? It means that the whole foundation of our traditional naval strategy, which served us

so well in the past, has been broken down! The foundation of that strategy was blockade. The fleet did not exist merely to win battles – that was the means not the end. The ultimate purpose of the fleet was to make blockade possible for us and impossible for our enemy.[30]

Despite considerable speculation about the likely impact of submarines, there was scant experience on which to base discussion. Submarines did not feature prominently in navy operations in the 1900s and early 1910s, for example the Russo-Japanese or Balkan Wars, and their potential had been greatly underestimated by most commanders.[31] Tirpitz indeed was a late convert to submarines. Nevertheless, Fisher was concerned about the vulnerability of battleships to torpedoes, and this led him to emphasise the use of flotillas of destroyers and light cruisers for the defence of home waters, while Britain, which had only launched its first submarine in 1901, had the largest number (89) at the outbreak of the First World War, although many were of limited value, in part because they were designed for harbour defence; while insufficient thought had been given to the defence of warships and merchantmen against submarines.[32]

THE FIRST WORLD WAR

The First World War was an appalling challenge to the societies of the countries that made up the Empire, although it did not have a direct disruptive impact on it comparable with that of the Second World War. This was not for want of effort, for the Germans sought to challenge the cohesion of imperial rule, and there was concern among British policymakers about the threat. In 1904, the Director of Military Operations had warned about the precariousness of the Empire,

> The fact cannot be too plainly stated that throughout Egypt and the Soudan, and throughout the great Protectorates of Uganda and British East Africa, our whole position depends entirely on prestige. We are governing with a mere handful of white officials vast populations alien to us in race, language and religion, and for the most part but little superior in civilization to savages. Except for the small, and from a military point of view inadequate, British force in Egypt, the authority of these officials is supported only by troops recruited from the subject races, whose obedience to their officers rests on no other basis than a belief in the invincibility of the British government and confidence in its promises. If that belief and confidence be once shaken, the foundations of all British authority between Cairo and Mombasa will be undermined, and at any moment a storm of mutiny and insurrection will sweep us into the sea.[33]

In The First World War, the German leadership indeed planned to destroy the British Empire, using revolution to extend the war to Egypt and India. Germany's Muslim ally, Turkey, was expected to provide the leadership for pan-Islamic revolts that, according to the German diplomat Rudolph Nadolny, were 'to light a torch from the Caucasus to Calcutta'. In the event, the German appeal to the 270 million Muslims of the world was undermined by the fact that in the Middle East some Muslims proved eager to revolt against Turkish rule. More generally, pan-Turkism was widely considered an unacceptable part of pan-Islamism, and this was readily apparent in Egypt where German promises of independence required Turkish troops to give effect to them. There was no supporting rising in Egypt and the Turkish advance was repelled by Gurkha and Indian units, supported by British and French warships.

In 1915, in the Gallipoli campaign, the Anglo-French attempt to force the Dardanelles and besiege Constantinople, the major amphibious operation of the war, failed. Initially, the emphasis was on the navy, but the attempt to force the Dardanelles on 18 March 1915 fell victim to mines, with three British or French pre-dreadnought battleships sunk. The naval experts had been aware of the hazards posed by the mines and shore batteries, not least because, before the war, the British naval mission had provided advice to the Turks on mine-laying, but their caution was thrust aside by Churchill, the First Lord of the Admiralty, who was a keen advocate of a bold naval advance on Constantinople.[34] With surprise lost, the Allies followed, on 25 April, with a landing of troops on the Gallipoli peninsula, but the Turks had strengthened local defences under German direction, the Allies failed to push their initial advantages and their advances were contained. The assault on the periphery of Europe had failed. The Allied withdrawal the following winter was one of the few well-managed aspects of the operation.

Turkish victories in 1915, which included a major defeat on the British at Kut in Mesopotamia (in modern Iraq), nevertheless did not have an impact on the prestige of the Empire comparable with the fall of Singapore to the Japanese in 1942, not least because they were defensive victories. In some respects, indeed, the war led to an intensification of British military control in the colonies. This was particularly the case near areas of conflict – the German colonies in Africa and the Turkish Empire; but, more generally, forces were also available to enforce imperial authority. In Sudan, the territory of Darfur was conquered, while in 1918 an expedition was launched against the Turkana of Kenya.

The successful articulation of the Empire was readily apparent in the war, for without the Empire Britain would have been unable to mount offensive operations in the Middle East, would have been largely reduced to the use of the navy alone against German colonies in Africa and the Pacific and would have been forced to introduce conscription, a contentious move, earlier than 1916. The use of imperial forces was helped by the absence of an enemy in East Asia, with the exception of the German base at Tsingtao in China, which was captured by Britain's ally Japan in 1914, although her activity in China contributed to growing British concern about her intentions, especially in India.[35]

More than 800,000 Indian soldiers fought for the British in the war, so that, far from the British having to garrison South Asia, it was a crucial source of manpower for them. Large numbers of Indians were at first used on the Western Front, while others captured Basra in 1914, protecting British oil interests in south-west Persia, and advanced into Mesopotamia the following year, this commitment a continuation of pre-war interest in increasing influence in the Persian Gulf. The impact of raising troops in India was particularly pronounced on the society of the Punjab, while India also provided large quantities of products for the war effort, including food and textiles.[36] In Africa, especially British East Africa, labour conscription was a heavy burden, with large numbers of carriers used to provide the logistics for Allied columns, and, as a result of disease, there were very high rates of casualties among the carriers.

The Dominions also raised large numbers of men, with the Canadians providing a substantial force for the Western Front. Forty per cent of the men of military age (i.e. between 19 and 45) in New Zealand, where conscription was introduced in 1916, served overseas, and of these 120,000 men, over 50,000 were injured and 18,000 died. These efforts and losses played a major role in the shared experience of empire, and were also important in developing attitudes towards the British connection. Thus, the war was seen as formative in the nationalism of the Dominions, although, in practice, this process was far more long-term. Heavy Australian losses, including 58,460 dead among the 332,000 troops who served overseas, were to play a potent role in a controversy focused on the argument that British self-interest and incompetence had led to unnecessary sacrifice, especially in the Gallipoli campaign,[37] although this argument rested on a less than secure reading of that campaign, particularly of the general surprise at the skill of the Turkish defence; and was less important at the time than when it became central to hostility towards the British link. During the war, tension in Canada was more evident. Whereas large numbers of Canadians volunteered (and 56,119 men died), the introduction of conscription was unpopular in Québec and led to riots. However, this was an indication of pre-existing strains, as many French Canadians felt only limited commitment to Canada, and did not extend to a fundamental rejection of the Empire.

Such a rejection did occur in Ireland in 1916, but the rapidly crushed extreme nationalist Easter Rising in Dublin enjoyed little support, and a far larger number of Irish Catholics volunteered to fight for George V on the Western Front and elsewhere. The firm British response to the Rising, however, served to radicalise much of Irish public opinion, although given the fact that Britain was then at war the execution of rebel leaders was scarcely surprising, and subsequent criticism of these executions reflects a failure to appreciate the embattled nature of the Empire at that moment. Other factors also helped increase nationalist support. Backers of Home Rule were alienated by the hostile role of the Conservatives in the British coalition government, and these constitutional nationalists anyway increasingly lost their ability to lead the Catholic community. A proposal to introduce conscription in March 1918 was particularly important in undermining both them and support for the Empire, although it was necessary because of opinion in Britain. Contingency was the key factor in Irish independence: the role of the war was crucial in that it destroyed the basis for the Home Rulers who, under John Redmond, the leader of the Irish Parliamentary Party, had been imperialists as well as nationalists. Redmond hoped to be the Irish equivalent of a Canadian or Australian Prime Minister: 'local but loyal', and his brother, an MP, died fighting for George V in the war.[38]

In some respects, albeit not in Ireland, the collective effort represented by the war led to a strengthening of empire. An Imperial War Cabinet, including representatives of the Dominions, met from 1917 and provided a welcome public sign of cohesion in decision-making that countered the emphasis on distinctive interests. The war also saw a measure of the economic union that had interested Chamberlain in the 1900s: schemes for an Imperial Customs Union were considered, while Britain's role as a market for imperial goods was fostered by military needs and political preference. The impact of the war on food imports to Britain from Continental Europe ensured that the British market increased for imperial exporters such as South Africa. Other recently conquered colonies were also affected, so that in Sudan food exports rose to meet wartime demand; but, at the same time, there and elsewhere, the war disturbed established economic patterns, even in areas not well integrated into the imperial economy, leading to both price and wage inflation.

The war seriously damaged Britain's economy, as most foreign investments were sold in order to finance the war effort, while the disruption of trade and the diversion, under state regulation, of manufacturing capacity to war production ensured that the economy was less able to satisfy international (and domestic) demand. This encouraged the growth of manufacturing elsewhere, both in colonies, such as India, and in areas, such as Latin America, that had traditionally taken British imports. Import substitution and industrial expansion was pushed in South Africa under a consolidated tariff for the entire Union introduced in 1914. The USA, which did not enter the war until 1917, benefited most of all, as the British war effort soon became heavily dependent on American financial and industrial resources, while the Americans were well-placed to replace British exports to Canada and Latin America.

THE NAVAL WAR

The outbreak of war led to a rush of naval patriotism. The Reverend J. Featherstone Stirling, Chaplain to the Forces, produced *1588 to 1914: Album-Atlas of British Victories on the Sea, 'Wooden Walls to Super-Dreadnoughts'*, a tribute to British heroism that was approved by the Official Press Bureau and included an autograph portrait of Winston Churchill, the First Lord of the Admiralty. On the inside page, 'Signatures of the Brave. A Place for the autographs of officers and men who served Britain by land and sea in the Great War of 1914', topped Shakespeare's lines 'This happy breed of men . . . this England'. The atlas, which had a picture of a bulldog on the back cover, included details on how to join the navy, and a note on Nelson:

> At this crisis of our destinies, there is no great dead Englishman to whom the nation's thoughts turn so surely and so proudly as to Nelson. Final victory or defeat for us is always and inevitably at sea, and the mere name of Nelson sums up all we have ever achieved there in the past, all we hold and win in the present . . . men and the sea are unchanging.

The British navy played a crucial role in Allied success in the war, although the outcome was not settled by the major battle sought by navalists. In the opening months of the war, there were two surface actions in the North Sea, but neither saw a clash between capital ships: in the battle of Heligoland Bight on 28 August 1914, British battle-cruisers played the decisive role in an engagement that had started as a clash between British and German squadrons of light cruisers and destroyers. The Germans lost three light cruisers and one destroyer, while, although one British light cruiser and two destroyers were badly damaged, the fact that none were lost helped ensure that the battle was presented as a striking victory; it certainly gave the British a powerful psychological advantage, which was underlined on 17 October 1914 when, in the battle of Texel, four German destroyers were sunk. In 1914, the loss of ships to German submarines and mines cost the British more men and major ships than the Germans lost in battle, but the impact was less dramatic in terms of the sense of relative advantage; indeed, these appeared to be the means to snipe at the British advantage rather than an effective counter to it. At the battle of Dogger Bank, on 24 January 1915,

British and German capital ships clashed for the first time, as battle-cruisers engaged in a pursuit action in which the retreating Germans lost an armoured cruiser but British gunnery suffered from poor fire control. On 4 February, the Germans responded to their limitations in surface operations by deciding on a new attack: unrestricted submarine warfare.

In 1916, the Germans again attempted to achieve a surface victory, by luring part of the British Grand Fleet into battle with the main force of their High Seas Fleet. The resulting battle of Jutland of 31 May to 1 June 1916 between the two fleets, the largest clash of battleships in history, was not the hoped-for Trafalgar, nor a repetition of the Japanese victory over the Russians at Tsushima in 1905: a total victory soon followed by the end of the war. The caution of Jellicoe, the British commander, concerned that German torpedoes would sink pursuing British ships, possibly denied the British the victory they might have obtained had the bolder Beatty, commander of the battle-cruiser squadron, been in overall command, and Kitchener had observed the previous year 'In the solution of the Dardanelles much I fear depends on the Navy. If we only had Beatty out there, I should feel very much happier'.[39] Nevertheless, although at Jutland the British suffered from inadequate training, for example in destroyer torpedo attacks, from unsafe handling of powder supplies and from command and communications flaws, and lost more ships (14, including three battle-cruisers, to 11, including one battle-cruiser) and men (6,097 to 2,551) in the battle, German ships were badly damaged in the big-gun exchange,[40] and their confidence was hit by the resilience and size of the British fleet.

This damage, combined with the maintenance of British naval superiority, ensured that, thereafter in the war, the German fleet sailed beyond the defensive minefields of the Heligoland Bight on only three occasions.[41] As in the pre-Jutland sortie that ended at Dogger Bank in 1915, three others in early 1916 that did not result in a battle, and that of Jutland itself, the Germans hoped to fall upon part of the British Grand Fleet with their entire High Seas fleet, but they failed to do so. As the Germans finished not one of the dreadnoughts or battle-cruisers they laid down during the war, compared with the five battle-cruisers laid down and completed by Britain, the Germans did not have the margin of safety of a shipbuilding programme to fall back upon; and nor did they have the prospect of support from the warships of new allies that the British benefited from with the entry of Italy into the war in 1915 and, more significantly, of the USA two years later. These additions more than nullified the success of German submarines in sinking Allied warships: in 1917, the British lost this way only one pre-dreadnought battleship and one armoured cruiser. The German failure in surface-ship warfare, and in the arithmetic of surface-ship strength, helped to accentuate the importance for them of submarines; although, in combating these, the British benefited from their wartime shipbuilding programme which included 56 destroyers and 50 anti-submarine motor launches.

Thanks to the navy, the British retained control of home waters, and therefore avoided blockade and invasion, maintained the flow of men and munitions to their army in France unmolested, retained trade links that permitted the mobilisation of British resources and blockaded Germany. German landings on the east coast were feared, but the inability of the German fleet to contest control of the North Sea blocked this possibility. German bombardment inflicted some damage, on Whitby, Lowestoft and Great Yarmouth, but, as a sign of things to come, air attack killed far more people in Britain. Without naval power, Britain's alliances could not have operated: the British would have lacked both the ability to move and use resources across the Channel and the Atlantic, and operational reach. Although Britain's allies made an important naval contribution, particularly the French in the Mediterranean, the British were dominant within the alliance at sea, and their role there contrasted with their less prominent, although in 1916 and even more in 1917–18, growing, part in the Allied order-of-battle on land.

Britain's supply system, that of a country that could not feed itself, an imperial economy that relied on trade and a military system that required troop movements within the Empire, was challenged by German surface raiders, but these were hunted down in the early stages of the war. The East Asiatic Squadron under Vice Admiral Maximilian Graf [Count] von Spee was the leading German naval force outside Europe at the outset of the war. In response to Japan's entry into the war, and the corresponding vulnerable nature of Germany's Chinese and Pacific positions, Spee sailed across the Pacific to Chile, where a weaker British force was defeated off Coronel on 1 November 1914, with the loss of two cruisers. Spee then sailed on to attack the Falkland Islands, but, using the speed and range of the warships, Fisher had sent two battle-cruisers there to hunt down Spee, and he was defeated on 8 December, although only after a prolonged chase that practically exhausted the magazines of the battle-cruisers: four German cruisers were sunk. Individual German warships elsewhere were eventually hunted down, although not before the *Emden*, which was lost to the combination of naval fire and a reef in the Cocos Islands on 9 November 1914, had inflicted some damage, and more disruption, to shipping in the Indian Ocean and had shelled Madras. By the end of 1914, foreshadowing events in the Second World War, the Allies, working in unusual concert, had cracked the three German naval codes, although, whilst the Germans seemed oblivious to this, the British navy, through slovenliness or mistrust, repeatedly failed to exploit this advantage to its full potential.

Submarines proved a more serious threat than surface raiders because it was very difficult to detect them once they submerged and depth charges were effective only if they exploded close to the hulls. The specifications of submarines, their range, seaworthiness, speed and comfort, and of the accuracy, range and armament of their torpedoes, improved during the First World War, and they came to play a major role in naval planning, both strategically, in terms of trying to deny bodies of water to opponents, and tactically, with the hope that, in engagements, opposing warships could be drawn across submarine lines, leading Jellicoe to observe 'I am most absolutely averse to moving the Battle Fleet without a full destroyer screen'.[42] It was felt necessary, in the face of the submarine threat, to withdraw the Grand Fleet from the North Sea and Scapa Flow in the Orkneys in 1914 to new bases on the north-west coast of Scotland: it did not return to Scapa Flow until 1915, when the base's defences had been strengthened, and the following year Balfour, then First Lord of the Admiralty, wrote 'the submarine has already profoundly modified naval tactics . . . It was a very evil day for this country when this engine of naval warfare was discovered', while Jellicoe argued that the greater size and range of submarines, and their increased use of the torpedo (as opposed to the gun), so that they did not need to come to the surface, meant that the submarine menace was getting worse.[43] After Jutland, losses in subsequent operations in August to November 1916 of warships to submarines encouraged first the British and then the Germans to restrict the sailing of capital ships in the North Sea.

Inexperience in confronting submarine attacks, and the limited effectiveness of anti-submarine weaponry, increased the vulnerability of British trade, and thus the danger that, despite its dreadnoughts and capacity for victory in battle, Britain would succumb to a form of blockade. Submarines promoted the German cause most effectively not by destroying warships but by sinking merchant vessels: during the war the Germans sank 11.9 million tons of Allied shipping, mostly commercial, at the cost of 199 submarines. On 2 February 1917, the Germans resumed the unrestricted submarine warfare they had already tried in 1915, as part of a deliberate campaign to starve Britain into submission, but which had been stopped on political grounds as likely to provoke American intervention. The resumption of such warfare was a reflection of the failure of the German surface navy to win victory at Jutland the previous year. The objective was total war, even if they lacked the submarine fleet to achieve this: although the Germans stepped up submarine production once war had begun, relatively few were ordered and most were delivered behind schedule, in part because of poor organisation and a concentration of industrial resources on the army. Nevertheless, greater numbers ensured that more damage was done than in 1915.[44]

In the spring of 1917, British leaders including Jellicoe were pessimistic about the chances of success against the submarines, and the initial rate of Allied shipping losses was sufficiently high to threaten defeat. From February to April 1917, 1,945,240 tons of shipping were sunk with only nine submarines lost. However, the attack helped bring the USA into the war on 6 April; and this added the world's strongest economy, and third largest navy, to the Allied war effort. American entry helped against the submarines for, from May 1917, American warships contributed to anti-submarine patrols in European waters. British efforts to manufacture imported goods at home and to enhance farm production also helped to combat the submarine menace. So, most importantly, did the introduction in May 1917 of a system of escorted convoys; it cut shipping losses dramatically and led to an increase in the sinking of German submarines. Convoys might appear such an obvious solution that it is surprising they were not adopted earlier, but there were counter-arguments, including the number of escorts required, the delays that would be forced on shipping and the possibility that convoys would simply offer a bigger target. They were also resisted by the Admiralty for some time as not sufficiently in line with the bold 'Nelson touch': such psychological pressures were important to the culture of naval power within which policy options were considered.

Convoys reduced the targets for submarines and ensured that, when they found them, they could be attacked by escorts, while convoys also benefited from the 'shoal' factor: when they found a convoy, submarines had time to sink only a limited number of ships. In coastal waters, convoys were supported by aircraft and airships, and this forced submarines to remain submerged, where they were much slower. Although in the first four months of the unrestricted submarine attacks in 1917 the British lost an average of 630,000 tons of shipping, the monthly tonnage lost fell below half a million in August 1917, while only 393 of the 95,000 ships that were to be convoyed across the Atlantic were lost, including just three troop transports. Convoys reduced the potency of German attack, but mines sank more submarines than other weapons, and mine barrages limited their options. Massive barrages were laid across the English Channel at Dover in late 1916, and across the North Sea between the Orkneys and Norway from March 1918, while, by the end of the war, magnetic mines had been developed and were being laid by the British. As yet, aircraft were not able to make a major contribution to anti-submarine operations, but Britain was the leader in naval air capability, with, by the close of the war, the only ship able to launch and land wheeled aircraft (as opposed to seaplane tenders) and 2,949 aircraft in the Royal Naval Air Service. At the end of the war, two aircraft carriers were under construction.

As the war came to a close, the redundancy of German naval operations became apparent. Submarine operations declined, so that, having sunk at least 268,000 tons of shipping each month from January to August 1918, only 288,000 tons were sunk in September and October combined. Submarine operations had not swayed the course of the war on land: Allied land forces were able to maintain the offensive launched that summer, while large numbers of American troops continued to cross the Atlantic. The German naval command's plan for a final sortie to begin on 29 October, leading to a fight to the finish with the Grand Fleet, was thwarted by the mutinous disobedience of the crews, and the German High Seas Fleet was no longer under control as the war ended on 11 November.

The war at sea was celebrated, not least on canvas. W. L. Wyllie, one of Britain's best maritime artists, produced works ranging across the diversity of British naval warfare, for example of the 'Q' ship HMS *Merope* in action with a U-boat, of the battle-cruisers *Tiger, Princess Royal, Lion, Warrior* and *Defence* going into action at Jutland, and of the loss there of HMS *Invincible*, which he had hoped to sail on. Wyllie's work on Jutland represented a continuation and updating of his celebration of the nation's naval enterprise, as his works included a panorama of Trafalgar, and a painting of HMS *Bellerophon* in Portsmouth with, in the background, HMS *Victory* which he had helped preserve for the nation.[45]

CONCLUSIONS

War with Germany had been far more exhausting than had been feared, and, despite comparisons with the French Revolutionary and Napoleonic Wars, it was also more difficult. Although Britain in the First World War was never as isolated as it had been on occasion during these earlier years, and German troops had not landed in the British Isles, as French ones had in Wales in 1797 and in Ireland in 1798, the submarine offensive was more deadly and immediate a form of economic warfare than the bar on trade attempted by Napoleon. Furthermore, in order to defeat Germany, Britain had both to play a role on land greater than she had during the Napoleonic wars, and to call on the assistance of the USA, the great power best placed to challenge her global position. The USA took part in the war, from 1917 until the close, but without being enervated to the same degree as Britain, while the build-up of the navies of both the USA and Japan, allies of Britain during the conflict, ensured that the war ended without Britain being in the dominant position at sea it had enjoyed at the close of the Napoleonic Wars when its key allies – Russia, Prussia and Austria – had neither possessed nor sought such power. Indeed, American and Japanese warships were deployed in European waters in co-operation with Britain: five American dreadnoughts joined the Grand Fleet in December 1917, four sailing with the Grand Fleet on 24 April 1918 when it failed to intercept a German sortie, while to assist convoying in the Mediterranean American warships were based in Gibraltar and Japanese ones in Malta.

In one respect, the war represented a shift in naval challenge for Britain: from Germany at the outset to the USA and Japan, and competition from these two was to be played out after the war in the diplomacy of naval limitation that led to the Washington Naval Treaty of 1922. However, wartime alliance followed by the success of these negotiations ensured that naval competition ceased to be the key theme that it had been prior to the outbreak of the First World War. Indeed, Britain did not lay down any battleships between January 1923 and December 1936, while the early lead in aircraft carriers was not maintained. Partly as a result of this situation, and of the lack of dramatic wartime success to compare with the victories of 1794–1805 – indeed Britain lost more capital ships than all the other combatants combined – the role of the navy in saving Britain in the First World War was underrated. The burden of the war on land had been far greater in terms of men committed and lives lost, but, strategically, the sea provided not only defence but also the means for offence, as, without maritime strength, land power could not have been applied by Britain. Allies helped at sea, particularly France and, eventually, Italy in the Mediterranean and the Americans in the Atlantic, but the British contribution at sea was proportionately greater than on land. Even if it lacked a dramatic victory, the navy was victorious and served successfully both national and coalition goals and achieved crucial strategic outcomes, particularly the defensive–offensive task of maintaining maritime links so that troops and supplies could be readily moved. Naval offensives and amphibious operations were far less successful, as Gallipoli showed, or remained on the drawing board: Fisher's plan for a Baltic expedition was not pursued (the fate, fortunately, that also befell Churchill's wish to do the same in the Second World War); but on the whole this limitation was the result of war with a continental power that could make little effort to protect its colonies. Thanks in part to the navy, Britain was, with a formidable effort, able to add being a continental power to its inherited position as a maritime empire.

8
New Threats, 1919–1945

The mutual inward and outward trade between the several possessions of the British People amounts annually to more than £600,000,000, and embraces every single article required for food, clothing, education, commerce, manufacture, or agriculture, and for all the pursuits, associations, and pleasures of every one of His Most Gracious Majesty's Loyal and Devoted Subjects in the United Kingdom and throughout the Empire. This great mercantile interchange is capable, moreover, of limitless expansion, by reason of the diversities of climate and geological conditions . . . Greater Britain that is the possessions of the British Peoples over the sea is one hundred and fifty-three times the size of Great Britain.
The Howard Vincent Map of the British Empire (21st edition, 1924)

The men are still very cheerful. They were all very cheered by the naval successes. It is remarkable how Britain reacts to naval news – it is in the blood.
General Sir John Dill, commander of the British Expeditionary Force's First Corps on the response to the destruction of the *Graf Spee*, 1939[1]

The Interwar Empire

The war was followed not by a retreat of empire but by its advance, as the imperial ethos remained strong, and the British, in particular, saw the events of the war outside Europe as reflecting the value of empire. The defeat of Germany and its allies indeed carried the British Empire to its maximum impact. Britain played a leading role in the peace conferences held in Paris, most importantly that with Germany which led to the Treaty of Versailles of 1919, and gained League of Nations mandates for Tanganyika (German East Africa), part of Togo and a sliver of Cameroon, all conquered German territories in Africa, and for Nauru Island in the Pacific, while Australia,

New Zealand and South Africa all made gains: German New Guinea as well as the Bismarck Archipelago, Western Samoa and South-West Africa respectively. The policies of racial control seen in South Africa were extended to South-West Africa. The partition of the Turkish Empire led to British mandates over Palestine, Transjordan and Iraq, while in 1914 Britain had already annexed Cyprus and made Egypt a protectorate, and in 1916 Qatar had become independent under British protection. British power along the Suez Canal route and in the Islamic world was now far stronger, while the British Empire made the greatest gains in Africa: France acquired mandates for most of Cameroon and much of Togo, and Belgium for some parts of German East Africa. The French also gained mandates over Lebanon and Syria, while Japan gained the Mariannas, Marshalls and the Carolines in the Pacific.

Ardent imperialists, such as Lord Milner and Leo Amery, pressed for the further strengthening of the Empire, partly in the hope that it would never be dragged into the Continental mire, and there were attempts to extend British influence and control. Hopes that Syria would be ruled by the pro-British Arab Hashemite dynasty, and that Britain would dominate 'Arabia' were thwarted, but British influence increased in both Persia and Turkey, in the latter of which the victorious Allies staked out zones of influence. Prior to the end of the First World War, British forces began to take a role against the Communists in the Russian Civil War that followed their coup in 1917. This continued after the end of the war. The British moved into the Caucasus, Central Asia and the White Sea region and were deployed in the Baltic and the Black Sea, and in 1919 Curzon, now Foreign Secretary, advocated control over parts of the former Russian Empire, a policy seen as a forward-defence for India.[2]

Such ambitions could not be sustained, and the high tide of empire was to ebb very fast. The strain of the war, the men lost, the money spent and the exhaustion produced by constant effort, was heavy enough, and it had left a burdensome debt, so that Britain had been transformed from the world's leading creditor nation to its greatest debtor. Britain's difficulties were exacerbated by political division, an absence of stable leadership and the re-emergence of pre-war problems, and, as a sign of insecurity and paranoia, there was also concern that Britain's imperial position was the target of wide-ranging conspiracies, both Communism and pan-Islamicism.[3] The expansion of imperial rule and Britain's international commitments both involved intractable problems. Armed intervention in Russia, which had been supported by Churchill, was a failure and was abandoned in 1919. It had been opposed by left-wingers, sympathetic to the Communists, and by conscripts eager for demobilisation, but failed, essentially, because of the difficulty of the task. The navy was extensively used in support of intervention, especially in the Baltic, Black and White Seas, and was important in securing the independence of the Baltic states, especially Estonia. In the Middle East, revolts in Egypt (1919) and Iraq (1920–21) helped lead Britain to grant their independence in 1922 and 1932 respectively, although she maintained considerable influence in both, in what was to be a successful exercise in informal empire.[4] The Third Afghan War, in 1919, underlined the difficult situation on the North-West Frontier, where there was a revolt in Waziristan, while there were also serious disturbances in the Punjab that year. British influence collapsed in Persia in 1921, when the pro-British Shah was overthrown by Reza Khan, who exploited nationalist sentiment and was to become the first of the new rulers of the Pahlevi dynasty, while, in the Chanak crisis of 1922, the government backed down in its confrontation with the nationalists in Turkey led by Kemal Ataturk.[5]

Arthur Griffith-Boscawen, Minister of Agriculture, wrote, during the Chanak crisis, 'I don't believe the country cares anything about Thrace', and, among the Dominions, only Newfoundland and New Zealand pledged help, a sign that British assumptions about the attitude of the Dominions required revision as they increasingly asserted their independence in policy-making. In Britain, the bulk of the Cabinet also rejected the willingness of Lloyd George and Churchill to risk war, and the crisis helped precipitate the fall of the coalition government headed by the former. His Conservative successor as Prime Minister, Andrew Bonar Law, who had been born in New Brunswick (his father was a Presbyterian clergyman from Ulster), argued that Britain 'cannot alone act as policeman of the world'.[6]

The loss of most of Ireland was also a major blow to imperial self-confidence: the Empire began at home. This was not a failure at the periphery, and at the hands of a totally alien population, but right at the centre, in what had been a part of Britain for centuries and had been represented at Westminster since the Act of Union of 1800, so that the weakness of British imperialism when confronted by a powerful nationalist movement was cruelly exposed. The First World War had destroyed the basis for the Irish Home Rulers, and in the 1918 general election, 47 per cent of the vote and 73 out of the 105 parliamentary seats, including most of those outside Ulster, were won by Sinn Féin, a party of nationalists who refused to attend Westminster and demanded independence. In 1919, a unilateral declaration of independence was issued, and fighting broke out. British refusal to accept independence led to a civil war that was ended by the Anglo-Irish Treaty of December 1921, which accepted both partition and effective independence (rather than Home Rule) for the new Irish Free State (Eire), which became the governing body over most of the island, excluding a large part of the province of Ulster in the North. The Irish Free State became a self-governing Dominion within the Empire, with a

Governor-General appointed by the Crown. This was the same status, in the 'Community of Nations known as the British Empire', as Australia, Canada, Newfoundland, New Zealand and South Africa, although in the constitution of the Irish Free State this was described as being 'a co-equal member of the community called the British Commonwealth of Nations'. Irrespective of the constitutional relationship, the new Dominion was far more alienated from Britain and the Empire than the others.

In India, the war had led to tension in the imperial relationship, in part because of resentment by some Indian soldiers of their treatment, as well as the impact in political and intellectual circles of notions of self-determination; but the disruption integral to war on this scale was more important, and there were also continued communal tensions. After the war, almost 400 people died in the Amritsar massacre of April 1919, when, in response to disturbances in the Punjab, General Dyer ordered (Indian) troops to fire on a demonstrating crowd. This further affected British authority by suggesting that it was inherently repressive. However, there were moves toward a less authoritarian system and practice of control. In 1919, under the Montagu-Chelmsford Reforms, a Government of India Act established the principle of dyarchy in the provinces. This Act, which reflected Liberal aspirations that were not shared by all Conservatives, allowed responsible self-government in certain areas of competence by Indian ministers under the supervision of provincial legislatures, while the British government retained finance and foreign policy in its competence.

Across the range of imperial interests and commitments, despite major efforts, there was a lack of resources and will to sustain international ambitions, particularly schemes for imperial expansion. Such schemes were expensive: it had cost £40 million to suppress the Iraq rising, and the garrison cost £25 million a year, and retrenchment and judging between commitments were increasingly the order of the day. The cuts recommended by the Geddes Committee in 1922 – the 'Geddes Axe' – hit military expenditure most heavily. Yet it would be inappropriate to focus only on problems, for, at one level, the picture was one of continued strength, certainly in comparison with the other European powers: France, and especially Germany and Russia, suffered even more from the war. The scuttling of the German High Seas Fleet at Scapa Flow on 21 June 1919 greatly increased the relative strength of the British navy, not least because, under the Versailles peace settlement, Germany was denied permission to build a new fleet, while the war also devastated the German merchant fleet, Britain's leading pre-war competitor. The Russian navy was badly affected by the civil war of 1917–22. The USA had now replaced Britain as the world's leading creditor, but American isolationism helped to mask the political consequences of the shift of financial and economic predominance to the

USA, while the commitment to the new international order advocated by President Woodrow Wilson was rejected by the Senate and was unwelcome to his two Republican successors.

It is also important to put problems in the Empire in perspective. The loss of the bulk of Ireland did not herald the collapse of other links within the British Isles, nor any serious pressures in them. The non-cooperation movement in India led by Mahatma Gandhi ebbed in effectiveness from 1922, the Indian army enabled Britain to discharge its military commitments, especially in Iraq, without conscription, and in Egypt, Britain retained control of the Suez Canal zone, as well as of defence and foreign affairs. Financial strength was suggested by Britain's return to the Gold Standard (convertibility of sterling with gold) in 1925, a measure actively pressed by Churchill, then Chancellor of the Exchequer, as a sign of imperial power, although the over valuing of sterling was a major burden on the economy. Britain also remained the world's leading shipper, but, during the 1920s, the limited increase in the volume of goods to be traded globally did not keep pace with the rise in the number of ships available to transport them: British shipping was hit hard by this world over capacity of shipping and the situation was to get much worse in the 1930s.

There was also a strengthening of empire, especially a deepening of imperial control as areas that, earlier, had been often only nominally annexed were brought under at least some colonial government. Thus, in southern Sudan, posts were established by Arab troops under British officers, and military patrols were launched, while road building improved the British position on the North-West Frontier of India. This deepening of control, however, challenged the processes of accommodation by which Britain had won local support for, or at least compliance with, imperial rule, and added an often unwelcome important political and administrative dimension to this rule. The stationing of a large garrison in Waziristan as part of the pacification that followed the 1919 revolt helped provoke a new, and more intractable, revolt in 1936.

There were also important economic changes in parts of the Empire, many of them linked to attempts to control the environment, for example by introducing irrigation schemes. In Sudan, the attempt to use the Gezira plain for the cultivation of cotton, which had begun in 1900, was pressed with the construction of an expensive irrigation scheme that was officially opened in 1926. This served to produce a cash crop designed to further the imperial economy, and was therefore an example of the process by which distant regions were more intensely integrated into the imperial economy. Prior to irrigation, the Gezira had been used to grow grain for the nearby city of Khartoum. There was also extensive investment in Indian irrigation. Much British foreign investment in the inter-war period took place in the

Empire, for example copper-mining in North Rhodesia (Zambia) and cotton and coffee production in Uganda, while in Kenya coffee had been grown commercially near Nairobi from 1901. In Africa, however, much of this investment was linked to the imposition of a white settler and company control that had a clear racial dimension, so that in Kenya both the African and the Indian population suffered discrimination, while white settlers extended their control over the land. The continuation in peacetime of the pass system introduced for Africans during the war was both indicative of attitudes and a cause of hostility.

In Malaya, in contrast, the development of a strong British presence in rubber and tin production was not affected by a white settler presence comparable with that in East Africa. British companies there benefited from the ready availability of investment capital and also from their easy access to international commercial networks, and the British role in industrial technology was also seen with the machinery used in tin production, especially for dredging. Similarly, in Ceylon (Sri Lanka) and Assam, there was no settler presence to accompany the development of tea production. They successfully focused on the distant metropolitan market and also benefited from the demand for tea elsewhere in the Empire, especially in the Dominions.

Economic and political integration within the Empire was further pressed forward by the extension of new communication systems, including the railways along which goods were moved to the ports and the harbour facilities developed there. In Africa, the creation of new links was at a greater scale than had been the case prior to 1914. The war itself had led to the extension of rail links, especially that in 1915 built to connect the rail system of South-West Africa with that of South Africa. After the war, the use of mechanical dredgers helped the already existing policy of clearing *sudd* (blockages of vegetation) from major Sudanese rivers. This made the rivers useable for the transport of goods and people. In Sudan, new port facilities were constructed at Port Sudan on the Red Sea and on the rivers, while the railway system, initially built to help the conquest, was greatly extended.

New air routes pioneered by Imperial Airways, a company founded with government support in 1924, linked the Empire to Britain, and the Britain to Australia airmail service began in 1932: it owed much to the development of the Cairo to Baghdad airmail service by the RAF. Weekly flights from London began to Cape Town (1932), Brisbane (1934) and Hong Kong (1936); in contrast, thanks to the problems of flying the Atlantic, they only began to New York in 1946. It took nine days to fly to Cape Town in 1936, and fourteen for Adelaide. These were far shorter journeys than sailing times,[7] but liner services remained crucial to imperial links. Regular air and sea services helped develop the integration of British and colonial elites, sustaining mutual interest, and ensuring the neo-Britishness that was characteristic of settler life. Thus, these services were used by sports teams and touring theatrical companies, as well as officials and businessmen. This integration of elites was also seen in India where, by the 1930s, tennis parties, some of the less exclusive clubs, and horse-racing provided venues where the upper levels of Anglo-Indian society mingled easily with their Indian counterparts.[8]

The social dimension of official British imperialism was captured by the Antarctic Place Names Committee established in 1932 in order to ensure that British maps at least reflected official views. The categories left out of their approved list of names for usage on maps included names of existing territories, towns or islands, names in any foreign language, names of sledge dogs, 'names in low taste' and 'names with obscure origins'.[9]

More prominent institutions sought to foster imperial links, as well as the Empire in British consciousness. On Empire Day every year, schools staged pageants and displays, souvenirs were issued and large parades were held in Hyde Park. The British Empire Exhibition in 1924–5, for which Wembley Stadium was built in 1923, was a major public occasion, celebrated in the press and the newsreels and commemorated by a set of stamps. Another Empire Exhibition followed in Glasgow in 1938. The Empire Marketing Board, created in 1926, sought to encourage trade within the Empire.

Other links included assisted emigration, especially by the Oversea Settlement Committee and the Society for the Oversea Settlement of British Women; it was hoped that these women would marry and produce children in whom a love of Britain would be instilled, and that they would ensure the purchase of British goods.[10] The settlement of demobilised soldiers in the Empire was seen as a means to reduce pressure on jobs in Britain. In relative terms, emigration to the Empire became more important, in part because of American restrictions on immigration enacted in 1921 and 1924, which hit trans-Atlantic passenger traffic and encouraged the passenger lines to try to develop cruising. In New Zealand, assisted immigration resumed after the First World War and continued until 1927, with the two categories most in demand being men ready to act as farm labourers and women ready to be domestic servants. In Canada, meanwhile, immigration revived after the war, although it did not match its 1909–13 peak and collapsed with the Great Depression of the 1930s. Although interwar immigrants from Britain added to the white population of South Africa, a high birth-rate caused the Afrikaner (Boer) population to grow even more quickly.[11]

The awarding of British university degrees through extension courses was another significant link and was particularly important for those seeking to use education in order to better themselves. Other educational links included the use of British school examination boards and the hiring of teachers trained in Britain, and these combined to focus educational advancement on British models and to ensure that what was seen as British civilisation was actively studied at schools and universities across the Empire. The British Whiggish notion of organic constitutional development and political change in stages could then by extension be applied to change within the Empire.

The royal family was more potent as a symbol of imperial partnership. Members of the royal family were linked closely to the ideal of imperial unity and to the role of Britain's navy in sustaining the Empire. The first fleet Colour was presented by George V in 1926. Writers such as Admiral G. A. Ballard in his *Rulers of the Indian Ocean* (1927) made much of George V's long naval experience, and the king associated himself with the naval heritage, not least by a visit in 1928 to HMS *Victory*, then being restored, while, as Prince of Wales, Edward VIII maintained the naval tradition. The accessions to the throne of Edward VIII and George VI successively in 1936, the first since that of George V in 1910, provided powerful images of continuity and were also used to define the Empire as a distinct political form. The abdication of Edward VIII in 1936 did not do much for imperial unity, however, except to the extent that the Dominion prime ministers exercised a veto over any possible morganatic marriage. Imperial tours by members of the royal family, such as that by George VI to Canada, were seen as important ways to sustain the spirit of empire. Another link with the Empire was provided by the Governors-General of the Dominions, such as Jellicoe, who served in New Zealand in 1920–24, and John Buchan, Lord Tweedsmuir, who served in Canada in 1935–40.

Imperial federation was an influential idea in this period. Its origins can be traced back to the late nineteenth century, and the development of the notion of a Commonwealth – unity in independence – proved useful in maintaining the support of the Dominions. Aside from Canada, New-foundland, Australia (1901) and New Zealand (1907), this group had been expanded when the search for reconciliation after the Boer War led to the formation of the Union of South Africa in 1910. The constitution gave power over the whole of South Africa to the Afrikaners, a form of responsible government that was very much a 'white' solution and which bitterly disappointed the hopes of the British Crown held by some black leaders. In contrast, in the 1920s, Maori leaders had greater success in obtaining redress for grievances when they approached the Crown, several, such as Tahupōtiki Wiremu Rātana in 1924, travelling to London. An imperial conference in 1926 defined the Commonwealth as 'the group of self-governing communities composed of Great Britain and the Dominions', and this formed the basis for the Statute of Westminster (1931), which determined that Commonwealth countries could now amend or repeal 'any existing or future act of the United Kingdom Parliament . . . in so far as the same is part of the law of this Dominion'. 'A common allegiance to the Crown' was seen as characteristic of the 'freely associated members of the British Commonwealth of Nations'. This notion of devolved empire did not, however, settle the question of India, which was not a Dominion, while Irish national sentiment was not satisfied with the Dominion status that followed the treaty of 1921.

These disparate elements interacted to create a sense of imperial partnership, camaraderie, even nationalism. Kipling, a keen defender of empire, found the celebration at Westminster Abbey in 1927 of the diamond jubilee of the Canadian Confederation a positive 'step on the threshold of a new life and self-knowledge for the Dominion and the Empire'.[12] Imperial partnership, however, was not free from tensions and the impact of other identities. These tensions varied, many stemming from activities that otherwise provided imperial links, not least the crisis in Anglo-Australian relations in 1932–3 over the 'bodyline' cricket tour, as aggressive English bowling roused Australian anger. However, the spread of cricket not only to the Dominions, but also to South Asia and the West Indies, in both of which there were few white settlers and where the sport spread beyond their number, indicated the way in which empire served to disseminate cultural norms and models.[13] More generally, acculturation worked best at the level of colonial elites, but was not effective only at that level.

Although pride in empire was strong, the psychological draw of the sea was lessened. Famous ocean-going liners, their speedy crossings much covered in the press and their lifestyle a subject for magazine articles and romantic fiction, received attention, but the popular imagination was far more engaged by the car and the plane. The ocean now had less of an impact than the seaside, and popular holidays there, a major development of the Victorian period, revived after the First World War, with new facilities added. In Lincolnshire, Cleethorpes was embellished with a bathing pool and a boating lake in the 1920s, and Skegness got both, as well as Butlin's Amusement Park; while, at Ingoldmells to the north of Skegness, Butlin opened his Luxury Holiday Camp in 1936.[14] The prosperity of those in work drove an expansion in leisure. Earlier in the century, nonconformists and early Socialists had condemned Blackpool and called instead for healthy outdoor pursuits, but their arguments had scant weight in the 1930s. Seaside holidays were in part sold on sex appeal, as Fortunito Matania's poster of about 1937 for the London Midland and Scottish Railway advertising Blackpool acknowledged. As in the Victorian period, those on the beaches, promenades and piers eyed each other up, rather than gazing out to consider the nation's maritime destiny.

Defence was an area of imperial co-operation, although it was not without tension. Visiting Australia in 1919, Jellicoe was made aware of opposition to subsuming the Australian navy into an imperial force and of Australian reluctance to spend more on the navy, but the Dominions benefited from the cover provided by British military strength, which enabled them to feel safe with only modest expenditure on defence, so that the Canadian navy was greatly run down after the First World War. At the imperial conferences of 1923 and 1926, the Canadian Prime Minister, William Mackenzie King, made it clear that his country would not fight in a war simply at Britain's behest, but, instead, that its interests had to be at stake and that the Canadian Parliament would play a crucial role in validating this. The limited provision by the Dominions for defence contributed greatly to the more general military vulnerability of the Empire that became apparent in the 1930s, while the Commonwealth failed to develop workable processes for effective co-operation on defence and international relations, and, although the threat posed by rising Japanese power was appreciated, there was no effective response.[15]

Economic relations between Britain and the Dominions were a major source of disagreement, not least because economic problems were encouraging a general move towards protectionism. This was seen as a way to develop the Commonwealth, and lobby groups, such as the Empire Industries Association launched in 1925, pushed the case for protectionism, but the relationship between Britain and the Dominions within such a system was a matter for controversy, as the latter wished to protect their industries from British competition and were concerned that free trade within the Empire would harm them. This was seen in shipping where non-Australian ships were banned from Australia's coastal trade.

The response was Imperial Preference, a cause championed from 1929 by the press baron Lord Beaverbrook in his 'Crusade' for Empire Free Trade, and eventually established in agreements reached at the Imperial Economic Conference held at Ottawa in 1932, which involved bilateral understandings on a large number of products;[16] although British exporters benefited less than Dominion producers, because, while the Dominions raised tariffs on non-British imports, they were unwilling to cut tariffs on British imports as they feared the impact on Dominion producers. The Ottawa agreement was a cautious arrangement that contrasted with the bold views of the Conservative politician Leo Amery, who pressed for a common economic policy and currency.[17] Nevertheless, it was promising, especially in light of rising protectionism elsewhere during the Depression. Furthermore, the tension and lack of warmth shown at Ottawa, an imperial conference that was far less harmonious than those of the 1920s, suggested that it would be difficult to achieve more. The protectionism introduced in Britain with the general 10 per cent tariff under the Import Duties Act of 1932 that brought an end to free trade was made more politically acceptable by Imperial Preference; but its essential thrust was concern about the economic position in Britain.

Thanks to Imperial Preference, the Empire became more important to Britain, although the growth of motor car and white goods manufacture in Britain in the 1920s and 1930s did not depend on colonial products or markets. A shift in Britain's economic relationship with the outside world, with manufacturing exports hit hard while consumer industries in Britain grew, can be seen by contrasting two events of 1936: the unemployed workers of Palmer's shipyard at Jarrow drawing attention to their plight and the continuing lack of shipyard orders with a march on London; and the opening of the new Carreras cigarette factory, employing 2,600 people at Mornington Crescent in London. Import substitution in some colonies, such as India, hit British export markets,[18] while in Canada this was related to the spread of American-owned branch-plant operations,[19] and British exports to the Empire fell in value; but, as those to the remainder of the world fell even more during the Depression, the Empire took 49 per cent of British exports in 1935–9, compared with 42 per cent a decade earlier. In the late 1930s, the British exported more to South Africa than to the more self-sufficient and protectionist USA.

Imperial trade was also more important to British shipping than hitherto, and led, for example, to the 'Empire food ships' bringing goods from Australasia, but shipping suffered with the decline in world trade in the early 1930s. The consequences of that decline were serious for British shipbuilding, which already endured the general problems of heavy industry as well as specific difficulties. For example, the decline of coal exports, that owed much to international competition, but something also to the increasing use of oil, hit a staple of British shipping and both shipbuilding and the training of sailors. Whereas the shipyards on the Tyne launched 238,000 tons of shipping in 1913, they launched fewer than 7,000 in 1933. Shipbuilding and shipping did not benefit from protectionism until the British Shipping (Assistance) Act (1935) offered tramp shipowners guaranteed freight rates.

The economic benefits stemming from empire helped justify imperial strategic commitments. These included interests in the Middle East, the presence in South-East Asia and the route to Australasia. As Correlli Barnett, however, has vigorously argued,[20] these commitments also represented a serious overreach that posed a problem in responding to particular crises. Instead of thinking primarily in terms of the global economy theoretically made possible by free trade, British policymakers were increasingly thinking in terms of an economic bloc, led by Britain with major contributions from the Dominions, that operated as a sterling area and that played a central role in strategic planning. Stanley Baldwin, Conservative Prime Minister in 1935–7, and Neville Chamberlain, his successor in 1937–40 and the Chancellor of the Exchequer in 1931–7, both thought in these terms. Until the 1967 devaluation of sterling, the currencies of most Commonwealth countries, bar Canada, were fixed in value relative to sterling, and they conducted their international trade in sterling, and many of these states held large sterling balances that helped support the currency and thus the financial stability of Britain and its government. This emphasis on the Empire was linked to a political assertiveness that presented the British Empire as a leading world power that possessed coherence and had distinct political interests.

The value of imperial control and association was indicated by the degree to which economic ties in the 'informal empire' faced serious difficulties in the interwar period. In Latin America, US businesses made major inroads, while in China, British cotton goods exports were affected by Japanese competition and the development of Chinese production. China had already become more assertive as a republic, with the rise of nationalism making foreign interests a conspicuous target, and was becoming harder to manage because of its acute divisions. In 1927, the British played a major role in the international deployment of warships and troops to protect the International Concession at Shanghai from Chinese nationalists, but the concessions in Hankou and Jiujiang were abandoned in 1927 after massive public protests overawed the local British military presence: a Chinese trade unionist was killed in each city by British troops, but, whereas in 1925 the position in Hankou had been underpinned by local warlords, in 1927 there was no such backing.[21] In Saudi Arabia, the negotiation in 1933 of an agreement with the American company Standard Oil was a vital step in the development of a powerful American presence.

There were also significant political problems in some parts of the Empire. The growth of anti-imperial feeling was related to indigenous notions of identity and practices of resistance, many of them central to a peasant culture of non-compliance with ruling groups. New organisations, such as the All-India Muslim League, founded in 1906, the National Congress of British West Africa (1920), the Young Kikuyu Association in Kenya (1921) and the African National Congress in South Africa (1923), fostered demands for change, and drew on the activism of individuals educated in new institutions established by the government, in part in order to provide officials. In colonies such as India and Jamaica, administrators and officers had for a long time been concerned as to how best to control populous territories with very small forces; and the military strength available was seen as the crucial support of a moral authority on which rule and control rested. The extent to which this authority was accepted by the colonised in the nineteenth century should not be exaggerated, but there is little doubt that it was under far more challenge by the interwar years, in part because the First World War had encouraged a sense of separate alongside imperial consciousness.[22]

British rule confronted serious problems in a number of colonies. In part, this was an aspect of the way in which empire was not a pacified or finished product, so that the imperial project and decolonisation were concurrent, or at least greatly overlapped. Thus, the deployment of a large garrison in Waziristan in the 1920s helped provoke a major rising in 1936.[23] In addition, the combination of opposition in the colonies and financial problems in Britain ensured that colonies became harder to administer and difficult to provide sufficient resources for. The Saya San rebellion in Burma was suppressed in 1932, while there was considerable trouble along and near the axis of British Empire in the Mediterranean. Greek Cypriot nationalists rioted in 1931, and in Malta the British were opposed by the Nationalist Party. Arab action in Palestine – a pogrom in 1929, a general strike in 1936 and a rebellion in 1937 – was largely directed against Jewish immigration. The rebellion was suppressed and did not have political consequences in Britain comparable with the question of the future of India, but there was concern about the impact of growing Arab nationalism, and in 1939 anxiety about the developing international crisis led to the issue of a White Paper designed to defuse this nationalism by rejecting the idea of partition for Palestine between Jews and Arabs. The use of force and of surveillance in Palestine indicated the extent to which policies of divide and rule and the co-option of elites were not sufficient to ensure political control,[24] and, to a varying extent, the same was true in other colonies.

The differing ability of local societies to cope with the pressures of change exacerbated contrasts between colonies and created problems for colonial governments, while in addition economic developments and tensions within the Empire helped cause political problems. In India, as elsewhere, rent disputes provided a link between economic troubles and political division, while in Burma tension owed much to the consequences of the spread of rice production geared for the Indian market, as well as to the fiscal demands of the British state; the response in the 1920s included a tax boycott.[25]

The world Depression of the 1930s reduced investment for colonial development, limiting the resources available to provide jobs at all levels, while the decline in markets for colonial goods – minerals, food and plantation products – hit local financial systems, cutting off credit and investment. As a result, social tensions became more potent: in the Gold Coast (modern Ghana), there were agrarian disputes linked to cocoa production in 1930–31 and 1937–8, and in Jamaica, where unemployment was high, labour tensions were linked to activism by the League of Coloured Peoples and in 1938 helped cause a serious crisis.[26]

In South Asia, the gravest difficulties arose not from Waziristan, although the major revolt that broke out in 1936 met with a formidable military response, but from the growing strength of the non-violent Indian National Congress Party. Gandhi's non-violent criticism of British rule, in particular his flouting of the tax on salt in 1930, led in Britain to uneasiness about the imperial position, although visual confidence was expressed in the majestic buildings designed by Sir Edwin Lutyens and Sir Herbert Baker for the official quarter in New Delhi finished in the 1930s. The British government sought a legislative response to pressures for change, and although designed to ensure British retention of the substance of power, the Government of India Act of 1935 moved towards self-government (and eventual dominion status), extending dyarchy to central government, while, as an aspect of modernisation, the Act proposed the creation of an All-India Federation, an incorporation of the hitherto autonomous princely states, although opposition by most of the princes ensured that this was not implemented.[27]

A section of the Conservative Party, led by Churchill, excluded from office from 1929, bitterly opposed the 1935 Act, seeing the moves towards self-government as a crucial step towards the abandonment of empire. For Churchill, the new policy on India was more than a tactical step, and he offered an apocalyptic vision of its consequences that appeared impractical and out of place to many. Churchill was not alone. The Indian Empire Society and the India Defence League campaigned vigorously. They were both under the presidency of John, Viscount Sumner (1859–1934). A key spokesman of the Conservative diehards, he had been one of the most out-spoken defenders of Dyer, had voiced unpopular views on Amritsar and had attacked the Anglo-Irish Treaty. Sumner, a fervent imperialist who was a contemporary of Curzon at Balliol when it was the seedbed of imperial mission, foresaw anarchy and bloodshed for the minorities if British rule was surrendered to Congress. He saw India as a trust, not to be frittered away, and said that he was not so enamoured of Western democracy as to seek to impose it on Orientals. Sumner had to face what he saw as successive betrayals over Ireland, Egypt and India, and was angered not only by Liberals but, to his greatest horror, by Conservatives who were willing to surrender British rule.

Baldwin, the Conservative leader, was no friend of the diehards, who he saw as living in the heyday of Victoria's Diamond Jubilee. The Viceroy of India, Lord Irwin, described Churchill as an 'Imperialist in the 1890–1900 sense of the word', and that sense now appeared less relevant. The bitter-ness of the parliamentary rebellion against the 1935 Act was a testimony to the continued pull of traditional notions of empire and the rebels' sense of danger, but also to their failure.[28] In the event, the provincial elections of 1937 were a success for the Indian National Congress.

Another sign of changing attitudes was provided by sensitivity to Indian opinion in the films shown there. In 1938, *The Relief of Lucknow*, a proposed film dealing with an iconic episode in the Indian Mutiny, was banned by the India Office, as were later moves to film stories from the Mutiny, and in 1939 the American film *Gunga Din* was prohibited following opposition to its showing by Indian newspapers. This led to the issue of guidelines by the India Office that banned films based on episodes in the history of British India, adaptations of Kipling and films that presented Indians as villains.[29] However, the market for empire among the British public was seen with films such as *The Drum* (1938) and *The Four Feathers* (1939), the latter, based on A. E. W. Mason's novel of 1902, a presentation of imperial endeavour in Sudan as a definition of manliness and heroism.

There was a general sense among policymakers that empire had to change, and that reform of the government of India was, alongside Imperial Trade Preference and more equal relations with the Dominions, the best means to strengthen the Empire. It was to that end that Leo Amery, an ardent imperialist, supported the legislation in 1935, while Lord Irwin (later Earl of Halifax), the Viceroy of India, backed eventual Dominion status for India. This was not the sole type of interest in imperial development. At Blickling Hall, Philip, 11th Marquess of Lothian, held regular meetings of the Round Table Movement, an influential body of idealists established in 1909 that sought what they saw as a modern future for the Empire based on greater unity and informed public support. More generally, the League of Nations' creation after the First World War of mandates for the colonies allocated to the victors had introduced the idea of an oversight of imperial rule from the outside and, although this did not amount to much, it contributed to a stress on such rule as a trust.

Empire was certainly changing at its closest point. In Ireland, relations between the Free State and Britain remained good until the Fianna Fáil party under Eamonn de Valera gained power after the 1932 election. He successfully pressed the British to recall the Governor-General, and the new one, nominated by de Valera, undertook no public duties, while the Executive Authority (External Relations) Act of 1936 limited the role of the Crown in the Free State to diplomatic formalities, and then only as advised by the Executive Council. After coming to power, de Valera set off an 'Economic War' with Britain by suspending the payment of land annuities from Irish farmers to the British government. A cycle of retaliation led to protectionism by both sides, hitting Irish agricultural exports to Britain, and the 'war' was ended by agreement in 1938. The previous year, a new constitution, passed after a referendum, asserted the Irish state's territorial claim to Northern Ireland, while the oath of allegiance to the Crown that MPs had been obliged to take under the Anglo-Irish Treaty of 1921 was abolished. The constitution was republican in essence, described the Irish State, now rechristened Eire (Ireland), as a 'sovereign independent, democratic state', and stipulated that the head of state was to be a directly elected President; Irish was to be the first language, an important declaration of cultural independence. De Valera did not want to go the whole way to independence: he hoped to keep open a bridge to the Ulster Unionists and was fearful of losing any remaining advantage of staying just inside the Commonwealth.

Although far less serious, there were also indications of tension in colonies ruled by the Dominions. In 1929, protest in Samoa owing to the suppression of the Fono of Faipule, Samoa's democratic assembly, and organised by the Mau movement, led to an armed police response in which the High Chief was killed and to the deployment of New Zealand troops.

THE NAVAL SITUATION

At sea, Britain was no longer in as strong a position as she had been prior to the First World War. She remained the strongest European naval power – under the Versailles agreement, the Germans lacked a battle fleet – but now had to consider the additional challenge of Japan with which relations deteriorated, although the Treasury proved reluctant to share the Admiralty's concerns.[30] In 1919, Jellicoe, who visited Australasia, pressed for a Far East Fleet including eight battleships and four carriers, to assuage his concerns about Japan, while an Admiralty memorandum warned that the navy was likely to be weaker than that of Japan in the Far East, suggested that using Hong Kong would expose the fleet to attack and argued, instead, that Singapore should be developed as a base, as it was sufficiently far from Japan to permit reinforcement without peril.[31] Hitherto, the challenge to Britain's position in Asia had been the land threat from Russian expansion, particularly across Central Asia toward Persia, Afghanistan and India, but also toward Manchuria, and the response had been military and diplomatic policies focused on the land mass, with the navy playing only a supporting role. The rise of Japanese power and its application to an expansionism judged unwelcome by Britain raised the prospect of a naval challenge in Far Eastern or even Indian waters that could not be countered by strength in home waters. In the First World War, Japan as an ally had deployed her navy to distant waters, as the USA had done, attacking German bases in the Pacific, escorting British convoys from Australia, hunting German surface raiders and in 1917 sending warships to assist the Allies in the Mediterranean. After the war, it was necessary for Britain to adjust to this capability, and this was done by a naval limitation agreement. Britain accepted naval parity with the Americans, the leading industrial and financial power in the world, and both states accepted the fact of Japanese naval power in the Pacific: a $5:5:3$ ratio in the capital ship tonnage of the three powers was agreed in the Washington Naval Treaty of 1922, which also included an agreement to scrap many battleships and to stop new construction for ten years. Extended by the London Naval Treaty of 1930, this agreement very much affected the force structure of the British navy.[32]

The Washington Naval Treaty had been accepted in the shadow of the build-up of the American navy ordered in 1916 which Britain lacked the economic and financial strength to match. She had won the naval race with Germany before the First World War, but could not win one with the USA, although the need to adjust to American power seen in naval ratios was eased by a *de facto* division of spheres of activity. The Americans took an interventionist role in the Caribbean, where they had conquered Puerto Rico from Spain in 1898 and bought St. Croix, St. Johns and St. Thomas from Denmark in 1917. Furthermore, the construction of the Panama Canal, and the American role in the Canal Zone, gave the American navy flexibility in deployment between the Atlantic and the Pacific, where American power was considerable, with the Philippines, Guam, Wake and Hawaii the major possessions. In contrast, the USA had no naval role in the Indian Ocean, while the British were more prominent in the South Atlantic and in East Asian waters. Although it was possible to settle Anglo–American naval ratios, there was tension in relations at the governmental level, and British politicians felt that their American counterparts were uncooperative.[33]

In Britain, the impact of difficult government finances posed a serious problem for the navy, as the Treasury repeatedly pressed for cuts in expenditure, while, in addition, there were the difficulties of adapting to developments in naval capability. Financial pressures caused a crisis in September 1931, when pay cuts imposed by the National Government led to the Invergordon Mutiny, in which sailors of 15 warships of the British Atlantic fleet, based at Invergordon in the Cromarty Firth, refused to go on duty. The Admiralty's willingness to revise the cuts ended the crisis in the fleet,[34] but the episode helped cause a run on sterling in the foreign-exchange markets, and the government had to come off the Gold Standard on 20 September.

The Admiralty regarded the demands of empire and trade as putting particular pressure on British naval requirements. Jellicoe argued that submarines destroyed the feasibility of close blockade of enemy naval bases, forcing a reliance for trade protection on convoys protected by cruisers, and was concerned that Britain had insufficient cruisers both to do this and to work with the battle fleet in a future war. Admiralty anxiety was also expressed by Admiral Sir Charles Madden, the First Sea Lord, in a meeting of the Cabinet Committee preparing for the 1930 London Naval Conference:

> The Admiralty required a sufficient number of cruisers to give security to the overseas trade of the Empire against raiding forces of the enemy and a battlefleet to give cover to the trade protecting cruisers . . . unlike any other nation, we had to dissipate our cruiser strength to protect our dominions and colonies, and our vital lines of communication.[35]

The serious Anglo-American dispute over cruiser numbers at and after the Geneva Naval Conference of 1927 reflected the difficulties American negotiators faced in accepting British concerns for the Empire; concerns that owed much to a British fear of Japanese naval superiority in Far Eastern waters. Worries about the naval situation were publicly voiced by Admiral G. A. Ballard in his *Rulers of the Indian Ocean* (1927), in which he argued that the rise in American and Japanese naval power had transformed the situation as it was no longer sufficient for Britain to prevail over European rivals in order to win naval dominance. Aside from seeing both Japan and the USA as threats, and drawing attention to rising nationalism in Asia, Ballard presented the Empire as vulnerable in the Indian Ocean, and argued that this made necessary the development of a strong base in Singapore:

> As regards its present form or fabric the Empire may be roughly divided into an occidental half – including the British Isles – and an oriental; which are held together commercially and strategically by the Imperial lines of communication across the Indian Ocean; the whole being kept in contact with foreign lands throughout the East by the trade routes traversing the same water-space. If those connections are cut, the two halves of the Empire will fall apart as surely as night follows day.[36]

As tensions mounted in the Far East in the 1920s and, even more, 1930s, with an increase in the size of the Japanese navy and Japanese expansionism more pronounced, so it was indeed necessary for Britain to reconcile commitments in both the Atlantic and Eastern waters. The British planned to send much of their fleet to Singapore in the event of war with Japan, and to proceed with the completion and defences of the naval base at Singapore.[37] Japanese intervention in China, first in Manchuria from 1931 and then more widely, particularly from 1937, challenged British interests, and the moves of the British China Squadron were harassed by larger Japanese forces. This not only intimidated the British in China,[38] but also affected naval planning as a whole as there was anxiety about the ability of the navy to

respond to its range of possible commitments.[39] In response to Treasury opposition in 1934 to sending a fleet to the Far East and, instead, concern about
Germany and support for a focus on air power, it was argued by both the
Admiralty and the Dominions Office that this was unacceptable because of
the impact on Australia and New Zealand of leaving them without support.[40]

At the same time as the Japanese became more aggressive, the development of the German and Italian navies in the 1930s suggested that both
powers might contest European waters, while German rearmament was used
by army and air force advocates to press for an emphasis on their services,
and not on the navy which was most concerned about Japan. Under the
Anglo-German Naval Treaty of 1935, an attempt to provide an acceptable
structure for German demands for rearmament that was criticised as an
example of unilateral appeasement, Germany was to have a surface fleet up
to 35 per cent the size of that of Britain, although the submarine fleet could
be the same size; but Hitler ignored these restrictions in his naval build-up.
The British were aware that any war would bring the threat of both air and
sea attacks on their communications. The February 1934 report of the
Defence Requirements Sub-Committee of the Committee of Imperial
Defence noted of the navy: 'The greatest potential threat lies in the
acquisition of submarines and aircraft by Germany'.[41] The German–
Japanese pact of 1936 accentuated Britain's vulnerability.

Imperial vulnerability was also readily apparent on land and in the air in
the 1930s, as the army and air force found that their range of commitments
made it difficult to respond to the growing threat posed by German rearmament. Under the Ten Year Rule adopted in 1919, it had been argued that
there would be no 'great war' involving the Empire for another ten years,
that therefore there was no need to prepare for one, a major restraint on
expenditure demands, and that the army and air force should focus on
imperial control. This Rule was renewed until suspended in March 1932,
and in 1934 the Committee of Imperial Defence noted 'It was under this
assumption, which became gradually untenable, that our present and exceed-
ingly serious deficiencies have accumulated'. Malta, for example, had only
12 anti-aircraft guns, and they were old and increasingly obsolete. In 1934,
the Committee also argued that preparations for a larger mechanised force
for warfare in Europe would hit the support of necessary imperial tasks,[42]
and, when such a war was forced on Britain in 1939, her ability to discharge
these tasks was greatly compromised.

Mussolini, the Fascist dictator of Italy, was eager to develop the Italian
navy and thus threatened the British position in the Mediterranean, the
crucial axis of the British Empire and one that was dependent on naval
power and related bases, for from bases in Gibraltar, Malta and Alexandria,
the navy protected the route to India and supported the military presence

in Cyprus and Palestine, and this naval role ensured that, although there was no maritime conflict in this period, the military basis of the Empire remained that of naval power. The Italian invasion of Abyssinia (Ethiopia) in 1935–6 led to the possibility of conflict with Italy, as the League of Nations condemned the invasion, and the Mediterranean Fleet assembled in force at Alexandria and was reinforced from other stations. Despite weaknesses, including a lack of sailors, reserves and anti-aircraft ammunition, the navy was confident that it could beat that of Italy, and the Italians were concerned on that front. Having unsuccessfully sought to settle the dispute by diplomatic means at the expense of Abyssinia, the government considered oil sanctions against Italy and closing the Suez Canal to Italian resupply ships, but France was willing to co-operate only if Britain undertook to guarantee the demilitarisation of the Rhineland, which it refused to do. In addition, the government wished to keep Italy separate from Germany, feared provoking Italian attacks on British shipping and bases in the Mediterranean, and did not wish to antagonise the Americans by stopping their tankers.[43] The failure to intimidate Italy was more a consequence of an absence of political will than of a lack of naval capability. This was true also of British neutrality during the Spanish Civil War of 1936–9, in which the navy was employed to protect trade routes threatened by Italian submarines acting on behalf of Franco's Nationalists.[44] The Mediterranean played an important role not only in imperial strategy, but also in British foreign policy, and the appeasement of Italy was a precursor to that of Germany,[45] which owed much to an awareness of the strategic problems of the British Empire: wide-ranging commitments that were incompatible with available resources.[46]

Under the pressure of growing German, Italian and Japanese naval strength, and increased doubts about the policies of all three powers, the navy was expanded as part of a general, and expensive, programme of rearmament, although this was affected by limitations in industrial capacity and capability, including a shortage of high-quality precision-engineering and of armourers, that led to weaknesses in a number of spheres, such as anti-aircraft fire-control, while the import of foreign technology strained the balance of payments.[47] A large number of carriers, cruisers and destroyers were laid down, while, after control over the Fleet Air Arm was transferred from the Royal Air Force to the Admiralty in 1937, it was greatly expanded. Anti-submarine methods and equipment were developed, although what could be achieved was widely misunderstood, while radar sets were installed in warships from 1938.[48] As Germany, Italy and the Soviet Union did not build carriers in the interwar period, and France had only one, Britain's carriers (four had been commissioned in 1923–30, having been converted from a battleship and three battle-cruisers) gave an important added dimension to her naval superiority over other European powers: four 23,000-ton carriers, the *Illustrious* class, each able to make over 30 knots and having a 3-inch armoured flight deck, were laid down in 1937, following the 22,000-ton *Ark Royal* laid down in 1935. The 23,450 *Implacable* was laid down in February 1939, although it was not commissioned until August 1944.[49] Furthermore, Britain had a clear lead over other European states in battleships, and although some theorists argued that battleships were now obsolete in the face of air power and submarines, big surface warships had a continued appeal, and British emphasis on battle-fleet tactics based on battleships and firepower was not simply a sign of conservatism: adaptability was displayed in tactics,[50] while in the Second World War, surface ships were crucial for conflict with other surface ships, not least because, although there were spectacular losses, many battleships took considerable punishment before being sunk by air attack.

Despite these strengths, Britain, thanks to a failure to build sufficient warships, lacked a navy capable of fighting Germany, Italy and Japan simultaneously.[51] This was the product of the stop on capital-ship construction under the Washington Naval Treaty, as well as the lack of sufficient industrial capability and fiscal strength. To expect the arithmetic of naval power to provide for conflict at once with all three powers was to anticipate a margin of superiority that was unreasonable given the state of the country, but also one that diplomacy sought to avoid. British naval strategy assumed that, if necessary, 'operations would be conducted sequentially in separate theatres by the Main Fleet to meet multiple threats arising simultaneously', a strategy that assumed that flexibility could help lessen the constraints posed by tough fiscal limits.[52] In addition, war was likely to bring Britain the support of allies, and thus Britain benefited from the increase in the naval power of a number of states. Italy did not enter the war until 1940 and Japan until December 1941, and although the loss of French naval support in 1940 was unexpected, Japanese entry led to an alliance with the USA that was crucial to the security of Australasia and to the maintenance of control over the Atlantic. British amphibious warfare capability was weak, but an invasion of France in a future war was not anticipated.

The Empire, however, was in a position to provide little naval support. In 1938, Australia had six cruisers and five destroyers, Canada only six destroyers and four minesweepers, New Zealand two light cruisers and India only eight small coastal ships. Co-operation was nevertheless eased by the extensive use of British or British-derived equipment and tactics. Under challenge, the Empire was developing its processes of consultation, and during the Munich crisis of 1938 Dominion leaders, such as William Mackenzie King, Prime Minister of Canada, expressed their views, mostly in favour of appeasement. Canada had earlier been opposed to supporting

Australia, New Zealand and, to a lesser extent, Britain as they searched for a response against Japanese aggression in China.[53] Meanwhile, British policy in India represented a stage between the traditional co-option of local support and democratisation. As with so much else, it is unclear what would have happened to the Empire but for the Second World War.

THE SECOND WORLD WAR

This sense of contingency continued during the conflict itself. In September 1944, Admiral Sir Geoffrey Layton, Commander-in-Chief Ceylon, wrote of

> the vital importance of our recapturing those parts of the Empire as far as possible ourselves. I would specially mention the recapture of Burma and its culmination in the recovery of Singapore by force of arms and not by waiting for it to be surrendered as part of any peace treaty . . . the immense effect this will have on our prestige in the Far East in post-war years. This and only this in my opinion will restore us to our former level in the eyes of the native population in these parts.

Lord Louis Mountbatten, the Allied Commander-in-Chief for South-East Asia, strongly agreed.[54]

The course of the war had dealt heavy blows to British power and prestige, and the prestige of the Empire throughout Asia was held to be fatally compromised by the humiliating surrender of Singapore to the Japanese in 1942, the culmination of the rapid conquest of Malaya, in which large numbers of British and Empire forces were outmanoeuvred and outfought by a smaller but more mobile Japanese army before surrendering. The Japanese had already captured Hong Kong in December 1941, and they were to go on to conquer Burma in the spring of 1942.

Defeats at the hands of Japan in 1941–2 pressed hard on an empire that had already been badly battered by Germany. Although the German attack on Poland in 1939 was the cause of the war, as Britain and France honoured the guarantees to Poland given earlier that year, the alliance was able to do nothing to stop the Germans quickly conquering the country.

At sea, the German navy attacked British trade routes. Instead of using their surface fleet as a unit and providing the British with a concentrated target, the Germans relied on raids by individual ships designed, in particular, to attack British shipping and to divert British warships from home waters. Such ships were hunted down, however. Thus, the 'pocket battleship' *Graf Spee*, which had sunk over 50,000 tons of British merchant shipping in the Atlantic, was damaged by British shelling off Buenos Aires in the battle of the River Plate (13 December 1939). In order to prevent the vessels from falling into British hands, its captain scuttled it on the 17th. Although the British force in the battle was less heavily gunned (by 11.1 inch to 8-inch guns) and badly outranged by over four miles, the clash was a significant indicator of British naval strength prior to the entry of Italy and Japan into the war and with France still allied to Britain. Aside from the availability of three cruisers for the battle, another was on hand to block-ade the *Graf Spee* in Montevideo, while the availability of a strategic reserve was seen with the dispatch of the battle cruiser *Renown* and the carrier *Ark Royal* to provide further reinforcement. The numerical strength of the navy had already been demonstrated when the Home Fleet with French assis-tance chased the *Scharnhorst* and *Gneisenau* back from a rapidly terminated hunt for merchantmen.

The *Graf Spee*'s cruise was responsible for one of the most memorable lines in British naval history, a morale-booster that had much significance for its generation. The warship captured 299 seamen who were then trans-ported to European waters on a supply ship, the *Altmark*, and treated harshly. Taking shelter from British pursuers in Norwegian territorial waters, the *Altmark* claimed freedom from Norwegian attempts to search the ship thor-oughly, leading a boarding party from the British destroyer *Cossack* to board and capture the ship on 16 February, the boarding officer shouting 'The Navy's here'. The episode appeared to show that the navy could fulfil its traditional roles in a glorious manner, and suggested continuity in a more troubled world in which aircraft and submarines took a prominent role. This episode, however, encouraged Hitler to press ahead with his plans for an invasion of Norway. Launched in April, this met with an inadequate British response. There was a general failure of naval manage-ment, as the mistaken conviction that the Germans were seeking to break out into the North Atlantic in order to attack trade routes ensured that poorly directed British warships failed to prevent the initial German land-ings. In addition, British warships were shown to be unable to cope effec-tively with German air power, and a doctrine of reliance on anti-aircraft fire was revealed as inadequate. Admiral Sir Dudley Pound, the First Sea Lord, remarked 'The lesson we have learnt here is that it is essential to have fighter protection over the Fleet whenever they are within reach of the enemy bombers'.[55]

The forces sent to Norway were unable to stem the German advance, and the launching of the major German offensive in the West undercut the British intervention and led to the withdrawal of the expeditionary force from Narvik. The navy also took hard knocks from the German surface warships, particularly when escorting the ships bringing back the Narvik force: HMS *Glorious* and two accompanying destroyers were sunk by the *Scharnhorst*, the only aircraft carrier ever sunk by battleships.

The German offensive launched on 10 May 1940 overran the Netherlands, Belgium and France swiftly, and cruelly exposed both the deficiencies of Allied strategy and the operational superiority of the Germans. The British were able to evacuate most of their isolated expeditionary force from Dunkirk, but defeat and the surrender of France left Britain exposed to invasion and greatly altered the naval balance of power by denying Britain the support of the French navy and by providing the Germans with nearby bases where they could accumulate barges, steamers, tugs and motorboats for their proposed landing. In response, the English coastline was hastily fortified, with anti-tank mines, concrete blocks, barbed-wire pillboxes and coastal-defence batteries. As a preparatory measure for their planned invasion, the Germans sought not only to seal the invasion route with minefields, but, more importantly, to gain air superiority over the Channel and southern England. Their failure, in the Battle of Britain, helped dissuade them from invasion, but, already, the absence of necessary preparations and the lure of war with the Soviet Union had ensured that there was not a viable window of opportunity.

Several leading politicians had felt it necessary, in the aftermath of defeat in France, to consider a negotiated peace. In May 1940, Viscount Halifax, the Foreign Secretary, was ready, if Hitler made one, 'to accept an offer which would save the country from avoidable disaster'. Hitler held out the possibility of peace on the basis of accepting German domination of Europe and returning the German colonies acquired as a result of the First World War, but Churchill, who had replaced Chamberlain as Prime Minister in May, as a result of widespread concern at the military situation, was understandably unwilling to trust Hitler and determined to fight on. He successfully outmanoeuvred his rivals in the government, but the military situation was still parlous, and late 1940 and early 1941 were the nadir of Britain's twentieth century. Effectively bankrupt, Britain was also faced with grave threats to her trade. The fall of France had increased British vulnerability, as German submarines were now based in the Atlantic ports of France, while British cities were under heavy air attack in the Blitz and Coventry, London and Southampton were devastated. These attacks failed to drive Britain out of the war, but they made it clear how far Britain had been pushed back onto the defensive. Ports attracted particular attention from the German air force both then and later in the war, and the damage done to London's docklands and to other harbour areas, particularly Plymouth and Southampton, destroyed much of the dockland townscape, especially the inter-connection of places of work and tightly packed terraced housing, and dispersed much of its population. When these cities were rebuilt after the war, the focus was not on recreating this world, nor indeed on utilitarian notions linked to harbour activities, but, instead, on applying generalised notions of progressive townplanning, the dire consequences of which can still be seen.[56]

Vulnerable and isolated in 1940–41, Britain had two crucial supports, the navy and the Empire, lending a pointed background to the publication in 1941 of J. A. Williamson's *The Ocean in English History*. The navy had played the major role in the evacuations from Dunkirk and elsewhere on the French coast, while British naval strength ensured that Hitler did not gain the full maritime benefit from his conquests that he might have done, especially by lessening the possibility of an invasion of England. In the North Atlantic, the British acted to limit the impact of the German conquest of Denmark by occupying the Faeroes, a strategic archipelago, in April 1940, and Iceland the following month.

The British had planned that, in the event of war with Japan, they would be able to rely on the French to protect their joint interests in the Mediterranean, while much of the British fleet sailed to Singapore. France's surrender to Germany in 1940 transformed the naval situation, and anxiety about the future of the French fleet moored at its North African base at Mers-el-Kébir near Oran led to a demand that it scuttle, join the British or sail to a harbour outside possible German control. When this was refused, the fleet was attacked on 3 July 1940, one battleship was sunk and two were damaged. In contrast, an attack proved unnecessary in order to ensure an acceptable oversight of the French warships in Alexandria, Plymouth and Portsmouth.[57] In some respects the attack at Mers-el-Kébir was a blunder, as it seriously weakened support within France for Charles de Gaulle and the cause of continued resistance to Germany, made it easier for the Vichy government to collaborate with the Germans and did not lead to the destruction of the most recent French battleships. It also demonstrated, however, the capability of the British navy; at least in the absence of hostile air attacks.

The most spectacular of the German warship raids, by the battleship *Bismarck* in May 1941, was designed to build on successful raids by the *Admiral Scheer*, the *Admiral Hipper*, the *Scharnhorst* and the *Gneisenau* between October 1940 and March 1941, and to show that surface warships could make a major impact on North Atlantic shipping; instead, it became one of the last unassisted victories for British naval power. British bombers failed to find the *Bismarck* as it sailed north through Norwegian waters, but she was spotted by patrolling warships as she approached the North Atlantic through the Denmark Strait, between Iceland and Greenland, on 23 May. The following day, the *Bismarck* and her sister ship, the cruiser *Prinz Eugen*, encountered a squadron sent to intercept her south-west of Iceland. In these difficult waters, ship radar helped the British shadow the German warships, but, in the subsequent gunnery exchange, the *Bismarck* sank the battle-cruiser *Hood*, one of the most prominent warships in the navy, with the loss of all bar three of her crew of 1,419. The battleship *Prince of Wales* was also damaged, but one of its shells hit the *Bismarck*, causing a dangerous oil leak that led the commander to set course for St-Nazaire in France and repairs. What had proved a terrible blow to British naval power and prestige was to be assuaged by a massive deployment of warships from the Home Fleet and the Gibraltar-based Force H, including five battleships, two battle-cruisers, thirteen other cruisers and two aircraft carriers. The *Bismarck* was eventually crippled by a hit on the rudder by an aircraft-launched torpedo on 26 May, a demonstration of the vulnerability of surface ships to air power, and, heavily damaged by a pounding by battleships, the *Bismarck* fell victim on the 27th to a cruiser-launched torpedo; although the Germans claimed that they scuttled the ship.[58] The torpedoing of the heavy cruiser *Lützow* off Norway by British air attack on 12 June ended the surface raiding of Atlantic sea routes.

The German submarine assault on British shipping was more serious and sustained. Submarines were less vulnerable than surface ships to blockade, detection and destruction, and could be manufactured quicker and in large quantities, but, owing to an overlong commitment to surface warships, the Germans did not focus their entire naval construction effort on submarines until the spring of 1943, after the failure on 31 December 1942 in the battle of the Barents Sea to use surface ships against less-heavily-gunned British cruisers to block the British supply route to the Soviet Union had led Hitler to change his naval commander.

Submarines were more sophisticated than in the First World War, and from 1940 the Germans had Norwegian and French bases, both of which they had lacked in the previous war. As a result, shipping sunk by U-boats rose from the summer of 1940, at a time when British warships were focused on home waters to cover the evacuation of forces from France and to retain control of the English Channel in the face of German invasion preparations. There were also severe losses in the winter of 1940–41, as the U-boats attacked Atlantic convoys and developed wolf-pack tactics. Aircraft forced U-boats to submerge where their speed was slower and where it was harder to maintain visual contact with targets, but neither the RAF, which was interested in strategic bombing and theatre fighters, nor the navy, which was primarily concerned with hostile surface shipping and content to rely on convoys and ASDIC (sonar) to limit submarine attempts, had devoted sufficient preparation to air cover against submarines, and the effectiveness of ASDIC was limited as submarines preferred to hunt on the surface. The British had used carrier-based planes against submarines at the start of the war, but the sinking by *U-29* of the carrier HMS *Courageous* on 17 September 1939 ended this practice, and the remaining fleet carriers were needed for operations against German and, from June 1940, Italian surface warships, while it took time to build escort aircraft-carriers: the first entered service in late 1941. In addition, the demands of the bomber offensive against Germany on available long-range aircraft restricted the numbers available for convoy escort, while land-based aircraft faced an 'Air Gap' across much of the mid-Atlantic.[59]

Although the stages by which the USA moved towards war tend to attract scholarly attention, it was the Empire that provided vital assistance for embattled Britain especially before American entry in December 1941 and also thereafter. The outbreak of war had been followed by the convoying of Australasian troops to Egypt, providing a vital fill-up to the British strategic reserve in the Middle East. The convoys were escorted by Australian warships, while the five destroyers in the Australian fleet had been sent to join the British fleet in the Mediterranean at the outset of the war. In 1940, at a time of threatened German invasion, the presence of Canadian forces, successfully convoyed across the Atlantic the previous winter, greatly strengthened the ability to repel attack. Canadian and New Zealand pilots played an important role in the Battle of Britain, while the Canadian navy also took the major role in convoying ships in the western Atlantic.[60] Over five million fighting troops were raised by the Empire during the war, the largest number in India; while the absence of large-scale sustained opposition within the colonies to British rule ensured that military resources could be concentrated on war with the Axis. The Empire also provided strategic depth. When, in the House of Commons on 4 June 1940, Churchill pledged to fight on, he added that, even if Britain was conquered, 'our Empire beyond the seas, armed and guarded by the British Fleet, would carry on the struggle' until the USA joined in. This echoed the assurance offered by Edward Gibbon in his *History of the Decline and Fall of the Roman Empire* (1776–88) that, in the unlikely event of civilisation collapsing in Europe before new barbarian inroads, it would be sustained 'in the American world'.[61]

Dominion and Empire forces were given a bigger role as a result of Italy's entry into the war on 10 June 1940 and Japan's on 7 December 1941. Mussolini sought gains from the British Empire, as well as from France and in the Balkans, and Admiral Domenico Cavagnari, the Chief of the Italian naval staff, had planned a fleet able to seize control of both ends of the Mediterranean, so that it could operate on the oceans. Mussolini's ambitions, however, were not based on a reasonable assessment of the capabilities of the Italian military machine, and Dominion and Empire forces played a major role in resisting Italian attacks, and then in invading Italian colonies.

In East Africa, the Italians overran British Somaliland in August 1940: larger Italian forces were able to outflank well-defended British positions and the far less numerous British garrison was evacuated by sea. However, on a larger scale, a poorly prepared and commanded invasion of Egypt from the Italian colony of Libya was mounted hesitantly, stalled and was then routed in December 1940 by the British forces. The Italians were then driven out of Egypt, before the British went on to conquer Cyrenaica (eastern Libya), taking large numbers of prisoners. The Australians played a prominent role in the operations in Libya, while the decision of Churchill to send tanks, which were a key part of Britain's strategic reserve, to Egypt was important to the success of operations in North Africa, and, like the movement of Dominion and Empire forces there, the Australians across the Indian Ocean and up the Red Sea, it reflected the benefit of controlling the sea-lanes. This was also seen in East Africa. In February 1941, British forces (mostly from East, South and West Africa) outfought the more numerous Italians in Italian Somaliland, and this was followed by the conquest of Eritrea and Ethiopia.[62] Although the advances were overland, maritime power was again important. For example the capture of the port city of Massawa in April 1941 was important to British logistics.

The Italians were also defeated at sea in the Mediterranean, in what was to provide the British navy with a glorious period that, in some respects, at least for British audiences, repeated the impression gained by eighteenth-century victories over France. Despite the numerical strength of the Italian navy, its superiority over the British in several types of warships and the success of individual Italian units, they were not to make a major impact on British naval strength, and instead the British repeatedly took the initiative. In a surprise night attack by 21 carrier-launched torpedo planes on Taranto harbour on 11 November 1940, three Italian battleships were badly damaged, while on 28 March 1941 off Cape Matapan, in Britain's last major high seas fleet battle, thanks to torpedo aircraft, battleship firepower and ships' radar, the navy sank three Italian cruisers and damaged a battleship.[63]

The situation was to deteriorate over the following year. Hitler had responded to Italian defeats, and to the possibility of weakening the British in the Mediterranean, by sending assistance to Mussolini, and from January 1941 the dispatch of German planes to Sicily helped make the central Mediterranean hazardous to British shipping, while German submarines were also to inflict serious damage after deployment from October 1941. Owing to German air power, British plans for amphibious attacks on Italian positions in the Mediterranean – Pantellaria or the Dodecanese – now seemed redundant, and the British were unable to prevent the transport of German troops to Libya. On land, the Germans both defeated the British in North Africa and successfully conquered Yugoslavia and Greece, and

British intervention in Greece proved fruitless, the Balkan campaign culminating in May 1941 with the capture of Crete by German parachute and glider troops. The vulnerability of sea power to air attack was amply demonstrated: in attempts to reinforce and eventually evacuate Crete, the Mediterranean Fleet took many losses, including three cruisers and six destroyers, and naval commanders were concerned about the way in which British policy was committing their ships to a vulnerable deployment.

There was also anxiety about German plans in the Atlantic. Hitler was interested in the idea of a league of Germany, Italy, Fascist Spain and Vichy France. Spain's entry would have led to an attack on Gibraltar that, if successful, would have destroyed the British ability to operate in the Western Mediterranean, not least as the Germans would have gained air bases in southern Spain. In addition there was concern in Britain that Spanish entry into the war would enable the Germans to gain submarine bases on Spain's Atlantic coast and in the Canary Islands, a Spanish territory, making the task of containing the U-boats even more difficult. There was, indeed, German interest in acquiring bases in the Atlantic, from where it would be possible to threaten British convoy routes, to increase German influence in South America and to challenge American power, an aspect of the interest of the Naval Staff in Germany becoming a power with a global reach provided by a strong surface navy. However, although Hitler wanted Germany to regain the overseas colonies it had lost in the First World War, an aspect of his general desire to reverse the losses and humiliations of that conflict, this was tangential to his central concern with creating a new Europe. British concern led to planning, in early 1941, for landings on the (Portuguese) Azores and Canaries to pre-empt possible German moves and to planning for the invasion of neutral Eire in order to ensure the use of the ports – Cobh, Castletown Bere and Lough Swilly – that the British had retained the right to use when Ireland gained independence, but which they had handed over in 1938. Irish neutrality was a powerful affirmation of independence from Britain and one that was much resented, not least by the 43,000 Irishmen who volunteered to fight for Britain, but it was deemed prudent not to occupy Eire.

American participation in the anti-submarine conflict with Germany pre-dated the German declaration of war on America in December 1941. As an important gesture, the USA provided 50 surplus destroyers (seven of them to the Canadian navy) in September 1940 in return for 99-year leases on bases in Antigua, the Bahamas, Bermuda, British Guiana, Jamaica, Newfoundland, St. Lucia and Trinidad. In practice, the deal was of limited value as the ships took time to prepare, but, aside from the psychological value at a time when Britain was vulnerable, no other power was in a position to provide such help. In March 1941, the passage by Congress of the Lend-Lease Act granted the American government the right to sell, lend or trade military *matériel* to any state vital to American security, opening the way for the shipping of American military supplies to Britain, and in July American forces replaced the British as the garrison of Iceland as part of their attempt to protect the Western Hemisphere, a policy outlined at the Havana conference of July 1940. During the Placentia Bay conference of 9–12 August 1941, Churchill and the American President, Franklin Delano Roosevelt, agreed to allocate spheres of strategic responsibility, with the Americans becoming responsible, alongside the Canadians, for escorting convoys in the western Atlantic. On 4 September, the *Greer*, an American destroyer, was attacked by a U-boat south-west of Iceland, leading Roosevelt to give the navy the authority to fire on German and Italian warships in waters protected by the Americans. That December, Hitler followed the Japanese attack on Pearl Harbor by declaring war on the USA, claiming that his decision was in response to American 'provocations' in the Atlantic, and he was indeed angered by American co-operation with the British against U-boat operations. The Germans appear to have been confident that the U-boats would weaken the USA, lessening the impact of its entry into the war.

The lesson of vulnerability to air attack was to be driven home off Malaya on 10 December 1941 when land-based Japanese naval bombers sank the battleship *Prince of Wales* and the battle-cruiser *Repulse*, the first ships of these types sunk at sea solely by air attack. Their loss demonstrated the susceptibility of capital-ships without air cover to enemy air attack, and arose primarily from the mistakes of the force commander, Admiral Sir Tom Phillips, but his poorly conceived and executed plan reflected wider problems: a lack of strategic foresight and operational weaknesses, including the problems of air–sea co-ordination.[64] Air support also helped the Japanese defeat a fleet made up of American, Australian, British and Dutch warships in the battle of the Java Sea from 27 February to 1 March 1942 without the loss of any of their own warships, greatly altering the naval balance in the south-west Pacific. Meanwhile the Japanese had rapidly overrun Malaya and Singapore, the last a particular humiliation, at the end of a badly mismanaged campaign and one that revealed serious deficiencies in British, Indian and Australian forces.[65]

Japanese naval capability was demonstrated anew in the spring of 1942 when a fleet that included six carriers moved into the Indian Ocean. A naval raid on Ceylon in April led to heavy damage to shore installations at Colombo and Trincomalee, and the sinking of two heavy cruisers and a carrier inadequately protected from dive bombers, while the Japanese lost no warships in the operation. In addition, a Japanese squadron mounted air raids on ports in east India and attacks on shipping in the Bay of Bengal, the Japanese occupied the Andaman and Nicobar Islands, and their army easily conquered Burma in another serious blow to British imperial power and prestige. In his War Diary, Layton pointed out that the British had been poorly prepared:

> Ceylon, on my arrival there on 21st January, was virtually defenceless . . . the problem of retaining control of the coastal waters of Burma was quite beyond our powers in the absence of either air superiority or fast patrol craft with good AA [anti-aircraft] armament so numerous that we could afford substantial losses.[66]

After the sinking of the British warships, the British withdrew their fleet from Ceylon to East Africa or Bombay, for Admiral Somerville was now having to think about the need to protect the Arabian Sea, and thus tanker sailings from the Persian Gulf, as well as the route from both the Gulf and the Red Sea down the coast of East Africa to the Cape of Good Hope. The clear need for carrier support led to the laying down of ten light fleet carriers between June 1942 and January 1943, as it was correctly anticipated that these would be finished more quickly than larger carriers.

Australia was left vulnerable by the Japanese advance into the East Indies and on 19 February 1942 Darwin was bombed, the first in a series of air attacks on northern Australia. There were only seven militia divisions available for home defence, and as a result there were plans to abandon northern Australia and to focus on defending a line north of Brisbane. Meanwhile, having seized Rabaul on New Britain on 23 January 1942, the Japanese had decided to press on to seize Port Moresby, New Caledonia, Fiji and Samoa in order to isolate Australia. This threat to Australia, New Zealand and British colonies in Oceania was thwarted by the American navy in the battle of the Coral Sea on 7–8 May 1942. American fighters had already arrived at Darwin on 17 March, providing protection for northern Australia. The build-up of American air support was important in lessening Australia's vulnerability and, alongside naval and land forces, was, subsequently, to play an important role in helping the Australians drive the Japanese back in New Guinea.

American entry into the war was indeed followed by very heavy losses to U-boat attacks in American coastal waters in the first half of 1942, but in May 1942 the situation improved considerably as effective convoying was introduced by the Americans. This led the U-boats from July to focus anew on the mid-Atlantic. Deciphered information (code-named ULTRA) had provided an ability to plot U-boat positions from May 1941, enabling the rerouting of convoys, but in February 1942 a new, more complex key was introduced. In 1942, 1,664 merchantmen amounting to nearly eight million tons were sunk by U-boats and the losses of U-boats were less than new

launchings – 58 lost in July–December 1942 when 121 were completed –
while, for the first time, there were enough U-boats to organise compre-
hensive patrol lines across North Atlantic convoy routes. The wartime peak
of tonnage sunk by the Germans (700,000) was reached in November 1942.
Allied shipping was particularly vulnerable then because many of the
destroyers and frigates that had escorted convoys were allocated to
Operation Torch, the successful American invasion of Morocco and
Algeria. However, after the summer of 1942, the effectiveness of individual
submarine patrols, in terms of tonnage sank, fell, reflecting the increase of
convoying and the greater strength of convoy escorts; and the majority of
merchantmen sunk in 1942 were sailing independently.

New emphasis was given to the submarine war in January 1943 when
Admiral Karl Dönitz, the head of the U-boat service, became commander
of the German navy, and particularly serious damage on Allied shipping was
inflicted in March. The Allies, however, responded with improved resources,
tactics and strategy. They introduced more powerful and forward-firing
depth-charges, ship-borne radar, and better ASDIC detection equipment.
Long-range aircraft also played a major role: land-based VLR Liberators
closed the mid-Atlantic air gap in May 1943. Furthermore, anti-submarine
air tactics became more effective, not only because of improved synchroni-
sation with convoy movements, but also because of a series of incremental
steps, such as better radar (and improved use of it), better search lights,
improved fuses for depth-charges, the use of white paint that made it harder
to spot aircraft and improved maintenance. Much of this stemmed from the
application of the findings of Coastal Command's Operational Research
Station. Aircraft operating against submarines were under naval operational
control, an important aid to effectiveness, while the greater availability of
escort carriers helped.[67] Similarly with convoy escorts, there were incremental steps, not only in numbers, detection equipment and weaponry, but
also in experience of operating together and thanks to the development of
effective formations and tactics. The success of stronger convoy defences had
been apparent from late 1941 and was now combined in a more effective
overall anti-submarine strategy.

The building of far more merchant shipping from 1942, particularly by
the Americans, was also very important to Allied victory, as was the
availability of more escort vessels, their improved armaments and the use of
communications intelligence to send them to reinforce convoys threatened
with attack: the German naval code was broken in December 1942.[68] In
May 1943, 41 U-boats were lost, on 24 May, Dönitz ordered a halt to attack
on convoys in the North Atlantic and the withdrawal of submarines to areas
where there was less Allied air power, and that year the ratio of ships sunk

to U-boats destroyed was 2 : 1, a rate of German success well down on the 14 : 1 of 1940–42.

May 1943 was not the end of the battle of the Atlantic, and should be seen as a turning point for the Allies only if the need to continue to overcome the submarine challenge is also stressed. A determined attempt by the Germans to regain the initiative in late 1943 was unsuccessful and they suffered heavy losses, including 37 boats in July. The German failure in the second half of the year confirmed and underlined their defeat that May, and although the loss of submarines per month never met May's figure, the aggregate total was far higher; while the number of convoyed ships sunk fell. The mid-Atlantic air gap was lessened in October 1943 when Portugal agreed to permit the British use of airbases on the Azores, closing what the Germans called the 'Black Pit' to the west of the islands.

In early 1944, the Germans fitted *schnorchel* devices to their submarines, allowing them to charge their batteries while submerged, thus reducing the vulnerability of the U-boats to air attack; the U-boats were becoming true submarines as opposed to just submersibles. However, this did not significantly increase attack capability vis-à-vis escorts, while the improvement in Allied escort capability and the application of communications intelligence outweighed submarine advances, and the Germans sank relatively few ships in 1944–5. Furthermore, the production of new types of submarine, especially the high-speed Type XXI 'Electro', was badly affected by Allied bombing.

The strategic failure of the U-boat offensive was clarified by Allied, especially American, shipbuilding. In the first quarter of 1943, the Allies built more ships than the U-boats sank, and by the end of the third quarter they had built more than had been sunk since the start of the war. The British played the leading role in defeating the U-boats, but the Americans and Canadians also took important parts, both at sea and in the air, and by 1945 the Canadian navy was the third largest in the world. The Allied success in the battle of the Atlantic was crucial to the provision of imports to feed and fuel Britain, as well as to the build-up of military resources there: only three Allied merchantmen convoyed across the Atlantic in the first three months of 1944 were sunk. This was the background to the Second Front sought by the Allies: the invasion of France.[69]

British air power also helped limit the role of German surface warships. Their vulnerability led the Germans to withdraw their major warships from Brest in February 1942, although the British were seriously humiliated when these ships successfully sailed up the Channel and through the Straits of Dover and the attempt to intercept them failed. Norway was an important base for operations against British convoys taking supplies to the Soviet

Union, but the major inroads by German aeroplanes and, in particular, submarines were not matched by surface ships. Instead, the German warships fell victim, the *Scharnhorst*, in the battle of the North Cape on 26 December 1943, to British warships escorting a westbound and an eastbound convoy, with the 14-inch guns of the *Duke of York* inflicting serious damage and torpedoes putting paid to the crippled ship; while the *Tirpitz*, which had sailed to Trondheim in Norway in January 1942, was sunk by British planes on 12 November 1944.

British warships played a key role in Allied amphibious operations. After failure against the Vichy base at Dakar in September 1940, there was a successful use of such operations when conquering Vichy-run Madagascar in May to November 1942. The campaign there indicated the potential of amphibious attacks when they could operate on a broad front, and the value to the British of enjoying carrier-borne air superiority, from two carriers initially, but also the problem that, once landed, troops could meet more serious opposition. In May, the port of Diego Suarez was captured and in September a full-scale attempt – both overland and with fresh landings – was launched to seize control of the rest of the island. Although this operation was peripheral to the main campaigns, it lessened the danger that the Allied world would be fractured by German and Japanese advances.

British naval support played a crucial role in the invasions of Sicily and mainland Italy in 1943, and that of Normandy in 1944, the British providing two carriers and eight battleships to support the Sicily landings. Accumulated experience in amphibious operations was important to these successes. The build-up and supply in, and from, Britain of the massive forces that landed in Normandy on 6 June 1944 and subsequently was a reflection of the failure of the U-boats to achieve strategic results, while the landings reflected the development of amphibious capability, the military theorist J. F. C. Fuller pointing out, in the *Sunday Pictorial* of 1 October 1944, that 'hitherto in all overseas invasions the invading forces had been fitted to ships. Now ships were fitted to the invading forces . . . by building various types of special landing craft' so that the forces 'could land in battle order on a wide front'.

As a reminder of the variety of means taken to ensure success, and of the range of activity on offer in naval bases, in January 1944, above a Portsmouth chemist shop, a naval officer, Stanley Worth, blew a whistle to summon the police to arrest Helen Duncan who was practising her skill in using ectoplasm in a 'materialisation' to conjure up the 'departed'. Duncan had attracted attention by publicising spirit messages about the sinking of warships before the news was released, and concern about her activities, not least in the run up to the Normandy invasion, led to her conviction under the Witchcraft Act.[70]

After the Allied breakout from Normandy, the Germans evacuated their submarine bases in western France and concentrated their force in Norway. From there, the U-boats focused on British waters, but they were no longer able to sink large numbers of merchantmen, and instead suffered serious losses as a result of air attacks on their bases and while at sea, and, even more, owing to convoy escorts and their use of forward-firing weaponry. However, the submarine threat remained potent, as U-boat construction maintained overall numbers, obliging the Allies to continue to devote considerable naval resources to escort duty and anti-submarine warfare. Given Allied, particularly American, shipbuilding capability and the resulting size of the Allied navies, this did not, however, limit or prevent other uses of Allied naval power, particularly the movement of British warships to the Indian Ocean and the Pacific.

From April 1944, the reinforced British Eastern Fleet attacked Japanese positions in what had been the Dutch East Indies, while, in the reconquest of Burma in 1944–5, the navy launched attacks on Japanese positions and shipping, and mounted amphibious operations. Despite logistical limitations, the Sydney-based British Pacific Fleet played a successful role alongside the Americans against Japan in 1945, although this was very much an American campaign, and indeed the fleet was organised like an American fast carrier task force and placed under overall American command. The British supported the invasion of Okinawa by attacking Japanese airfields from which the garrison could have been supported, taking considerable damage from kamikaze suicide planes, although, thanks to their armoured decks, none was lost. Subsequently, the British fleet joined in attacks on Japan itself: both air raids and coastal bombardment. The presence of warships in Asian waters enabled the British to regain control of their colonies soon after the end of the war: they returned to Hong Kong on 27 August and to Penang a day later.

If victory over Japan, particularly at sea and in the air, was primarily an American triumph, and a key aspect of the way in which the USA dominated the Anglo-American alliance,[71] this had important implications for Australasia and the British colonies in the Pacific, as throughout the war there was a marked increase in the American military presence in the Dominions and the colonies. This was a matter not only of bases and the presence of troops, warships and planes, but also of defence-planning. Although there was tension, not least over the role of the USA in the southwest Pacific,[72] the war ended with closer strategic relations between the USA and both Australia and Canada. Economic as well as strategic links between the Dominions and Britain became less important. The development of industries in Canada and Australasia was linked to a longer-term decline in dependence on imports of British manufactures, while, more generally, their

economies and societies changed. Although they stemmed from the imperial war, the growing size of the economies and governments of the Dominions lessened the role of Britain. Thanks to production for the war, Canadian
gross national product more than doubled in 1939–45, while federal government expenditure rose from $680 million in 1939 to $5,136 million in
1945. War also brought a fluidity in assumptions and relations and a decline
in deference in the latter that affected attitudes towards imperial links.

More seriously for Britain, the Roosevelt administration was opposed to
colonial rule and, instead, in favour of a system of 'trusteeship' as a prelude
to independence. Roosevelt pressed Churchill on the status of both Hong
Kong (which he wanted returned to China) and India, and British officials
were made well aware of a fundamental contradiction in attitudes. In 1943,
at the Tehran conference, Roosevelt told Churchill that Britain had to adjust
to a 'new period' in global history and to turn their back on '400 years of
acquisitive blood in your veins'.[73]

There were indeed major changes in the colonies. In India, which provided the bulk of the troops for the Malaya and Burma campaigns, there
was an upsurge in volunteering: the Indian Army became a million strong
in 1942, and two and a half million strong by 1945, the largest volunteer
army in history, although this drove up the cost of supporting it. In addition, the British changed their military policies to encourage both the
recruitment of traditional 'non-martial' races and a degree of Indianisation
of the officer corps. At the same time, the war witnessed an increase in agitation for independence. The Quit India movement of 1942 spearheaded by
Congress was a serious crisis for British rule, with a series of rural rebellions, mainly in eastern India. The British responded by arresting senior
Congress leaders, after which the movement became more violent, hinder-
ing the operation of British authority. However, the Quit India movement
did not encompass all of India and it was suppressed. India in 1942–5 was
no repeat of the Thirteen Colonies in 1775–83: there was less dissidence and
the Japanese could not play the role of the French. The Japanese-backed
Provisional government of Free India that was formed by the Indian nationalist Subhas Chandra Bose in October 1943, was granted administrative
control of the Andaman and Nicobar islands the following month; while a
pro-Japanese government was granted titular independence in Burma in
August 1943; Bose's Indian National Army, however, made little impact.[74]
The Viceroy, Field Marshal Wavell, who had responded promptly to serious
food shortages, wrote in July 1944 'On the whole, India is getting along
reasonably well in spite of the lack of interest in it on the part of the
War Cabinet . . . Once the Japanese war is over, our troubles out here really
will begin'.[75]

Aside from active dissidence, if not, on occasion, treason, war more generally encouraged native politicisation in colonies, for example Sudan. Furthermore, the experience of military service expanded horizons. The range of such service saw the repetition of accustomed tasks that in some respects affirmed racial and social hierarchies, for example the use of Basuto mule drivers for British mountain-artillery units in Italy, and, at the same time, a challenging of such hierarchies. Thus, officers from Bechuanaland found that their orders could be ignored by British NCOs, but such discrepancies led to tension and pressure for change.[76] More generally, participation in the war altered relations within the Empire, those between Britain and the Dominions and colonies, and those within each of these.

The 'informal empire' was also greatly affected by the war. The assertive British role in Egypt, which included the intimidation of the king in 1942, in order to make him accept a change in government, increased hostility to Britain's role. Japan destroyed the treaty port system in China and, thereafter, Communist triumph in the Chinese Civil War (1946–9) cemented the rejection of Western influence. In Latin America, British economic and political influence lessened as the USA became more powerful, while the war led to the slackening of economic links with Britain, which encouraged a measure of industrialisation.

Alongside the argument that Japanese success fatally undermined the British Empire in Asia (as well as the Dutch and French Empires there) and crucially destroyed the Empire's prestige, it is necessary to focus on the overall political and resource costs of the two world wars; as a result, Britain's post-war decision to abandon its colonial presence in South Asia can be seen as stemming in part from conflict within the European system, rather than as simply a response to the war with Japan or to growing indigenous pressure on Britain to 'quit India'. Shrewd observers at the end of the Second World War saw the weaknesses of empire, especially as Britain was financially exhausted. Difficulties over naval strength played a major role in a bitter debate in March 1944 over how best to re-establish the Empire in South-East Asia. To that end, Churchill instructed the Chiefs of Staff to delay sending naval help to the Americans in the Pacific:

It is in the interest of Britain to pursue what may be termed the 'Bay of Bengal Strategy' at any rate for the next twelve months ... All preparations will be made for amphibious action across the Bay of Bengal against the Malay Peninsula and the various island outposts by which it is defended, the ultimate objective being the reconquest of Singapore. A powerful British fleet will be built up based on Ceylon, Adu Atoll and East India ports.

In response, the Chiefs of Staff argued that there was a lack of necessary resources, unless they were lent by the Americans, and claimed 'we shall not have sufficient British aircraft to equip the full number of fighter carriers required . . .'. They also argued that Churchill's plan required an unrealistic degree of administrative and logistical flexibility, and argued that a focus on the Pacific would make it easier to bring the war to a speedy conclusion.[77] In the end, the British warships were sent to the Pacific: when the Eastern Fleet was divided in November 1944, the British Pacific Fleet got the best capital ships, including the fleet carriers, while the new East Indies Fleet made do with escort carriers and only one battleship.

The exchange in March 1944 underlined the extent to which the reconquest of empire in the mid-twentieth century entailed, as its conquest had done, the need to reconcile different strategic commitments and to allocate scarce resources. All comparisons and contrasts are problematic, but, whereas in 1899–1902, Britain had been able to confront a difficult distant challenge, in the shape of the Boers, without opposition closer to home, the situation was very different with Japan. British imperial overreach in the Second World War was most problematic in shipping, as that provided the way to move and apply resources. Whereas, thanks to shipbuilding, the British had replaced most of their merchantmen sunk during the First World War, they were unable to do so in the Second World War. Instead, the merchant fleet in 1945 was 70 per cent the size it had been in 1939, and it was American shipbuilding with its more effective pre-fabrication and flow production methods that played the crucial role. The pre-war problems of British shipbuilding and shipping had led to a lack of skilled workers and modern machinery, which contributed to the shipping crisis that affected British logistics and helped oblige the British to heed American views on strategy.[78] The British were far less prominent within the alliance than they had been in the First World War.

9
LOSS AND LEGACY, 1945–1972

It is impossible yet to see the shape of the post-war world, but one thing is clear. The British Commonwealth, tried and tested in the fire of adversity, can form 'a core of stability', and in association with the USA, the USSR and China can lay the foundations of a system which can make future aggression impossible and promote equality of opportunity for all peoples, large and small.

> V. T. Harlow, 'The Dominions', in *The British Way and Purpose, III: The Growth of Empire*, booklet prepared by the Director of Army Education, 1943.[1]

IMPERIAL RECOVERY?

Naval power and military capability had been of great importance in helping to channel the products of nineteenth-century technological change and economic and demographic growth, to British economic and political advantage. However, from the perspective of the early twenty-first century, the resulting imperial hegemony proved shortlived: less than 70 years across most of Africa and South-East Asia. In the place of such colonial control, Western states focused in the late twentieth century on economic and financial strength, and on military power without permanent territorial conquests. This was the model of American imperialism, but Britain found the transition more difficult.

Britain's Empire was largely to disappear within two decades of the end of the Second World War, one of the most significant shifts of authority in global history, as well as an important aspect of the more general decline of Europe's place in the world; but such a result had seemed far from obvious, for, just as the First World War had ended with an expansion of empire, so it appeared likely that the Second World War would be followed by the same, and, at least, that most of the Empire would be retained. During the war, the French feared British designs on their Empire, the USA was con-

cerned that British military planning was overly directed to imperial goals
and the British occupied Italian Somaliland and Libya, both of which were
seen as important for protecting the route to India. Churchill indeed considered the annexation of the latter, and there were hopes that it would be
able to maintain wartime gains under the equivalent of League of Nation
mandates. Italian Somaliland remained under British administration until
1950, while control over Libya was partitioned between Britain and France
with Britain gaining the lion's share: Cyrenaica and Tripolitania, which both
gave Britain a military presence to the west of Egypt and extended her
control over the shores of the Mediterranean to a greater extent than hitherto. Had the Germans had overseas colonies they would doubtless have
met with a similar fate.

There were also hopes of a recovery of imperial military greatness, as the
surrender of Japan was followed by the reimposition of control in occupied
areas, including Malaya, Singapore and Hong Kong, and the return of the
navy to Chinese waters,[2] while Britain joined Australia, India and New
Zealand in contributing troops to the American-dominated occupation of
Japan. British power in Asian waters also ensured that the British played a
major role in the reintroduction of Dutch and French power into the Dutch
East Indies and Vietnam respectively, although the former commitment,
which lasted until November 1946, led to conflict with Indonesian nationalists. Similarly, in the closing stages of the war, the British had sent troops
to Greece, in part to prevent a Communist takeover, and British support of
the royalist government continued after the war. British policy in Antarctica and the South Atlantic also indicated a continued desire to act as an
imperial power: the creation of the Falkland Islands Dependencies Survey
in 1945 signalled a determination to use scientists to consolidate influence,
and the mapping of the Antarctic peninsula and nearby areas carried out by
the Survey was designed to underline Britain's title to the area. British maps
omitted names found on Argentine and Chilean maps of the Antarctic
peninsula, and the cruiser HMS *Nigeria* was dispatched to Antarctic waters
in 1948 in order to support British claims, while Britain's presence was
validated that year by the release of the film *Scott of the Antarctic*.[3]

There were also plans for the extension of British power in South
Asia. In 1946, Sir Francis Tucker, Head of Eastern Command in India, was
concerned about threats to India from the north and proposed a British
protectorate over what he termed Mongol territory from Nepal to Bhutan.
Sir Claude Auchinleck, Commander-in-Chief India, had to explain that the
idea was not realistic;[4] and this was also true of ideas about extending British
influence in Tibet, and even Xinjiang, in order to maintain them as buffers
between India and China; the China then seen as a threat was Kuomintang
(Nationalist) China.[5]

Imperial expansion now seemed anachronistic; at least when practised overseas by Western European powers. The dominant role in the victorious coalition had been taken by the USA and the Soviet Union, both of which, albeit from different perspectives, had anti-colonial ideologies and saw no reason to view the expansion of the British Empire with any favour. Churchill's imperial perspectives had enabled him in 1943–5 to see the danger of Soviet domination of Eastern Europe, but Roosevelt could not grasp it and he thwarted Churchill's call for Allied military advances into south-east Europe. Under American pressure, the Atlantic Charter, issued by Churchill and Roosevelt in the Placentia Bay conference in August 1941, had declared 'the right of all people to choose the form of government under which they will live', and the United Nations, which was founded in 1945, was to show favour for the notion of national self-determination. For example, in 1946, it renewed the authority New Zealand had wielded in Western Samoa under a League of Nations mandate, after New Zealand agreed on eventual independence for the territory, and, indeed, Western Samoa became independent in 1962 after a plebiscite sponsored by the United Nations.

The British Empire was also challenged by internationalism from a different direction. The new international economic order was American-directed and a challenge to the protectionism of the sterling bloc, deliberately so. The Bretton Woods conference, held in the USA in 1944, produced plans for post-war co-operation that led to the foundation of the International Monetary Fund and the International Bank for Reconstruction and Development (World Bank), both of which had American headquarters. Free trade was also actively supported as part of an American-directed liberal economic order, and the General Agreement on Tariffs and Trade (GATT), signed in 1947, began a major cut in tariffs that slowly established or established anew a measure of free trade.

Despite these challenges, there was an attempt to protect, if not revive, the British Empire – important not least because while the age of imperial greatness in the nineteenth century has faded from memory, impressions of empire in this post-war period continue to play a role for people who are alive today. Empire was seen in the late 1940s as a crucial economic sphere and resource: oil from the Middle East was increasingly valuable to the economy, the discriminatory tariffs of imperial preference were crucial to trade and financial links helped maintain sterling.[6] Ernest Bevin, the influential Foreign Secretary in the Labour government from 1945 until 1951, was determined to preserve British military strength in the Middle East, and hoped to use imperial resources to make Britain a less unequal partner in the Anglo-American alliance.[7] There was an attempt to develop the economy of Tanganyika (now mainland Tanzania), with an ambitious, and ultimately unsuccessful, Groundnuts Scheme, designed to increase the supply of vegetable oils and fats within the sterling area, in order to cut imports from non-sterling areas, and thus to help maintain the level of the currency. Similar hopes were built on African mineral resources, and these encouraged the belief that Britain did not need to join schemes for economic co-operation in Western Europe. There was also an ethical dimension to the furtherance of empire, for although support for Indian independence played an important role in Labour Party circles, there was also a conviction, which drew on aspects of the liberal tradition, not least the nonconformist belief that there was a duty of care to protect the less fortunate, that imperial rule could serve the interests of the colonial peoples; and most were not regarded as as developed and ready for independence as the Indians.

INDEPENDENCE FOR INDIA

In India, the Second World War had helped undermine British rule, and post-war political volatility made it impossible to provide a level of stability sufficient to serve as the basis for a restoration of the processes of accommodation that ensured widespread consent. The rise of the Congress Party had challenged the British position, not least by hitting the effectiveness, business and morale of government, while the increased sectarianism of Indian politics, particularly with the rise of the Muslim League, made imperial crisis-management, let alone control, impossible. To the Muslims, in turn, the cause of Indian independence was compromised by Hindu sectarianism, and they called for partition. In response to the Muslim League's 'Direct Action Day' of 16 August 1946, Field Marshal Wavell, the Viceroy, pressed for a show of consistency: a commitment to ten more years of rule, or the fixing of a date for withdrawal. His replacement, Mountbatten, concurred. The timing of independence owed much, however, to the fact that Labour under Clement Attlee, not the Conservatives under Churchill, was in power. It was agreed, in early 1947, that the British would transfer power in June 1948. The British hope for a quasi-federation of Muslim and Hindu India fell victim to an inability to reach compromises, leading to a reluctant agreement to partition; and the decision to bring forward withdrawal to August 1947 made it harder to contain communal violence. The end of empire in South Asia was marked by large-scale violence, and left a lasting dispute over Kashmir, although it is too easy to blame deep sectarian divides on British rule.[8]

India had been the most populous and important part of the Empire, and the area that most engaged the imaginative attention of the British, although it was not important to British emigration, and, once India had been granted independence, it was difficult to summon up much popular interest in the retention of the remainder of the empire. There had been talk of India being given independence only if it agreed to help in the defence of other imperial possessions, specifically Aden, Burma and Malaya, and an expectation that an independent India would accept a continued presence by British forces, or at least co-operate closely in military matters, but such hopes were misplaced, and unlike Britain India was to be neutral in the Korean War (1950–53). In 1944, when post-war Indian independence seemed already likely, there had been consideration of separating the Andaman Islands in the Bay of Bengal, so that imperial control and a naval base could be retained there, but this option was not pursued; as Britain still had bases at Mombasa and Singapore, it scarcely seemed necessary.

Indian independence greatly affected British military options. India was important to British trade routes, especially to the Persian Gulf and the Strait of Malacca, but, more significantly, Indian troops were important to Britain's expeditionary capacity around the Indian Ocean and in the Middle East. The loss of those troops removed an important mainstay of the military dimension of the Empire, so that, for example, whereas in 1941 Indian forces had played a major role in the successful invasion of Iraq, a decade later, when Britain was in dispute with the Nationalist government in Iran over its nationalisation of British oil interests, Plan Y, the plan for a military intervention by the seizure of Abadan, was not pursued, in large part because, without Indian troops and with British forces committed in Germany and Korea, it no longer seemed militarily viable. The warships that were deployed, however, were crucial to the successful British economic blockade of the newly nationalised industry.

FROM INDIAN INDEPENDENCE TO THE SUEZ CRISIS

Independence was also granted to Burma and Ceylon in 1948, as, with India independent, it seemed pointless to hang on to either. The result in Burma was unhappy from the British point of view, with regional separatism, political instability, military rule and poor relations with Britain all rapidly following independence. The situation was happier in Ceylon (Sri Lanka), as democratic rule was established and British interests maintained; and Ceylon was subsequently held up as a model of decolonisation, although, by the 1990s, Tamil separatism had undermined this conviction.

In Palestine, it proved impossible to suppress violence and to negotiate a peaceful end to the mandate, and the British presence was brought to a close in 1948, with the government keen to get an embarrassing problem off its hands. Tensions between Arabs and Jews, which the British were unable to contain, were made harder to manage by pressure on Britain from the pro-Zionist American government. The mandate posed a particular problem for the navy as it had to intercept illegal immigrants, most of whom were Holocaust survivors, understandably determined to leave Europe.[9]

Less controversially, after a referendum in 1948 that led on the second poll to a small majority (52.3 per cent to 47.7 per cent) for confederation with Canada, the British-appointed commission that had administered bankrupt Newfoundland since 1934 came to an end in 1949. Also in 1949, Eire became a republic: the previous year, vestigial British authority had been tackled by the Republic of Ireland Act, which repealed the External Relations Act of 1936 and took Eire out of the Commonwealth. Proposing the Bill in the *Dáil*, John Costello, the Prime Minister, claimed it would 'end forever, in a simple, clear and unequivocal way this country's long and tragic association with the institutions of the British Crown'.

Unlike after the loss of America in 1783, that of India was not to be followed by imperial recovery, and instead the weakness of Britain as an imperial power was readily apparent. The war had exhausted her public finances and seriously damaged the economy, and this left her in a weaker position to sustain imperial commitments, while the wartime sale of overseas investments ensured that it would not be possible to use 'invisible exports' in order to finance the serious trade deficit. In addition to these sales, part of the heavy cost of the war had been financed on credit, but, unlike after 1815, there was to be no period of maritime dominance, imperial hegemony and an absence of expensive foreign challenge, that would help ensure renewed fiscal stability. Instead, after 1945 there were a series of imperial crises and a confrontation with the Soviet Union, both of which posed serious financial burdens. Furthermore, the American loan given to assist Britain when wartime Lend-Lease help ended in 1945 had been provided on condition that the pound be made convertible into the dollar, a measure that caused pressure on the Bank of England's reserves. The sterling crises of 1947, when the currency's convertibility was hit hard, and April 1949, when there was a devaluation of 30 per cent, underlined British weakness.

Owing to these problems, the British had little to offer those whose cooperation they sought, for example in the Middle East, and it was felt necessary to seek American assistance in resisting Communist pressure in Greece and Turkey (1947) and in South-East Asia (1949). The foundation of NATO in 1949 was similarly a response to the need to rely on the USA in the face of Britain's concern to resist Soviet expansionism in the absence of effective Western European assistance. Pushed onto the defensive, the British were also not in a good position to reassert themselves in areas of earlier imperial influence, such as China, although there the destruction of the

Kuomintang (Nationalists) by the Communists in the Civil War of 1946–9 was the key element.[10] The Chinese Civil War involved the navy in the familiar task of protecting nationals and other interests. The frigate *Amethyst* was fired upon in the Yangzi River by Communist forces in 1949, but the British response was restricted to refloating the ship, which had run aground, and escaping down-river to the sea – a dramatic escape, but not one that maintained economic or political interests.[11] The response offered to the provocation that had led to the First Opium War seemed a world away, and indeed there had been a fundamental shift in Britain's political attitudes and military capability, and in the international context.

British warships had also been fired upon by Communist forces in 1946, in this case by Albanians in the Corfu Channel, an international waterway, and when, later that year, the British tried to enforce their rights and to intimidate the Communists by sending two destroyers down the Channel, both were heavily damaged by mines. Other naval operations in the late 1940s included attempts to shore up the British position in Palestine and Malaya, in the first case by blocking Jewish immigration and gun supplies, while, more mundanely, the navy had to cope with the consequences of the Second World War, including the sweeping of large numbers of mines and the demobilisation of much of the fleet. In 1950, Britain contributed the second largest contingent to the American-dominated United Nations force that resisted Communism in the Korean War (1950–53), with the navy providing important carrier air support.

When Churchill regained power at the head of a Conservative government in 1951 (the year in which the British withdrew from Libya), he had no intention of dismantling the Empire, and indeed the Conservatives had fought the 1950 election by urging the electors to 'make Britain great again'. In 1952, Britain became a nuclear power, as a policy initiated by the Labour government in order to give Britain an independent nuclear role was brought to fruition. More generally, there was a sense of greatness. The accession in 1952 and coronation in 1953 of Queen Elizabeth II led to talk of a 'New Elizabethan Age', which was celebrated with a Coronation Review of the fleet, and the ascent of hitherto unclimbed Mount Everest in 1953 by an imperial team contributed to this excitement, not least because the planned coincidence of timing ensured that the achievement was focused on the new monarch, and reign. Ironically, mountaineering in the Himalayas was linked to attempts to keep an eye on Chinese moves in Tibet, another stage of the Great Game.

Although global commitments were reduced in some areas in the early 1950s, elsewhere they were maintained, and even expanded, in order to demonstrate that Britain was not weak, to protect British interests and to enhance military capability in the event of war with the Soviet Union, but these commitments put serious pressure on Britain's ability to maintain force levels in Europe, a goal that in turn challenged Britain's role as a military power outside Europe.[12] From 1948, a major and successful military effort was made to resist a Communist insurrection in the economically crucial colony of Malaya[13] which, it was hoped, would serve as the basis for a Dominion of South-East Asia that would also include Sarawak, Singapore and North Borneo. British assertiveness also included, in late 1952, RAF overflights of Buraimi oasis, an oil-rich part of the Arabian peninsula, then in dispute between British-backed Sultan Said bin Taimur of Oman and Saudi Arabia, which looked to American support, while, in Antarctica, the Churchill government funded expeditions to consolidate territorial claims.

No more colonies were granted independence under the Churchill ministry (1951–5), although, in 1954, the government abandoned its military commitment over Buraimi, while, that year, British troops were withdrawn from the Suez Canal Zone, after fighting two years earlier had indicated the cost of staying on. Also in 1954, Britain had to accept the liquidation of its oil interests in Iran, but, further east, Britain underlined its willingness to take an active role in collective defence when it became a founder member, with the USA, Australia, New Zealand, Pakistan, France, Thailand and the Philippines, of the South-East Asia Treaty Organisation (SEATO).

In 1955, Britain agreed to transfer the Simonstown naval base from British to South African control, a measure that Churchill had strongly opposed. Under the agreement, however, Britain retained important naval advantages, including South African agreement to make the base available to Britain in war, even if South Africa itself was neutral, as well as South African responsibility for the maintenance of the base, orders for warships from British yards and acceptance of British views on the development of the South African navy. Significantly, the British had earlier hoped to win a South African commitment to the defence of the Middle East, but this did not play a role in the agreement.[14] The assertive British policy in the Middle East, directed against the Soviets and the challenge from Arab nationalism, and intended to impress the Americans, led to the creation of the British-backed Baghdad Pact in 1955 which, by the end of the year, linked Britain, Iran, Iraq, Pakistan and Turkey. This policy also led to plans for intelligence operations designed to overthrow the governments of Egypt, Syria and Saudi Arabia, plans that culminated with the unsuccessful Suez invasion of 1956 directed against Egypt.[15]

In sub-Saharan Africa, the most important confrontation occurred in Kenya, where the British suppressed the Mau-Mau uprising in 1952–7. In this, the British benefited from a wide-ranging social reform policy, including land reform, in which the government distanced itself from the white colonists, as well as from the assistance of loyal Africans, including former insurgents. Force was also applied in Cyprus from 1955, in response to communal tensions between Greek and Turkish communities, and the development among the former of the EOKA (Ethniki Organosis Kyprion Agoniston) – a Greek Cypriot terrorist movement that sought union with Greece. The new governor, Field-Marshal Sir John Harding (who had replaced a civilian), saw the situation in large part in a military light, a response that appears anachronistic from the perspective of imminent decolonisation, but that did not seem so to many in the 1950s; indeed there was a parallel between policies then and those in the interwar period.

Maritime themes continued to play a major role in the national self-image: of the four high-value definitive stamps issued in 1951, one depicted HMS *Victory* and another the White Cliffs of Dover with sailboats in the foreground, but security policies were increasingly set without reference to empire. Canada was a founder member of the North Atlantic Treaty Organisation (NATO) established in 1949, but it was a security framework for Western Europe, not one focused on the Empire, and, although both Britain and Canada wanted NATO to have a North Atlantic identity, this goal was undermined by successive enlargements: Greece and Turkey in 1952, and West Germany in 1955.[16] As a more obvious sign of Britain's lesser role and prestige for the Dominions, in 1951, Australia and New Zealand, concerned about possible challenges from China, Indonesia and Japan, independently entered into a defence pact with the USA: ANZUS, a pact that Britain objected to and that marked a major departure from the alignment outlined by the Australia–New Zealand Agreement of 1944 which Britain had encouraged as a way to increase the Australasian contribution to imperial defence. From 1949, in response to British overstretch, the Australian navy became largely responsible for the defence of sea communications in the ANZAM (Australia, New Zealand and Malaya) region, and in 1951 the Radford-Collins agreement underlined co-operation between the American and Australian navies.

In the event, the USA was unwilling to heed the views of Australia and New Zealand: it wanted ANZUS to be part of a range of security agreements, not a partnership, and this helped to maintain Australian and New Zealand interest in continued good relations with Britain, although they were unwilling to heed British requests for a military commitment to the Middle East. South Africa unsuccessfully sought to supplement its naval links with Britain by others with Western powers.

The Americans were unwilling to let Britain join ANZUS because, in 1950, the British government had recognised the Communist government of China, beginning a pattern of difference with the USA over policy towards China that, in part, reflected clashing conceptions of the role of ideology and the nature of pragmatism in international politics.[17] This was not the limit of differences between the two powers, for the British wish to preserve the Empire, seen by both the Labour and Conservative leaderships as the basis for Britain's international and economic position, contrasted with American interest in a new world order of capitalist democracies, an order that challenged imperial rule as much as Communism. For example, the CIA-supported 'Asia Foundation' produced anti-imperialist propaganda in Singapore on the model of the anti-Soviet 'Radio Free Europe'. While British governments saw the Empire as a way to demonstrate to the USA the value of the 'special relationship', the Americans both encouraged what they saw as orderly decolonisation and sought to manage it as a means of thwarting Communism and increasing informal American control.[18] Thus, former colonies received American military assistance, as Pakistan did from 1953. There were also different views between Britain and the USA on the liberalisation of trade and air routes, while the USA had taken an unwelcome position on Palestine, and had helped to weaken Britain's position in Iran

Nevertheless, the two powers were united in opposition to Communism, especially in the establishment of NATO, while in 1950 the British contributed the second largest foreign contingent (after the Americans) to the American-led United Nations army that resisted the Communist North Korean invasion of South Korea, a departure from pre-war imperial geopolitics and one that was expensive. The cost of the military build-up of these years lessened the resources available both for economic development and for social welfare, while Britain lacked the resources to sustain the Colonial Office policies outlined in the successive Colonial Development and Welfare Acts of 1940, 1945, 1949, 1950 and 1959, and government action was able to provide only a portion of the investment necessary for colonial economic development. In 1956, Harold Macmillan, then Chancellor of the Exchequer, revealed anxiety about the cost of colonial aid, while other ministries opposed colonial industrialisation as a threat to British economic interests.

THE SUEZ CRISIS

In 1956 Britain granted independence to the largest remaining colony, Sudan, as well as suffering a major crisis in imperialism. The weakness of the imperial response to challenges and the limited domestic popularity of empire were exposed in the Suez Crisis, when Britain and France attacked Egypt, in an intervention publicly justified as a way of safeguarding the Suez Canal, which had been nationalised by the aggressive Egyptian leader, Gamal Abdel Nasser. His Arab nationalism was also seen as a threat to Britain's Arab allies, and to the French position in Algeria, while the Prime Minister, Anthony Eden, saw Nasser as another Fascist dictator. Eden saw

Nasser's takeover of the Suez Canal Authority as a personal betrayal in the aftermath of the agreement to withdraw British troops from the Canal Zone that he had reached with Egypt's leader in 1954. In 1956, Britain and France secretly encouraged Israel to attack Egypt and then intervened ostensibly to protect the Suez Canal.

Although poorly planned, in part a reflection of the lack of operational capability that arose from the failure to create a strong doctrine, an institutional focus for amphibious forces and adequate appropriate shipping and forces,[19] the invasion was a major display of military power, with a large force sent to the eastern Mediterranean and the extensive use of warships and air attack, including helicopter-borne troops. The abandonment of the invasion was in large part because of American opposition. President Eisenhower was already dubious about many aspects of the 'special relationship' between Britain and the USA, especially in the Middle East, and had made this clear to Churchill in 1953. Concerned about the impact of the invasion on attitudes in the Third World, the American government refused to extend any credits to support sterling, blocked British access to the International Monetary Fund until she withdrew her troops from Suez and refused to provide oil to compensate for interrupted supplies from the Middle East.

American opposition, which underlined the vulnerability of the British economy, was crucial in weakening British resolve and led to a humiliating withdrawal. The Suez Crisis can be seen as marking the end of Britain's ability, or at least resolve, to act independently, and has been aptly termed the lion's last roar;[20] from then on, there was an implicit reliance on American acceptance, as in the Falklands War of 1982.[21] The crisis also strained British relations with other powers, both Commonwealth, such as Canada, and non-aligned. As at the time of the Munich crisis, the British government, in 1956, displayed a failure to understand the nature of political opinion in the Dominions, and the decline in the latter's relations with Britain was apparent in the crisis and was accentuated by it; although the Canadian role in organising the creation and deployment of a United Nations Emergency Force to oversee the withdrawals helped provide a face-saving device that brought a close to the Suez episode. Although there was no immediate relationship with the crisis, 1956 was also the year in which Britain ceded its position as the leading shipbuilding country to Japan.

DECOLONISATION

Eden's career was one of the victims of Suez. His successor as Prime Minister, Harold Macmillan, set out to restore relations with the USA, rather than to preserve, let alone try to strengthen, the Empire. He put much effort into this task, but he was a supplicant, as American policy over the provision of missiles for Britain's nuclear bombs was to demonstrate,[22] and, in 1960, Macmillan described the British 'as Greeks in the Roman Empire of the Americans', in other words providers of wisdom, not power. Even wisdom was to be provided on terms: American reluctance to alienate other NATO members had helped by the spring of 1959 to lead to the lapse of the Anglo-American working groups created in 1957.[23] In Ian Fleming's short story 'The Hildebrand Rarity', published in 1960 in the collection *For Your Eyes Only*, James Bond is told by Milton Krest, an obnoxious and brutal American,

> Nowadays there were only three powers – America, Russia and China. That was the big poker game and no other country had either the chips or the cards to come into it. Occasionally some pleasant little country . . . like England would be lent some money so that they could take a hand with the grown-ups. But that was just being polite like one sometimes had to be to a chum in one's club who'd gone broke.

In the story, however, it was still possible to present Britain as an imperial power: Bond was in the Seychelles to check out security conditions, because the Admiralty needed a safe fall-back position in the Indian Ocean for the naval facilities at Gan in the Addu Atoll in the Maldives. Naval strength, in short, was still apparently crucial to the projection of British power.

When he became Prime Minister in January 1957, Macmillan sought a profit and loss assessment for each of the colonies, an instrumentalist approach that summed up a lack of conviction in the imperial idea, and while he was Prime Minister (1957–63) there was a wave of decolonisation and much of the Empire was dismantled, especially in Africa but also in South-East Asia. Churchill and Eden would have been far less willing to abandon the Empire at this rate, for to them independence was gradual, an organic process that was in large part unwelcome, or in which the unwelcome process could be lessened by dilution over a long timescale. This was the approach taken toward the African colonies by Churchill, Eden and Alan Lennox-Boyd, the Colonial Secretary from 1954 until 1959, prior to what in practice was to be a very speedy granting of independence.

Decolonisation, which brought to an end all the Western European territorial empires, was a varied process, with the British government having very different plans for particular colonies, and the context and chronology were often determined by local and regional factors rather than a common drive.[24] Nevertheless, decolonisation was hastened by a strong upsurge in colonial nationalist movements,[25] particularly in West Africa, which policymakers did not know how to confront, as the educated local elites, who had become more prominent, proved far more eager to embrace change than the tribal chiefs that the British had had close relations with. In addition, nationalism caused problems in countries where Britain was influential: the overthrow of the pro-British Iraqi government in 1958 underlined the limitations of British power, and was followed by Britain encouraging the USA to help with or take over some of its former responsibilities in the Middle East; although Britain did act militarily to support its ally Jordan when it was threatened by Egyptian pressure in July 1958.

By departing from colonies, the British were also able to abandon their position as unwilling mediators of local divisions, the situation in Palestine. In Malaya, tension between the prosperous Chinese minority and the Malay majority burst into violence in 1969, but Britain had ceased to be the colonial power in 1957, not least because it was felt that independence offered the best way to resist Communism there. In contrast, because Northern Ireland was a part of the United Kingdom with directly elected MPs at Westminster, sectarian tensions there had far less happy consequences for Britain.

Decolonisation proceeded on the assumption that Britain would withdraw from those areas that it could no longer control, or where the cost of maintaining a presence was prohibitive. Although criticised by some right-wing Conservatives, especially the Suez Group and the Marquess of Salisbury, Chairman of the Cabinet Colonial Policy Committee, who resigned in 1957 over the matter, decolonisation was not a central issue in British politics, in part because the Empire was seen as being transformed into the Commonwealth, so that the management and presentation of colonial withdrawal lessened both the controversial possibilities of decolonisation and reduced the domestic perception of decline.[26] The British view of empire was important, as the proclaimed logic of Britain's imperial mission, bringing civilisation to backward areas of the globe, allowed Britain to present the granting of self-government as the inevitable terminus of empire, and this view was shared in the Dominions, the contribution of which to British interests remained readily apparent in Canada's membership of NATO. The retention of the role of the Crown also made it seem as if the Empire was being maintained, in the shape of daughter nations within the Commonwealth, rather than ended. The British hoped they could manage decolonisation in order to wield renewed influence and to maintain their reach well beyond the confines of NATO, so that, in 1956, the government advanced the idea of a free trade area for manufactured goods that would encompass Western Europe and the Commonwealth, and therefore preserve both agricultural imports from the Commonwealth to Britain and an economic basis to imperial links. Rejected by the French

President, Charles de Gaulle, in November 1958, this scheme was an aspect of the British determination to retain an identity and role outside Europe.[27]

The contraction of empire was relatively painless at the imperial centre, because public interest in much of it, and support for its retention, was limited, although the absence of consultation within the British political system was such that this limit was not tested. The Colonial Office and the Ministry of Defence were keener to retain empire than the Foreign Office and the Treasury,[28] but this debate was not tested by the electorate. Some traditional Conservative interests, such as the military, were concerned about empire, but this was less the case with much of the party's middle-class support, and the latter was increasingly prominent in constituency associations and at party conferences. The young, who were playing an ever more assertive cultural and consumerist role, manifested little enthusiasm for empire. Films such as *West of Zanzibar* (1954), *Pacific Destiny* (1956) and *North West Frontier* (1959) now seemed dated,[29] although *Zulu* was to enjoy considerable success in 1964. For many in the older generations, there was more of a sense of loss. Much of the working-class support that the Conservative Party attracted in Scotland may have been connected with that Party's support for the Empire. As the Empire disappeared so did such support, and the Conservatives, who had won 50.1 per cent of the popular vote in Scotland in the 1955 general election, won no seats there in the election of 1997. Although the link between imperial sentiment and working-class support for the Conservatives is largely suggestive, it is significant that, in Scotland, Conservative support declined from the 1959 election and that working-class Scottish Conservatism/Unionism was particularly badly hit.

Fearful for their position, white settlers and landowners in the colonies were vociferous critics of decolonisation. Settlement had increased after 1945, in part because the high tax regime of the Labour governments of 1945–51 encouraged emigration. The dominant position of white settlers in Southern Rhodesia (now Zimbabwe) helped make contentious the future of the Central African Federation (of Rhodesia, both Northern and Southern, and Nyasaland), created in 1953. Lord Malvern, who had been Prime Minister of Southern Rhodesia from 1933 to 1953, made threatening reference in the House of Lords to action by the Federation's army and air force. This looked toward the eventual Unilateral Declaration of Independence by Southern Rhodesia in 1965, as did the Federation's support for White secessionism in the neighbouring Katanga region of Congo.[30]

At the same time, criticisms by settlers and their supporters in the Lords simply underlined the importance of an absence of colonial representation in the Commons, as, whereas Ireland's representation there gave it a crucial role in the arithmetic of parliamentary power prior to independence, there was no equivalent for any other colony. Furthermore, the pattern of earlier emigration was important. There were far more 'kith and kin' in the USA and the Dominions than in the African colonies, and many of the latter, for example in Kenya, were landowners and did not strike a popular resonance in British politics. There was no equivalent to the major French presence in Algeria or that of the Portuguese in Angola. Within the Commonwealth, South Africa, a state based on white-minority rule, was isolated, and its departure in 1961 did not lead to the collapse of that body. The failure of federation in Central Africa was matched by that in the West Indies: political and economic rivalries between the colonies could not be overcome, and Britain's plan to include Singapore in Malaysia was also to fail.

Decolonisation was also encouraged by defence issues, particularly the commitment to NATO.[31] This indeed led to criticism by the British government of the implications for NATO of the French focus on their retention of Algeria. Britain's colonies now appeared less necessary in defence terms, not only because of alliance with the USA but also because Britain had, in 1957, added the hydrogen to the atomic bomb. In addition, the declining role of the colonies in the British economy was a factor: many of them appeared less valuable than the areas where informal empire, in the shape of influence tipped with military power, continued, particularly the Persian Gulf and South-East Asia.

In Malaya, where the British did not allow the struggle with Communist insurgents to deter them from their political course, independence was granted in 1957, while in West Africa, the Gold Coast, which had a troublesome nationalist movement and a buoyant export economy based on world demand for cocoa, gained independence the same year under the name Ghana, the first British sub-Saharan African colony other than South Africa to gain independence. This reflected the relative wealth of the colony and the absence of a powerful white settler community; in colonies with such communities, such as Kenya, there was interest in ways to retain an important political role for the settlers, although it was also hoped that economic growth and constitutional provisions would ease racial differences.

In 1960, British Somaliland, Nigeria, the most populous of the African colonies, and Cyprus followed, the last especially significant as it had been said that Cyprus, which was bitterly divided between a Greek majority and a Turkish minority, would 'never' be independent, and because, with a small population, it set the precedent for the cession of independence for such territories. Independence was granted in the aftermath of a bitter struggle from 1955 with EOKA, and the confusion and violence of this process reflected the degree to which the British were not always able to manage decolonisation effectively.[32] Indeed, there was at least an undercurrent of violence to much of decolonisation. The granting of independence by

France to its remaining sub-Saharan colonies in 1960 drove forward the process of decolonisation, and its pace was particularly rapid in the early 1960s, which helped to make it normative. Sierra Leone, Southern Cameroon (as part of Cameroon) and Tanganyika gained independence in 1961, Jamaica, Trinidad (with Tobago) and Uganda in 1962, British North Borneo (as Sabah), Sarawak, Singapore, Zanzibar and Kenya in 1963 and Malawi, Zambia and Malta in 1964. In Kenya, the whites were too few to prevent independence on the basis of majority (African) rule, and the British government supported a multiracial settlement in the shape of the Kenya African Democratic Union, although the Kenya African National Union proved far more powerful.

Direct representation for Malta in Westminster had been considered, but this course was followed neither there nor in Gibraltar, despite a large majority in favour of integration in the referendum held in Malta,[33] and there was thus no comparison with the representation in the French Parliament of territories such as Martinique. Nevertheless, there were areas where popular support for remaining part of the Empire was expressed, and in 1959 the Cayman Islands, which were officially part of Jamaica, voted in a plebiscite to remain a colony, as they still are.

The list of colonies granted independence should not lead to a neglect of those areas where imperial rule or influence remained important, especially South-West Asia, with both formal empire in Aden and informal in the Persian Gulf. In 1955, 1957 and 1959, rebellions in Oman, an allied state where British influence was strong, were put down with the help of British troops, and in 1962 the government declared that British troops would be based in Aden 'permanently'. This was not to be. In the face of a nationalist revolt that broke out in 1963, independence for Aden for 1968 was promised in 1964, although the colony was to be abandoned in November 1967. As late as 1970, the British played a key role in the change of ruler in Oman, where they also made a major effort to help suppress the separatist Dhofari rebellion. However, John Darwin has drawn attention to the extent to which British imperialism imploded because informal imperialism proved a difficult option for a declining power.[34]

The departure from empire lent added force to Macmillan's unsuccessful bid to join the European Economic Community (EEC) in 1961–2, and was encouraged by it; rather as the Labour government's decision in 1967 to reapply for membership preceded the decision to withdraw from east of Suez. Anglo-American relations were more important to Macmillan than imperial links, and he wished to preserve the special relationship by showing that Britain could play a key role in Europe.[35]

The departure from empire also provided one of the might-have-beens of post-war British history. There was fighting in the last stages of empire, including in Malaya, Kenya and Aden, but nothing on the scale that the French and Portuguese confronted in their colonies: the heroic defence of imperial pretensions depicted in *Zulu*, a popular film in 1964, was an incident from 1879. It is unclear how far a major nationalist rising in, or foreign invasion of, a British colony would have led to a substantial response that might have proved bitterly divisive within Britain, but neither occurred until Aden (1967) and the Falklands (1982), respectively, and these episodes did not lead to a serious questioning of government policy. Certainly, decolonisation did not prove as divisive for the Conservatives as relations with the European Union were to be from the late 1980s.

The abandonment of empire also entailed conflict in protecting the newly independent Commonwealth and other overseas interests. In 1961, in Operation Vantage, the British successfully deployed forces to dissuade the Iraqis from invading Kuwait, with which relations remained very close after the end of the British proctectorate: Royal Marine Commandoes were landed from HMS *Bulwark*. The Americans supported the intervention, but it was very much a British action, and the British only withdrew their forces that October when, in large part owing to British pressure, there was a sufficient Arab force in place to deter Iraqi attack.[36]

In December 1962, an Indonesian-based rebellion in Brunei by the 'North Borneo Liberation Army' led to a major naval response that included the carrier HMS *Albion*, and helicopter-backed troops swiftly suppressed the rising. This was followed in 1963–6 by a successful confrontation with Indonesia in support of Malaysia, which had been formed from Malaya, Singapore, Sarawak and British North Borneo (now Sabah) partly in order to group together for security after the end of imperial control: the creation of Malaysia was seen as a way to manage the process of British withdrawal, and thus to maintain British interests while cutting defence costs. In the event, Indonesian hostility was followed by attacks. The Indonesians had good weapons, especially anti-personnel mines and rocket launchers, but the British, Australian and New Zealand troops were well-led, well-trained and versatile, and benefited from complete command of sea and air, a good nearby base at Singapore, excellent intelligence and an absence of significant domestic opposition in Britain. Anglo-Malaysian firmness prevented the situation deteriorating until a change to government in Indonesia in 1965 led to negotiations.[37] The navy played a major role: defensive, by blocking Indonesian incursions, offensive, with its helicopters and aircraft, and in terms of force projection and logistics. This confrontation was used by the British government as a reason for not helping the USA in Vietnam, and it helped ensure that the two powers supported each other diplomatically. It was cited as one of the three reasons for the refusal of the formal request for military assistance, particularly a token troop deployment, made by President Johnson,

when Harold Wilson made his first visit as the newly elected Prime Minister to Washington in late 1964.[38]

The military commitment to Malaysia showed the 'east of Suez' policy
providing political and economic value. An additional sign was provided in
January 1964 when mutinies by military units in newly independent Kenya,
Tanganyika and Uganda led to a successful British response, which included
the transport of troops by sea from Aden and their helicopter landing at
Dars-es-Salaam in Tanganyika.

Wilson hoped to maintain Britain's role as a major independent power,
and sought to act as a leading figure on the international stage. In support
of India against China, and, reflecting concern about the consequences of
China's easy victory over India in their border war of 1962, Wilson declared
that 'Britain's frontiers are on the Himalayas'. The possibility that this victory
would be followed up appeared to threaten the stability of the Indian Ocean
rim and, with it, British interests in South-West and South-East Asia and
in the Indian Ocean. British strategic thinking, which owed much to the
geopolitical ideas of Halford Mackinder, discerned a tension between the
Eurasian heartland and the oceanic rim, and thus saw the stability of South
Asia and the Indian Ocean, in which Britain was the leading naval power,
as closely linked. Already, in November 1960, the carrier HMS *Victorious*
had joined the Far East station with a complement of planes capable of
dropping nuclear bombs and several nuclear bombs aboard; this in furtherance of a decision to have two carriers east of Suez. Subsequent planning
called for the use of a carrier in the Indian Ocean for nuclear strikes on
southern China, and for a second carrier to be deployed in 1964. These carriers were to complement RAF planes based in Singapore.[39]

In contrast, the American role in the Indian Ocean in the early
1960s was minor, with only a small squadron showing the flag in the
Persian Gulf, while, until the late 1960s, the Indian navy was equipped
with surplus British warships, and links between the two navies were close.
This was an aspect of the use of arms sales and military training in order
to maintain imperial links, a process that was particularly prominent in
Africa, so that, in the Nigerian Civil War of 1967–70, the British provided
the federal government with weaponry including Saladin and Saracen
armoured cars.[40]

When Wilson came to power in October 1964, Britain had more troops
'east of Suez' than in Germany, and he initially maintained that commitment, thus both underlining Britain's claim to be a power in South Asia and
supporting American interests in maintaining stability in the Indian Ocean
and the Persian Gulf.[41] Planning for the new Polaris-armed submarines
included firing stations in the Indian Ocean designed both to block
Himalayan passes, through which the Chinese could advance on India, and

to reach targets in southern Russia. Wilson also sought to be a peacemaker: to end the unilateral declaration of independence (UDI) by the white settlers in Southern Rhodesia, as well as what was seen as the damaging conflict between Pakistan and India in 1965, to mediate in the Vietnam War and to try to ease Cold War tensions, the last following a course set by Churchill, Eden and Macmillan.

However, the attempt to act as an independent power brought scant benefit. Wilson failed to end the Vietnam War, irritating the Johnson administration by his repeated efforts, and Pakistan and India turned to Soviet mediation. Britain lacked the necessary diplomatic strength to further its goals, and the varied commitments to Europe, represented by NATO and by the wish to join the EEC, affected the consideration of other interests. The Commonwealth, which had changed greatly with the entry of newly independent former colonies, was not able or willing to provide support for Britain's international goals; the rival to the European Economic Community, the European Free Trade Association (EFTA), of which Britain was the leading member, was not intended as a political force, and, anyway, was weak; and Britain faced intractable problems, including a Southern Rhodesian government unwilling to abandon white supremacy. The British government was insistent that independence there was not an option unless the democracy that permitted black majority rule was established, the line earlier taken in Kenya. The bulk of the settlers, however, preferred to look to South Africa's apartheid government as a model, and in 1965 announced UDI. British diplomatic efforts failed to end the Rhodesian crisis, and the use of the navy to impose sanctions – prohibitions on trade, particularly in oil – also failed. A patrol was mounted off the Mozambique port of Beira in 1966–75 in order to support the oil embargo on Rhodesia ordered by the United Nations. Paralleling attitudes towards far tighter limits on immigration, UDI was supported in some right-wing circles, but not by the leadership of the Conservative opposition.

More generally, Britain's attempt to act as a major power had to be abandoned in the face of the country's severe financial problems, which led to a major devaluation of sterling in October 1967, gravely weakening Britain's prestige and also hitting her position as a major power. As a result, under pressure from the Chiefs of Staff, who were concerned about the mismatch between commitments and resources, the government announced in January 1968 that it was abandoning Britain's military position 'east of Suez'. This breached the understanding reached with the Johnson administration, but the financial situation pointed in this direction, while the much greater parliamentary majority that Wilson had secured as a result of the general election of 1966 meant that he did not need to fear opposition from Conservatives and Labour mavericks.

Forces were withdrawn from Aden when independence was granted in November 1967, from the Persian Gulf in 1971, and from Singapore in 1975 (they had been much scaled down in 1971). The withdrawal from the Gulf took place against the wishes of the local sheikhs, but, to the British government, it no longer seemed a viable presence, not least because of the withdrawal from Aden and the sterling crisis, but also owing to a lack of government commitment to Britain's imperial position.[42] The Conservative opposition criticised the decision to withdraw from the Gulf, and this encouraged Lee Kuan Yew of Singapore to persuade the Labour government to delay the withdrawal of most of the forces from Singapore until 1971, but he was disappointed, as once in power under Edward Heath in 1970–74, the Conservatives implemented the policy of withdrawal. Although, under the Commonwealth Five-Power Defence Arrangement (which replaced the Anglo-Malaysian Defence Agreement), Britain joined Australia and New Zealand in a limited commitment to Malaysia and Singapore, this proved only a transitional arrangement.

As a consequence of withdrawal, Britain became less important in the Indian Ocean, while the concern that had been expressed in 1947 that partition would weaken India's potential as an ally had been doubly vindicated, for the rivalry between Pakistan and India, which led to war again in 1971, provided opportunities for both China and Russia to win local support, and this further challenged Western interests, as it was feared that China and Russia would be able to develop important naval facilities. To a certain extent, Britain countered this by encouraging the American naval build-up in the Indian Ocean, and making Diego Garcia available to the USA as a naval base;[43] it is still a significant American military asset, including being used as an important air base for attacks on Iraq. In late 1974, an American carrier entered the Persian Gulf, the first such deployment since 1948.[44] The Americans had provided aid to the Pakistani army from 1954.

Unlike Australia and New Zealand, and despite, early on, providing encouragement and some support,[45] Britain did not come to the assistance of the USA in Vietnam: for Britain, Vietnam was to be no second Korea. Instead, Australia and New Zealand fought without Britain, which, combined with the withdrawal from east of Suez, represented a major shift. Britain became increasingly less relevant to Pacific states. When, in 1985, there was a major crisis within the ANZUS alliance over the New Zealand government forbidding the visit of an American warship that might carry nuclear arms, this was not a dispute in which there was any role for Britain.[46]

The political and strategic changes discussed above led to a major shift in British naval procurement. A planned 50,300-ton fleet carrier, the CVA-01, was cancelled in February 1966, leading to the resignation of both the Navy Minister and the Chief of Naval Staff. The carrier, and the sister ship that had also been projected, had been seen as crucial to maintaining British military viability east of Suez, not least because bases on land had been lost or compromised by independence or instability, the fate in particular of bases in Kenya and Aden, and although Fremantle in Western Australia remained an accessible naval base, it was distant from the Persian Gulf, while in 1966 the Australian government made it clear that they did not want to provide Britain with a substitute base for Singapore. The RAF, however, argued that they could achieve the task allocated to the CVA-01 less expensively from island bases. There was also a belief that vertical short take-off and landing (VSTOL) aircraft, the first of which had flown in 1960, made large carriers less necessary, while Denis Healey, the Defence Secretary, was concerned about the cost and manning requirements of the CVA-01. He subsequently wrote

> our political commitments would not be affected if we renounced the option of landing or withdrawing troops against sophisticated air opposition, outside the range of friendly land-based aircraft. I asked the navy to invent a plausible scenario in which the carrier would be essential. The only one they could conceive was a prolonged naval battle in the straits of Sumatra, in which the enemy had Russian MIGs on the adjoining coast, but we had given up our bases in the area.

Having noted that there was no reference in the scenario to the Falklands War in 1982, where the carrier would have been useful, Healey closed his self-congratulatory account:

> I imagine historians will best remember my six years at the Ministry of Defence [1964–70] for the liquidation of Britain's military role outside Europe, an anachronism which was essentially a legacy from our nineteenth-century empire.[47]

Published in 1989, this confidence looks less well-grounded in light of subsequent military challenges and commitments.

In the 1960s, British defences became more clearly dependent on American weaponry, not only the Polaris missile that had been bought after the cancellation of the American land-based Blue Streak inter-continental missile system, but also the F-111 jet that had been ordered in 1965 to fill the gap after the cancellation of the projected British TSR 2 strike-reconnaissance plane, which was over-budget and late. The purchase of the F-111, in turn, was cancelled in 1968 as the result of a further defence review. In 1962, the Australian government bought two American guided missile destroyers, their first major warships not to be built in Britain or Australia and a purchase made in preference to British class warships.[48]

Decolonisation meanwhile continued. Gambia and the Maldives gained independence in 1965, Bechuanaland (as Botswana), Basutoland (as Lesotho), Barbados and British Guiana (as Guyana) in 1966, Aden in 1967, Mauritius, Nauru and Swaziland in 1969 and Tonga and Fiji in 1970. In most cases, this process posed few problems for Britain, but the withdrawal from Aden was far from bloodless and, from the British perspective, there was a failure to create an acceptable successor government. Nevertheless, Aden was no longer a key point on shipping routes and, by delaying their departure until after Egypt had been defeated by Israel in the Six Day War, the British lessened their concern about exploitation of this move by Egypt, then the leader of pan-Arab nationalism.[49]

There was soon little left in the Empire, apart from such far-flung outposts as the Falkland Islands, Gibraltar and Hong Kong. The last was the only colony with a substantial population not en route for independence, and this was largely because of Chinese irridentinist interest in the colony, which compromised the possibility of independence, and to poor British relations with Communist China. The mainland portion of Hong Kong was scheduled, by treaty, to be returned to China in 1997.

A sense of empire as anachronistic was captured in the public reaction in 1969 when the Wilson government sent two frigates, a detachment of parachutists and a group of London policemen to invade the Caribbean island of Anguilla, which had rejected membership in the St. Kitts-Nevis-Anguilla federation. There was governmental concern that the island would become a base for drug smugglers, but the bloodless invasion was treated as a farce by much of the British press. In 1967, the year in which the British withdrew from Aden, the running aground of the *Torrey Canyon* supertanker off the Scilly Isles led to the military action that engaged most domestic attention as efforts were made to stem the spread of oil, while, also that year, the plan to create an airfield on the uninhabited Indian Ocean island of Aldabra (part of the Seychelles) was thwarted by environmentalists concerned about giant tortoises. The attitudes surrounding empire were very different from those of two decades earlier.

Although part of the United Kingdom, Northern Ireland was also a legacy of empire. Following sectarian tension that led to fighting in 1968 and a breakdown in law and order in 1969, troops were deployed there in August 1969. Their very presence became an issue, however, and in 1971 the first major offensive by the Provisional Irish Republican Army (RA), which had been founded in 1970, occurred. The Catholic population and the army increasingly saw each other as enemies. In response, the British government made a determined attempt to re-impose control, increasing the number of troops to 20,000 in 1972 and forcibly reopening IRA 'no-go' areas for military and police patrols. That March, the intractability of the situation led to the imposition of 'direct rule' from London: the Unionist regional government and the Stormont Assembly were suspended.

THE DECLINE OF MARITIME AND NAVAL STRENGTH

The maritime strand, as well as the imperial one, became far less prominent in British history during this period. This reflected changes stemming from the spreading role of air power and transport, as well as Britain's changing geopolitics, and the decline of British naval power and the merchant marine. The last was important, because the sea had provided employment for many, and ports and shipping had been part of the detailed configuration of British geography and society. In 1900, the UK owned about 50 per cent of the merchant shipping afloat, and, in 1914, 39.3 per cent. Thereafter, there was a serious decline, to 29.9 per cent in 1930, and 26.1 per cent in 1939, but the percentage in 1948 was still 22.4. This was in part thanks to destruction during the Second World War of the shipping of other countries, especially France, Germany, Italy, Japan, the Netherlands and Norway, and in part because the USA, which in 1945 had had 56 per cent of the world's merchant fleet, sold or laid up much of that shipping. By 1960, however, the UK share was down to 16.3 per cent. This was due not only to the growth in the shipping of other countries, but also to serious problems in the British industry, especially labour disputes, anachronistic working practices, poor management and under-investment. Although Britain's merchant fleet was not to reach its post-war peak until 1975, in 1967 she lost her position as the world's leading shipper to Liberia, which operated as a flag of convenience for the USA, helping to provide American-owned shipping with lower taxation and cheaper crews. This competition hit British shippers hard. In addition, the British were poor at taking advantage of new opportunities and were particularly unsuccessful in developing independent tanker tonnage for the rapidly growing oil trade, while they were also slow to move into bulk carriers, although they were to respond rapidly to the use of container ships in the 1960s. More generally, the profits obtained from shipping as a percentage of the capital employed were poor compared with other sectors of the British economy, particularly in the 1960s. This led to a reluctance to order replacement tonnage, let alone new tonnage, which greatly affected British shipbuilding as the majority of its orders by 1960 were from British shipowners.

In the late 1940s and early and mid-1950s, British shipyards benefited from rising world demand, but, by 1960, they were losing orders to the lower charges of foreign yards. In addition, the latter were able to promise earlier and more reliable delivery dates, a consequence of the absence in Britain of modern yards able to offer flow-line production, and the consequent higher productivity. As with shipping, this absence reflected poor management, problematic labour relations and a lack of investment, born of short-term attitudes and limited planning for the longer term.

As the market became more competitive from the 1960s, the decline of British competitiveness in this sphere hit hard. Business was lost and shipyards were closed, so that, whereas the UK had delivered 12.4 per cent of the ships that entered service in 1962, by 1971 the percentage was down to 5.1; although, in terms of tonnage, this represented a larger figure.[50] The Suez Crisis of 1956 had exposed a particular problem in British shipbuilding capacity, as it led to a shift towards super-tankers (designed to round Africa rather than to go through the Suez Canal) that British yards, with their limited facilities on narrow rivers, could not build. It was indicative that there was nothing maritime in the stamp set on 'British Discovery and Invention' that appeared in 1967, while, of the six ships depicted in the series of British ships two years later, only one, *Queen Elizabeth II*, was at sea, and the series was largely one of historical celebration.

The decline of naval power had a different cause, course and consequence, but, it shared with that of merchant shipping and shipbuilding, a linkage with a wider economic malaise. Despite a protracted period of economic recovery and growth until 1973, with an annual average growth rate of real GDP of 2.8 per cent for 1951–73, low levels of unemployment and no major recessions, Britain was less competitive than other leading Western economies and her relative economic position deteriorated. There were particular problems with heavy industry.[51] Economic problems caused a strain on public finances that exposed the navy to the reiterated pressures of defence cuts; although other issues, especially rising national expenditure on social welfare, also played a major role.

Geopolitics and air power were particular problems facing the navy. The focus on the Cold War initially meant a lesser need for it, as, from the late 1940s, defence anxieties centred on a Soviet advance across the North European Plain, and this, alongside continued imperial commitments, helped ensure the retention of conscription and consequent heavy expenditure on the army. The development of a British atomic bomb programme furthered the relative neglect of the navy, as the bomb was designed to be dropped from the air,[52] so that in the event of war with the Soviet Union, whether conventional or nuclear, there appeared to be only a minor function for the navy. Anti-insurgency campaigns in the colonies, for example Kenya and Malaysia, did not greatly alter this. Warships were useful for coastal interdiction in Malaya, but not for operations in the hinterland. Instead, air-attack and mobility, thanks to aircraft and helicopters, were of importance, and although naval aircraft did play a role, the navy had only a limited part in the defence of empire. This was even more the case because colonial insurgency focused on rural areas, not on port cities, lessening the deterrent impact of warships.

Warships, nevertheless, still had a valuable role to play in conventional operations, although these were not against other fleets. Instead, in both the Korean War and in the Suez Crisis, the navy essentially provided firepower support for land operations, by means of shore bombardment and, more widely, air power. Thanks to a rotation of carriers, one light carrier was on station at any given time during the Korean War (in 1952–3, two were on station); and the British Fleet Air Arm flew close to 23,000 operational sorties, while Canadian, Australian and New Zealand warships also took part in the Korean War: like the British, under the authority of the United Nations. At Suez, attacks by the RAF from Cyprus and Malta and from two French and three British (*Eagle*, *Albion* and *Bulwark*) carriers destroyed the Egyptian Air Force, preparing the way for an airborne assault that included the first helicopter-borne assault landing from the sea: 415 marines and 23 tons of supplies landed by 22 helicopters from *Ocean* and *Theseus*.

Nevertheless, naval forces were not central to British defence planning. Mountbatten, then First Lord of the Admiralty, wrote in 1956, 'The Navy has begun to assume its new streamline form for the atomic age',[53] but streamlining was followed by repeated adjustments downwards owing to financial stringency. In 1957, the Defence White Paper increased the emphasis on nuclear deterrence, recommended the end of conscription and declared that 'the role of naval forces in total war is uncertain'. The Reserve fleet, including four of the surviving five battleships, was scrapped, and the number of naval personnel cut, although Mountbatten successfully lobbied to save the carriers in the face of a Minister of Defence who regarded them as expensive and outmoded. The Chiefs of Staff had reported that it was crucial to retain the Fleet Air Arm as it offered a way to deploy air power in regions where ground-based planes could not be used.[54] Nevertheless, of the light carriers, *Ocean*, *Glory* and *Theseus* were transferred to reserve, before being broken up in 1961–2, while *Triumph* became a maintenance ship.

The combination of retrenchment, an emphasis on NATO and nuclear deterrence and the beginnings of decolonisation also affected the global network of Britain's naval bases. Independence for Malaya in 1957 was followed, in 1959, by the ending of the East Indies Station and the closure of the Hong Kong dockyard. Also that year, the naval dockyard in Malta was privatised. In European waters, there was not the prompting of competition with the French or with other allied Western European navies. Instead, there was a more general trend of naval retrenchment in Western Europe. After their wartime losses, the French navy and its infrastructure were revived in the early 1950s, in part with American help, but this was compromised by Franco-American differences and French naval construction and deployment were reduced in the late 1950s.

The naval situation was to change for two reasons. First, the build-up of the Soviet fleet that began in the 1950s under Admiral Sergei Gorshkov quickly made the Soviet Union the world's number two naval power (the USA was number one), a position facilitated by the wartime destruction of the Japanese navy and the post-war decline of its British counterpart: the tonnage of the Soviet navy exceeded that of Britain in 1959. The traditional doctrine of Soviet naval power had emphasised support of land forces in the Baltic and Black Seas, and the quest for naval superiority in these areas, but Soviet forces based in these seas could gain access to the oceans only through straits and shallow waters, where they were vulnerable, and a similar problem affected the naval base of Vladivostok on the Sea of Japan. As a result, the Soviet navy developed their Northern Fleet based at Murmansk, and it became the largest Soviet fleet, with a particularly important submarine component.[55] This obliged NATO powers to develop nearby patrol areas for submarines and underwater listening devices, and also a similar capability in the Denmark Strait between Iceland and Greenland and in the waters between Iceland and Britain, through which Soviet submarines would have to travel en route to the Atlantic.

As a consequence, the British navy built up a focus on anti-submarine warfare, specifically the protection of maritime routes across the North Atlantic.[56] As a result, 46 frigates were laid down in 1952–9, while the Type 22 *Broadsword* class frigates of the 1980s lacked a main gun armament as this was seen as irrelevant for their anti-submarine duties. This role was as part of Standing Naval Force Atlantic, a NATO force established in 1967. More generally, much of the fleet was allocated to NATO responsibilities, the Atlantic naval command of which, despite Churchill's efforts, has been under an American since the first appointment in 1952, and multilateralism diminished the independent role of British naval strategy. In the North Atlantic, again under NATO, the Canadians similarly developed the anti-submarine capability their navy had been rapidly expanded to provide during the Second World War,[57] the lessons of which dominated much naval doctrine and planning.

British naval power, however, also developed in a different direction as a result of the second major change. The cancellation of the land-based Blue Streak inter-continental missile system helped ensure that the second generation of British nuclear warheads would be sea-based. In this, the British followed the Americans. In July 1960, the USS *George Washington* was responsible for the first successful underwater firing of a Polaris missile, and the following year the Americans commissioned the USS *Ethan Allen*, the first true fleet missile submarine. In December 1962, in what became known as the Nassau Agreement, Macmillan and Kennedy decided that the Americans would provide Polaris for a class of four large nuclear-powered British submarines that were to be built, although American agreement was dependent on the British force being primarily allocated for NATO duties. On 15 February 1968, the first British Polaris test missile was fired from HMS *Resolution*, the Royal Navy's first nuclear-powered ballistic missile submarine, which had been laid down in 1964 and commissioned in 1967, and which was to arrive in its patrol area in July 1968. Initially, the Polaris force led to a renewed interest in imperial fragments, because, prior to the development of satellite systems, communications with submarines were dependent on transponder stations, so that, in the Indian Ocean, there was interest in islands such as Adu Atoll.

Despite this role, the navy had been sceptical from the outset about the extent to which the atom bomb had altered the parameters of naval warfare. The limited availability of atom bombs encouraged initial caution on this head, and was followed by the equations of deterrence, which sustained the view that the navy had an important conventional role to play, whether alongside or instead of a nuclear conflict. Interest in sea control remained central to naval planners,[58] and the volatility of the Middle East increased concern about sea routes from the Persian Gulf which were crucial to British oil supplies. These routes lengthened with the closure of the Suez Canal owing to Egyptian–Israeli hostilities in 1967 and with the growing size of oil tankers that, irrespective of the politics of the Middle East, forced more tankers to use the route round the Cape of Good Hope.

Although less dramatic than Polaris submarines, there were also important developments in surface shipping, one of the most important being the introduction of a new propulsion system, the gas turbine, which meant a major shift from coaling. Combined steam and gas turbines were introduced in frigates in the 1960s, and were followed in the 1970s by gas turbines, and subsequently the new system was introduced more generally. Other major changes included the introduction of helicopters and jets to the navy: the navy's first operational helicopter squadron was formed in 1952 in order to help anti-guerrilla operations in Malaya, while the navy played a major role in the development of carrier capability. The first successful carrier landing of a jet aircraft took place on HMS *Ocean* in December 1945, carrier trials of the navy's first operational jet began in 1947, and the navy responded to the increased weight of aircraft by introducing steam catapults (first used in 1951) and angled decks (experiments began in 1952), while the mirror landing system was first employed in 1953. All three were swiftly emulated by American carriers.

Major changes in British warships were seen in 1960: HMS *Devonshire*, the first British guided missile destroyer was launched, as was HMS *Dreadnought*, the navy's first nuclear submarine, and the first of a series of 12 nuclear attack submarines. The choice of the name *Dreadnought* was significant, as was the date of the launch – Trafalgar Day – and the launching by the Queen. Also in 1960, HMS *Bulwark*, formerly a light fleet carrier, was, after conversion, commissioned as a 'Commando' carrier, able to carry a Royal Marine Commando, their arms, stores and vehicles, the necessary assault craft and a squadron of helicopters. As another sign of change, the age of the British battleship was brought to a close when the 44,500-ton HMS *Vanguard* was scrapped: laid down in 1941 and commissioned in 1946, she was the largest battleship built for a European navy, as well as the sole European battleship commissioned after the war.

Naval planning in the 1960s continued to place a heavy focus on the distant strike capability brought by fleet carriers, but the cancellation in February 1966, following a Defence Review, of the planned CVA-01 carrier led to a focus on a less ambitious naval force structure. In particular, it was envisaged that, after the existing carriers came to an end of their service, which was projected to be in the 1970s, naval air power would amount essentially to helicopters designed to act against submarines in the NATO sphere of operations. An ability to support amphibious operations with carriers no longer seemed necessary. This represented a major shift from established patterns of British unilateral force projection: although British naval power had been concentrated in home, European or, at the most, North Atlantic waters earlier in the century, both then and in the nineteenth century there had also been a capability elsewhere based on squadrons in distant seas. The cancellation of the carrier also led to the building of only one of the four projected Type 82 class destroyers that had been designed to escort it.

Britain's international commitments were increasingly centred on Western Europe with other interests, especially east of Suez, playing a lesser role. Defence priorities were focused on deterring a Soviet invasion of Western Europe, and the Mediterranean, a traditional sphere of British naval activity, became an area of American–Soviet confrontation. Indeed, in a symbolic act, the Queen's Colour of the Mediterranean Fleet was laid up in 1967. Britain's options from the late 1960s seemed no longer to be those of independence or alliance from a position of strength, but, instead, to be those of centring political interests and defence undertakings on American or European systems. Although lessened by the role of NATO, this tension between American and European alignments was to be the theme of British power politics thereafter. Defence interests outside Europe, however, also continued to play a role, and these revived after the end of the Cold War, encouraging a renewed interest in distant force-projection.

ECONOMIC SHIFTS

After the Second World War, there was a major decline in economic links between Britain and her former colonies, owing to the dynamism of the American economy, the growing sophistication of those of the Dominions, the impact of the world wars on the British economic and fiscal systems, and the consequences for British investment capital of high rates of taxation, and of practices of state control and direction of economic and financial resources initiated under the Labour governments of 1945–51, 1964–70 and 1974–9. Thus, nationalisation of much of the economy in the late 1940s focused investment (under state control) on domestic goals, and this was underlined anew by the National Plan introduced by Labour in 1965. Meanwhile, the willingness of sterling-zone countries to direct their fiscal policies to support sterling declined, and, with it, went imperial economic ideology. The 'gentlemanly capitalism' that had played a major role in the development of Britain's imperial system in the eighteenth and nineteenth century was undermined by the reduced status of sterling as an international currency and by political and fiscal changes, in Britain and overseas, that affected Britain's capacity to act as a financial power.[59]

Britain's declining role as a financier and an exporter of capital was readily apparent in the Dominions. The USA replaced Britain as the biggest source of foreign investment in Canada in the 1920s, and as Canada's biggest export market after the Second World War: the British share of this foreign investment in Canada fell from 85 per cent in 1900 to 15 per cent in 1960, while the American share rose from 14 per cent to 75 per cent. The Canadian assets of American insurance companies already exceeded those of British companies by 1911. After the war, especially from the 1960s, Australia came increasingly to look to East Asia, particularly Japan, for economic partners, and, by 1970, 49 per cent of Australian exports went to Asia. In 1963, a stamp bearing the logo 'Commonwealth Cable' was issued in Britain to commemorate the opening of the Trans-Pacific Telephone Cable, but, in practice, the Pacific was now very much part of the American world.

Combined with high growth rates in the European Economic Community (EEC), these factors encouraged renewed efforts to join it. Wilson was unsuccessful in this, but Edward Heath, Conservative Prime Minister in

1970–74, made a third effort, and a treaty of accession, finally signed in Brussels on 22 January 1972, came into effect at the start of the following year. Convinced that British membership was crucial to the modernisation of Britain, and not keen on close co-operation with the USA, Heath was prepared to surrender much in order to obtain membership. He accepted the EEC's Common Agricultural Policy, although it had little to offer Britain: cheap food from the Commonwealth, especially New Zealand lamb, was to be excluded in order to ensure a market for more expensive, subsidised Continental products.

Shifting trade routes were linked to changes in the relative success of British ports, although industrial relations were also important. Ports that focused on the Continent and where a more flexible workforce welcomed container loads, for example Dover, Harwich and, particularly, Felixstowe, flourished, while trans-oceanic ports with militant workers, especially Liverpool and Southampton, lost business. The percentage of British trade tonnage that operated deep-sea fell with the re-orientation of trade routes and by 1986 it was down to 28 per cent, a fall from 59 per cent in 1971. This was linked to a decline in the absolute and relative size of the British merchant fleet from 30.1 million gross tons in 1973, then third largest in the world after Liberia and Japan, to 19.1 million in 1983 and eighth largest.[60]

The varied economic shifts in the 1970s shared as a common element a declining role for former imperial interests and links. New Zealand agriculture was badly hit by Britain's entry into the EEC, with the number of sheep falling from about 60 million to about 55 million from the late 1960s to the mid-1970s. For Britain, entry into the EEC also led to a loss of national control over nearby fishing grounds, and contrasted with the extension of territorial limits to 12 miles in 1965. Combined with the exhaustion of fish stocks, which led the European Union (as the EEC became) to impose quotas under the Common Fisheries Policy, and with the sale of some fishing quotas (permission to fish) by private interests, this was to help destroy much of the fishing industry. Deep-sea fishing also declined: the failure to defend fishing interests in the Cod Wars with Iceland (1958, 1973 and 1975–6) led to the exclusion of trawlers from waters claimed by Iceland, and indicated the inability of naval force to offer sustained protection for maritime interests. Further afield, already in 1958 the UK had only caught 0.7 per cent of the total catch in the area covered by the International Commission for the Northwest Atlantic Fisheries, an area that included the Newfoundland Grand Banks, compared with 6.4 per cent by France and 6.2 per cent by Spain.

As distant-water trawling was badly hit, there was a major decline in fishing from once leading centres in the 1970s, including Aberdeen,

Fleetwood and Hull, and fishing ceased at once major centres, for example at Lowestoft in the 1960s, Great Yarmouth in the late 1960s, and at Grimsby in the 1980s; although a focus on home waters helped sustain the south-west's fishing industry, especially at Newlyn and Brixham.[61] Fishing was also hit in Canada, with the share that fishing contributed to the gross domestic product falling, as did fishing's labour force.

In a very different industry, energy, the development of oil and natural gas production from the North Sea lessened interest in energy sources from further afield. Thanks to this production, the sea became an important source of national power, but this was scarcely an instance of imperial navalism, and although the navy had to consider its protection, the new industry was maritime largely only in the sense that the oil and natural gas came from under the sea. The focus that North Sea energy brought on nearby waters was symbolic of a wider shift of hopes and interests. As oil for Britain increasingly meant the North Sea, not the Middle East, so hopes of economic renewal and political strength were based not on the Empire, as they had been in the late 1940s, but on Western Europe.

10

THE REMAINS OF EMPIRE, 1973–2004

On my wall the colours of the maps are running
From Africa the winds they talk of changes coming
. . .
In the islands where I grew up
Nothing seems the same
It's just the patterns that remain,
An empty shell

On The Border, Al Stewart, 1976.

'End of an Era' proclaimed the British satirical journal *Private Eye* on its front cover on 2 April 1976. It marked the resignation of Harold Wilson as Prime Minister by depicting a largely submerged battleship with only the superstructure showing. The bubble coming from the boat had Wilson saying to James Callaghan 'Alright, Jim, you can take over now', but the legacy he was being offered was of a wrecked state. The photograph, ironically, was of a German dreadnought scuttled in Scapa Flow in 1919, but shipwreck appeared an appropriate metaphor for a country that had lost direction and a state that could no longer function adequately. Both Labour and Conservative hopes of modernisation had failed and British prestige was in marked decline. Hit hard by the oil price shock of 1973–4 and by a failure to control inflation and trade union militancy, the Labour government had to turn, in 1976, to the International Monetary Fund for a loan, and to accept cuts in government spending in return. Indeed, in 1977, the Central Policy Review Staff suggested sweeping reductions in diplomatic representation, with most diplomacy handled from London. In 1978–9, in the 'Winter of Discontent', the economic and trade-union crises of the decade appeared to culminate in a political and social breakdown. Outside Europe, the Labour governments of 1974–9 took a much less assertive stance than their predecessors of 1964–70 had done. Britain participated in the

CENTO naval exercise, Midlink 74, in the Arabian Sea in 1974, but the last forces were withdrawn from Singapore, SEATO was dissolved in 1977, the military presence in Malta was withdrawn in 1979 and there was no pretence that Hong Kong could be defended. James Callaghan, Prime Minister in 1976–9, nevertheless ordered a continued naval presence in the South Atlantic in order to deter the Argentinians from action against the Falklands, and in 1977 allegedly ordered that Argentinian naval intelligence be informed of the deployment of ships to protect the islands.

Imperial fragments continued to gain independence – the Bahamas in 1973, Grenada in 1974, the Solomon Islands, Ellice Island and Dominica in 1978, the Gilbert Islands (as part of Kiribati), St. Lucia and St. Vincent in 1979, Antigua and British Honduras in 1981 and St. Kitts–Nevis in 1983, while Brunei, hitherto a protectorate, with Britain responsible under a 1971 treaty for defence and foreign policy, became fully independent in 1984. The abandonment of the overseas system of bases continued in 1975 with the termination of the Simonstown agreements and with the departure of the navy from Malta, where it had continued to use facilities after independence under the Military Facilities Agreement. The Empire briefly expanded when independent white rule in Southern Rhodesia was undermined by the loss of South African support, and, with the collapse of UDI, British control was reintroduced, but this was a prelude to democratic elections that were followed by the grant of independence in 1980 to what became Zimbabwe.

The failure to reconcile European and global interests was a more serious issue. Although the British government had hoped that it would be possible to bridge Commonwealth and the EEC, not least by making the latter more 'outward-looking', British entry into the EEC was understandably seen by many former colonies as a deliberate rejection of their interests; indeed, prior to entry, British trade with the Commonwealth was greater than that with Europe. Links were further frayed because of serious divisions within the Commonwealth over British government policy towards South Africa and Southern Rhodesia, which provided the occasion and spark for disagreements within an already problematic system. Newly independent states had developed their own views, and the non-aligned movement sapped the willingness of some to follow the British lead. India was more interested in the non-aligned movement than the Commonwealth, while Mahathir bin Mohamad, Prime Minister of Malaysia from 1979, did not attend the Commonwealth Heads of Government meetings in 1981 and 1983, as he claimed to prefer to 'look east' to Japan.

Although the Commonwealth Secretariat was established in 1965, while the first Commonwealth Heads of Government meeting was held in Singapore in 1971, the Commonwealth amounted to little in the international system, or even in British foreign policy. Its rapid expansion to include a large number of newly independent colonies also affected the position within the Commonwealth of the Dominions. Successive British governments did not appreciate pressure to take action against white minority regimes in southern Africa, and this difference reached a high point with Margaret Thatcher's refusal in the 1987 and 1989 meetings of Commonwealth Heads of Government to accept the Commonwealth policy on sanctions against South Africa and the conference communiqués' resulting clause was 'with the exception of Britain'. More generally, the Commonwealth did not meet British hopes that it would serve as a continuation of imperial cohesion, not least because of a reluctance to follow the British lead that reflected a scepticism about British intentions and moral authority,[1] while the British were unable or unwilling to compensate for estrangement by large amounts of economic aid and financial support.[2] The creation of an equal partnership proved a goal that was incompatible with British leadership. The displays in the Commonwealth Institute in London seemed increasingly tired.

There had been a major shift in naval force-structure in the 1970s, with a move from the large, fixed-wing plane, fleet, strike-carriers (*Victorious* was sold in 1969, *Eagle* went into reserve in 1972 and was broken up in 1978 and the last, *Ark Royal*, was decommissioned in 1978) and, instead, the development of a new type of carrier designed for anti-submarine duty equipped for operating VSTOL aircraft. The first one, the 16,000-ton HMS *Invincible*, laid down in 1973 and commissioned in 1980, was the largest vessel built for the British navy since the Second World War, and was followed by the *Illustrious*, built in 1976–82, and a new *Ark Royal*, built in 1978–85, both of which were also designed for Sea Harrier fighter-bomber VSTOL planes, a process aided by the fitting of a 'ski-jump' ramp to assist take-off; the first one was tested in 1976. The light fleet carrier *Hermes*, which had been converted to a helicopter carrier in 1971–3, was, in turn, fitted with a ski-jump bow ramp in 1980–81.

In some respects, the Conservative government of Margaret Thatcher, which was elected to power in 1979, represented a self-conscious return to earlier values and interests, but there was to be no revival of imperial concerns. Thatcher sought a clear alignment with the USA in the Cold War, and this dominated her view of the world. East–West tensions had revived markedly with the Soviet intervention in Afghanistan at the close of 1979, although the USA, not Britain, took the major role in supporting opposition there. However, anxiety about Soviet plans led the British to return in strength to the Indian Ocean in 1980, to participate in 'Beacon Compass', a joint exercise with the American navy. The settlement of the Southern Rhodesia dispute further helped ensure the focus on the Cold War, while British concern in 1983 about the American intervention on Grenada, a

Caribbean island and member of the Commonwealth that had been violently taken over by a hard-line left-wing group, did not have a major impact on Anglo-American relations. The British government did not take a major role when Fiji had two coups in 1987.

THE FALKLANDS WAR, 1982

That Britain was to fight a last imperial war in 1982 was totally unexpected. The Falklands had been under British control from 1833, but were claimed, as the Malvinas, by the Argentinians, whose ruling military junta was convinced that because the British government was uncertain of the desirability of holding onto the colony it would accept the seizure. The decision, in 1981, to withdraw the Antarctic patrol ship *Endurance* was seen as a sign of British lack of interest in the South Atlantic, and, on 2 April 1982, the virtually undefended islands were successfully invaded. Assured that the navy could fulfil the task, and determined to act firmly in what was seen as a make-or-break moment for the government, Thatcher decided to respond with Operation Corporate: an expeditionary force, dispatched from 5 April, that included most of the navy: 51 warships were to take part in the operation. As another sign of British maritime strength, 45 ships were 'taken up from trade', including the cruise ships *Queen Elizabeth II* and *Canberra*, which were used to transport troops, and the container ship *Atlantic Conveyor*, which was sunk by an Exocet missile, taking a large amount of stores to the bottom. American mediation attempts that would have left the Argentinians in control were rejected.

As a result of the shift from large fleet carriers, not least the cancellation of the CVA-01 project in 1966, the expeditionary force lacked a large aircraft carrier, and therefore airborne early warning of attacks, but it had two smaller carriers, *Hermes* and *Invincible*, each with Sea Harriers. Furthermore, the Argentinian aircraft carrier, *25 de Mayo*, built in the Second World War as HMS *Venerable* and sold to the Dutch in 1948 before being taken out of service by them in 1968 and sold to Argentina, had not been refitted to operate the Super Etendard aircraft Argentina had bought from France, and, as a result, it was unable to play a role in the war. On 25–6 April, the British recaptured the subsidiary territory of South Georgia, and, on 2 May, large-scale hostilities began when HMS *Conqueror*, a nuclear-powered submarine, sank the Argentine cruiser *General Belgrano* with 321 fatalities, a step that was crucial to the struggle for command of the sea, as it led the Argentinian navy to desist from threatening attack.

However, air-launched Exocet missiles and bombs led to the loss of a number of British ships, showing that modern anti-aircraft missile systems were not necessarily a match for manned aircraft and revealing a lack of adequate preparedness on the part of the British navy. An Exocet was responsible for the loss of the destroyer *Sheffield* and bombs for that of the destroyer *Coventry*. However, the Argentinians did not sink the two carriers that provided vital air support (but not superiority) for both sea and land operations. Designed for anti-submarine warfare in the North Atlantic, the carriers' Sea King helicopters and Harriers demonstrated their versatility, the Harriers both in the combat air patrol and the close air support roles. They were more effective in both thanks to the ski-jump ramp, because of the fuel savings and increased payloads it allowed.

The Argentinians on the Falklands outnumbered the British force, and also had both aircraft and helicopters, while the British were short of ammunition because they had underestimated requirements. Nevertheless, landing on 21 May, British troops advanced on the capital, Port Stanley, fighting some bitter engagements on the nearby hills and forcing the isolated, demoralised and beaten Argentinians to surrender on 14 June. American logistical and intelligence support aided the British, but in the end it was a matter of bravely executed attacks, the careful integration of infantry with artillery support, and the ability to continue without air control.[3]

The gut patriotism released and displayed in 1982 made many commentators uncomfortable, but Thatcher knew how to respond, and war helped give her leadership a dynamic reputation enjoyed by no Conservative leader since Churchill and cemented her already strong relations with party activists. Thatcher's defence of national interests struck a chord across party boundaries and most of the Labour Party supported the recovery of the Falklands.

The war led to a re-examination of the policy of naval force structure and procurement that the Conservative government had earlier introduced with the defence review *The Way Forward* (1981), which had implied that the navy was not concentrating on what should be its core mission and, instead, that there was an anachronistic emphasis on the surface fleet. Indeed, in 1979, HMS *Blake*, the last active cruiser, had been decommissioned, while *Bulwark* had been laid up in 1981. HMS *Invincible* was about to be sold to Australia in early 1982 when the Falklands war broke out. The war, however, revealed the continued importance of the fleet for the tackling of unexpected tasks, leading to the retention of the carrier and amphibious capability and to the ordering of new ships. Although *Bulwark* was broken up in 1984 and *Hermes* was sold to India in 1986, *Ark Royal* entered service that year, while 17 frigates were laid down in 1982–91. However, the most important commitment was to the 16,000 *Vanguard* class submarines armed with Trident missiles, the replacement to Polaris; four were laid down in 1986–93, and the first, HMS *Vanguard*, was commissioned in 1993.

Nevertheless, thanks to the end of the Cold War with the collapse in 1989–91 of the Soviet Union, the major naval commitment of the 1990s, the Gulf War of 1990–91 was both outside the NATO area and a surface fleet operation. Furthermore, in 1994, the government decided to reduce the number of warheads to be carried on each Trident submarine, and also reached an agreement with Russia that matched the American–Russian one ending the missile-targeting of each other's territory.

The Falklands War led, among much of the population, to an imperial glow that helped the Conservatives win re-election in 1983, but to many it seemed anachronistic. This was even more true of the former Empire. New Zealand had offered naval support, a welcome step, but Britain fought alone. For logistical and timing reasons, the provision of troops by former colonies would not have been of much value, but had Canada maintained its earlier naval strength and been willing to help that would have been useful. However, under Pierre Trudeau, Prime Minister from 1968 to 1979 and 1980 to 1984, there was a stronger neutralism in Canadian policy. After the war, the Falklands were developed, at considerable expense, as a military base.

In contrast, Hong Kong, which unlike the Falklands was not 300 miles off the coast of a militarily far weaker power, was turned over to China in 1997 after a negotiated settlement. There was no attempt to hand the issue over for decision to local views, and, despite concern about the authoritarian nature of Chinese rule, the desire to win the goodwill of the Chinese government, and an acceptance of the dominant position of China, prevailed. Relations with China had improved considerably after the death of its radical leader Mao Zedong in 1976.

China also became influential in the naval affairs of former British colonies. The Chinese developed a naval base at Gwadar on the Baluchi coast for Pakistan, from which it could overlook the approaches to the Persian Gulf, and they also played a role on the Burmese coast, developing an offshore listening station to keep an eye on Indian naval moves, while Chinese territorial claims in the South China Sea were seen as threatening by Malaysia and Singapore and, as they could not rely on British assistance, encouraged development of their naval power.

Yet, as an instance of the continued importance of the British navy's traditional function of protecting trade, in 1980 the outbreak of the Iran–Iraq war led to the establishment of the Armilla patrol in the Persian Gulf which continued until responsibilities broadened in 1990 with the outbreak of the Gulf War. The navy played a prominent role, though very much secondary to that of the Americans, both in the blockade of Iraq and in Operation Desert Storm in 1991. For the latter, Britain committed three destroyers, four frigates, three minehunters and two submarines, and navy helicopters destroyed 15 Iraqi vessels. As an indication, nevertheless, of the deficiencies of maritime support, many of the merchantmen chartered to take British troops and material both to the Persian Gulf and, subsequently, during peacekeeping intervention in conflicts in what had been Yugoslavia were foreign.[4]

ECONOMIC DEVELOPMENTS

Despite the Falklands War, the developments and debates of the 1980s continued to focus on the Cold War or on domestic economic issues, while relations within the European Economic Community became more politically divisive in the late 1980s. The economic importance to Britain of links with the former Empire continued to decline, and, with them, deep-sea trade. In 1961, 51 per cent of New Zealand's exports went to Britain, but, in 1991, only 6 per cent went there and Australia, Japan, the USA and the rest of the European Union took larger shares. The New Zealand assembly of Japanese cars began in the 1970s. In 1966–7, Britain was replaced by Japan as Australia's leading market, and the percentage of Australian exports that went to Asia increased from 49 in 1970 to 67 per cent in 1991. In 2001, the USA exported $163 billion worth of goods to Canada, making Canada by far America's largest export market. The USA had also become the dominant economic power in former Caribbean colonies, and its political clout was displayed in 1993 when 266 troops from Barbardos, Belize, Jamaica and Trinidad accompanied the 20,000 Americans that invaded Haiti, lending a regional respectability to the forcible return of the President Jean–Bertrand Aristide.

Britain's economic role in Asia was substantially reduced in the second half of the century. This was the case both in former colonies, such as Malaya, where British companies lost control of the palm oil, rubber and tin production they had developed, and in India, where British firms were hit by the discriminatory policies of the Indian government, including exchange controls and taxation, and by the development of multinational and Indian competition;[5] as well as in other countries where Britain's role had been important: China, Iran and Japan. Successive British governments devoted only limited effort to the protection of these overseas interests, although to have done more would not have been easy. British investments in Egypt were expropriated in 1956, as a result of the Suez Crisis, while British Petroleum's interests in Libya were seized in 1971. More generally, links with the former 'informal' Empire had declined. By the late 1980s, Latin America, once a major field of British trade and investment, supplied only 1.5 per cent of British imports and took only 1.4 per cent of its exports, and investments in the region totalled only 6 per cent of British foreign investment. With both the former Empire, for example in India and Pakistan, and the former 'informal' Empire, for example Latin America, British shipping lines encountered problems from protectionism as countries sought to develop national shipping lines.[6]

CULTURAL LINKS

Cultural influence in former imperial possessions also declined. The percentage of the Australasian and Canadian populations who can claim British descent has fallen markedly since 1945, and this has also ensured that fewer Britons have had siblings or children living in former colonies, although 'fewer' can conceal the large number who still have these links. British emigration to former colonies, with their greater economic opportunities, was still very important in the 1950s and, to a lesser extent, 1960s. Indeed, thanks in part to American limitations on immigration, the percentage of British emigrants going to Australia, Canada and New Zealand rose from about 59 in 1900–14 to 82 in 1949–63. Committed to a White Australia policy and anxious about the demographic strength of Asia, Australia encouraged British and Dutch immigrants, although post-war Displaced Persons from Eastern Europe were also important.[7] Of New Zealand's immigrants in 1951–61, 190,000 were British and only 44,600 were non-British, including some Dutch under the assisted immigration begun in 1950. As a result, 18.3 per cent of the population of Northern Auckland in 1971 was British born and 12.3 per cent of that of Wellington. In Canada, Britain remained the largest individual source of immigrants in the 1950s, although it was now considerably less important than the remainder of Europe combined. Immigrants continued to come by sea.

However, especially from the 1970s, there was a decline in British emigration to former colonies that reflected a number of factors. First, it became more common to emigrate elsewhere, particularly to France or Spain, for retirement. Second, restrictions on immigration and work permits were put in place by former colonies, especially Canada and Australia, while, in New Zealand, economic difficulties led to the imposition of controls in 1974. Third, former colonies, particularly Australia, became more open to immigration from other countries, especially Mediterranean Europe and South and East Asia. All these shifts became more pronounced from the 1970s. Furthermore, the reduced 'draw' of Britain was shown by emigration from South Africa and Zimbabwe in the late 1990s and early 2000s, much of which was to Australia, although considerable numbers from Zimbabwe went to Britain. Much emigration from Hong Kong in the 1990s was to Vancouver.

America came to play a more important cultural role in both Australasia and Canada with, for example, American soap operas being shown frequently on the television. Thus, 40 per cent of the programmes shown on New Zealand television in November–December 1985 were made in the USA, with New Zealand being responsible for 35 per cent and the UK for 19 per cent. The proportion of records in the New Zealand top 20 by country of origin, fell from over 50 per cent from the UK in 1966 to 40 per cent, while, for 1985, of the top 100 albums, 43 per cent were from the UK, but 46 per cent from the USA. There was nothing to compare with the impact of the Beatles' 1964 tour to New Zealand. More generally, after Britain entered the EEC, New Zealand increasingly reconceptualised itself as a South Pacific state. Similarly, republican sentiment grew markedly in Australia from the 1980s, a reaction not only to changing views about the British connection, but also to altered perceptions of Australia, not least the need to find a new international role and national identity after the decline of the British Empire.[8]

Across the former Empire, constitutional links with Britain, for example the right of appeal to the Judicial Committee of the Privy Council in Britain from the superior courts of Commonwealth countries, were severed or diminished in importance. The British refusal to support the death penalty was an issue reflecting different cultural norms in relations with former Caribbean colonies plagued by drug crime, and in 2003 the Jamaican Parliament voted for the creation of a Caribbean Court of Justice, a step also supported by Barbados, Guyana, and Trinidad and Tobago.

The ending or weakening of former aspects of imperial power and connection were not however the sole legacy of empire, and, in terms of influence, the imperial experience continued to have an important role, both for Britain and for her former colonies, although the situation in the latter varied greatly. In particular, there were major differences depending on whether the states had been extensively settled during the colonial period, and on how far British rule was simply part of a sequence of imperial episodes. Another variable was provided by whether or not British imperial rule had been responsible for the original unification of the country, and thus for giving it lasting territorial shape.

IRELAND

Within Britain, empire's legacy was most apparent in two respects: Ireland and migration. The Heath government (1970–74) had wanted to establish the conditions under which Northern Ireland could become self-governing again, but on a different basis than before: this time there would be a genuine cross-community government in Northern Ireland. The government sought, with the Sunningdale Agreement of 1973 and the creation of a non-sectarian power-sharing Executive, which took office in 1974, to negotiate a settlement, but they did not command sufficient cross-community support, and the Protestant Ulster Workers' strike of May 1974 led rapidly to the resumption of direct rule that spring.

IRA terrorism continued, even after the government of the Republic of Ireland was brought into the equation through the Anglo-Irish Agreement of 1985, which gave the Irish government a formal role in the affairs of Northern Ireland through an Anglo-Irish Secretariat and an Inter-Governmental Conference. In 1993, new talks between the two governments led to the Downing Street Declaration: the two Prime Ministers agreed to a shared sovereignty that would guarantee the rights of Nationalists, while Unionists were assured that they would not be forced into a united Ireland. A paramilitary ceasefire, declared in 1994, breached in 1996 and resumed in 1997, provided a basis for negotiations.

The difficult relations between Unionists, Nationalists and the British government were shot through with attitudes and tensions that derived from perceptions of empire, leading Tony Blair, who became Prime Minister, to complain about the burden of history. In 1998, however, the Good Friday Agreement laid the basis for the resumption of provincial self-government. After the agreement was endorsed by a referendum, an Assembly and a Northern Ireland Executive were both created, but the Agreement was weakened by a fundamental problem: that the Nationalists regarded it as a stage towards further gains, while many of the Unionists found it difficult to accept even the Agreement. The situation in Northern Ireland continued to be one of the Empire's most troubling legacies.

MIGRATION

Migration, both emigration and immigration, linked the British with former colonies. Immigration played a more prominent role in the national consciousness from the late 1950s when it was dominated by former colonies, especially the West Indies, Cyprus, Pakistan and India, although, also, with important strands from other former colonies, for example Uganda. Immigration, however, was not solely an issue of ex-empire, and major strands in the early 2000s came from Eastern Europe, for example Albania, and from peoples able to claim political asylum, for example Afghans and Iraqi Kurds.

Successive changes in immigration legislation affected links between Britain and former colonies. The British Nationality Act of 1948 guaranteed freedom of entry from the Commonwealth and colonies, and this immigration was clearly different from that from elsewhere in the world. The Act was followed in the 1950s by large-scale immigration, including from the West Indies, although many of the immigrants intended only a limited stay. A temporary labour shortage in unattractive spheres of employment, such as transport, foundry work and nursing, led to an active sponsorship of immigration that accorded with Commonwealth idealism, but there was public concern about the scale of immigration and growing racial tension, especially over jobs and public housing. This led to alarmist newspaper reports, so that on 14 September 1953 the headline of the populist *Daily Sketch* proclaimed GUNMEN AT LARGE: DOPE, DAGGERS AND TERROR IN THE STREETS. THE FACTS. It introduced an exaggerated account of the problems of Tiger Bay in Cardiff and a misleading attempt to link them to the black population of the Butetown area of Cardiff. Anxieties were exploited by Fascists and there was a shift, on the paranoid right and in wider circles, from the anti-Semitism of the 1930s to a stress on black immigrants. The League of Empire Loyalists was founded in 1954 by A. K. Chesterton, brother of the novelist G. K. Chesterton and, earlier, one of Sir Oswald Mosley's lieutenants in the British Union of Fascists. The League never had many members, and the four candidates it ran in parliamentary elections in 1957–64 all did very badly; but it put forward ideas that the bulk of the population had not quite sloughed off. The League merged with the National Front when the latter was formed in 1967 and Chesterton became its president.

Racial tension and concerns about the impact of immigration on unemployment levels led to a redefinition of nationality, seen with the Commonwealth Immigration Acts of 1962 and 1968, the Immigration Act of 1971, the British Nationality Act of 1981 and the Immigration Act of 1988, which progressively reduced Commonwealth immigration. For example, the Act of 1968 deprived East African Asians with British passports of the automatic right to entry, which they had been promised when Kenya gained its independence from Britain.[9] After the 1971 Act, there were few differences between the rights of Commonwealth and foreign immigrants. In the 1971 census, 707,100 people were recorded as what would be described as having New Commonwealth origins. Partly thanks to immigration, Churchill's 1956 description of the British as an 'island race' increasingly appeared anachronistic, although that did not prevent Margaret Thatcher from echoing it at the time of the Falkland Crisis in 1982.[10]

Alongside restrictions on immigration, the rights of those who had legally immigrated were strengthened. Race Relations Acts in 1965, 1968 and 1976 prohibited discrimination and established a Commission for Racial Equality to deal with general problems of discrimination as well as individual cases. This legislation failed to convince many immigrants that they were not the victims of a racialist system, but it marked a major advance on the earlier legal situation.

More significantly, despite often vicious racialism, British society became less racist in the sense that fewer people formally challenged racial diversity. The success of immigrants and their descendants in sport was particularly important in changing attitudes. Thus, in November 1999 Lennox Lewis became world heavyweight boxing champion, while in 2002 Paul Boateng became Chief Secretary to the Treasury and the first 'black' man in the Cabinet, and the Pakistani-born Michael Nazir-Ali, Bishop of Rochester, was much (although unsuccessfully) touted as a possible Archbishop of Canterbury.

Immigration affected a country no longer confident of its role in the Commonwealth, let alone the world, and this influenced the response. This is one of the ways in which decolonisation had an important cultural res-onance and affected the self-image of both the British and their country,[11] but it is difficult to distinguish the impact of empire and its loss from other influences. For example, de-industrialisation and social change have to be considered alongside changes linked to the end of empire. To turn, for example, to the social consequences of empire, it is possible to dwell on the extent to which curry has become a British national dish, to comment on the numbers employed in Indian restaurants and, more generally, to talk of the way in which the legacy of empire has transformed national diet. In such an approach, we move on from curry to West Indian foodstuffs sold in markets, and so on. All this is true, but it has to be seen as part of a wider cosmopolitan exposure to foreign foods and ways of preparing meals that does not focus on former colonies, so that, alongside curry can be placed pizza, chop suey, sushi, hamburgers and fried chicken. Indeed, in the case of diet, it can be argued that the legacy of empire has been over-played, in that, after a burst of interest in Indian cuisine, that in large part reflected its ready and inexpensive availability through plentiful restaurants in most urban localities, has come a relative decline that has owed something to the rise of other cuisines, such as Japanese food, and has more generally been the product of a more mobile consumer market.

CONCLUSIONS

To pursue the theme of the limited current impact of empire within Britain, many people today know little of Britain's earlier history, and, if they have an image of empire, it is limited, simplistic and largely negative. 'Abroad' is far more focused on the USA and Europe. There is a particular lack of interest in Africa and Oceania, other than as holiday destinations, such as

Gambia or Kenya. It would surprise most readers to know that the British had had a colony in Somaliland.

Alongside this, the disputed character of empire has led to a contest over its image that has become particularly pronounced during the last decade. In part this revolves around the issue of imperial guilt, with specific foci on the slave trade, the Irish Famine and Amritsar, demands for apologies, if not compensation, and more generally a powerful critique of empire as a whole and of Britain, past and present, as a result. Much of this criticism is naïve, and most of it is ahistorical, but that does not lessen its weight.

As a related issue, in Australia, Canada and New Zealand, the indigenous populations have become increasingly assertive culturally and politically, and have actively pressed for the redress of grievances dating both to the period of settlement, much of which involved the expropriation of land, and subsequently. The response has varied, being more positive in Canada and New Zealand than in Australia. In New Zealand, the Waitangi Tribunal was founded by the government to probe breaches of the Treaty of Waitangi, and, from the late 1980s, legislation, such as the State-Owned Enterprises Act of 1986, the Maori Fisheries Act of 1989 and the Resource Management Act of 1991, took account of Maori interests.[12]

Furthermore, as Jack Straw, the British Foreign Secretary, complained in November 2002, the legacy of empire, for Britain and for other powers, can be held responsible for disputes across much of the world. In particular, the baneful consequences of British imperialism, or of the circumstances of its departure, have been traced in disputes in South Asia and the Middle East, both between states such as India and Pakistan, and also within them, as with the relations between the communities in Sri Lanka (Ceylon). Britain itself has become involved in a territorial dispute with Spain over Gibraltar as a consequence of an imperial conquest.

If the legacy is fraught, there are also more beneficial consequences of empire. These range from the emphasis on freedoms and the rule of law in British constitutionalism, to the extent to which the English language has opened the world to many; and one obvious legacy is the ability to debate the value of empire with people around the world, with most of them being free to express their views.

CONCLUSIONS

We must begin by recognising how different is the part played by our Navy from that of the navies of every other Country. Alone among the great modern States, we can neither defend the soil upon which we live nor subsist upon its produce . . . The food of our people, the raw material of our industries, the commerce which constitutes our wealth, have to be protected as they traverse thousands of miles of sea and ocean from every quarter of the globe . . . The burden of responsibility laid upon the British Navy is heavy, and its weight increases year by year.

Churchill as First Lord of the Admiralty, introducing the Naval Estimates, House of Commons, 17 March 1914.

There is no central narrative to the seaborne empire. It involved trade and war, fishing and shipbuilding, piracy and seaborne settlement, emigration, immigration and a myriad of other links. To provide a last chapter that offers coherence would be to underrate the open-ended character of these continuing relationships. Instead, there is deliberately an eclectic approach that focuses on important recent and current developments in a number of different spheres, without pretending to a central theme other than change. At the close, there is a discussion of the impact of empire, but the invitation to readers is to let it prompt them to other reflections, and that would be an appropriate result of the diversity of the imperial experience and impact.

At the start of 2004, Britain had an empire that was still far larger in extent than her overseas possessions had been in 1500. Alongside islands in and near the West Indies – Anguilla, Bermuda, the Cayman Islands, Montserrat, the Turks and Caicos Islands and the British Virgin Islands – there were possessions in the mid-Atlantic – Ascension Island, St. Helena and Tristan de Cunha; in the Pacific – the Pitcairn Islands; the Indian Ocean – the British Indian Ocean Territory; and in and close to Antarctica – the British Antarctic Territory, South Georgia, the South Orkney, South Sandwich and South Shetland Islands and the Falklands. In the Mediterranean, aside from Gibraltar, the British bases in Cyprus were also sovereign territories. Some of the territories were unoccupied, but in others there was no support for independence. Bermuda voted against it in 1995. Similarly, the Cook Islands achieved self-government from New Zealand in 1965 with a continuing right to choose independence, which they have not exercised. Niue, the world's largest coral island, followed the same route in 1974, and, again, has not chosen independence from New Zealand. Such fragments of empire led to commitments by the former imperial power in order to sustain their isolated societies. In some cases, emigration, and its consequences in the shape of unwelcome immigration from these fragments to the metropole, encouraged this role. Thus, large-scale emigration by Pacific Islanders to New Zealand from the 1950s led it to provide economic aid, for example to Niue.

The determination shown in a referendum in 2002 organised by the inhabitants of Gibraltar, in defiance of the British government, to remain British rather than be party to any agreement between the governments of Britain and Spain to introduce a measure of Spanish control, struck a resonance in British domestic opinion. Gibraltar itself became, in 2003, the only UK Overseas Territory to commemorate the martyrdom of St. George, the patron saint of England, on a postage stamp. As an instructive sign of the potentially incorporating nature of empire, the three stamps issued on St. George's Day also commemorated the Constantinian Order of St. George, a Christian military order intended for the propagation of the Catholic Church.

In Britain, however, the Empire was no longer seen as a community, and instead the ambiguities of its past and heritage were increasingly stressed. Nor was there much interest in the assets, strategic and economic, that it offered. Gibraltar still had importance as a military base, and there was interest in the resources of the Falklands and surrounding seas, but there was scant commitment to the remaining territories. Furthermore, the symbolic role of the sea in British life has been undermined.

DEFENCE

Owing to the development of the Polaris fleet, the navy had become the strategic force of last resort for Britain, but this was a military arm that was not dependent on any conventional understanding of empire. Based in

Britain, at Faslane on the Clyde and Devonport, nuclear submarines could cruise for long distances without needing refuelling or other port facilities. The structure of maritime empire provided by coaling stations and, earlier, watering and re-supply anchorages, had gone. So also had the imperative of protecting trade: anti-submarine capability remained important during the Cold War, but Polaris, until 1995, and its successor from 1993, Trident, were not designed for maritime tasks. Instead, the targets they aimed at, and the attacks they sought to deter, were land-based.[1] Similarly, after the Cold War, as the navy sought to find a new role, not least in response to the cuts suggested in the government's *Options for Change* (1991), it developed a doctrine of amphibious assault and power projection into the littoral, using helicopter-borne forces and cruise missiles, so that targets and goals remained land-based. In 1998, the submarine HMS *Splendid* achieved Britain's first live firing of a Tomahawk cruise missile, the latter a weapon bought from the USA. The following year, *Splendid* fired these missiles at Serb targets in Kosovo as part of the NATO operations there. In Operation Allied Force, the British also launched sorties from *Invincible*, while they deployed the 22,000-ton helicopter carrier *Ocean*, completed in 1998, and the assault ship *Fearless* to provide the capability for a marine assault, although, in the event, one was not launched. Earlier, in support of the pressure on Iraq, the *Invincible* had been deployed to the Persian Gulf on three missions in 1996–9.

To return to an issue raised in the Introduction, transformation of power, as well as end of empire, were at stake. With hydrogen bombs and Trident missiles, the British state wielded more power than ever before, and, depending on the criteria for measurement and shifts in economic success, Britain was the fourth, fifth or sixth most important economy in the world: in 2003, its position as the fourth-wealthiest economy was challenged by France, as a result of the fall of sterling against the euro and differing growth rates. Not to be the leading power in the world was not necessarily to be without an empire of some type. Indeed, throughout history, most empires have been in this position, and that remained the case after Western expansion ensured that empires across the world came into contact with each other.

This is an approach that differs from the empire as leading power thesis, but that thesis has serious limitations, as it employs empire to describe something that is different, namely the hegemonic power, which is inherently a state in an eccentric position. Britain was in that position, particularly in the nineteenth century, and it moulded the British perception of empire, both its own and those of others, but most empires have never been in this hegemonic position, nor been able to aspire to it. The approach of adopting the empire as leading power ensures that the history of Britain in the twentieth century becomes an account of decline, the dominant theme in much of the scholarly literature, in British self-image and one given greater force in 2003 by Niall Ferguson's television series and books on the Empire which received considerable attention. Ferguson drew eloquent attention to the long-term benefits of the Empire – 'no organisation in history has done more to promote the free movement of goods, capital and labour . . . and . . . to impose Western norms of law, order and governance around the world',[2] leading to criticism that he had failed to give due weight to its disadvantages, but, aside from this, his account of the Empire in the second half of the twentieth century was more mixed (and far shorter).

While it would be foolish to ignore the extent to which decline and failure have been prominent themes in British history in this period, it would be mistaken to argue that economic problems and decolonisation meant the end of imperial power. To take simply the focus of naval strength, there was no longer need for a network of coaling stations. Furthermore, as maritime trade was increasingly concentrated on large deep-draught vessels, such as super-tankers, so its protection did not require control over coastal waters around the world. Control over territory against the wishes of its population was no longer viable for Britain at the close of the twentieth century, but the strength demonstrated in the Falklands conflict in 1982 represented imperial power, even if it was not in pursuit of imperial expansion, but, instead, as a war of self-defence, if not a liberation struggle on behalf of the Falklanders. At the start of the third millennium CE, commentators referred to the American Empire, although, with the exception of its Pacific possessions and Puerto Rico, it was not an empire expressed through rule over territory. On this criterion, it is worth reconsidering the end of empire notion, not least through considering the continued capability of imperial powers for power projection.

For Britain, as for the USA and France, this projection in large part took a naval form. The Americans deployed troops into Afghanistan in 2002 from carriers and other warships in the Arabian Sea: helicopters lifted troops into combat at Kandahar, a distance of 450 miles, most of it across a former British colony, Pakistan. Britain itself contributed cruise missiles fired from *Trafalgar* and *Triumph* to the initial bombardment of Afghanistan in October 2001. American carriers played a major part in the attack on Iraq in 2003, and British warships provided an important supporting role. The previous winter, British warships played a major part in Operation Resinate, the Anglo-American attempt to stop Iraqi oil smuggling.

The navy itself was changing. The *Options for Change* White Paper outlined a cut in naval personnel of 3,000 while the submarine fleet was to be reduced from 27 to 16. Under *Frontline First* (1994), naval personnel was to be cut by another 1,900, the smallest reduction, but the navy contained fewer personnel than the army or the air force. In 1998, the Strategic Defence Review outlined cuts in warship and submarine numbers, although it included a provision for the construction of two super-carriers, capable of acting as a platform for aircraft in a way that the anti-submarine carriers they were designed to replace had not been able to. This ran the risk of investing in an out-dated force structure, as carriers provide readily identifiable targets for missiles, and their protection in wartime would require the use of other warships. At the same time, the plan for a new generation of warships centred on carriers capable of operating around the world was a reminder of the continuing close relationship between British power and naval strength. This strength was presented as justifying Britain's continued claims to great power status, for example her permanent seat on the United Nations Security Council. The carriers were designed for multiple roles: fighting naval battles, launching ground strikes and mounting amphibious missions.

At the same time, Britain was most likely to act in collaboration with other powers. There was a stress on inter-operability with the American military, but also a stated determination to breathe life into ideas of European military collaboration. Thus, in 2003, Britain joined with France, Italy and Spain in agreeing to collaborate over maintaining the readiness of their aircraft carriers (of which Britain then had three, the others one each), in order to ensure that one was on station at all times. In addition, a European Capabilities Agency was to be established. The value of sea power was further demonstrated in the 2003 crisis with Iraq as the deployment of British aircraft to the region was affected by the reluctance of states, particularly Jordan, to provide overflying permission and refuelling facilities.

British naval capability was seen in joint terms not only with regard to other powers but also because of an emphasis on co-operation with land and air forces. The establishment of the Permanent Joint Headquarters for the conduct of joint operations by Britain was followed, after the 1998 Strategic Defence Review, by that of the Joint Doctrine and Concepts Centre. The impact of this was seen with the decision that the 1999 second edition of *British Marine Doctrine* would be the last written under the auspices of the Naval Staff, as all future editions would be written and published under that of the new Centre. The second edition indeed declared:

The maritime environment is inherently *joint* . . . Naval forces themselves exist to influence events ashore; they have never operated strategically in an exclusively naval environment . . . the sea is a pre-eminent medium because, above all, it provides access at a time and place of political choice. By history, tradition and skill the UK is better placed, certainly than any other European nation, to exploit this medium and to develop a strategic doctrine of warfare based on the joint use of the sea . . . Ultimately, maritime forces can only realise their considerable potential when integrated fully into a joint force.[3]

Britain was indeed better placed than other European states to deploy naval power. This was enhanced from 1990 by the acquisition of HMS *Ocean* (the largest warship in the fleet), 16 'Duke' class frigates and two 32,300-ton Fleet Replenishment Ships, each able to carry five helicopters and, if necessary, Sea Harriers. Critics focused on the decline in overall warship numbers. On 5 June 2000, Iain Duncan Smith, the Shadow Defence Secretary, complained in the House of Commons that the number of frigates and destroyers had fallen from 35 in 1997 to 27 and of submarines from 15 to 10, while Gordon Prentice, a Labour MP, reported that 'we are flogging off at a knock-down price ships that are perfectly serviceable, that were only commissioned maybe 12 or 13 years ago'. In reply, John Spellar, the Armed Forces Minister, noted that the Strategic Defence Review had shown that the requirement for major surface vessels had 'altered', and three years later, in the *Delivering Security in a Changing World* White Paper, there were provisions for fresh changes: 'Some of our older vessels contribute less well to the pattern of operations that we envisage, and reductions in numbers will be necessary'. As a result, in January 2004, it was decided to mothball four destroyers, not previously due to be decommissioned until 2007–10. This would reduce the number of escort ships to 28, compared with 32 French counterparts. The destroyers to be mothballed had, with their Sea Dart missiles, an important air defence capability, but this no longer appeared so necessary. The sense of betrayed heritage was readily apparent in the editorial of the *Daily Telegraph* on 6 January 2004, which began 'What would Nelson have said?' It was argued that Britain would no longer be able to mount major naval operations unless alongside the USA or France.

The decline of the former Soviet navy in the 1990s nevertheless increased the relative importance of British naval power, not least as the weakness of Russian governmental systems was abundantly shown in the failure to sustain the operational effectiveness of both warships and bases. Assessment of the nature of the British Empire at the start of the new millennium requires a focus not on territorial control but on the maritime potency that was so important a strand in Western imperial history.

BRITISHNESS

If debates over naval tasking represented one legacy of the British seaborne empire, another was provided by a growing cultural diversity within Britain and, also, in some of her former colonies, particularly Australia, which contains the largest Greek community outside Greece, but also Canada, where there was a large influx to Vancouver from Hong Kong. Britishness became a container for many nationalities: one can be British and Pakistani, Ghanian and Greek, as well as Scottish, English or Welsh. The relationship between Englishness and these categories was less clear. With the prospect of Cyprus and Malta, both former colonies, joining the European Union, after enlargement of the Union was agreed in 2003, a further note of variety will be added, as their inhabitants will acquire rights to work in Britain. The ability of Britishness to retain value alongside the nationalities it contained receded, just as it had previously done in the Dominions. Whether the earlier imperial role bore some responsibility for this failure was a matter of debate for scholars who enjoyed considering discourses of identity.

Religion and ethnicity posed particular issues of adaptation, both for immigrants and for those born in Britain. By 2001, there were two million Muslims in Britain, and a poll in December 2002 revealed that eight per cent of a sample amongst them claimed to be willing to support terrorist acts against Britain, in other words the slaughter of their fellow citizens. As a separate issue, there were serious tensions over the position of ethnic minorities, especially, but not only, in the early 2000s in Lancashire and Yorkshire. However, although public discussion about racism cast in terms of 'black and white' addresses the issue of 'institutional' racism, it tends to posit a non-existent unitary 'black community' and a dubious notion of 'whiteness'. Instead, multi-cultural Britain sees a myriad of tensions and alliances in which place, ethnicity, religion, class and other factors both clash and co-exist, for example church-going people of Caribbean descent versus criminous Jamaican Yardies. This was also true of former colonies, although, nevertheless, there were readily apparent rifts, many arising from immigration during the period of imperial ascendancy, for example between Chinese and Malays in Malaya, and Indians and Fijians in Fiji.

In Britain and elsewhere, the interest in, and response of, immigrant groups and individuals to imperial legacies varied greatly, as did those of the population as a whole. One of the most arresting instances was provided by television, which played a central role in societies increasingly dominated by visual images. Although a few of the period-costume dramas that enjoyed considerable prominence in the closing decades of the twentieth century and in the early twenty-first century were accounts of empire, for example *The Jewel in the Crown*, they were not heroic sagas, and the majority of the programmes were dramatisations of stories set within Britain. Empire indeed was often castigated as racist, or was mocked with characters such as Private Widdle, an epicene soldier, Sir Sidney Roughdiamond, the sexually adventurous governor, and the roguish missionary in *Carry On Up the Khyber* (1968), a film in fact shot in North Wales.

Similarly, the list of one hundred Great Britons produced by popular choice for the BBC in 2002 was singularly low on imperial heroes. Martial figures as a whole were in short supply: only Nelson and Cromwell made the last ten, and if the winner, Churchill, can be seen as the greatest, as well as the last, of the imperial heroes, he was presented, as were Nelson and Elizabeth I, as a defender of an endangered country/people/culture, rather than as an exponent of empire. The theme of defence not expansionism was similarly present in the television treatment of C. S. Forester's Hornblower saga. Furthermore, as also was the case when Forster's novels first appeared (from 1937, when *The Happy Return* was published), the television reflected a preference for the billowing sails and creaking timbers of the age of sail, rather than for the world of steam, a preference repeated with the success in 2003 of *Master and Commander*, the first filmed version of Patrick O'Brian's maritime novels.

The shift away from empire was not simply a matter of television audiences. The furore over exhibitions, especially on the slave trade, at the National Maritime Museum and the new Museum of the British Empire at Bristol, revealed signs of strong sensitivity in some circles to Britain's imperial past. The celebratory mural on the New Palace Theatre in Plymouth's Union Street showing the defeat of the Spanish Armada in 1588 now looks out on a world for which such events are drained of meaning and resonance.

This is particularly the case in Scotland, Wales and Northern Ireland where nationalist traditions have defined Britishness and the British Empire in alien terms and, indeed, as actively hostile to the interests of the Scots, Welsh and Irish. In each case, there are important variations. In Northern Ireland, this definition has long been offered by Catholic nationalists, and this underlines the unionism of the Protestant majority which includes a more positive account of the British Empire. In Scotland, there is pride in the major contribution of Scots to the Empire, but this is less prominent than hitherto and increasingly seen in terms of nineteenth-century entrepreneurship and industry, such as shipbuilding, rather than as also comprehending the major role of the Scots in imperial conquest. The 22 per cent of Scottish votes cast in the 1997 general election for the Scottish National Party (SNP) was a comment on the decline of Britishness in Scotland, but that decline involved more than simply support for the SNP.

Apologists for empire now appear dated, especially in light of the modern preference for cultural relativism. Thus, to turn to Admiral Ballard's *Rulers of the Indian Ocean* (1927), his theme of the beneficial consequences stemming from 'the establishment of a reign of law and order by British power in the Indian Ocean' is now more acceptable than his statement, 'If the teachings of past history are any guide to the future it will be helpful to the continued progress of civilisation throughout the eastern hemisphere that the supremacy of that force should long remain effective'.[4] Interest in empire is frequently decried now as reprehensible nostalgia or inappropriate anachronism, but, for many Britons, the results of empire provide a taproot of identity, the consequences of which include a reluctant attitude towards closer relations with Europe. In addition, for many in the world, the experience of British control marks the importance and relevance of British history.

Empire and the sea are not coterminous in British history and experience, even if empire and oceans have a closer relationship. It is instructive to note how the role of the sea in national interests and consciousness has become less prominent, if not downright inconspicuous, in recent decades. For example, despite its origins on Merseyside, with the Beatles, Cilla Black, Gerry and the Pacemakers, and the Swinging Blue Jeans, the popular music explosion that began in the 1960s made scant reference to the sea. Instead, it was firmly rooted in city streets, although in the 1976 song *Lord Grenville* Al Stewart made reference to maritime themes in his account of rootless questing:

> Go and tell Lord Grenville that the tide is on the turn
> It's time to haul the anchor up and leave the land astern
> . . .
> . . . our dreams have run aground
> . . .
> Go and fetch the captain's log and tear the pages out
> . . .
> Send a message to the fleet, they'll search for us in vain
> We won't be there among the reaches of the Spanish Main.

The influence of former colonies on popular music was limited in the 1960s, although from the 1970s, Bob Marley had a major impact, and Afro-Caribbean influence, in part also through American intermediaries, remained important with 'rap' sound.

Over the twentieth century, the sea played scant role in the two major images of national identity that were offered: ruralism and the city. The former became prominent from the late nineteenth century, as there was a reaction against the cities, and as the comfortable, as well as the affluent, increasingly sought to adopt a rural or suburban lifestyle, which were seen as quintessentially English. The ideal was also taken up by many, although by no means all, twentieth-century reformers, so that the development of suburbia drew on the ideas of social improvement advanced by the garden city movement. The strength and endurance of the relationship between the ruralist tradition and Englishness derived from the fact that it was not just conservative but also able to accommodate and place the apparently irreconcilable ideals of the Romantic right (country house, country church, squire, parson and deferential society), and the Romantic left (folk society, the village, rural crafts and honest peasantry): that there are in short several ruralist traditions which co-exist. The rural ideal was taken up by such leading interwar politicians as Stanley Baldwin, Conservative Prime Minister 1923–4, 1924–9 and 1935–7, whose speeches were littered with respectful eulogies to the English countryside and the sons of the soil, and who, despite being from an industrial 'ironmaster' background, used his native Worcestershire to conjure up wonderfully evocative images of the rural England he loved so much.[5]

The commitment to the rural landscape was especially strong in this period. It took many forms, in music in the positive response to Vaughan Williams, and in painting in the popularity of 'authentic', rather than modernist, works. In fiction, there were ruralist writers such as Henry Williamson, whose works included *Tarka the Otter* (1927), and who, in *The Linhay on the Downs* (1938), referred to 'the harmony of nature', a central theme in much interwar culture. Similar ruralist themes echoed in the second half of the century, although not continually, in the 1950s rather than the 1960s for example, and the rural life, including the rural 1950s, were celebrated again in television programmes in the early twenty-first century. This was an account that had no real place for the sea apart from in minor roles, for example as a background to scenes of the South Downs.

There was an urban alternative to this tradition, but it also had little role for the sea. This was a tradition that looked back to pragmatic, liberal, puritan and utilitarian accounts of identity and history, and was developed on the left. This tradition had powerful cultural advocates and resonances, as in the work of H. G. Wells and the Vorticists, although, as also with left-wing views on patriotism,[6] there was a tension between cosmopolitan cultural resonances in liberal and left-wing thought and those that could be defined as more clearly national, whether British, English or Scottish. Alongside the pastoral tradition of the 1930s and 1940, other writers were open to urban life, and although, for much of the century, the rural conception of England was the one that dominated domestic artistic and popular images, and was not eclipsed by urban constructions of identity, toward the close of the century the image of England as a 'green and pleasant land' was increasingly overtaken by the city, where the bulk of the population lived or worked.

In Scotland and Wales, there had not been a garden ruralism to compare with that in England and the urban experience had been more central throughout. Given the urban character of major ports and shipbuilding centres, this might suggest a stronger emphasis on aspects of seaborne activity, but this was not the case other than on the Clyde. North Sea oil provided Scottish nationalists with another issue with which to berate the

British connection, but, although it provided jobs for many Scots and helped greatly in the development of Aberdeen, it did not lead to a particular cultural engagement with the sea.

SHIPBUILDING AND DOCKS

The urban centres of maritime activity did not seem to offer a positive account of their maritime legacy. Across the British Isles, shipbuilding was in decline from the 1960s, and in terminal crisis from the 1970s, and it was associated with embittered groups of unionised manual workers, rather than with the images of urban enterprise, culture and style that were being propagated. The growing difficulties of the industry in the 1960s had led to government intervention, but that by the Labour ministries of 1964–70 had deleterious consequences. In a pattern subsequently familiar in universities, intervention took the form of structural change, particularly the creation of larger groupings, rather than the reform of practices. This led, in 1971, to the occupation, by their workers, of yards on the Upper Clyde threatened by closure. The Conservative government backed down in 1972, later claiming that it feared large-scale civil violence, although this was probably not the sole major factor.[7]

Subsequently, the economic crisis caused by the quadrupling of oil prices in 1973 hit British shipbuilding as tanker orders fell dramatically, although it was also responsible for the major development of the North Sea energy industry. A major collapse in order books between 1973 and 1975 hit Britain alongside the rest of the world. The UK launched 1,281,000 gross registered tonnage of ships in 1974, 813,000 in 1978 and 527,000 in 1983, although, in the percentage of the world output, the position was different and the decline far less steep: 3.7 to 5.2 to 3.5. The Labour government responded by nationalising the industry in 1977 and creating British Shipbuilders. The Belfast yard of Harland and Wolff, which had already been nationalised in 1975 in order to prevent bankruptcy, remained outside the new company.

The auguries were not auspicious for successful reorganisation. Orders remained low. In response, the number of building sites was cut, by the close of 1981, from 27 to 15, and employment from 87,000 to 66,000. Trading losses continued heavy, £117 million alone in the financial year 1982–3, and the recession of the early 1980s inflicted further damage, with British shipbuilding suffering both absolute and relative decline. The gross registered tonnage launched fell from 191,000 in 1984 to 46,000 in 1987, before recovering to 250,000 in 1992, the relevant percentages of world output being 1.1, 0.5 and 1.2. This, however, was not the only criterion, for, in the mid-

1980s, there were heavy financial losses in merchant shipbuilding and in the work on offshore rigs for the rapidly growing North Sea gas and oil industry.

British Shipbuilders was also under great pressure from the Conservative government elected in 1979. It was opposed to state ownership and public subsidy, and psychologically out of sympathy with heavy industry and what was seen as a world dominated by militant trade unionism and inadequate management. These hostile views, in fact, were no longer appropriate, as design was now informed by computers, and restrictive working practices had been greatly reduced, but ministers maintained views born in an earlier age of militancy. As a consequence, there was a lack of interest in ensuring that privatisation led to the creation of an effective industry, and, instead, a conviction that shipbuilding was a 'sunset', 'smokestack', industry. In 1984, privatisation was formally announced as a policy, but, in achieving the doctrinal objective, there was a lack of interest in practical consequences. Privatisation was completed by the end of 1988, but at the cost of the loss of UK volume shipbuilding: the closures of yards on the Tees and at Troon and of the Wallsend engine works were announced in 1986, and the Sunderland-based North East Shipbuilders Ltd followed two years later. The combination of a European Union policy of limiting subsidies in order to reduce capacity, and of a maladroit handling of the situation by the government, was fatal. By 2002, the only remaining merchant yards were in Belfast, Appledore in Devon and on the Clyde. There had also been serious redundancies in the oil platform yards at Ardersier and Nigg in 1999–2000.[8] Faced with serious financial problems in 2003, the Appledore yard announced large-scale redundancies and put its remaining workers on a four-day week. It appeared inconceivable that in 1955 Britain was still the world's biggest shipbuilder.

The effect of the closure of shipyards on towns such as Birkenhead and Sunderland was very serious. Aside from high unemployment, there was the knock-on impact on suppliers and on other local activities. These combined to ensure a decline in the local urban fabric, with pubs named after great ships and naval heroes gazing forlornly over derelict yards and empty streets, as well as in local tax revenues, and a shift towards the expedients of retraining and welfare.

Docks and, even more, dockers also suffered from a negative image, not least owing to strikes, as in 1945–50, 1960, 1970, 1972 and the 1995–8 dispute over sacked dockers at Liverpool. Maritime trade was increasingly conducted from container ports that were often separate from traditional harbours. The containerisation of freight introduced on shipping in 1956, was, significantly, developed by the Americans. It increased the speed, and decreased the cost, of freight movement, and was linked to the needs for labour productivity and product predictability that played a major role in Western manufacturing and helped it to sustain a powerful competitive edge. British dockers, however, did not respond well to the change in working practices required by containerisation, and this was a major reason for an industrial militancy that further encouraged a shift in freight business, for example to Rotterdam, which proved a more adaptable port. The first British container ship sent to Australia, the *Encounter Bay*, sailed from Rotterdam in 1969 because of an industrial dispute at the Tilbury terminal. The ship itself had been built in Hamburg. Aside from containerisation, there was a rise in roll-on roll-off trade, with lorries driving directly onto ferries. This benefited ports such as Dover, Felixstowe and Harwich. By 1975, Ipswich, Felixstowe and Harwich together ranked second only to London in both the value and tonnage of non-fuel exports and, by 1994, Felixstowe handled nearly half the country's deep-sea container traffic.[9]

In London, the docks below the Tower were all closed apart from those at Tilbury, which was 26 miles downstream from Tower Bridge: the first deep-water oceanic container berth there was opened in 1968. Among the major London docks, the Surrey Commercial Docks were closed in 1970 and the Royal Docks in 1981. The resulting opportunities and problems of this large tract of what had been the maritime hub of empire were tackled by the creation of the London Docklands Development Corporation in 1981, and of an Enterprise Zone the following year. Up-river dock areas in Bristol, Glasgow and Liverpool were also abandoned. The standard theme that cities turned their backs on the rivers and estuaries on which they had been built – on Thames and Mersey, Clyde and Tyne, Humber and Wear, Avon and others, was largely true in terms of land values, commercial activity and urban ambience.

Over the last two decades there has been a return to the riverside, as in Bristol, Newcastle, Sunderland or Exeter, and a revitalisation of docklands, especially in London and, to a lesser extent, Liverpool. However, this has been a case of finding a particular segment of urban real-estate attractive, rather than engaging with Britain's maritime heritage, let alone trying to revive it. The current state of London's former docks, dominated by the office towers at Canary Wharf or, less prominently, the shipping centre in the former Surrey Docks, is an apt indicator of the passing of seaborne interests, while once major centres of naval shipbuilding, such as Devonport, or naval bases, such as Portland, have lost these functions or been greatly run down. Naval shore training establishments have also been closed or run down. The aquariums opened in Birmingham, Blackpool, Brighton, Great Yarmouth, Hull, London, Newquay, Oban, Plymouth, St. Andrews, Sheffield, Southsea, Torbay and elsewhere are a very different response to the sea to that offered by fishing, while the Sealife centre at Portsmouth is primarily a celebration of naval heritage. Many of the anchorages that are busy now are so as a result of yachting and other marine leisure pursuits, rather than trade. The popularity of cruise holidays since the 1990s throws an unwelcome light on British maritime industries as the passenger lines prefer to commission new ships from foreign yards, for example the *Queen Mary II* built in St. Nazaire, and to repair them there, while much of the crew are also foreign.

NAVAL AND MARITIME REPUTE

At a more symbolic level, the fate of the Royal Navy was in part bound up with the reputation of the royal family. This was seen in the review of the fleet at Spithead by Elizabeth II on 15 June 1953. The Royal Navy ships present included a battleship (*Vanguard*), five fleet carriers (*Eagle, Illustrious, Implacable, Indefatigable* and *Indomitable*), two light carriers, eight cruisers, 23 destroyers, the names of several of which echoed naval victories (*Barfleur, Camperdown, Trafalgar*), 40 frigates, 16 ocean-going minesweepers, 28 submarines and three surveying vessels, as well as an Australian carrier, a Canadian Squadron including a carrier, and warships from India, Pakistan and Ceylon (Sri Lanka). About 300 aircraft were involved in the fly-past, while the representatives of the merchant navy included three tankers and eleven large ocean-going merchantmen. One of the latter was the *Empire Windrush*,[10] best known for its prominence in bringing West Indian immigrants to Britain. Although occurring only 51 years ago, the entire occasion very much appears one from an age that has passed.

Prominent members of the royal family by birth, and connections by marriage, played a conspicuous role in the navy during the twentieth century, especially Lord Mountbatten, who headed the Admiralty, Edward VIII as Prince of Wales, the Duke of Edinburgh, who saw war service in the Second World War, and Prince Andrew, who served as a helicopter pilot during the Falklands War. The lessened impact of the royal family in national identity thus influenced responses to the Royal Navy, with which, in turn, the royal family became less associated. Whereas there was a full-scale royal review to mark Elizabeth II's Silver Jubilee in 1977, the Golden Jubilee of 2002 saw no such celebration, and the royal 'yacht' *Britannia* was not replaced, an important practical and symbolic shift in the relationship between the royal family and the sea. In 2003, however, the Queen presented a new Colour to the navy at Plymouth, the occasion being marked by the presence of 18 ships from the fleet. In her speech, the Queen referred to herself as 'a daughter, wife and mother of naval officers'. The previous presentation of a new Colour to the navy was at Plymouth in 1969. Also in 2003, names were chosen for the two new planned aircraft carriers: *Queen Elizabeth II* and *Prince of Wales*.

The decline in the role of naval heroes and history is also instructive, for names rich in the resonance of victory, such as Anson, Collingwood, Hawke and Rodney, are now forgotten. They have left a residue in the names of pubs, streets and the houses of public schools, but this is not a residue that is being enriched by fresh names. Admirals and warships of the First World War and, even more, the Second, did not have this impact on everyday townscapes. Whereas schoolboys once collected cigarette packet cards of naval heroes and warships, now there are other mementos, most of them international in their scope. The names that are still remembered reflect their ability to represent new values: thus, Nelson still attracts attention, but as a Byronic Romantic hero, not a master of naval tactics and leadership, and this attention is one he shares with Emma Hamilton. Drake, the naval hero of the Elizabethan age, appears as a secondary figure in costume dramas, such as the *Blackadder* saga. Beatty and Jellicoe are largely forgotten, and, thus, at least are spared the obloquy meted to the commanders on land in the First World War, especially Haig. There has been no naval novel to match Nicholas Monsarrat's *The Cruel Sea* (1951), which was based on his war experience.

If naval heroes are forgotten, naval history is undervalued. The excellent first volume of Nicholas Rodger's three-volume *Naval History of Britain, The Safeguard of the Sea* (1997), sold very well, but its impact in the academic world was far less than it should have been, and the history of war as a whole, and the popular approach of war and society, are both dominated by studies of land warfare. Far fewer scholars work on naval or maritime history, and courses on either are taught at few British or Dominion universities.

As an instance of the world that has gone, it is instructive to consider the image of rivers. For modern children, this is primarily the 'rural' and idyllic portrayal provided by *The Wind in the Willows* by Kenneth Grahame. Although published in 1908, this has been kept alive, not least in performances of A. A. Milne's play *Toad of Toad Hall* (1929). A very different, and far more vigorous, account is that of the Thames in Charles Dickens's *Great Expectations* (1860–61), particularly when Pip and his roommate Herbert Pocket run down from the Temple stairs to collect Magwitch and help get him out of the country by steamer. Dickens was able to depict a scene of energy and to present shipping as becoming more advanced and impressive: 'At that time, the steam-traffic on the Thames was far below its present extent . . . Of barges, sailing colliers, and coasting traders, there were perhaps as many as now; but of steamships, great and small not a tithe or a twentieth part so many'. Below the Tower of London, they were soon in among the tiers of shipping. Here, were the Leith, Aberdeen, and Glasgow steamers, loading and unloading goods . . . here, were colliers by the score and score . . . hammers going in ship-buildings' yards, saws going at timber, clashing engines going at things unknown, pumps going in leaky ships, capstans going, ships going to sea, and unintelligible sea-creatures roaring curses over the bulwarks at respondent lightermen.

This immediacy, the pressure of the sea, ships and commerce on the senses, captured by Dickens[11] is not one that engages the imaginative attention of modern writers. The sea still appears in paintings, but the ships on it are yachts not traders, while the harbours depicted tend to be mellow anchorages, not the ports of international commerce. The same is true of music: the most powerful opera with a maritime setting, Benjamin Britten's *Billy Budd* (1951), was set in the world of sail.

IMPERIAL IMPACT

Empire and the imperial experience are at the close as much about the impact on other peoples as that on Britain. Manifestations range from the trivial to the more profound; the former including hobbies and foodstuffs, whether playing cricket in the Ionian Islands, or drinking gin on Minorca, or the bread and butter pudding I was given on Hawaii in January 2003, which was attributed to British influence during the nineteenth century (this has also left the Union Jack on the state flag). As with much of this influence, the flavour had been 'cut' or fractured, in this case to produce bread and butter pudding with a tropical taste that I can recommend.

The more profound effects of the British Empire vary. They include the spread of English, major demographic movements and the creation of states. The growth of English as the global language of business and of international political and cultural links has been of major importance in global integration, and has also helped disseminate not only English-language culture, but also political, economic and social suppositions. This owed much to British imperial rule, especially in Africa, the Middle East and South Asia, but, over the last half-century, has more clearly been an aspect of American influence. This was taken further by technology. The Intel 4004, the first microprocessor chip, was created in the USA in 1971. The spread of the Internet as a worldwide interactive medium, and the dominance of computing by American operating systems, ensured that English became more prominent as a language than ever before. Although, by 2003, English was still only known by a minority of the world's population (and this was particularly apparent in East Asia and Latin America), it was, nevertheless, a larger minority than ever before. Furthermore, the impact of the language spread in countries where Britain had never been the colonial power. There was also a class and age dimension. The affluent and younger had more knowledge of English than the poorer and older, and that increased its influence. The pattern and language of international telephone calls reflects these linguistic links and also bears the imprint of empire, echoing the maps of British trade a century ago. Thus, in 1991, Britain was, after Australia, the destination of the second biggest number of telephone calls made from New Zealand, with the USA coming third. This is a reminder of one particular shift in the former empire, the extent to which Australia, Canada, New Zealand, the UK and the USA now collectively represent an important sphere of interaction, although it does not define the interests of these states nor exhaust their axes of interaction.

The impact of language is one of the many ways in which it is appropriate to think of a symbiotic transfer of imperial hegemony from Britain to the USA. Symbiosis and transfer do not, however, mean sameness: whereas much of the spread of the English language prior to the mid-twentieth century arose as a result of territorial control, and its impact on government and education, since then, under American hegemony, it has largely been due to economic advantage outside the context of any such control.

In the case of the British Empire, however, it is repeatedly difficult to differentiate between the impact of empire, in the shape of territorial control, and that of external influence during the period of imperial dominance. The latter would have been profound without formal control, as the role of the USA today indicates. To use informal empire as a term to describe this is not without value, but, aside from its somewhat elastic, if not, at times, nebulous meaning and application, there is a problem that it focuses on one power, rather than the range of external influences that might well exist. Thus, for example, while Britain was the most important external force commercially in China in the 1920s, and was dominant in Chinese external and coastal shipping, it was not the sole non-Chinese power wielding influence and able to apply pressure.

Formal or informal, Britain was the dominant imperial power across much of the globe in the nineteenth and early twentieth century, the period of the onset of modernity, as defined by such criteria as large-scale industrialisation, urbanisation and the spread of literacy. The pressures and problems stemming from this process of modernisation could be accentuated by foreign rule, but it was not the root cause of change. This is not a welcoming reflection for many, not only because it challenges the facile habit

of blaming outsiders for unwelcome developments, but also because it questions the ability of post-imperial regimes to cope with the continued effects
of globalisation.

If the British Empire is blamed for many of the aspects of modernisation and globalisation, it also serves as a way of offering historical depth to
a critique of American power, and, in part, this is at issue when British
imperialism is criticised. As with the British, particularly in the nineteenth
century, American global policy developed with a pursuit of morality linked
to the furtherance of imperial goals. There was a quest for an open world,
in the shape of free trade and the unfettered movement of money, and a
confidence that technology endorses as much as it underlines a privileged
position in the international order. The power of the British and American
Empires can be presented in instrumental terms, as protection systems for
economic practices, but, for both Britain and the USA, the idea of empire
included the pursuit of a benign and mutually beneficial world order, and,
in each case, there was a willingness to use major efforts to engage with
rival empires that were also, correctly, seen as tyrannies: Napoleonic France,
Wilhelmine and Nazi Germany, and Second World War Japan. The terms of
the mutual benefit offered by the British and American Empires were
unwelcome to many, more particularly in the British case as its empire rested
more clearly on control, constraint and coercion. In contrast, there was a
democratic objective at the heart of American capitalism that was seen as
in America's and the world's interest,[12] and that helped foster American
opposition to the European colonial empires. The Americans hoped that
newly independent peoples would support democratic capitalism and thus
look to the USA.

If the British Empire seemed both alien and redundant from this perspective (and, as a minor echo, British accents and actors seemed obvious
trademarks of villainy through the democratising lens of Hollywood), that
has not prevented a conflation of British and American imperialism in some
quarters; and this offers another way in which the experience of British rule
can be seen as unwelcome. More generally, criticism, if not caricature, of
the British Empire is freely offered, and few defenders are to be seen. This
criticism would be more impressive if it could be shown that the British
were worse than other imperialists. Although they were not alone in being
seaborne, the seaborne character, global range and association with particular
commercial and, eventually, industrial developments of the Western Empires
over the last half-millennium, gave them a particular character, but they
scarcely invented long-distance commerce, slavery, war, external rule and
racism. Instead, imperial pretensions and power, not self-determination, were
the norm, and still are in parts of the world such as Tibet and Xinjiang,
both still under Chinese control. Furthermore, 'the underlying centrality of

slavery in the historical relationship between Egypt and the Sudan' was such that anti-colonial nationalism in Egypt was compatible with a determination to regain power over Sudan.[13]

At this level of abstraction, it is all too easy to forget that people were involved in making empire and in the web of connections and relationships that sustained it. However much the military who were responsible for the initial conquests might be perceived as automata, and even be trained to act thus, they were not a uniform mass of unthinking humanity. This is true both of sailors[14] and of soldiers. The journals and letters of the British soldiers in the Seven Years' War reveal that their number included men of considerable intelligence and perception. They also had a clear sense of rights, which led, in 1763, to serious complaints about pay deductions for provisions. The mutineers' methods were similar to those in labour disputes in England: mass demonstrations backed by the threat of violence. The conditional aspect of military service was also seen in the fleet, most conspicuously with mutinies, such as that on the frigate *Hermione* when the unpopularity of the brutal captain Hugh Pigot led to the killing of him and nine other officers. The navy responded with more than the vigour displayed for example in hunting down some of the *Hermione*'s crew.[15] In 1806, the punishment of Running the Gauntlet was abolished; in 1809 the practice of 'starting' (the unofficial punishment beating about the back and head) was forbidden, possibly in response to a mutiny on HMS *Nereide*;[16] on HMS *Winchester* in Hong Kong in 1853, when the admiral's refusal to grant leave led to hostility and a refusal to obey an order to quarters, control was enforced, but the admiral was recalled.

Such episodes were part of a culture of mutual respect that was important to successful command and service. Military service also helped to engender a 'brand' of Britishness[17] that was distinctive, as important as the writings that tend to engage scholarly attention, and a reminder of the wide-ranging impact of empire. The general precariousness of employment among labourers and artisans, as well as the sheer drudgery of civilian life, that were important for recruitment were harnessed to the furtherance of empire on sea and land, but to treat this as a simple mechanistic process – hardship at home leading to its imposition abroad – is to ignore the way in which British imperial pretensions and power interacted with those of others around the world. If the British Empire is central to much of world history over the last four centuries, that was in part because its character stemmed from all the peoples and countries that were affected.

NOTES

Unless otherwise stated, publication place is London.

PREFACE

1. *Oxford History of the British Empire, vol. i: The Origins of Empire*, ed. N. Canny (Oxford, 1998); ii: *The Eighteenth Century*, ed. P. J. Marshall (Oxford, 1998); iii: *The Nineteenth Century*, ed. A. Porter (Oxford, 1999); iv: *The Twentieth Century*, ed. J. Brown and W. R. Louis (Oxford, 1999); v: *Historiography*, ed. R. Winks (Oxford, 1999).

INTRODUCTION

1. C. Rouillard, *The Turk in French History: Thought and Literature, 1520–1660* (Paris, 1938); A. Cirakman, 'From Tyranny to Despotism: The Enlightenment's Unenlightened Image of the Turks', *International Journal of Middle East Studies*, 33 (2000), pp. 49–68; D. Goffman, *The Ottoman Empire and Early Modern Europe* (Cambridge, 2002).
2. A. G. Jamieson, *Ebb Tide in the British Maritime Industries: Change and Adaptation, 1918–1990* (Exeter, 2003), p. 177, n. 86.
3. An excellent introduction is provided by G. V. Scammell, *The World Encompassed: The First European Maritime Empires, c. 800–1650* (1981).

4. T. J. Barfield, 'The Shadow Empires: Imperial State Formation along the Chinese-Nomad Frontier', in S. E. Alcock, T. N. D'Altroy, K. D. Morrison and C. M. Sinopoli (eds.), *Empires: Perspectives from Archaeology and History* (Cambridge, 2001), p. 29.
5. Barfield, 'Shadow Empires', pp. 33, 35–6.
6. E. Manche, 'Negotiating an Empire: Britain and Its Overseas Peripheries, c. 1550–1780', in C. Daniels and M. V. Kennedy (eds.), *Negotiated Empires: Centers and Peripheries in the Americas, 1500–1820* (2002), p. 236.
7. B. Harris, '"American Idols": Empire, War and the Middling Ranks in Mid-Eighteenth-Century Britain', *Past and Present*, 150 (Feb. 1996), pp. 138–9.
8. D. Armitage, 'Literature and Empire', in N. Canny (ed.), *The Origins of Empire: British Overseas Enterprise to the Close of the Seventeenth Century* (Oxford, 1998), p. 114.
9. N. A. M. Rodger, 'Seapower and Empire: Cause and Effect?', in B. Moore and H. van Nierop (eds.), *Colonial Empires Compared: Britain and the Netherlands, 1750–1850* (Aldershot, 2003), pp. 97–111, esp. p. 100.
10. Carmarthen to Robert Liston, envoy in Spain, 9 Ap. 1787, Edinburgh, National Library of Scotland, vol. 5546 fol. 109. The literature can be approached through three recent studies: F. G. Dawson, 'William Pitt's Settlement at

Black River on the Mosquito Shore: A Challenge to Spain in Central America, 1732–87', *Hispanic American Historical Review*, 63 (1983), pp. 702–4; B. Potthast, *Die Mosquitoküste im Spannungsfeld britischer und spanischer Politik 1502–1821* (Cologne, 1988), pp. 295–302; R. A. Naylor, *Penny Ante Imperialism: The Mosquito Shore and the Bay of Honduras, 1600–1914: A Case Study in British Informal Empire* (1989), pp. 64–7.

11. D. K. Bassett, *British Trade and Policy in Indonesia and Malaysia in the Late Eighteenth Century* (Hull, 1971), pp. 85–96, 106–7; R. Bonney, *Kedah 1771–1821: The Search for Security and Independence* (Oxford, 1971), p. 100; P. N. Tarling, *Anglo-Dutch Rivalry in the Malay World, 1780–1824* (St. Lucia, Queensland, 1962), p. 13.

12. H. Mackinder, *Britain and the British Seas* (1902), p. 358.

13. K. M. Panikkar, *India and the Indian Ocean: An Essay on the Influence of Sea Power on Indian History* (1945), p. 7.

14. Gordon to John, 4th Earl of Sandwich, 2 Aug. 1764, PRO. SP. 81/107.

15. B. D. Hunt, 'The Strategic Thought of Sir Julian S. Corbett' in J. B. Hattendorf and R. S. Jordan (eds.), *Maritime Strategy and the Balance of Power: Britain and America in the Twentieth Century* (1989), pp. 110–35; J. Goldrick and J. B. Hattendorf (eds.), *Mahan is not Enough: The Proceedings of a Conference on the Works of Sir Julian Corbett and Admiral Sir Herbert Richmond* (Newport, R. I., 1993).

16. J. S. Corbett, *The Seven Years War* (1907; Folio Society edition, 2001), pp. 300–57, quote p. 356.

17. The seventh Stephen Roskill Memorial Lecture, given at Cambridge, 4 Feb. 1997. See also S. Palmer, *Seeing the Sea: The Maritime Dimension in History* (Greenwich, 2000), p. 8. For a book that appeared after mine was written, I. Friel, *Maritime History of Britain and Ireland* (2003).

18. The posters are reproduced in S. Constantine, *Buy and Build: The Advertising Posters of the Empire Marketing Board* (1986).

19. M. H. Fisher (ed.), *The Travels of Dean Mahomet: An Eighteenth-Century Journey Through India* (Berkeley, 1997), p. 55.

20. BL. Add. 56088 fol. 5.

21. A. J. Bacevich, *American Empire: The Realities and Consequences of U.S. Diplomacy* (Cambridge, Mass., 2002), pp. 6, 224.

I THE ORIGINS OF EMPIRE

1. N. Canny (ed.), *The Origins of Empire: British Overseas Enterprise to the Close of the Seventeenth Century* (Oxford, 1998), p. xi.

2. B. Cunliffe, *Facing the Ocean: The Atlantic and its Peoples, 8000 BC–AD 1500* (Oxford, 2001).

3. C. Martin, 'Water Transport and the Roman Occupations of North Britain', in T. C. Smout (ed.), *Scotland and the Sea* (Edinburgh, 1992), pp. 6–8.

4. A valuable note of caution is sounded by N. A. M. Rodger in his excellent treatment of *The Safeguard of the Sea: A Naval History of Britain, 1, 660–1649* (1997), pp. 10–18.

5. Rodger, *Safeguard*.

6. F. Barlow, *Edward the Confessor* (1970), pp. 136–7.

7. J. Muldoon, *Empire and Order: The Concept of Empire, 800–1800* (Basingstoke, 1999).

8. R. Davies, *Domination and Conquest: The Experience of Ireland, Scotland, and Wales, 1100–1300* (Oxford, 1990).

9. S. Rose, *Southampton and the Navy in the Age of Henry V* (Winchester, 1998).

10. R. H. Britnell, *The Commercialisation of English Society, 1000–1500* (1992).

11. G. V. Scammell, 'English Merchant Shipping at the End of the Middle Ages', *Economic History Review*, 2nd ser., 13 (1961), pp. 327–41, and 'Shipowning in England, c. 1450–1550', *Transactions of the Royal Historical Society*, 5th ser., 12 (1962), p. 106.

12. R. Koebner, '"The Imperial Crown of this Realm": Henry VIII, Constantine the Great and Polydore Vergil', *Bulletin of the Institute of Historical Research*, 26 (1953), pp. 29–52; F. Yates, *Astraea: The Imperial Theme in the Sixteenth Century* (1977); W. Ullmann, 'This Realm of England is an Empire', *Journal of Ecclesiastical History*, 30 (1979), pp. 175–203.

13. G. V. Scammell, 'The British North-East Coast Fisheries, c. 1500–1750', *Durham County Local History Society Bulletin*, no. 65 (2002), pp. 37–66.

14. D. Hussey, *Coastal and River Trade in Pre-Industrial England: Bristol and Its Region, 1680–1730* (Exeter, 2000).

15. E. M. Carus Wilson, 'The Iceland Trade', in E. Power and M. M. Postan (eds.), *Studies in English Trade in the Fifteenth Century* (1933), pp. 155–82; S. Pawley, 'Maritime Trade and Fishing in the Middle Ages', in S. and N. Bennett (ed.), *An Historical Atlas of Lincolnshire* (2nd edn., Chichester, 2001), p. 56.

16. D. Burwash, *English Merchant Shipping, 1460–1540* (Toronto, 1947); I. Friel, *The Good Ship: Ships; Shipbuilding and Technology in England, 1200–1520* (1995).

17. D. B. Quinn, 'Edward IV and Exploration', *Mariner's Mirror*, 21 (1935), pp. 275–84, and 'The Argument for the English Discovery of America between 1480 and 1494', *Geographical Journal*, 127 (1961), pp. 227–85.

18. J. A. Williamson, *The Cabot Voyages and Bristol Discovery under Henry VII* (Cambridge, 1962); D. B. Quinn, *England and the Discovery of America, 1481–1620* (1974); P. E. Pope, *The Many Landfalls of John Cabot* (Toronto, 1997).

19. See, for example, Canny, *Origins of Empire*, pp. 3, 149.

20. G. T. Cell, *English Enterprise in Newfoundland* (Toronto, 1969).

21. J. Scantlebury, 'John Rashleigh and the Newfoundland cod fishery, 1608–20', *Journal of the Royal Institution of Cornwall*, 8 (1978), pp. 61–71.

22. G. R. Elton, 'Piscatorial Politics in the Early Parliaments of Elizabeth I', in N. McKendrick and R. B. Outhwaite (eds.), *Business Life and Public Policy: Essays in Honour of D. C. Coleman* (Cambridge, 1986), pp. 1–20; F. C. L. Sgroi, 'Piscatorial Politics Revisited: The Language of Economic Debate and the Evolution of Fishing Policy in Elizabethan England', *Albion*, 35 (2003), pp. 1–24.

23. D. J. Starkey, 'The West Country-Newfoundland Fishery and the Manning of the Royal Navy', in R. Higham (ed.), *Security and Defence in South West England before 1800* (Exeter, 1987), pp. 93–101.

24. B. Lavery, *The Arming and Fitting of English Ships of War, 1600–1815* (1987).

25. R. Gardiner and R. W. Unger (eds.), *Cogs, Caravels and Galleons: The Sailing Ship, 1000–1650* (1994).

26. G. V. Scammell, 'War at Sea under the Early Tudors: Some Newcastle upon Tyne Evidence', *Archaeologia Aeliana*, 4th ser., 38 (1960), p. 80.

27. G. Parker, 'The Dreadnought Revolution of Tudor England', *Mariner's Mirror*, 82 (1996), pp. 269–300.

28. K. DeVries, 'The Effectiveness of Fifteenth-Century Shipboard Artillery', *Mariner's Mirror*, 84 (1998), pp. 389–99, esp. p. 396.

29. A. B. Caruana, *The History of English Sea Ordnance, 1523–1875, I, The Age of Evolution, 1523–1715* (Rotherfield, 1994). For the list, review by G. Parker in *Sixteenth Century*, 24 (1993), p. 1022.

30. T. Glasgow, 'The Shape of the Ships that Defeated the Spanish Armada', *Mariner's Mirror*, 50 (1964), pp. 177–88; G. V. Scammell, 'Ship Owning in the Economy and Politics of Early Modern England', *Historical Journal*, 15 (1972), pp. 385–407.

31. T. Glasgow, 'The Navy in Elizabeth's First Undeclared War, 1559–60', *Mariner's Mirror*, 54 (1968), pp. 23–37.

32. N. Canny, *The Elizabethan Conquest of Ireland: A Pattern Established, 1565–1576* (1976); S. G. Ellis, *Tudor Ireland* (1985).

33. C. A. Bayly, *Imperial Meridian: The British Empire and the World, 1780–1830* (Harlow, 1989).

34. J. M. Hill, *Fire and Sword: Sorley Boy MacDonnell and the Rise of Clan Ian Mor, 1538–90* (1993).

35. N. Canny, *Making Ireland British, 1580–1650* (Oxford, 2001).

36. T. Glasgow, 'The Navy in Philip and Mary's War, 1557–1558', *Mariner's Mirror*, 53 (1967), pp. 321–42.

37. P. E. H. Hair, 'Protestants as Pirates, Slavers and Proto-Missionaries: Sierra Leone 1568 and 1582', *Journal of Ecclesiastical History*, 21 (1970), pp. 203–24; D. Loades, *England's Maritime Empire: Seapower, Commerce and Policy, 1490–1690* (Harlow, 2000), p. 87.

38. K. R. Andrews, *Elizabethan Privateering: English Privateering during the Spanish War, 1585–1603* (Cambridge, 1964) and *Trade, Plunder and Settlement: Maritime Enterprise and the Genesis of the British Empire, 1480–1630* (Cambridge, 1984).

39. N. J. W. Thrower (ed.), *Sir Francis Drake and the Famous Voyage, 1577–1580* (Berkeley, 1984).

40. H. Kelsey, *Sir Francis Drake: The Queen's Pirate* (New Haven, 1998).

41. C. Martin and G. Parker, *The Spanish Armada* (1988); M. J. Rodríguez-Salgado, *Armada, 1588–1988* (1988); F. Fernandez-Armesto, *The Spanish Armada: The Experience of War in 1588* (Oxford, 1988); M. J. Rodríguez-Salgado and S. Adams (eds.), *England, Spain and the Grand Armada, 1585–1604* (Edinburgh, 1991); Rodger, *Safeguard*, pp. 254–71.

42. R. T. Spence, *The Privateering Earl: George Clifford, 3rd Earl of Cumberland, 1558–1605* (Stroud, 1995).

43. G. V. Scammell, 'War at Sea under the Early Tudors – Part II', *Archaeologia Aeliana*, 4th ser., 39 (1961), p. 203; J. Glete, *Warfare at Sea, 1500–1650: Maritime Conflicts and the Transformation of Europe* (2000), esp. pp. 71–3; N. A. M. Rodger, 'The New Atlantic: Naval Warfare in the Sixteenth Century', in J. B. Hattendorf and R. Unger (eds.), *War at Sea in the Middle Ages*

and Renaissance (Woodbridge, 2002), p. 243.

44. D. Loades, *The Tudor Navy: An Administrative, Political and Military History* (Aldershot, 1992).

45. S. A. Skilliter, *William Harborne and the Trade with Turkey, 1578–1582: A Documentary Study of the First Anglo-Ottoman Relations* (Oxford, 1977).

46. G. D. Ramsay, *English Overseas Trade during the Centuries of Expansion* (1957) and *The City of London in International Politics at the Accession of Queen Elizabeth* (Manchester, 1975); T. K. Rabb, *Enterprise and Empire, 1575–1630* (New Haven, 1967); R. Brenner, 'The Social Basis of English Commercial Expansion, 1550–1650', *Journal of Economic History*, 32 (1972), pp. 361–84.

47. K. N. Chaudhuri, *The English East India Company: The Study of an Early Joint-Stock Company, 1600–1640* (1965).

48. T. S. Willan, *The Early History of the Russia Company, 1553–1603* (Manchester, 1956).

49. T. H. B. Symons, *Meta Incognita: A Discourse of Discovery. Martin Frobisher's Arctic Expeditions, 1576–1578* (Hull, Québec, 1999); J. McDermott, *Martin Frobisher: Elizabethan Privateer* (New Haven, 2001).

50. T. Gray, 'Devon's Fisheries and Early Stuart Northern New England', in M. Duffy et al. (eds.), *The New Maritime History of Devon I* (1992), pp. 139–44, and 'Fisheries, Exploration, Shipping and Mariners in the Sixteenth and Seventeenth Centuries', in R. Kain and W. Ravenhill (eds.), *Historical Atlas of South West England* (Exeter, 1999), p. 380.

51. G. T. Cell (ed.), *Newfoundland Discovered: English Attempts at Colonisation, 1610–1630* (1982).

52. D. B. Quinn (ed.), *The Roanoke Voyages, 1584–1590* (2 vols., 1955); K. O. Kupperman, *Roanoke: The Abandoned Colony* (Savage, Maryland, 1984).

53. K. O. Kupperman, 'Apathy and Death in Early Jamestown', *Journal of American History*, 66 (1979), pp. 24–40.

54. N. Salisbury, *Manitou and Providence: Indians, Europeans, and the Making of New England, 1500–1643* (New York, 1980).

55. H. C. Porter, *The Inconstant Savage: England and the North American Indian, 1500–1660* (Cambridge, 1979).

56. W. Cronon, *Changes in the Land: Indians, Colonists, and the Ecology of New England* (New York, 1983).

57. N. E. S. Griffith and J. G. Reid, 'New Evidence on New Scotland, 1629', *William and Mary Quarterly*, 3rd ser., 39 (1992), pp. 492–508.

58. C. and R. Bridenbaugh, *No Peace beyond the Line: The English in the Caribbean, 1624–1690* (New York, 1972).

59. H. McBeckles, '"Black Men in White Skins": The Formation of a White Proletariat in West Indian Slave Society', *Journal of Imperial and Commonwealth History*, 15 (1986), pp. 5–21, and *White Slavery and Black Servitude in Barbados, 1627–1715* (Knoxville, 1989).

60. J. F. Richards, *The Unending Frontier: An Environmental History of the Early Modern World* (Berkeley, 2003), p. 419.

61. L. Cormack, *Charting an Empire: Geography at the English Universities, 1580–1620* (Chicago, 1997).

62. C. A. Fury, *Tides in the Affairs of Men: The Social History of Elizabethan Seamen, 1580–1603* (Westport, 2002).

63. T. Marshall, *Theatre and Empire: Great Britain on the London Stages under James VI and I* (Manchester, 2000).

64. W. B. Patterson, *King James VI and I and the Reunion of Christendom* (Cambridge, 1997).

65. J. Hemming, *The Search for El Dorado* (1978); A. Sinclair, *Sir Walter Raleigh and the Age of Discovery* (1984); J. Lorimer (ed.), *English and Irish Settlement on the River Amazon, 1550–1646* (1989).

66. T. Gray, 'Turkish Piracy and Early Stuart Devon', *Transactions of the Devonshire Association*, 121 (1989), pp. 159–71.

67. B. Quintrell, 'Charles I and His Navy in the 1630s', *The Seventeenth Century*, 3 (1988), pp. 159–79; D. D. Hebb,

Piracy and the English Government, 1616–1642 (Aldershot, 1994).

68. K. R. Andrews, *Ships, Money and Politics: Seafaring and Naval Enterprise in the Reign of Charles I* (Cambridge, 1991), p. 5.

69. W. F. Craven, 'The Earl of Warwick, a Speculator in Piracy', *Hispanic American Historical Review*, 10 (1930), pp. 457–79; K. O. Kupperman, *Providence Island, 1630–1641: The Other Puritan Colony* (Cambridge, 1993).

70. G. V. Scammell, 'England, Portugal and the *Estado da India, c.* 1500–1635', *Modern Asian Studies*, 16 (1982), pp. 177–92, esp. pp. 187–8.

71. V. T. Harlow (ed.), *The Voyages of Captain William Jackson, 1642–1645* (1924).

72. A. Games, *Migration and the Origins of the English Atlantic World* (Cambridge, Mass., 1999), p. 216.

73. D. Goffman, *Britons in the Ottoman Empire, 1642–1660* (Seattle, 1998).

74. D. W. Waters, *The Art of Navigation in England in Tudor and Early Stuart Times* (1958).

75. R. Law, 'The First Scottish Guinea Company, 1634–9', *Scottish Historical Review*, 76 (1997), pp. 185–202; D. Armitage, 'Making the Empire British: Scotland in the Atlantic World', *Past and Present*, 155 (May 1997), pp. 34–63.

2 GROWING STRENGTH, 1650–1750

1. William Cobbett, *Parliamentary History of England from 1066 to . . . 1803* (36 vols., 1806–20), XIV, column 801.

2. I. K. Steele, *The English Atlantic, 1675–1740: An Exploration of Communication and Community* (Oxford, 1986).

3. C. J. French, 'Computerizing London's Eighteenth-Century Maritime Activity', *Archives*, 22 (1997), p. 135.

4. J. F. Shepherd and G. M. Walton, *Shipping, Maritime Trade and the Economic Development of Colonial North America* (Cambridge, 1972).

5. J. Bannister, *The Rule of the Admi-*

rals: *Law, Custom, and Naval Government in Newfoundland, 1699–1832* (Toronto, 2003).

6. G. Jackson, *The British Whaling Trade* (1978); T. Barrow, *The Whaling Trade of North-East England, 1750–1850* (Sunderland, 2001).

7. N. Zahedieh, 'Overseas Expansion and Trade in the Seventeenth Century', in N. Canny (ed.), *The Origins of Empire: British Overseas Enterprise to the Close of the Seventeenth Century* (Oxford, 1998), p. 399.

8. D. Ormrod, *The Rise of Commercial Empires: England and the Netherlands in the Age of Mercantilism, 1650–1770* (Cambridge, 2003), p. 342.

9. J. Scott, '"Good Night Amsterdam": Sir George Downing and Anglo-Dutch Statebuilding', *English Historical Review*, 118 (2003), pp. 355–6.

10. P. G. E. Clemens, 'The Rise of Liverpool, 1665–1750', *Economic History Review*, 29 (1976), p. 212.

11. C. Wilson, *Profit and Power: A Study of England and the Dutch Wars* (1957), pp. 97–102; R. Conquest, 'The State and Commercial Expansion: England in the Years 1642–1688', *Journal of European Economic History*, 14 (1995), pp. 155–72.

12. W. Minchinton (ed.), *The Growth of English Overseas Trade in the Seventeenth and Eighteenth Centuries* (1969).

13. N. Zahedieh, 'The Merchants of Port Royal, Jamaica, and the Spanish Contraband Trade, 1655–1692', *William and Mary Quarterly*, 3rd ser., 43 (1986), pp. 570–93; G. V. Scammell, '"A Very Profitable and Advantageous Trade": British Smuggling in the Iberian Americas, c. 1500–1750', *Itinerario*, 24 (2000), p. 167.

14. G. Pagano de Divitiis, *English Merchants in Seventeenth-Century Italy* (Cambridge, 1997), pp. 62, 184.

15. C. J. French, 'Productivity in the Atlantic Shipping Industry: A Quantitative Study', *Journal of Interdisciplinary History*, 17 (1987), pp. 613–38.

16. R. Davis, *The Rise of the English Shipping Industry in the Seventeenth and Eighteenth Centuries* (1962); G. V. Scammell,

'British Merchant Shipbuilding c. 1500–1750', *International Journal of Maritime History*, 11 (1999), pp. 27–52, esp. pp. 41–2.

17. P. K. O'Brien and S. L. Engerman, 'Exports and the Growth of the British Economy from the Glorious Revolution to the Peace of Amiens', in B. L. Solow (ed.), *Slavery and the Rise of the Atlantic System* (Cambridge, 1991), pp. 177–209.

18. BL. Evelyn 49 fol. 37; K. Wrightson, *Earthly Necessities: Economic Lives in Early Modern Britain* (New Haven, 2000), p. 298; A. J. O'Shaughnessy, *An Empire Divided: The American Revolution and the British Caribbean* (Philadelphia, 2000), p. 72.

19. R. B. Sheridan, 'The Molasses Act and the Market Strategy of the British Sugar Planters', *Journal of Economic History*, 17 (1957), pp. 62–83; W. A. Speck, 'Britain and the Atlantic World', in H. T. Dickinson (ed.), *A Companion to Eighteenth-Century Britain* (2002), pp. 447–8.

20. G. V. Scammell, *Seafaring, Sailors and Trade, 1450–1750* (Aldershot, 2003), not paginated continuously, but chapter 7, esp. p. 5.

21. D. Richardson (ed.), *Bristol, Africa and the Eighteenth-Century Slave Trade to America: 1, The Years of Expansion 1698–1729* (Gloucester, 1986).

22. J. Walvin, *Fruits of Empire: Exotic Produce and British Taste, 1660–1800* (1997), p. 16; M. Morineau, 'The Indian Challenge: Seventeenth to Eighteenth Centuries', and D. Rothermund, 'The Changing Pattern of British Trade in Indian Textiles, 1701–1757', in S. Chaudhury and M. Morineau (eds.), *Merchants, Companies and Trade: Europe and Asia in the Early Modern Era* (Cambridge, 1999), pp. 243–86.

23. P. Gauci, *The Politics of Trade: The Overseas Merchant in State and Society, 1660–1720* (Oxford, 2001). For merchant MPs, see also I. R. Christie, *British Non-Elite MPs, 1715–1820* (Oxford, 1995).

24. D. J. Starkey, *British Privateering*

Enterprise in the Eighteenth Century (Exeter, 1990).

25. J. S. Bromley, 'The French Privateering War, 1702–13', in H. F. Bell and R. L. Ollard (eds.), *Historical Essays Presented to David Ogg* (1963), pp. 203–31; C. Swanson, *Predators and Prizes: American Privateering and Imperial Warfare, 1739–1748* (Columbia, S. C., 1991).

26. Delaval to Lord Dartmouth, Secretary of State, 15 Ap., 18 July 1713, PRO. SP. 89/22; Captain John Blankett to Marquess of Shelburne, 9 Feb. 1784, BL. Bowood Mss., papers of 2nd Earl, vol. 11; M. S. Anderson, 'Great Britain and the Barbary States in the Eighteenth Century', *Bulletin of the Institute of Historical Research*, 29 (1956), pp. 87–107.

27. K. Morgan, *Slavery, Atlantic Trade, and the British Economy, 1660–1800* (Cambridge, 2000).

28. C. A. Palmer, *Human Cargoes: The British Slave Trade to Spanish America, 1700–1739* (1981).

29. Thomas Burnett, Consul in Lisbon, to John, Lord Carteret, 6 June 1723, Thomas Lumley, envoy to Lisbon, to Carteret, Secretary of State, 31 May 1723, (PRO. SP. 89/30 fols. 213–19).

30. W. Minchinton, 'Characteristics of British Slaving Vessels, 1698–1775', *Journal of Interdisciplinary History*, 20 (1989), pp. 53–81; D. Richardson, 'The British Empire and the Atlantic Slave Trade, 1660–1807', in P. J. Marshall (ed.), *The Oxford History of the British Empire, II: The Eighteenth Century* (Oxford, 1998), pp. 442.

31. M. Dresser, *Slavery Obscured: The Social History of the Slave Trade in an English Provincial Port* (New York, 2001); N. Tattersfield, *The Forgotten Trade, comprising the log of the Daniel and Henry of 1700 and accounts of the Slave Trade from the Minor Ports of England, 1698–1725* (1991); D. Richardson and M. M. Schofield, 'Whitehaven and the Eighteenth-Century British Slave Trade', *Transactions of the Cumberland and Westmorland Antiquarian and Archaeological Society*, 102 (1992), pp. 183–204.

32. M. Elder, *The Slave Trade and the Economic Development of Eighteenth-Century Lancaster* (Preston, 1992).

33. D. Richardson (ed.), *Bristol, Africa and the Eighteenth-Century Slave Trade to America: II, The Years of Ascendancy, 1730–1745* (Gloucester, 1987).

34. D. H. Sacks, *The Widening Gate: Bristol and the Atlantic Economy, 1450–1700* (Berkeley, 1991).

35. S. D. Behrendt, 'The Captains in the British Slave Trade from 1785 to 1807', *Transactions of the Historic Society of Lancashire and Cheshire*, 140 (1991), p. 115.

36. D. Hancock (ed.), *The Letters of William Freeman, London Merchant, 1678–1685* (2002), p. xl.

37. J. Thornton, *Africa and Africans in the Making of the Atlantic World, 1400–1800* (2nd edn., Cambridge, 1998) and *Warfare in Atlantic Africa, 1500–1800* (1999).

38. K. N. Chaudhuri, *The Trading World of Asia and the English East India Company* (Cambridge, 1978).

39. C. A. Palmer, 'From Africa to the Americas: Ethnicity in the Early Black Communities of the Americas', *Journal of World History*, 6 (1995), p. 236.

40. P. D. Morgan, *Slave Counterpoint: Black Culture in the Eighteenth-Century Chesapeake and Lowcountry* (Chapel Hill, 1998).

41. T. Burnard, 'European Migration to Jamaica, 1655–1780', *William and Mary Quarterly*, 3rd ser., 53 (1996), pp. 791–3.

42. J. E. Chaplin, *An Anxious Pursuit: Agricultural Innovation and Modernity in the Lower South, 1730–1815* (Chapel Hill, 1993).

43. P. H. Wood, *Black Majority: Negroes in Colonial South Carolina from 1670 through the Stono Rebellion* (New York, 1974), pp. 314–23.

44. G. Metcalf, *Royal Government and Political Conflict in Jamaica, 1729–1783* (1965), pp. 33–79; O. Patterson, 'Slavery and Slave Revolts: A Socio-historical Analysis of the First Maroon War – Jamaica, 1655–1740', *Social and Economic Studies*, 19 (1970); M. Craton, *Testing the Chains: Resistance to Slavery in the British West Indies* (1982),

pp. 61–96; M. Campbell, *The Maroons of Jamaica, 1655–1796: A History of Resistance, Collaboration and Betrayal* (Trenton, N. J., 1990).

45. A. R. Ekirch, *Bound for America: The Transportation of British Convicts to the Colonies, 1718–1775* (Oxford, 1987).

46. D. M. Hockedy, 'Bound for a New World: Emigration of Indentured Servants via Liverpool to America and the West Indies, 1697–1707', *Transactions of the Historic Society of Lancashire and Cheshire*, 144 (1995), pp. 124–5.

47. A. Games, *Migration and the Origins of the English Atlantic World* (Cambridge, Mass., 1999).

48. R. V. Wells, *The Population of the British Colonies in America before 1776: A Survey of Census Data* (Princeton, 1975); B. Bailyn, *Voyagers to the West: Emigration from Britain to America on the Eve of the Industrial Revolution* (1987) and *The Peopling of British North America: An Introduction* (1987); A. Gogleman, 'Migrations to the Thirteen British North American Colonies, 1700–1775: New Estimates', *Journal of Interdisciplinary History*, 22 (1992), pp. 691–709; K. Morgan, *Slavery and Servitude in North America, 1607–1800* (Edinburgh, 2000).

49. T. Burnard, 'Prodigious Riches: The Wealth of Jamaica before the American Revolution', *Economic History Review*, 54 (2001), pp. 506–24.

50. T. Burnard, ' "The Countrie Continues Sicklie": White Mortality in Jamaica, 1655–1780', *Social History of Medicine*, 12 (1999), pp. 45–72.

51. A. L. Karras, *Sojourners in the Sun: Scottish Migrants in Jamaica and the Chesapeake, 1740–1800* (Ithaca, 1993). For the situation in the British Isles, I. D. Whyte, *Migration and Society in Britain, 1550–1830* (Basingstoke, 2000).

52. M. S. Wokeck, *Trade in Strangers: The Beginnings of Mass Migration to North America* (University Park, Penn., 1999).

53. W. E. Washburn, 'The Moral and Legal Justifications for Dispossessing the Indians', in J. M. Smith (ed.), *Seventeenth-Century America: Essays in Colonial History* (Chapel Hill, 1959), pp. 24–32; B. Arneil, *John Locke and America* (Oxford, 1996).

54. R. Legg, *A Pioneer in Xanadu: Denys Rolle, 1725–1797* (Whitchurch, Hampshire, 1997).

55. D. H. Usner, *Indians, Settlers and Slaves in a Frontier Exchange Economy: The Lower Mississippi Valley before 1783* (Chapel Hill, 1992).

56. R. White, *The Middle Ground: Indians, Empires and Republics in the Great Lakes Region, 1651–1815* (Cambridge, 1991); C. G. Calloway, *Crown and Calumat: British-Indian Relations, 1783–1815* (Norman, Okla., 1971); E. Hinderaker, *Elusive Empires: Constructing Colonialism in the Ohio Valley, 1673–1800* (Cambridge, 1997); M. L. Oberg, *Uncas: First of the Mohegans* (Ithaca, 2003).

57. K. Y. Daaku, *Trade and Politics on the Gold Coast, 1600–1700* (Oxford, 1970), pp. 96–114.

58. P. D. Morgan, 'Encounters between British and "Indigenous" Peoples, c. 1500–c. 1800', in M. Daunton and R. Halpern (eds.), *Empire and Others: British Encounters with Indigenous Peoples, 1600–1850* (1999), p. 64.

59. J. D. Drake, *King Philip's War: Civil War in New England, 1675–1676* (Amherst, Mass., 1999), p. 198.

60. C. Bridenbaugh and R. Bridenbaugh, *No Peace beyond the Line: The English in the Caribbean, 1624–1690* (New York, 1972); R. C. Ritchie, *Captain Kidd and the War against the Pirates* (Cambridge, Mass., 1986); P. Earle, *The Pirate Wars* (2003).

61. M. Rediker, *Between the Devil and the Deep Blue Sea: Merchant Seamen, Pirates, and the Anglo-American Maritime World, 1700–1750* (Cambridge, 1987); P. Linebaugh and M. Rediker, *The Many-Headed Hydra: Sailors, Slaves, Commoners, and the Hidden History of t he Revolutionary Atlantic* (2000), quote p. 327.

62. L. Gragg, 'Englishmen Trans-

planted': The English Colonization of Barbados, 1627–1660 (Oxford, 2003).

63. D. W. Galenson, White Servitude in Colonial America: An Economic Analysis (Cambridge, 1981); M. S. Quintanilla, 'Late Seventeenth-Century Indentured Servants in Barbados', Journal of Caribbean History, 27 (1993).

64. D. H. Akenson, If the Irish Ran the World: Montserrat, 1630–1730 (Montréal, 1997); P. Griffin, The People With No Name: Ireland's Ulster Scots, America's Scots Irish, and the Creation of a British Atlantic World, 1689–1764 (Princeton, 2001).

65. W. Holton, Forged Founders: Indians, Debtors, Slaves, and the Making of the American Revolution in Virginia (Chapel Hill, 1999).

66. J. Horn, Adapting to a New World: English Society in the Seventeenth-Century Chesapeake (Chapel Hill, 1994); P. D. Morgan, 'The Caribbean Islands in Atlantic Context, circa 1500–1800', in F. A. Nussbaum (ed.), The Global Eighteenth Century (Baltimore, 2003), p. 53.

67. R. Bliss, Revolution and Empire: English Politics and the American Colonies in the Seventeenth Century (Manchester, 1993).

68. D. S. Lovejoy, The Glorious Revolution in America (New York, 1972).

69. W. E. Washburn, The Governor and the Rebel: A History of Bacon's Rebellion in Virginia (Chapel Hill, 1957); S. S. Webb, 1676: The End of American Independence (New York, 1984).

70. Dudley to John, 1st Duke of Marlborough, 28 Dec. 1703, BL. Add. 61306 fol. 144.

71. C. E. Clark, The Public Prints: The Newspaper in Anglo-American Culture (Oxford, 1994).

72. F. Felsenstein (ed.), English Trader, Indian Maid: Representing Gender, Race, and Slavery in the New World: An Inkle and Yarico Reader (Baltimore, 1999).

73. V. Dickenson, Drawn From Life: Science and Art in the Portrayal of the New World (Toronto, 1998), pp. 148–9.

74. D. Howse and N. J. W. Thrower,

A Buccaneer's Atlas: Basil Ringrose's South Sea Waggoner (Berkeley, 1992).

75. B. Hooker, 'Identifying "Davis's Land" in Maps', Terrae Incognitae, 21 (1989), pp. 55–61.

76. C. Lloyd, William Dampier (1966); G. Williams, The Great South Sea: English Voyages and Encounters, 1570–1750 (New Haven, 1997).

77. G. Williams, 'The Inexhaustible Fountain of Gold: English Projects and Ventures in the South Seas, 1670–1750', in J. E. Flint and G. Williams (eds.), Perspectives of Empires: Essays Presented to Gerald S. Graham (1973), pp. 27–53; D. Reinhartz, 'Shared Vision: Hermann Moll and His Circle and the Great South Sea', Terrae Incognitae, 19 (1987), pp. 1–10; D. Howse (ed.), Background to Discovery: Pacific Exploration from Dampier to Cook (Berkeley, 1990).

78. G. Williams, Voyages of Delusion: The Quest for the Northwest Passage (New Haven, 2003); W. Barr and G. Williams (eds.), Voyages to Hudson Bay in Search of a Northwest Passage, 1741–1747, I: The Voyage of Christopher Middleton, 1741–1741; II: The Voyage of William Moor and Francis Smith, 1746–1747 (1995).

79. J. E. D. Williams, From Sails to Satellites: The Origin and Development of Navigational Science (Oxford, 1992).

3 COLONIAL EXPANSION AND THE STRUGGLE FOR MARITIME DOMINANCE, 1650–1750

1. H. Erskine-Hill, The Augustan Idea in English Literature (London, 1983), pp. 214–18.

2. Maynard, Consul in Lisbon, to Lord Arlington, Secretary of State, 17 September 1670, PRO. SP. 89/10 fol. 306.

3. A. J. Smithers, The Tangier Campaign: The Birth of the British Army (Stroud, 2003).

4. R. J. Barendse, The Arabian Seas: The Indian Ocean World of the Seventeenth Century (Armonk, N. Y., 2002), p. 454.

5. B. Capp, *Cromwell's Navy: The Fleet and the English Revolution* (Oxford, 1989).

6. S. C. A. Pincus, *Protestantism and Patriotism: Ideologies and the Making of English Foreign Policy, 1650–1685* (Cambridge, 1996).

7. R. Harding, *Seapower and Naval Warfare 1650–1830* (1999), pp. 73–5; W. Maltby, 'Politics, Professionalism and the Evolution of Sailing Ship Tactics', in J. A. Lynn (ed.), *Tools of War: Instruments, Ideas and Institutions of Warfare, 1445–1871* (Chicago, 1990), pp. 53–73; M. A. J. Palmer, 'The Military Revolution Afloat: The Era of the Anglo-Dutch Wars', *War in History*, 4 (1997), pp. 123–49, and '"The Soul's Right Hand": Command and Control in the Age of Fighting Sail, 1652–1827', *Journal of Military History*, 61 (1997), pp. 679–706.

8. D. Armitage, 'The Cromwellian Protectorate and the Languages of Empire', *Historical Journal*, 35 (1992), pp. 537–8.

9. J. R. Powell, *Robert Blake* (1972); T. Venning, *Cromwellian Foreign Policy* (Basingstoke, 1995).

10. R. Ollard, *Man of War: Sir Robert Holmes and the Restoration Navy* (1969).

11. J. R. Jones, *The Anglo-Dutch Wars of the Seventeenth Century* (1996).

12. D. Davies, 'James II, William of Orange, and the Admirals', in E. Cruickshanks (ed.), *By Force or By Default? The Revolution of 1688–89* (Edinburgh, 1989), pp. 82–108; A. Pearsall, 'The Invasion Voyage: Some Nautical Thoughts', in C. Wilson and D. Proctor (eds.), *1688: The Seaborne Alliance and Diplomatic Revolution* (1989), pp. 166 71.

13. T. G. Coad, *The Royal Dockyards 1690–1850* (Aldershot, 1989), pp. 7–10, 92–7; M. Duffy, 'The Establishment of the Western Squadron as the Linchpin of British Naval Strategy', in M. Duffy (ed.), *Parameters of British Naval Power, 1650–1850* (Exeter, 1992), pp. 61–2; M. Duffy, 'The Creation of Plymouth Dockyard and its Impact on Naval Strategy', in *Guerres Maritimes, 1688–1713* (Vincennes, 1990), pp. 245–74.

14. J. Ehrman, *The Navy in the War of William III* (Cambridge, 1953); E. B. Powley, *The Naval Side of King William's War* (1972); P. Aubrey, *The Defeat of James Stuart's Armada 1692* (Leicester, 1979).

15. S. F. Gradish, 'The Establishment of British Seapower in the Mediterranean, 1689–1713', *Canadian Journal of History*, 10 (1975), pp. 1–16.

16. D. W. Jones, *War and Economy in the Age of William III and Marlborough* (Oxford, 1988).

17. P. Dickson, *The Financial Revolution in England* (1967).

18. H. C. Owen, *War at Sea under Queen Anne* (Cambridge, 1934).

19. J. B. Hattendorf, 'Admiral Sir George Byng and the Cape Passaro Incident, 1718: A Case Study in the Use of the Royal Navy as a Deterrent', in *Guerres et Paix* (Vincennes, 1987), pp. 19–38; J. D. Harbron, *Trafalgar and the Spanish Navy* (1988), p. 31.

20. Tyrawly to Admiral Sir Charles Wager, 10 May 1738, Washington, Library of Congress, Manuscript Division, Wager papers, reel 91.

21. P. Woodfine, *Britannia's Glories: The Walpole Ministry and the 1739 War with Spain* (Woodbridge, 1998).

22. R. Harding, *Amphibious Warfare in the Eighteenth Century: The British Expedition to the West Indies, 1740–1742* (Woodbridge, 1991).

23. D. Baugh, *British Naval Administration in the Age of Walpole* (Princeton, 1965); D. Crewe, *Yellow Jack and the Worm: British Naval Administration in the West Indies, 1739–1748* (Liverpool, 1993).

24. H. W. Richmond, *The Navy in the War of 1739–1748* (3 vols., Cambridge, 1920); F. McLynn, 'Sea Power and the Jacobite rising of 1745', *Mariner's Mirror*, 67 (1981), pp. 163–72.

25. P. M. Malone, *The Skulking Way of War: Technology and Tactics among the New England Indians* (Baltimore, 1993).

26. J. A. Sainsbury, 'Indian Labor in Early Rhode Island', *New England Quarterly*, 48 (1975), pp. 378–93.

27. A. Deshpande, 'Limitations of Military Technology: Naval Warfare on the West Coast, 1650–1800', *Economic and Political Weekly*, 25 (1992), pp. 902–3.

28. R. Rolt, *The Conduct of the Several Powers of Europe* (1750), III, p. 1.

29. Woodfine, *Britannia's Glories.*

30. K. Wilson, 'Empire, Trade and Popular Politics in Mid-Hanoverian Britain: The Case of Admiral Vernon', *Past and Present*, 121 (Nov. 1988), pp. 74–109; G. Jordan and N. Rogers, 'Admirals as Heroes: Patriotism and Liberty in Hanoverian England', *Journal of British Studies*, 28 (1989), pp. 201–24.

31. [S. Johnson], *London: A Poem, In Imitation of the third Satire of Juvenal* (1738), lines 25–30.

32. P. Griffin, *The People with No Name: Ireland's Ulster Scots, America's Scots Irish, and the Creation of a British Atlantic World, 1689–1764* (Princeton, 2001).

33. Amidst the massive literature on this topic see, B. Bradshaw and J. S. Morrill (eds.), *The British Problem, c. 1534–1707: State Formation in the Atlantic Archipelago* (Basingstoke, 1996); B. Bradshaw and P. Roberts (eds.), *British Consciousness and Identity: The Making of Britain, 1533–1707* (Cambridge, 1998); C. A. Whatley, *'Bought and Sold for English Gold': Explaining the Union of 1707* (Edinburgh, 1994).

34. M. Fry, *The Scottish Empire* (East Linton, 2001).

35. This paragraph draws heavily on D. Armitage, *The Ideological Origins of the British Empire* (Cambridge, 2000). See also L. Colley, *Britons: Forging the Nation, 1707–1837* (New Haven, 1992); K. Wilson, *The Sense of the People: Politics, Culture and Imperialism in England, 1715–1785* (Cambridge, 1995).

36. J. Hart, *Comparing Empires: European Colonialism from Portuguese Expansion to the Spanish–American War* (Basingstoke, 2003), p. 90.

37. R. Chandler (ed.), *The History of Proceedings of the House of Commons from the Restoration to the Present Time* (1743) XI, cols. 32–3.

38. G. Williams, *'The Prize of all the Oceans': The Triumph and Tragedy of Anson's Voyage round the World* (1999).

39. G. Quilley, '"All Ocean is Her Own": The Image of the Sea and the Identity of the Maritime Nation in Eighteenth-Century British Art', in G. Cubitt (ed.), *Imagining Nations* (Manchester, 1998), pp. 132–52.

40. B. Harris, 'Patriotic Commerce and National Revival: The Free British Fishery Society and British Politics, c. 1749–58', *English Historical Review*, 14 (1999), pp. 285–313, and *Politics and the Nation: Britain in the Mid-Eighteenth Century* (Oxford, 2002), pp. 254.

41. K. A. Rasler and W. R. Thompson, *The Great Powers and Global Struggle, 1490–1990* (Lexington, Ky, 1994), p. 15. See also G. Modeslski and W. R. Thompson, *Seapower and Global Politics, 1494–1993* (1988).

42. P. C. Perdue, 'Culture, History and Imperial Chinese Strategy: Legacies of the Qing Conquests', in H. van de Ven (ed.), *Warfare in Chinese History* (Leiden, 2000), p. 277.

43. S. Chaudhury and M. Morineau (eds.), *Merchants, Companies and Trade: Europe and Asia in the Early Modern Era* (Cambridge, 1999).

44. R. Bin Wong, *China Transformed: Historical Change and the Limits of European Experience* (Ithaca, 1997); K. Pomeranz, *The Great Divergence: China, Europe and the Making of the Modern World Economy* (Berkeley, 1999); P. K. O'Brien, 'Making the Modern World Economy', *History*, 87 (2002), p. 552.

4   THE BATTLE FOR PRIMACY,
1750–1815

1. P. D. Chase (ed.), *The Papers of George Washington: Revolutionary War Series*, X (Charlottesville, 2000), p. 507.

2. Dundas to Charles, 2nd Earl Corn-

wallis, Governor General and Commander-in-Chief in India, 29 July 1787, PRO. 30/11/112, fol. 201.

3. M. Duffy, 'Contested Empires', in P. Langford (ed.), *The Eighteenth Century, 1688–1815* (Oxford, 2002), p. 231.

4. L. H. Gipson, *Zones of International Friction: North America, South of the Great Lakes Region, 1748–1754* (New York, 1937).

5. G. Le Moing, *La Bataille Navale des Cardinaux, 20 novembre 1759* (Paris, 2003).

6. C. Buchet, *Marine, Économie et Société, Un exemple d'interaction: l'Avitaillement de la Royal Navy Durant la guerre de sept ans* (Paris, 1999).

7. J. M. Black, *Pitt the Elder* (Stroud, 1999).

8. P. M. Kennedy, *The Rise and Fall of British Naval Mastery* (1976), pp. 115–16; J. Brewer, *The Sinews of Power: War, Money and the English State 1688–1783* (1989), p. 178.

9. C. Ross (ed.), *Correspondence of Cornwallis* (2 vols., 1859), I, 201

10. N. Tracy, *Manila Ransomed: The British Assault on Manila in the Seven Years War* (Exeter, 1995).

11. L. W. Labaree et al., *The Papers of Benjamin Franklin* (New Haven, 1959–), XXII, pp. 520–21.

12. S. Brumwell, *Redcoats: The British Soldier and War in the Americas, 1755–1763* (Cambridge, 2002); E. M. Spiers, 'Army Organisation and Society in the Nineteenth Century', in T. Bartlett and K. Jeffery (eds.), *A Military History of Ireland* (Cambridge, 1996), pp. 335–41.

13. J. M. Black, *America or Europe? British Foreign Policy, 1739–63* (1998).

14. J. C. Beaglehole, *The Exploration of the Pacific* (3rd edn., Stanford, 1966) and *The Life of Captain James Cook* (1974); O. H. K. Spate, *Paradise Found and Lost: The Pacific since Magellan*, III (1988); D. A. Baugh, 'Seapower and Science: The Motives for Pacific Exploration', in D. Howse (ed.), *Background to Discovery: Pacific Exploration from Dampier to Cook* (Berkeley, 1990), pp. 32–42.

15. K. Wilson, *The Island Race: Englishness, Empire and Gender in the Eighteenth Century* (2003), pp. 58–91.

16. P. J. Marshall, 'The Great Map of Mankind: The British Encounter with India', in A. Frost and J. Samson (eds.), *Pacific Empires: Essays in Honour of Glyndwr Williams* (Carlton South, 1999), p. 240.

17. K. Wilson, *The Sense of the People: Politics, Culture and Imperialism in England, 1715–1785* (Cambridge, 1995), pp. 38–40; P. Lawson, '"Arts and Empire Equally Extend": Tradition, Prejudice and Assumption in the Eighteenth-Century Press Coverage of Empire', in P. Lawson, *A Taste for Empire and Glory: Studies in British Overseas Expansion, 1660–1800* (Aldershot, 1997), pp. 119–46.

18. T. J. Hatton, J. S. Lyons and S. E. Satchell, 'Eighteenth-Century British Trade: Homespun or Empire Made', *Explorations in Economic History*, 20 (1983), pp. 163–82.

19. J. Thomas, *The East India Company and the Provinces in the Eighteenth Century, I: Portsmouth and the East India Company, 1700–1815* (Lewiston, 1999).

20. A. Currie, *Henleys of Wapping – A London Shipowning Family, 1770–1830* (1988); C. J. French, '"Crowded with Traders and a Great Commerce": London's Domination of English Overseas Trade, 1700–1775', *London Journal*, 17 (1992), pp. 27–35; D. Hancock, *Citizens of the World: London Merchants and the Integration of the British Atlantic Community, 1735–1785* (Cambridge, 1995).

21. J. J. McCusker and R. R. Menard, *The Economy of British America, 1607–1789* (Chapel Hill, N. C., 1991).

22. A. Smith, *An Inquiry into the Nature and Causes of the Wealth of Nations* (1776; Oxford, 1979 edn.), II, p. 755.

23. K. Morgan, 'Mercantilism and the British Empire, 1688–1815', in D. Winch and P. K. O'Brien (eds.), *The Political Economy of British Historical Experience, 1688–1914* (Oxford, 2002), pp. 180–81.

24. D. Richardson, 'The British Empire and the Atlantic Slave Trade,

1660–1807', in P. J. Marshall (ed.), *The Oxford History of the British Empire, II: The Eighteenth Century* (Oxford, 1998), p. 446; J. E. Inikori, *Africans and the Industrial Revolution in England: A Study in Interna-tional Trade and Economic Development* (Cambridge, 2002), esp. pp. 479–82.

25. R. R. Rea, 'Urban Problems and Responses in British Pensacola', *Gulf Coast Historical Review*, 3 (1987), p. 56.

26. M. A. Ali, 'Recent Theories of Eighteenth-Century India', *Indian Historical Review*, 13 (1987), pp. 101–10; H. Hossain, *The Company Weavers of Bengal: The East India Company and the Organization of Textile Production in Bengal, 1750–1813* (Delhi, 1988); S. Chaudhuri, *From Prosperity to Decline: Eighteenth-Century Bengal* (New Delhi, 1995). The debate is reviewed in P. J. Marshall, 'Reappraisal: The Rise of British Power in Eighteenth-Century India', *South Asia*, new ser., 19 (1996), pp. 71–6.

27. P. J. Marshall, 'Britain and the World in the Eighteenth Century: IV, The Turning Outwards of Britain', *Transactions of the Royal Historical Society*, 6th ser., 11 (2001), pp. 6–7; S. Sen, *Empire of Free Trade: The East India Company and the Making of the Colonial Marketplace* (Philadelphia, 1998).

28. M. H. Fisher (ed.), *The Travels of Dean Mahomet: An Eighteenth-Century Journey through India* (Berkeley, 1997), p. 58.

29. L. Vorsey, *The Indian Boundary in the Southern Colonies, 1763–1775* (Chapel Hill, 1996), pp. 162–4.

30. H. V. Bowen, 'British Conceptions of Global Empire, 1756–83', *Journal of Imperial and Commonwealth History*, 26 (1998), pp. 1–27; P. J. Marshall, 'Britain and the World in the Eighteenth Century, I: Reshaping the Empire', *Transactions of the Royal Historical Society*, 6th ser., 8 (1998), pp. 1–18.

31. H. V. Bowen, *Revenue and Reform: The Indian Problem in British Politics, 1757–1773* (Cambridge, 1991); Macpherson to 2nd Earl of Shelburne, 6 Dec. 1782,

BL. Bowood Mss., papers of 2nd Earl, Box 56.

32. B. Speck and M. Geiter, *Colonial America, 1585–1776* (Basingstoke, 2002).

33. E. Gould, *The Persistence of Empire: British Political Culture in the Age of the American Revolution* (Chapel Hill, 2000).

34. A. J. O'Shaughnessy, *An Empire Divided: The American Revolution and the British Caribbean* (University Park, Penn., 2000); P. Lawson, *The Imperial Challenge: Quebec and Britain in the Age of the American Revolution* (Montreal, 1989); F. M. Greenwood, *Legacies of Fear: Law and Politics in Quebec in the Era of the French Revolution* (Toronto, 1994).

35. N. R. Stout, *The Royal Navy in America, 1760–1775: A Study of Enforcement of British Colonial Policy in the Era of the American Revolution* (Annapolis, 1973).

36. R. Buel Jr., *In Irons: Britain's Naval Supremacy and the American Revolutionary Economy* (New Haven, 1999).

37. D. Syrett, *The Royal Navy in American Waters, 1775–1783* (Aldershot, 1989); N. A. M. Rodger, *The Insatiable Earl: A Life of John Montagu, Fourth Earl of Sandwich* (1993), pp. 266–300.

38. Anon. account, Bristol Record Office Mss. 17839.

39. R. Cavaliero, *Admiral Satan: The Life and Campaigns of Suffren* (1994).

40. A. Stockley, *Britain and France at the Birth of America: The European Powers and the Peace Negotiations of 1782–1783* (Exeter, 2001).

41. Narrative of engagement off Cape Dobbs, 1–2 Feb. 1775, Hughes's journal, 8 Dec. 1780, BL. India Office H/Misc.126, pp. 6–18, Mss. Eur., F. 27, p. 174; Macpherson to 2nd Earl of Shelburne, 17 Ap. 1783, Bowood Mss., papers of 2nd Earl, Box 56.

42. Watson to Holdernesse, 7 Oct. 1755, 15 Feb., 10 Mar. 1756, BL. Eg. 3488 fols. 81–2, 140–41, 157–8.

43. S. L. Engerman, 'France, Britain and the Economic Growth of Colonial

North America', in J. J. McCusker and K. Morgan (eds.), *The Early Modern Atlantic Economy* (Cambridge, 2000), p. 248.

44. D. Hancock, 'The British Atlantic World: Co-ordination, Complexity, and the Emergence of an Atlantic Market Economy, 1651–1815', *Itinerario*, 23 (1999), pp. 107–26.

45. R. A. Burchell (ed.), *The End of Anglo-America: Historical Essays in the Study of Cultural Divergence* (Manchester, 1991). Over the longer timescale, H. Temperley, *Britain and America since Independence* (Basingstoke, 2002).

46. J. Kelly, *Prelude to Union: Anglo-Irish Politics in the 1780s* (Cork, 1992).

47. P. J. Marshall, '*A Free though Conquering People': Eighteenth-Century Britain and its Empire* (Aldershot, 2003), chapter x, p. 18 (book not paginated continuously).

48. N. Leask, *British Romantic Writers and the East: Anxieties of Empire* (Cambridge, 1993).

49. Liston to Auckland, 14 Sept. 1790, BL. Add. 34433 fol. 117.

50. W. Cobbett, *Parliamentary History*, xxviii, pp. 916–18.

51. A. Frost, 'Nootka Sound and the Beginnings of Britain's Imperialism of Free Trade', in R. Fisher and H. Johnston (eds.), *From Maps to Metaphors: The Pacific World of George Vancouver* (Vancouver, 1993), p. 123.

52. W. K. Lamb (ed.), *The Voyages of George Vancouver, 1791–1795* (1984); D. Mackay, *In the Wake of Cook: Exploration, Science, and Empire, 1780–1801* (1985); R. Fisher and H. Johnston (eds.), *From Maps to Metaphors: The Pacific World of George Vancouver* (Vancouver, 1993).

53. W. A. Spray, 'The Surveys of John McCluer', *Mariner's Mirror*, 60 (1974), pp. 233–50, esp. pp. 242–6.

54. G. Martin (ed.), *The Founding of Australia* (Sydney, 1978); A. Frost, *Botany Bay Mirages: Illusions of Australia's Convict Beginnings* (Melbourne, 1994).

55. G. Williams, 'The First Fleet and After: Expectation and Reality', in T. Delamothe and C. Bridge (eds.), *Interpret-ing Australia* (1988), pp. 24–40; B. Reece, *The Origins of Irish Convict Transportation to New South Wales* (Basingstoke, 2001).

56. A. Peyrefitte, *The Collision of Two Civilisations: The British Expedition to China, 1792–4* (1993).

57. S. J. Braidwood, *Black Poor and White Philanthropists: London Blacks and the Foundation of the Sierra Leone Settlement, 1786–1791* (Liverpool, 1994); M. J. Turner, 'The Limits of Abolition: Government, Saints and the "African Question", c. 1780–1820', *English Historical Review*, 122 (1997).

58. M. Postlethwayt, *Universal Dictionary* (4th edn., 2 vols, 1774), I, no pagination, entry for Africa.

59. K. Wilson, 'The Island Race: Captain Cook, Protestant Evangelicalism and the Construction of English National Identity, 1760–1800', in T. Claydon and I. McBride (eds.), *Protestantism and National Identity: Britain and Ireland, c.1650–c.1850* (Cambridge, 1998), p. 284.

60. D. Turley, *The Culture of English Anti-slavery, 1780–1860* (1991); J. R. Oldfield, *Popular Politics and British Anti-Slavery: The Mobilisation of Public Opinion Against the Slave Trade, 1787–1807* (Manchester, 1995); J. Jennings, *The Business of Abolishing the British Slave Trade, 1783–1807* (1997).

61. M. Duffy, *Soldiers, Sugar and Seapower: The British Expeditions to the West Indies and the War against Revolutionary France* (Oxford, 1987).

62. G. Mowbray, *Remarks on the Conduct of Opposition during the Present Parliament* (1798), p. 115.

63. P. Geoghegan, *The Irish Act of Union* (Dublin, 1999); D. Keogh and K. Whelan (eds.), *Acts of Union: The Causes, Contexts, and Consequences of the Act of Union* (Dublin, 2001).

64. J. Mistler, 'Hambourg sous l'occupation française: observations au sujet du blocus continental', *Francia*, 1 (1973), pp. 451–66.

65. P. Crimmin, 'A Community of Interest and Danger: British Naval Power in the Eastern Mediterranean and the

Levant, 1783–1815', in W. Cogar (ed.), *New Interpretations in Naval History* (Baltimore, 1990), pp. 61–73; P. Krajeski, *In the Shadow of Nelson: The Naval Leadership of Admiral Sir Charles Cotton, 1753–1812* (Westport, 2000).

66. Aberdeen to Wellesley, 15 Feb. 1810, BL. Add. 37309 fol. 344.

67. D. D. Horward, 'British Seapower and its Influence on the Peninsular War, 1810–18', *Naval War College Review*, 21 (1978), pp. 54–71; C. D. Hall, 'The Royal Navy and the Peninsular War', *Mariner's Mirror*, 79 (1993), pp. 403–18.

68. P. Webb, 'The Rebuilding and Repair of the Fleet, 1783–93', *Bulletin of the Institute of Historical Research*, 50 (1977); R. J. W. Knight, 'The Royal Navy's Recovery after the Early Phase of the American Revolutionary War', in G. J. Andreopoulos and H. E. Selesky (eds.), *The Aftermath of Defeat: Societies, Armed Forces, and the Challenge of Recovery* (New Haven, 1994), pp. 10–25; J. E. Talbot, *The Pen and Ink Sailor: Charles Middleton and the King's Navy, 1778–1813* (1998).

69. R. Morriss (ed.), *The Channel Fleet and the Blockade of Brest, 1792–1801* (Aldershot, 2001), p. 21; R. Morriss, *The Royal Dockyards during the Revolutionary and Napoleonic Wars* (Leicester, 1983).

70. D. Crossley and R. Savage (eds.), *The Fuller Letters: Guns, Slaves and Finance, 1728–1855* (Lewes, 1991).

71. C. Gill, *The Naval Mutinies of 1797* (Manchester, 1963).

72. C. D. Hall, *British Strategy in the Napoleonic War, 1803–15* (Manchester, 1992).

73. G. W. Shaw, 'Printing by the British in Sri Lanka at the End of the Eighteenth Century', *Factotum*, 32 (1990), pp. 21–3.

74. Colonel John Brathwaite to James Bland Burges, 28 July 1792, Oxford, Bodleian Library, Bland Burges papers, vol. 31 fol. 114. See, more generally, C. A. Bayly, *Imperial Meridian: The British Empire and the World, 1780–1830* (Harlow, 1989).

For an emphasis on the role of British credit in the Indian military labour market, R. G. S. Cooper, *The Anglo-Maratha Campaigns and the Contest for India: The Struggle for Control of the South Asian Military Economy* (Cambridge, 2004), pp. 299–312.

75. H. Moyse-Bartlett, *The Pirates of Trucial Oman* (1966).

76. Stevenson to Earl of Liverpool, Secretary for War and the Colonies, 1 Feb. 1812, Exeter, Devon Record Office, Addington papers, 152M/C 1812/OF27.

77. C. N. Ponsford (ed.), *Shipbuilding on the Exe: The Memoranda Book of Daniel Bishop Davy (1799–1874) of Topsham, Devon, with a Biography of Robert Davy, 1762–1862* (Exeter, 1988).

78. J. Fowler, 'The Philanthropy of Fish: Sir Thomas Bernard and the Salt Duties', *Consortium on Revolutionary Europe: Selected Papers* (2000), pp. 386–95, esp. 391–2.

79. J. D. Mack, *Matthew Flinders, 1774–1814* (1966).

80. B. Smith, *Imagining the Pacific: In the Wake of the Cook Voyages* (New Haven, 1992).

81. A. Griffin, 'London, Bengal, the China Trade and the Unfrequented Extremities of Asia: The East India Company's Settlement in New Guinea, 1793–95', *British Library Journal*, 16 (1990), pp. 151–73, esp. 131–4, 164.

82. R. Anstey, *The Atlantic Slave Trade and British Abolition, 1760–1810* (1975).

83. A. J. Barker, *Slavery and Antislavery in Mauritius, 1810–33: The Conflict between Economic Expansion and Humanitarian Reform under British Rule* (1996).

84. B. W. Higman, *Slave Populations of the British Caribbean, 1807–1834* (Baltimore, 1984).

85. L. Ryan, *The Aboriginal Tasmanians* (Brisbane, 1981).

86. M. Turner, *Slaves and Missionaries: The Disintegration of Jamaican Slave Society, 1787–1834* (Urbana, 1982); E. V. d'Costa, *Crowns of Glory, Tears of Blood: The Demer-*

ara Slave Rebellion of 1823 (New York, 1994).

87. J. T. Burke, 'The Iconography of the Enlightenment in English Art', *Australian Academy of the Humanities: Proceedings*, 1 (1970), p. 56.

88. Royal Academy of Arts, exhibition catalogue, *France in the Eighteenth Century* (London, 1968), p. 45.

5 THE WORLD POWER, 1815–1901

1. J. Lean and T. Burnard, 'Hearing Slave Voices: The Fiscal's Reports of Berbice and Demerara-Essequebo' [now Guyana], *Archives*, 27 (2002), p. 127.

2. B. Vale, *A War Betwixt Englishmen: Brazil Against Argentina on the River Plate, 1825–1830* (2000).

3. C. N. Parkinson, *Edward Pellew, Viscount Exmouth, Admiral of the Red* (1934), pp. 419–72.

4. N. A. M. Rodger, 'Seapower and Empire: Cause and Effect?', in B. Moore and H. van Nierop (eds.), *Colonial Empires Compared: Britain and the Netherlands, 1750–1850* (Aldershot, 2003), p. 110.

5. P. W. Schroeder, *The Transformation of European Politics, 1763–1848* (Oxford, 1994), p. 523.

6. D. J. Lolmes, 'British Naval Problems at Halifax during the War of 1812', *Mariner's Mirror*, 59 (1973), pp. 324–5.

7. L. Maloney, 'The War of 1812: What Role for Sea Power?', in K. J. Hagan (ed.), *This People's Navy: The Making of American Sea Power* (New York, 1991), pp. 46–62; R. Morriss, *Cockburn and the British Navy in Transition: Admiral Sir George Cockburn, 1772–1853* (Exeter, 1997), pp. 83–120.

8. For the years 1783–1812, J. Gascoigne, *Science in the Service of Empire: Joseph Banks, the British State and the Uses of Science in the Age of Revolution* (Cambridge, 1998), pp. 168–9.

9. C. H. D. Howard, *Splendid Isolation* (1967). In 1834, William IV was convinced 'that we shall besy succeed in lowering its

[Russia's] arrogance and in defeating its duplicity, by preparing for [an] easy and vigorous exertion of our maritime superiority', William to Sir James Graham, 1st Lord of the Admiralty, 16 March 1834, BL., Add. 75956.

10. J. A. de Moor, ' "A very Unpleasant Relationship": Trade and Strategy in the Eastern Seas: Anglo-Dutch Relations in the Nineteenth Century from a Colonial Perspective', in G. J. A. Raven and N. A. M. Rodger (eds.), *Navies and Armies: The Anglo-Dutch Relationship in War and Peace, 1688–1988* (Edinburgh, 1990), pp. 49–69.

11. O. Pollak, *Empires in Collision: Anglo-Burmese Relations in the Mid-Nineteenth Century* (Westport, 1979), esp. pp. 4–5; D. M. Peers, 'Rediscovering India under the British', *International History Review*, 12 (1990), pp. 560–61.

12. N. Thompson, *Earl Bathurst and the British Empire* (Barnsley, 1999), pp. 167–8.

13. J. S. Guest, *The Euphrates Expedition* (1992).

14. R. V. Kubicek, 'The Role of Shallow-Draft Steamboats in the Expansion of the British Empire, 1820–1914', *International Journal of Maritime History*, 6 (1994), pp. 86–106.

15. M. P. Gautier, *Captain Frederick Marryat: L'Homme et L'Oeuvre* (Paris, 1973). William IV refused to give Marryat a knighthood because he had published a book opposing impressment, William to Sir James Graham, 1st Lord of the Admiralty, 30 August 1833, BL. Add. 79596.

16. M. Lincoln, *Representing the Royal Navy: British Sea Power, 1750–1815* (Aldershot, 2003), pp. 201–2.

17. T. L. Hunt, *Defining John Bull: Political Caricature and National Identity in Late Georgian England* (Aldershot, 2003), p. 165.

18. M. Lincoln, *Representing the Royal Navy: British Sea Power, 1750–1815* (Aldershot, 2003), p. 197.

19. For a classic statement, E.

Williams, *Capitalism and Slavery* (Chapel Hill, 1944).

20. S. Drescher, *Econocide: British Slavery in the Era of Abolition* (1977).

21. I. Gross, 'The Abolition of Negro Slavery and British Parliamentary Politics, 1832–3', *Historical Journal*, 23 (1980), pp. 63–85.

22. C. Shammas, 'The Revolutionary Impact of European Demand for Tropical Goods', in J. J. McCusker and K. Morgan (eds.), *The Early Modern Atlantic Economy* (Cambridge, 2000), p. 183.

23. J. R. Ward, *British West Indian Slavery, 1750–1834: The Process of Amelioration* (1988).

24. R. Coupland, *The Exploitation of East Africa, 1856–90: The Slave Trade and the Scramble* (1939).

25. P. M. Kielstra, *The Politics of Slave Trade Suppression in Britain and France, 1814–48: Diplomacy, Morality, and Economics* (Basingstoke, 2000); M. Kale, *Fragments of Empire: Capital, Slavery and Indian Indentured Labor Migration in the British Caribbean* (Philadelphia, 1998).For another form of control that kept alive existing power relations, H. Altink, 'Slavery by another Name: Apprenticed Women in Jamaican Workhouses in the period 1834–81', *Social History*, 26 (2001), pp. 40–59.

26. P. J. Cain, 'Economics and Empire: The Metropolitan Context', in A. Porter (ed.), *The Oxford History of the British Empire, III: The Nineteenth Century* (Oxford, 1999), pp. 34–5.

27. M. McLaren, *British India and British Scotland, 1780–1830: Career Building, Empire Building, and a Scottish School of Thought on Indian Governance* (Akron, 2001).

28. R. MacLeod and M. Lewis (eds.), *Disease, Medicine and Empire: Perspectives on Western Medicine and the Experience of European Expansion* (1988).

29. E. Quin, *Historical Atlas in a Series of Maps of the World* (1830).

30. M. Bowden, *The Life and Archaeological Work of Lieutenant-General*

Augustus Henry Lane Pitt Rivers (Cambridge, 1991).

31. J. M. MacKenzie, *The Empire of Nature: Hunting, Conservation and British Imperialism* (Manchester, 1997).

32. H. Ritvo, 'Destroyers and Preservers: Big Game in the Victorian Empire', *History Today* (Jan. 2002), p. 34.

33. R. V. Kubicek, 'The Colonial Steamer and the Occupation of West Africa by the Victorian State, 1840–1900', *Journal of Imperial and Commonwealth History*, 18 (1990), pp. 9–32.

34. M. H. Edney, *Mapping an Empire: The Geographical Construction of British India, 1765–1843* (Chicago, 1997) and 'Bringing India to Hand: Mapping an Empire, Denying Space', in F. A. Nussbaum (ed.), *The Global Eighteenth Century* (Baltimore, 2003), pp. 65–78; I. J. Barrow, *Making History, Drawing Territory: British Mapping in India, c. 1756–1905* (Oxford, 2004). I would like to thank Sudipta Sen for sending a copy of his paper 'Invasive Prospects: Uses of the Cartographic Image in Early Colonial India'.

35. S. Ryan, *The Cartographic Eye: How Explorers Saw Australia* (Cambridge, 1996).

36. G. J. Alder, 'Standing Alone: William Moorcroft Plays the Great Game, 1808–1825', *International History Review*, 2 (1980), pp. 172–215.

37. I. Jones and J. Joyce, *Oceanography in the Days of Sail* (Sydney, 1992).

38. D. Headrick, *When Information Came of Age: Technologies of Knowledge in the Age of Reason and Revolution, 1700–1850* (Oxford, 2001).

39. D. Clayton, 'On the Colonial Genealogy of George Vancouver's Chart of the North-West Coast of North America', *Ecumene*, 7 (2000), p. 392, and *Islands of Truth: The Imperial Fashioning of Vancouver Island* (Vancouver, 2000); B. Cohn, *Colonialism and its Forms of Knowledge: The British in India* (Princeton, 1996).

40. S. Thorne, *Congregational Missions and the Making of an Imperial Culture in*

Nineteenth-Century England (Stanford, 1999).

41. J. Wyld, *Notes to Accompany Mr Wyld's Model of the Earth, Leicester Square* (1851).

42. J. Civin, 'Slaves, Sati and Sugar: Constructing Imperial Identity through Liverpool Petition Struggles', in J. Hoppit (ed.), *Parliaments, Nations and Identities in Britain and Ireland, 1660–1850* (Manchester, 2003), p. 193.

43. P. L. Schuyler, *The Fall of the Old Colonial System: A Study in British Free Trade, 1770–1870* (New York, 1945).

44. J. R. Davis, *Britain and the German Zollverein, 1848–66* (1997).

45. P. T. Marsh, *Bargaining on Europe: Britain and the First Common Market, 1860–1892* (New Haven, 2000).

46. R. Perkins, 'The "Coastguard Stations" at Babbacombe and Torquay, 1818–1826', *Devon Historian*, 50 (1995), pp. 11–17.

47. W. R. Louis (ed.), *Imperialism: The Robinson and Gallagher Controversy* (New York, 1970).

48. D. C. M. Platt, *Latin America and British Trade, 1806–1914* (1972); R. Miller, *Britain and Latin America in the Nineteenth and Twentieth Centuries* (1993).

49. K. Gallo, *Great Britain and Argentina: From Invasion to Recognition, 1806–1826* (Basingstoke, 2002).

50. C. M. Lewis, *British Railways in Argentina, 1857–1914* (1983).

51. B. Gough, *The Falkland Islands/ Malvinas: The Contest for Empire in the South Atlantic* (1992).

52. R. Cave, '"To instruct and enlighten the Negro", the West Indian (1838) and its Failure', *Journal of Newspaper and Periodical History*, 1 (1984), pp. 12–28.

53. Pearson to his parents, 19 July 1857, BL. IO., MSS Eur C 231, p. 57.

54. P. J. Cain and A. G. Hopkins, *British Imperialism: I, Innovation and Expansion, 1688–1914* (1993);

55. R. Burt, 'British Investment in the American Mining Frontier', *Business and Economic History*, 26 (1997), pp. 515–25.

56. L. E. Davis and R. E. Gallman, *Evolving Financial Markets and International Capital Flows: Britain, the Americas, and Australia, 1865–1914* (Cambridge, 2001).

57. P. Parry, 'The Dorset Ports and the Coming of the Railways', *Mariner's Mirror*, 53 (1967), pp. 243–9.

58. F. C. Danvers, 'The Persian Gulf Route and Commerce', *Asiatic Quarterly Review* (1888), pp. 413–14; G. N. Curzon, *Persia and the Persian Question* (2nd edn., 1966) II, pp. 557–7; T. J. Bennett, 'The Past and Present Connection of England with the Persian Gulf', *Journal of the Society of Arts* (1902), pp. 645–6; C. Issawi (ed.), *The Economic History of the Middle East, 1800–1914* (1966), p. 350. I would like to thank Ferej Ahmadi for these references.

59. D. C. North, 'Ocean Freight Rates and Economic Development, 1750–1914', *Journal of Economic History*, 17 (1958), pp. 537–55.

60. There is much on work practices and social structure in J. Field, *Portsmouth Dockyard and its Workers, 1815–1875* (Portsmouth, 1994).

61. F. Broeze, 'The External Dynamics of Port City Morphology: Bombay, 1815–1914', in I. Banga (ed.), *Ports and Their Hinterlands in India* (New Delhi, 1992), pp. 245–72.

62. D. G. Bovill, 'The Industrial Training Ship "Wellesley" and the Training Ship Movement', *Durham County Local History Society Bulletin*, 41 (1988), p. 18.

63. M. Kearney, *The Indian Ocean in World History* (2004), p. 139.

64. F. Harcourt, 'British Oceanic Mail Contracts in the Age of Steam, 1838–1914', *Journal of Transport History*, 3rd ser., 9 (1988), pp. 1–18.

65. V. T. Harlow, *The Founding of the Second British Empire, 1763–1793: II, New Continents and Changing Values* (1964), p. 265.

66. S. Palmer, *Politics, Shipping and the Repeal of the Navigation Acts* (Manchester, 1990).

67. H. J. M. Johnston, *British Emigration Policy, 1815–1830: 'Shovelling out Paupers'* (Oxford, 1972).

68. H. I. Cowan, *British Emigration to British North America: The First Hundred Years* (Toronto, 1961); J. C. Robert, 'An Immigrant Population', in R. L. Gentilcore (ed.), *Historical Atlas of Canada, II: The Land Transformed, 1800–1891* (Toronto, 1993), p. 22.

69. L. Robson, *The Convict Settlers of Australia* (Melbourne, 1981).

70. C. Anderson, *Convicts in the Indian Ocean: Transportation from South Asia to Mauritius, 1815–1853* (Basingstoke, 2000).

71. O. MacDonagh, *A Pattern of Government Growth, 1800–1860: The Passenger Acts and their Enforcement* (1961).

72. O. MacDonagh, 'Irish Emigration to the United States of America and the British Colonies during the Famine', in R. D. Edwards and T. D. Williams (eds.), *The Great Famine: Studies in Irish History, 1845–1852* (Dublin, 1962), pp. 319–90.

73. W. Nugent, *Crossings: The Great Transatlantic Migrations, 1870–1914* (Bloomington, 1992).

74. T. M. Devine, *The Great Highland Famine: Hunger, Emigration and the Scottish Highlands in the Nineteenth Century* (Edinburgh, 1988); T. M. Devine (ed.), *Scottish Emigration and Scottish Society* (Edinburgh, 1992).

75. B. Deacon, 'How Many Went? The Size of the Great Cornish Emigration of the Nineteenth Century', *Devon and Cornwall Notes and Queries*, 36 (1987), pp. 5–8.

76. P. Payton, *The Cornish Miner in Australia* (Redruth, 1984).

77. A. Graves, *Cane and Sugar: The Political Economy of the Queensland Sugar Industry, 1862–1905* (Edinburgh, 1993).

78. K. Saunders, *Indentured Labour in the British Empire, 1834–1920* (1984); D. Northrup, *Indentured Labor in the Age of Imperialism* (Cambridge, Mass. 1995).

79. D. Northrup, 'Migration from Africa, Asia, and the South Pacific', in A.

Porter (ed.), *The Oxford History of the British Empire, III: The Nineteenth Century* (Oxford, 1999), pp. 88–90.

6   NAVAL STRENGTH AND IMPERIAL
EXPANSION, 1815–1901

1. N. Tarling, *Piracy and Politics in the Malay World: A Study of British Imperialism in Nineteenth-Century South-East Asia* (Melbourne, 1963).

2. C. White, 'The Long Arm of Seapower: The Anglo-Japanese War of 1863–1864', in P. Hore (ed.), *Seapower Ashore: 200 Years of Royal Navy Operations on Land* (2001), pp. 153–62.

3. P. Hore, 'Lord Melville, the Admiralty and the Coming of Steam Navigation', *Mariner's Mirror*, 86 (2000), pp. 157–72.

4. R. V. Kubicek, 'The Role of Shallow-Draft Steamboats in the Expansion of the British Empire, 1820–1914', *International Journal of Maritime History*, 6 (1994), pp. 86–106.

5. Cockburn memorandum, 9 June 1845, BL. Add. 40458 fols. 63–4.

6. A. Lambert, ' "Within Cannon Shot of Deep Water": The Syrian Campaign of 1840', in Hore, *Seapower Ashore*, pp. 79–95.

7. B. Brodie, *Sea Power in the Machine Age* (Princeton, 1941); C. I. Hamilton, *Anglo-French Naval Rivalry, 1849–1870* (Oxford, 1993); D. K. Brown, *Warrior to Dreadnought: Warship Development, 1860–1905* (1997).

8. G. S. Graham, *The Politics of Naval Supremacy: Studies in British Maritime Ascendancy* (Cambridge, 1965).

9. N. Tarling, 'The Establishment of the Colonial Régimes', in N. Tarling (ed.), *The Cambridge History of Southeast Asia* (2nd edn., 4 vols., Cambridge, 1999), III, 41.

10. BL. Add. 40458 fol. 57.

11. A. T. Patterson, *Palmerston's Folly: The Portsdown and Spithead Forts* (Portsmouth, 1985); M. S. Partridge, *Military Planning for the Defense of the*

United Kingdom, 1814–1870 (Westport, 1989).

12. J. B. Kelly, Britain and the Persian Gulf, 1795–1880 (Oxford, 1968); M. al-Qasimi, The Myth of Arab Piracy in the Gulf (1986).

13. R. J. Gavin, Aden under British Rule, 1839–1967 (1975).

14. D. Clayton, 'The Creation of Imperial Space in the Pacific Northwest', Journal of Historical Geography, 26 (2000), p. 343.

15. F. M. Carroll, A Good and Wise Measure: The Search for the Canadian-American Boundary, 1783–1842 (Toronto, 2001).

16. S. W. Haynes, 'Anglophobia and the Annexation of Texas: The Quest for National Security', in S. W. Haynes and C. Morris (eds.), Manifest Destiny and Empire: American Antebellum Expansionism (College Station, 1997), pp. 115–45; E. D. Adams, British Interests and Activities in Texas (Gloucester, 1963).

17. J. C. Arnell, 'Trooping to the Canadas', Mariner's Mirror, 53 (1967), pp. 143–60.

18. PRO. WO. 6/86, pp. 300–01.

19. H. Jones, To the Webster-Ashburton Treaty: A Study in Anglo-American Relations, 1783–1843 (Chapel Hill, 1977); H. Jones and D. Rakestraw, Prologue to Manifest Destiny: Anglo-American Relations in the 1840s (Wilmington, Del., 1997).

20. P. Statham-Drew, James Stirling: Admiral and Founding Governor of Western Australia (Crawley, Western Australia, 2003), pp. 500–02.

21. J. Y. Wong, Deadly Dreams. Opium and the Arrow War (1856–60) in China (Cambridge, 1998).

22. H. Reynolds, The Other Side of the Frontier: Aboriginal Resistance to the European Invasion of Australia (Ringwood, 1982); N. Loos, Invasion and Resistance: Aboriginal-European Relations on the North Queensland Frontier, 1861–1897 (Canberra, 1982); J. Grey, A Military History of Australia (2nd edn., Cambridge, 1999), pp. 25–37.

23. J. Cowan, The New Zealand Wars (Wellington, 1983).

24. D. Killingray, 'The British and Asante, 1870–1914', in J. A. de Moor and H. L. Wesseling (eds.), Imperialism and War: Essays on Colonial Wars in Asia and Africa (Leiden, 1989), pp. 158–67.

25. D. Bates, The Abyssinian Difficulty (Oxford, 1979).

26. H. Jones, Union in Peril: The Crisis over British Intervention in the Civil War (Chapel Hill, 1992).

27. R. J. M. Blackett, Divided Hearts: Britain and the American Civil War (Baton Rouge, 2001).

28. PRO. FO. 5/879 fols. 52–7.

29. J. F. Beeler, British Naval Policy in the Gladstone-Disraeli Era, 1866–1880 (Stanford, 1997), pp. 199–200.

30. D. C. Gordon, The Dominion Partnership in Imperial Defense, 1870–1914 (1965); D. M. Schurman, Imperial Defence, 1868–1887 (2000), pp. 26–7.

31. Beeler, British Naval Policy in the Gladstone-Disraeli Era.

32. I. Beckett, The Victorians at War (2003), pp. 105–12.

33. J. Bach, The Australia Station: A History of the Royal Navy in the South West Pacific, 1821–1913 (Sydney, 1986).

34. R. Brooks, 'March into India: The Relief of Lucknow, 1857–1859', in Hore, Seapower Ashore, p. 131.

35. G. Fox, British Admirals and Chinese Pirates, 1832–1869 (Westport, 1940), pp. 107–8.

36. H. Preston and J. Major, Send a Gunboat! (1967); M. Rodman and M. Cooper (eds.), The Pacification of Melanesia (Ann Arbor, 1979).

37. B. M. Gough, Gunboat Frontier: British Maritime Authority and North-West Coast Indians, 1846–1890 (Vancouver, 1984).

38. J. Belich, The New Zealand Wars and the Victorian Interpretation of Racial Conflict (Auckland, 1986).

39. H. Carr, 'Modernism and Travel, 1880–1940', in P. Hulme and T. Youngs (eds.), The Cambridge Companion to Travel Writing (Cambridge, 2002), p. 71.

40. Warren, Reminiscences, BL. IO. Mss Eur. C 607, pp. 188–96.

41. E. M. Spiers, *Wars of Intervention: A Case-Study – The Reconquest of the Sudan, 1892–99* (Camberley, 1998), pp. 46–7.

42. R. Robinson (ed.), *Railway Imperialism* (Westport, Conn., 1991); I. J. Kerr, *Building the Railways of the Raj, 1850–1900* (Oxford, 1995).

43. P. J. Hugill, *Global Communications since 1844: Geopolitics and Technology* (Baltimore, 1999), pp. 29–46; D. R. Headrick, *The Invisible Weapon: Telecommunications and International Politics, 1851–1945* (New York, 1991).

44. R. D. Long (ed.), *The Man on the Spot: Essays on British Empire History* (1995).

45. R. I. Rotberg, *Cecil Rhodes and the Pursuit of Power* (Oxford, 1988).

46. M. Hooper, 'The Naval Defence Agreement of 1887', *Australian Journal of Politics and History*, 14 (1968); J. Grey, *A Military History of Australia* (2nd edn., Cambridge, 1999), pp. 20, 22–4, 40, 45.

47. R. Johnson, *The Penjdeh Crisis and its Impact on the Great Game and the Defence of India, 1885–1897* (Ph.D., University of Exeter, 1999).

48. J. G. Darwin, 'Imperialism and the Victorians: The Dynamics of Territorial Expansion', *English Historical Review*, 112 (1997), pp. 614–42.

49. D. Munro and S. Firth, 'Towards Colonial Protectorates: The Case of the Gilbert and Ellice Islands', *Australian Journal of Politics and History*, XXXII (1980), pp. 66–7.

50. J. Meriwether, 'The Intricacies of War Office Administration: Civilians, Soldiers and the Opening of the South African War, October–December 1899', *Archives*, 28 (2003), p. 52.

51. A. Porter, 'The South African War and Imperial Britain: A Question of Significance?', in G. Cuthbertson, A. Grundlingh and M.-L. Suttie (eds.), *Writing a Wider War: Rethinking Gender, Race, and Identity in the South African War, 1899–1902* (Athens, Ohio, 2002), p. 296.

52. L. Field, *The Forgotten War: Australian Involvement in the South African Conflict* (Melbourne, 1979).

53. B. Nasson, *The South African War* (1999); D. Omissi and A. S. Thompson (eds.), *The Impact of the South African War* (Basingstoke, 2002).

54. D. M. Schurman, *The Education of a Navy: The Development of British Naval Strategic Thought, 1867–1914* (1965) and *Julian S. Corbett, 1854–1922: Historian of British Maritime Policy from Drake to Jellico* (1981).

55. R. A. Johnson, 'The Penjdeh Incident, 1885', *Archives*, 24 (April 1999), pp. 28–48, esp. pp. 28, 44; King's College, London, Liddell Hart Archive, Hamilton papers, 1/3/3.

56. J. Fisher, 'On the Baghdad Road: On the Trail of W. J. Childs: A Study of British Near Eastern Intelligence and Historical Analysis, c. 1900–1930', *Archives*, 24 (Oct. 1999), p. 55.

57. P. Smith, 'Ruling the Waves: Government, the Service and the Cost of Naval Supremacy, 1885–99', in P. Smith (ed.), *Government and the Armed Forces in Britain, 1856–1990* (1996), pp. 21–52, esp. pp. 51–2.

58. P. M. Kennedy, *The Rise and Fall of British Naval Mastery* (1983), pp. 193, 209.

59. T. Benady, *The Royal Navy at Gibraltar* (Liskeard, 1985), p. 108.

60. D. M. Schurman, *Imperial Defence, 1868–1887* (2000), pp. 152–3.

61. M. Burrows, *The History of the Foreign Policy of Great Britain* (1895), pp. vi–vii.

62. E. F. Biagini, 'Exporting "Western and Beneficient Institutions": Gladstone and Empire, 1880–1885', in D. Bebbington and R. Swift (eds.), *Gladstone Centenary Essays* (Liverpool, 2000), pp. 202–24.

63. L. Kitzan, *Victorian Writers and the Image of Empire: The Rose-Colored Vision* (Westport, 2001).

64. G. Dawson, *Soldier Heroes: British Adventure, Empire and the Imagining of Masculinities* (1994).

65. J. M. MacKenzie (ed.), *Popular Imperialism and the Military, 1850–1950* (Manchester, 1992).

66. R. H. Macdonald, *Sons of the Empire: The Frontier and the Boy Scout Movement, 1890–1918* (Toronto, 1993).

67. S. J. Potter, *News and the British World: The Emergence of an Imperial Press System, 1876–1922* (Oxford, 2003).

68. *Julian Browning Autographs and Manuscripts*, catalogue 24 (2001), p. 7, item 55.

69. J. S. Bratton et al., *Acts of Supremacy: The British Empire and the Stage, 1790–1930* (Manchester, 1991); P. H. Hoffenberg, *An Empire on Display: English, Indian, and Australian Exhibitions from the Crystal Palace to the Great War* (Berkeley, 2001).

70. H. Kelsey, *Sir John Hawkins: Queen Elizabeth's Slave Trader* (New Haven, 2003), pp. 275–6.

71. D. Gilmour, *The Long Recessional: The Imperial Life of Rudyard Kipling* (2003), p. 108; J. M. MacKenzie (ed.), *Imperialism and Popular Culture* (Manchester, 1987).

72. A. D. Lambert (ed.), *Letters and Papers of Professor Sir John Knox Laughton, 1830–1915* (Aldershot, 2002).

73. D. Cannadine, *Ornamentalism: How the British Saw Their Empire* (2001).

74. For this concept, see J. J. L. Gommans, 'The Silent Frontier of South Asia, c. 1100–1800 AD', *Journal of World History*, 9 (1998).

75. Selborne to Curzon, 19 Ap. 1901, D. G. Boyce (ed.), *The Crisis of British Power: The Imperial and Naval Papers of the Second Earl of Selborne, 1895–1910* (1990), p. 115.

7   EMPIRE UNDER CHALLENGE, 1901–1918

1. BL. Add. 49710 fol. 140.

2. A. Roberts, *Eminent Churchillians* (1994).

3. B. Porter, 'Edward Elgar and Empire', *Journal of Imperial and Commonwealth History*, 29 (2001), p. 11.

4. D. McLean, 'Finance and "Informal Empire" before the First World War', *Economic Historical Review*, 29 (1976), pp. 291–305.

5. L. Johnman and H. Murphy, *British Shipbuilding and the State since 1918: A Political Economy of Decline* (Exeter, 2002), p. 9.

6. G. Morton and R. J. Morris, 'Civil Society, Governance and Nation, 1832–1914', in R. A. Houston and W. W. J. Knox (eds.), *The New Penguin History of Scotland* (2001), p. 372.

7. R. Malster, 'The Herring Fishery', in D. Dymond and E. Martin (eds.), *An Historical Atlas of Suffolk* (3rd edn., Ipswich, 1999), p. 138.

8. M. H. Edney, 'Cartographic Confusion and Nationalism: The Washington Meridian in the Early Nineteenth Century', *Mapline*, 69–70 (1993), p. 48.

9. M. Jones, *The Last Great Quest: Captain Scott's Antarctic Sacrifice* (Oxford, 2003).

10. B. Ramirez, *Crossing the 49th Parallel: Migration from Canada to the United States, 1900–1930* (Ithaca, 2001).

11. Chamberlain addressing the Imperial Conference of 1902, J. Amery, *The Life of Joseph Chamberlain* (6 vols., 1956), IV, p. 421.

12. J. Amery, *Joseph Chamberlain and the Tariff Reform Campaign* (1969); A. Sykes, *Tariff Reform in British Politics, 1903–1913* (Oxford, 1979).

13. A. Thompson, *Imperial Britain: The Empire in British Politics, c. 1880–1932* (Harlow, 2000).

14. For example, A. Burton, *Politics and Empire in Victorian Britain: A Reader* (Basingstoke, 2001).

15. J. Bush, *Edwardian Ladies and Imperial Power* (1999).

16. G. K. Peating, 'Home Rule for England, English Nationalism, and Edwardian Debates About Constitutional Reform', *Albion*, 35 (2003), pp. 71–90.

17. F. Coetzee, *For Party or Country:*

Nationalism and the Dilemmas of Popular Conservatism in Edwardian England (New York, 1990); D. G. Boyce (ed.), *The Crisis of British Sea Power: The Imperial and Naval Papers of the Second Earl of Selborne, 1895–1910* (1990).

18. P. Gibb, 'Selling out Canada? The Role of Sir Julian Pauncefote in the Bering Sea Dispute, 1889–1902', *International History Review*, 24 (2002), pp. 817–44.

19. B. Perkins, *The Great Rapprochement: England and the United States, 1895–1914* (1969).

20. P. M. Kennedy, *The Rise of Anglo-German Antagonism, 1860–1914* (1980).

21. P. M. Kennedy, 'The Development of German Naval Operations Plans against England 1896–1914', *English Historical Review*, 89 (1974), pp. 48–76.

22. R. Hobson, *Imperialism at Sea: Naval Strategic Thought, the Ideology of Sea Power, and the Tirpitz Plan, 1875–1914* (Leiden, 2002).

23. J. Gooch, *The Plans of War: The General Staff and British Military Strategy, c. 1900–1916* (1974); S. R. Williamson, *The Politics of Grand Strategy: Britain and France Prepare for War* (Cambridge, Mass., 1969); J. McDermott, 'The Revolution in British Military Thinking from the Boer War to the Moroccan Crisis', in P. M. Kennedy (ed.), *The War Plans of the Great Powers* (1979), pp. 108–10.

24. C. McKee, *Sober Men and True: Sailor Lives in the Royal Navy, 1900–1945* (Cambridge, Mass., 2002), p. 33.

25. P. P. O'Brien, 'The Titan Refreshed: Imperial Overstretch and the British Navy before the First World War', *Past and Present*, no. 172 (Aug. 2001), p. 153.

26. C. H. Fairbanks, 'The Origins of the *Dreadnought* Revolution: A Historiographical Essay', *International History Review*, 13 (1991), pp. 246–72; N. Lambert, *Sir John Fisher's Naval Revolution* (1999). For a powerful revisionist argument, J. T. Sumida, *In Defence of Naval Supremacy: Finance, Technology, and British Naval Policy, 1889–1914* (Boston, Mass., 1989) and 'Sir John Fisher and the Dreadnought: The

Sources of Naval Mythology', *Journal of Military History*, 59 (1995), pp. 619–38.

27. M. Lincoln, 'Naval Ship Launches as Public Spectacle, 1773–1854', *Mariner's Mirror*, 83 (1997), pp. 466–72.

28. I have benefited from hearing a presentation on this subject by Jan Rüger.

29. BL. Add. 50294 fol. 6, 49710 fol. 2.

30. BL. Add. 48993 fol. 86.

31. M. Wilson, 'Early Submarines', in R. Gardiner (ed.), *Steam, Steel and Shellfire: The Steam Warship 1815–1905* (1992), pp. 147–57.

32. N. Lambert (ed.), *The Submarine Service, 1900–1918* (Aldershot, 2001).

33. BL. Add. 50300 fol. 176.

34. G. Penn, *Fisher, Churchill and the Dardanelles* (1999); T. Travers, *Gallipoli, 1915* (Stroud, 2002).

35. A. Best, *British Intelligence and the Japanese Challenge in Asia, 1914–1941* (Basingstoke, 2002).

36. D. Omissi, *The Sepoy and the Raj: The Indian Army, 1860–1940* (1994); T. Tai-Yong, 'An Imperial Home-Front: Punjab and the First World War', *Journal of Military History*, 64 (2000), pp. 371–410.

37. J. Laffin, *Damn the Dardanelles! The Agony of Gallipoli* (1980).

38. K. Jeffery, *Ireland and the Great War* (Cambridge, 2000); A. Gregory and S. Pašeta (eds.), *Ireland and the Great War: 'A War to Unite Us All'?* (Manchester, 2002).

39. Kitchener to Balfour, 6 Nov. 1915, PRO. 30/57/66.

40. N. M. Campbell, *Jutland: An Analysis of the Fighting* (1986).

41. A. Gordon, *The Rules of the Game: Jutland and British Naval Command* (1996), pp. 514–15.

42. BL. Add. 49714 fol. 29.

43. BL. Add. 49715 fol. 210; BL. Add. 49714 fol. 145.

44. H. H. Herwig, 'Total Rhetoric, Limited War: Germany's U-Boat Campaign, 1917–1918', in R. Chickering and S. Förster (eds.), *Great War, Total War: Combat and Mobilization on the Western Front, 1914–1918* (Cambridge, 2000), p. 205.

45. N. Grundy, *W. L. Wyllie, R. A.: The Portsmouth Years* (Portsmouth, 1996).

8 New Threats, 1919–1945

1. Dill to Field Marshal Montgomery-Massingberd, retired Chief of the Imperial General Staff, 23 Dec. 1939, King's College, London, Liddell Hart Archive (hereafter KCL. LH), Montgomery-Massingberd papers, 10/14.

2. J. Fisher, *Curzon and British Imperialism in the Middle East, 1916–1919* (1999).

3. J. Fisher, 'Major Norman Bray and Eastern Unrest in the British Empire in the Aftermath of World War I', *Archives*, 27 (2002), pp. 39–56, esp. 45–52.

4. E. Monroe, *Britain's Moment in the Middle East, 1914–1956* (Baltimore, 1963); B. C. Busch, *Britain, India and the Arabs, 1914–21* (1971); J. Darwin, *Britain, Egypt and the Middle East: Imperial Policy in the Aftermath of War, 1918–1922* (1981); B. Westrate, *The Arab Bureau: British Policy in the Middle East, 1916–1920* (University Park, Penn., 1992).

5. B. Gokay, *A Clash of Empires: Turkey between Russian Bolshevism and British Imperialism, 1918–1923* (1997).

6. K. O. Morgan, *Consensus and Disunity: The Lloyd George Coalition Government, 1918–1922* (Oxford, 1979), pp. 323, 325, 342.

7. R. Higham, *Britain's Imperial Air Routes, 1918–1939* (Hamden, Conn., 1960); R. L. McCormack, 'Imperialism, Air Transport and Colonial Development: Kenya 1920–1946', *Journal of Imperial and Commonwealth History*, 17 (1989), pp. 374–95.

8. E. M. Collingham, *Imperial Bodies: The Physical Experience of the Raj, c. 1800–1947* (Cambridge, 2001).

9. K. Dodds, *Pink Ice: Britain and the South Atlantic Empire* (2002), pp. 26–7.

10. D. Kennedy, 'Empire Migration in Post-War Reconstruction: The Role of the Oversea Settlement Committee, 1919–1922'; B. L. Blakeley, 'The Society for the Oversea Settlement of British Women and the Problems of Empire Settlement, 1917–1936', *Albion*, 20 (1988), pp. 403–44, esp. 432–3.

11. A. Thompson, 'The Languages of Loyalism in Southern Africa, c. 1870–1939', *English Historical Review*, 118 (2003), p. 648.

12. D. Gilmour, *The Long Recessional: The Imperial Life of Rudyard Kipling* (2003), p. 297.

13. K. A. Sandford and B. Stoddart, *The Imperial Game: Cricket, Culture and Society* (Manchester, 1998).

14. D. N. Robinson, *The Book of the Lincolnshire Seaside* (Buckingham, 1981).

15. E. M. Andrews, *The Writing on the Wall: The British Commonwealth and Aggression in the East, 1931–1935* (1967).

16. I. M. Drummond, *Imperial Economic Policy, 1917–1939* (1974).

17. W. R. Louis, *In the Name of God, Go! Leo Amery and the British Empire in the Age of Churchill* (New York, 1992), pp. 106–8.

18. B. R. Tomlinson, *The Political Economy of the Raj, 1914–1947: The Economics of Decolonization in India* (1979).

19. S. Clarkson, *Uncle Sam and US Globalization, Neoconservatism, and the Canadian State* (Toronto, 2002), p. 20.

20. C. Barnett, *The Collapse of British Power* (1972).

21. R. Bickers, *Britain in China: Community, Culture and Colonialism, 1900–49* (Manchester, 1999); S. K. Fung, *The Diplomacy of Imperial Retreat: Britain's South China Policy, 1924–1931* (Oxford, 1991).

22. A. Draper, *The Amritsar Massacre: Twilight of the Raj* (1985); D. G. Boyce, 'From Assaye to the *Assaye*: Reflections on British Government, Force, and Moral Authority in India', *Journal of Military History*, 63 (1999), pp. 643–68; G. D. Howe, *Race, War and Nationalism: A Social History of West Indians in the First World War* (Oxford, 2002).

23. P. Warren, 'Archives and the Indian Army in Waziristan, *Archives*, 22 (1997), p. 46.

24. M. Kolinsky, *Britain's War in the Middle East: Strategy and Diplomacy, 1936–42* (New York, 1999); N. Shepherd, *Ploughing Sand: British Rule in Palestine, 1917–1948* (Piscataway, N.J., 2000).

25. P. Ghosh, *Brave Men of the Hills: Resistance and Rebellion in Burma, 1823–1932* (Honolulu, 2000).

26. T. C. Holt, *The Problem of Freedom: Race, Labor, and Politics in Jamaica and Britain, 1932–1938* (Baltimore, 1992).

27. B. R. Tomlinson, *The Indian National Congress and the Raj, 1929–1942: The Penultimate Phase* (1976).

28. K. Robbins, *Churchill* (Harlow, 1992), p. 108; G. Peele, 'Revolt over India', in G. Peele and C. P. Cook (eds.), *The Politics of Reappraisal, 1918–1939* (1975), pp. 114–45; C. Bridge, *Holding India to the Empire: The British Conservative Party and the 1935 Constitution* (1986). I have benefited from information from Tony Lentin in the section on Sumner.

29. P. Chowdhry, *Colonial India and the Making of Empire Cinema: Image, Ideology and Identity* (Manchester, 2000).

30. J. Ferris, '"It is our business in the Navy to Command the Seas": The Last Decade of British Maritime Supremacy, 1919–1929', in K. Neilson and G. Kennedy (eds.), *Far Flung Lines: Studies in Imperial Defence in Honour of Donald Mackenzie Schurman* (1997), pp. 124–70.

31. J. Moretz, *The Royal Navy and the Capital Ship in the Interwar Period: An Operational Perspective* (2002), p. 37; BL. Add. 49045 fols. 1–2.

32. S. Roskill, *Naval Policy between the Wars: 1, The Period of Anglo-American Antagonism, 1919–1929* (1968); E. O. Goldman, *Sunken Treaties: Naval Arms Control Between the Wars* (University Park, Penn, 1994); E. Goldstein and J. H. Maurer, *The Washington Naval Conference: Naval Rivalry, East Asian Stability, and the Road to Pearl Harbor* (Ilford, 1994); P. P. O'Brien, *British and American Naval Power: Politics and Policy, 1900–1936* (Westport, 1998).

33. J. Charmley, 'Churchill and the American Alliance', *Transactions of the Royal Historical Society*, 6th ser., 11 (2001), pp. 353–4.

34. A. Carew, *The Lower Deck of the Royal Navy: The Invergordon Mutiny in Perspective* (1981).

35. PRO. CAB. 29/117 fols. 78, 19; R. W. Fanning, *Peace and Disarmament: Naval Rivalry and Arms Control, 1922–1933* (Lexington, Ky, 1995); C. M. Bell, *The Royal Navy, Seapower, and Strategy between the Wars* (2000).

36. G. A. Ballard, *Rulers of the Indian Ocean* (1927), pp. 309–16, quote p. 311.

37. W. D. McIntyre, *The Rise and Fall of the Singapore Naval Base, 1919–1942* (1979); J. Neidpath, *The Singapore Naval Base and the Defence of Britain's Eastern Empire, 1919–1941* (Oxford, 1941); O. C. Chung, *Operation Matador: Britain's War Plans against the Japanese, 1918–1941* (Singapore, 1997); M. H. Murfett et. al., *Between Two Oceans: A Military History of Singapore from First Settlement to Final British Withdrawal* (Oxford, 1999).

38. M. H. Brice, *The Royal Navy and the Sino-Japanese Incident* (1973).

39. M. H. Murfett, '"Are We Ready?" The Development of American and British Naval Strategy, 1922–1939', in R. S. Jordon and J. B. Hattendorf (eds.), *Maritime Strategy and the Balance of Power: Britain and America in the Twentieth Century* (1989), pp. 214–42.

40. K. Neilson, 'The Defence Requirements Sub-Committee, British Strategic Foreign Policy, Neville Chamberlain and the Path to Appeasement', *English Historical Review*, 118 (2003), p. 675.

41. PRO. CAB. 16/109 fol. 9; J. Maiolo, *The Royal Navy and Nazi Germany, 1933–9* (1998).

42. PRO. CAB. 16/109 fols. 7, 15; J. Holland, *Fortress Malta: An Island under Siege, 1940–1943* (2003), p. 25.

43. A. Marder, 'The Royal Navy and the Ethiopian Crisis of 1935–36', *American Historical Review*, 75 (1970), pp. 1327–56.

44. J. Cable, *The Royal Navy and the Siege of Bilbao* (Cambridge, 1979).

45. R. M. Salerno, *Vital Crossroads: Mediterranean Origins of the Second World War, 1935–1940* (Ithaca, 2002), esp. p. 214.

46. D. Dutton, *Neville Chamberlain* (2001).

47. G. C. Peden, *British Rearmament and the Treasury, 1932–1939* (Edinburgh, 1979); A. Gordon, *British Seapower and Procurement between the Wars: A Reappraisal of Procurement* (1988); C. Barnett, *Engage the Enemy More Closely: The Royal Navy in the Second World War* (1991) and 'British Economic Decline, 1900–1980', in P. K. O'Brien and A. Clesse (eds.), *Two Hegemonies: Britain 1846–1914 and the United States 1941–2001* (Aldershot, 2002), p. 143.

48. S. Roskill, *Naval Policy between the Wars, II: The Period of Reluctant Rearmament, 1930–1939* (1976); G. Franklin, *Britain's Anti-Submarine Capability, 1919–1939* (2003), esp. p. 190.

49. G. Till, 'Adopting the Aircraft Carrier: The British, American, and Japanese Case Studies', in W. Murray and A. R. Millett (eds.), *Military Innovation in the Interwar Period* (Cambridge, 1996), pp. 191–226; T. C. Hone, N. Friedman and M. D. Mandeles, *American and British Aircraft Carrier Development, 1919–1941* (Annapolis, 1999).

50. J. Sumida, ' "The Best Laid Plans": The Development of British Battle-Fleet Tactics, 1919–1942', *International History Review*, 14 (1992), pp. 682–700.

51. C. Barnett, 'The Influence of History upon Sea Power: The Royal Navy in the Second World War', in N. A. M. Rodger (ed.), *British Naval Power in the Twentieth Century* (1996), p. 122.

52. J. Moretz, *The Royal Navy and the Capital Ship in the Interwar Period: An Operational Perspective* (2002), p. 253.

53. R. Ovendale, *Appeasement and the English-Speaking World: Britain, the United States, the Dominions and the Policy of Appeasement, 1937–39* (Cardiff, 1975); J. D. Meehan, 'Steering Clear of Great Britain: Canada's Debate over Collective Security

in the Far Eastern Crisis of 1937', *International History Review*, 25 (2003), pp. 253–81.

54. Layton to First Sea Lord, 13 Sept., Mountbatten to Layton, 15 Sept. 1944, BL. Add. 74796.

55. Pound to Admiral Cunningham, 20 May 1940, BL. Add. 52560 fol. 120.

56. P. J. Larkham and K. D. Lilley, *Planning the 'City of Tomorrow': British Reconstruction Planning, 1939–1952* (Pickering, 2001).

57. A. Tute, *The Deadly Stroke* (1973).

58. G. Rhys-Jones, *The Loss of the Bismarck: An Avoidable Disaster* (1999); D. J. Bercuson and H. H. Herwig, *The Destruction of the Bismarck* (Woodstock, N.Y., 2001); R. Chesneau, *Hood: Life and Death of a Battlecruiser* (2002).

59. J. Terraine, *Business in Great Waters: The U-Boat Wars, 1916–45* (1989).

60. J. L. Granatstein, *Canada's Army: Waging War and Keeping the Peace* (Toronto, 2002), p. 186; M. Milner, *North Atlantic Run: The Royal Canadian Navy and the Battle for the Convoys* (Toronto, 1985).

61. E. Gibbon, *The History of the Decline and Fall of the Roman Empire*, ed. J. B. Bury (7 vols., 1897–1901), IV, p. 166.

62. M. Glover, *An Improvised War: The Abyssinian Campaign of 1940–1943* (1987).

63. J. Greene and A. Massignani, *The Naval War in the Mediterranean, 1940–1943* (Rockville, N.Y., 1999).

64. C. M. Bell, 'The "Singapore Strategy" and the Deterrence of Japan: Winston Churchill, the Admiralty and the Dispatch of Force Z', *English Historical Review*, 116 (2001), pp. 604–34, esp. p. 633.

65. A. Warren, *Singapore 1942, Britain's Greatest Defeat* (2002).

66. BL. Add. 74806.

67. C. H. Waddington, *O. R. in World War 2: Operational Research against the U-Boat* (1973); A. Price, *Aircraft Versus Submarine: The Evolution of Anti-submarine Aircraft, 1912 to 1980* (2nd edn., 1980); K. Poolman, *Allied Escort Carriers of World War Two in Action* (1988); J. Buckley, *The RAF and Trade Defence 1919–1945: Constant*

Endeavour (Keele, 1995); C. Goulter, 'Sir Arthur Harris: Different Perspectives', in G. Sheffield and G. Till (eds.), *Challenges of High Command in the Twentieth Century* (Camberley, 1999), pp. 78–80.

68. D. Syrett, 'Communications Intelligence and the Battle of the Atlantic, 1943–1945', *Archives*, 22 (1995), pp. 56–7; W. J. R. Gardner, *Decoding History: The Battle of the Atlantic and Ultra* (Basingstoke, 1999).

69. J. Rohwer, *The Critical Convoy Battles of March 1943: The Battle for HX229/SC122* (1977); S. Howarth and D. Law (eds.), *The Battle of the Atlantic, 1939–1945* (1994); D. Syrett, *The Defeat of the German U-Boats: The Battle of the Atlantic 1939–1945* (1994); F. Barley and D. Waters, *The Defeat of the Enemy Attack on Shipping* (2nd edn., Aldershot, 1997).

70. M. Gaskill, *Hellish Nell: Last of Britain's Witches* (2001).

71. B. J. C. McKercher, *Transition of Power: Britain's Loss of Global Pre-eminence to the United States, 1930–1945* (Cambridge, 1999).

72. P. Orders, *Britain, Australia, New Zealand and the Expansion of American Power in the South-West Pacific, 1941–46* (Basingstoke, 2002).

73. Quote, N. Smith, *American Empire: Roosevelt's Geographer and the Prelude to Globalization* (Berkeley, 2003), p. 360; W. R. Louis, *Imperialism at Bay: The United States and the Decolonisation of the British Empire, 1941–1945* (New York, 1978); A. J. Whitfield, *Hong Kong, Empire, and the Anglo-American Alliance at War, 1941–45* (Basingstoke, 2001).

74. M. Hauner, *India in Axis Strategy: Germany, Japan and Indian Nationalists in the Second World War* (Stuttgart, 1981).

75. Wavell to Field Marshal Brooke, Chief of the Imperial General Staff, 4 July 1944, KCL. LH, Alanbrooke papers 6/4/12.

76. A. Jackson, *Botswana, 1939–1945: An African Country at War* (Oxford, 1999).

77. Churchill to Brooke, 20 Mar., Chiefs of Staff to Churchill, 28 Mar. 1944, KCL. LH, Alanbrooke papers 6/3/8–9.

78. K. Smith, *Conflict over Convoys: Anglo-American Logistics Diplomacy in the Second World War* (Cambridge, 1996).

9   Loss and Legacy, 1945–1972

1. King's College London, Liddell Hart Archive, Misc 33/2.

2. M. H. Murfett, 'Old Habits Die Hard: The Return of British Warships to Chinese Waters after the Second World War', in M. H. Murfett and J. B. Hattendorf (eds.), *The Limitations of Military Power* (1990), pp. 203–17.

3. K. Dodds, 'Screening Antarctica: Britain, the FIDS and *Scott of the Antarctic* (1948)', *Polar Record*, 38 (2002), pp. 1–10.

4. Manchester, John Rylands Library, Auchinleck papers, nos. 1136, 1143 and 1155.

5. P. J. Brobst, 'Sir Olaf Caroe and the Question of British Grand Design', *Commonwealth and Comparative Politics*, 36 (1998), p. 95.

6. F. McKenzie, *Redefining the Bonds of Commonwealth, 1939–1948* (Basingstoke, 2002); G. Krozewski, *Money and the End of Empire: British International Economic Policy and the Colonies, 1947–58* (Basingstoke, 2001).

7. A. Bullock, *Ernest Bevin, Foreign Secretary, 1945–51* (Basingstoke, 1999).

8. R. J. Moore, *Escape from Empire: The Attlee Government and the Indian Problem* (Oxford, 1983).

9. W. R. Louis and R. W. Stookey (eds.), *The End of the Palestine Mandate* (Austin, 1986); N. Stewart, *The Royal Navy and the Palestine Patrol* (2002).

10. Z. Feng, *The British Government's China Policy, 1945–50* (Keele, 1994).

11. M. H. Murfett, *Hostage of the Yangtze: Britain, China and the Amethyst Crisis of 1949* (Annapolis, 1991) and *In Jeopardy: The Royal Navy and British Far Eastern Defence Policy, 1945–1951* (1995).

12. M. J. Cohen, *Fighting World War Three from the Middle East: Allied Contingency Plans, 1945–54* (1997); R. Gregorian, *The British Army, the Ghurkhas and Cold War Strategy in the Far East, 1947–1954* (Basingstoke, 2002).

13. T. Mockaitis, *British Counter-Insurgency, 1919–60* (1990); T. Jones, *Postwar Counterinsurgency and the SAS, 1945–1952: A Special Type of Warfare* (2001).

14. R. Hyam and P. Henshaw, *The Lion and the Springbok: Britain and South Africa since the Boer War* (Cambridge, 2003), pp. 236–49.

15. D. R. Devereux, *The Formulation of British Defence Policy towards the Middle East, 1948–56* (1990); P. Darby, *British Defence Policy East of Suez, 1947–1968* (Oxford, 1973).

16. M. Smith, *NATO Enlargement during the Cold War: Strategy and System in the Western Alliance* (Basingstoke, 2000).

17. V. S. Kaufman, *Confronting Communism: US and British Policies toward China* (Columbia, Mo., 2001).

18. C. Fraser, 'The "New Frontier" of Empire in the Caribbean: The Transfer of Power in British Guiana, 1961–1964', *International History Review*, 22 (2000), pp. 583–610.

19. I. Speller, *The Role of Amphibious Warfare in British Defence Policy, 1945–1956* (Basingstoke, 2001).

20. S. Lucas, *Britain and Suez: The Lion's Last Roar* (Manchester, 1996).

21. W. R. Louis and R. Owen (eds.), *Suez 1956: The Crisis and Its Consequences* (1989); W. S. Lucas, *Divided We Stand: Britain, the US and the Suez Crisis* (1991).

22. M. Dockrill, 'Restoring the "Special Relationship": The Bermuda and Washington Conferences, 1957', in D. Richardson and G. Stone (eds.), *Decisions and Diplomacy: Essays in Twentieth-Century International History* (1995), pp. 205–23; I. Clark, *Nuclear Diplomacy and the Special Relationship: Britain's Deterrent and America, 1957–1962* (Oxford, 1994).

23. M. Jones, 'Anglo-American Relations after Suez, the Rise and Decline of the Working Group Experiment, and the French Challenge to NATO, 1957–59', *Diplomacy and Statecraft*, 14 (2003), pp. 49–79.

24. J. Mohamed, 'Imperial Policies and Nationalism in the Decolonization of Somaliland, 1954–1960', *English Historical Review*, 117 (2002), p. 1177.

25. H. G. Gelber, *Nations out of Empires: European Nationalism and the Transformation of Asia* (Basingstoke, 2001).

26. Amidst the extensive literature on the subject, see J. G. Darwin, *Britain and Decolonisation: The Retreat from Empire in the Post-War World* (Basingstoke, 1988); W. R. Louis and R. E. Robinson, 'The Imperialism of Decolonization', *Journal of Imperial and Commonwealth History*, 22 (1993), pp. 462–511; W. D. McIntyre, *British Decolonization, 1946–1997* (1998); D. G. Boyce, *Decolonization and the British Empire, 1775–1997* (Basingstoke, 1999); K. Fedorowich and M. Thomas (eds.), *International Diplomacy and Colonial Retreat* (2001).

27. J. Ellison, *Threatening Europe: Britain and the Creation of the European Community, 1955–1958* (Basingstoke, 2000).

28. S. Howe, *Anti-Colonialism in British Politics, 1918–1964* (Oxford, 1993); S. Ward, *British Culture and the End of Empire* (Manchester, 2001); F. Heinlein, *British Government Policy and Decolonisation, 1945–1963: Scrutinising the Official Mind* (2002).

29. J. Richards, 'Imperial Heroes for a Post-Imperial Age: Films and the End of Empire', in S. Ward (ed.), *British Culture and the End of Empire* (Manchester, 2001), pp. 128–44.

30. M. Hughes, 'Fighting for White Rule in Africa: The Central African Federation, Katanga, and the Congo Crisis, 1958–1965', *International History Review*, 25 (2003), pp. 592–615.

31. M. Thomas, *The French North Africa Crisis: Colonial Breakdown and Anglo-French Relations, 1945–1962* (2000).

32. R. Holland, *Britain and the Revolt in Cyprus, 1954–1959* (Oxford, 1998).

33. J. G. Darwin, 'Decolonization and End of Empire', in R. W. Winks (ed.), *The Oxford History of the British Empire, v: Historiography* (Oxford, 1999), p. 551.

34. J. G. Darwin, 'The Fear of Falling: British Politics and Imperial Decline since 1900', *Transactions of the Royal Historical Society*, 5th ser., 36 (1986), p. 42.

35. J. G. Giauque, *Grand Designs and Visions of Unity: The Atlantic Powers and the Reorganization of Western Europe, 1955–1963* (Chapel Hill, 2002).

36. S. C. Smith, *Kuwait, 1950–1965: Britain, the al-Sabah, and Oil* (Oxford, 1999); N. Ashton, 'Britain and the Kuwaiti Crisis, 1961', *Diplomacy and Statecraft*, 9 (1998), pp. 163–81.

37. J. and D. S. Small, *The Undeclared War: The Story of the Indonesian Confrontation, 1962–1966* (1971); P. Dennis and J. Grey, *Emergency and Confrontation: Australian Military Operations in Malaya and Borneo 1950–1966* (St. Leonards, New South Wales, 1990).

38. K. Haack, *Defence and Decolonisation in Southeast Asia: Britain, Malaya and Singapore, 1941–68* (2001); M. Jones, *Conflict and Confrontation in South East Asia, 1961–1965: Britain, the United States, Indonesia, and the Creation of Malaysia* (Cambridge, 2002).

39. M. Jones, 'Up the Garden Path? Britain's Nuclear History in the Far East, 1954–1962', *International History Review*, 25 (2003), pp. 325–7; P. Darby, *British Defence Policy East of Suez, 1947–68* (1973).

40. M. Phythian, *The Politics of British Arms Sales since 1964: 'To Secure Our Rightful Share'* (Manchester, 2000).

41. M. Jones, 'A Decision Delayed: Britain's Withdrawal from South East Asia Reconsidered, 1961–8', *English Historical Review*, 117 (2002), pp. 569–95.

42. J. Pickering, *Britain's Withdrawal from East of Suez* (Basingstoke, 1998); S. Dockrill, *Britain's Retreat from East of Suez: The Choice between Europe and the World?* (Basingstoke, 2002); W. R. Louis, 'The British Withdrawal from the Gulf,

1967–71', *Journal of Imperial and Commonwealth History*, 31 (2003), p. 83.

43. M. A. Palmer, *On Course to desert Storm: The United States Navy and the Persian Gulf* (Washington, 1992), pp. 83–4. I have benefited greatly from discussing this and related topics with John Brobst.

44. L. Sondhaus, *Navies of Europe* (2002), p. 295.

45. P. Busch, *All the Way with JFK? Britain, the US, and the Vietnam War* (Oxford, 2003).

46. M. McKinnon, *Independence and Foreign Policy: New Zealand in the World since 1935* (Auckland, 1993).

47. D. Healey, *The Time of My Life* (1990), pp. 276–7.

48. A. Cooper, 'At the Crossroads: Anglo-Australian Naval Relations, 1945–1971', *Journal of Military History*, 58 (1994), p. 709.

49. K. Pieragostini, *Britain, Aden and South Arabia: Abandoning Empire* (1991).

50. L. Johnman and H. Murphy, *British Shipbuilding and the State since 1918: A Political Economy of Decline* (Exeter, 2002), p. 192.

51. P. Clarke and C. Trebilcock (eds.), *Understanding Decline: Perceptions and Realities of British Economic Performance* (Cambridge, 1997); R. Middleton, *The British Economy since 1945: Engaging with the Debate* (1999).

52. S. J. Ball, *The Bomber in British Strategy: Doctrine, Strategy, and Britain's World Role, 1945–1960* (Boulder, 1995).

53. Southampton, University Library MB1/I 149.

54. M. Navias, *Nuclear Weapons and British Strategic Planning, 1955–1958* (Oxford, 1991); S. J. Ball, 'Harold Macmillan and the Politics of Defence: The Market for Strategic Ideas during the Sandys Era Revisited', *Twentieth Century British History*, 6 (1995), pp. 79–100, and ' "Vested Interests and Vanished Dreams": Duncan Sandys, the Chiefs of Staff and the 1957 White Paper', in P. Smith (ed.), *Government and the Armed Forces in Britain, 1856–1990* (1996), pp. 217–34, esp. pp. 232–3.

55. B. Ranft and G. Till, *The Sea in Soviet Strategy* (1983).

56. P. Nitze et al., *Securing the Seas: The Soviet Naval Challenge and Western Alliance Options* (Boulder, 1979); J. D. Watkins, *The Maritime Strategy* (Annapolis, 1986).

57. M. Milner, *Canada's Navy: The First Century* (Toronto, 1999), pp. 219–20.

58. R. Hope, *A New History of British Shipping* (1992), p. 448; A. G. Jamieson, *Ebb Tide in the British Maritime Industries: Change and Adaptation* (Exeter, 2003), p. 43.

59. R. Moore, *The Royal Navy and Nuclear Weapons* (2001).

60. P. J. Cain and A. G. Hopkins, *British Imperialism, II: Crisis and Deconstruction, 1914–1990* (1993).

61. R. Robinson, *Trawling: The Rise and Fall of the British Trawl Fishery* (Exeter, 1996).

10 THE REMAINS OF EMPIRE,
1973–2004

1. R. J. Moore, *Making the New Commonwealth* (Oxford, 1987); W. D. McIntyre, *The Significance of the Commonwealth, 1965–90* (Basingstoke, 1991).

2. D. A. Low, *Eclipse of Empire* (Cambridge, 1991), p. 332.

3. D. K. Brown, *The Royal Navy and the Falklands War* (1987); R. A. Burden et al., *Falklands: The Air War* (1986); M. Clapp and E. Southby-Tailyour, *Amphibious Assault Falklands: The Battle of San Carlos Water* (1996), D. Rice and A. Gavshon, *The Sinking of the Belgrano* (1984); S. Woodward, *One Hundred Days: The Memoirs of the Falklands Battle Group Commander* (1992).

4. J. Cable, *The Political Influence of Naval Force in History* (Basingstoke, 1998), pp. 167–8.

5. M. Misra, *Business, Race and Politics in British India, c. 1850–1960* (Oxford, 1999).

6. A. G. Jamieson, 'Facing the Rising Tide: British Attitudes to Asian National Shipping Lines, 1958–1964', *International Journal of Maritime History*, 7 (1995), pp. 135–48.

7. N. Peters, *Milk and Honey – But No Gold: Postwar Migration to Western Australia, 1945–1964* (Perth, 2001).

8. D. Goldsworthy, *Losing the Blanket: Australia and the End of Britain's Empire* (Melbourne, 2002).

9. K. Paul, *Whitewashing Britain: Race and Citizenship in the Post-war Era* (Ithaca, N.Y., 1994).

10. W. Churchill, *A History of the English-Speaking Peoples* (4 vols., 1956–8); M. Thatcher, *The Downing Street Years* (1994), p. 183.

11. S. Ward, *British Culture and the End of Empire* (Manchester, 2001).

12. M. P. K. Sorrenson, 'Towards a Radical Reinterpretation of New Zealand History: The Role of the Waitangi Tribunal', *New Zealand Journal of History*, 21 (1987), pp. 173–88; J. Evans, P. Grimshaw, D. Philips and S. Swain, *Equal Subjects, Unequal Rights: Indigenous Peoples in British Settler Colonies, 1830–1910* (Manchester, 2003), pp. 182–92.

CONCLUSIONS

1. E. J. Grove, *Vanguard to Trident: British Naval Policy since World War Two* (1987).

2. N. Ferguson, *Empire: How Britain Made the Modern World* (2003), p. xxi.

3. *British Maritime Doctrine* (2nd edn., 1999), pp. 3, 171. I have benefited from discussing this with the author, Captain Peter Hore.

4. G. A. Ballard, *Rulers of the Indian Ocean* (1927), pp. 293, 319.

5. P. Williamson, *Stanley Baldwin: Conservative Leadership and National Values* (Cambridge, 1999).

6. P. Ward, *Red Flag and Union Jack: Englishness, Patriotism and the British Left, 1881–1924* (Woodbridge, 1998).

7. J. Foster, 'The Twentieth Century,

1914–1979', in R. A. Houston and W. W. J. Knox (eds.), *The New Penguin History of Scotland* (2001), p. 476.

8. L. Johnman and H. Murphy, *British Shipbuilding and the State since 1918: A Political Economy of Decline* (Exeter, 2002), pp. 158–243.

9. A. G. Jamieson, *Ebb Tide in the British Maritime Industries: Change and Adaptation, 1918–1990* (Exeter, 2003), pp. 119, 157.

10. Liddell Hart Archive, Misc. 45/1.

11. C. Dickens, *Great Expectations* (Everyman edn., 1907), pp. 412–13.

12. A. J. Bacevich, *American Empire: The Realities and Consequences of U.S. Diplomacy* (Cambridge, Mass., 2002).

13. E. M. T. Powell, *Egypt, Great Britain, and the Mastery of the Sudan* (Berkeley, 2003), quote p. 219.

14. N. A. M. Rodger, *The Wooden World: An Anatomy of the Georgian Navy* (1986); J. D. Davies, *Gentlemen and Tarpaulins: The Officers and Men of the Restoration Navy* (Oxford, 1991); B. Lavery (ed.), *Shipyard Life and Organization, 1731–1815* (Aldershot, 1998), dealing largely with 1786-1815; C. A. Fury, *Tides in the Affairs of Men: The Social History of Elizabethan Seamen, 1580–1603*(Westport, 2002); C. McKee, *Sober Men and True: Sailor Lives in the Royal Navy 1900-1945* (Cambridge, Mass., 2002).

15. D. Pope, *The Black Ship* (1963).

16. C. Lloyd, 'The Mutiny of the Nereide', *Mariner's Mirror*, 54 (1968), pp. 245–51.

17. S. Brumwell, *Redcoats: The British Soldier and War in the Americas, 1755–1763* (Cambridge, 2002), p. 310.

INDEX